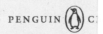

THE RISE OF ROME

PLUTARCH (*c.* AD 45–*c.* 120) was a writer and thinker born into a wealthy, established family of Chaeronea in central Greece. He received the best possible education in rhetoric and philosophy, and travelled to Asia Minor and Egypt. Later, a series of visits to Rome and Italy contributed to his fame, and it was said that he had received official recognition by the emperors Trajan and Hadrian. Plutarch rendered conscientious service to his province and city (where he continued to live), as well as holding a priesthood at nearby Delphi. His voluminous surviving writings are broadly divided into the 'moral' works and the Lives of outstanding Greek and Roman leaders. The former (*Moralia*) are a mixture of rhetorical and antiquarian pieces, together with technical and moral philosophy (sometimes in dialogue form). The Lives have been influential from the Renaissance onwards.

IAN SCOTT-KILVERT was Director of English Literature at the British Council and editor of *Writers and Their Works*. He translated Cassius Dio's *The Roman History* as well as Plutarch's *The Rise and Fall of Athens: Nine Greek Lives*, *Makers of Rome* and *The Age of Alexander* for Penguin Classics. He died in 1989.

JEFFREY TATUM is Professor of Classics at Victoria University of Wellington. He is the author of *The Patrician Tribune: Publius Clodius Pulcher* (1999), *Always I am Caesar* (2008) and *A Caesar Reader* (2012), as well as numerous articles and chapters on Roman history and culture and Latin literature.

CHRISTOPHER PELLING is Regius Professor of Greek at Oxford University. He has published a commentary on Plutarch's *Life of Antony* (1988) and a commentary on Plutarch's *Life of Caesar* (2011). His other books include *Literary Texts and the Greek Historian* (2000). Most of his articles on Plutarch were collected in his *Plutarch and History: Eighteen Essays* (2002).

The Rise of Rome

Twelve Lives by Plutarch

Romulus · Numa · Publicola · Coriolanus
Camillus · Fabius Maximus · Marcellus · Aratus
Philopoemen · Titus Flamininus · Elder Cato
Aemilius Paullus

Revised Edition

Translated by
IAN SCOTT-KILVERT, JEFFREY TATUM
and CHRISTOPHER PELLING

Introductions and Notes by
JEFFREY TATUM

With Series Preface by
CHRISTOPHER PELLING

PENGUIN BOOKS

PENGUIN CLASSICS

Published by the Penguin Group
Penguin Books Ltd, 80 Strand, London WC2R 0RL, England
Penguin Group (USA) Inc., 375 Hudson Street, New York, New York 10014, USA
Penguin Group (Canada), 90 Eglinton Avenue East, Suite 700, Toronto, Ontario, Canada M4P 2Y3
(a division of Pearson Penguin Canada Inc.)
Penguin Ireland, 25 St Stephen's Green, Dublin 2, Ireland (a division of Penguin Books Ltd)
Penguin Group (Australia), 707 Collins Street, Melbourne, Victoria 3008, Australia
(a division of Pearson Australia Group Pty Ltd)
Penguin Books India Pvt Ltd, 11 Community Centre, Panchsheel Park, New Delhi – 110 017, India
Penguin Group (NZ), 67 Apollo Drive, Rosedale, Auckland 0632, New Zealand
(a division of Pearson New Zealand Ltd)
Penguin Books (South Africa) (Pty) Ltd, Block D, Rosebank Office Park,
181 Jan Smuts Avenue, Parktown North, Gauteng 2193, South Africa

Penguin Books Ltd, Registered Offices: 80 Strand, London WC2R 0RL, England

www.penguin.com

This collection first published in Penguin Classics 2013

014

Translations of *Coriolanus*, *Fabius Maximus*, *Marcellus* and *Elder Cato* copyright © Estate of Ian
Scott-Kilvert, 1965
Revisions to translations of *Coriolanus*, *Fabius Maximus*, *Marcellus* and *Elder Cato*, and new
translations of *Romulus*, *Numa*, *Publicola*, *Camillus*, *Aratus*, *Aemilius Paullus* and their *Comparisons*
copyright © Jeffrey Tatum, 2013
Translations of *Philopoemen*, *Titus Flamininus* and their *Comparison*
copyright © Christopher Pelling, 1997
Introduction and Notes copyright © Jeffrey Tatum, 2013
Series Preface copyright © Christopher Pelling, 2005
All rights reserved

The moral right of the translators and editor has been asserted

Set in 10.25/12.25 pt Postscript Adobe Sabon
Typeset by Jouve (UK), Milton Keynes
Printed in Great Britain by Clays Ltd, Elcograf S.p.A.

Except in the United States of America, this book is sold subject
to the condition that it shall not, by way of trade or otherwise, be lent,
re-sold, hired out, or otherwise circulated without the publisher's
prior consent in any form of binding or cover other than that in
which it is published and without a similar condition including this
condition being imposed on the subsequent purchaser

ISBN: 978-0-140-44975-4

www.greenpenguin.co.uk

MIX
Paper from
responsible sources
FSC® C018179
www.fsc.org

Penguin Books is committed to a sustainable
future for our business, our readers and our planet.
This book is made from Forest Stewardship
Council™ certified paper.

Contents

Penguin Plutarch, by Christopher Pelling   viii
Preface to the New Edition   xi
Abbreviations   xii
General Introduction   xiv
List of Surviving Lives by Plutarch   xlii
Further Reading   xliii

THE RISE OF ROME

ROMULUS
Introduction to *Romulus*   5
Life of Romulus   10
Comparison of Theseus and Romulus   48

NUMA
Introduction to *Numa*   57
Life of Numa   61
Comparison of Lycurgus and Numa   92

PUBLICOLA
Introduction to *Publicola*   101
Life of Publicola   105
Comparison of Solon and Publicola   130

CORIOLANUS

Introduction to *Coriolanus*   137
Life of Coriolanus   146

CAMILLUS

Introduction to *Camillus*   191
Life of Camillus   200

FABIUS MAXIMUS

Introduction to *Fabius Maximus*   247
Life of Fabius Maximus   256
Comparison of Pericles and Fabius Maximus   289

MARCELLUS

Introduction to *Marcellus*   295
Life of Marcellus   304
Comparison of Pelopidas and Marcellus   341

ARATUS

Introduction to *Aratus*   347
Life of Aratus   356

PHILOPOEMEN

Introduction to *Philopoemen*   407
Life of Philopoemen   416

TITUS FLAMININUS

Introduction to *Titus Flamininus*   441
Life of Titus Flamininus   450
Comparison of Philopoemen and
Titus Flamininus   473

ELDER CATO

Introduction to *Elder Cato*   479
Life of Elder Cato   489
Comparison of Aristeides and Elder Cato   524

AEMILIUS PAULLUS

Introduction to *Aemilius Paullus*   533
Life of Aemilius Paullus   543

Maps

1. Rome   586
2. Latium   587
3. Italy   588
4. Greece   590
5. East Mediterranean   592
6. Spain and Africa   593

Notes   595

Penguin Plutarch

The first Penguin translation of Plutarch appeared in 1958, with Rex Warner's version of six Roman Lives appearing as *Fall of the Roman Republic*. Other volumes followed steadily, three of them by Ian Scott-Kilvert (*The Rise and Fall of Athens* in 1960, *Makers of Rome* in 1965 and *The Age of Alexander* in 1973), and then Richard Talbert's *Plutarch on Sparta* in 1988. Several of the moral essays were also translated by Robin Waterfield in 1992. That left only fourteen of the forty-eight Lives untranslated. The new edition now includes these remaining Lives, along with revised versions of those which appeared in the first edition.

This has also given an opportunity to divide up the Lives in a different way, although it is not straightforward to decide what that different way should be. Nearly all Plutarch's surviving biographies were written in pairs as *Parallel Lives*: thus a 'book' for Plutarch was not just *Theseus* or *Caesar* but *Theseus and Romulus* or *Alexander and Caesar*. Most, but not all, of those pairs have a brief epilogue at the end of the second Life comparing the two heroes, just as many have a prologue before the first Life giving some initial grounds for the comparison. Not much attention was paid to this comparative technique at the time when the Penguin series started to appear, and it seemed natural then to separate each Life from its pair and organize the volumes by period and city. The comparative epilogues were not included in the translations at all.

That now looks very unsatisfactory. The comparative technique has come to be seen as basic to Plutarch's strategy, underlying not only those brief epilogues but also the entire pairings. (It is true, though, that in the last few years scholars have become increasingly alert to the way that *all* the Lives, not just the pairs, are crafted to complement one another.) It is very tempting to keep the pairings in this new series in a way that would respect Plutarch's own authorial intentions.

After some agonizing, we have decided nevertheless to keep to something like the original strategy of the series, though with some refinement. The reason is a practical one. Many, perhaps most, readers of Plutarch will be reading him to see what he has to say about a particular period, and will wish to compare his treatment of the major players to see how the different parts of his historical jigsaw fit together. If one kept the pairings, that would inevitably mean buying several different volumes of the series; and if, say, one organized those volumes by the Greek partner (so that, for instance, *Pericles–Fabius, Nicias–Crassus* and *Coriolanus–Alcibiades* made one volume), anyone primarily interested in the Roman Lives of the late Republic would probably need to buy the whole set. That is no way to guarantee these finely crafted works of art the wide reading that they deserve. Keeping the organization by period also allows some other works of Plutarch to be included along with the Lives themselves, for instance the fascinating essay *On the Malice of Herodotus* along with the Lives of Themistocles and Aristides and (as before) several Spartan essays along with the Spartan Lives.

Of course the comparative epilogues must now be included, and they will now be translated and printed along with the second Life of each pair, just as the prologues are conventionally printed before the first Life. Each volume will now also usually include more extended introductions to each Life, which will draw attention to the importance of the comparison as well as other features of Plutarch's technique. This is a compromise, and an uncomfortable one; but it still seems the better way.

These volumes do, however, sort the Lives into more logical groups.

The early Roman figures are now grouped together in this single volume *The Rise of Rome*; the Life of Agesilaus has

migrated from *The Age of Alexander* to join the rest of the
Spartan Lives, and *Artaxerxes* has joined *The Age of Alexander* collection; the rest of the new translations of Roman Lives
have joined those of the Gracchi, Brutus and Antony in the new
Rome in Crisis volume. The introductions and notes are being
fully revised. In due course we hope to include the *Moral Essays*
in the project as well.

In a bibliometric study (*Ancient Society*, 28 (1997), 265–89),
Walter Scheidel observed that the proportion of scholarly articles devoted to most classical authors had remained more or
less constant since the 1920s. The one author to stand out with
an exceptional rise was Plutarch. That professional pattern has
been matched by a similar surge in the interest in Plutarch
shown by the general reading public. The Penguin translations
have played a large part in fostering that interest, and this new,
more comprehensive project will surely play a similar role in
the future.

Christopher Pelling
2004

Preface to the New Edition

The original translations of *Coriolanus*, *Fabius Maximus*, *Marcellus* and *Elder Cato* were by I. Scott-Kilvert. Each has been revised by me, without, it is hoped, spoiling the lovely cadences for which they are justly admired. Chris Pelling translated *Philopoemen*, *Titus Flamininus* and their *Comparison*, originally as part of the project that led to his Rizzoli commentary on this pairing: C. Pelling and E. Melandri, *Plutarco, Vite Parallele: Filopemene e Tito Flaminino* (1997). Translations of the remaining Lives and *Comparisons* (*Romulus*, *Numa*, *Publicola*, *Camillus*, *Aratus* and *Aemilius Paullus*) are mine.

Chris Pelling has been an inspiration from the start, and his support throughout has been characteristically generous. I am also grateful to Jon Hall, Hans Mueller and Robin Seager for reading extensive sections of this volume and offering detailed and very helpful comments. David Rosenbloom was kind enough to answer several difficult questions, and Hannah Webling provided valuable assistance of a technical kind. The contribution made by this volume's superb copy editor, Monica Schmoller, must not go unrecognized. Alexander Cambitoglou gave me an opportunity to present some of my views on these Lives in a lecture and a seminar hosted by the Australian Archaeological Institute at Athens, and I have received generous support from the Committee on Research of the Faculty of Humanities and Social Sciences at Victoria University of Wellington. My greatest debt lies with Diana Burton, who read the whole of this book, suggested many improvements for it and, more crucially, made life outside and beyond it so much fun.

Jeffrey Tatum
2013

Abbreviations

ANRW: *Aufstieg und Niedergang der römischen Welt* (1972–)

Beard, *Roman Triumph*: M. Beard, *The Roman Triumph* (2007)

CAH The Cambridge Ancient History: vol. vi (1994), D. M. Lewis, J. Boardman, S. Hornblower and M. Ostwald (eds.); vol. vii. 1 (1984), F. Walbank, A. E. Astin, M. W. Frederiksen and R. M. Ogilvie (eds.); vol. vii. 2 (1990), F. W. Walbank, A. E. Astin, M. W. Frederiksen, R. M. Ogilvie and A. Drummond (eds.); vol. viii (1989), A. E. Astin, F. W. Walbank, M. W. Frederiksen and R. M. Ogilvie (eds.); vol. xi (2000), A. K. Bowman, P. Garnsey and D. Rathbone (eds.).

Cornell, *Beginnings of Rome*: T. J. Cornell, *The Beginnings of Rome: Italy and Rome from the Bronze Age to the Punic Wars (c. 1000 BC–264 BC)* (1995)

CQ: *Classical Quarterly*

Dion. Hal.: Dionysius of Halicarnassus, *Roman Antiquities*

DK: H. Diels and W. Kranz, *Fragmente der Vorsokratiker* (6th edn, 1952)

Duff, *Plutarch's Lives*: T. Duff, *Plutarch's Lives: Exploring Virtue and Vice* (1999)

Festus: W. M. Lindsay, *Sexti Pompei Festi: De verborum significatu quae supersunt cum Pauli epitome* (1913)

FGrH: F. Jacoby, *Fragmente der griechischen Historiker* (1923–)

Forsythe, *Early Rome*: G. Forsythe, *A Critical History of Early Rome from Prehistory to the First Punic War* (2005)

GRBS: *Greek, Roman, and Byzantine Studies*

Hammond–Walbank: N. G. L. Hammond and F. W. Walbank, *A History of Macedonia*, vol. 3 (1988)

HRR: H. Peter, *Historicorum Romanorum Fragmenta*, 2 vols. (1906, 1914)

Humble, *Plutarch's Lives*: N. Humble (ed.), *Plutarch's Lives: Parallelism and Purpose* (2010)

ILS: H. Dessau, *Inscriptiones Latinae Selectae* (1892–1916)

JHS: *Journal of Hellenic Studies*

Jones, 'Chronology': C. P. Jones, 'Towards a Chronology of Plutarch's Works', in Scardigli, *Essays*, pp. 106–14

Jones, *P&R*: C. P. Jones, *Plutarch and Rome* (1971)

JRS: *Journal of Roman Studies*

Lintott, *Constitution*: A. Lintott, *The Constitution of the Roman Republic* (1999)

Pelling, *P&H*: C. Pelling, *Plutarch and History: Eighteen Essays* (2002)

Pelling, 'Roman heroes': C. Pelling, 'Plutarch: Roman heroes and Greek culture', in M. Griffin and J. Barnes (eds.), *Philosophia Togata I* (1989), pp. 199–232

Scardigli, *Essays*: B. Scardigli (ed.), *Essays on Plutarch's Lives* (1995)

Skutsch: O. Skutsch, *The Annals of Quintus Ennius* (1985)

Swain, 'Culture': S. Swain, 'Hellenic Culture and the Roman Heroes of Plutarch', in Scardigli, *Essays*, pp. 229–64

Swain, *H&E*: S. Swain, *Hellenism and Empire: Language, Classicism, and Power in the Greek World*, AD 50–250 (1996)

Syll.: W. Dittenberger, *Sylloge Inscriptionum Graecarum* (3rd edn, 1915–24)

TAPhA: *Transactions of the American Philological Association*

Walbank, *Commentary*: F. W. Walbank, *A Historical Commentary on Polybius*, vols. 1–3 (1957–79)

General Introduction

I. *Man of the World*

During the first and second centuries of our era, Greece enjoyed a brilliant recrudescence of literary genius that is often described, filching a phrase from the Greek biographer Philostratus, as the Second Sophistic (*Lives* 1.19).[1] Imperial Greece was indeed a time of talented, and frequently flamboyant, orators, writers and intellectuals, of whom the unglamorous Plutarch was simply the best. He was born sometime in the mid-forties of the first century AD, in the Boeotian town of Chaeronea. His family belonged to the local aristocracy, and Plutarch was sufficiently wealthy to study rhetoric and philosophy in Athens, to travel to Alexandria in Egypt and to visit Italy more than once. Most of his life, however, he spent in his native city: 'I live in a small town, and owing to my affection for it I prefer to remain there, lest it become even smaller' (*Demosthenes* 2). Although his occupations took him beyond Chaeronea – Plutarch became a citizen of Athens and of Delphi, where he held an important priesthood – it was there nevertheless that he gave instruction to his own pupils and, mostly in his mature years, became the author of a vast body of literary work that made him famous in antiquity and influential in the history of European letters.[2]

We sort Plutarch's writings into two unequal piles. One, the Lives, consists of his biographies, and the other, the *Moralia* or *Moral Essays*, includes everything else. Plutarch was a prolific writer: the *Catalogue of Lamprias*, a fourth-century list of his works, includes more than 200 titles. Many of these works have been lost, but quite enough of Plutarch survives to make him one of the best represented of all the writers of antiquity. Of Plutarchan biography, more presently. But no reader of the Lives should overlook the astonishingly variegated body of work subsumed under the heading *Moral Essays*. Plutarch was an orator, rhetorician and – most importantly – a philosopher, and these diverse roles are reflected in his *Moralia*.

Plutarch studied philosophy and remained a committed Platonist for the whole of his life. He was the author of numerous philosophical works, including highly technical, specialist treatises, but he also composed more accessible pieces, of the kind we might describe as popularizing, on such topics as *How to Tell a Friend from a Flatterer* (*Moralia* 48e–74f) and *Advice on Marriage* (*Moralia* 138a–146a). Sometimes Plutarch composed traditional philosophical dialogues, at others more experimental pieces, like the *Amatorius*, in which, by way of a tale about a widow who abducts a young man she desires to wed, Plutarch analyses the nature of homosexual and heterosexual love. Equally remarkable is his *Table Talk* (*Moralia* 612c–748d), a lengthy account of learned and graceful conversations on the part of powerful and cultivated Romans and sophisticated Greeks. Plutarch also wrote numerous essays on religion as well as didactic pieces on literature, including *On the Malice of Herodotus* (*Moralia* 854e–874c), a still important contribution to ancient historiography. Antiquarianism, another Plutarchan interest, resulted in his *Roman Questions* (*Moralia* 263d–291c) and *Greek Questions* (*Moralia* 291d–304f). Of a different nature altogether are Plutarch's set speeches, composed largely for the purpose of aesthetic display: these, too, are bundled into the *Moralia*. The best specimens are *The Fortune of Rome* (*Moralia* 316c–326c) and *The Glory of Athens* (*Moralia* 345c–351b); the latter surprisingly or perhaps provocatively insists that Athens' true glory lay in her military rather than her cultural achievements.

The Rise of Rome is concerned with Plutarch's contributions to biography. In this genre, too, he was highly inventive. In addition to several stand-alone biographies (one of which, *Aratus*, is included here), Plutarch composed two important

biographical collections. Sometime during the reign of the
Flavians (AD 69–96), he completed his *Lives of the Caesars*, a
series of sequential imperial biographies beginning with Augustus and concluding with Vitellius, whose defeat and death
ushered in the Flavian dynasty. Only *Galba* and *Otho* subsist.
This was a first in imperial biography: no one, so far as we
know, had previously recorded the lives of emperors in this
way, collapsing history into imperial biography. Suetonius, of
course, soon reinvented the genre for himself, and his version
proved far more influential, but that reality should not distract
us from Plutarch's originality. More significant – and in fact the
masterpiece of all Plutarch's literary efforts – is his *Parallel
Lives of Greeks and Romans*, biographical pairings each of
which conjoins the life of an eminent Greek with a famous
Roman political figure.

Plutarch's Lives, like all of his writings, proved very popular.
Much of their attraction resided in their style.[3] In Plutarch's
day, Greek authors strove to use only the language and mannerisms of the literary world of the fifth and fourth centuries
BC, the period, in their view, that represented Greek writing at
its best. Plutarch shares this archaizing tendency, but he is not
bound by it: his undeniably fine Attic prose admits, more than
occasionally, contemporary vocabulary and syntax, the effect
of which is a Greek that is always meticulous, respectable and
suitable to its subject but almost never stodgy. Plutarch delights
in metaphor and imaginative imagery, and he entertains his
reader with frequent allusions to poetry and philosophy (which
only seldom become pretentious). He exhibits an impressive
narrative flair: his visual descriptions are vivid, his dramatic
sense acute – and his capacity for depicting complexities and
nuances of character is advanced. And the stories he tells are all
superb stuff: the public and private lives of the greatest men of
the Greek and Roman past, hallowed figures who made history
and about whom Plutarch records 'what is noblest and most
important to know' (*Aemilius* 1).

Plutarch died a famous man. And yet we know remarkably
little about his life and career. In his writings, he often and
affectionately mentions his family, especially his wife, Timox-

ena, herself an author (*Moralia* 145a) and the object of her husband's devotion. Plutarch was the father of at least five children, three of whom died very young, and in his Lives he is alert to the pain felt by fathers who suffer such losses. And he is keen, especially in the *Moralia*, to mention his intercourse with friends, Romans and Greeks alike, with whom he shares common tastes in literary and philosophical discourse.

It was an obligation for a man of Plutarch's class to participate in public life – he makes the point himself more than once (*Moralia* 793c–d, 794b, 811 a–c, 813c–d) – but rarely does he divulge much about his own career as a man of affairs. Still in his twenties, he successfully represented Chaeronea in an embassy to the Roman proconsul governing Greece (*Moralia* 816c–d). During the reign of Vespasian (AD 69–79), Plutarch made a visit to Rome where he impressed the Romans with his philosophical acumen – and his curiosity about Roman history. He quizzed the orator Julius Secundus about the emperor Otho and travelled throughout northern Italy with the distinguished Lucius Mestrius Florus, a friend of the emperor and consul in AD 75.[4] Whether there was a political purpose to his visit – upon his ascension, Vespasian had rescinded many of Nero's concessions to the Greek cities of the east – must remain unknown. Nonetheless, it was Mestrius Florus who secured Roman citizenship for Plutarch (*Syll.* 829a), a politically as well as socially important acquisition which Plutarch himself never mentions. Plutarch also received Athenian citizenship, and he was a long-serving priest at Delphi: after his death, the Delphians and the Chaeroneans together erected a statue in his honour (*Syll.* 843a). Trajan, we are told (but not by Plutarch), granted him the honorary trappings of a consul (*ornamenta consularia*), and in his old age he accepted from Hadrian an appointment as imperial procurator in Achaea (Syncellus 659 Dindorf), a distinction that indicates that he had earlier been enrolled in the equestrian order at Rome. Again, Plutarch says nothing of this, and some scholars are disinclined to believe in any of these imperial laurels.[5] Nevertheless, it is clear enough that Plutarch was a man of practical accomplishments, who understood the realities of Roman power and personally benefited from it.

He certainly enjoyed the acquaintance of many important Romans.[6] In addition to Mestrius Florus, Plutarch mentions grandees like Quintus Junius Arulenus Rusticus (consul in AD 92) and Gaius Minicius Fundanus (consul in AD 107). He dedicated several of his compositions, including the *Parallel Lives*, to Quintus Sosius Senecio, an honoured associate of Trajan who was a distinguished military commander and held the consulship twice (in AD 99 and 107). There is even good reason to believe that Plutarch could, in communicating with Trajan, denominate the emperor as his friend.[7] This was illustrious company, though in each instance Plutarch represents his Roman associates not as powerbrokers but rather as deeply cultured men, thoroughly at home in the world of Greek literature and learning: it is their conspicuous philhellenism – not political or practical affairs – that unites Plutarch with his Roman friends.

Plutarch became an instant and lasting classic, not least because his Lives provided (and continue to provide) a welcome, and for us an essential, window to the past. In late antiquity he was deemed a consummate scholar, and even the Church Fathers read him. The survival of so much of his work is itself testimony to his popularity. He was not forgotten in the Middle Ages, and regained a wide readership in the Renaissance, though almost exclusively in Latin (and later in vernacular) translations. His prominence became even more conspicuous in the sixteenth century, when he was rendered into elegant and lively French by Jacques Amyot (first the Lives, in 1559, followed by the *Moralia* in 1572). Thereafter Plutarch remained a profound and pervasive influence in French letters. In Thomas North's translation of Amyot, in 1579, Plutarch at last became available in English, and it was North's Plutarch who inspired Shakespeare's *Coriolanus*, *Julius Caesar*, *Antony and Cleopatra* and *Timon of Athens*.

II. *Plutarch and Biography*

Plutarch's biographies are intended to illuminate the personality and character of each subject, an inquiry that necessitates an exposition of his (always *his*) historical actions within their

historical context. But this account is not meant to be a historian's narrative of events. Plutarch insists on this distinction in
the prologue to his *Lives of Alexander and Caesar*:

> My preamble shall consist of nothing more than this one plea: if
> I do not record all their most celebrated achievements or describe
> any of them exhaustively, but merely summarize for the most
> part what they accomplished, I ask my readers not to complain
> about this. For I am writing biography, not history, and the truth
> is that the most brilliant exploits often tell us nothing of the vir-
> tues and vices of the men who performed them, whereas a chance
> remark or a joke may reveal far more of a man's character than
> the mere feat of winning battles in which thousands fall, or of
> marshalling great armies, or laying siege to cities.
>
> (*Alexander* 1)

Now it is hardly the case that Plutarchan biography eschews
battles or sieges, or political contests of great moment, nor
does every biography teem with personal details. Nonetheless,
it was never Plutarch's purpose to narrate events in their broad-
est sweep. Instead, everything included in one of his biographies
is there in order to help the reader to appreciate its hero's struggle to live a virtuous life, so that the reader, too, can make
progress towards virtue. It is on this basis that Plutarch puts
together a subject's Life: 'I . . . select from the events of his career what is noblest and most important to know' (*Aemilius* 1).
This is because our encounter with the nobility of the past has
the potential for making us better in the present (*Pericles* 1–2).
So Plutarch scrutinizes his subjects' lives in order to explicate
their virtues – and their lapses from virtue, inasmuch as few
men can sustain perfection over the course of an entire life.
This inspection, although exacting, is not harsh. Plutarch
likens the literary representation of his heroes to the work of
the best portrait painters, who neither conceal nor exaggerate
unflattering features (*Cimon* 2). Plutarch does not believe a single failure or even several failures need vitiate an entire career,
and so his moralizing examinations are invariably conducted
with a remarkable generosity of spirit.[8]

But what did it mean to imitate the virtues of a Plutarchan hero? The figures he wrote about were all of them great men, in Thomas Carlyle's sense of the phrase: valorous men of war and domineering politicians who held the highest positions in their states – in short, men at the top who, if they did not transform history, nonetheless played a major role in shaping it. Now it is true that the *Parallel Lives* was dedicated to a man who was both a political grandee and a distinguished military commander, but even Sosius Senecio served Rome as an official of the emperor and not as an independent statesman or general like Marcellus or the Elder Cato. And it is obvious that Plutarch's intended audience consisted mostly of men like himself, that is, highly educated Greeks.[9] The contrast between *their* political and social situation and the circumstances of Plutarch's ancient heroes was unmistakable.

Plutarch himself emphasizes, in his essay *Advice on Public Life* (*Moralia* 798a–825f), how much the conditions of imperial Greece differ from those of its classical past. In an age when Greek leaders no longer command armies or vanquish tyrannies (*Moralia* 805a), there is folly in confusing the present with the past:

We laugh at small children when they try to pull on their fathers' boots and wear their crowns. But what of leaders in the cities, when they foolishly excite the multitude by encouraging them to imitate their ancestors' achievements and spirit and deeds, even though those are all quite impossible under the present circumstances? Their behaviour may be laughable, but the consequences they suffer are no laughing matter. There are many other actions of the Greeks of old which one may recall in order to mould the character of the Greeks of today and give them wisdom. At Athens, for example, one might remind them not of their exploits in war but of their decree of amnesty after the rule of the Thirty, or how they fined Phrynichus for his tragedy about the fall of Miletus, or how they put on crowns when Cassander refounded Thebes, but, when they learned that at Argos the Argives clubbed to death 15,000 of their fellow-citizens, they gave orders that their entire assembly should be purified, or how, during the

Harpalus affair, as they were searching all the houses, they passed
by the one of the newly wedded bridegroom. Even now one can
imitate these things, and in doing so make oneself like one's
ancestors; as for Marathon and Eurymedon and Plataea and all
such examples as inspire the multitude with pride and fill them with
pointless boasting, we should leave them to the rhetoricians.

(*Moralia* 814a–c)

The modern Greek, Plutarch observes, need no longer exert
himself in war, and Roman administration makes it unnecessary as well as unwise to be so assertive in politics as to open
the door to faction:

Consider the greatest goods which a city can enjoy – peace, freedom, prosperity, a thriving population and social harmony. As
for peace, we have no real need of politicians at the present time,
for every war, Greek and barbarian, has vanished. We have as
much freedom as the ruling power allows us, and perhaps more
than that would not be a good thing.

(*Moralia* 824c)

Public service remains a crucial duty, but it is no longer the
same as it was in Greece's grand and glorious past. As for old-
style eminence, Plutarch asks, 'what influence, what glory can
be won by a man whose power is easily undone by an edict of
a Roman proconsul?' (*Moralia* 824e). As he makes clear elsewhere, factionalism within a Greek city can attract unwelcome
and dangerous Roman attentions (*Moralia* 813e–f).[10] The celebration and appropriation of the past, still important and
beneficial, is no longer a simple matter in the imperial age for
any Greek engaged in public life.[11]

It is perhaps worth observing that it was not only in Greece
that there existed this sense of belatedness and discontinuity
with the past. The *Satires* of Juvenal and the *Annals* of Tacitus
betray the same anxiety. In his *Dialogue on Oratory* (36), one
of Tacitus' speakers, in explaining the disparity between contemporary orators and the likes of Cicero, observes how

Orators of today have obtained all the influence that it would be right for them to be allowed in a state that is settled and peaceable and prosperous, whereas their predecessors, living in times of unrest and unrestraint, seemed to achieve more, in those days of complete disorder lacking the guidance of a single ruler.

It is no accident that this sounds very much like Plutarch, since a Roman senator, no less than any Greek public figure, was, as Plutarch puts it, 'both ruler and ruled' (*Moralia* 813e). Tacitus, like Plutarch, was a biographer, and in his *Agricola* he explores the challenges of preserving republican virtue under imperial restrictions. For all public figures in the empire, their classical heritage was as much a problem as it was a source of pride or inspiration.[12] Even a Roman, then, could learn something from Plutarch about the true value of the past.

This brings us back to the moral purpose of Plutarch's biographies, from which one should learn the right things to imitate and 'in doing so make oneself like one's ancestors' (*Moralia* 814c). This is an explicit theme in *Aratus*, probably an early biography. There Plutarch, addressing a youthful Greek audience, invites and implores his readers to emulate this great man of the past. Not that Plutarch's readers are asked to overthrow tyrants or seize the Acrocorinth, as Aratus did, but they are urged to match him in moderation and magnanimity. The same kind of ethical imitation is the point of the *Parallel Lives*, though there Plutarch's literary design, like his demands on the reader, is more sophisticated.

The *Parallel Lives* is a series of paired biographies, in each of which a Greek is matched with a Roman parallel. Plutarch began to compose these Lives early in the reign of Trajan (AD 98–117) and continued, it seems, for the rest of his life.[13] In all, he completed forty-eight biographies, of which we possess forty-six. We have unfortunately lost the first pairing, which joined *Epaminondas*, a Life of the philosophically inclined Boeotian (d. 362 BC) who defeated the Spartans at the battle of Leuctra (371 BC) and who dominated Greek politics in his day, with *Scipio Africanus*, probably not a Life of the victor at Zama (202 BC) but rather of Scipio Aemilianus, the Roman philhellene who conquered and destroyed Carthage in 146 BC.[14]

Each pairing exhibits more or less the same design. There is usually a prologue, sometimes quite elaborate, explaining Plutarch's selection of heroes. For instance, Timoleon is paired with Aemilius Paullus because the influence of fortune was so deeply implicated in the career of both (*Aemilius* 1), whereas, in the case of Marcellus and his match, Pelopidas, each was a valiant general ultimately undone by his recklessness (*Pelopidas* 1). After the prologue comes the biography of the Greek subject, then the Roman, though this order is occasionally reversed.[15] At the end Plutarch supplies a *Comparison* (*Synkrisis*) of his two heroes in which he sorts out their comparative strengths and failings, sometimes coming to an explicit conclusion about which was the better man, at others leaving it to his readers to make their own determination.[16]

Within each Life one finds, despite modest variation, a fairly uniform pattern. Plutarch usually begins by introducing his subject's family, after which he observes conspicuous features of his personality and physical appearance. A description of his early education (or its absence) routinely follows. After these preliminaries, the subject's career is the focus, reviewed largely though not entirely in chronological sequence. This narrative is punctuated by relevant digressions or clusters of telling anecdotes, which also help to mark out important phases in the hero's life. The circumstances of his death are described when they are known, and this event typically elicits a commentary on the hero's legacy, sometimes through noticing how deeply he was missed, sometimes by way of an observation on the fate of his enemies.

It is important to recognize in each of Plutarch's pairings an organic literary unity.[17] Plutarch does not simply compose two discrete Lives which he fits together by means of a prologue and suffixed *Comparison*. Instead, Lives are made parallel by means of common themes and issues that permeate and consequently integrate the two biographies within each pairing. For instance, in *Philopoemen–Flamininus*, the Greek hero, portrayed throughout as a champion of Greek freedom, is honoured in that role at the Nemean festival (*Philopoemen* 11), an event that must be read over against Flamininus' proclamation of the Greeks' freedom during the Isthmian games

(*Flamininus* 10), the moment in which the Roman becomes the liberator of Greece. Each episode is, independently, a milestone for its protagonist, but together they raise important and unsimple questions about the nature of Greek freedom and its dependence both on Greek character and Roman power, and these issues recur throughout the pairing.[18]

The finely textured parallelism in each pairing is there in order to assist the reader's moral improvement. It was Plutarch's conviction, inspired by his Platonism, that the best way to apprehend virtue is by seeing *through* superficial differences in its specific manifestations in such a way that one gets at its essential reality, an approach to moral analysis he explains in his essay *Virtues of Women*:

> There is no better way to learn the similarity and difference between the virtue of women and the virtue of men than by setting lives beside lives and deeds beside deeds ... For the virtues, on account of [individual] natures, take on certain differences, personal colours one might say, as they assimilate themselves to the habits, physical temperaments, education and way of life of the individual ... But let us not on this account create many different courages, wisdoms and justices, provided only that individual dissimilarities do not drive from any of the virtues its proper definition.
>
> (*Moralia* 243b–d)

By examining the lives of famous women when they have been set in parallel, the reader of this essay is able to perceive the reality of their shared virtue, and it is a proper understanding of *that* virtue which is the real point of the exercise. Similarly, in the *Parallel Lives*, the true subject of each pairing is, in a sense, the virtue manifested in the careers of different men in different cultural situations.[19] Parallelism thus guides the attentive reader towards moral verity, and this is how the *Parallel Lives* is able to make its readers better people. They will never imitate the specific deeds of Camillus or Fabius Maximus, but the same moral excellence *is* within their grasp, and because virtue is virtue whatever its particular setting, by behaving justly or moderately or honestly they can enact the ethical greatness of these historical figures.

Despite Plutarch's original design in the *Parallel Lives*, his biographies are usually published separately instead of in parallel. This stems from practical considerations, since most modern readers of Plutarch's Lives are interested in a specific period of Greek or Roman history, and this volume conforms to that practice.[20] However, in this collection his pairing of Philopoemen and Flamininus, who were contemporaries, appears in its entirety, including its closing *Comparison*, as Plutarch intended.

III. *The Plutarchan Hero*

Plutarch's fundamental sensibilities are aristocratic, and this perspective naturally colours his attitude towards his heroes. Consequently, high birth counts to their credit, as does the martial valour that aristocrats in Greece as well as Rome never ceased to admire. Indeed, even if Plutarch plainly prefers peace to war, it remains the case that most of his heroes are lethal warriors. As statesmen, he expects them to guide and care for the masses but not to pay heed to their shifting and mercurial moods, except to take whatever measures are needed for their conciliation and persuasion – though this should never come at the cost of irresponsible policies. For Plutarch, demagogy is always a vice.[21]

Plutarch's moralism draws on Platonic and Aristotelian ethics in conventional ways that could hardly surprise or offend his contemporaries. And so his heroes, when at their best, display courage and patriotism, are industrious and generous, and rely on intelligence and reason. They are truthful and honest in every transaction, and are consistently indifferent to wealth, luxury or sensuality. They are good family men. In politics they are committed to justice – and to freedom, even if they are kings. Plutarch especially prizes the virtue of gentleness or moderation – *praotes* – which, far from making a man weak, affords him the strength to exhibit justice and mercy: *praotes* furnishes self-restraint and leaves its possessor unaffected by injury or jealousy or the debilitating vice of anger. Another quality esteemed by Plutarch, not unconnected with *praotes*, is *philanthropia*, that is, a sense of humane civilization, which in his view is essential for attaining moral perfection.[22] Plutarch's idea of a humane civilization is a specific one, and although an inclination to *philanthropia* can occur naturally (as it does in the case of Marcellus), to flourish properly it requires the presence of Greek high culture and a philosophical Greek education.

This, for Plutarch, is a vital matter. No amount of natural talent can compensate for the absence of a properly philosophical education. Indeed, men endowed with marvellous capacities are often those at the greatest risk of veering into ethical failure if they lack the moral training required for curbing the force of their emotions and ambitions. Such is the case, in this volume, for Coriolanus, whose great nature remains untempered by philosophy, for the simple if regrettable reason that a thorough Greek education – *paideia* – was impossible for any Roman in his day. *Paideia*, for Plutarch, is almost the sine qua non of the perfect man, and its absence constitutes Plutarch's readiest diagnosis whenever any of his heroes, Roman or Greek, proves deficient.[23]

It is clear, then, that, although the subjects of Plutarch's Lives derive from different cultures and nearly always exist in different times and places, they nevertheless inhabit the same moral universe as they enact the same virtues or vices. And the criteria defining that moral universe are Greek ones. This in no way excludes Romans from the attainment of moral perfection, but it does require them to embrace the values of Greek civilization. Which, for Plutarch, was an important part of the rise of Rome. Although Numa, allegedly a pupil of Pythagoras, was a suitably learned man, an appreciation for Greek high culture came to Rome only with Marcellus and was welcomed by the Romans only gradually after that, a development unfolded in the Lives included in this volume and culminating in Aemilius Paullus, who was, according to Plutarch, an authentic philhellene.

For all its concentration on the nature of virtue, however, the *Parallel Lives* attracts readers owing to the excitement, drama and charm of its stories, those superficial enactments of virtue that nevertheless rivet our attention – and provoke our judgement. Our inclination to make our own assessment of Plutarch's heroes is stimulated by the *Comparison* that concludes each pairing. There the heroes are pitted against one another. The *Comparisons*, set next to the complexities of the twinned Lives, seem unsophisticated, and it is odd how they sometimes include information not mentioned in the relevant Life or sometimes view previously narrated events in a drastically different way. Even their Greek, while not without flourishes, is in a different and less ambitious register than the biographies they conclude. These peculiarities once led scholars to doubt their Plutarchan authorship, an extreme view that has long been abandoned.[24] Nonetheless, the *Comparisons* continue to perplex critics, who cannot agree on why it is Plutarch elected to find closure for his pairings in this remarkable device. One view is that Plutarch intended, through the inconsistencies and want of sophistication that mar the *Comparisons*, to bring to the fore the impediments that hamper simple moral judgements.[25] Another approach prefers to take the *Comparisons* at face value: after the Lives have investigated the essential quality of the virtues manifested in the pairing, the *Comparisons* urge the reader to try to decide which of Plutarch's protagonists was in fact the better man.[26] Whatever one's take on the *Comparisons*, however, it is obvious how, unlike the parallelism that structures the twinned biographies, their emphasis on contrasts signals the potential for rivalry even between very similar Romans and Greeks.

IV. *Greek and Roman in the Imperial Age*

What did it mean to be a Greek in imperial Rome? And what was the role of Greek culture in a world dominated by Roman power? By Plutarch's day, as his own career demonstrates, Greece and Rome were hardly separate worlds. This was obviously true politically, as Plutarch more than once reminds his readers in his *Advice on Public Life*, but it was also the case that, in cultural terms, there was no strict divide. Elite Romans had long immersed themselves in Greek high culture, and not even Juvenal's rants about the Orontes flowing into the Tiber can decisively distract anyone from the humane world of Plutarch's *Table Talk*, which discloses a cosmopolitan society of Romans and Greeks bound together by their common devotion to Greek literature and Hellenic values. And, on the other side of the equation, even the staunchest proponent of Hellenism had to concede that 'nowadays nearly everyone uses some Latin' (*Moralia* 1010d).

Some Greeks went further than that. By Plutarch's day, the Roman senate included Greek aristocrats, not all of whom are obvious to modern scholars because at least some of them preferred, in Roman public life, to use their Roman names instead of their Greek ones.[27] These men were Roman citizens, spoke Latin as well as Greek and carried out their duties for the greater glory of Rome. Although specific figures are elusive, Plutarch regards it as an uncontroversial observation that senatorial ambitions pervade the Greek high society of his day (*Moralia* 470c). It has even been suggested that Sosius Senecio, the dedicatee of the *Parallel Lives*, originated in the Greek east.[28] A splendid illustration of this Graeco-Roman complexity is Julius Celsus, a contemporary of Plutarch. A native of Asia Minor, Celsus was a tribune of the soldiers in a Roman legion, then a senator and finally consul in AD 92. He later held the lofty position of proconsul of Asia. His distinguished career was memorialized by his son, himself consul in AD 110, in the famous Library of Celsus in Ephesus. There Celsus' service to the empire was recorded in both Greek and Latin inscriptions, and statues of Celsus exhibited him in his Roman offices. At the same time, Celsus' monument was a *Greek* library, and his personal qualities, represented in the building's ornamentation, were expressed as *Greek* virtues.[29]

Celsus' library, like the *Parallel Lives*, raises more questions than it answers. Does it symbolize cultural unity, or is its hybridism its most conspicuous feature and therefore its most significant message? It was once natural to view Plutarch's age as a time when, as Gibbon puts it, 'the nations of the empire insensibly melted away into the Roman name and people'. The

Parallel Lives were adduced as evidence of this conciliatory spirit by Ronald Syme, who observed how they 'proclaimed the harmony and parity of the two peoples in a sequence of historical biographies, Roman worthies paralleled with Greek'.[30] Such views, however, fail to account for the predominately Greek atmosphere of Plutarch's literary project, in which Roman history has been appropriated as a part of Hellenic culture, to the extent that Plutarch can claim of Rome, in response to the Elder Cato's hostility towards Hellenic values, that 'in the age when the city rose to the zenith of her greatness, her people had made themselves familiar with Greek learning and culture in all its forms' (*Elder Cato* 23). The moral universe of the *Parallel Lives*, as we have seen, is a Greek one, in which Romans must find their fit if they are to arrive at true virtue. From this perspective, it is now commonly asserted, the *Parallel Lives* has little to do with harmony or reconciliation but is instead a statement of cultural resistance in response to Roman power.[31]

That, too, may be a bit reductive. Matters remain untidy in the *Parallel Lives* not least because Plutarch exhibits a somewhat paradoxical response to the Roman empire. On the one hand, it reflects a divine providence. On the other, it brought an end to real Greek freedom, a reality which Plutarch plainly regrets even if he accepts it.[32] Plutarch comes back to this concern more than once, especially, in this volume, in his *Philopoemen–Flamininus*, a pairing which centres around issues of power, liberation and lost independence. And so Plutarch, a loyal and dutiful citizen of Rome, remains its critical and independent subject.

Plutarch's independence, however, is hardly a hostile or antagonistic reflex. His characteristic generosity and fairness are lavished on his Roman as well as his Greek heroes, and it is important that, in the world of the *Parallel Lives*, it is very often the Roman who excels the Greek in a particular virtue. Men like Claudius Marcellus, Titus Quinctius Flamininus and Aemilius Paullus win his deep admiration – even as they bring Roman legions into places once governed by Greeks. If all this seems a bit untidy, it must be remembered that Plutarch's was an age in which controversies over cultural identity and the correct response to Roman authority were topical and unsettled matters. It should not surprise us to find Plutarch investigating these issues in a manner too thoughtful to lend itself to a simple or easy formulation.[33]

V. *Plutarch's Historical Research*

In the introduction to each biography in this volume there is a brief discussion of its historical setting and Plutarch's sources. But certain issues, and certain writers, are relevant to every Life included here. The period spanning from Romulus to Aemilius Paullus was a vast one, and it is testimony to Plutarch's deep reading and industry that he can cover so much historical territory. Plutarch read widely, taking detailed notes and also relying on what was undoubtedly a capacious memory. When it came to writing his biographies, however, his practice, sensible in a world constrained to use cumbersome scrolls instead of more easily accessible books or databases, was for long stretches to follow a single source which he then supplemented or corrected on the basis of his comprehensive research. Modern scholars are naturally interested in Plutarch's sources and the uses to which he puts them.

Plutarch is responsible for his own ethical observations, and he is very fond of digressions, which he supplies out of his own erudition. Nor, even when he is guided by a single source, is Plutarch a mere copyist. He expresses every episode in his own distinctive literary style, shaping it to suit the moral purpose of the Life in which it appears. It is owing to this preoccupation that Plutarch sometimes abridges his sources, or conflates certain historical episodes, or violates the chronology of his narrative by displacing material from various periods of his subject's life in order to illustrate what he deems an important aspect of the man's character, all practices that occasionally frustrate or irritate modern historians.[34]

But how good were Plutarch's sources? Any casual reader of Livy or Dionysius of Halicarnassus could feel justified in drawing the conclusion that the history of early Rome was fairly well known to the Romans and therefore reasonably accessible to Plutarch – and to us. This, however, would be a serious error. Although eventually the Romans worked out a cohesive – and very exciting – account of their origins and their rise as an Italian power, it was based on a good deal of legend, surmise and guesswork. Which is why their account of their early history creaks a bit. For instance, the Romans once believed, on the basis of Greek authorities going back to the fifth century BC, that their city was founded after the fall of Troy, late in the second millennium, which made sense if Rome was founded by Aeneas or any other refugee from the Trojan War.[35] Later, however, they came to the view, again on the basis of Greek scholarship, that their city was more or less the same age as Carthage, Rome's greatest rival. And so the city's foundation date was shifted to the eighth century BC. Still, the Romans' Trojan connection was preserved, and in the end, in one version at least, Aeneas brought the Trojan remnant to Italy, where he founded the city of Alba Longa. Generations later, Romulus and Remus, true princes of Alba Longa, after expelling tyranny from their native city, founded Rome. This account, which probably also owes itself to Greek invention,[36] never entirely succeeded in stifling its numerous competitors: they could still be studied well into the empire, as Plutarch amply demonstrates in his long rehearsal of them in the opening chapters of his *Romulus* (1–2).

It is remarkable but true that in many ways we know more about early Rome than did Roman historians of the republic or the empire. The material evidence of the city, for instance, makes it plain that Rome was never founded in a single go. Instead, early inhabitations ultimately congealed into an urbanized settlement, the understandable disorder of which the Romans explained by appealing to the haste with which the survivors of the Gallic sack rebuilt their ruined city (*Camillus* 32).[37] To take another example, the Romans very early on forgot that, after the fall of the monarchy, their government was first led by a single magistrate called the *praetor maximus* (literally, 'the chief leader'), a post soon replaced by two consuls.[38] Livy and Dionysius of Halicarnassus, however, speak of consuls from the start. And the Romans' own accounts of the expulsion of the Tarquins and the establishment of the republic were so cluttered by competing stories that, in the end, they settled on a tradition whereby, in the first year of the republic, they were governed by no fewer than five consuls, whose stories sit together uncomfortably.[39]

This early period was poorly known because the writing of history came late to Rome. As we have seen, on the topic of Roman history, the Romans were anticipated by the Greeks, who began making observations about Rome as early as the fifth century BC. The first true historians of Rome were the Greeks Hieronymous of Cardia (c. 360–c. 256 BC) and Timaeus of Tauromenium (c. 356–260 BC).[40] Hieronymus, in writing about the invasion of Italy by Pyrrhus of Epirus (319–272 BC), included a detailed account of early Rome. Timaeus, who composed an influential history of the western Mediterranean world in thirty-eight books, integrated the history of Rome into the established chronology of Greek events, a project he furthered in his own narrative of the Pyrrhic War (280–278 and 275 BC). The beginnings of Roman history, then, lay outside Rome.

Quintus Fabius Pictor, a senator active in the Second Punic War (218–201 BC), was Rome's first historian.[41] Writing shortly before 200 BC, and writing in Greek, he gave his readers an account of Roman history from the mythical days of Hercules down to his own time. He set a fashion of senatorial historiography – in Greek – that continued until the Elder Cato (234–149 BC), late in his life, composed his *Origines* (*Origins*). This was the first Roman history ever written in Latin, and it was only afterwards that the Romans embraced the practice of writing their history in their own language.

But what were *their* sources? It will be obvious how much historians of early Rome depended on Greek sources, whose methods for recovering the facts of the monarchy or early republic we cannot now evaluate. Of archival material for early Rome, there was little. Legends and antiquarian speculations, by contrast, were ample and no doubt credited. Family traditions, boastful and unverifiable, also enlarged and aggrandized

Roman traditions, even if some Romans were inclined to take them with a pinch of salt (see Cicero, *Brutus* 62; Livy 8.40.2). Nor were Roman historians shy in trying to recreate their past by way of applying the events of their recent history to ancient situations: the narratives in Livy that recount early republican discord rely heavily on the social conflicts experienced during the late republic, not on contemporary evidence. There is not much here to inspire unqualified confidence.[42]

The Romans themselves were sceptical about their history prior to the Gallic sack of 390 BC, a point made explicitly by Livy (6.1.1–3) as soon as he gets past that point in his narrative. And we must remain dubious about Roman history before the invasion of Italy by Pyrrhus of Epirus, when, at last, contemporary witnesses began to shape available accounts. Matters improve significantly thereafter. Fabius Pictor, however partisan, was a contemporary or near contemporary of the events he narrated in his later books. The Punic Wars and Rome's expansion into the eastern Mediterranean attracted the attention of numerous historians, Greek and Roman alike, writing from more than one perspective, and so from the third century BC onwards we possess histories that, while imperfect and incomplete, can be deemed satisfactorily grounded in reliable research.

The most important of these sources, for many of the biographies in this volume, is Polybius (*c.* 200–118 BC). He was a rising statesman in the Achaean League, as a consequence of which he found himself among the prominent Achaeans deported to Rome in the aftermath of the Third Macedonian War (171–168 BC). There he became friendly with several important senators, most crucially with Aemilius Paullus, who became his patron, and Paullus' sons, Quintus Fabius Maximus and Scipio Aemilianus. While in Rome, Polybius directed his energies towards literary composition, the most important result of which was his *Histories*, a work in forty books that attempted to explain how, in the period between the end of the First Punic War (264–241 BC) and the conclusion of the Third Macedonian War, the Romans acquired, for better or worse, their worldwide dominion. He later expanded his project down to the year 145 BC – just to investigate whether it *was* better or worse. Polybius was a universal historian, that is, his account included important events conducted by Carthaginians and Greeks as well as by Romans. In the end, his detailed, impeccably researched and knowledgeable treatment of this period isolated several causes for Rome's success, one of them being a world historical force he identifies with *tyche*, fortune.[43]

Polybius became the essential source for later writers interested in any aspect of Roman history covered in the *Histories* as well as in the rise of the Achaean League (he unsurprisingly pays a great deal of attention to the history of his native state). Consequently, his treatment of events strongly influenced Livy – and it makes a crucial contribution to Plutarch's narratives in various Lives, including those of Fabius Maximus, Marcellus, Aratus, Philopoemen, Flamininus and Aemilius Paullus. Furthermore, it is increasingly clear that Plutarch saw in Polybius an important antecedent to his own intellectual project. Polybius, like Plutarch, was a Greek expert in Roman society, and his *Histories*, by way of its universality, elevated Greek affairs to a rough equivalence with Roman ones. It is also the case that Polybius, like Plutarch, though with less philosophical rigour, intended his exposition of the past to contribute to the moral improvement of his readers (Polybius 1.1.2). Polybius was much honoured by the Romans and in his native Greece, and in him Plutarch detected a model of dignified and scholarly compliance with the political realities of Roman power.[44]

For the Lives in this volume, Plutarch often draws on Dionysius of Halicarnassus, a Greek rhetorician, critic and historian resident in Rome during the late first century BC. His *Roman Antiquities*, in twenty books, begins with the origins of Rome and carries down to the time of the First Punic War. It is a work very much in dialogue with Polybius (an author who writes so poorly, Dionysius complains in a critical essay, no one can bear to read him all the way through: see his essay *On the Arrangement of Words* 4.30). Dionysius concentrates on the earliest stages of Roman history, observing with emphasis that, in the beginning, the Romans *were in fact Greeks* (e.g. Dion. Hal. 1.5.1; 1.89.2). Hence, in his view, the acceptability of their governance of the world, in the execution of which the Romans will naturally want to take advantage of the culture of their forebears (4.26.2).[45]

Dionysius writes in Greek and primarily though not exclusively for a Greek audience. By contrast, Livy (59 BC–AD 17), who covered Roman history in 142 books from its origins to 9 BC, wrote in Latin for Roman consumption. His purpose was moral, and the chief attraction of his work was literary. Livy's account of Roman history became an instant classic and soon eclipsed all his sources and predecessors, with the exception of Polybius. Livy, although a diligent reader as well as a gifted writer, was only as good a historian as his sources permitted. Nonetheless, for later generations his became the orthodox summary of early Roman history, and so naturally Plutarch turned to Livy for the authentic Roman perspective on Rome's conquest of Carthage and of Greece. Plutarch confesses that he never became entirely proficient in Latin, but he knew he needed to know enough to read his most important Roman sources – and for Plutarch's purposes Livy was quite simply indispensable.[46]

VI. *Magistracies, Money and Measurements – and Roman Names*

Plutarch assumes his readers are more or less familiar with Roman political offices, and so a brief introduction here may lend some clarity later. Each year the people elected two *consuls*, the city's supreme magistrates and the chief commanders of its armies. They also elected *praetors*, the number of whom eventually reached six by the second century BC. Although obliged to defer to the consuls, they shared the same powers, commanding in the field and, in Rome, routinely managing the courts and summoning the senate to its duties. The remaining magistracies were *aediles*, who looked after the material fabric of the city and managed its festivals, and *quaestors*, financial officers and administrative assistants to the consuls and praetors. It was the duty of the *tribunes of the people* to ensure that no legislation or senatorial decree was passed that diminished the rights of the people (these they could block with their veto) and to protect the rights of individual citizens when they were jeopardized by magisterial excesses. Tribunes could also propose legislation. Every five years or so, the Romans elected two *censors*, who conducted a census, issued public contracts for significant building projects, like roads or aqueducts, selected the senate, exercised moral supervision over the leading classes and performed a ritual purification of the city. When the authority of any magistrate was extended beyond his term of office, which was often the case for consuls and praetors, they became promagistrates, and so were called proconsuls or propraetors. There was also an extraordinary magistrate, the *dictator*, appointed in states of emergency. The dictator held absolute power, unchecked by any colleague. His task was to restore the city's order and safety, often simply by conducting elections when there was no authority competent to do so, but at other times by taking charge of the army in situations so dire that any divisions in command were deemed dangerous. The dictator was assisted by a magistrate called *master of the horse* (*magister equitum*), his cavalry commander. It was routine for Romans to proceed through the magistracies by way of a quaestorship, followed, if they were successful, by the praetorship and consulship. The aedileship was never obligatory, nor was the tribunate, from which patricians were excluded.

The most important Roman monetary terms for this volume are the *as*, *sesterce* and *denarius*, tariffed at the rate of 10 asses = 4 sesterces = 1 denarius (around 140 BC the denarius was re-tariffed and became worth 16 asses). The denarius was in fact only introduced in 216 BC, but is often used by ancient writers to describe values and costs even in earlier periods. Plutarch equates the Roman denarius with the Greek *drachma*, with the result that 6,000 denarii (or 24,000 sesterces) = 1 *talent*. Modern equivalences can be misleading, but it is perhaps helpful to recognize that, by the late republic, an ordinary labourer could expect to earn 3 to 6 sesterces for a day's effort, while a Roman soldier was paid 1,200 sesterces each year. By contrast, a Roman knight was worth at least 400,000 sesterces and a senator at least a million.

Greek writers measure distances in *stades*. One stade consists of 6 *plethra*; a plethron is 100 Greek feet but Greek feet varied significantly: an Olympic foot, for instance, was 320 mm (12.6 inches), whereas an Attic foot was 297.7 mm (11.64 inches). It is not obvious that Plutarch was very troubled about consistency in this matter. A Roman mile was 5,000 Roman feet (1,480 m or 4,855.5 modern feet). Plutarch tends to equate 1 Roman mile with 8 stades.

All Romans had two names, a personal first name (*praenomen*) and a clan (or gentile) name (*nomen*), to which was often added a third name or *cognomen* which, in combination with the *nomen*, defined one's family (one's branch of the larger clan). For instance, Marcus Porcius Cato was a member of the clan of Porcii but his specific family were the Porcii Catones. Plutarch is inconsistent in his use of Roman names: Cato is always Cato, but Titus Quinctius Flamininus is always Titus (this use of the first name in narratives is very much a non-Roman habit). Romans also employed honorific names, the most common in this volume being the name given Publius Cornelius Scipio, who, after defeating Hannibal at Zama, was called Publius Cornelius Scipio Africanus. Plutarch (incorrectly) believed that Coriolanus was so-called for a similar reason.

NOTES

1. Philostratus, *Lives* 1.19. Philostratus, a Greek writer popular in imperial circles, lived in the third century AD. The expression *Second Sophistic* is used both to refer to the renaissance of Greek literature, especially oratory, during this early imperial period, and, more generally, to the Greek cultural scene of the early empire. There is an excellent introduction by T. Whitmarsh, *The Second Sophistic* (2005); see also the chapters by G. Woolf, E. Bowie and J. M. Dillon in *CAH* xi (2000), pp. 875–942.

2. The best account of Plutarch's career is Jones, *P&R*; see also Swain, *H&E*, pp. 135–86.

3. A lucid introduction to Plutarch's style is provided by D. A. Russell, *Plutarch* (1973), pp. 18–41.

4. For a description of Roman magistracies, see General Introduction VI.

5. Swain, *H&E*, pp. 171–2.

6. On Plutarch's network of distinguished friends, see Jones, *P&R*, pp. 39–64, and B. Puech, *ANRW* 2.33.6 (1992), 4831–93.

7. See the important paper by M. Beck in P. A. Stadter and L. Van der Stockt (eds.), *Sage and Emperor: Plutarch, Greek Intellectuals, and Roman Power in the Time of Trajan (98–117 AD)* (2002), pp. 163–73.

8. Duff, *Plutarch's Lives*, pp. 13–51, examines in detail the programmatic statements in Plutarch's biographies.

9. Although Plutarch naturally hoped for a wide readership, including Romans – see P. A. Stadter in A. G. Nikolaides (eds.), *The Unity of Plutarch's Work* (2008), pp. 123–35 – he nevertheless assumes his audience is Greek. The indications for this are several, but the most obvious sign in his biographies is his habit of explaining Roman institutions or translating Latin words, whereas he tends to take for granted a familiarity with all aspects of Greek culture; see Duff, *Plutarch's Lives*, pp. 299–300.

10. Plutarch's family knew, from the experiences of his great-grandfather, how dangerous the Romans could be (*Antony* 68): 'My great-grandfather Nicarchus used to relate how all the citizens of our native town of Chaeronea were forced [by the Romans] to carry on their shoulders a certain quantity of wheat down to the sea ... and how they were urged on by the whip.'

11. This strong consciousness of belatedness was a feature of the Second Sophistic: see G. Woolf, *Proceedings of the Cambridge Philological Society* 40 (1994), pp. 121–32, and T. Whitmarsh, *Greek Literature and the Roman Empire: The Politics of Imitation* (2001), pp. 41–89.

12. On imperial Rome's response to its discontinuity with the republic, see A. M. Gowing, *Empire and Memory: The Representation of the Roman Republic in Imperial Culture* (2005). Belatedness in imperial Latin literature is discussed by P. Hardie, *The Epic Successors of Virgil: A Study in the Dynamics of a Tradition* (1993), pp. 105–19.

13. See Jones, 'Chronology', pp. 106–14.

14. Publius Cornelius Scipio Africanus (235–183) brought the Second Punic War to an end by defeating Hannibal in the battle of Zama; Scipio Aemilianus (185–129), a son of the Aemilius Paullus included in this volume, was victorious in the Third Punic War. Aemilianus was adopted by Africanus' son and so was called Scipio Africanus.

15. The Roman Life comes first in *Sertorius–Eumenes*, *Aemilius Paullus–Timoleon* and *Coriolanus–Alcibiades*.

16. Some pairings lack a closing *Comparison*: *Themistocles–Camillus*, *Alexander–Caesar*, *Phocion–Younger Cato* and *Pyrrhus–Marius*. The *Comparison* is sometimes treated by editors as a continuation of the Life it immediately follows and, consequently, the numeration of its chapters simply continues that of the Life preceding it: for instance, the first chapter of the *Comparison Theseus–Romulus* is, in some editions, *Romulus* 30 instead of *Comparison Theseus–Romulus* 1. In this volume, chapters in the *Comparisons* display both numerations.

17. This point was made long ago by H. Erbse, *Hermes* 84 (1956), pp. 398–424, and is now well established; see further Duff, *Plutarch's Lives*, pp. 243–86, and Pelling, *P&H*, pp. 349–64.

18. See Introductions to both Lives.

19. On Plutarch's technique for apprehending virtue and its Platonic origins, see P. A. Stadter, *Plutarch's Historical Methods: An Analysis of the Mulierum Virtutes* (1965).

20. The practice of publishing the Lives separately is as old as the Renaissance: see N. Humble's essay in Humble, *Plutarch's Lives*, pp. 237–65.

21. For instance, at *Moralia* 813a–c Plutarch stresses the importance of aristocratic unity in dealing with the natural deficiencies of the multitude; on Plutarch's political views, see Swain, *H&E*, pp. 161–86.

22. On the values prized by Plutarch in his heroes, see H. M. Martin, *GRBS* 3 (1960), pp. 65–73; H. M. Martin, *American Journal of Philology* 82 (1961), pp. 164–75; and Duff, *Plutarch's Lives*, pp. 72–98.

23. Pelling, 'Roman heroes'; Swain, 'Culture'; and Duff, *Plutarch's Lives*, pp. 74–8.

24. On the *Comparisons* and their peculiarities, see W. J. Tatum in Humble, *Plutarch's Lives*, pp. 1–22.

25. Duff, *Plutarch's Lives*, pp. 243–86.

26. Tatum in Humble, *Plutarch's Lives*, pp. 1–22.

27. H. Halfmann, *Die Senatoren aus dem östlichen Teil des Imperium Romanum bis zum Ende des 2. Jh. n. Chr.* (1979); A. R. Birley, *Zeitschrift für Papyrologie und Epigraphik* 116 (1997), pp. 209–45; and O. Salomies in O. Salomies (ed.), *The Greek East in the Roman Context* (2001), pp. 141–87.

28. Jones, *P&R*, pp. 55–7.

29. See the discussion of the Library of Celsus by B. Burrell in W. J. Johnson and H. N. Parker (eds.), *Ancient Literacies: The Culture of Reading in Greece and Rome* (2009), pp. 69–96. A similarly complex monument is unpacked by M. Gleason in T. Whitmarsh (ed.), *Local Knowledge and Microidentities in the Imperial Greek World* (2010), pp. 125–62.

30. R. Syme, *Tacitus* (1958), p. 504, restating a view that goes back to K. Ziegler, in A. Pauly, G. Wissowa and W. Kroll, *Real-Encyclopädie der klassischen Altertumswissenschaft* 21.2 (1951), p. 897, and is shared by Jones, *P&R*, p. 107.

31. See e.g. Duff, *Plutarch's Lives*, pp. 301–9; Whitmarsh, *Greek Literature and the Roman Empire*, pp. 117–29; and S. Goldhill, *Who Needs Greek? Contests in the Cultural History of Hellenism* (2002), pp. 254–61.

32. See Swain, *H&E*, pp. 151–61 (Roman rule and divine providence) and 145–50 (the Greeks' loss of independence).

33. It must also be remembered that Plutarch's was an age of intense cultural competitiveness *between individuals*: see Whitmarsh, *Second Sophistic*, pp. 38–40.

34. On Plutarch's methods of historical research, see Pelling, *P&H*, pp. 1–44 and 91–116.

35. Cornell, *Beginnings of Rome*, pp. 48–80; and D. Feeney, *Caesar's Calendar: Ancient Times and the Beginning of History* (2007), pp. 88–100. There was persistent disagreement in antiquity about the date of the fall of Troy and the foundation of Carthage and of Rome. Feeney makes a compelling case for Timaeus as the source for the synchronization of Rome and Carthage.

36. Rome's first historian, Fabius Pictor, learned it from the Greek writer Diocles of Peparethus, who probably lived in the third century BC.

37. Cornell, *Beginnings of Rome*, pp. 48–57; Forsythe, *Early Rome*, pp. 78–124.

38. The traces appear at Livy 3.5–7.

39. T. P. Wiseman, *Greece & Rome* 45 (1998), pp. 19–26.

40. J. Hornblower, *Hieronymus of Cardia* (1981); and T. S. Brown, *Timaeus of Tauromenium* (1958).

41. *HRR*, vol. 1, pp. 5–39; *FGrH* 809.

42. A useful introduction to the problems of the historiography of early Rome is Forsythe, *Early Rome*, pp. 59–77. A more optimistic view of the reliability of early Roman traditions is maintained by Cornell, *Beginnings of Rome*, pp. 1–25, and S. P. Oakley, *A Commentary on Livy, Books 6–10*, vol. 1 (1997), pp. 21–108.

43. See Introduction to *Aemilius Paullus*.
44. Excellent introductions to Polybius include F. W. Walbank, *Polybius* (1972), and B. McGing, *Polybius' Histories* (2010). The influence of Polybius on Plutarch is discussed, with guidance to previous scholarship on the matter, in W. J. Tatum, *Historia* 59 (2010), pp. 448–61.
45. C. Pelling in J. Marincola (ed.), *A Companion to Greek and Roman Historiography* (2007), pp. 252–8.
46. On Plutarch's Latin, see *Demosthenes* 2. A concise but superb introduction to Livy is provided in C. S. Krauss and A. J. Woodman, *Latin Historians* (1997), pp. 51–81.

List of Surviving Lives by Plutarch

Lives included in this volume are marked with an asterisk.

PARALLEL LIVES

Theseus and Romulus*
Lycurgus and Numa*
Solon and Publicola*
Themistocles and Camillus*
Aristides and Elder Cato*
Cimon and Lucullus
Pericles and Fabius
    Maximus*
Nicias and Crassus
Coriolanus* and Alcibiades
Lysander and Sulla
Agesilaus and Pompey
Pelopidas and Marcellus*
Dion and Brutus

Aemilius Paullus* and
    Timoleon
Demosthenes and Cicero
Phocion and Younger Cato
Alexander and Caesar
Sertorius and Eumenes
Demetrius and Antony
Pyrrhus and Marius
Agis & Cleomenes and
    Tiberius & Caius Gracchus
    (a double pair)
Philopoemen* and Titus
    Flamininus*

STAND-ALONE LIVES

Artaxerxes
Aratus*

LIVES OF THE CAESARS

Galba
Otho

Further Reading

Recommended reading specific to each Life is given in the endnotes.

Good general introductions to Plutarch include D. A. Russell, *Plutarch* (1973), A. Wardman, *Plutarch's Lives* (1974) and R. Lamberton, *Plutarch* (2001). Plutarch's historical and cultural circumstances are well explained by Jones, *P&R*, and Swain, *H&E*. The most important critical studies of Plutarch's Lives are Duff, *Plutarch's Lives*, and Pelling, *P&H*. When reading the Lives, it is often helpful to consult G. J. D. Aalders, *Plutarch's Political Thought* (1982). There is a valuable critical edition of Plutarch's Lives, with French translation and concise but illuminating introductions and annotations, by R. Flacelière and E. Chambry, *Plutarque, Vies*, 16 vols. (1957–93). Of the many collections of essays dealing with Plutarch, the most important is B. Scardigli (ed.), *Essays on Plutarch's Lives* (1995). Recent collections include J. Mossman (ed.), *Plutarch and his Intellectual World* (1997), P. A. Stadter and L. Van der Stockt (eds.), *Sage and Emperor: Plutarch, Greek Intellectuals, and Roman Power in the Time of Trajan (98–117 AD)* (2002), L. de Blois, J. Bons, T. Kessels and D. M. Schenkeveld (eds.), *The Statesman in Plutarch's Lives*, 2 vols. (2004), and N. Humble (ed.), *Plutarch's Lives: Parallelism and Purpose* (2010). On questions concerning Plutarch's sources in his Roman Lives, the best place to begin is B. Scardigli, *Die Römerbiographien Plutarchs: Ein Forschungsbericht* (1979). A superb introduction to the habits of ancient historians more generally is L. Pitcher, *Writing*

Ancient History: An Introduction to Classical Historiography (2009).

There are several very fine investigations of the Second Sophistic and the Greek response to imperial Rome, any sampling of which must include T. Whitmarsh, *Greek Literature and the Roman Empire* (2001), S. Goldhill (ed.), *Being Greek under Rome: Cultural Identity, the Second Sophistic and the Development of Empire* (2001), E. N. Ostenfeld (ed.), *Greek Romans and Roman Greeks: Studies in Cultural Interaction* (2002), and D. Konstan and S. Saïd (eds.), *Greeks on Greekness: Viewing the Greek Past under Roman Rule* (2006). A useful examination of the political and cultural setting of the time is C. Ando, *Imperial Ideology and Provincial Loyalty in the Roman Empire* (2000).

The Rise of Rome

ROMULUS

INTRODUCTION TO
ROMULUS

Myth, Legend and History

In the beginning, Rome was ruled by kings. In canonical succession they were Romulus, Numa Pompilius, Tullus Hostilius, Ancus Marcius, Tarquinius Priscus, Servius Tullius and Tarquinius Superbus – Tarquin the Proud. To this list one could add Titus Tatius, the Sabine king who shared Rome's throne with Romulus, and the mysterious Mastarna, whom the Romans sometimes, for the sake of tidiness, identified with Servius Tullius. Romulus, it is obvious, is an eponymous fiction, as much a myth as the notion of the city's instant foundation, as if it were a Greek settlement, when in reality the site of Rome was gradually developed over a very long time. That, however, is a conclusion we draw from archaeological evidence. Reliable literary sources for early Rome simply do not exist – and did not exist for the first Greeks and Romans who took an interest in Roman origins. Not that the absence of a historical record did anything to impede their early speculations: we get a glimpse of the Greeks' and the Romans' intellectual industry and ingenuity simply by consulting Plutarch's brief review, at *Romulus* 1–2, of only a few of their theories explaining how Rome got its name.[1]

The Romans fleshed out the legends of their early rulers by making each into a repository for institutional developments and national characteristics. Romulus founded his city, it was ultimately agreed, in 753 BC, and in his person and character he exemplified Rome's natural belligerence, its native sense of justice and the valour of its people. His tale is by turns inspiring and disturbing. He and his twin brother, Remus, were taken from their mother and left to die on the orders of Amulius, the tyrant of Alba Longa who had usurped the throne of its rightful king, Numitor, who was also the boys' grandfather. The truth about the twins' birth, whether they were indeed the sons of Mars, is unsurprisingly left doubtful in historicizing versions of their story but was obviously essential to their original myth. Plutarch handles the matter delicately (chs. 2 and 4), as did his principal sources. Grown to manhood, the twins led a rebellion that restored Numitor to his throne and afterwards, owing to their robust personal ambitions, left Alba Longa to found a new city. Rivalry between the two brothers, however, led to the death of Remus, a baleful sign of the Romans' proclivity for bloodshed, although Plutarch like other writers introduces exculpating evidence on Romulus' behalf (ch. 10). Despite its violent beginnings, Rome managed to thrive, even if its first steps also exhibited a good deal of brute force: the Romans stole their wives from the neighbouring Sabines (an event still known as the Rape of the Sabine Women) and they thereafter expanded their domains through unrelenting warfare. In the end, Romulus' reign was marred when the king's disposition began to exhibit autocratic traits. But he never became a tyrant: he was either assassinated by his senate or vanished to become the god Quirinus.

Romulus always sustained his vitality as an exemplar for Roman authority. He appealed to Caesar and to Augustus,[2] and even in Plutarch's day the emperor could burnish his image by appealing to the legend of Rome's first king.[3] Owing to such continuing imperial interest, any biography of Romulus required delicacy.[4] His incipient autocracy when at the height of his power, for instance, was liable to be misconstrued unless handled deftly. And because accounts of his death invariably evoked the assassination of Caesar, that part of the Life was also likely to attract a close reading. So, too, Plutarch's treatment of the legend of Romulus' ultimate apotheosis, which could only activate modern concerns in imperial Rome, when emperors anticipated divine honours for themselves. In this Life, however, Plutarch is at pains to emphasize Romulus' antiquity, his sheer distance from the contemporary Roman society of which he was the founder. Although by Roman reckoning, as we have seen, Romulus was a figure of the eighth century, he is paired by Plutarch with Theseus, a denizen of the mythological past lying far beyond the grasp of authentic history.

Out of History

The pairing of Romulus with Theseus is not a neat one. The Greek was not the founder of Athens but rather the figure associated with its *synoecism*, that is, with the political unification of Attica which constituted the true beginning of Athens' political identity. For all that, however, Theseus was and remains better known as the slayer of the Minotaur and the hero who battled Amazons and Centaurs and who journeyed to the underworld. This is very different territory from any other Plutarchan pairing, and, in its Prologue, Plutarch acknowledges the anomaly. He observes how, after extending his historical range back to Lycurgus and Numa, 'there seemed to be nothing unreasonable in going back a step further to Romulus'. Except that, in taking this further step, Plutarch found himself in a world in which his ideas about history did not always apply:

> Let us hope, then, that I shall succeed in purifying fable, and make her submit to reason and take on the appearance of history. But when she obstinately defies probability and refuses to admit any element of the credible, I shall throw myself on the indulgence of my readers and of those who can listen with forbearance to the tales of antiquity.
>
> (*Theseus* 1)

One consequence of Plutarch's reaching back into the realm of mythology is that this pairing becomes something of a demonstration of his historicizing techniques. Greek and Roman scholars were keen to rationalize or contextualize myths in

order to align them with modern expectations: indeed, this
practice was essential for maintaining any continuity between
the present and the distant but still meaningful mythological
past, with events like the Trojan War or the founding of Rome.
In writing biographies of Theseus and Romulus, then, Plutarch
situated himself in a long-standing and highly respectable tradition of Greek historiography and antiquarianism.[5]

Myth and Moralism

For Plutarch, his universalizing moralism applies even in the
world of myth. And so this pairing, like the others, centres on
familiar moral themes. Romulus is both legislator and warrior,
and, as is frequently the case in Plutarch, his Life underscores
the importance of combining might with intelligence and self-
control.[6] Indeed, Romulus' final communication to the Romans
makes this very point:

> Farewell, and tell the Romans that if they cultivate self-restraint
> together with valour they will not fail to attain the utmost degree
> of human power.
>
> (*Romulus* 28)

Neither Theseus nor Romulus is an ideal monarch, however,
and, through their errors and successes alike, each serves as a
vivid reminder of how monarchical government relies on the
moral virtue of the king himself. Plutarch was keenly interested
in the extent to which any statesman's character affected his
administration,[7] and the issue was by no means irrelevant in a
world governed by emperors.

Sources

It is obvious that, in writing this Life, Plutarch turned to both
Dionysius of Halicarnassus and Livy.[8] Historians of early Rome
had no choice but to exploit antiquarian research and speculation, and Plutarch was no different: he seems to have read
Marcus Terentius Varro (116–27 BC), a Roman officer and

intellectual who rose (at an uncertain date) to the rank of praetor. He was famous for his prodigious learning, and two of his
many compositions were useful to Plutarch: *On the Latin Language* (*De Lingua Latina*, in twenty-five books, of which Books
5 to 10 are partially preserved) and *Antiquarian researches into
matters human and divine* (*Antiquitates rerum humanarum et
divinarum*, in 41 books which are now lost). Plutarch also cites
several leading authorities for early Rome, such as Diocles of
Peparethus (*FGrH* 840), a third-century BC Greek historian
who was Fabius Pictor's main source for his account of the
foundation of Rome, Fabius Pictor himself and Promathion[9]
(*FGrH* 817), the obscure author of a work on Italy. He also
mentions Juba, the learned king of Mauretania and friend of
Augustus who composed a now lost history of Rome in Greek
(*FGrH* 275). He is apparently familiar with Valerius Antias,[10]
the first-century BC Roman historian whose history of Rome
from its origins to 91 BC celebrated, perhaps tendentiously, the
achievements of the Valerian family. And it should not be forgotten that Plutarch had erudite friends from whom he could
seek advice on Roman history and antiquarianism: at *Romulus*
15 he acknowledges the help of Sextius Sulla, also a figure in
Plutarch's *Table Talk* and a distinguished man whom Plutarch
had visited in Rome (*Moralia* 727b).

LIFE OF ROMULUS

[reigned 753–716 BC]

1. Scholars disagree about the origins of the great name of Rome, the fame of which has spread among all peoples. After whom was the city named, and why? Some claim that the Pelasgians, after they had wandered over most of the known world and had overpowered most of its inhabitants, chose that spot to settle and, on account of their military might, named their city Rome.[1] Others relate a different story. When Troy was captured, a few escaped and found ships and, blown by strong winds until they reached the territory of the Etruscans, lay at anchor in the River Tiber. By this point the women were bewildered and distressed at the prospect of another sea voyage, when one of them, a woman of distinguished family and superior intelligence, whose name was Rome, proposed burning the ships. This was done, and, at first, the men reacted with fury. Afterwards, out of sheer necessity, they settled around the Palatine, where they were soon faring better than they might have hoped, for they found that the land was good and their neighbours proved friendly. At that time, they paid a distinct honour to Rome and named their city after her, since it was because of her that it had been founded. And this explains, we are told, why it is customary for Roman women to greet their kinsmen with kisses,[2] because these women, after they had burnt the ships, greeted their husbands in just this affectionate manner as they entreated with them and induced them to lay aside their anger.

2. There are others who say that the Rome who gave her name to the city was a daughter of Italus and Leucaria[3] and that she was married to Aeneas; others, however, make her a daughter

of Telephus, the son of Heracles – and still others say she was the wife not of Aeneas but of Ascanius, his son. Others again claim that the city was founded by Romanus, a son of Odysseus and Circe, while others mention the son of Emathion, Rhomus, who was sent to Italy from Troy by Diomedes.[4] Still others insist that Rome was founded by Romis, a tyrant of the Latins,[5] after he had driven off the Etruscans, who had themselves made their way from Thessaly to Lydia and then from Lydia to Italy.[6]

Not even those scholars who specify Romulus as the city's eponym, which is the version found in the best accounts, can agree about his lineage. It is claimed by some that he was a son of Aeneas and Dexithea, the daughter of Phorbas.[7] While still a baby, he was brought to Italy along with his brother Remus. But the travellers' boats were all destroyed by the floodwaters of the Tiber, except the one carrying the two boys, which was gently guided to a grassy place along the river's edge. Since the boys had been so unexpectedly saved, the site was named Rome. But others have it that Rome, a daughter of that Trojan woman I mentioned earlier,[8] was married to Latinus, son of Telemachus,[9] and bore Romulus to him. There are others who maintain that Aemilia, Aeneas' daughter, bore Romulus to Mars.[10] Still others insist that it was Lavinia[11] who bore him to Mars.

And some authors relate the most fantastic tales about his origins. Here is an example. A divine apparition visited the house of Tarchetius, the savage and cruel king of Alba Longa.[12] It took the form of a phallus rising out of his hearth, and it remained there for many days. Now in Etruria there was an oracle of Tethys.[13] When Tarchetius consulted this oracle, he received the revelation that a virgin must have intercourse with the apparition and should bear a son destined to be famous for his bravery and superior in both fortune and might. Tarchetius explained this prophecy to one of his daughters and ordered her to have intercourse with the phallus. She, however, deemed it too degrading, so she sent in a servant. Tarchetius, when he discovered this, was so outraged that he arrested both women with the intention of putting them to death. But Vesta[14] appeared to him in his sleep and warned him not to carry out the executions.

He instead instructed the imprisoned girls to busy themselves at the loom, on the pretext that, once they had completed their weaving, they should be given in marriage. Day after day they laboured at weaving, but, by night, other women, on Tarchetius' orders, unravelled their work. When at last the servant, who had been impregnated by the phallus, gave birth to twins, Tarchetius handed them over to a certain Teratius, whom he commanded to do away with them. This man carried the infants to the bank of the river and left them there. Afterwards, a she-wolf watched over them and suckled them, while birds of every species brought morsels of food, which they fed to the babies. This continued until a cowherd caught sight of the boys. Though he was astonished by what he saw, he ventured to approach the children so he could carry them away. Such was the story of their rescue, and, when the boys became men, they attacked Tarchetius and defeated him. This is the account given by a certain Promathion,[15] who compiled a history of Italy.

3. But the account of Rome's founding that possesses the greatest credibility and is most widely attested was first published among the Greeks by Diocles of Peparethus,[16] whom Fabius Pictor for the most part follows.[17] Even this version exhibits numerous variations, but the essential narrative runs as follows. The descendants of Aeneas reigned as kings in Alba Longa, and the succession eventually fell upon two brothers, Numitor and Amulius. Amulius divided their inheritance into two parts: on one side he set the throne, on the other their ancestral wealth, which included gold that had been brought from Troy. Numitor chose the throne. Consequently, Amulius took possession of the wealth, by means of which he soon came to have greater power than Numitor and easily deprived him of his kingdom. Because he was frightened that his brother's daughter might one day have children, Amulius appointed her a priestess of Vesta, which meant that she should always remain unmarried and a virgin. Some give her name as Ilia, others as Rhea, others as Silvia.

It was not long after this had taken place that she was found to be pregnant, a violation of the established law for priestesses of Vesta. The daughter of the king, Antho, pleaded with her father and persuaded him not to put his niece to death. She was instead placed in solitary confinement, so that she could not give birth without Amulius' knowledge. She bore two sons who were extraordinary for their size and beauty, an event that caused Amulius even greater alarm than he had felt before. So he ordered a servant to dispose of the boys. Some say that this servant's name was Faustulus, but others insist that it was not this man but the boys' rescuer who bore that name. This servant placed the boys in a basin and went down towards the river, where he intended to pitch them into the water. But when he saw the river in a violent flood, he was too afraid to go near it. He left the boys on the bank and departed. The inundation of the rising river lifted up the basin and bore it gently along until it came to rest at a quite comfortable place, which the Romans now call Cermalus but in the past called Germanus, no doubt because *germanus* is the Latin word for brother.[18]

4. Near this place was a wild fig tree, called the Ruminal fig, either from Romulus, as most people believe, or from the ruminating of animals that once gathered under its shade in the heat of the day, or, what is the best explanation, from the fact that there is where the infants were suckled. For the ancient Romans used the word *ruma* to refer to the nipple, and there is a goddess, still called Rumina, who looks after the rearing of young children. When sacrificing to her the Romans do not use wine but instead pour libations of milk[19] over her victims. In any case, it was here the infants lay, and, according to the historians, here is where a she-wolf nursed them and where a woodpecker came to help to feed and watch over them. These animals are deemed sacred to Mars, and the Latins especially worship and venerate the woodpecker. Consequently their mother was widely taken at her word when she claimed that her children were fathered by Mars. However, others say that she was deceived in this and that in reality it was Amulius himself who deflowered her, when he came to her dressed in armour and violated her.

In the view of some, this fable arose from the ambiguity of the name of the infants' nurse. The Latins use the word *lupa* not only for a she-wolf but also for any woman who is a prostitute, and the wife of Faustulus, the man who took in and reared the children, whose name was Acca Larentia, was such a woman. Still, the Romans offer sacrifices to her, and in the month of April the priest of Mars pours libations in her honour, at a feast called the Larentalia.[20]

5. There is another Larentia whom the Romans also honour, and the explanation is as follows. The custodian of the temple of Hercules, when once, it seems, he had nothing else to occupy his time, proposed a game of dice to the god. The terms of their wager were that, if he should win, he would gain something valuable from the god, whereas if he should lose, he would furnish the god with a sumptuous banquet and with a beautiful woman for his pleasure. He then threw the dice, first for the god and then for himself, and found that he had lost. Inasmuch as he wished to keep faith and thought it only just to meet the terms of their wager, the custodian prepared a feast for the god and hired Larentia, who, though not yet famous, was in the full bloom of her beauty. He served her dinner in the temple, where he had also placed a bed, and after the meal he closed her within, as if the god would actually embrace her. Even so, it is reported that the god did in fact come to her, and he instructed her to go early in the morning to the forum, where she should greet the first man whom she met and befriend him. Now there she was met by a citizen of mature years, who was very wealthy but childless and a lifelong bachelor, whose name was Tarratius. This man took Larentia as his lover and became so fond of her that, when he died, he named her as heir to his many precious possessions, most of which she bequeathed to the people in her will. Furthermore, so the story goes, after she had become famous, being esteemed because she was the god's beloved, she suddenly vanished at the very spot where the previous Larentia lay buried. This place is now called Velabrum,[21] because, when the river overflowed, as in the past it often did, it was there that people crossed over to the forum by way of ferries, and the

Latin word for a ferry is *velatura*. Others, however, prefer the view that this place's name is derived from *velum*, which is the Roman word for sail, for the street leading from the forum to the Circus Maximus is, from that point onwards, hung with sails by those who exhibit public spectacles. In any case, it is for these reasons that this second Larentia is honoured by the Romans.

6. Returning to the infants, Faustulus, a swineherd of Amulius, brought them up without anyone knowing of it. Or, as some record with greater likelihood, Numitor was not only aware of it but secretly aided these foster-parents as they reared the children. When they were boys, it is said, they were taken to Gabii,[22] where they were educated in literature as well as all other studies suitable for anyone of aristocratic birth. Furthermore, as the historians inform us, they were given names based on *ruma*, the Latin word for nipple, namely, Romulus and Remus, because, when they were first discovered, they were being suckled by a wild beast. Even when they were infants, the nobility of their appearance, owing to their size and beauty, indicated their genuine nature, and, as they matured, each of them proved courageous and manly. Their dispositions inclined towards dangerous actions and both were possessed of a boldness that nothing could intimidate. Still, Romulus seemed to have the better judgement and a keen political intelligence. Even in his dealings with their neighbours, in matters relating to the grazing of flocks or to hunting, he gave the strong impression of being a man born to rule rather than obey. For this reason, they remained on very friendly terms with their equals and inferiors, but despised the royal overseers and inspectors as well as the chief herdsmen, for they considered them in no respect their superiors and consequently took no notice of their threats or anger. Moreover, they devoted themselves to liberal pursuits and occupations, which in their view had nothing to do with idleness or sloth but rather consisted in physical exercise, hunting and running – as well as in repelling bandits or capturing thieves or coming to the rescue of any who were violently wronged. Thus they came to be celebrated far and wide.

7. It so happened that, when a dispute broke out between the herdsmen of Numitor and of Amulius, during which quarrel Amulius' cattle were driven off, Romulus and Remus refused to stand for it and so fell upon the robbers, putting them to flight and recovering most of the stolen cattle. This angered Numitor, but the brothers paid him little regard. Instead, they collected a following consisting of many poor men and many slaves, thereby displaying the first signs of their spirited and seditious brazenness. But while Romulus, who was devoted to sacrifice and divination, was busy in making an offering to the gods, some herdsmen of Numitor fell upon Remus as he was strolling with a few of his companions. A fight ensued, in which blows and wounds were suffered on both sides, at the end of which, however, the herdsmen of Numitor proved the stronger and took Remus prisoner. He was brought before Numitor and denounced, but Numitor did not punish him, for he feared his own brother's harshness. Therefore he went to Amulius and asked him for justice, on the grounds that, although he was the brother of the king, he had been insulted by the king's servants. The people of Alba Longa were likewise angry, for they felt that Numitor had been treated outrageously and unfairly, which led Amulius to hand Remus over to Numitor to treat him however he thought fit.

And so Numitor took him away, but, when he had reached his own home, he began to marvel at the young man's distinct superiority in stature and physical strength, and he discerned from his countenance that the courage and vigour of his mind were neither subdued nor affected by his current circumstances. Even despite this, however, it was owing chiefly to the inspiration of some divinity, busy shaping this prelude to momentous events, that Numitor was seized with the truth and prompted by a fortunate intuition to ask Remus who he was and what were his origins. His gentle voice and kindly demeanour encouraged Remus and made him hopeful, and as a result he replied boldly: 'I shall conceal nothing from you, for in your conduct you are more like a king than Amulius. You listen and weigh the evidence before punishing, whereas he surrendered me for punishment without first judging my case. In the past, my twin brother and I believed we were the children of Faustulus and Larentia, who are servants of the king. Now, however, since we have been accused and denounced before you and we stand in peril of our lives, we hear great things about ourselves. Whether or not they are true will probably be decided in this present danger. Our birth is said to have been secret, our infant nurture fabulous. For although we were abandoned as prey to the birds and to the beasts, we were actually fed by them, from the milk given by a she-wolf and morsels brought to us by a woodpecker, as we lay in a basin alongside the great river. The basin exists still: it is preserved, made of bronze bands, and on it there is an inscription, now nearly entirely effaced, which will perhaps, after our deaths, help to inform our parents what became of us.'

When Numitor heard these words, and after he had calculated, on the basis of the young man's appearance, how long ago these things must have happened, he embraced a very gratifying hope. But first he had to devise a means of discussing these matters in secret with his daughter, for she was still kept under close guard.

8. When Faustulus heard that it was Remus who had been captured and handed over to Numitor, he called on Romulus to go to his aid. It was then, for the first time, that he gave him a complete account of his origins. Previously he had spoken of them only enigmatically, though he had revealed just enough for the twins, when they pondered the matter, to entertain elevated ambitions. Faustulus himself then took up the basin and rushed to see Numitor, for he was seized by fear and dreaded that he might arrive too late. His manner aroused the suspicions of the king's sentries, and when he was questioned by them his answers were confused, nor did he manage to conceal the basin under his cloak. Now it happened that one of these sentries had been a member of the detachment that had taken the boys to cast them in the river and so had played a part in their exposure. As soon as he saw the basin, he recognized its construction and its inscription and so began to realize what was actually taking place. He immediately informed the king

and brought Faustulus before him for interrogation. Beset by
so many grave dangers, Faustulus' resolution was broken, and
yet even then he did not allow everything he knew to be forced
from him. The boys, he confessed, were alive, but he said that
they lived as herdsmen far away from Alba Longa; as for himself, he was taking the basin to Ilia, who often desired to see it
and touch it, as a reassurance of her hopes for her children.

Amulius now behaved just as men typically do when they
are perplexed and are motivated by fear or anger. He selected a
man who was thoroughly upright – and one of Numitor's
friends – to go and inquire of Numitor whether he had received
any report of the children's remaining alive. When this man
arrived and saw that Numitor was all but holding Remus in an
affectionate embrace, he immediately confirmed the hopes of
each and exhorted them to take swift action. He straightaway
joined in their cause and acted alongside them, for the critical
moment had come and, even had they wished it, there could be
no delay. Romulus was now very near, and he was being joined
by the many citizens who hated and feared Amulius. He was
also leading a large force of his own, which was divided into
units of a hundred men. The man who led each of these detachments carried aloft a bundle of hay and shrubs tied around the
end of a pole. Now the Latin word for a bundle is *manipulus*,
and it is on this account that, to this very day, the Romans call
the soldiers who serve in these companies *manipulares*. At the
same time that Remus was inciting revolt within the city, Romulus attacked it from outside. As for the tyrant, still perplexed
and confused, he did nothing. He did not even form a plan for
his personal safety, and so was captured and put to death.

Most of this narrative is reported by Fabius and by Diocles
of Peparethus, who appears to have been the first man to publish an account of Rome's foundation. There are some, however,
who remain suspicious of its dramatic and fabulous quality.
But we must believe it when we recognize how creative a poet
Fortune can be, and when we accept that the grandeur of the
Romans could never have been raised to such a peak had their
origins not been divine and attended by profound marvels.

9. After the death of Amulius and when public order had been restored, Romulus and Remus were unwilling to dwell in Alba Longa unless they were its rulers, nor would they consent to take power while their grandfather lived. Consequently, they handed the government of the city over to Numitor. They also paid their mother every suitable honour. They then decided to dwell apart and found a city in the region where they had been nourished as infants. This, in any case, was the most seemly of their possible motives. Perhaps, however, they had little choice, now that they had been joined by many slaves and fugitives, but to dismiss the whole of their following by dispersing them here and there or to live separately with these men. For it is undeniable that the inhabitants of Alba Longa would not permit the fugitives to intermarry with themselves, nor would they grant them citizenship. This is made clear, in the first place, by the Romans' seizure of the Sabine women,[23] an action they undertook, not owing to brazenness but rather to sheer necessity when they could not win consent to find wives among their neighbours (as evidenced by how, after the Romans carried off these women, they showed them every honour). The second proof is this: soon after their city was founded, the Romans established a sanctuary where fugitives could take refuge, which they called the temple of the god Asylum. There they received anyone, and none was handed over, not slave to master, not debtor to creditor, nor murderer to magistrate. Instead, they declared this place a secure asylum for all men, which they had created in accordance with an oracle delivered by the Pythian.[24] The result of this is that the city was very soon well populated, for it is said that at first there were no more than a thousand houses in Rome. But more on these matters presently.

No sooner had they set out to found their city than a controversy arose over its location. Romulus established the site called Roma Quadrata (the latter word meaning square) and wished to build the city in that place.[25] Remus, however, laid out a defensible precinct on the Aventine Hill, which was given the name Remorium, after his own name, but is now called Rignarium.[26] They agreed to settle their dispute by looking to the flight of sacred birds, and so, when each had taken a position distant from the other, we are told that six vultures were seen by Remus, but twice that number by Romulus. Some authorities, however, report that, whereas Remus in fact saw six, Romulus actually lied about the twelve, but, when Remus came to report his observation, at that very moment twelve birds did appear to Romulus. This is why, to the present day, the Romans, whenever they take auguries from the flights of birds, pay the most regard to vultures.

Herodorus Ponticus[27] makes the point that even Heracles rejoiced whenever a vulture appeared to him while he was engaging in some exploit. This is because the vulture is, of all animals, the least destructive to human concerns, for it does no harm to grain or fruit-trees or cattle. Instead, it feeds on carrion. It does not kill, nor will it even harm another living creature. And, as for other birds, a vulture will not touch them, even when they are dead, on the grounds that they are kindred species – unlike eagles and owls and hawks, which peck at their own kind, even when they are alive, and kill them. And yet, as Aeschylus puts it, 'how could a bird that feeds on another bird be pure?'[28] Furthermore, all other birds rally round our eyes, so to speak, and let themselves be seen constantly, whereas a vulture is a rare sight, and we scarcely ever come upon a vulture's young. In fact, some men entertain the strange notion that vultures come here from some distant and alien land, so rarely and infrequently do they appear, which is of course the very quality that soothsayers deem characteristic of any apparition that does not occur naturally or spontaneously but only through divine agency.[29]

10. When Remus learned of his brother's trick, he was very angry. Now Romulus was at work digging a trench along the course he intended the city's wall to run. Remus ridiculed some of these works, others he obstructed. Finally, when he leapt over the trench, he was struck down, by Romulus himself according to some authorities, by Celer, one of Romulus' companions, according to others. Faustulus also fell during this struggle, along with his brother Pleistinus, who, we are told,

had aided him in bringing up Romulus. Celer then removed himself to Etruria, and it is because of him that Romans call men who are fast or swift *celeres*. Quintus Metellus is an example. Only a few days after the death of his father he exhibited gladiatorial games in his honour. Everyone was amazed by the speed at which these preparations were made and so they gave him the surname *Celer*.[30]

11. Romulus buried Remus in the Remoria,[31] along with his two foster-fathers. Thereafter he turned to the foundation of his city. He first summoned men from Etruria, who guided and instructed him in every detail, so that everything was done in strict accordance with sacred rites and formulas, as if in a religious ceremony. And so a circular trench was dug around what is now the Comitium[32] and in it they deposited the first fruits of all things that are essential to life or deemed precious by custom. Finally, each man brought a small portion of earth from his native land and threw it in among the first fruits, so that everything was mixed together. The Romans call this trench by the same word they use to describe the heavens, which is *mundus*.[33] With this as its centre, the Romans then laid out their city around it in a circle. The founder fitted a bronze ploughshare to a plough and yoked to it a bull and a cow, and with this he drove a deep furrow around the limits of the city. Meanwhile, it was the task of those following him to turn any clods of earth thrown up by the plough inwards, towards the city, and to leave none turned outwards. By means of this boundary the Romans defined the course of their city wall, and it is called, in a contracted form, *pomerium*, which means behind or next to the city wall.[34] Wherever they decided to make a city gate, at that point they lifted the plough from the earth and carried the ploughshare, thus leaving a space that was not ploughed. This is why the Romans regard the city wall as sacred, but not its gates. Indeed, if they believed that the gates were sacred, they could not, without fear of offending the gods, bring into the city, or remove from the city, those things which, though necessary, are nevertheless ritually unclean.[35]

12. It is agreed that the city was founded on the eleventh day before the Calends of May,[36] and the Romans celebrate this day with a religious festival which they call the birthday of their country. When this festival first began, so they say, it included the sacrifice of no living creature. This was because they believed that this occasion, which marked the birth of their country, ought to remain pure and undefiled by blood. But, even before the city was founded, they celebrated, on the same day, a pastoral festival known as the Parilia.[37]

It is still the case that Roman months do not correspond with Greek ones, but it is reported that the day on which Romulus founded his city was precisely the thirtieth day of the month[38] and, on that day, the conjunction of the moon and sun produced an eclipse, which is believed to be the one observed by Antimachus,[39] the epic poet of Teos, during the third year of the sixth Olympiad.[40] Now, in the time of Varro the philosopher,[41] a Roman who was superbly well read in history, one of his companions was a philosopher and mathematician named Tarutius.[42] This man's speculative instincts had brought him to the study of astrology, in which subject he was regarded as an expert. Varro once suggested to him that he deduce the moment of Romulus' birth, down to the day and the hour, drawing his conclusions from the recorded events of the man's life, just as if he were solving a problem in geometry. After all, he said, the same science that can predict the events of a man's life on the basis of the time of his birth must be able, on the basis of the actual events of a man's life, to calculate the time of his birth. Tarutius undertook this assignment, and, after a close study of Romulus' experiences and actions, as well as an examination of the length of his life and the manner of his death, pronounced, with a bold and even daring confidence, that Romulus had been conceived in his mother's womb during the first year of the second Olympiad, on the twenty-third day of the Egyptian month of Choeac,[43] in the third hour, during a total eclipse of the sun. He furthermore concluded that Romulus was born on the twenty-third day of the month of Thoth,[44] at sunrise, and that Rome was founded by him on the ninth day of the month of Pharmuthi,[45] between the second and the third hour –

for the fortune of a city, like that of a man, is believed by astrologers to be governed by a specific moment in time, which is determined by the position of the stars when the city is founded. Perhaps it will be the case that these conclusions, and other reports of their like, will, on account of their novelty and peculiarity, attract readers more than they offend them, owing to their fantastic quality.

13. After the founding of the city, Romulus' first act[46] was to select from the multitude those men who were of a suitable age and divide them into military companies, each of which consisted of 3,000 infantrymen and 300 cavalry. Each company was called a *legion*[47] because its soldiers were selected from the whole of the populace. The remainder of the population he then established as the people, and in Latin this multitude is called *populus*. He appointed a hundred of the best men to be his advisers, and he designated them *patricians*[48] and their assembly as the *senate*. The word *senate* literally means a council of elders,[49] and, according to some sources, these senators were described as patricians because they were fathers of legitimate offspring. Others, however, attribute this title to the fact that each of these men could demonstrate his own legitimacy, by adducing the identity of his father, which few among those who first streamed into the city were able to do. Still others derive the word from *patronage*, the word they used then – and use to this day – to describe the protection of the weak by the powerful, for they believe that among the companions of Evander[50] there was a man named Patron[51] who defended and protected the poor and the needy and who left his own name as the word for this institution. By far the likeliest explanation, however, is that Romulus deemed it a duty of the most distinguished and powerful men in the city to look after the lowly with fatherly care and concern. At the same time, he taught the rest of the populace neither to fear their superiors nor to resent their honours, but rather to think of them fondly and regard them and even address them as fathers. Hence their designation. For, even today, whereas non-Romans refer to men who are in the senate as *authorities*, the Romans themselves call

them *conscript fathers*,[52] a title conveying the highest honour and dignity but inciting the least degree of envy. At first they were called simply *fathers*, but, later, as more men were enrolled in their number, they were addressed as *conscript fathers*, and this more solemn title was employed by Romulus to distinguish the senate from the common people. He found other means as well for discriminating between the powerful and the common people: the former he called *patrons* (which is Latin for *protectors*), the latter *clients* (which means *dependants*). At the same time, he inspired in each class an astonishing degree of goodwill for the other, and this became the basis for important rights and obligations. Patrons advised their clients in legal matters, defended them in court and offered them counsel and assistance in all their affairs. For their part, clients displayed their devotion to their patrons not simply by holding them in high esteem but also, should their patron fall on hard times, by contributing to his daughter's dowry or helping him to pay his debts. And neither the law nor any magistrate could compel a patron to give evidence against his client, nor a client against his patron. This relationship persists, and it is felt by the Romans to be base and dishonourable for the powerful to take money away from men in humble circumstances. This, however, is a sufficient discussion of these matters.[53]

14. It was during the fourth month after the founding of the city, according to Fabius, that the Romans audaciously carried off some of the Sabine women. Some authorities say that this event took place because Romulus was, owing to his very nature, disposed to warfare and because he had come to believe, on account of certain oracles, that Rome was destined to be increased and made great by war, until she became the greatest of all cities. Consequently, he initiated hostilities against the Sabines. This is why so few maidens were seized by the Romans – only thirty in fact – because Romulus wanted war instead of marriages. But this is improbable. Instead, because he observed that his city was quickly becoming filled with newcomers, few of whom had wives and most of whom amounted to a contemptible rabble of poor and obscure men unlikely ever

to form themselves into a unified and strong society, Romulus devised this injury in the hope that it might, once the Romans had won the affections of the women they carried away, lead to some sort of confederation and community with the Sabines. And so he undertook this exploit in the following way.[54]

He began by spreading a report that he had discovered, hidden under the earth, an altar of a certain god, whom they called Consus. He is either a god of counsel, for *consilium* is the Latin word for *counsel* and the Romans call their chief magistrates *consuls*[55] (which means *counsellors*), or he is Poseidon the god of horses,[56] for his altar is located in the Circus Maximus, where it remains hidden, except during horse races, when it is uncovered. Some, however, make the simple assertion that, inasmuch as counsel is given secretly and in private, it is perfectly reasonable for an altar to the god of counsel to remain hidden. In any case, when the altar was discovered, Romulus announced a splendid sacrifice and a public festival to honour the occasion, with contests and spectacles. The event attracted a great throng of celebrants, and Romulus, wearing a purple cloak and seated with his chief men, presided over the festival. A signal had been devised for marking the right moment to seize the women. Romulus would rise to his feet, fold a part of his cloak and twist it behind him. Many of the Romans were armed and were watching Romulus closely. Once the signal was given, they drew their swords and rushed forward with a great cry. They carried off the daughters of the Sabines, but allowed the men to escape and offered no pursuit. Some sources report that only thirty women were seized, and that the *curiae* were named after them.[57] Valerius Antias, however, says that 527 women were taken, while Juba puts the number at 683, all of them virgins.[58] This latter fact was Romulus' best defence of his actions, for the Romans captured only one married woman, Hersilia, and she was taken in error, for the Romans did not seize these women in order to violate them or to do them an injustice but rather to unite and affiliate Romans and Sabines through the most compelling of all bonds. As for Hersilia, according to some accounts she was given in marriage to Hostilius,[59] one of the most distinguished men in Rome. In others,

however, she was given to Romulus himself[60] and bore him
children: a daughter named Prima, from the order of her birth,
and only one son, whom Romulus named Aollius on account
of the large number of citizens whom he ruled. Later he was
called Avillius. This information, however, is taken from
Zenodotus[61] of Troezen, and there are many authorities who
contradict him.

15. The story is told that, among those who were carrying off
the Sabine women, there happened to be some men of mean
status who were dragging along a maiden who far excelled the
others in beauty and stature. When some men of higher rank
appeared and attempted to take her away, they cried out that
they were taking the girl to Talasius, a young man who was
already distinguished for his merit. The other party, when they
heard this, registered their approval with shouts and applause.
Some of them, motivated by goodwill and a desire to please
Talasius, went so far as to follow along, crying out his name.
This is why, down to the present day, the Romans shout
talasius at weddings, just as Greeks cry *hymenaeus*, for the story
goes that Talasius was very fortunate in his wife.[62]

Sextius Sulla of Carthage,[63] however, a man of deep culture
and elegance, told me that Romulus supplied this name as the
watchword for seizing the Sabine women, and so all those who
carried the maidens off cried out *talasius* and this is the reason
for the custom that prevails at weddings. But most authorities,
and Juba is one of them, believe the cry is an exhortation and
an encouragement to industry – especially to spinning wool,
the Greek word for which is *talasia*,[64] for in those days Greek
words had not been entirely supplanted by Italian ones. Now if
this is correct and the Romans did, in those days, use the word
talasia as we do, then a more believable explanation of this
custom can be conjectured. When the Sabines, after their war
against the Romans, agreed to be reconciled with them, it was
stipulated that the Romans' Sabine wives should undertake no
other task for their husbands apart from those associated with
spinning. Thereafter it became customary at weddings for those
who gave the bride away or accompanied her to her new home

or simply were present on the occasion to cry out *talasius* playfully, in this way attesting that the woman was being led away
to perform no other service than spinning wool. Even today,
after all, it remains the custom that no Roman bride steps
across the threshold of her new home but instead is lifted up
and carried in, because long ago the Sabine women were carried into their new homes by force and did not enter voluntarily.
Some writers add that the custom of parting a bride's hair with
the head of a spear symbolizes how the first Roman marriages
involved fighting and warfare. These are subjects I have com-
mented on more fully in my *Roman Questions*.[65] In any case,
the seizing of the Sabine women took place on the eighteenth
day of the month that was once called Sextilis but is now called
August, on which day the festival known as the Consualia is
celebrated.[66]

16. The Sabines were a numerous and belligerent nation who
lived in unwalled villages, for they thought it only fitting that,
being Lacedaemonian colonists, they remain proud and fearless.[67] Nevertheless they were now impeded from fighting on
account of the precious hostages held by the Romans, for they
were afraid for their daughters. Consequently, they sent ambassadors to Romulus with fair and moderate proposals: he should
restore the maidens, make amends for his violent action, and
then, through customary diplomacy, establish a friendly alliance
between the two peoples. But Romulus would not return the
women and instead demanded that the Sabines accept a union
with the Romans. In reaction to this, the Sabines applied themselves to long deliberations and extensive preparations for going
to war – with the exception of Acron, the king of Caenina,[68] a
bold man who was skilled in warfare. From the beginning he
had been suspicious of Romulus' daring acts, and what happened to the women made him certain that Romulus was now
a threat to everyone and would remain intolerable if he were
not punished.[69] Therefore he went to war, advancing against
Romulus with a great army. Romulus marched out to meet him.
After they came within sight of one another and each had taken
the other's measure, the two men accepted one another's

challenge to single combat, while their armies stood by under arms. Romulus then made a vow that, if he should vanquish and slay his adversary, he would carry the man's armour to Rome, where he would dedicate it to Jupiter. And Romulus did defeat Acron and slay him, after which he routed his army in battle and captured his city as well. He did no harm to the captured Sabines beyond ordering them to destroy their homes and follow him to Rome, where they would become citizens with rights equal to those of all other Romans. And it is this more than anything else that has made Rome great: Rome always annexes and incorporates the peoples whom she conquers.[70]

Romulus now considered carefully how he might fulfil his vow in a manner most pleasing to Jupiter and with a spectacle that would delight the citizens of Rome. Accordingly, he cut down a gigantic oak tree growing in the camp, fashioned it into the shape of a trophy[71] and fastened to it all of Acron's armour, each piece in its proper position. He then donned a special garment[72] and wreathed himself in laurel, after which he lifted the trophy onto his right shoulder, where he held it erect, and set forth, leading a paean of victory which was sung by his army as it followed him under arms. This procession was welcomed by the citizens with joy and wonder, and it is the origin and model for all subsequent Roman triumphs.[73] The trophy was consecrated as a dedication to Jupiter Feretrius,[74] for the Latin word *ferire* means *to smite*, and Romulus had prayed to smite his enemy and to slay him. Varro claims that these spoils are called *opima* because *opes* is the Latin word for wealth. A more plausible explanation of the expression would derive it from the valiant deed involved, for *opus* is the Latin word for an exploit, and it is only a general who has slain an enemy general with his own hand who is permitted to dedicate the *spolia opima*.

Only three Roman generals have achieved this distinction. Romulus was the first, for slaying Acron the king of Caenina. After him came Cornelius Cossus,[75] who slew Tolumnius the Etruscan. And finally Claudius Marcellus, who vanquished Britomartus,[76] who was king of the Gauls. Now Cossus and Marcellus each entered the city in a chariot driven by four horses, although both of them carried their own trophies.

Dionysius of Halicarnassus, however, is incorrect when he reports that Romulus employed a chariot,[77] for historians agree that Tarquinius,[78] the son of Demaratus, was the first of the kings to elevate the triumph to such a pitch of pomp and magnificence, although other authorities name Publicola as the first man who celebrated a triumph in a chariot.[79] In any case, one can inspect the statues in Rome that depict Romulus bearing his trophy. Each of them represents him on foot.

17. After the city of the Caeninenses had been taken and while the rest of the Sabines continued making their preparations for war, the inhabitants of Fidenae, Crustumerium and Antemnae[80] joined their forces against the Romans. They, too, were defeated in the ensuing battle. They surrendered their cities for destruction, their lands to be divided and themselves to be transferred to Rome. Romulus distributed among his citizens all the lands that were taken, except for any property belonging to fathers of the maidens who had been carried off, which he allowed the owners to keep for themselves.

These events so angered the rest of the Sabines that they appointed Tatius[81] their general and marched on Rome. Now the city was securely protected by a steep fortress, which today is the Capitol, on which the Romans stationed a garrison whose captain was named Tarpeius – not a maiden named Tarpeia, as some sources report, thereby making Romulus seem foolish. Instead, Tarpeia was a daughter of this captain of the guard and it was she who betrayed the place to the Sabines because she coveted the golden bracelets which they wore on their left arms. Indeed, she demanded what they wore on their left arms as the price for her treachery. Tatius agreed to this, whereupon she opened one of the city's gates during the night and allowed the Sabines to enter. Antigonus,[82] I suppose, is not the only man who has said that, whereas he loved men who were willing to betray their side to him, he hated the men who actually did so. Caesar, too, in speaking of Rhoemetalces[83] the Thracian, said that he loved treachery but loathed a traitor. And this is the general feeling held against wicked men by those who require their services. Just as they need certain savage beasts in order to exploit their poisonous bile, so they welcome such people only as long as they are useful, but, after getting what they want from them, despise their wickedness. This is exactly how Tatius felt about Tarpeia when he gave the order to the Sabines, in observance of their agreement, not to deny her anything which they wore on their left arms. He acted first, removing from his arm not only his bracelet but also his shield, both of which he threw at her. His soldiers did the same, and the girl, struck by the gold bracelets and buried beneath the shields, perished owing to their quantity and weight. Tarpeius was also condemned for treason, after he was prosecuted by Romulus. This is the account of Sulpicius Galba,[84] as reported by Juba.

There are other traditions about Tarpeia, none of them credible, alleging that she was the daughter of Tatius, the leader of the Sabines, and that, because she had been forced to live with Romulus, she acted as she did and was punished by her own father. Antigonus[85] is one of these authors. And the poet Simylus[86] is simply talking nonsense when he writes that Tarpeia betrayed the Capitol not to the Sabines but to the Gauls, because she was in love with their king. This is how he puts it:

> Tarpeia, who dwelt hard by the steep Capitoline,
> Ushered in destruction for the walls of Rome;
> In her desire for the marriage bed of a Celtic chief[87]
> She betrayed the homes of her fathers.

And, somewhat later in his poem, he writes of her death:

> In their exultation, neither the Boii nor the myriad Celtic
>   tribes,
> Did cast her into the streams of the Po;
> But they hurled upon the hated maiden shields from their
>   warlike arms,
> And with their ornaments they slew her.

18. In any event, Tarpeia was buried on the Capitol and the place was called the Tarpeian Hill until King Tarquinius,[88] who

consecrated it to Jupiter and removed her remains, after which time the name was forgotten, except for the cliff on the Capitol that is still called the Tarpeian Rock, from which the Romans throw evildoers.[89]

When he discovered that the citadel had been occupied by the Sabines, Romulus angrily challenged them to fight, and Tatius boldly accepted, since he knew that, should they suffer a defeat, the Sabines had a secure refuge. The space between them, where the battle was to be fought, was restricted by many hills, which meant that, owing to the difficulty of the terrain, their battle would be bitter and hard for both armies, for there was little room for flight or pursuit. Only a few days before this, moreover, the river had overflowed and had left in the plain where the forum now is a deep but indistinct layer of mud. This hazard, mucky underneath its surface and so very dangerous, was at once hard to detect and hard to avoid. The Sabines, completely unaware of it, were rushing towards this very place when they were saved by a stroke of good fortune. Curtius, a distinguished man who was bold and eager for fame, galloped far ahead of the rest, only for his horse to become mired in the mud. For some time he tried, both with his whip and with cries of encouragement, to goad his horse to free itself, but when this failed he abandoned his horse and saved himself. On account of this episode, the place is to this day called the Lake of Curtius.[90]

Because of this, the Sabines avoided the hazard. Still, though they fought staunchly, the battle remained undecided. Indeed, many fell, including Hostilius, who, some report, was the husband of Hersilia and who was the grandfather of Hostilius, the king who succeeded Numa.[91] As the battle raged, there were many struggles within a short time, as one would expect. The most memorable of these was the final one, when Romulus was struck on the head with a stone and nearly fell to the ground, unable to fight on against the Sabines. At that the Romans gave way and retreated in flight towards the Palatine, since they had been ejected from the plain. Soon, however, Romulus recovered from the blow and sought to recall his fleeing troops, and so he cried out in a great voice that they should stand firm and

fight. But all around him was panic, and not a single man had
the boldness to turn and do battle. Romulus then raised his
hands to heaven and prayed that Jupiter stay the army and not
allow the Roman cause to fall but lift it up instead. No sooner
had he completed his prayer than the Romans were overcome
by reverence for their king and the fugitives' fear was replaced
by courage. The place where they first made their stand is now
the site of the temple of Jupiter Stator, an epithet which one
could interpret as *Stayer*.[92] The Romans then closed their ranks
and drove the Sabines back to the place where the Regia and
the temple of Vesta[93] now stand.

19. There, as both sides were preparing to renew their struggle,
they were transfixed by a sight that was strange to behold – a
spectacle beyond all description. For they saw the daughters of
the Sabines, the women who had been carried off by the
Romans, rushing in from all directions, amid cries and lamentations. Like women divinely possessed, they charged past
armed men and corpses to find their husbands and fathers.
Some of them bore infants in their arms; others covered their
faces in dishevelled hair; all of them called, with tender names,
now upon the Sabines, now upon the Romans. Both armies
were deeply affected, and they drew apart so the women could
come between their battle-lines. All began to weep, and a profound degree of pity was stirred by the sight of these women
and still more by their words, which passed from just and candid upbraiding to supplication and entreaty.

'What terrible injury have we done you', they said, 'that we
have had to suffer, and must continue to suffer, such cruel evils?
Although we were carried off, violently and lawlessly, by the
men to whom we now belong, nevertheless, after being carried
off, we were neglected by our brothers and fathers and kinsmen for so long a time that we are now united, by the strongest
of ties, with those whom we had previously hated. And so now
we are fearful for these same men, who treated us violently and
lawlessly, whenever they go out to battle, and we mourn for
them if they are slain. For, while we were still maidens, you did
not come to exact revenge against the men who wronged us,

yet now you seek to force wives from their husbands and mothers from their children, a rescue of our wretched selves that is more deplorable than your previous neglect and abandonment. Such is the love shown us by these men! Such is the compassion shown us by you! Even if you had gone to war for another reason, it is only right that you halt for our sakes, for you are now fathers-in-law and grandfathers and kinsmen to one another. But if this war is being waged on our behalf, then lead us away together with your sons-in-law and your grandchildren and in this way restore to us our fathers and our kinsmen, but do not deprive us of our children and husbands. We beg you, do not make us captives a second time!'

Hersilia made many such appeals as this and was joined in her entreaties by the rest of the women. Consequently, a truce was declared and the leaders from both sides convened a summit. During this time, the women introduced their husbands and children to their fathers and brothers. They also took food and drink to any who needed it, and carried the wounded to their houses, where they nursed them. It was soon obvious that they were indeed mistresses in their own homes, with husbands who were attentive and gladly showed them every honour. Accordingly, terms were agreed between the Romans and the Sabines, whereby any woman who wished to do so might continue living with her husband, although, as I remarked earlier, she must be exempt from every form of service to her husband except spinning wool.[94] It was also agreed that the city should be the common property of Romans and Sabines, and should be called Rome, after Romulus, while all citizens of Rome should be called Quirites, after the native city of Tatius.[95] Moreover, Romulus and Tatius should be joint kings and joint commanders of the army. The place where these agreements were made is even now called the Comitium,[96] for in Latin the word *comire* means *to meet*.

20. Thus the city of Rome was doubled in population, and a hundred of the Sabines were selected to become patricians,[97] while the legions were expanded to 6,000 infantrymen and 600 cavalrymen each. The people were divided into three

tribes, one of which was called Ramnes, after Romulus, the second Tities, after Tatius, and the third Luceres, from the sacred grove into which many had fled, during the time of asylum, after which they had become citizens (the Latin word for *grove* is *lucus*).[98] That there were originally three tribes is demonstrated by their Latin designation, for even now they are called *tribes*[99] and the chief of a tribe is called a *tribune*. Each tribe is divided into ten phratries,[100] which some claim were named for the thirty Sabine women who were abducted. But this seems untrue, since many phratries have topographical names. However, the Romans did accord these women many concessions and honours, among which are the following: men must yield to them when they are walking in the street; men may not utter any indecency in the presence of a woman; no man may be seen naked by a woman, and if he is, he is liable to prosecution in the courts that try homicide.[101] Furthermore, their children wear what the Romans call a *bulla*,[102] a kind of necklace that takes its name from its shape since it looks like a bubble, and a robe bordered with purple.

At first the two kings did not meet in a single council. Instead, each met separately with his own hundred senators and only subsequently did they join the two assemblies into a common body, as is still the case today. Tatius made his home where today stands the temple of Moneta,[103] while Romulus made his beside the Steps of Cacus,[104] which are near the descent from the Palatine to the Circus Maximus. This is where they say there once grew a sacred cornel tree, and the following legend is told about it. In order to test his strength, Romulus once hurled a spear, whose shaft was made of cornel wood, from the Aventine. Its head sank so deep into the ground that no one could pull it out, though many tried. Instead, the fertile earth supported and nourished the shaft of the spear, producing fresh shoots, until it became an immense cornel tree. The generations after Romulus preserved and venerated this tree as if it were the most sacred of objects, and they constructed a wall around it. If anyone noticed that the tree was not flourishing and green, but instead appeared withered or dying, he cried out in alarm to all whom he met, and everyone would shout

'water! water!', just as if there were a fire, and would rush to
the tree from all sides, bringing buckets of water. But when
Gaius Caesar,[105] so they say, was repairing the steps around the
enclosure, some of the workers dug too close to the tree, inadvertently injuring the roots, which caused the tree to wither
away.

21. Now the Sabines adopted the Roman calendar, a topic I
have discussed extensively in my *Life of Numa*.[106] For his part,
Romulus began to employ the Sabines' long, oblong shields.
Furthermore, he changed his own armour and the armour of
all the Romans, who previously had used round shields like
those of the Argives. The two peoples shared in one another's
festivals and sacrifices, abolishing none of them and instituting
new ones as well. One of these is the Matronalia,[107] founded in
honour of the women who put a stop to the war. Another is the
Carmentalia.[108] In the opinion of some, Carmenta is the Fate
who presides over the birth of children and for this reason is
honoured by mothers. Others, however, claim that she was the
wife of Evander the Arcadian[109] and that she was a prophetess
who, when inspired by Phoebus, uttered oracles in verse. Thus
she came to be known as Carmenta, for in Latin verses are
called *carmina*.[110] Her actual name was Nicostrate,[111] and on
that point there is no disagreement. Nevertheless, there are also
authorities who offer a more plausible explanation of the name
Carmenta, which they interpret as meaning *demented*, or *out
of one's mind*, a reference to her prophetic raptures, since
carere is Latin for *be deprived* and *mens* for mind.

I have already discussed the Parilia.[112] As for the Lupercalia,
judging from the time of its celebration, it seems to be a festival
of purification, because it is observed during the inauspicious
days of February, and the name of that month can be interpreted to mean *purification*.[113] And, in ancient times, the very
day of the festival was called Febrata. The name of this festival,
however, evokes the Greek Lycaea,[114] or Feast of the Wolves,
which suggests that its origins are very early and go back to the
Arcadian followers of Evander. This is at least a common opinion, though the name of this festival could derive from the

legendary she-wolf,[115] and in fact we see that the Luperci[116] begin their run around the city at the place where Romulus is said to have been exposed. Still, the actual ceremonies of this festival make its origins difficult to deduce. Goats are sacrificed, after which two young men of noble birth are brought forward. Certain men are assigned to touch the forehead of each with a bloody knife, and at once others wipe away the stain with wool that has been dipped in milk. After their foreheads are wiped, the youths must laugh out loud. They then cut the goats' skins into strips and, after that, they run around, naked except for a loincloth, lashing everyone they meet with the strips of goatskin. Young brides make an effort to receive this lashing, for they believe it renders them fertile and will make their labour an easy one. An oddity of this festival is that the Luperci also sacrifice a dog.

A certain Boutas has composed poems in elegiac verse about the legendary origins of Roman customs.[117] He says that after their victory over Amulius the followers of Romulus ran joyfully to the place where the she-wolf had suckled the twins when they were babies and that this festival is conducted in imitation of this event. Thus the two noble youths run

> Striking all whom they meet, as once Romulus and Remus
> Came down from Alba Longa, swords in hand.

Boutas goes on to say that the bloody knife applied to their foreheads commemorates the slaughter and peril of that day, while the cleansing of their foreheads with milk recalls their nourishment by the she-wolf. Gaius Acilius[118] offers a different explanation. According to him, before the founding of the city, Romulus and his followers once lost their flocks. And so, after offering prayers to Faunus,[119] they rushed forth in search of them. They ran naked so as not to be troubled by sweating, and this is why the Luperci ran around the city naked.

As for the dog, if the sacrifice is carried out for the purpose of purification, then one may say that it is a suitable victim for rituals of this nature, for the Greeks too, in their ceremonies of purification, offer up puppies, and in many places they employ rites that are called *periskylakismoi*, a name which refers to carrying around and sacrificing puppies.[120] On the other hand, if these ceremonies commemorate the she-wolf who nourished and saved Romulus, it is perfectly reasonable that a dog is sacrificed, since a dog is a natural enemy to wolves – unless of course the creature is sacrificed as a punishment for obstructing the Luperci as they run their course.

22. According to some authorities, it was Romulus who first consecrated fire and appointed the sacred virgins, who are called Vestals.[121] Others, however, attribute this institution to Numa, though they concede that in all respects Romulus was decidedly religious. Furthermore, historians record that he was adept in divination, and for this purpose carried with him what the Romans call a *lituus*, a crooked staff employed in marking out the precincts of the sky whenever one engages in divination from the flight of birds.[122] This staff was later preserved on the Palatine, but is said to have disappeared when the city was sacked by the Celts. Afterwards, however, when the barbarians had been driven from Rome, it was discovered beneath a deep layer of ash. It was unharmed by the fire, although everything around it had been utterly destroyed.[123]

Romulus also enacted several laws, one of which was severe. It forbade a woman's divorcing her husband, but permitted a husband to divorce his wife if she was found to have poisoned her children or counterfeited his keys or committed adultery. If, however, a man divorced his wife on any other grounds but these, the law stipulated that half his property should be given to his wife, while the other half should be consecrated to Ceres. Furthermore, any man who divorced his wife was required to make a sacrifice to the gods of the underworld. A peculiarity of Romulus' legislation is that it established no specific penalty for parricide. Instead, any homicide was denominated parricide,[124] and while the former was deemed an abomination, the latter was considered unimaginable. And for much of Rome's history Romulus seemed quite correct in not having prescribed a specific form of indictment for this crime, for no one committed such an act for almost 600 years. It was after the war with

Hannibal,[125] according to historians, that Lucius Hostius[126] became Rome's first parricide. This, however, is a sufficient discussion of these matters.

23. In the fifth year of Tatius' reign it happened that, when some friends and relations of his encountered ambassadors from Laurentum who were on their way to Rome, they attempted to rob them and, when they met with stout resistance, killed them. This was an act at once terrible and brazen, and Romulus believed it was essential to punish the wrongdoers immediately. Tatius, however, resorted to delay, protracting matters. Only on this one occasion was there open disagreement between the two monarchs. Otherwise they had always conducted themselves in such a way as to exhibit complete unity and concord in their administration of public affairs. The slain ambassadors' kinsmen, after they had been blocked by Tatius from pursuing any legal action, fell upon him as he and Romulus were performing a sacrifice in Lavinium.[127] They killed Tatius, but Romulus they escorted on his way, praising him as a just man. Romulus had the body of Tatius brought to Rome, where he was buried with full honours on the Aventine near the place called Armilustrium.[128] Romulus did nothing, however, to exact justice from Tatius' murderers. Several historians tell us that the city of Laurentum, seized by fear, actually handed the assassins of Tatius over to Romulus, whereupon he released them, saying that murder had been paid for with murder. This action led some to suspect and even to suggest that Romulus was not at all displeased to be rid of his colleague. Still, this episode led to no disruption of public business, nor did it incite the Sabines to any seditious actions. Quite the contrary, all continued to venerate their king, some on account of affection, others because they stood in fear of his power, and still others because they saw in him a benefactor who was favoured by the gods. Many foreign peoples also paid their respects to Romulus. Indeed, the Latins of those early times sent ambassadors to him in order to establish friendship and alliance.

Romulus captured Fidenae, a city near Rome.[129] According

to some, he attacked the city without provocation, ordering a sudden charge by his cavalry, who cut away the hinges of the city's gate, after which he unexpectedly made his appearance. Others, however, maintain that it was the men of Fidenae who first invaded Roman territory, despoiling and devastating the countryside as far as the outskirts of Rome itself. Romulus then ambushed these men, killed many and took their city. He did not, however, destroy the city or raze it to the ground. Instead, he made it into a Roman colony, where, on the Ides of April,[130] he settled 2,500 colonists,

24. Soon after this a plague broke out that caused men to expire suddenly although they had not previously been ill. It afflicted the crops, which became unfruitful, and the cattle, which became barren. Drops of blood rained down in the city, and this added superstitious terror to the people's unrelieved suffering. When similar horrors befell the inhabitants of Laurentum, everyone soon recognized that both cities were being visited by divine wrath owing to their neglect of justice in the case of Tatius' murder as well as that of the slain ambassadors. The murderers from both cities were therefore delivered up and punished, after which the pestilence abated. Romulus then purified the cities with expiatory rituals that, even today, according to historical authorities, are performed at the Ferentine Gate.[131] Before the plague had ceased, the Camerians[132] attacked the Romans and overran their lands, for they were convinced that, owing to their misfortunes, the Romans were powerless to defend themselves. At once, however, Romulus marched out and defeated them in a battle in which 6,000 Camerians fell. He also captured their city, and of the remaining survivors he settled half in Rome. From Rome he sent as colonists to Cameria twice as many men as he had left there. This took place on the first of August. One can see in this how great the population of Rome had become after not quite sixteen years of existence. Among the spoils of this war Romulus brought home from Cameria a bronze four-horse chariot, which he dedicated in the temple of Vulcan.[133] He had already placed there a statue of himself being crowned by Victory.

25. Thus did Rome wax ever stronger, a reality conceded by her weaker neighbours, who were pleased simply to find themselves unmolested. Fear and jealousy, however, led the stronger ones to conclude that they could no longer remain mere spectators but must stand up to Romulus and put a stop to his growing power. The people of Veii[134] were the foremost of the Etruscans. Their territories were extensive and they inhabited a great city. It was they who took the initiative in waging war against the Romans, using as their pretext a claim that Fidenae should belong to them. This was not only unjust, it was ridiculous, for Veii had not assisted Fidenae when that city undertook to hazard war against the Romans, but instead had allowed the men of Fidenae to perish. Now, however, Veii was demanding that the Romans surrender the houses and lands of Fidenae, which they had taken after their conquest. When Romulus contemptuously dismissed these claims, the men of Veii divided their forces into two armies, one of which attacked the garrison at Fidenae, the other of which moved against Romulus. Although they were victorious at Fidenae, where they slew the 2,000 Romans who fought against them, they were defeated by Romulus with a loss of 8,000 men. Another battle was fought near Fidenae, and it is universally agreed that Rome's victory in this engagement was due almost entirely to Romulus himself, for he exhibited consummate skill and boldness and appeared to fight with superhuman strength and speed. A few writers, however, advance a claim that is wholly fabulous, or, put better, simply unbelievable, namely, that of the 14,000 who fell in this battle more than half were struck down by Romulus himself. After all, it is obvious that even the Messenians were making an inflated boast when they claimed that Aristomenes[135] three times sacrificed a hecatomb in commemoration of the number of Lacedaemonians he had slain.

After routing the enemy, Romulus allowed the survivors to escape and advanced against the city, which, after so serious a reverse, could not hold out against him but instead sought and obtained a treaty of friendship for a hundred years. Veii surrendered a large parcel of its territory, which is called Septem Pagi, meaning the Seven Districts.[136] They likewise abandoned

their salt-works along the river and supplied fifty of their leading citizens as hostages. Romulus celebrated a triumph for this
victory on the Ides of October.[137] Among the captives led by
him was the general of the Veientes,[138] an old man who seemed
to have conducted his campaign foolishly and without the prudence expected from a man of his age and experience. It is for
this reason that the Romans, down to this very day, whenever
they offer sacrifice for victory, lead an old man through the
forum to the Capitol. He wears the purple-bordered toga of a
boy, along with a child's bulla, while a herald cries 'Sardians
for sale!'. For the Etruscans are believed to be colonists from
Sardis, and Veii was an Etruscan city.[139]

26. This was the final war waged by Romulus. Thereafter, like
most men, or, more precisely, like nearly all men who have
risen to power and importance by way of striking and unexpected good fortune, he, too, was deeply affected by the
experience. His accomplishments increased his boldness and he
became haughty, abandoning his popular manner and taking
on in its place the airs of an autocrat, and this change was
made odious and offensive from the start on account of the
apparel he donned. For he dressed in a scarlet tunic, over which
he wore a toga bordered in purple,[140] and he gave audiences
while seated on a reclining throne. He was always attended by
young men, who were called Celeres[141] owing to their swiftness
in serving him. There were other attendants who walked ahead
of him and were equipped with staffs, which they employed in
holding back the crowd. They also wore leather straps so that
they could bind on the spot anyone he commanded to be
bound.

The Latin for *to bind* was once *ligare*, but it is now *alligare*.
Consequently, the attendants who carry these staffs are called
lictores,[142] and the staffs themselves are called *bacila*,[143] because
in those days the Romans used rods.[144] At the same time, there
is another plausible explanation: the *c* in the word *lictores*, as
they are now called, could be an addition, and originally these
attendants were called *litores*, which is the same as *leitourgoi*,
the Greek word for public servants. In fact the Greeks still call

a public building a *leïton*, and refer to the public with the word *laos*.[145]

27. When Romulus' grandfather, Numitor, died in Alba Longa, the royal succession fell to him. However, in order to win over its people, he put the city's government in their hands and appointed a chief magistrate whose term of office would last only one year. In so doing, he taught the leading men of Rome to desire for themselves a state that could also govern itself without a king, one in which they would be subjects and rulers in their turn. For by this point not even the so-called patricians played a part in public affairs. Instead, they merely enjoyed a prestigious title and dignified dress, and it was simply owing to custom – and not in order to give advice – that they attended the senate. There they listened in silence to the king's commands, and, when they had departed, their sole advantage over the common people lay in having learned of his decrees before they did. The senate suffered numerous affronts, but each of them seemed minor next to this one. Romulus distributed the lands that Rome had taken by conquest and restored to Veii the hostages this city had handed over to Rome – all on his own authority and without any consent or approval by the senate. This was deemed an outrageous insult, which is why, when Romulus unaccountably disappeared a short time afterwards, a cloud of suspicion and calumny hung over the patricians.[146] He vanished on the Nones of July,[147] as the month is now called, or Quintilis, as it was called then.[148] Nothing about the matter is certain, nor is there any widely accepted tradition concerning the circumstances of his death apart from its date, which I have just reported. For even now that day is marked by many ceremonies that recall what took place then.[149]

This uncertainty need occasion no surprise. After all, although Scipio Africanus[150] died after dinner in his own home, the manner of his death remains unexplained to everyone's satisfaction. Some say he died a natural death, the fault of his unhealthy constitution, others that he poisoned himself. Still others claim that he was stifled by his enemies, who broke into his house during the night. Furthermore, the body of Scipio was exposed to public view, which allowed everyone who inspected it to form his own suspicions and draw his own conclusions as to what had happened. By contrast, Romulus vanished suddenly, nor did a single part of his body or clothing remain to be seen. Some have conjectured that the senators fell upon him in the temple of Vulcan[151] and, after they had killed him, cut his body into pieces small enough for each of them to conceal a part in the folds of his toga and thus carry it away. Others, however, do not believe that he disappeared in the temple of Vulcan or that only the senators were present at the time. Instead, they maintain, Romulus was conducting a public assembly outside the city near the so-called Goat's Marsh[152] when suddenly the air was filled with bewildering and inexplicable phenomena and unfathomable transformations. The light of the sun was eclipsed, and the day was turned into night, not a gentle or quiet night, moreover, but one disturbed by terrible thundering and furious gales driving rain in all directions. At this, the multitude dispersed and fled, but the leading men drew close to one another. When the storm had ceased and the sun again shone, the multitude returned to this same place. Noticing his absence, they began to look for their king, but the senators refused to allow them to seek their king or even to concern themselves with his disappearance. They urged them to honour Romulus and to venerate him, for he had been taken up to join the gods and now, instead of being their king, had become a propitious divinity. Most of the people believed these things and so went away with joy and gladness to offer him worship. There were some, however, who rejected this claim and in a bitter and hostile temper provoked the patricians by accusing them of having beguiled the public with a silly story while in reality they had murdered their king.

28. At this very moment, one of the patricians, Julius Proculus, a man of excellent birth who was highly esteemed for his character, a close and trusted friend of Romulus and a man who had joined him when first he left Alba Longa to found Rome, entered the forum.[153] In the presence of all the people he placed his hand on the city's most sacred objects and swore a solemn

oath that, as he was making his way along the road, he had
seen Romulus coming to meet him. He appeared grand and
handsome, more so than ever he had done before, and he wore
armour as brilliant as fire. Proculus confessed that he was
astonished by the sight and asked: 'Why, my king, and for what
purpose have you forsaken us, so that we patricians are objects
of unjust and wicked accusations while the entire city is bereft
and plunged into deep sorrow?' To this Romulus replied: 'It
was the will of the gods, Proculus, that I should be among mortals for only a fixed time, for I came to you from the gods and
I have founded a city that is destined to be the greatest of all in
its power and glory. Now I must again dwell in heaven. Farewell, and tell the Romans that if they cultivate self-restraint
together with valour they will not fail to attain the utmost
degree of human power.[154] As for me, I shall hereafter be the
god Quirinus,[155] and I shall favour you always.' This report
seemed credible to the Romans owing to the character of the
man who gave it and to the nature of the oath he had sworn.
But these were not the only reasons they believed Proculus.
They were touched by some kind of divine influence, not unlike
holy inspiration, for not a single man contradicted him. Instead,
everyone cast aside his suspicions and detractions alike and,
offering up prayers to Quirinus, invoked him as a god.

Now this account is like the myths told by the Greeks about
Aristaeus[156] of Proconnesus and Cleomedes[157] of Astypaleia.
For they say that Aristaeus died in a fuller's workshop but
when his friends came to collect his body it had vanished. Soon
afterwards, however, certain men, returning from abroad,
reported that they had met Aristaeus as he was making his way
towards Croton. As for Cleomedes, he was a man of enormous
size and strength, but his disposition was impulsive and even
wild, and as a consequence he committed many acts of violence. At last, in a schoolhouse, he struck with his fist a pillar
that supported its roof. The pillar was broken and the building
fell in, killing the children within. Cleomedes was then pursued, but he took refuge in a chest, the lid of which he shut and
held so fast that even a large number of men was unable to
force it open. So they broke the chest into pieces, but, when

they did so, could not find the man, alive or dead. Bewildered by this, they sent a delegation to consult the oracle at Delphi,[158] where the Pythian priestess gave them this response: 'Last of the heroes is Cleomedes the Astypalaean.' There is also the story that the body of Alcmene[159] vanished as it was being carried forth for burial and a stone was found in its place on the bier. To put it simply, many myths of this kind are recorded by writers who seek to ascribe divinity not only to the gods but also to that which is mortal by its nature. Admittedly, there is something impious and base about rejecting the divine essence of human virtue. At the same time, it is silly to unite earth with heaven. If one wishes for certainty in this matter, then let him agree with Pindar that

> The body of every man yields to an incontestable death,
> But yet there remains still living an image of his life,
> For this alone is from the gods.[160]

Indeed, this comes from the gods and returns to them – not, however, together with its physical body but only when it is entirely released and separated from its body and has become completely purified, incorporeal and undefiled. For 'a dry soul is best',[161] as Heracleitus puts it, which flies from the body like a flash of lightning from a cloud, whereas a soul which is suffused throughout a physical body, and is thus defiled by its physical body, remains difficult to release and slow to ascend, like a thick and cloudy vapour.

29. The name Quirinus, which was given to Romulus, is explained by some as meaning Enyalius.[162] Others think its meaning is *citizen* on the grounds that the Romans called their citizens Quirites. Still others, however, observe how the ancients called the tip of a spear, or a spear itself, by the word *curis*,[163] and described the statue of Juno leaning on a spear as Juno Curitis.[164] Furthermore, they note, there is a spear in the Regia that is consecrated to Mars,[165] and it was a Roman practice to honour men who distinguished themselves in warfare with a spear as their prize. Consequently, they maintain that Romulus

was called Quirinus because he was a martial god, or a god
armed with a spear. His temple was built on the hill that, on
account of his name, is called Quirinalis,[166] and the day on
which he vanished is known as the Flight of the People[167] and
the Capratine Nones,[168] because they make sacrifice outside the
city at the Goat's Marsh and *capra* is the Latin word for she-
goat. On this occasion, as the Romans leave the city for the
sacrifice, they cry out many of their native names, like Marcus,
Lucius or Gaius, imitating thereby the manner in which they
called to one another in fear and perturbation at the time of
Romulus' disappearance.

According to other authorities, however, this practice does
not imitate the people's flight at that time but instead, they
explain, originates in their haste and hurry on a different occasion. After the Celts who had captured Rome[169] had been
expelled from the city by Camillus, while Rome was still too
weak to arrive at a full recovery from its destruction, a large
force of Latins, under the command of Livius Postumius,
marched against the city. The general set up his camp near
Rome and sent a herald who announced that the Latins wished
to revive their ancient, but now obsolete, affinity with the
Romans by contracting new marriage ties between the two
peoples; if the Romans should send them a large number of
virgins and widows, they would enjoy peace and friendship
with the Latins on terms similar to the ones that had existed in
the past between Romans and Sabines. When the Romans
heard this, although they were afraid to fight, they nevertheless
felt that handing over their women in this way would render
them little better off than captives seized in war. Thus the
Romans were at a loss as to how to proceed, when a servant
girl named Philotis,[170] or, in some versions, Tutula, advised
them not to choose either of these actions but by resorting to a
ruse avoid both war and surrendering hostages. And this was
the ruse. They should hand Philotis herself over to the enemy,
along with other servant girls who were beautiful and dressed
like freeborn women. Then, during the night, Philotis would
raise up a torch as a signal for the Romans to come forth in
arms and deal with their enemies while they lay asleep. This is

exactly what was done and the Latins were deceived, and, from a certain wild fig tree, Philotis held up a torch, which she hid from behind with curtains and draperies, so that its light could not be seen by the enemy but was distinctly visible to the Romans. As soon as the Romans saw it, they rushed through the gates in a great hurry and, because of their haste, called out to one another again and again. They fell upon their enemies unexpectedly and defeated them, a victory commemorated in this festival. The day on which it is celebrated is called the Capratine Nones because the Latin word for a wild fig tree is *caprificus*, and on this day the women of Rome are honoured with a feast outside the city during which they are shaded by the branches of a fig tree. The maidservants gather together and run about playfully, after which they strike and throw stones at one another, recalling how on that day they aided the Romans and joined with them in battle.

Many historians agree on this account of the origin of this festival. Still, the practice of calling out to one another by name when it is daylight and of walking out to the Goat's Marsh in order to make sacrifice seems to favour a commemoration of Romulus' disappearance, unless of course both events took place on the same day although in different periods of time.[171] Romulus is said to have been fifty-four years old, and in the thirty-eighth year of his reign, when he vanished from the sight of mortals.

COMPARISON OF
THESEUS AND ROMULUS

1 (30). These, then, are the memorable facts that I have been
able to learn about Romulus and Theseus. The first point to be
made, and it is an obvious one, is that Theseus, although he
was heir to a splendid kingdom at Troezen,[1] where he could
have reigned as king in complete serenity, nevertheless took it
upon himself, in the absence of any compulsion, to strive for
even greater things. Romulus, by contrast, in order to escape
his condition as a slave and evade the baleful prospect of punishment, became, to put it neatly, 'brave on account of his
fear',[2] to employ Plato's phrase, and, because he was frightened
of suffering the worst of penalties, was driven to do great deeds.
The second point is this: Romulus' greatest exploit came when
he cut down a single tyrant in Alba,[3] whereas, in the case of
Theseus, when he slew Sciron, Sinis, Procrustes and Corynetes,[4]
these actions were little more than sidelines and a prelude to his
real career; indeed, he freed Greece from these terrible tyrants
before he was even known to those whom his adventures had
liberated. Theseus, to press the point, could have made his way
to Athens by sea,[5] safely and unmolested by brigands such as
these, while in the case of Romulus, so long as Amulius lived,
he could not avoid danger. Of this assertion there is a compelling proof. Theseus attacked these wicked men on behalf of
others, when he had not himself been wronged by any of them,
whereas Romulus and Remus, so long as they were unharmed
by the tyrant, left him free to abuse others.

And if it was a great thing for Romulus to be wounded when

fighting against the Sabines, and to slay Acron, and to conquer many enemies in battle, one can set these deeds alongside Theseus' clash with the Centaurs and his campaign against the Amazons.[6] However, if one considers Theseus' daring in regard to the Cretan tribute, when he voluntarily sailed off with the virgins and young boys, whether it was to become food for some monster or a sacrifice on the tomb of Androgeus or to suffer what of all versions of this story involved the least dangerous fate for him, namely, vile and degrading slavery at the hands of insolent and cruel masters,[7] in each case words fail to express his boldness, his high-mindedness or his sense of universal justice – or his desire for glory and virtue. This is why I am convinced that philosophers have done well in defining love as 'a labour of the gods in the care and salvation of the young'.[8] For it looks as if Ariadne's love was, more than anything else, the work of a god and a means to this hero's salvation. And it would be wrong to fault her for falling in love with Theseus; on the contrary, we must be astonished that he was not held in the same affection by all men and all women. And if it was she alone who felt such a passion for him, then, in my view, she was indeed worthy of a god's love, for she was a lover of nobility and of goodness and of the finest qualities.[9]

2 (31). Theseus and Romulus were each of them natural statesmen, but neither succeeded in maintaining himself as a true monarch and instead each made constitutional alterations, Theseus by inclining towards democracy, Romulus towards tyranny. In this way, each leader, though influenced by different dispositions, committed the same error, for the first duty of a ruler is to preserve the very constitution by which he governs, and this is accomplished as much by avoiding unseemly practices as it is by embracing attractive ones. If, however, he too greatly surrenders or extends his authority, then he is no longer a king or a ruler but becomes instead either a demagogue or a despot and inspires hatred or contempt in his subjects. Still, the one error seems to arise from a sense of fairness and humane sensibilities, whereas the other is the result of self-centred arrogance and harshness.

3 (32). If we can agree that men's misfortunes are not always attributable to the agency of the gods but in fact are sometimes best explained on the basis of their differing characters and emotions, then it is impossible to pardon Romulus for his treatment of his brother or Theseus for his actions against his son,[10] for each of them was guilty of irrational anger and precipitate and uncontrollable rage. However, if we consider the circumstances of each one's anger, we are likely to be more understanding of the man who was overcome by the more grievous provocation, as if he had been struck a heavier blow. Now Romulus was involved in deliberation and in making plans for the welfare of the state when he quarrelled with his brother, and it is unimaginable that, under those conditions, anyone could suddenly become so furious. By contrast, Theseus was induced to wrong his son by influences that hardly any man could escape: love, jealousy and a woman's lies. More importantly, Romulus' wrath realized itself in an action and a deed the outcome of which was truly terrible, whereas Theseus' fury remained confined to words – insults and an old man's curse – for what befell his son afterwards seems to owe itself to misfortune. For all these reasons, then, one could give one's vote of preference to Theseus.

4 (33). Turning to Romulus, however, the first point in his favour is the fact that, despite his base origins, he elevated himself to a position of great power. He and his brother are said to have been slaves and the sons of a swineherd, and yet not only did they gain their own freedom, they also liberated nearly all the Latin people, acquiring in a single moment the most honorific of titles: slayers of their enemies, saviours of their family and friends, kings of nations and founders of cities. They were not simply consolidators of existing communities, as was Theseus. He joined numerous peoples into one, but in so doing eliminated many cities that bore the names of ancient kings and heroes.[11] Admittedly, Romulus did these things too, but at a later time, when he forced his enemies to demolish and abandon their homes and become citizens in the same city as their conqueror. In the beginning, however, Romulus neither resettled nor enlarged an existing city but instead created a new one

from nothing, acquiring along with this territory a homeland, a kingdom, families, wives and alliances. In the founding of his city, he neither subjugated nor killed anyone. On the contrary, he was a benefactor to men lacking home or hearth and longing to become citizens in a recognized community. He did not slay brigands and criminals,[12] but he annexed to Rome the nations he conquered in warfare, he subdued cities and he triumphed over kings and generals.

5 (34). There are further points on Romulus' side. For instance, where the death of Remus is concerned there remains some controversy over his actual killer, and in some versions the responsibility for his death is attributed to others and not to Romulus.[13] What is not in doubt is how Romulus rescued his mother from certain death and how he restored his grandfather, who had endured a servile existence, bereft both of reputation and honour, to the throne of Aeneas.[14] Romulus did him many additional kindnesses, all voluntarily, and did him no harm whatsoever, not even inadvertently. Theseus, by contrast, owing to forgetfulness and negligence regarding his father's instructions about the sail,[15] is in my view guilty of the crime of parricide, a verdict he could escape neither by way of an extended defence nor even through lenient jurors. There is, of course, a certain Athenian author who, because he perceives how very difficult a task it must be for anyone to try to defend Theseus in this matter, has concocted the story that, as the ship was approaching, Aegeus, anxious to catch sight of it, hastened up to the acropolis but stumbled and fell to his death[16] – as if it could be the case that he lacked a royal escort or rushed down to the sea without a single servant.

6 (35). As for Theseus' abductions of women, these are wrongs that cannot easily be excused. In the first place, there are so many of them. After all, he carried off Ariadne, Antiope, Anaxo of Troezen and, last of all, Helen, who at the time was not yet an adult but remained an immature child, whereas he was old and past any age for legitimate wedlock.[17] The second objection to these actions lies in their motive, for he did not marry

the daughters of the Troezenians or the Spartans or the Amazons, nor were they more worthy to be mothers of his children
than the Athenian women who were descended from Erechtheus and Cecrops.[18] Instead, one must suspect that he
perpetrated these acts out of a passion for violence and sexual
pleasure. Romulus presents a very different case. First of all,
although he carried off nearly 800 women,[19] he did not marry
them all but only one, whom the sources name as Hersilia. The
rest he distributed among the unmarried citizens. Second, in
the respect, love and equity shown these women, Romulus
made it clear that his action, for all that it was violent and
illegal, had a very noble purpose and was designed for the
political advantage of his community. For this was the means
by which he joined and amalgamated two peoples with one
another, thereby providing Rome with a source of future goodwill and might. And history bears witness to the modesty,
affection and stability of Roman marriages,[20] which he helped to
establish. In the course of 230 years, there was not a single
man who undertook to put away his wife, nor any woman her
husband, and just as the most erudite of the Greeks can name
the first parricide or matricide, so every Roman knows that
Spurius Carvilius was the first to divorce his wife,[21] which he
justified on the grounds that she was barren.

The immediate consequences of Romulus' actions join with
the long record of history as witnesses in his behalf, for, after
these marriages took place, the two kings[22] shared in a common government and their two peoples shared in a common
citizenship. The liaisons of Theseus, however, brought the
Athenians nothing in the way of new friendships or alliances,
but only hostility, wars and the deaths of their citizens. In the
end, Aphidnae was captured, and it was only owing to the piety
and compassion of the Athenians' enemies, whom the Athenians reverenced and called upon as if they were gods, that they
avoided the fate which Troy suffered on account of Alexander.[23] Even the mother of Theseus was in danger and actually
suffered the fate of Hecuba[24] when she was forgotten and abandoned by her son, unless the story of her captivity is a fiction,

and it may well be untrue, as are most of the other tales told about Theseus.[25] Even in the matter of the myths regarding the intervention of the gods into their lives, there are significant differences between them. Romulus owed his salvation to the unmistakable goodwill of the gods, whereas the oracle given to Aegeus,[26] which forbade his approaching any woman while he was in a foreign land, apparently makes it clear that the birth of Theseus was against the will of the gods.

NUMA

INTRODUCTION
TO NUMA

Prince of Peace

Numa Pompilius was remembered for his wisdom and piety –
and for his profound commitment to peace. He was a Sabine
citizen of high repute who was offered the throne after the
death of Romulus (the Romans believed, perhaps correctly,
that their kings had been chosen by election). He instituted the
ceremonies of Roman public religion, reformed the calendar
and introduced changes to Rome's social order, innovations
that promoted social harmony and brought an end to the incessant warfare that had dominated the career of his predecessor.
It was a golden age that never returned, not even in Plutarch's
day, when, as he puts it elsewhere, owing to Rome, 'every war,
Greek and barbarian, has vanished' (*Moralia* 824c).

Although Numa's life was less eventful than that of Romulus, he, too, attracted legends, most of which were efforts to
explain his almost superhuman insight into religion and statecraft. It was commonly reported by early writers that Numa
had been a student of Pythagoras, though by Cicero's day the
chronological impossibility of this had been made clear (Cicero,
The Republic 2.28). Nevertheless, the opinion persisted, and
a connection with Pythagoras, despite its lack of historicity,
is actually Plutarch's preferred explanation of the Roman's
wisdom. There was also a tale that the king had become the
lover of a goddess, who, by way of a special brand of pillow
talk, revealed to him truths about the gods – and who helped
Numa to parley successfully even with an angry Jupiter. In the

light of that story, one begins to understand why Plutarch preferred to look for philosophical influences on the Roman king.

Numa is paired with the legendary Spartan lawgiver, Lycurgus, whose constitution was widely admired in antiquity, not least by Plato, who in his *Republic* makes much use of it when discussing the principles and practicalities of an ideal society. For Plutarch, each man became king at a moment when his city was affected with a political and moral fever, a common theme he emphasizes by employing explicitly Platonic language in each Life.[1] To each state its new king brought a tonic. Rome suffered from excessive belligerence, Sparta from decadence. Numa imposed philosophical religiosity, Lycurgus martial discipline. For each the result was an admirably well-ordered community characterized by justice. Plutarch plainly esteems both figures – there is little criticism or qualification in this pairing – but in their *Comparison* he makes the startling observation that, if it is true that Lycurgus was responsible for the Spartans' harsh treatment of their serfs, 'we must then concede that, as a lawgiver, Numa – far more than Lycurgus – conformed to Greek ideals' (*Comparison Lycurgus–Numa* 1).

Numa's standing as a venerable example of a truly good man was an enduring one. From Ennius through late antiquity, he is mentioned again and again.[2] Even the emperor Hadrian, it seems, looked to Numa as a kind of predecessor.[3] Only in the works of the Christian Fathers does Numa's reputation take a change for the worse, understandably enough inasmuch as, in their view, he was responsible for inculcating false religious practices in Rome. And yet even in these writers there remains a grudging respect for Numa's integrity.[4] Plutarch's admiration is unmistakable, and, like most ancient Greek intellectuals, he is perfectly comfortable with the idea that parts of Numa's sacred legislation were more or less noble lies, the purpose of which was to introduce discipline and justice among the multitude (ch. 4). For him, that is simply another dimension of Numa's wisdom.

War and political strife were the natural stuff of ancient history. The life of the peaceable Numa, however admirable, offered little in the way of narrative interest. This is why he is given such short shrift by Livy. Dionysius of Halicarnassus is, as always, more expansive, not least because he offers lengthy (and, for us, very useful) explanations of Numa's institutional innovations. Plutarch, like Dionysius, is untroubled by the absence of exciting adventure in Numa's life. It is in fact Numa's concentration on study, reflection, good order and peace that constitutes the focus of Plutarch's biography, because, in Plutarch's view, Numa was the realization of Plato's hopeful dream that the world would one day see a state governed by a philosopher-king.[5] This is not a conclusion that requires subtle criticism on the part of the reader:

> Numa was in any case an unmistakable example and a convincing proof of an opinion which, many generations later, Plato dared to express about the nature of government. For he insisted that respite and rescue from human ills would come only when, thanks to a stroke of good fortune sent by the gods, the power of a king should be joined in one person with the understanding of a philosopher.

>   (ch. 20)

Plutarch's Numa comes very close to being the kind of philosopher-king described by Plato in his *Laws* or in book six of his *Republic*, a representation reinforced in this Life by an abundance of Platonic allusions. Numa possesses all the best virtues, especially *philanthropia*, the sense of civilized humanity, closely associated with Greek values, that Plutarch regarded as essential for moral perfection.[6]

It is sometimes objected that, in this pairing, Plutarch is in reality offering his reader a subtle critique of the Platonic ideals found in the *Laws* and *Republic*.[7] Lycurgus' constitution did not elevate Sparta to a state of philosophical perfection, nor, it is argued, could Rome have prospered or even survived under a pacifist king. Now there is no doubting Plutarch's capacity for independent philosophizing, but, in this instance, he seems Platonic enough. After all, the deficiencies of the historical Sparta actually illustrate the need at the top for a philosopher-king and not simply military commanders, as Lycurgus' successors proved mostly to be. And as for Numa, in Plutarch's account he is no pacifist. He establishes the priestly college of the Fetiales not to banish the reality of war but rather to ensure its justice and thereby minimize its occurrence (ch. 12). Not that he required their services during his own reign, marked as it was by an unbroken peace:

> This can be explained by the fact that it was not only the Roman people who were charmed and rendered peaceable by the justice and mildness of their king. The surrounding cities, as if a gentle zephyr were wafting from Rome, or a salubrious breeze, also began to change their habits, for all were filled with a desire to live in peace under good laws, to cultivate their lands, to rear their children in quiet and to honour the gods. Throughout Italy there were festivals and banquets, while everyone, whatever his city, made friendly visits to other cities, frequently and without fear.
>
> (ch. 20)

Such, in Plutarch's view, is the practical influence of a true philosopher-king.

Sources

In composing this Life, Plutarch largely relied on the same sources he used in writing *Romulus*. Although he corrects him more than once (evidence of his wide and independent reading), Plutarch plainly turned to Dionysius of Halicarnassus, whose account of Numa was more expansive than Livy's, which he will also have consulted. Furthermore, he cites numerous other historians of early Rome, like Juba and Valerius Antias (see Introduction to *Romulus*) as well as Lucius Calpurnius Piso,[8] the consul of 133 BC whose *Annals* (now lost) dealt with Roman history from its origins to his own day. It is clear that Plutarch has also exploited authorities on antiquarian and etymological learning, like Varro, and doubtless experts among his contemporaries (see Introduction to *Romulus*).

LIFE OF NUMA

[reigned 715–674 BC]

1. There persists a sharp controversy over the time at which King Numa lived, notwithstanding the existence of apparently accurate modern genealogies that, whatever their contemporary starting point, trace themselves back to Numa's own time.[1] A certain Clodius,[2] however, in his *Chronological Investigations* (for that is the title he gave his book), argues vigorously that any ancient documents were lost when the city was sacked by the Celts[3] and that such records as we now possess were counterfeited by authors seeking to gratify certain men wishing to push their way into the traditions of Rome's foremost families and most illustrious houses,[4] although in reality they had no right to be included. Consequently, despite the common report that Numa was a close friend of Pythagoras, there are others who insist that Numa had nothing in the way of a Greek education.[5] Either he attained to virtue owing to his natural capacities and his own exertions, or the king received his education from a barbarian who was superior to Pythagoras.[6] Other writers claim that Pythagoras in fact lived as many as five generations after Numa, but draw attention to another Pythagoras, a Spartan who won the sprint in the sixteenth Olympiad, which took place during the third year of Numa's reign.[7] Accordingly, it was this Pythagoras who, when he was travelling in Italy, became familiar with Numa and assisted him in putting the Romans' constitution in order. This is why so many Spartan customs find a place in Roman society, for it was this Pythagoras who taught them to Numa. But then again, Numa was of Sabine origins, and the Sabines claim to be colonists from Sparta.[8] Thus it is difficult to find exact dates for

Numa's life, and this is especially the case for any chronology
based on the names of Olympic victors because that list was
drawn up at a rather late date by Hippias of Elis,[9] whose
sources were by no means unquestionably reliable. As for me, I
have chosen a natural beginning for relating what I have found
to be the most noteworthy aspects of Numa's life.[10]

2. Thirty-seven years had elapsed since Rome had been founded
and Romulus had become its king. On the fifth day of the
month, a day which the Romans now call the Capratine
Nones,[11] as Romulus was making a public sacrifice outside the
city near the so-called Goat's Marsh in the presence of the senate and a majority of the Roman people, there was suddenly a
great change in the air, and a cloud, discharging blasts of wind
and rain, fell upon the earth. The common people fled in fear
and were dispersed, and Romulus vanished. When he could not
be found, either alive or dead, hostile suspicions arose against
the patricians and rumour was soon rife among the public,
who were inclined to believe that, wearied of monarchy, the
patricians had plotted to seize power for themselves and so had
done away with the king. Nor had it escaped anyone's notice
that Romulus had lately behaved harshly, even imperiously,
towards the patricians. In order to blunt these suspicions, the
patricians paid divine honours to Romulus and attempted to
persuade the people that he was not dead but had been elevated
to a better condition. A distinguished man named Proculus
went so far as to swear an oath that he had seen Romulus
ascending into heaven in full panoply and had heard his voice
commanding that he henceforth be named Quirinus.

Dissension and faction again gripped the city, however, over
the appointment of a new king, for the more recent inhabitants
had not yet been entirely integrated with Rome's original citizens. Instead, the people continued in a state of agitation, while
the patricians, animated by their mutual jealousies, remained
divided. Although everyone agreed that there should be a new
king, they disagreed and quarrelled, not only over which individual to choose but also over which community should be the
one to furnish the new leader. The followers of Romulus who

had been Rome's original settlers could not abide the idea of the Sabines, who had been allowed to share in the city and its territories, forcing their way into a position of power over the very men who had admitted them. As for the Sabines, they too could advance a sound argument: after the death of their king, Tatius, they did not rebel against Romulus but permitted him to reign as the sole king, which is why they now insisted that the new king be selected from their number.[12] Nor would they concede that, when they had joined themselves to the Romans, they had come as inferiors to their superiors, for it was their contribution to Rome's numbers and strength that had advanced it to the status of a true city. It was on account of these issues, then, that the Romans were divided into factions.

The patricians, however, in order to keep the city's factionalism from turning into complete disorder owing to a lack of government during this time of constitutional uncertainty, decided that each of them (there were 150 patricians[13]) should take a turn donning the insignia of the king, offering the customary sacrifices to the gods and managing state affairs for six hours each night and six hours each day. Confining each patrician's tenure of power to these limits, so the leading men concluded, was the best means of promoting equality between the two factions. Furthermore, transferring power in this way would preclude any envy on the part of the people, when they observed the same man, in the course of a single day and night, first elevated to the status of a king and then returned to the rank of a private citizen.[14] The Romans call this form of government an *interregnum*.

3. Although the patricians governed Rome with civility and moderation, they nonetheless remained the object of suspicion and complaint, for the public accused them of changing the state into an oligarchy and making themselves into guardians of the constitution solely in order to avoid being ruled by a king. Finally, the two factions agreed that the most effective means of ending their current strife was for one of them to appoint as king someone from the other's membership. Any king elected in this way would be impartial, for he would be as

fond of the party that chose him to be king as he would be friendly to the other owing to his kinship with them. When the Sabines left it to the original citizens of Rome to choose their option in this matter, they decided that it was better to have a Sabine king whom they had appointed themselves than to have a Roman king selected by the Sabines. After taking counsel among themselves, they elected Numa Pompilius, a Sabine who had not yet taken residence in the city of Rome but who enjoyed such a reputation for virtue that, when he was named, the Sabines accepted him with an enthusiasm even greater than that of his Roman electors. After this decision was announced to the people, ambassadors chosen from the leading figures in each faction were sent to Numa to entreat him to move to Rome and become its king.

Numa was from Cures, a famous Sabine city. It was from the name of this city that the Romans, after their union with the Sabines, had designated themselves Quirites.[15] Numa was a son of Pompon, an illustrious man, and was the youngest of four brothers. He was born, by divine providence, on the very day on which Rome was founded by Romulus and his followers, the twenty-first day of April.[16] His character was so admirably constituted by nature that it inclined towards every virtue, and by means of education, austerity and philosophy Numa had made himself even more disciplined. He did not merely preserve his soul from the passions that incur disgrace, he also kept it free from those which are admired among the barbarians, that is, from violence and greed, for he judged that true courage consisted in subjecting one's passions to reason. Consequently he banished all luxury and extravagance from his home. Any citizen or stranger who sought his services found in him a blameless judge and adviser, while he devoted his leisure not to amusements or money making but instead to the worship of the gods and to the philosophical contemplation of their nature and power. He acquired such fame and reputation that Tatius, who was Romulus' royal colleague in Rome and who had only one daughter, Tatia, chose him as his son-in-law.[17] This marriage, however, did not induce him to take up residence with his father-in-law. Instead, he remained among the Sabines and looked after his aged father along with Tatia, who preferred the tranquillity of her husband's private life to the honour and esteem which she had enjoyed at Rome on account of her father. Tatia, it is reported, died in the thirteenth year of her marriage.

4. Numa then gave up city life, spending much of his time in the countryside, where it became his habit to wander alone in the groves of the gods and in sacred meadows and holy places. It was this more than anything else that gave rise to the tale about the goddess. According to this story, Numa did not forsake the company of men on account of anguish or eccentricity but because the pleasure of more august associations had come his way, for he had been judged worthy of a divine marriage. He shared, it was said, in the passion as well as the companionship of the goddess Egeria,[18] a relationship that brought him both happiness and wisdom in matters pertaining to the gods. This is a tale, however, that all too clearly resembles many of the very ancient fables told by various peoples who welcome legends of mortal men blessed by the love of the gods, like the myth of the Phrygians concerning Attis,[19] or of the Bithynians concerning Rhodoetes,[20] or the Arcadians concerning Endymion.[21]

Now there is every reason to believe that the gods, inasmuch as they are not lovers of horses or of birds but rather of humanity, should be pleased to be present among men of extraordinary virtue and that they would neither dislike nor disdain the companionship of a man who was holy and wise. The suggestion, however, that the beauty or gracefulness of a mortal's body should arouse a god or a divinity to have sexual intercourse with him is very difficult to credit. The Egyptians, however, introduce to this controversy a subtle distinction that is far from implausible. In their view, it is possible for the spirit of a god to infuse itself into a woman, thereby initiating her pregnancy, but sexual activity and corporeal association between a man and a goddess, they insist, is impossible. In making this argument, however, they still fail to recognize that, in sexual intercourse, each party plays an equal role in the physical encounter. Nevertheless, it is entirely natural that a god should love a mortal, and it would be understandable if that love should be inaccurately described in terms of passion when it manifested itself as a concern for his character and virtue. It is in this sense that we can say that the poets do not err when they tell fables of Apollo's passion for Phorbas,[22] Hyacinthus[23] or Admetus[24] – as well as Hippolytus of Sicyon,[25] of whom it is said that, whenever he happened to sail from Sicyon to Cirrha,[26] the Pythia,[27] as if the god knew of his journey and rejoiced because of it, would pronounce this heroic verse: 'Once more does my beloved Hippolytus take to the sea.' The tale is also told of Pan's falling in love with Pindar and his poems.[28] Moreover, after their deaths, Archilochus and Hesiod[29] were honoured by the gods for the sake of the Muses. During his lifetime, so goes a story that is much attested down to the present day, Sophocles entertained Asclepius as his guest, and, after the playwright died, a different god helped him to obtain his tomb.[30] If we admit these accounts, is it right to doubt that the gods likewise visited Zaleucus,[31] Minos,[32] Zoroaster,[33] Numa and Lycurgus, men who governed kingdoms and drew up constitutions? Is it unlikely that gods should associate themselves with such men as these in order to provide serious instruction and guidance on the noblest of matters, if it is true that, simply for their own pleasure, they appreciated the singing of lyric poets? To the man who disagrees, however, I reply with Bacchylides that 'the road is broad'.[34] Indeed, there is another explanation of the divine connections of Lycurgus and Numa and leaders like them, and it is a very compelling one. Since these men were endeavouring to bring discipline to headstrong, obstinate multitudes and were introducing extensive innovations to the constitutions of their states, they pretended that their undertakings enjoyed the sanction of the gods, and this sanction proved the salvation of the very men who were deceived by this ruse.

5. Now Numa was already a man of forty[35] when the ambassadors arrived from Rome to summon him to the throne. Speeches were made for the occasion by Proculus[36] and

Velesus.[37] It had been expected that one of these men would be the Romans' choice as their new king, for the people of Romulus strongly favoured Proculus while the people of Tatius felt the same about Velesus. Each man spoke briefly, for both assumed that Numa would welcome his stroke of luck. It turned out, however, that theirs was no trivial task. On the contrary, many arguments and entreaties were required in order to persuade this man, who had lived in peace and quiet, to change his mind and agree to govern a city that had in large measure come into existence and seen itself prosper through war. This, then, was Numa's reply, which he delivered in the presence of his father and one of his relations, a man named Marcius:[38]

'Every change in the life of a mortal is dangerous, but, for a man who is lacking in nothing and who finds no fault in his present circumstances, it is utter folly to make changes and quit his customary pursuits. For even if these have no other advantage, the security they offer is superior to the uncertainties of the unknown. And yet one can hardly describe the exigencies of a royal career as uncertain, if the experiences of Romulus are any indication, for his reputation was tarnished by the slander that he had plotted against his colleague Tatius, and a similarly base claim was made against his nobles, who were accused of having assassinated their king. Romulus, however, is celebrated in song and legend as a child of the gods, and men tell us how, when he was an infant, he was nourished supernaturally and miraculously rescued from death. I, by contrast, was born a mortal, and I received my nourishment and education from men who are well known to you. In addition, the very aspects of my character for which you praise me are entirely unsuitable in a man destined to be your king. I speak of my retiring nature and my cultivation of private studies, my keen and inveterate passion for peace and unwarlike occupations – and for the company of men, like farmers or herdsmen, who meet only to worship the gods and join in friendly society but otherwise keep to themselves. But to you, Romans, Romulus has left a legacy of abundant warfare, even if it is not what you wished for, and your city requires an experienced king who is as resolute as he is vigorous. For the people of Rome have become accustomed to war, and their victories have made them eager for more of it. Their desire to amplify their power and rule over others is obvious to everyone, and I should become a laughing-stock if I strove to serve the gods, teaching the city to honour justice and hate violence and warfare, when what Rome truly desires is not a king but a general for its armies.'

6. These were the kinds of arguments Numa employed in refusing to accept the kingship he was offered.[39] For their part the Romans did all they could do to meet his objections, and they begged him not to allow them to collapse once more into factional strife or even into civil war, since there was no other man who could unite both of the city's factions. After the ambassadors departed, Numa's father and Marcius also put forward their own arguments and tried to persuade him to accept this exalted – and providential – gift: 'Although you have no desire for wealth – for you are independent and require no more than what you have, nor do you covet office or power, for you enjoy the greater distinction of possessing virtue – you should nevertheless recognize that the essential duty of a king lies in his hard labour in service to the gods.[40] Indeed, it is a divine force that now summons you to eminence and refuses to allow you, endowed as you are with such profound righteousness, to remain in retirement. And so you must not flee or try to escape this office, which, for a wise man, offers an arena for splendid and noble achievements. For with you as king the worship of the gods will be elevated to a suitable grandeur, and the people will easily and quickly, as their natures are transformed by the character of their ruler, become disposed towards piety. The Romans loved Tatius, though he was a foreign ruler, and Romulus they commemorate with divine honours. Who knows whether the Roman people, for all their victories, have not had their fill of war? Abounding in triumphs and spoil, they may now desire a mild leader, a friend of justice, who can add order and peace to their martial attainments. Should it prove otherwise, if the Romans are instead possessed of a violent and mad longing for war, is it not far better that you, holding in your

hands the reins of power, should turn their ardour in another direction, and that your native city, along with all the Sabine people, should have – through you – a bond of goodwill and friendship with a city so vigorous and mighty?' These arguments, we are told, were reinforced by favourable omens as well as by the earnest zeal of his fellow-citizens, who, when they learned of the embassy, begged him to go to Rome and become king there in order to establish unity and harmony among Romans and Sabines.

7. Numa decided that this advice was best, and so he sacrificed to the gods and departed for Rome. He was met on the way by the senate and people, whose enthusiasm and affection for Numa were marvellous, while the women greeted him with seemly acclamations. Sacrifices were offered in the temples, and everyone was joyous, as if the city were gaining not simply a king but a kingdom. When they reached the forum, Spurius Vettius,[41] for it was his turn at that hour to be *interrex*, put the matter to a vote, and all the people elected Numa their king. When the royal insignia were brought to him, however, Numa ordered a delay and declared that his regal authority must first be sanctioned by the gods. Taking with him the augurs and the priests, he climbed the Capitol, which in those days the Romans called the Tarpeian Hill.[42] There the chief of the augurs turned Numa's head, which had been covered, towards the south. He then stood behind Numa and, touching Numa's head with his right hand, uttered a prayer. Next, looking about in all directions, he searched for signs from the gods, in the shape of birds or other omens. An astonishing silence gripped the vast multitude in the forum below, who waited in eager suspense for the result, until auspicious birds appeared from the right.[43] Only then did Numa don his royal robes and descend from the citadel to the forum. There he was welcomed with jubilation and applause, as the Romans saluted him as the most pious of men and the most beloved by all the gods.

Numa's first action after he became king was to disband the corps of 300 men that Romulus always kept as his bodyguard and whom he called Celeres, which means *the swift men*.[44] His

reason for doing so was that he did not think it right to distrust
men who trusted him, nor to reign over men who did not trust
him. His second act was to add to the priests of Jupiter and
Mars a third priest, dedicated to Romulus, whom he called the
flamen Quirinalis. The Romans called their ancient priests
flamines.[45] This name is derived from the hats, which are essentially skull caps, that they wear on top of their heads, the full
name for which, we are informed by reliable authority, was
actually *pilamenes*,[46] for in the past Greek words were used
more frequently by Latin speakers than is now the case. Another
instance is the cloak called a *laena*, which is worn by priests; its
name, according to Juba,[47] comes from the Greek word for
cloak, namely *chlaena*.[48] Furthermore, the Romans use the
term *camillus* to describe the boy, each of whose parents must
be alive, who assists the priest of Jupiter, just as some of the
Greeks call Hermes by the name Cadmilus[49] on account of his
role as an attendant to Zeus.

8. These changes in the administration of Rome earned Numa
the people's goodwill and gratitude, and so immediately he
seized the opportunity to transform his harsh and bellicose city
into one that was more mild and just, as if Rome were iron to
be softened. Rome, at that time, was the very essence of what
Plato describes as a 'city swollen with fiery phlegm',[50] for it had
burst into existence through the bold and reckless courage of
men whose daring and warlike natures had urged them to
make their way to this city, whatever their origins. Then, nourished by frequent campaigns and constant warfare, the city
increased its power, gathering strength from its dangers the
way a stake, when planted in the earth, is more firmly fixed in
the ground by the blows it receives. Now, because Numa realized it was no small or unworthy undertaking to refashion a
people so spirited and violent by introducing a disposition
towards peace, he availed himself of the assistance of the gods.
Thus he conducted many sacrifices, processions and dances,
practices which he himself organized and supervised in person.
These activities combined solemnity with charming amusements and civilizing pursuits, all of which won over the public

and at the same time curbed its headstrong and belligerent instincts. In addition, from time to time, he announced the occurrence of terrifying signs from the gods, such as strange apparitions or dreadful sounds, thus subduing and humbling the Romans' minds through their fear of the gods.

These were the innovations that did the most to establish the tradition that Numa's wisdom and education owed themselves to his deep acquaintance with Pythagoras. For the philosophy of the one, like the political administration of the other, devoted a great deal of attention to studying the gods and establishing the right relationship with them. It is also said that the majestic and dignified manner which Numa cultivated was derived from a habit of mind he shared with Pythagoras. Indeed, this philosopher is thought to have trained an eagle to stop in its flight and come down to him whenever he called it. He is also said to have exhibited his golden thigh when he passed through the crowd at the Olympic Games.[51] And there are other reports of his marvellous devices and deeds, which stimulated Timon the Philasian to write:

> Pythagoras, who stoops to win the reputation of a charlatan,
> Casts his decoys at men, enamoured of solemn speech.[52]

In Numa's case there was the fiction of the love of a goddess or mountain nymph and her secret meetings with him, as I mentioned before.[53] He also claimed to have intimate conversations with the Muses, and he went so far as to attribute most of his revelations to them. He taught the Romans to venerate one Muse in particular and her above all the others, whose name, he said, was Tacita, which means *the silent* or *speechless one*.[54] He did this, it appears, in order to commemorate and honour the Pythagorean precept of maintaining one's silence.

His ordinances regulating statues of the gods are also in close agreement with the teachings of Pythagoras, for this man taught that the First Principle of Being was neither perceptible nor sensible, that it was invisible and uncreated and could be apprehended only by the mind, while Numa, for his part, forbade the Romans from representing divinity in any human or animal form. Indeed, the Romans of this early period did not represent the divine in painting or in sculpture. Although during the first 170 years of their history they busied themselves in constructing temples and setting up shrines, the Romans refused to make graven images for them owing to their conviction that it was impious to assimilate higher beings to inferior ones and that it was impossible to apprehend the divine by any other means than the intellect.[55] Even the Romans' sacrificial rites were strongly reminiscent of Pythagorean cultic practices in that they rarely involved the shedding of blood.[56] Instead, the Romans made offerings of meal, of wine and of other uncostly things.

These are not the only proofs adduced by those who insist that these two men were closely acquainted with one another. There is, for instance, the argument that the Romans enrolled Pythagoras as a citizen of their city, information which is transmitted by Epicharmus[57] the comic poet in a work he addressed to Antenor[58] and for which there is a claim to credibility because its author is a figure from antiquity and belonged to the Pythagorean sect. Furthermore, and this is a second argument, one of King Numa's four sons was named Mamercus, after a son of Pythagoras. It is widely believed that the patrician Aemilii took their name from this son of Numa, for Numa affectionately called him Aemilius on account of the endearing charm of his speech.[59] Finally, when I was in Rome, I listened to many who spoke about how, when once there was an oracle instructing the Romans to honour the most intelligent and courageous of the Greeks by erecting monuments to them, they set up two bronze statues in the forum, one of Alcibiades, the other of Pythagoras.[60] Nevertheless, this is a topic teeming with controversy, and any prolonged attempt at making a convincing case risks the imputation of juvenile disputatiousness.

9. Both the institution of high priests, whom the Romans call *pontifices*, as well as the assignment of their responsibilities are attributed to Numa, who, we are told, was himself the first to be enrolled in their order. They are called *pontifices*, according to some authorities, because they serve the gods, who are

powerful and are the lords of all things, and the Latin word for powerful is *potens*. Others, however, derive the word from the nature of the legislator's prescriptions regarding the performance of their duties, for they maintain that he enjoined upon these priests an obligation to carry out their sacred duties when it was possible to do so but did not hold them responsible should any serious impediment prevent them from actually doing so.[61] Most sources, however, accept an absurd explanation of the priests' designation. Simply put, they are called *bridge-builders* (the Latin word for bridge is *pontem*) on account of the rituals they perform on the bridge,[62] rituals which are deeply sacred and very ancient. These writers add that, along with all their other inviolable and ancestral observances, the priests are responsible for looking after and repairing this bridge, for the Romans believe not only that the demolition of their wooden bridge is sacrilegious but that such an event must result in divine punishment. It is also said that this bridge, in obedience to an oracle, was constructed entirely without iron and is held together by wooden fastenings. The stone bridge was built much later, when Aemilius[63] was quaestor. However, there are also sources claiming that the wooden bridge belongs to a time later than Numa's and was finished in the reign of Ancus Marcius, Numa's grandson by his daughter.

The *pontifex maximus* is responsible for explaining and interpreting divine matters, or, more precisely, for giving instruction in correct ritual practice.[64] Not only does he supervise public ceremonies, he also oversees private sacrifices in order to ensure that no one diverges from established custom, and he teaches everyone the necessary rites for honouring and propitiating the gods. He is also the overseer of the sacred virgins, called Vestals by the Romans, for Numa is credited with the consecration of the Vestal Virgins and the establishment of all the sacred practices associated with the preservation and veneration of the eternal fire,[65] which the Vestals watch over. He did this either out of the belief that, inasmuch as the nature of fire is pure and incorruptible, it should be entrusted to persons whose bodies are chaste and unsullied, or because he associated with virginity the sterile and unproductive qualities of fire. In Greece, wherever a perpetual fire is tended, at Delphi or Athens,[66] to take two examples, its care is entrusted not to virgins but to widows who are past a marriageable age. It sometimes happens that these fires go out. In Athens, they say, the sacred lamp was put out during the tyranny of Aristion,[67] while at Delphi its fire was extinguished when the temple was burned down by the Medes and later, during the Mithridatic War, as well as during the Romans' civil wars, when the altar was destroyed.[68] Under such circumstances it is reportedly forbidden to rekindle the fire from any other fire. Instead, a new and fresh fire must be made by lighting a pure and undefiled flame from the rays of the sun. This is usually accomplished by employing concave mirrors, which have been hollowed out by forming the shapes of right-angled isosceles triangles converging from the periphery of the hollowed space towards a unique central point. When these mirrors are made to face the sun in such a way that its rays are reflected from all sides and concentrated towards the centre, this renders the air in the hollow of the mirror extremely rarefied and, as a result, materials that are very light and very dry, if placed there, quickly ignite owing to their resistance to the sun's rays, which in this environment take on the substance and effect of fire.[69] Returning to the Vestals themselves, there are some who believe that it is only the eternal fire that they watch over, whereas others claim that they also guard certain sacred objects, which they alone are permitted to gaze upon. I have recorded in my *Life of Camillus* what one may rightfully know – and report – about these matters.[70]

10. According to our sources, Gegania and Verenia were the first to be consecrated as Vestals by Numa, who later added Canuleia and Tarpeia. Later still, during the reign of Servius, two more were enrolled,[71] and this is the number of Vestals that has been maintained to the present day. The king decreed that the sacred virgins should preserve their chastity for thirty years, during which time they should spend their first ten years learning what was required of them, their second ten actually performing what they had learned, and their last ten years giving instruction to novices. When these thirty years had elapsed,

any Vestal who so desired it was free to marry and take up a different way of life, once she had quit her holy office. There were few, so we are informed, who took advantage of this indulgence, and those who did so found no happiness in their choice but rather lifelong regret and sorrow, and this had the effect of inspiring in the rest a superstitious fear that bound them to their virginity until they reached old age and death.

Numa granted the Vestals important privileges, including the right to make a will while their fathers were still alive and the right to manage their own affairs without a legal guardian, like mothers of three children.[72] Whenever they go out in public, they are preceded by lictors[73] bearing fasces, and should one of them accidentally encounter a criminal who is being led away for punishment, his life is spared, although she must first swear on her oath that the meeting was involuntary and owing to chance instead of design. If anyone passes beneath a Vestal's litter as she is being transported, he is put to death.

The Vestals' offences are punished, in all instances save one, by whipping. Sometimes when the *pontifex maximus* scourges an errant Vestal, she is naked, although this takes place in a dark confined place obscured by a curtain. But if a Vestal violates her vow of chastity, she is buried alive near the Colline Gate, inside the city where, extending alongside the wall, there is a little ridge of earth which is designated by the Latin word for a rampart.[74] A small subterranean chamber, which can be entered from above, is constructed there. Inside it are a bed equipped with cushions and covers, a lighted lamp and modest provisions of the things necessary for sustaining life, like bread, a bowl of water, milk and oil – as if the Romans thereby sought to acquit themselves of responsibility for starving to death someone who had been consecrated to an exalted sacred office. She who is to be punished is then placed on a litter that is so thoroughly covered and so tightly secured by cords that it is impossible to hear any sound from within. She is then carried through the forum. Everyone makes way for this litter in total silence and, without uttering a sound, follows it in a state of terrible sadness, for no other spectacle is more terrifying than this one, nor is any other day more grievous for the city. When this litter reaches its destination, its attendants loosen its bonds while the chief priest lifts up his hands to the gods and recites mysterious prayers, after which he turns to the fatal moment. He brings the Vestal forth from the litter – she is closely veiled – and he puts her on the steps leading down to the chamber below. Then he looks away, as do the other priests, until she has made her descent. The steps are then taken up and the opening is filled with great quantities of earth, until the site is level with the rest of the mound. This is how the Romans punish any Vestal who violates her vow of virginity.[75]

11. Numa is credited with giving the temple of Vesta,[76] in which the perpetual fire is secured, its circular form. He did this, not to imitate the shape of the earth, as if Vesta were to be identified with the earth,[77] but rather to imitate the structure of the universe, in the centre of which the Pythagoreans place fire and call it Hestia and Monad.[78] As for the earth, the Pythagoreans do not believe that it sits motionless, nor that it exists in the centre of the revolution of the rest of the world. Instead, they maintain that the earth revolves around this central fire and is not included among the most impressive or important parts of the cosmos. Plato is reported to have held this view of the earth when he was an old man, that is, he believed that the earth occupies a secondary space, while the central and dominant space belongs to some other – and better – entity.[79]

12. The pontiffs also give instructions, to any who consult them, on the correct ancestral form of funeral rituals. Numa taught the priests to believe that there was absolutely no trace of pollution in these practices, but instead to venerate, by way of their traditional ceremonies, the gods of the underworld, as if it were they who receive the most important part of ourselves.[80] The Romans especially honour the goddess called Libitina,[81] the divinity who presides over the rites sacred to the dead, whether she is to be identified with Proserpina or, as the most learned of the Romans insist, with Venus, a belief that wisely connects our birth and our death with the power of one and the same goddess. Numa also regulated the duration for

mourning the dead according to the age of the deceased. For a child of fewer than three years,[82] no mourning was permitted. For a child older than that, the number of months given over to mourning could not excel the number of years the child had lived and in no case could exceed ten months. In fact, no deceased person, of whatever age, could be mourned for more than ten months, which was the longest legitimate period for mourning. Ten months is also the length of time that women who have lost their husbands must remain widows. A woman who marries before this interval has elapsed is obliged by the laws of Numa to sacrifice a pregnant cow.

Numa went on to establish many other priesthoods, of which I shall discuss only the Salii and the Fetiales,[83] for these offer unmistakably clear illustrations of his piety. The Fetiales are, as it were, the guardians of peace, and it is my opinion that even the name of their order is derived from this function, for they endeavour to put a halt to disputes by means of negotiation,[84] nor will they permit a military campaign to commence before every other hope of obtaining justice has been eliminated. Among the Greeks, the word for peace refers to two parties settling their disputes by means of deliberation instead of violence.[85] Whenever any party treated the Romans unjustly, the Fetiales paid them several visits during which they tried to persuade them to act fairly. If these requests were ignored, the Fetiales then summoned the gods as witnesses and invoked, upon themselves and upon their country, many terrible curses if there was any injustice in their decision to march out against their enemies. Only then did they declare war. If, however, the Fetiales forbade it or simply refused to give their consent, then it was unlawful for a soldier or even for the king of Rome himself to take up arms. It was only after the Fetiales had declared that the undertaking of a war was just that the ruler, when he received this verdict, could begin to devise his plans for how best to carry out the war.

The dreadful calamity inflicted on the Romans by the Celts is attributed to a failure to observe the judgements of these priests. For once, when the barbarians were besieging Clusium,[86] Fabius Ambustus was sent to their camp as an ambassador in order to obtain a cessation of hostilities. His appeal was rejected, however, at which point, in Fabius' view, he had fulfilled and completed his duty as an ambassador. Then, in the rashness of youth, he took up arms on behalf of the Clusians and went so far as to challenge the most valiant of the barbarians to single combat. The contest went Fabius' way, and he unhorsed his enemy and stripped him of his armour. When the Celts recognized who he was, they sent a herald to Rome who accused Fabius of treacherously violating the truce under which he had come to them and of fighting against them when no war had been declared. At that time, the Fetiales tried to persuade the senate to hand Fabius over to the Celts, but he took refuge with the multitude and, owing to popular favour, escaped the punishment he deserved. Soon thereafter the Celts marched on Rome and sacked the city, except for the Capitol. But these are events I have narrated in more detail in my *Life of Camillus*.[87]

13. As for the priesthood of the Salii,[88] its institution is explained in the following way. In the eighth year of Numa's reign, a plague afflicted the whole of Italy, including Rome. According to our sources, it was when the people were deep in despair that a bronze shield fell from the sky and was delivered into Numa's own hands. A miraculous account of this shield's origin was disclosed by the king, who claimed that he learned it from Egeria and the Muses. The arrival of this shield, he said, ensured the salvation of the city, and it must be protected by making eleven other shields just like it in appearance, size and shape, so that, owing to their resemblance, no one who wished to steal the shield that fell from the sky would be able to recognize which it was. It was also necessary, Numa explained, to consecrate to the Muses the spot where the shield had fallen to earth along with the surrounding meadows, places in which Numa claimed he had often spent time in the Muses' company. In addition, the spring[89] flowing in this spot must be declared holy and reserved for the use of the Vestal Virgins, who should, every day, purify their temple by sprinkling it with this water. The truth of all this, so the story goes, was verified by the sudden

end to the plague. Numa exhibited the shield to the artisans and ordered them to fashion others like it, but all refused except Veturius Mamurius. He was a superb craftsman and was so successful in reproducing the design of the shield that not even Numa could distinguish his eleven copies from the original. So it was to watch over these shields[90] and to care for them that Numa established the priesthood of the Salii.

The Salii[91] are not, despite the assertions of several authorities, named for a certain Salius, a man from Samothrace or Mantinea[92] who was the first to teach dancing performed in armour. They take their name from the dance itself, which is characterized by leaping. They perform this dance whenever they make their way with their shields through the streets of the city, which they do in the month of March.[93] They wear purple tunics, broad belts made of bronze and bronze helmets. They also carry bronze daggers, which they use to strike their shields. The dance itself consists mostly in movements of their feet, which they execute gracefully, moving in varying and shifting steps that display both force and agility, all to a rapid and recurring rhythm.

These shields are called *ancilia* on account of their shape, which is neither round nor oval, like most shields, but instead each shield is cut out so that it has a sinuous outline, the edge of which is rounded, and, where the shield is thick and there are protrusions, the edges are bent so that they form a curve. Or alternatively it may be that these shields are named for the elbow on which they are carried. These, at least, are the suggestions of Juba, in his attempt to derive their name from Greek. But these shields could also have received their name because the first of their number fell from on high, or because it brought a cure to those who were suffering from the plague, or because it put an end to the drought, or because it brought a cessation to the Romans' terrible afflictions,[94] explanations that are analogous to the Athenians' calling the Dioscuri the Anakes[95] – if, that is, we feel obliged to explain the name of the shields by way of the Greek language.

Mamurius, according to some authorities, was compensated for his exquisite workmanship by the inclusion of his name in the song sung by the Salii when they perform their war dance, although there are others who insist that the Salii do not sing about Veturius Mamurius but instead are saying *veterem memoriam*, which means *ancient memorial*.[96]

14. After Numa had regulated the priesthoods, he built, near the temple of Vesta, the building which is called the Regia, which means the royal dwelling.[97] Most of his time was spent there, occupied either in carrying out sacred duties or instructing the priests or in private meditation devoted to the gods. He had another house on the Quirinal Hill and even today the Romans can point out its location.[98] Whenever there was a solemn procession by the priests, or on any ceremonial occasion, heralds were sent ahead to go through the city commanding the people to lay aside their work and be at leisure. For just as the Pythagoreans are said to forbid worshipping the gods or offering them prayers merely in passing, but make it their doctrine that whenever men leave their houses to perform sacred ceremonies they should go forth with their minds concentrated[99] entirely on this one purpose, so too Numa believed that it was wrong for his citizens to hear or watch any religious service when they were busy or concerned with other matters. Consequently, he required that on such occasions the public quit all other activities, concentrating their attention on holy observances as if nothing were more important. By putting a stop to all the noise and clatter and clamour made whenever menial or manual labour is carried out, the people purified the city's streets during the performance of sacred rituals. The Romans preserve a trace of these scruples even today, for whenever a magistrate is taking auspices or sacrificing, there is a cry of *hoc age*,[100] a phrase that means *attend to this* and focuses the attention of bystanders, instilling in them a proper sense of order and decorum.

Many other of Numa's prescriptions resemble the Pythagoreans'. Their teachings, for instance, include 'do not sit on a quart of grain' and 'do not stir a fire with a sword', and 'when setting out on a journey, do not turn back', and, as a final example, 'to the gods above sacrifice an odd number, but an even number to the gods below', all sayings the true meaning of which remains concealed except to a few.[101] So, too, in the case of some of Numa's precepts, the significance is hidden, as is illustrated in maxims like 'do not offer the gods a libation of wine from unpruned vines' or 'do not make a sacrifice without barley', or, again, in the instruction to turn around when worshipping[102] and to sit down after one has worshipped. Now the first two of Numa's directions seem to teach us that cultivating the land is an aspect of piety. As for turning oneself around when worshipping, that action is regarded by some authorities as an imitation of the rotation of the universe, but I rather think that, because temples face east, which means that anyone who enters in order to worship must turn his back to the rising sun, the action of turning oneself first in that direction and then continuing to turn until one is again facing the god of the temple, a move which describes a full circle, has the effect of connecting every divinity with the fulfilment of one's prayer. Unless, by Zeus! this movement has some mysterious association with Egyptian wheels[103] and is therefore meant to teach us that there is no stability in human affairs and so, however the divine may twist and turn our lives, we must accept it and even welcome it. The instruction to sit down after worshipping is explained by pointing out that doing so is a sign that one's prayers have been accepted and that the blessings to be granted will endure. The observation has also been made that pausing in this way distinguishes one sacred act from another, which means that, by sitting in the presence of the gods, a worshipper can conclude one ritual before commencing a second one in the presence of the same gods. This precept, too, can be understood along the lines of my previous discussion of Numa's regulations, for in putting forward this rule the legislator seeks to prevent us from offering our petitions to the gods hastily and in passing, as if we were in a hurry, but instead urges us to do so only when we have sufficient time and leisure.

15. It was because of this training in religion that the city became manageable, and the people were so astounded by Numa's sacred authority that they accepted his strange and

unusual stories and deemed nothing incredible or impossible if Numa wished them to believe it or do it. An example of this is the following story. He once invited a large number of citizens to join him for a meal, at which he placed before them simple dishes and quite ordinary food, but then, just as everyone was beginning to eat, he insisted that the goddess with whom he spent his time had just arrived and suddenly showed them a room filled with expensive goblets and tables laden with every kind of meat and rich furniture.[104] But nothing that is recorded about Numa is more bizarre than the tale of his conversation with Jupiter. Now, according to this story, two minor divinities, Picus and Faunus,[105] dwelt in the region of the Aventine Hill, which in those days was a place of many springs and shaded recesses, not yet a part of the city and so uninhabited by mortals. These divinities were not unlike satyrs or even titans, but what distinguished them was their skill in using powerful drugs and magical spells by means of which they performed, as they travelled up and down Italy, the same marvels as the beings whom the Greeks call the Idaean Dactyls.[106] Numa is said to have gained mastery over Picus and Faunus by adding wine and honey to the spring from which it was their habit to drink. After he captured them, they transformed themselves out of their natural shape into a multitude of different forms, manifesting themselves as monstrous and frightening apparitions. However, when they recognized they were caught fast and escape was impossible, they revealed to Numa many things about the future. And most important of all they taught him the expiatory ritual that must be used when lightning strikes, a ritual the Romans practice to this day and which is performed with onions and hair and sprats.[107]

But some writers tell a different tale, that the ritual was not revealed by these divinities but instead they used their magic to call down Jupiter, who angrily decreed that expiation demanded heads – 'of onions', inserted Numa, by way of completing the phrase. 'Heads of men,' said Jupiter. 'With hair?' asked Numa, again trying to avert the horror of the commandment, but the god answered him, 'with living –' 'sprats', added Numa. Egeria had instructed Numa to say these things. Then Jupiter became kindly disposed to Numa and departed, and this is why the place is called Ilicium,[108] and this is why the expiatory ritual is performed in this way. Fables like this, however ridiculous, reveal the religious disposition of the Romans of that time, a disposition they acquired from habituation. As for Numa, our authorities tell us that his confidence in the divine was so profound that once, when it was reported to him that enemies were marching against the city, he smiled and said, 'Yes, and I am sacrificing.'

16. Numa is also described as the first to raise a temple to Faithfulness[109] and a temple to Terminus.[110] Furthermore, he decreed that among the Romans the oath by Faithfulness should be their most solemn oath, and this remains their practice to this very day. The god Terminus, whose name means *boundary*, is worshipped in both public and private ceremonies wherever the Romans' fields are defined by boundaries. Nowadays this worship involves the sacrifice of living animals, but in the past these rites were bloodless, for Numa in his wisdom recognized that, inasmuch as the god of boundaries was the protector of peace and a witness for justice, he ought to remain pure of any kind of killing.[111] And it is quite clear that it was this king who set limits to the territory of Rome, for Romulus was unwilling to define the extent of his own territory and thereby make it clear how much he had seized from others. After all, borders, when they are respected, act as a curb on the exercise of military power, and if they are not, stand as proofs of injustice. Indeed, at the time of its origin the territory of Rome was not extensive, but through conquest Romulus greatly expanded it. All of this captured land Numa distributed among the poor, for he wished to eliminate the neediness that compels men to behave criminally and instead to turn the people towards agriculture so that they might become settled along with their lands. For there is no other occupation that engenders a passion for peace so keen and so instant as does the life of a farmer, for while it preserves a martial boldness sufficient to protect one's own property, it curtails the urge to act unjustly or greedily. This is why Numa administered

farming to his citizens as if it were a peace-potion, and welcomed this vocation as a means of instilling in his people skills
that made them better men rather than simply richer men. He
then divided this territory into districts, which he called *pagi*,[112]
and for each of them he appointed an overseer, to whom he
assigned attendants. Sometimes, however, he visited these districts in person, and he formed an estimation of the character
of each of his citizens on the basis of the work they had done
on their farms. Some he elevated to positions of honour and
trust, but others he faulted for their sloth and carelessness, correction which he hoped would bring them to their senses.[113]

17. Of all his institutional reforms, by far the most admired was
his division of the common people along the lines of their trades
and crafts.[114] For, although ostensibly the city was defined by the
union of two nations, a situation I described earlier,[115] in reality
it was divided between these two nations, which refused to join
with one another or to put aside their differences. Instead, inter-
minable conflicts and quarrels persisted. Numa took a lesson
from material substances that are hard and by nature difficult to
combine. When these are crushed and reduced to particles, they
become easy to mix together owing to the smallness of their elements. So he decided to increase the number of divisions among
the common people and, by creating many new distinctions, dissolve the original and fundamental division keeping them apart,
which would disappear amid so many minor ones. Therefore he
divided them by their trades and crafts into flautists, goldsmiths,
carpenters, dyers, leatherworkers, curriers, blacksmiths and pot-
ters. As for the remaining occupations, these he united into a
single organization. Furthermore, he established meetings and
assemblies and even religious ceremonies suitable for each of
these newly formed associations. Then, for the first time, the
habit of describing or regarding some citizens as Sabines and
others as Romans vanished from the city, nor did anyone any
longer describe some men as subjects of Tatius, others as subjects
of Romulus. Thus did Numa's new classifications result in the
harmonious union of all with all.

Another of Numa's measures that is praised is his reform of

the law allowing fathers to sell their sons into slavery. He introduced an exception for sons who had married either with their father's approval or in obedience to their father's commandment, the reason being that it seemed unfair that a woman who had married a free man should find herself living with a slave.[116]

18. Numa also applied himself to the study of the calendar, not with scientific exactness but with a respectable degree of careful observation. During the reign of Romulus, the Romans had arranged their months with neither reason nor regularity, allocating fewer than twenty days to some, to others thirty-five days, and still more days to others. Nor had they any idea of the inequality obtaining between the annual courses of the sun and the moon. They had instead only one rule, which was that the year should last 360 days. But Numa calculated that the inequality between the sun's and the moon's courses was eleven days, since the lunar year lasted 354 days whereas the solar year lasted 365. Consequently, he doubled this number and in every other year inserted, after the month of February, an intercalary month, which the Romans call Mercedonius and which lasts twenty-two days. This solution, however, later entailed other and greater changes in the calendar.[117]

He changed the order of the months. March, which had been the first month, he put third, whereas January, which during the reign of Romulus had been the eleventh month, he now put first.[118] February, which had been the twelfth and final month of the year, now became the second. However, there are many authorities who insist that Numa added January and February to the calendar and that originally the Roman calendar had only ten months, as, among some barbarians, there are only three months in the year and, among the Greeks, the Arcadians have four[119] and the Acarnanians six. Scholars tell us that the Egyptians at first had a year with only a single month in it, though afterwards they increased the number to four. This explains why, although they inhabit a land that is very new, the Egyptians appear to be an ancient people whose genealogies go back an inconceivable number of years, for they count their months as if they were years.

19. The proof that the Romans originally had only ten months
in their year is the name of their last month, which they still call
the Tenth Month.[120] And it can be shown that March used to
be their first month by examining the sequence of months that
follow it, for the name of the fifth month after March[121] was
derived from the Latin word for fifth, the name of the sixth
month after March[122] from the Latin word for sixth, and so on
for all the remaining months. When the Romans added January and February before March, the result was that what was
now their seventh month was still named the Fifth Month.
Besides, it is only reasonable to conclude that Romulus would
put March first, since it is the month that is sacred to Mars, and
April second, because it is named after Aphrodite,[123] which is
why the Romans sacrifice to this goddess in April[124] and why,
on the first day of this month, their women bathe wearing
garlands of myrtle. Some commentators disagree with this
derivation, arguing that the name of the month is not pronounced as *Aphril* but – without aspiration – as *April*.[125] They
prefer to derive the name of this month from the fact that it
marks the height of spring, when the buds and shoots of plants
are opened, because the name of the month signifies opening in
Latin.[126] The next month in succession is called May, a name
derived from Maia, the mother of Mercury, to whom the month
is sacred, and this month is followed by June, which is named
for Juno. A different tradition derives the names of these
months from stages of life, one meaning older and the other
younger, for in Latin *maiores* is the word for older men and
iuniores the word for younger men.[127] The remaining months
the Romans named solely on the basis of their order, as if they
were counting them. In other words, they named them fifth,
sixth, seventh, eighth, ninth and tenth.[128] Subsequently, the
fifth month was renamed July after the Caesar who vanquished
Pompey. The sixth month was named August, after Caesar's
successor, who received the name Augustus. Domitian imposed
new names on the seventh and eighth months,[129] but that was
not for long, inasmuch as, after his assassination, their previous names were restored. Only the last two months in this

sequence have preserved the names they were first given without any change whatsoever.

Of the months which Numa added or transposed, February may fairly be deemed a month of purification, for that is more or less the meaning of the name of the month, and it is in this month that the Romans make sacrifices to the dead and celebrate the Lupercalia, which in most respects resembles a purification.[130] The first month, January, takes its name from Janus.[131] Now I believe that Numa deprived the month named for Mars of its place at the start of the year because he wished in every respect to prefer civil values to martial ones. For in ancient times, it is said, this Janus, who was either a demi-god or a mortal king, devoted his political and humanitarian qualities to elevating the condition of mankind, which in those days was bestial and savage. This is why Janus is represented with two faces, because he brought to men's lives a new outlook and way of living, which replaced what existed before.

20. Janus also has a temple in Rome that consists mostly of two doors, which the Romans call the Gate of War.[132] It is their custom to open this gate during times of war and to close it whenever there is peace. Closing this gate has occurred rarely and only with difficulty, because, as the Romans' dominion expanded, they continually came into conflict with fresh barbarian tribes dwelling nearby, and, as a consequence, found themselves always at war. In the time of Augustus Caesar the gate was closed after his victory over Antony.[133] Before that it was closed for a brief time when Marcus Atilius and Titus Manlius were consuls.[134] In each case, however, war broke out once more and the gate was opened. During the reign of Numa, by contrast, this gate was not seen open for even a single day. Instead, it remained closed for forty-three years, so lasting and universal was the disappearance of war in that time. This can be explained by the fact that it was not only the Roman people who were charmed and rendered peaceable by the justice and mildness of their king. The surrounding cities, as if a gentle zephyr were wafting from Rome, or a salubrious breeze, also

began to change their habits, for all were filled with a desire to live in peace under good laws, to cultivate their lands, to rear their children in quiet and to honour the gods. Throughout Italy there were festivals and banquets, while everyone, whatever his city, made friendly visits to other cities, frequently and without fear. The wisdom of Numa was like a spring out of which noble feelings and a sense of justice poured into all, while his serenity spread everywhere. Even the hyperbole of poets, we are told, falls short of the reality of those days, even lines like

> On shield handles shod with iron, rust-coloured spiders weave
>   their webs

or

> Spear points and two-edged swords are consumed by decay,
> No more the blast of brazen trumpets,
> Nor are the eyes despoiled of sweet sleep.[135]

Indeed, historians record neither war nor sedition nor revolution during the reign of Numa. No one hated or envied the king, nor did ambition for power stimulate plots or conspiracies against his throne. Whether it was owing to fear of the gods, who seemed to protect him, or respect for his virtue, or perhaps even his good fortune, which was itself divine in origin and kept the men of his time pure of any wickedness, Numa was in any case an unmistakable example and a convincing proof of an opinion which, many generations later, Plato dared to express about the nature of government. For he insisted that respite and rescue from human ills would come only when, thanks to a stroke of good fortune sent by the gods, the power of a king should be joined in one person with the understanding of a philosopher, thereby assuring that virtue would remain lord and master over vice. 'For blessed is he', this man who is truly wise and temperate, 'and blessed, too, are they who hear the words of wisdom and temperance issuing from his mouth.'[136] As soon as this happens, there will be no need for coercion or threats in dealing with the multitude, for, when the people witness in the life of their ruler a conspicuous and splendid model of virtuous conduct, they will of their own accord behave wisely and temperately, and they will unite in friendship and concord in order to lead blameless and blessed lives shaped by justice and moderation. In this lies the noblest purpose of any government, and he is most worthy to be a king who can inspire in his subjects this way of life and this disposition. It is obvious how, more than anyone else, Numa understood these things.

21. On the topic of Numa's children and his wives, authorities disagree. According to some,[137] Tatia was his only wife and Pompilia his only child. Others, however, attribute to Numa, in addition to his daughter, four sons. These are Pompon, Pinus, Calpus and Mamercus, each of whom is the ancestor of a distinguished family. From Pompon the Pomponii are descended, from Pinus the Pinarii, from Calpus the Calpurnii and from Mamercus the Marcii, who on account of their origins assume the surname Reges, which means *kings*.[138] There also exists a third class of writers. They accuse their rivals of fabricating genealogies going back to Numa in order to flatter these great families.[139] They also claim that Pompilia was not the daughter of Tatia but instead of Lucretia, another woman whom Numa married after he became king. Still, all our sources agree that Pompilia was married to Marcius, who was a son of the Marcius who persuaded Numa to accept the throne.[140] That Marcius came to Rome with Numa, where he was honoured with membership in the senate. After Numa's death, he competed with Hostilius[141] for the succession, but he lost and consequently starved himself to death. His son, however, the Marcius who was married to Pompilia, remained in Rome and was the father of Ancus Marcius, who was king of Rome after Tullus Hostilius. Ancus Marcius, we learn, was only five years old when Numa died. His death was neither swift nor sudden. Instead, according to Piso, he died gradually of old age and the effects of a debilitating malady.[142] At the time of his death he was slightly more than eighty years old.

22. The enviable quality of Numa's life was revealed even in his funeral. All the nations that were allies or friends of Rome assembled at these rites, bearing offerings and crowns. His bier was carried by senators, who were accompanied by the priests of the gods. The rest of the people, including the women and the children, followed them, yet not like subjects marching in the funeral cortège of an aged king but instead with weeping and lamentations, as if each was laying to rest a loved one taken in the very flower of life. On his own instructions, it is reported, they did not cremate his corpse. They made two stone coffins, which they buried beneath the Janiculum.[143] One of these coffins contained his body, the other the sacred books he had written himself, just as Greek lawgivers make their own tablets. While he was living Numa had taught the priests what he had written and fixed in their minds both the practices prescribed in his books as well as their purposes. Consequently, he commanded that his books be buried at the same time as his body, for he deemed it wrong to entrust sacred mysteries to lifeless writings. It is, they say, for this same reason that the Pythagoreans do not commit their doctrines to writing but instead, through oral instruction, teach them to those who are worthy of receiving them. Once, they say, when they taught the solution to certain abstruse and secret geometrical problems to an unworthy person, who then divulged these mysteries to others, the gods threatened to punish this profanation and impiety with a severe public calamity. This is why one must forgive anyone who is keen to argue, on the basis of the many resemblances between them, that Numa and Pythagoras knew one another. Antias[144] reports that in this stone coffin there were twelve books dealing with priestly matters and twelve more that discussed various topics in Greek philosophy.

About 400 years later, when Publius Cornelius and Marcus Baebius were consuls,[145] there was a great storm during which a violent torrent washed away the earth, dislodging the coffins, the lids of which fell off. One could see that one coffin was entirely empty, without any trace of a corpse, but in the other one Numa's books remained. The praetor Petilius[146] is said to have read them, after which he brought them before the senate

and declared that, in his opinion, it was counter to human and
divine law for these texts to be shared with the public. Consequently, the books were taken to the Comitium[147] and burned.

It is the fate of all good and just men to receive more praise
after their deaths than when they are alive, for the envy they
inspire does not long survive them, and sometimes even dies
before they do. And, indeed, the misfortunes of the kings who
succeeded Numa added lustre to his reputation. Of the five
kings who came after him, the last one was overthrown and
grew old in exile,[148] and, of the remaining four,[149] none died a
natural death. Three were plotted against and murdered. As for
Tullus Hostilius, who was the next to be king after Numa, he
jeered at Numa's noble qualities, especially his religious devo-
tions, which, he claimed, left men lazy and effeminate. He
turned his citizens to war instead. But not even he could persist
in his childish insolence, for, when he was afflicted with a grave
and intractable malady, he gave himself over to superstitions
that were nothing like the seemly piety of Numa. In the end, he
led the Romans to even more extreme forms of superstition,
for, we are told, he perished when he was struck by lightning.

COMPARISON OF
LYCURGUS AND NUMA

1 (23). Now that I have recounted the lives of Numa and Lycurgus, each of whom has been clearly depicted for the reader, I must not shrink from the task, however difficult it may prove, of collecting their differences. For it is unmistakable, from the evidence of their deeds, how much they have in common: their moderation, their piety, their talents as statesmen and teachers. And each of them predicated his legislation on a divine source.[1] Still, each can boast noble achievements all his own. To begin with, Numa received but Lycurgus resigned a kingdom.[2] One got his kingdom without asking for it, the other had his kingdom but gave it up. Although Numa was a private citizen and a foreigner, he was chosen by others to be their sovereign, whereas Lycurgus, who was a king, elected to become a private citizen. It is unquestionably a noble thing to acquire a kingdom because one is just, but it is also noble to hold justice in higher regard than a kingdom. It was virtue that made the one so illustrious that he was deemed worthy of a kingdom, just as it was virtue that made the other so great that he could despise a kingdom.

Let us turn to a second distinction. Just as a musician tunes his lyre by tightening or loosening its strings, so Lycurgus tightened the strings of a decadent Sparta, while for his part Numa loosened the strings of a Rome whose pitch was too high.[3] Lycurgus' task was harder to achieve. After all, he had to persuade his countrymen not to remove their breastplates and put down their swords, but instead to surrender their gold and silver and to cast away their expensive beds and tables, not to stop waging wars in order to celebrate festivals and make sacrifices but to leave off feasting and drinking in order to toil and train as soldiers and athletes. This is why Numa easily persuaded his people, owing to the favour and honour in which they held him, while Lycurgus suffered danger and actual wounds and even then barely managed to succeed.[4]

Numa's muse, however, was civilized and humane, and he converted his people to peace and justice by calming their violent and ardent dispositions. Furthermore, if, in assessing Lycurgus, we must take into consideration the Spartans' treatment of their helots,[5] which is an extremely savage and lawless practice,[6] we must then concede that, as a lawgiver, Numa – far more than Lycurgus – conformed to Greek ideals. For Numa allowed men who were slaves plain and simple to enjoy a taste of dignity and freedom by establishing the custom whereby slaves feast with their masters during the Saturnalia. This is recorded as one of Numa's institutions, and it allows anyone who has contributed to producing a year's fruits some share in their enjoyment. Others, however, turn to myth as an explanation of this custom and consider it a reminder of the equality that existed during the age of Saturn,[7] when there was neither slave nor master and all men regarded one another as kinsmen and equals.

2 (24). In general, it is obvious how both Numa and Lycurgus led their peoples to self-sufficiency and temperance. Of the remaining virtues, one was more enamoured of valour, the other of justice – unless, by Zeus! it was the case that these two societies, which were characterized by different natures and habits, demanded different measures from their lawgivers. For Numa did not put a halt to the waging of war out of cowardice but rather to stop injustice. Nor did Lycurgus make the Spartans more belligerent in order to promote injustice but rather to stop them from suffering injustice at the hands of others. Both kings, then, in order to eliminate their citizens' excesses and correct their deficiencies, were forced to introduce major reforms.

In so far as the division and classification of the citizenry is concerned, Numa's arrangement was populist and favourable to the masses, for he made his people into a diffuse and variegated community of goldsmiths and musicians and shoemakers,[8] whereas Lycurgus' was strictly aristocratic: he considered crafts like these impure[9] and assigned them to slaves and resident aliens, while he directed citizens to take up shields and spears and thereby become experts in the craft of warfare, servants of Ares[10] whose only occupation lay in obedience to their commanders and in overpowering Sparta's enemies. Lycurgus did not allow free men to engage in any profitable business, in order to keep them free in each and every respect. Consequently, all commerce was the responsibility of slaves and helots, a chore they carried out just as they looked after the preparation and serving of the citizens' meals. No such distinction was made by Numa, who, although he curbed the soldiers' rapacity, did nothing to prohibit other means of making money. Nor was he bothered by economic inequalities: the acquisition of wealth he left unrestricted, and he remained unconcerned as rising poverty crept into the city. And yet he had a moral duty from the very beginning – before disparities became deep and widespread and while most people shared more or less the same means – to put a stop to avarice. This is what Lycurgus did, and in this way he prevented the harm that avarice can cause, which has shown itself to be far from trifling and has in fact proved to be the origin and very seed of history's most serious and devastating evils.

It is wrong, in my view, to find fault with Lycurgus for making a redistribution of land or with Numa for not doing so. In Lycurgus' case, the equality gained by redistributing land was the very foundation of his state's constitution,[11] and, as for Numa, inasmuch as the land had recently been allocated, there was no pressing reason to make new allotments or for upsetting what was very likely the original assignment of the city's land.[12]

3 (25). Lycurgus and Numa, each of them for sound and statesmanlike reasons, endorsed shared marriages and shared offspring,

and with this in mind endeavoured to get rid of the jealousies that husbands naturally feel regarding their wives. However, they approached the matter in quite different ways. A Roman husband who had enough children might be persuaded by another man, who was in want of children, to relinquish his wife: the Roman might give her up entirely, or he might give her up but thereafter marry her once again.[13] The Spartan, by contrast, although he would keep his wife in his home and his marriage would carry on as it always had, might nonetheless offer his wife to another man, if that man could persuade him to share her for the purpose of getting children. And there were many husbands, as I have already observed,[14] who would invite and introduce into their homes such men as they thought likeliest to father handsome and brave sons. What, then, is the difference between these customs? Do we not see how the Spartan exhibits a complete and total indifference to his wife and to those emotions that disturb and anger most men by consuming them with jealousy, whereas, in the case of the Roman, his discretion lends a modest cover to the reality of this arrangement, as if it were a wedding veil, all of which indicates that he finds sharing his wife difficult to do?

Furthermore, Numa was vigilant in his efforts to maintain the femininity and decorum of young girls,[15] whereas they were not a bit restrained by Lycurgus, which was not merely unsuitable to their sex but provoked commentary from the poets.[16] Ibycus referred to Spartan maidens as 'thigh-flaunters',[17] and Euripides criticized them as man-crazy in lines like these:

> Never at home, they are always with young men,
> Their thighs are naked and their robes unfastened.[18]

In fact young girls in Sparta did wear tunics the sides of which were not sewn together below the waist, and so, when they walked, their tunics flew back and completely revealed their thighs. Sophocles depicts this vividly in the following lines:

> And that young girl, whose still unsewn tunic
> Falls round her exposed thigh, is Hermione.[19]

This is why Spartan wives were said to be too presumptuous, acting the part of men not least in the presence of their husbands, since they ruled their households like autocrats, and in public affairs they expressed their views – without inhibition – on the weightiest matters.

As for Numa, although he scrupulously preserved for married women the courtesies and respect from their husbands that had been prescribed by Romulus when he granted them honours as compensation for their abduction,[20] he nevertheless insisted on their behaving with the utmost modesty: he forbade their meddling in other people's business, taught them sobriety and trained them to keep silent.[21] Thus they abstained from wine and from discussing important matters unless their husbands were present. It is in fact reported that when once a woman pleaded her own case in the forum,[22] the senate sent envoys to an oracle to ask what this prodigy portended for the city. The most convincing proof of the obedience and mildness of Roman wives lies in the nature of our evidence for such women as were disagreeable. For just as our historians record for us the names of those men who were the first to murder a kinsman or to wage war against a brother or to slay a father or mother, so the Romans preserve the fact that Spurius Carvilius was the first man to divorce his wife, and he did this 230 years after the founding of Rome,[23] when nothing of the like had ever before occurred. We also learn that Thalaea, the wife of Pinarius, was the first woman to quarrel with her mother-in-law,[24] whose name was Gegania, and this took place in the reign of Tarquinius Superbus. This makes it clear how well and how suitably Roman marriages were regulated by their lawgiver.

4 (26). When it comes to the marriageability of young girls, the practices of the two peoples are consistent with methods they use in rearing their daughters. Lycurgus allowed them to marry only when they were mature enough to desire sexual relations, so that intercourse with their husbands, coinciding with their natural cravings, might be a source of affection and love instead of hatred and fear, which could result if they were forced to

have sex before it was natural to them.[25] He also wanted their bodies to be vigorous enough to be able to endure the strains of pregnancy and childbirth, for he believed that marriage served no other purpose than the production of children. By contrast, the Romans give their daughters in marriage at the age of twelve or even younger, the idea being that this would ensure that, when they married, they were pure in body and character.[26] It is clear, then, how one approach is mostly concerned with the question of the girls' physical development and is focused on the procreation of children, whereas the other gives greater consideration to the girls' moral development, focusing on the quality of conjugal life.

However, in his careful attention to boys, by way of their organization into groups, their instruction and their communal upbringing, and in his exacting regulations for their meals and exercises and games,[27] Lycurgus makes it clear how Numa was no better than any other lawgiver. For Numa left it up to their fathers to determine, according to their preferences or needs, how best to raise their sons.[28] If he wished, a father might make his son a farmer or shipbuilder, or teach him to become a blacksmith or a flautist, as if the right thing to do were not to train them all for one purpose and to mould all their characters in the same way. Instead, Numa's Romans grew up to be like passengers on a ship, each taking part in its voyage for very different reasons and therefore only coming together for the common good if a danger should arise (because everyone is afraid of suffering a private loss) but otherwise each looking only to his own interest. Granted it is pointless to find fault with most lawgivers who fail owing either to ignorance or incapacity, but, in the case of a man who is wise and has been chosen king by a people with no long-standing institutions and who can thus refuse him nothing, what priority could come before educating boys and training young men with the goal of eliminating disruptive differences in their characters, so that, shaped and moulded in one and the same virtue from the very beginning, they might remain in harmony? It was this system of education that, in addition to all its other advantages, helped to preserve the laws of Lycurgus. The Spartans' oaths to abide by Lycurgus' legislation would not really have counted for much had this system of educating and training the young not instilled his laws into their character by making the love of his constitution an element of their upbringing.[29] As a consequence, for more than 500 years the principal and most important of his laws persisted unchanged, like the pigments of a strong and indelible dye. Although Numa's constitution was designed to ensure that the Romans continued in peace and amity, all that ceased at the end of his reign. After his death, the two gates of the temple he had kept closed, as if he really kept war itself confined and imprisoned within, were opened, and the Romans filled Italy with blood and corpses.[30] Not even for a brief time, then, did Numa's institutions persist, although they were truly noble and just, and this came about because they lacked an adequate foundation in the education of the young.[31]

'But wait,' someone will say, 'is it not true that Rome advanced to a better condition by way of her wars?' That is a question that will require a long answer if one is speaking with men for whom what is better consists of riches, luxury and domination instead of security, mildness and independence tempered by justice.[32] Nevertheless, even this objection seems to speak in Lycurgus' favour, for it was only after they had given up Numa's constitution that the Romans increased their power, whereas, in the case of the Lacedaemonians, no sooner did they abandon the regulations instituted by Lycurgus than they fell from the highest to the lowest condition, lost their domination of Greece and were in danger of being utterly destroyed.[33]

Still, there remains one great and truly divine dimension to Numa's career, the fact that, although he was a foreigner, he was sent for to be king and proceeded to bring about major reforms strictly through persuasion, maintaining his mastery over a reluctant and demurring city without recourse to arms or violence – unlike Lycurgus, who led his nobles against the common people – but instead, Numa won over his citizens and brought them into harmony owing to his wisdom and justice.

PUBLICOLA

INTRODUCTION TO PUBLICOLA

The Civic Hero

Ideally, the Roman emperor was possessed of every talent essential for success in war and in peace. On campaign, his supreme command was grounded in his superior martial valour, whereas, in matters pertaining to the political administration of the empire or the society of his fellow-aristocrats, he should, for all his natural majesty, exhibit a welcoming and courteous degree of moderation and civility – an imperial virtue the Romans designated as *civilitas*. All emperors enjoyed unexcelled authority, but only base ones behaved like raw autocrats – and even the worst of Rome's emperors shared with their subjects the opinion that tyranny was an abomination and a thing utterly un-Roman in its nature. Instead, so insisted imperial panegyrists and moralists alike, the good emperor was a figure who employed his might in ensuring the freedom and security – and the dignity – of his subjects, not least by way of his commitment to justice.[1] It is from the perspective of this imperial ideology that we must read Plutarch's Life of Publius Valerius Publicola.

Publicola was a founding father and a champion of the new republic established in 509 BC after the tyrannical king, Tarquinius Superbus, had been driven into exile. The significance of this event in Roman history cannot be overestimated, and the political and social values which the Romans associated with their republic persisted long after its constitution had been replaced by the rule of emperors.[2] The republic, so the Romans believed, was marked by a wise and responsible leadership responsive to its public. The fall of the monarchy and the establishment of the republic – and its subsequent defence from the exiled Tarquinius and his Etruscan allies – were events that attracted the exploits of many legendary heroes. Tarquinius was overthrown in an aristocratic coup led by Lucius Junius Brutus, Lucius Tarquinius Collatinus, Spurius Lucretius, Marcus Horatius Pulvillus and Publius Valerius Publicola – all of them said to have been consuls in the first year of the republic, magisterial clutter that suffices to demonstrate the unreliability of Rome's early historical narrative. Furthermore, the defence of the republic required the exertions of legendary figures like Mucius Scaevola, Horatius Cocles, even Cloelia, each of whom makes an appearance in this biography.

Plainly, then, Publicola was only one of many heroes of the early republic, and hardly its most eminent figure. That, surely, was Brutus, the striking fluctuations of whose career, in combination with the man's fierce severity in service to Rome, ought to have made for a fascinating, even exciting, and yet satisfactorily moralizing read. Publicola's Life, by contrast, while not short of adventure and accomplishment, is marked by numerous chapters in which its hero vanishes from the scene or is only obliquely connected to it. Put differently, there is room in Publicola's Life for the achievements of others. And that, of course, is part of its point.

Publicola was consul in 509 BC, including a brief period in which he was sole consul. He was again consul in 508, 507 and 504. He was credited with two triumphs but was equally celebrated for negotiating a peace with Lars Porsenna, the king of Clusium, which brought to an end Tarquinius' attempts at rousing the Etruscans in support of his restoration to the Roman throne. It was also he, in this Life at least, who succeeded in bringing to Rome one of its most brilliant families, the Claudians. Publicola was especially remembered as a legislator who made the new order agreeable to the Roman people by establishing enduring popular rights, which is why Plutarch matches him with the iconic Athenian legislator Solon (c. 638–558 BC). In their pairing, each exhibits a genius for resolving dangerous social conflicts, which for Plutarch represents the highest form of political skill.

Reconciling others came naturally to Publicola, and early in his Life he displays, even during Tarquinius' tyranny, boldness in defence of justice, evidence for Plutarch that 'should Rome ever become a democracy, he would certainly be one of its leading men' (ch. 1). Now, this early introduction of democracy is explicable on account of Publicola's being matched with Solon. But it must not be overlooked that, for Greek writers of the imperial period, *democratic* (*demotikos*), when applied to governors and magistrates and especially to the emperor, served as the Greek equivalent of *civil* (*civilis*), the imperial virtue cited above. And, for Plutarch, Publicola is the embodiment of civility and moderation, a conclusion he draws in chapter 12: 'Publicola, then, revealed himself to be a lawgiver who was sensitive to popular rights [*demotikos*], as well as moderate.' During his first consulship, when after Brutus' death he was Rome's sole consul and was dwelling in a grand house on the Palatine, Publicola was accused of having tyrannical aspirations. These suspicions he allayed by demolishing his mansion and by displaying before the people a proper respect for its sovereignty, actions that instilled a popular appreciation for his high-mindedness, that is to say, his *megalophrosyne*, another imperial virtue that registered a ruler's unwillingness to descend into tyranny. These qualities of Publicola mark a striking contrast with the one emperor who is mentioned in this Life, the wicked Domitian, whose appetite for luxurious building, including the furnishing of his own Palatine mansion, reveals his baseness as well as his tastelessness (ch. 15).

Nothing in Plutarch's analysis of Publicola's statesmanlike behaviour should be mistaken for idealizing sentimentality. He knew very well that it was through exercising the virtues of moderation and civility that Publicola, like any leader in similar circumstances, enhanced his real political authority:

Now, it was hardly the case that in doing this Valerius actually abased himself, as the multitude was mistakenly inclined to believe, but rather, by exercising moderation, he checked and

eliminated the people's envy of his authority, thereby adding as
much to his real influence as he appeared to be giving up in political power. It was because of this that the public submitted to
him gladly, and willingly obeyed him.

(ch. 10)

Thus the quality of good leadership remains the same, be the
government republican or imperial, and Publicola is nothing
less than an exemplary specimen of its ideal practice. This Life,
then, is an essay on sound statesmanship.

Naturally, the Publicola of Plutarch's Life, like the Publicola
he found in his sources, is a figure more legendary than historical. In 1977, however, an inscription was discovered near
Borgo Montello at the site of ancient Satricum (for which reason it is known as the *lapis Satricum*). It dates from around
500 BC and records a dedication made to Mars by 'the companions of Poplios Valesios'. Now this figure is unquestionably
to be connected with our Publius Valerius Publicola, but *this*
Valerius, the leader of a band of loyal fighters, was a local war-
lord and plainly nothing like the Roman consul whose fame lay
in forging the good government of the republic.[3] In this instance,
a fragment of realia from Rome's early history helps us to
appreciate the profound gap between what our sources report
and what was actually the case at the time.

Sources

Doubtless Plutarch consulted Dionysius of Halicarnassus and
Livy. And for this Life he unquestionably turned to Valerius
Antias (on whom see Introduction to *Romulus*). Of course,
Plutarch's interests in early Rome and antiquarianism led him
to read widely, and it is impossible to identify his every source.
For instance, at *Brutus* 40, Plutarch cites the memoirs of
Valerius Messala Corvinus, the great general and statesman of
the Augustan age: his account of the civil war[4] may also have
included notices of his illustrious ancestry, including the great
Publicola, which Plutarch took up (even though Messala's
work is never mentioned in this Life).

LIFE OF PUBLICOLA

[consul in 509 BC]

1. Such a man as this was Solon.[1] For his parallel, we turn to
the life of Publicola, who received this name as an honour from
the Roman people.[2] Prior to that he was called Publius Valerius.
He was reputed to be a descendant of the Valerius who, in
ancient times, had been chiefly responsible for the reconciliation between Romans and Sabines that led to their becoming
a single people, for it was he who persuaded their kings to meet
with one another in order to settle their differences.[3] This is
what our sources tell us about Valerius' origins. During the
period when Rome was still ruled by kings, he became distinguished for his eloquence and wealth,[4] always using the one in
truthfully and openly defending justice and the other in offering liberal and humane assistance to the needy. These practices
made it clear that, should Rome ever become a democracy, he
would certainly be one of its leading men.

Now inasmuch as Tarquinius Superbus[5] had acquired his
power ignobly through impiety and injustice, and did not govern like a king but like a violent and arrogant tyrant, the people
found him odious and intolerable. Consequently, when Lucretia[6] took her own life after she had been raped, the people
seized the moment to rise in rebellion. Lucius Brutus,[7] taking
charge of this revolution,[8] went first to Valerius and, with his
fervent cooperation, expelled the monarchy.

So long as it seemed likely that the people would select a
single magistrate to replace their king, Valerius was content to
remain quiet, for he believed it more than fitting that Brutus,
who had taken the lead in the cause of freedom, hold the office.
The people, however, disliked the idea of putting all political

authority in the hands of one man, believing instead that, by dividing this power, it would be easier to endure. For this reason, they proposed and demanded that two men be elected.[9] At this point, Valerius began to hope that he would be elected after Brutus and share the consulship with him. He was disappointed, however, when, despite his receiving an endorsement from Brutus, Valerius was passed over and Tarquinius Collatinus, the husband of Lucretia, was elected Brutus' colleague. Collatinus was by no means Valerius' superior in merit, but the leading men of the city were still afraid of the king, who, although in exile, continued to exert himself in striving to regain the city's favour. For this reason they wished to have a leader who was one of the king's bitterest enemies on the grounds that he would be unrelenting in his opposition to the monarchy.[10]

2. Valerius, indignant when his capacity to do everything he could for his country was put in doubt simply because he had suffered no personal injury during the tyranny, withdrew from the senate, ceased pleading in the courts, and renounced public affairs altogether. This gave rise to anxious murmuring on the part of the multitude, who worried that, owing to his anger, Valerius might attach himself to the party of the king and subvert the new government, which was not yet securely established. However, when Brutus, because he was suspicious of the loyalties of other prominent men, wanted the senate to take a sacrificial oath[11] and fixed a day for it, Valerius came cheerfully down to the forum and was the first man to swear that he would never yield or submit to the Tarquins but would fight for freedom with all his might. This pleased the senate and encouraged the consuls. And at once Valerius' oath was confirmed by his deeds. For Tarquinius sent envoys[12] bearing conciliatory letters as well as appealing proposals which they believed would seduce the multitude, for they were offered by a king who gave the impression of abandoning his pride and seeking only modest concessions.[13] The consuls took the view that these men had to be allowed to appear before a public assembly, but Valerius would not allow it. On the contrary, he

was absolutely opposed to supplying opportunities or pretexts for overthrowing the new government to men whose poverty would render revolution an even more grievous burden than tyranny.

3. Afterwards, there came new envoys who announced that Tarquinius had renounced his throne and given up his war against Rome. He sought instead, on his own behalf as well as that of his friends and relations, the return of their riches and goods, for they needed these to sustain themselves in exile. Many were inclined to allow this, not least Collatinus, who joined in supporting the proposal.[14] Brutus, however, whose nature was harsh and unbending, rushed to the forum, where he accused his colleague of treason on the grounds that he favoured handing over to men for whom it would be danger-ous to vote even basic subsistence during their exile material resources sufficient for resuming war or even restoring their tyranny. The citizens were then assembled, and the first man to address them was a private citizen named Gaius Minucius.[15] He exhorted both Brutus and the Roman people to see to it that the wealth of the Tarquins remained the people's ally in their fight against tyranny and not be allowed to take the tyr-ant's side against the Roman people. In spite of this, however, the Romans decreed that, since they now possessed the free-dom they had fought for, they would not, for the sake of Tarquinius' property, reject peace. They decided instead to rid themselves simultaneously of the tyrants and the tyrants' riches.[16]

But Tarquinius was not concerned about his property. His request for its return had in reality been a ruse for sounding out public opinion in Rome and for laying the groundwork for the city's betrayal.[17] His agents, by busying themselves in disposing of the king's wealth – selling one part of it, retaining another, sending the rest of it abroad – found excuses for extending their stay in Rome. In the end, they succeeded in corrupting two of the noblest families in the city, the Aquillii, three of whom were members of the senate, and the Vitellii, of whom two were senators. All of these men, through their mother, were nephews of Collatinus.[18] The Vitellii were also related to Brutus, for he had married one of their sisters[19] and she had borne him several sons. Two of Brutus' sons[20] were young men. They were not merely close kinsmen but actually close companions of the Vitellii, who persuaded them to join in their conspiracy to betray the city. This they managed by urging the young men to attach themselves to the grand family – and the royal expectations – of the Tarquins and by doing so deliver themselves from the stupidity and cruelty of their father. Cruelty was their word for Brutus' inflexibility in punishing criminals. As for his stupidity, Brutus, it appears, had kept up just that pretence for a long time in order to keep himself safe from the tyrants, and even later he never lost this surname.[21]

4. And so, when Brutus' sons had been persuaded and after they and the Vitellii had conferred with the Aquillii, it was agreed by them all to swear a solemn and terrible oath. A human sacrifice was to be performed, and as each conspirator touched the dead man's entrails, he would pour a libation of his blood.[22] To carry this out, they met in the home of the Aquillii.[23] Now the house in which this ritual was to be performed was, as one might expect, dark and nearly deserted, which is why the conspirators did not perceive that a slave named Vindicius hid himself there. He had not done this on purpose or because he had any idea of their intentions. Instead, it was simply by chance that he was in the house and, when he saw them dash in, was afraid of being noticed and consequently hid behind a chest. From there he was able to witness their actions and overhear their scheming.[24] They decided to murder the consuls and wrote letters to Tarquinius informing him of their plot, letters which they handed over to his agents, who were houseguests of the Aquillii and had been present when this conspiracy was formed.

After all these things had taken place and the conspirators had departed, Vindicius crept away in secret. He was entirely at a loss as to what he should do about what he had discovered, for he rightly recognized how dreadful a matter it would be to denounce the sons of Brutus before their father, or the nephews of Collatinus before their uncle, especially when the accusations involved were so abominable in nature. At the same time, he hesitated to entrust so important a secret to a private citizen. And yet it was absolutely impossible for him to remain silent, plagued as he was by his knowledge of these intrigues. Finally he sought out Valerius, drawn to him by the man's affability and kindness and because he made a point of being accessible to anyone who needed him. Indeed, his house remained open even to the humblest person who wanted to speak with him or ask for a favour.

5. So it was that Vindicius went to Valerius and revealed everything to him[25] as well as to his wife and his brother, Marcus,[26] who were the only other persons present. Valerius was at once shocked and frightened by what he heard. He refused to allow Vindicius to leave, closing him up in a room and posting his wife as a guard at the door, while he ordered his brother to surround the royal residence, seize whatever letters he found there and arrest the slaves. For his part, he made his way to the house of the Aquillii. He was accompanied by the many clients and friends who were always with him, as well as a large number of his slaves. The Aquillii were not at home, but, to everyone's astonishment, Valerius burst through the doors of their house and found the letters to Tarquinius[27] in the rooms where the king's envoys were lodged. Even as Valerius was so occupied, the Aquillii rushed home and there was a struggle at the door of the house as they tried to recover the letters. Valerius' men fought back, throwing their togas around the necks of their adversaries, and finally, after a fierce brawl, they managed to drag the Aquillii through the streets and into the forum. At the same time, similar actions were taking place at the royal residence, where Marcus had taken possession of other letters that were meant to be carried to Tarquinius in the king's baggage and had seized as many as he could of the king's agents, whom he brought to the forum.

6. After the consuls had quietened the tumult, Valerius ordered that Vindicius be brought from his house. When he was delivered to the forum, accusations were lodged against the

conspirators and their letters were read aloud. The accused did not dare offer a defence. Nearly everyone present hung his head in silence, but a few, out of regard for Brutus, proposed exile as the penalty, and the tears of Collatinus, like the silence of Valerius, gave the accused some hope of clemency. Brutus, however, addressed each of his sons by name. 'Come, Titus, come, Tiberius, why do you not defend yourselves against this charge?' When they did not respond, although he put the question to them three times, Brutus turned his face to the lictors and said, 'It is now your duty to do what remains to be done.' Immediately the lictors took hold of the young men, stripped them of their clothes, bound their hands behind their backs and, with rods, scourged their bodies. No one could bear to look upon this spectacle, but Brutus, we are told, did not remove his gaze, nor did any pity soften his angry and severe countenance as he watched the dreadful punishment of his sons.[28] Finally, the lictors threw them on the ground and, with their axes, cut off their heads. Only then did Brutus rise and depart, leaving the punishment of the rest to his colleague. He had done a deed which one can neither praise nor blame in the right measure, for either it was his superior virtue that let his soul transcend the limitations of human feelings or, owing to the enormity of his outrage,[29] he became utterly callous. Each disposition is extraordinary, nor is either of them natural for a human being, for the one is characteristic of a god, the other of a beast. Still, it is just that our verdict be guided by the man's glorious reputation and that his virtue not be put into question on account of our own limitations as judges, for the Romans believe that even Romulus' achievement in creating their city is not so great as Brutus' in founding and establishing their republican constitution.

7. For a long time after Brutus quitted the forum, everyone was gripped by bafflement, horror and grim silence as they contemplated what had just taken place. Then, observing the weakness and indecision of Collatinus, the Aquillii regained their boldness. They demanded time in which to prepare their defence and insisted that Vindicius be handed over to them on the

grounds that he was their slave and it would be wrong to leave him with their accusers. Collatinus was disposed to acquiesce in these requests and thus dissolve the assembly. But Valerius was no longer in a position to surrender Vindicius, because the man had melted into the surrounding crowd. He also refused to allow the people to release the traitors, nor would he allow the assembly to be broken up. Finally, he arrested the Aquillii himself and called for Brutus to return. He complained that Collatinus was acting unnaturally, for, after putting his colleague in a situation in which he was constrained to put his own sons to death, he was now acting as if it were right to restore to their wives these traitors, who were the enemies of their country. The consul then flew into a rage, commanding that Vindicius be handed over to the Aquillii, whereupon his lictors, shoving their way into the crowd, attempted to seize the slave while landing blows on anyone who tried to rescue him. At that, however, Valerius' friends rushed forward to protect Vindicius, as the people cried out for Brutus, who turned back and returned to the forum. When there was silence, Brutus said that, whereas it was fitting for him to act as the judge of his own sons,[30] the fate of the other men was a different matter and must be determined by the votes of the citizenry. 'Let anyone speak who wishes to do so,' he urged, 'and let him try to persuade the people.' There was no longer any need for speeches, however, and the matter went to a vote in which the conspirators were condemned unanimously. They were then beheaded.[31]

As for Collatinus, it appears that even before this he had begun to attract suspicion on account of his kinship with the royal family.[32] Furthermore, because the people loathed Tarquinius, they found the very sound of Collatinus' other name vexatious. But his behaviour in this most recent affair left him unpopular with everyone. Consequently, he resigned his office and withdrew from the city in secret. When new elections were held, Valerius was gloriously elected consul, a fitting reward for his civic spirit. He decided that Vindicius ought to have a share in this reward, and so he passed a decree that made him the first freedman in Rome to become a citizen and entitled him to vote in whatever *curia*[33] he chose to enrol. At a much later time,

other Roman freedmen were granted the right to vote by
Appius,[34] when he was trying to win popular favour. To this
day, according to some authorities, the Romans call full manumission *vindicta* on account of this very Vindicius.[35]

8. After these events, the properties of the royal family were
handed over to the Roman people to pillage. The king's house
and the whole of his estate were razed to the ground. The most
agreeable part of the Campus Martius,[36] which had also
belonged to Tarquinius, the Romans consecrated to the very
god for whom it was named. Now it happened that this land
had just been harvested and its grain still lay upon the ground.
Because this field had been consecrated, however, they believed
it would be wrong to thresh the grain or to put it to any other
use, so they agreed to throw the sheaves into the river. In the
same way, they also cast into the river any trees that had been
cut down. Thus they left in the god's possession an uncult-
ivated, unproductive land.

The river's current could not carry such enormous heaps of
grain and wood very far. The first of these stuffs to be thrown
in soon ran into shallows and began to accumulate in a large
deposit. The material that followed could not float by but
instead combined and joined with this mass, which was quickly
made firm and hardened by the stream as it carried along great
quantities of mud, thus adding to the size and increasing the
solidity of this aggregation. This was because the water flowed
along the mound gently, not forcefully, and in this way moulded
and shaped everything into a single whole. Owing to its size
and situation, this mass quickly doubled itself, becoming a
tract of land capable of capturing most of the materials carried
downstream by the river. It is now a sacred island and part of
the city of Rome, where it is home to temples and covered
walks and in Latin is called *Between the Two Bridges*.[37]

Some writers, however, insist that this did not happen when
Tarquinius' land was consecrated but much later, at a time when
Tarquinia consecrated a neighbouring field.[38] This Tarquinia
was a Vestal Virgin and, in recognition of her generosity, received
great honours, including the privilege, shared with no other

woman, of giving testimony in court. The Roman people also voted that she be allowed to marry, but she refused. Such, at least, is the legend they report.

9. By now Tarquinius had despaired of regaining his throne by seditious means. And so he turned to the Etruscans,[39] who, keen to aid him, dispatched a great army to restore him to power. In reaction to this, the consuls led forth the Romans and arrayed them for battle in two sacred precincts, one of which is called the Horatian wood,[40] the other the Naevian meadow.[41] Not long after the fighting began, Aruns, who was Tarquinius' son, and Brutus, the consul of Rome, fell upon one another.[42] This did not happen by chance, for each man was driven by hatred and anger, the one intent on exacting vengeance from a tyrant and an enemy of his country, the other striking out in retaliation for his exile. They rode swiftly at one another, but both men fought with rage rather than intelligence, heedless of mortal danger, and the result was that each was struck down by the other. Nor was the conclusion of this battle any better than this terrible prelude. After inflicting and suffering losses in equal measure, the two armies were parted by a storm.

Valerius was now at a loss. He did not know the true outcome of the battle, so indiscriminate was the carnage, but could see only that his soldiers were simultaneously discouraged by their own casualties yet heartened by the losses of the enemy. Nevertheless, each side, because its own dead were near and visible while the enemy fallen could only be a matter of conjecture, was more inclined to believe itself defeated than victorious. There soon followed such a night as one might expect in the case of men who had suffered through combat of this kind and silence prevailed in both camps. Suddenly, according to tradition, the wood began to shudder and a loud voice issued forth declaring how, in this battle, the Etruscans had lost one more man than the Romans. This was plainly the voice of a god,[43] and it inspired the Romans to raise their war cry loud and bold even as it terrified the Etruscans. Most of them deserted their camp in confusion and fled, while those who remained, barely 5,000 men, were attacked and taken prisoner by the Romans, who also plundered the camp. When the dead were counted, it was found that 11,300 Etruscans had fallen. Roman losses were fewer by only one man. This battle is reported to have taken place on the day before the Calends of March.[44]

Valerius celebrated a triumph for this victory. He was the first consul to enter the city in a chariot[45] pulled by four horses, the occasion of a magnificent and majestic spectacle that was not, as some authorities claim, in any way hateful or offensive to the public as it looked on. Had that been the case, a triumph could not have remained the object of emulation and ambition on the part of the Romans for so many years thereafter. Valerius also won approval for the honours he accorded his colleague, whose funeral he marked with pomp and grandeur. He delivered a speech at Brutus' funeral that was so pleasing and gratifying to the Romans that ever since that day, on the death of one of Rome's great men, a funeral oration[46] is pronounced by a distinguished citizen. Some believe that Valerius' funeral oration anticipated the Greek practice,[47] unless the custom originated with Solon, as the rhetorician Anaximenes reports.[48]

10. Valerius did in fact incur the displeasure and hostility of the people, but for a different reason. Brutus, whom the Romans regarded as the father of their liberty, did not think it right that he govern the city alone, which is why he – not once, but twice – chose a colleague to share his power. 'But this man,' the people complained, 'by concentrating all political authority in his own person, is heir not to Brutus' consulship, to which he has no claim, but rather to the tyranny of Tarquinius. Why has he praised Brutus in words, when in deeds he imitates Tarquinius? For he descends alone to the forum, escorted by all the rods and axes, from a house every bit as grand as the royal residence that he tore down.' And it was true that Valerius lived in a highly theatrical fashion, inhabiting an ostentatiously large house on a hill called the Velia.[49] It hung over the forum and from it one could view everything. The path to this house was steep and difficult, and it was owing to his house's situation that, whenever Valerius walked down, his lofty procession gave an impression of regal arrogance. Now it is a good thing when

powerful men, in charge of great affairs, keep their ears open to frank and truthful words instead of flattery, as subsequent events demonstrated. For when Valerius heard from his friends that, in the opinion of the multitude, he was behaving incorrectly, he did not argue the point or grow angry,[50] but quickly assembled a large crew of workmen who, that very night, demolished his house and razed it to the ground.[51] When it was day, the Romans gathered in crowds to view what had taken place. They were at once pleased and amazed by Valerius' high-mindedness, and yet they also were pained by the loss of the house, whose beauty and stateliness they missed, as if it were an actual person whom the envy of others had unjustly brought to ruin. They were also distressed that their consul, like a man without a hearth of his own, was reduced to sharing the houses of others. Indeed, Valerius accepted the hospitality of his friends until the people gave him a site and on it built him a house. This house was more modest than the one he had torn down and it was located in the place where today stands the temple of Vica Pota.[52]

It was not enough for Valerius that the public see in him a man who was conciliatory and agreeable instead of intimidating. He wanted them to hold a similar view of the consulship itself. For this reason, he detached the axes from his fasces and, whenever he came into the assembly, instructed his lictors to lower the fasces[53] in the presence of the people, a gesture that increased the majesty of popular authority. This is a custom observed by the consuls to this day. Now, it was hardly the case that in doing this Valerius actually abased himself, as the multitude was mistakenly inclined to believe, but rather, by exercising moderation, he checked and eliminated the people's envy of his authority, thereby adding as much to his real influence as he appeared to be giving up in political power. It was because of this that the public submitted to him gladly, and willingly obeyed him. They called him Publicola, a name which means *he who is concerned for the people*. And since he was ultimately better known by this name than by his original ones, it is this name I shall use in writing the remainder of his biography.[54]

11. He permitted anyone who desired the office to put himself forward as a candidate for the consulship. Before elections took place, however, Publicola took advantage of his being sole consul to enact many excellent and important political reforms. He did this because he did not know who his new colleague would be and was afraid that, owing to jealousy or ignorance, that man might prove obstructionist.

His first act was to replenish the senate's membership,[55] for its numbers had been sorely diminished. Some had been put to death by Tarquinius, while others had recently fallen in battle against the Etruscans. He enrolled, historians tell us, 164 new senators. After this, Publicola enacted several laws, one of which considerably strengthened the power of the multitude by giving anyone who was accused before the consuls the right to appeal his case to the judgement of the people.[56] A second law made it a capital offence to hold any magistracy unless it was bestowed by the people. A third measure was designed to bring relief to the poor: it abolished the taxes[57] paid by the common people in order to provide an incentive for all of them to be more industrious in their occupations. Even Publicola's law against disobeying the consuls seemed populist in nature, inasmuch as its terms were drafted in the interest of the many and not of the powerful, for it punished disobedience with a fine of five oxen and two sheep.[58] The value of a sheep was 10 obols,[59] while that of an ox was 100, for in those days the Romans rarely used coined money and instead their wealth was constituted in their flocks and herds. This is why, even today, the Romans refer to their property as *peculia*, a word derived from their expression for herds, and their oldest coins were struck with figures of an ox, sheep or pig.[60] Indeed, the Romans go so far as to name their sons Suillus, Bubulcus, Caprarius and Porcius (they call goats *caprae* and pigs *porci*).[61]

12. Publicola, then, revealed himself to be a lawgiver who was sensitive to popular rights,[62] as well as moderate. In the matter of an offence the enormity of which violates the very idea of moderation, however, he made the punishment extreme. He enacted a law that permitted killing without a trial anyone

plotting to make himself a tyrant. Furthermore, he stipulated that the killer be pronounced innocent of murder provided he could furnish evidence of the would-be tyrant's crime. Now it is impossible for a man endeavouring to make himself tyrant to escape all notice, but it is not at all impossible for him to become so powerful that, by the time his actions attract scrutiny, it is too late to bring him to trial, inasmuch as committing the actual crime of making oneself a tyrant precludes the possibility of being brought to trial for having done so. This is why Publicola authorized, in the case of anyone capable of doing so, the right to carry out the verdict of such a trial.

Publicola is also acclaimed for his law establishing the quaestorship. When it became necessary for Roman citizens to contribute from their own means to defray the costs of their war against the Etruscans, Publicola did not wish to administer these funds himself, nor was he willing to allow his friends to do so – nor did he believe that public monies should be deposited in a private house. Consequently, he made the temple of Saturn a public treasury,[63] as it remains to this day, and entrusted the people with the election of two young men as quaestors[64] or treasurers. The first men to be elected to this office were Publius Veturius and Marcus Minucius,[65] under whose supervision large sums of money were collected, for the tax rolls included the names of 130,000 citizens, not including widows and orphans.[66]

After introducing these regulations, Publicola received Lucretius,[67] the father of Lucretia, as his colleague in the consulship. Inasmuch as Lucretius was the older man, Publicola conceded him priority and handed over the rods which the Romans call fasces. Since that day it has remained the practice that this honour is granted to the senior consul. Lucretius, however, died only a few days afterwards, and another election was held at which Marcus Horatius was chosen as the new consul.[68] For the remainder of the year he was Publicola's colleague.

13. Meanwhile Tarquinius was in Etruria pressing for another war against the Romans. At this time, so it is reported, there

occurred a momentous prodigy. While he was still king and had nearly completed building the temple of Capitoline Jupiter,[69] Tarquinius, either acting on an oracle or because the idea struck him in some other way, commissioned Etruscan craftsmen in Veii[70] to make a chariot of terracotta that he planned to place on the roof of the temple. Not long afterwards he was expelled from Rome. Still, the Etruscans fashioned the chariot and put it in the furnace, but, during the firing, the clay did not contract and shrink, as clay normally does when its moisture evaporates. Instead, it expanded and as it grew its fabric increased in strength and hardness, until it reached proportions that prevented its being easily removed even after the roof and walls of the furnace itself had been torn down. Unsurprisingly, the seers recognized in this event a portent of good fortune and power for whoever possessed this chariot. For this reason, the people of Veii decided to keep it when the Romans asked for it, insisting that it belonged to the Tarquins and not to those who had expelled the Tarquins. Only a few days later, there were chariot races in Veii, and this spectacle took place with the usual degree of excitement and interest. When, however, the winner, freshly crowned, was leading his victorious chariot out of the hippodrome, his horses took fright for no obvious reason – perhaps it was caused by some divinity or owing merely to chance – and they ran off at top speed towards Rome, taking along their charioteer. He struggled in vain to rein in his horses or calm them down, but, overpowered by their sheer force and velocity, he was carried along until they reached the Capitol, where they threw him off at the gate which is today called the Ratumena.[71] The Veientines were astounded and frightened by this event, and so allowed the craftsmen to deliver the chariot to the Romans.

14. This temple of Capitoline Jupiter was vowed by Tarquinius,[72] the son of Demaratus, when he was waging war against the Sabines, but it was Tarquinius Superbus, his son or grandson,[73] who built it. He did not, however, have an opportunity to consecrate the temple because it was not quite finished when he was driven out of Rome. Now that it was completed and suitably adorned, Publicola very much wanted to be the one

who performed its dedication. Many of Rome's leading men, however, were jealous of Publicola, and although they could just tolerate his other honours, which as a legislator and a general he truly deserved, they considered this distinction a different matter. In their view, it ought to be awarded to someone else. Therefore they strongly encouraged Horatius to lodge his own claim to perform the dedication. When later it happened that Publicola's military duties obliged him to be absent from the city, these men, convinced that they would be foiled if Publicola were actually present in Rome, seized the occasion to secure legislation assigning the temple's consecration to Horatius. They then led him up to the Capitol. Some authorities, however, claim that the two consuls simply drew lots and that Publicola, despite his preference, received the military command, while Horatius was allotted the dedication.[74] In any case, it is easy to see how the matter stood between the two men on the basis of what took place during the actual consecration. It was the Ides of September,[75] which very nearly coincides with the full moon of the month of Metageitnion.[76] All the people were assembled on the Capitol and ritual silence prevailed. Horatius, after performing the appropriate ceremonies, put his hand on the temple's door, as is the custom, and began to pronounce the ritual formula for consecration. At that moment, Marcus, the brother of Publicola, who had been standing by the door for a long time just waiting for this opportunity, said, 'Consul, your son in the Roman camp has perished from sickness.' This report afflicted all who heard it, but Horatius remained unperturbed and gave only this reply: 'Cast the body where you like, for I am not submitting to grief.' He then completed the dedication. Marcus' announcement was untrue, but he had hoped, by telling this lie, to deter Horatius from performing the consecration.[77] But Horatius exhibited admirable resolution, and this remains true whether he had perceived Marcus' deceit or actually believed the report but remained undisturbed by it.

15. The circumstances of the dedication of the second temple of Capitoline Jupiter were not entirely unlike that of the first.

The first temple, as I have said, was vowed by Tarquinius but consecrated by Horatius. This temple was destroyed during the civil wars.[78] The second temple was built by Sulla but was dedicated, after Sulla's death, by Catulus,[79] whose name was inscribed on its front. This temple was also destroyed, in the turbulence associated with the reign of Vitellius.[80] The third temple was begun and completed by Vespasian, who enjoyed good fortune in all his undertakings. Furthermore, he both lived to see his temple finished and died before seeing it destroyed, as that took place shortly after his death. In this respect, he was luckier even than Sulla,[81] for Sulla did not live to see his temple consecrated, whereas Vespasian died before his met with destruction. This happened almost immediately after Vespasian's death, when the Capitol was consumed by fire.[82]

The present temple, the fourth, was completed and dedicated by Domitian.[83] Now Tarquinius is reported to have spent 40,000 pounds of silver for the foundations of his temple.[84] By contrast, the wealth of the richest man in Rome would not suffice to pay the cost just of the gilding on the modern temple, which ran to more than 12,000 talents. Its columns were hewn from Pentelic marble[85] and, in thickness and height, were once perfectly proportioned, as I know for I saw them at Athens. In Rome, however, they were cut again, and smoothed, but they did not gain as much in polish as they lost in symmetrical beauty, and now they appear far too thin. If anyone, after being astounded at the enormous expense of Domitian's rebuilding of the Capitol, also looked at even a single portico in his palace, or a single basilica or bath, or at the apartment for his concubines, he would recall what Epicharmus[86] once said to a man who was unrestrainedly lavish:

> It is not generosity that stirs you but a disease;
> You extract pleasure simply from giving.

He would then be moved to address Domitian along similar lines: 'It is not piety or a passion for honour that stirs you, but a disease; you extract pleasure simply from building; like the notorious Midas,[87] you wish that you could change everything into gold or marble.' But that is enough on this topic.

16. After the great battle in which his son fell in single combat with Brutus,[88] Tarquinius took refuge in Clusium[89] and sought help from Lars Porsenna, the most powerful of the kings in Italy, who was reputed to be a valiant man devoted to the pursuit of honour.[90] Porsenna promised Tarquinius his aid. His first step was to send a delegation to Rome demanding Tarquinius' restoration as king. When the Romans refused, Porsenna declared war, announced the time and the location of his invasion, and proceeded there with a large force. Publicola, although absent from the city, was elected consul for the second time, and Titus Lucretius was his colleague.[91] Publicola then returned to Rome and, because he wanted to make it clear that his own confidence excelled that of Porsenna, he chose that moment to found the city of Signuria,[92] even though his enemy was already very near. He first fortified the place at great expense and then sent 700 colonists to occupy it, all in order to show how unconcerned and unafraid he was in the matter of the war with Porsenna.[93] However, during a vigorous assault on the Janiculum,[94] Porsenna dislodged its defenders, who, in their flight, nearly brought the enemy into the city along with themselves. But Publicola came to their aid[95] by charging out of the city gate and joining battle alongside the river. Although the enemy surged against him in great numbers, Publicola held out until he was grievously wounded and carried from the battle in a litter. When his colleague Lucretius suffered a similar injury, the Romans lost courage and fled for the city in an attempt to save themselves. By then the enemy had forced their way towards the wooden bridge over the Tiber[96] and there was now a great risk that Rome would be captured. Horatius Cocles[97] was the first to take a stand in defence of the bridge, and with him two of the city's most illustrious men, Herminius and Larcius.[98] Horatius was surnamed Cocles because he had lost an eye in combat.[99] Other sources, however, record a different reason. Because his nose was sunken and very flat, there was nothing separating his eyes and his eyebrows ran together.

Consequently, most people called him Cyclops,[100] but they mispronounced the word and instead he was popularly known as Cocles. In any case, it was this man who stood before the bridge, warding off the enemy until his companions succeeded in cutting it down behind him. Then, although he was in full armour, he leapt into the river and swam to the other side, in spite of being wounded in the buttock by an Etruscan spear.[101] Publicola was filled with admiration for Horatius' valour and proposed that the Romans all bestow on him as much food and drink as they consume in a day,[102] and that, later, he be granted as much land as he could plough in a day. They also erected a bronze statue of him in the temple of Vulcan in order to console him, by means of this honour, for the lameness he suffered on account of his wound.[103]

17. Porsenna proceeded to lay siege to the city, and very soon the Romans were afflicted by famine. At that same time, another Etruscan army, independent of Porsenna's,[104] also invaded Roman territory. Publicola was now consul for the third time[105] and he decided that the best way to defend the city from Porsenna was to remain watchful from within the walls. As for the other Etruscan army, Publicola sallied out in secret against it. This battle ended in the enemy's being routed and losing 5,000 men.[106]

The exploit of Mucius has been recorded in different versions by various authors.[107] Here I must report the account I find most credible. Mucius was an excellent man, possessed of every virtue, and in war he was without a superior in valour. He devised a plan for assassinating Porsenna and therefore infiltrated his camp dressed as an Etruscan and speaking their language. For some time he milled around the tribunal where the king was sitting, but he could not distinguish Porsenna from the others who were sitting with him and was afraid to ask anyone to point him out. So he drew his sword and cut down the man in this group whom he thought most likely to be the king. He was seized at once. As he was being interrogated, a burning brazier was brought to Porsenna so that he could perform a sacrifice. At that moment, Mucius thrust his right hand over the fire and, although his flesh was burning, merely stood before Porsenna, gazing at him with a bold and resolute expression until the king, overcome by admiration, ordered his release and returned his sword, which he personally handed down to him from the tribunal. Mucius reached out with his left hand to take the sword. This is the reason, according to our sources, that he received the surname Scaevola, which means *left-handed*. Then Mucius said that, although he had overcome whatever fear Porsenna inspired, he was nonetheless vanquished by the king's nobility and therefore out of gratitude would reveal what he could never have been forced to disclose: 'Three hundred Romans, with the same mission as mine, are present in this camp and awaiting their opportunity. I was chosen by lot to make the first attempt on your life, but I am not distressed that I was foiled by chance and failed to kill a noble man who would make the Romans a far more fitting friend than enemy.' Porsenna believed what Mucius told him and decided to come to terms, not so much, I think, because he was afraid of the 300 but because he admired the spirit and the courage of the Romans.[108] Now, all authorities agree in describing this Mucius as Scaevola, with the exception of Athenodorus,[109] the son of Sandon, who, in a work dedicated to Octavia, the sister of Caesar Augustus, says that he was also named Cordus.[110]

18. Publicola came to the conclusion that Porsenna, although a redoubtable enemy, should be made into a friend and ally of Rome, and so proposed that the king act as arbitrator between himself and Tarquinius. Again and again he challenged Tarquinius to plead his cause, so certain was Publicola that he could demonstrate how Tarquinius was the most wicked of men and thus rightly overthrown. Tarquinius, however, responded harshly, insisting that he would accept no one as his judge, least of all Porsenna, who was now vacillating in his commitment to their alliance. This displeased Porsenna, who turned against Tarquinius.[111] At the same time, Porsenna's son, Aruns, who favoured the Roman cause, pleaded with his father on their behalf. Consequently, Porsenna ended the war on

condition that the Romans surrender any Etruscan territory they had captured, return their prisoners of war and take back their own deserters. To guarantee the terms of this treaty, the Romans handed over as hostages ten young men, all of them patricians, and the same number of virgins, one of whom was Valeria, a daughter of Publicola.

19. Even as the terms of this treaty were still being carried out, Porsenna abandoned his warlike posture on account of his confidence in the Romans' trustworthiness. At this time, the Roman girls who were his hostages went down to bathe at a place where a pool is formed by a bend in the river and the water is very still and placid. When they saw that they were unguarded, nor was anyone passing by or crossing the stream, they were seized by a desire to swim out into the full current and deep eddies of the river. Some writers tell us that one of them, named Cloelia, crossed on horseback, exhorting and encouraging the others as they swam. When, however, they had safely made their way to Publicola, he, far from giving them his admiration or approval, worried instead that Porsenna might think him untrustworthy because of this and consider the girls' bold act proof of the Romans' perfidy. Therefore he arrested them and returned them to Porsenna. The partisans of Tarquinius learned of this, however, and waited in ambush for the party that was leading the girls back. As the girls were being taken across the river, they attacked in superior numbers. Despite this, the Romans put up a fight, and Valeria, the daughter of Publicola, managed to make her way through the combatants and flee, thanks to the efforts of three servants who shoved their way through the melee and thus got Valeria to safety. The remaining girls, however, were trapped by the struggle and in great danger, when Aruns, Porsenna's son, became aware of what was happening and rushed to save them. He drove away their enemies and rescued the Romans.

The girls were led before Porsenna and he asked which of them had incited the others to attempt their escape. When he was told that it was the one named Cloelia, he gazed at her with a look that was at once beneficent and radiant. He commanded that one of his royal horses be brought out, magnificently caparisoned, which he then presented her as a gift. This is the evidence adduced by those authorities who claim that Cloelia and only Cloelia crossed the river on horseback, whereas others dispute this point and maintain that this present was simply the token by which the Etruscan king honoured the girl's courageousness.[112] An equestrian statue of her was set up on the Sacred Way[113] as one heads towards the Palatine, though some insist that it is not a statue of Cloelia but of Valeria.[114]

Thus was Porsenna reconciled with the Romans. He gave the city further proof of his magnanimity when he ordered the Etruscan troops, when they broke camp, to take nothing with them except their weapons, leaving the Romans an abundance of provisions as well as valuables of every description. This is why, down to our day, whenever the Romans conduct a sale of public goods, Porsenna's are named as the first to be auctioned in honour and in perpetual remembrance of his generosity.[115] A bronze statue[116] of the man was also erected near the senate-house, an unadorned example of archaic craftsmanship.

20. After these events, the Sabines invaded Roman territory and Marcus Valerius, Publicola's brother, was elected consul along with Postumius Tubero.[117] All the most important actions of this war were conducted with Publicola's advice and cooperation,[118] and the result was that Marcus won two great battles. In the second of these victories he did not lose even a single man, whereas he slew 13,000 of the enemy. As a mark of honour, in addition to his triumphs, a house was built at public expense for Marcus on the Palatine. In those days, the exterior doors of all houses opened inwards, in the direction of the rooms within, but the Romans constructed the outer door of Marcus' house, and his alone, so that it opened outwards. By granting him this distinction, they believed, Marcus might always enjoy his portion of public honour.

In the past, we are told, all Greek doors used to open outwards in this same way. That is an inference one can draw from comic dramas, in which any character wishing to exit a house beats on the inside of its door and makes a noise loud enough to be noticed by passers-by, who are then not taken by surprise when the doors open into the street and someone emerges.[119]

21. In the following year Publicola was elected to his fourth consulship.[120] At this time, it was feared that there would soon be war against a coalition of Sabines and Latins. The city was also in the grip of superstitious anxiety, introduced when all the pregnant women gave birth prematurely to babies who were deformed. Publicola, therefore, consulted the Sibylline Books[121] and made propitiatory offerings to Dis.[122] He also celebrated games that had been advised by the Delphic oracle.[123] These acts improved the city's morale and rendered its citizens hopeful of divine favour. Publicola then turned his attention to quelling such fears as are inspired by mortals, for the city's enemies, it was obvious, were forming a powerful alliance and making formidable preparations for war.

Now among the Sabines there was a certain Appius Clausus, a man whose riches made him influential, whose impressive physical strength and valour made him famous, but who above all was pre-eminent for his virtue and eloquence. Like all great men, Clausus was an object of envy. Consequently, when he opposed going to war, his detractors seized upon this as a pretext for accusing him of magnifying the power of the Romans as part of a plot to make himself tyrant and enslave his country. When he saw how the populace was disposed to believe these charges, and since he found himself so acutely at odds both with the war's supporters and with the soldiers, he feared he would be brought to trial. Nevertheless, relying for protection on his extensive and powerful network of friends and kinsmen, Clausus persisted in his opposition. This caused the Sabines to delay initiating the war.

As for Publicola, not only did he make it his business to stay well informed about these matters, he also worked hard stimulating and exacerbating the Sabines' factiousness. He kept sending friends to Clausus to speak with him and convey sentiments like these: 'Publicola believes that a man like you, who is righteous and just, should not use violence in defending himself against his fellow-citizens, even when he is being treated unjustly. But should you ever wish to guarantee your safety by fleeing those who hate you and emigrating, he will receive you with public and private honours that are worthy of your own virtue and the glory of Rome.' Clausus reflected at length on this offer before deciding that, in consideration of his difficult circumstances, accepting it was his best course of action. So he summoned his friends to join him, and they in their turn persuaded many others to come along as well, with the result that he led to Rome 5,000 families with their wives and children. These were the most peaceable of the Sabines, devoted to leading gentle and untroubled lives, and Publicola, who knew beforehand that they were coming, graciously and enthusiastically welcomed them as full Roman citizens. He immediately incorporated these families into the Roman state, and to each he gave two square plethra[124] of land along the River Anio.[125] To Clausus he gave 25 square plethra[126] of land and enrolled him in the senate, where he conducted himself so wisely that he quickly rose to the highest rank and acquired great influence.[127] This man is the ancestor of the Claudian family, the glory of which remains uneclipsed in Rome.[128]

22. The emigration of Clausus and his followers brought an end to the Sabines' political divisions. Nevertheless, the immigrants were not left alone to settle down in peace. Instead, Sabine demagogues complained that Clausus, now that he was an exile and an enemy, would still bring to pass the very thing he had not been able to persuade the Sabines of while he was still one of them, namely, that the Romans should not be punished for their outrages. And so the Sabines set out with a great army and pitched their camp near Fidenae.[129] A force of 2,000 infantry was assigned to lie in wait as an ambuscade in a wooded ravine not far from Rome. It was their intention to send out at daybreak a small detachment of their cavalry, who would make a show of plundering the Romans' livestock. They had been given orders that, whenever they drew near the city, they should then withdraw little by little until they lured the enemy into the ambuscade. On that very day, however, Publicola

learned of this plan from deserters, and in order to make provisions to counter it he immediately divided his army. While it was still evening, Postumius Albus, Publicola's son-on-law,[130] set out with 3,000 soldiers and occupied the hills below which the Sabines were lying in ambush. There they kept watch on the enemy. Lucretius, Publicola's fellow-consul, remained in the city in command of men who were lightly armed and very young. Their assignment was to attack the enemy cavalry while it was plundering the countryside. As for Publicola himself, he took the rest of the army and encircled the enemy's camp. It just so happened that, at the dawn of the next day, there was a thick fog under the cover of which – all at the same moment – Postumius, with a great cry, fell upon the ambuscade from the heights above, while Lucretius launched his men against the cavalry as it rode near the city and Publicola attacked the enemy in its encampment. On every front the Sabines were routed and slaughtered. None of the enemy stood his ground. Instead, they fled straight away and the Romans slew them. It was their very hope of survival that proved most lethal to them. For neither of the army's divisions, because each believed that the other was safe, made any attempt to stay and fight. The men who were encamped rushed towards the ambuscade, while those who had been lying in ambush raced for the protection of their comrades in the camp. As a result, fugitive met fugitive and desperate men in want of help encountered desperate men seeking help from them. The only reason the Sabines did not perish altogether is that a few managed to make it to the nearby city of Fidenae, especially those who escaped from the camp when it was captured. Any who failed to reach Fidenae, however, were either killed or taken prisoner.[131]

23. Although the Romans were accustomed to attributing all their great successes to the gods, *this* victory they credited exclusively to the achievement of their general. The soldiers were heard to say how Publicola had delivered them their enemies lame, blind and all but bound, and thus easily struck down by their swords. The people also acquired a good deal of money from the spoils and from the sale of the prisoners. But

no sooner had Publicola celebrated his triumph and handed the government of the city over to the consuls designated to succeed him[132] than he died, thereby completing a life characteristic of the best and noblest men. The people, as if they had done nothing in the way of showing him honour while he was alive in exchange for all the gratitude owed him, decreed that he should be buried at public expense[133] and that every man should contribute a quadrans[134] towards this mark of popular esteem. The women decided privately among themselves to mourn for him for an entire year, also an enviable honour.[135] He was buried, in accordance with a law passed by the citizens, inside the city near the so-called Velia, and all his descendants were granted the privilege of burial in that place.[136] Today, however, none of the family is interred there. Instead, the corpse is carried to the spot and set down; then someone, taking up a burning torch, holds it beneath the body for a moment but then immediately removes it, attesting by this action that the deceased has a right to this honour but has renounced it. Afterwards, the body is carried outside the city.

COMPARISON OF
SOLON AND PUBLICOLA

1 (24). There is something quite singular in this *Comparison*, something unprecedented in anything I have written so far, and it is this: of our two subjects, one modelled himself on his predecessor, and the earlier man is himself an advocate for the later one.

Consider Solon's opinion on happiness, which he delivered to Croesus. Clearly it applies more to Publicola than it does to Tellus.[1] Although Solon pronounced Tellus the happiest of men on account of his good fortune, his virtue and his excellent offspring, Solon did not mention him as a good man in any of his poems, nor did any of Tellus' children hold a public office through which he acquired a glorious reputation. Publicola, by contrast, was, so long as he lived, the foremost man among the Romans, both in influence and in reputation, on account of his virtue, and, since his death, the most illustrious of our families, the Publicolae, the Messalae and the Valerii,[2] whose genealogies reach back 600 years, ascribe the dignity of their noble birth to him. Furthermore, Tellus fell in battle, though he fought bravely and never retreated, whereas Publicola cut his enemies to pieces, which is a better fortune than being struck down by them. And after he saw his country victorious because of his exertions as consul and general, and after he had celebrated honours and triumphs, he came to that end which Solon had judged happiest and most enviable.

Even Solon's own desire, expressed in his response to Mimnermus[3] on the topic of how long we should live:

> Leave me not to an unlamented death, but, when I die,
> Let me be a source of sorrow and grieving to my friends[4]

portrays Publicola as a happy man. For, when he died, it was not only his friends and family but the entire city in its tens of thousands who wept, grieved and mourned his loss. The women of Rome lamented as if they had all lost the same son or brother or father.[5]

Solon also said:

> I want to have wealth, but to acquire it unjustly
> I do not desire,[6]

on the grounds that punishment would supervene. Now, not only did Publicola come to his wealth honestly, he employed it nobly in giving assistance to the poor.[7] Therefore, if Solon was the wisest of men, then Publicola was the happiest, for all the good things sought by Solon because they were best and noblest were the very things Publicola had and preserved until the end of his life.

2 (25). In this way, then, Solon himself confirms Publicola's fine reputation. Similarly, Publicola, through his statesmanship, advances the cause of Solon by marking him out as the best model for anyone trying to organize a democratic state, for he subtracted from the consulship its most arrogant features, and in doing so rendered this magistracy attractive and acceptable to everyone in Rome.[8] And he adopted many of Solon's laws.

Thus he granted the people the right to elect their own rulers, and defendants were allowed to plead their cases before the people, just as Solon permitted them to plead before juries.[9] Publicola did not, as Solon did, establish a new senate, but he doubled the membership[10] in the existing one. The idea of appointing quaestors to be in charge of official funds was also inspired by Solon. Publicola wished to release honest consuls from routine financial business, so they could concentrate on great affairs, and at the same time deny dishonest consuls opportunities for perpetrating grave injustices if they had in

their power both matters of state and the administration of
public finances.[11] Publicola was fiercer in his hatred of tyranny
than Solon was, for, under Solon's law, if anyone attempted to
seize power, he must first be tried before he could be punished,
whereas Publicola made it lawful to kill such men without a
trial.[12]

Solon correctly and justly praises himself[13] for his refusal to
accept absolute power at a time when circumstances urged his
doing so and his fellow-citizens would have been glad of it.
Still, it was no less noble on Publicola's part that, when he was
invested with tyrannical authority, he made his office more
democratic in character and did not make use of all the powers
that he actually possessed.[14] Solon seems to have appreciated
the soundness of this policy even before Publicola carried it
out, for he says of the people:

> They will be best at following their leaders
> When they are neither unrestrained nor oppressed.[15]

3 (26). Unique to Solon was his remission of debts, the chief
means by which he secured the freedom of his fellow-citizens.[16]
After all, equality under the law means nothing if the poor are
in effect deprived of it by their debts. For it is in the very situations where their freedom is most in evidence – in the courts, in
the exercise of the magistrates' duties, in public debates – that
the poor are actually in the greatest subjection to the rich.
More importantly, although the abolition of debts is invariably
followed by sedition, Solon's reform is the sole exception to
this rule: by applying, at just the right moment, a bold but efficacious remedy, he instead brought an end to the sedition that
was already present in Athens, and his own virtue and reputation prevailed over the disrepute of his measure and the calumny
it provoked.

Now, as for their political careers, Solon's started off more
brilliantly than Publicola's, for he acted on his own authority
and not as anyone's subordinate, and it was through his own
agency – not as a colleague of others – that he realized most of

his greatest public achievements. At the end of his career, by contrast, Publicola was the more fortunate and enviable of the two, for Solon lived to see undone the constitution he had established, while Publicola's preserved his city's sound government down to the time of the civil wars.[17] After he had enacted his laws, Solon left them inscribed on wooden tablets, bereft of any champion, and he removed himself from Athens.[18] But Publicola remained in Rome, holding the consulship and continuing in public affairs, thereby strengthening his constitution and assuring its stability. Moreover, although Solon knew in advance of Peisistratus' intrigues, not only did he fail to stop them but ultimately acquiesced in the tyranny they imposed.[19] By contrast, Publicola overthrew and abolished a powerful and long-standing monarchy. His virtue was the equal of Solon's, and his purpose identical; in addition, he enjoyed good fortune and the capacity to realize his virtue's ends.

If we turn to their military accomplishments, we find that, according to Daimachus of Plataea,[20] Solon did not play the part in the war against the Megarians that I described earlier,[21] whereas Publicola, both as a warrior and a commander, was victorious in the greatest battles.[22] Let us return again to their political acts. Solon, as if he were playing a game, pretended to be mad so that he could come forward and argue for recovering Salamis,[23] whereas Publicola willingly ran the greatest of risks in opposing the Tarquins and in detecting the treason of their supporters. It was he who was chiefly responsible for capturing and punishing these criminals, and so not only did he expel the tyrants from the city, he also eliminated any prospect of their restoration. Clearly, then, his resolution was bold and steely in affairs that demanded a courageous and vigorous struggle. He excelled still further in situations requiring peaceful diplomacy and gentle persuasion, which is how he won over Porsenna, a man who was an invincible and daunting enemy but whom Publicola made a friend of Rome.[24]

Someone, however, might object that Solon regained Salamis for the Athenians after they had given it up, whereas Publicola surrendered territories that the Romans had already conquered.[25] But actions must be judged on the basis of the

circumstances in which they take place. An intelligent statesman approaches each situation in such a way as to win the
greatest advantage possible: sometimes, by giving up a part, he
saves the whole, and by making light concessions secures
greater advantages. This is why Publicola, in that instance,
renounced some foreign territory in order to preserve his own
country, with the result that, although the Romans had had to
struggle hard to protect their city, they thereby secured its
safety and even gained the camp of the enemy who had besieged
them.[26] By making his enemy his judge, Publicola won his case,
and through this success acquired for the Romans what they
would gladly have surrendered for the sake of victory. For
Porsenna ended the war and left behind all his provisions for
prosecuting it on account of the virtue and nobility which he
attributed to all the Romans because of the actions of their
consul.

CORIOLANUS

INTRODUCTION TO CORIOLANUS

History and Legend

The story of Coriolanus is the stuff of legend. A hero of the Volscian Wars, he gained his renown after displaying unmatched courage in the Romans' capture of the town Corioli. However, the fierceness of his defence of the patrician order in its struggle with the plebeians for political dominance incurred general hostility, and he was eventually prosecuted by the tribunes of the people, who succeeded in driving him into exile. The embittered Coriolanus then retaliated by lending his bravery to Rome's enemies, to the very Volscians fighting against whom he had previously won his reputation for valour. He led their armies in victory to the gates of Rome, where only the pleas of his mother could turn him back from destroying the city.

Coriolanus' was a familiar story by the time Plutarch came to tell it. As an example of a great man exiled by an ungrateful people, he was viewed, at least by the late republic, as an apt Roman parallel for the Athenian Themistocles[1] – often unfavourably. Extended accounts of Coriolanus' story can be found in Livy (2.33.5–2.40.12) and Dionysius of Halicarnassus (6.92–8.62). In each there is heavy emphasis on Coriolanus' natural superiority, his profound connection with the patrician cause in its struggle against an emerging plebeian role in Roman government and his unwillingness to compromise when confronted by tribunician aggression, the unjust result of which was his exile. Coriolanus' transfer of his loyalty to the Volscians and his subsequent campaign against Rome are duly reported, but for each author the climax lies in Coriolanus' confrontation with his mother, who persuades her son not to conquer his native city. In the pages of Livy (who here defers to the authority of Fabius Pictor: 7.40.12, 28.29.1) Coriolanus ends his life a broken man, and in later books he emerges as a negative example from the past. For Dionysius, however, who catalogues Coriolanus' failings along with his virtues (8.61–2), the Roman remains a righteous man, single-mindedly committed to justice but unkindly buffeted by fate (8.62.1), whose reputation as 'a pious and just man' (8.62.3) is rightly celebrated. Dionysius is Plutarch's principal source for his *Coriolanus*. He may well have consulted other writers, of course, and it is obvious that he has delved into antiquarian literature in order to deepen his and his readers' understanding of Coriolanus' historical moment. Still, this biography represents Plutarch's own, highly creative, adaptation of the material recorded by Dionysius.[2]

The Conflict of the Orders

The story of Coriolanus, like the career of Camillus, takes place against the background of the Conflict of the Orders. Roman society comprised two kinds of citizens, patricians and plebeians, categories determined by birth. During the republic, the order of the patricians comprised a few hundred wealthy families; plebeians were everyone else and thus the vast majority of Romans. How the patriciate came to be a distinct caste remains unclear, but it is plain enough that in the early republic this order enjoyed a near monopoly on the highest magistracies and played a dominating role in the senate. Unsurprisingly, this state of affairs was resented by those plebeians rich enough, valorous enough and ambitious enough to insist on having their share of honour and political influence. This friction was exacerbated because, during this early period, when Rome was beset by war and by economic crises resulting from its military struggles, poorer Romans often found themselves victims of crushing debts as well as food shortages, for which they held the patricians principally responsible. It was these difficulties that opened a way for plebeian leaders to challenge the paramountcy of the patricians.[3]

The plebeians, their plight unheeded by the senate, created an independent assembly which selected its own leaders, called tribunes of the people. All plebeians swore an oath to protect their tribunes from harm, thereby conferring a privileged status which these officers could employ in rescuing vulnerable citizens from magisterial injustices and in striving to check senatorial excesses. As a result of continual plebeian pressure, by the fourth century BC, if not actually earlier, most of the patricians' exclusive rights were abolished, and a new elite, called nobles (*nobiles*), composed of patricians and plebeians whose families had reached the consulship, began to emerge. The social struggles subsumed under the rubric of the Conflict of the Orders were real enough but remain hard to recover owing to the unreliability that characterizes all ancient narratives of early Roman history.[4]

Coriolanus' legendary career, marred by his antagonistic relationship with the common people of Rome, who are plebeians, comes at the beginning of the Conflict of the Orders. And Coriolanus is always depicted as a patrician exponent of patrician supremacy, which is very odd because, although his family, the Marcii, could and did claim descent from Ancus Marcius, the fourth king of Rome, they were, in the historical period at least, plebeian.[5]

Great Nature, Great Perils

Plutarch rejects the Themistoclean parallel. By the time he came to write this Life, he had already matched Themistocles with Camillus – the saviour of Greece with the saviour of Rome (and each of them an exile).[6] Coriolanus he paired with Alcibiades.[7] The match comes as something of a surprise, the rude and primitive Roman (so Plutarch at ch. 1) set in parallel with the chic and cosmopolitan Athenian. Still, like the Roman, Alcibiades was an orphan and a talented general. He, too, was exiled and offered his services to the enemies of his country, whom he ultimately let down. In Plutarch's telling, each man was hounded by the envy of others and each came to a violent

end in a foreign land. This decision to link Coriolanus with
Alcibiades entailed important implications for the texture of
the Roman Life. To a serious Platonist like Plutarch, Alcibiades
was a classic example of the truth of the master's claim that
great natures (*megalai phuseis*), if unequipped with sufficient
education or reason, although capable of extraordinary accomplishments, ultimately do great harm to their cities. Plato
discusses this phenomenon in his *Republic* (491d–492a), after
which he proceeds to analyse a single specimen that clearly
reflects the career of Alcibiades (494b–495a).[8] Plutarch shared
this view of Alcibiades: in his moral essays, he explicitly adduces
him as an example of a man with a great nature (*Moralia*
552b), and in his *Alcibiades* he examines the difficulties of
understanding his great nature.[9] Coriolanus' Life, drawn in
broader strokes, prepares the reader for this investigation.[10]

Coriolanus is noble and good but, lacking a proper education, he also lacks the reason necessary to temper his passions:
he's vengeance proud, as Shakespeare puts it, and entirely lacking in moderation. This is made plain in the opening of the Life
(ch. 1: 'Gaius Marcius' career bears witness to the truth of the
view that a naturally generous and noble disposition, if it lacks
education, will produce both good and evil fruits at once') and
is emphasized in one of its defining moments, Coriolanus' failure in the consular elections,

> he revealed that he was quite incapable of patience or self-control
> when faced with a reverse. He had always given free rein to the
> impulses of spirit and contentiousness in his nature, as if there
> were some inherent grandeur and nobility in these qualities . . . it
> never occurred to him that it might be a symptom of effeminate
> weakness to be unable to restrain the anger which bursts out like
> an abscess from the wounded and suffering spirit, and so he went
> away full of indignation and rancour towards the people.
>
> (ch. 15)

Plutarch's diagnosis of Coriolanus' character in this passage
is thoroughly Platonic (cf. *Epistles* 4.321c; and *Republic*
375b–376c, 440d–442d).

Plutarch's Coriolanus, then, is, like Alcibiades, a man with a great nature who will do harm as well as good to his city. But the two heroes enact their natures in strikingly different contexts and actions. Coriolanus' want of a proper education, for instance, was unavoidable:

> we must remember that the Romans of those days prized above all else the kind of virtue which finds its expression in warlike and military achievements . . . the Romans made courage [*virtus*] stand for virtue in all its aspects, though it only denotes one of them.[11]
>
> (ch. 1)

Alcibiades' circumstances are conspicuously different. His philosophical tendencies are hampered and interrupted by his political ambitions and by the flattery and provocation of others, all illustrated in his uneven and inconsistent relationship with Socrates (*Alcibiades* 1 and 3–6). Both Alcibiades and Coriolanus are men of deep passions. The Roman is unable to temper the spirited and contentious aspects of his personality.[12] And so he is obstinate. And easily overcome by anger. Alcibiades, too, is contentious, but he is neither obstinate nor angry – quite the opposite. He is motivated by love of honour and glory (*Alcibiades* 2), but also by physical passions, like luxuriousness, sensuality and sexual desire (*Alcibiades* 8, 11–12, 16, 23, 39), none of which touches Coriolanus. The Roman is 'always a simple man' (ch. 15), whereas the Greek is always unpredictable and entirely, perhaps excessively, adaptable (*Alcibiades* 2, 6, 16, 23).

Anger and Exile

Although an irresistible warrior and impeccable general, Coriolanus fails to manage the complexities of political life: his strength and bravery, like his indifference to pleasure, pain and riches, inspire admiration, but in politics he rejects compromise or accommodation, not owing to an acute sense of justice or lofty principles but instead due to obstinacy and anger. It was

Plutarch's view, expressed in his essay *On the Avoidance of Anger* (*Moralia* 452e–464d), that one must understand how anger 'is not magnificent or manly, and that it has neither dignity nor grandeur. Nevertheless, most people mistake its turmoil for effectiveness, its menace for courage, its inflexibility for strength' (*Moralia* 456e), a misapprehension that affects Coriolanus' view of the world, as we have seen. At the time of his exile, he appears indifferent to his misfortune, but 'this apparent composure was based neither upon logic, equanimity, nor any intention of enduring his fate meekly. It was the product of a concentrated fury'. In exile, Coriolanus' thoughts are 'urged on by his anger'. He is not inspired by any 'praiseworthy or constructive purpose, but simply by the desire to revenge himself on the Roman people' (ch. 21).[13]

Exile and anger combine to exhibit Coriolanus' fundamental inadequacies. First anger, perhaps the most analysed of passions in antiquity. For Plato and for most intellectuals, Greek and Roman alike, not all anger was to be deemed objectionable, and the spirit that could manifest itself in rage, when instead managed by reason, was regarded as an element of masculine courage (e.g. Plato, *Republic* 411b; *Laws* 731b–d; Aristotle, *Nicomachean Ethics* 1125b26–1126b10). As we have seen, however, Plutarch, in *On the Avoidance of Anger*, allows no connection between manliness and bravery on the one hand and anger on the other, nor does he here recognize the legitimacy of righteous anger (his views are somewhat less absolute elsewhere: e.g. *Moralia* 443c, 451d, 452a–b; *Aratus* 45). Plutarch's seething Coriolanus, although he does not lack intelligence or concentration, is nevertheless untethered to logic or reason. Consequently, he falls short of anyone's expectations of a man motivated by righteous anger – and he remains entirely outside the scope of Plutarch's prescriptions.[14]

Plutarch's open criticisms of Coriolanus' state of mind during his exile signal for his readers a contemporary intellectual concern: how ought a reasonable man to respond to exile? There was no shortage of advice, including Plutarch's own essay on the topic (*On Exile*: *Moralia* 599a–607f). Although Plutarch there underlines the consolations of life that survive exile, such as friendship and freedom, and observes the Platonic reality that we are all, in a sense, exiles so long as our souls dwell within their mortal coil, several of his contemporaries introduce the additional assertion that exile presents a man with an opportunity to refashion himself, not least through an elevated engagement with philosophy. Exile, then, was potentially empowering – and far from destructive, either to the exiled themselves or to others.[15] The contrast with Coriolanus is unmistakable, and Coriolanus' failure owes itself, again unmistakably, to his lack of education.

The End of Coriolanus

It was Plato's view that a man with a great nature who is poorly educated can only be rescued from doing great evil by the intervention of a god (*Republic* 492a), and in this Life it is only as a result of divine influence that Coriolanus is finally confronted by his mother and persuaded not to destroy Rome (chs. 32–6), a miraculous touch that is at once Platonic and highly flattering to the traditions of Roman religiosity. Still, Coriolanus is not saved from personal ruin: he is murdered by a conspiracy of Volscian demagogues (ch. 39). Their foolishness, however, is soon revealed, for, as soon as the Volscians are deprived of Coriolanus' military talents, they are quickly vanquished by their Roman enemies, who subject them to humiliating terms (ch. 39). It is not uncommon for Plutarch to report the events supervening on the death of his protagonist, and the tenor of this posthumous commentary is important for grasping the essentials of the Life one has just read.[16] Here the signals are mixed. Coriolanus' death was all but ignored by the Romans, who at least permitted his mother and wife the dignity of mourning his loss. The Volscians, however, buried Coriolanus with full honours, as if he were a hero.

Coriolanus is by no means an attractive moral exemplar, for all his good qualities, and here Plutarch diverges from the simple moral assessment of Dionysius. Still, in important respects he seems to excel his Greek parallel. Alcibiades was murdered in sordid circumstances and was buried by a courtesan,

Timandra, wrapped in her own garments (*Alcibiades* 39), a demise that occasions no further commentary from Plutarch. The *Comparison* between the two has a similarly unbalanced quality. Coriolanus' obstinacy, anger and ambition are castigated, but his excellent qualities, and especially his incorruptibility, render him, according to Plutarch, comparable to the best of the Greeks – not to Alcibiades (*Comparison Coriolanus–Alcibiades* 5).

Shakespeare's Coriolanus

For his *Coriolanus*, Shakespeare turned principally (though not exclusively) to Plutarch's Life in its translation by Thomas North.[17] But Plutarch's essential story – and its essential values – subsist even in Shakespeare's dramatic recreation. Unsurprisingly, certain unmistakable differences attract attention. The plebeians' complaints about indebtedness (*Coriolanus* 5–7), for instance, are eliminated in order to underscore their conflict with the patricians over the dearth of grain, a contemporary issue in England when the play was written and one that effectively subverts Menenius Agrippa's fable of the belly and its body (I.1.110–46 = *Coriolanus* 6).[18] Coriolanus' death, including his passionate refusal to be dismissed either in the moment or in history's memory (V.6.115–19), rewrites Plutarch's treatment in important ways. And Shakespeare devotes far more attention than does the biographer to Coriolanus' actual canvass (Plutarch dilates on antiquarian and moral concerns at chs. 14–15), inventing scenes that nonetheless exhibit key Plutarchan themes: Coriolanus' political incapacities, his obstinacy and his devotion to Volumnia.

Coriolanus, as critics have observed, is perhaps Shakespeare's least introspective protagonist. Instead, he relentlessly and, in the event, virulently enacts Plutarch's observation that 'Marcius . . . was always a simple man as well as an obstinate one, and believed that it is under all circumstances a brave man's duty to bear down and overwhelm all opposition' (ch. 15).[19] This is behaviour that, in the play, leads Coriolanus to confound constancy and obstinacy, a muddled principle that offends the plebeians, entails his exile and inspires his march on Rome. For all that, he is driven to abandon even this brand of constancy in his climactic encounter with Volumnia, though in despite of himself: 'Let it be virtuous to be obstinate' (V.3.26), Coriolanus cries in vain. Still, he very soon recovers his true nature, thereby providing (Tullus) Aufidius – who understands him well (it is he who tells us how it is Coriolanus' nature 'Not to be other than one thing': IV.7.42) – with the means of bringing about his destruction. He provokes Coriolanus to anger when he taunts him as 'thou boy of tears' (V.6.100), and the Roman's subsequent outburst outrages the Volscians, who then slay him. The lesson is fundamentally Plutarchan, even if it lacks his Platonic perspective.

It is Plutarch who emphasizes Coriolanus' psychological dependency on his mother (ch. 4). In Shakespeare's tragedy, this relationship is vastly expanded: Coriolanus' upbringing is rehearsed in fantastic detail, and with it we are impressed by the sheer domination of his formidable mother, who embodies in this play the Roman *virtus* that, according to Plutarch, had in Coriolanus' day not yet yielded a place for a liberal education (ch. 1). Her character is larger than her son's, on any interpretation or staging of the play: she triumphs as 'our patroness, the life of Rome!' (V.5.1), and in so doing annihilates the boy who – to his dying breath – Coriolanus resists remaining.[20] Heroic individuality has rarely been made so simultaneously terrible and small: the poetry is Shakespeare's, but the idea is already there in Plutarch.[21]

LIFE OF CORIOLANUS

[*fl.* 490 BC]

1. The patrician house of the Marcii[1] at Rome produced many
men of distinction. One of them was Ancus Marcius,[2] the grandson of Numa on his daughter's side, who succeeded to the
throne after the death of Tullus Hostilius.[3] Publius and Quintus
Marcius, the men who provided Rome with its best and most
abundant supply of water,[4] also belonged to this family, as did
Censorinus,[5] who, after he had twice been appointed censor by
the Roman people, persuaded them to pass a law which prohibited any man from holding this office for a second term.

Gaius Marcius,[6] the subject of this Life, lost his father when
he was young, and was brought up by his mother, who never
remarried.[7] His example shows us that the loss of a father, even
though it may impose other disadvantages on a boy, does not
prevent him from living a virtuous or a distinguished life, and
that it is only worthless men who seek to excuse the deteriora-
tion of their character by pleading neglect in their early years.
On the other hand, this Gaius Marcius' career bears witness to
the truth of the view that a naturally generous and noble disposition, if it lacks education, will produce both good and evil
fruits at once, in the same way as a naturally fertile soil, if it
does not receive the proper tilling. Coriolanus' energy of mind
and strength of purpose constantly led him to attempt ambitious exploits, the results of which were momentous for Rome,
but these qualities were combined with a violent temper and an
uncompromising self-assertion, which made it difficult for him
to cooperate with others. People could admire his indifference
to hardship, to pleasure and to the temptations of money –
which they dignified by the names of courage, moderation and

probity – but, when he displayed the same qualities in his dealings with his fellow-citizens, they were offended and found him
harsh, ungracious and overbearing. It is my belief that of all the
blessings which men enjoy through the favour of the Muses,
there is none so great as that process of taming and humanizing
the natural instincts which is wrought through education and
study, so that by submitting ourselves to reason we acquire balance and learn to avoid excess. On the other hand, we must
remember that the Romans of those days prized above all else
the kind of virtue which finds its expression in warlike and
military achievements. We have an interesting piece of evidence
for this in the fact that there is only one word in the Latin
vocabulary which signifies virtue, and its meaning is *manly
valour*:[8] thus the Romans made courage stand for virtue in all
its aspects, though it only denotes one of them.[9]

2. Marcius was passionately fond of warlike feats and contests
and began at once to handle arms even in his early boyhood.
He believed that mere weapons are of little value in themselves,
unless the soldier's natural capacities and physique are first
properly developed and always kept ready for use.[10] Accordingly, he trained his body so thoroughly for every type of
combat that he acquired not only the speed of an athlete, but
also such muscular strength for wrestling[11] and close combat
that few opponents could escape his grasp. At any rate those
who from time to time tested their prowess against his in feats
of courage and daring used to attribute their defeat to his
immense physical strength, which they found impossible to
overcome and which no amount of exertion could wear out.

3. He served in his first campaign while he was still little more
than a boy. This was at the time when Tarquinius Superbus,[12]
after he had been expelled from the kingship of Rome and had
fought many unsuccessful battles, resolved to stake everything
upon a final throw.[13] Tarquinius' army had been recruited mainly
from the tribes of Latium, but many men from other districts of
Italy had rallied to his cause and were marching against Rome,
not so much because of any personal attachment to Tarquinius,

but through fear and jealousy of the growing power of the Romans. In the battle which followed,[14] during which fortune changed sides several times, Marcius, who was fighting bravely under the eye of the dictator,[15] saw a Roman soldier struck down close by. He immediately ran up, placed himself in front of the wounded man and killed his assailant. Later, after the Romans had won the battle, Marcius was one of the first to be crowned by the general with a garland of oak leaves.

This is the civic crown,[16] which, according to Roman custom, is awarded to a man who has saved the life of a fellow-citizen in battle. There are several possible explanations for the choice of this tree. It may have been intended as a compliment to the Arcadians, the tribe led by king Evander,[17] who, according to an oracle of Apollo,[18] were known as acorn eaters. Or it may have been a matter of mere convenience, because the Romans could easily find plenty of oak trees wherever they fought a campaign. Again, it may have been considered that an oaken wreath, which is sacred to Jupiter as the guardian of Rome, was the most fitting reward for a man who had saved the life of a fellow-citizen. Besides this, the oak bears the most shapely fruit of any wild tree, and it is the strongest of all those that grow under cultivation. In the early days of the human race, it supplied both food and drink from its acorns and from the honey found inside them,[19] and it enabled men to catch a great number of grazing creatures and of birds for their meat, since it produced the mistletoe from which they made bird-lime for their snares.

Legend has it that in this battle which I have described, Castor and Pollux appeared in the field, that immediately after the fighting they were seen in the forum, their horses foaming with sweat, and that they announced the victory by the fountain where their temple now stands.[20] For this reason the fifteenth of July, the day of the victory, was afterwards declared a festival dedicated to the Dioscuri.[21]

4. It would seem that to win distinction and high honours too early in life is apt to stifle the ambitions of young men in whom

the desire to excel does not go very deep, for then their thirst or appetite for fame, never very intense, is quickly satisfied. But for those strong-willed spirits, with whom ambition is a ruling passion, the honours they receive serve only to spur them to greater efforts: the fire within them glows, and they respond as if some mighty wind were urging them on in pursuit of their ideal. They do not think of themselves as being rewarded for what they have already achieved, but rather as pledging themselves to the future: in this way they feel ashamed of the possibility of falling short of the reputation they have already won, and constantly strive to make their latest actions excel it.[22] It was in this spirit that Marcius set himself to surpass his own record in courage. And since he was always eager to attempt fresh exploits, he added one deed of valour to another and heaped spoils upon spoils, so that his later commanders found themselves vying with their predecessors in the effort to commend him in ever higher terms and to pay him the honours he deserved. And indeed, of all the many campaigns and battles which the Romans fought at that time, there was not one from which Marcius returned without laurels or some mark of distinction.

But while other men displayed their courage to win glory for themselves, Marcius' motive was always to please his mother.[23] The delight that she experienced when she saw him crowned, and the tears of joy that she wept as she embraced him – these things were for him the supreme joy and felicity that life could offer. And this, no doubt, was the feeling which Epaminondas[24] wished to express when he said, so the story goes, that he counted it the greatest blessing of his whole career that his father and mother should have lived to hear of his victory at Leuctra. But he was fortunate enough to have had both his parents to rejoice and share in his triumph, whereas Marcius, who believed that he ought to lavish on his mother all the filial affection which would normally have belonged to his father, could never do enough to praise and honour Volumnia.[25] It was his mother's will and choice which dictated his marriage, and he continued to live in the same house with her, even after his wife had borne his children.

5. Marcius' prowess as a soldier had already earned him a great reputation and influence in Rome when a serious political conflict broke out. The quarrel was between the senate, which supported the interests of the rich, and the common people, who complained of the many grievous injustices which they had suffered at the hands of the money-lenders. Those who possessed a modest income had their property seized as security or compulsorily sold and suddenly found themselves destitute, while those who had no means at all were arrested and imprisoned, and this was done regardless of the many wounds and hardships they had suffered in the wars fought to defend their country. The last of these campaigns had been against the Sabines: the people had gone out to fight after their richest creditors had expressly assured them that they would be treated with consideration, and the senate had passed a decree that this undertaking would be guaranteed by the consul Marcus Valerius.[26] But after they had fought with great courage and defeated the enemy, their creditors showed themselves as remorseless as ever, while the senate did not even pretend to remember its promises, but again allowed them to be seized as security for their debts and dragged off to prison. It was not long before violent demonstrations and riots began to break out in the city, and the enemy soon took advantage of these disturbances to invade and devastate the countryside. But when the consuls called upon all those who were of military age to take up arms, not a man responded.

In this crisis the ruling class were again divided among themselves as to how they should act. Some believed that they ought to make concessions to the poor, and that the state of the law was too strict and ought to be relaxed. Others opposed any leniency of this kind, and one of them was Marcius. He did so not because he attached any great importance to the matter of the people's debts, but rather because he regarded this as an insolent and presumptuous attempt on the part of the common people to overthrow the laws, and he sternly warned the magistrates that if they had any foresight they would put a stop to this threat without further ado.

6. The senate held a number of meetings within the space of a few days to debate this question, but they failed to reach a decision. Thereupon the people suddenly assembled in a body, and after encouraging each other in their resolution marched out of the city,[27] seized the hill which is now known as the Sacred Mount and established themselves beside the River Anio.[28] They did not attempt any violence or revolutionary action, but merely shouted aloud as they marched along that they had long ago been driven out of their own city by the wealthy classes. Any part of Italy, they said, would provide them with air to breathe, water to drink and a place to lay their bones, and this was all they possessed if they stayed in Rome, except for the privilege of being wounded or dying in wars fought for the protection of the rich.

These proceedings frightened the senate, and they therefore selected from among their older members those who were the most moderate and reasonably disposed towards the people, and sent them out to negotiate. Their chief spokesman was Menenius Agrippa.[29] He began by appealing to the people to come to terms; next he put before them a frank defence of the senate's position, and he concluded his speech with a well-known fable.[30] Once upon a time, he told them, all the parts of the human body revolted against the belly. They accused it of being the only member which sat idly in its place and contributed nothing to the common good, while the others suffered great hardships and performed great services, all for the sake of keeping the belly's appetites supplied. But the belly only laughed at them for being so simple as not to understand that while it received all the body's nourishment, it also sent it out again and distributed it to every organ. 'So you see, my fellow-citizens,' he went on, 'this is exactly the part that the senate plays. It is there that the various proposals and affairs of state are studied and transformed into action, and the decisions which we take bring results which are useful and profitable to you all.'

7. In the end they succeeded in resolving their difference, but only after the people had asked and been granted by the senate the right to elect five men to act as protectors of any citizen

who might be in need of help. It is these officers who are now known as the tribunes of the people.[31] The first men to be elected to this office were Junius Brutus and Sicinius Vellutus,[32] who had led the people when they marched out of Rome. Then as soon as the city had been restored to unity, the people immediately hurried to enlist and enthusiastically offered the consuls[33] their services for the war. Marcius was vexed that the people should have won a political victory at the expense of the aristocracy, but when he saw that many of the nobility shared his feelings, he reminded them that they must on no account be outdone in patriotism by common people. On the contrary, they should prove that their superiority to the people lay in their valour rather than in their political strength.

8. At this time Rome was at war with the Volscian people,[34] and the most important city in their territory was Corioli.[35] Cominius the consul laid siege to it, whereupon the Volscians became alarmed that it might be captured, and they gathered their forces from all quarters to defend it, their intention being to force a battle in front of the city and then attack the Romans from both sides at once. To counter this plan Cominius divided his army into two groups. He himself advanced to meet the relieving force, while Titus Larcius,[36] one of the bravest Roman soldiers of that time, was left in charge of the siege operations. The men of Corioli, who now felt contemptuous of the weakness of the besieging force, made a sortie, attacked the Romans and in the first engagement routed them and chased them back to their entrenchments.

At this point Marcius collected a small body of men and hurried to the rescue. He cut down the leading ranks of the enemy, checked their advance and in a loud voice summoned the Romans to return to the fight. Marcius went into action, as Cato insisted that a soldier should do,[37] not only with a strong sword-arm, but with a powerful voice and a ferocious expression, so that his very appearance struck terror into the enemy and made him an almost irresistible opponent. Many of the Romans now rallied to support him and the enemy fell back in panic. Not content with this, Marcius pressed on and finally drove the men of Corioli in headlong flight up to the very gates of their city.

Here he saw the Romans beginning to slacken their pursuit. They had now come within range of a shower of missiles which were being discharged from the walls, and none of them dared to think of mingling with the crowds of fugitives and so forcing their way into the city. But Marcius stood firm and exhorted them to make the attempt, cheering on his companions and shouting out that fortune had now thrown open the city to the pursuers no less than to the pursued. Only a handful of men volunteered to follow him, but putting himself at their head he fought his way through the enemy, rushed the gates and broke into the city before a single man dared to oppose him. However, when the Volscians saw that only a handful of Romans all told had made their way inside, their courage returned and they attacked the intruders. In the hand-to-hand fighting that followed, Marcius, finding himself surrounded by a struggling mass in which friend and foe were inextricably intermingled, hewed his way out with a speed, a daring and a sheer fury of attack which passed all belief. He bore down all resistance before him, so that some of these opponents took refuge in the farthest parts of the city, while other threw down their arms, and finally Larcius was able to lead in his troops without striking a blow.

9. After Corioli had been captured in this way, many of the Roman soldiers fell to looting and pillaging the city. This enraged Marcius and he declared angrily that it was disgraceful for these soldiers, at the very moment when the consul Cominius and their fellow-citizens might be engaged in a battle with the Volscian army, to be roaming the streets of Corioli looking for plunder or hiding from danger under the pretext of collecting the spoils of war. Only a few paid any attention to his protest, whereupon he gathered together those who were willing to follow him and started out along the road which he had learned Cominius' army had taken. As they marched, he urged on his companions, begged them not to slacken their pace and offered up prayer after prayer to the gods that they might not

be too late for the battle, but arrive in time to share the trials
and dangers of their fellow-countrymen.

In those days it was a custom among the Romans, when they
were on the point of going into action and were preparing to
gird up their tunics and take their shields in their hands, to
make at the same time an unwritten will[38] by naming their heirs
in the presence of three or four witnesses, and this was what
Cominius' soldiers were doing when Marcius came upon them.
Some of the men were dismayed at first, when they saw him
arrive covered in blood and sweat and leading no more than a
handful of men. But when he ran up to the consul with a jubilant expression, stretched out his hand and gave him the news
that Corioli had been captured, and when Cominius embraced
him and kissed him, the soldiers took courage. Some of them
actually heard him speak of the victory, while others guessed
what had happened, and finally they all shouted to the consul
to lead them into action. Marcius then asked Cominius what
was the enemy's order of battle and where their best troops had
been stationed. The consul said he believed that the finest and
bravest soldiers in the Volscian army were the men of Antium,[39]
and that they were posted in the centre, whereupon Marcius
answered: 'I beg and demand of you to place us opposite them.'
The consul was filled with admiration at his spirit and granted
his request.

As soon as the armies came within range of each other and
spears began to fly, Marcius ran out ahead of the Roman line.
The Volscians opposite him could not face his charge, and the
Romans broke through at the point where he had attacked. But
the troops on either side wheeled inwards and surrounded him
with their weapons, so that the consul became alarmed for his
safety and dispatched his best men to the rescue. A furious battle raged around Marcius and men fell thick and fast, but
Cominius' troops never slackened the pressure of their attack
and finally drove the enemy from the field. When they started
in pursuit, they urged Marcius, who by this time was stumbling
with fatigue and the pain of his wounds, to retire to the camp.
His only reply was that the victor has no business to be weary,
and he immediately set off on the heels of the flying enemy. In

the end the entire Volscian army suffered a crushing defeat, many were killed and large numbers taken prisoner.

10. On the following day Lartius' troops joined them and the whole army was paraded before the consul. Cominius then mounted the speaker's platform,[40] and after offering up the thanks that were due to the gods for two such glorious successes, he addressed himself to Marcius. He began by paying tribute to Marcius' extraordinary exploits, some of which he had seen for himself in the battle, while the others had been reported to him by Larcius. An enormous quantity of booty as well as prisoners and horses had been captured, and out of these spoils he ordered Marcius to choose a tenth share for himself before anything was distributed to the rest of the army, and over and above all this he presented him with a charger equipped with a splendid harness as a special prize for his valour.[41] The Romans cheered this speech, whereupon Marcius stepped forward and declared that he gladly accepted the horse and was grateful for the consul's words of praise. But he felt that he must decline the other rewards because they seemed to him to represent not so much an honour as a payment for his services, and so he would be content to take his single share like the rest. 'But there is one special favour', he went on, 'which I beg may be granted me. There is a friend of mine among the Volscians, whose guest I have been. He is a just and kindly man, but now he has become a prisoner, and so has lost all his wealth and happiness and has been reduced to the condition of a slave. He has suffered many misfortunes, but I should like to rescue him from one at least – the fate of being sold into slavery.'

These words were greeted with louder applause, for there were even more admirers of Marcius' indifference to personal gain than of the courage he had shown on the battlefield. The very men who had felt a certain jealousy towards him on account of the extraordinary honours which he had been paid, now considered that he deserved great rewards for the very reason that he would not accept them, and they were more impressed by the virtue which enabled him to despise such prizes than by the exploits for which he had earned them. For it is a nobler achievement to have mastered the use of wealth than the use of weapons, but it is nobler still to have no need for it.

11. When the cheers which followed Marcius' speech had died down, Cominius spoke again and said: 'Fellow-soldiers, we cannot force a man to accept these gifts against his will, but there is another reward which he can scarcely refuse when it is offered him. I propose that we give him this and pass a vote that he shall henceforth be named Coriolanus, although you might think that his gallantry at Corioli had already earned him the title.' This was the origin of his third name, Coriolanus, and the story makes it clear that Gaius was his personal name, that his second name, in this instance Marcius, was the common name of his family or clan, while the third was added afterwards and was given because of some exploit, stroke of fortune, physical peculiarity or notable virtue.[42]

In the same way, the Greeks in times past used to give men names that were derived from some action, for example Soter and Callinicus; or from a physical feature, such as Physcon and Grypus; or from some outstanding excellence, such as Euergetes or Philadelphus; or from a stroke of good fortune, such as Eudaemon, the name give to the second Battus.[43] On the other hand, some of the Greek rulers have had names given them in irony, such as Antigonus Doson and Ptolemy Lathyrus.[44] The Romans used surnames of this kind even more frequently. For example, one member of the Metellus family was named Diadematus[45] because he suffered for a long time from a running sore and was always to be seen with a bandage wrapped around his forehead like a diadem. Another member of this same family was named Celer[46] because he so hastened to provide the public with funeral games in which gladiators took part – within days after his father's death – that the speed and urgency of his preparations were considered extraordinary. To this day, some Roman children take their name from the circumstances of their birth. Thus a boy may be called Proculus[47] if he is born while his father is away from home, or Postumus if his father is dead, or, if twins are born of whom one survives while the other dies, he is called Vopsicus. Again the Romans often give names because of physical peculiarities, and they choose not only such epithets as Sulla, Niger and Rufus, but also Caecus and Claudius.[48] And indeed, it is a wise practice to accustom men not to regard blindness or any other physical disability as a disgrace or a matter for reproach, but to answer to these names as if they were their own. However, this is not the place for me to pursue this subject.

12. The war was no sooner over than the leaders of the popular party began to stir up fresh quarrels. They had no fresh cause for complaint nor any just ground for making accusations, but they exploited the various evils which had inevitably grown out of the earlier disputes and disturbances, and made these their excuse for opposing the patricians. The greater part of the countryside had been left unplanted and untilled, and the war had allowed no opportunity to arrange for supplies to be imported from other territories. The result was a severe shortage of food, and when the popular leaders saw that there were no provisions in the market, and that even if there had been the people had no money to buy them, they spread malicious stories to the effect that the rich had deliberately created the famine to revenge themselves on the people.

At this moment there arrived a delegation from the people of Velitrae,[49] who offered to hand over their city to the Romans and begged them to send out colonists to live in it. They had been attacked by a plague which had ravaged their country so terribly that barely a tenth of the whole population had survived. Those who could consider the matter without prejudice thought that this appeal from the people of Velitrae had come at a most fortunate moment, since the scarcity of food made it necessary to reduce the population at Rome, and at the same time they hoped that this seditious agitation would be broken up if the unruly elements and those who were most easily roused by the popular leaders could be purged away like some unhealthy discharge from the body. Accordingly, the consuls selected a number of citizens of this type, who were known to be discontented, and ordered them to go and colonize Velitrae,

while others were conscripted for a campaign against the Volscians. The consuls' intention was to keep them too well
occupied to create disturbances at home, but they also hoped
that when patricians, plebeians – rich and poor alike – once
more found themselves bearing arms together in the same camp
and exerting themselves for the common good, they would
learn to show more goodwill and to treat one another with
greater tolerance.

13. However, Sicinius and Brutus, the popular leaders, immediately intervened. They protested bitterly that this apparently
harmless scheme of sending out a colony was the cover for a
most dastardly outrage. In reality the authorities were thrusting these poor citizens into a plague pit by sending them to a
city where the air was full of infection and the stench of
unburied corpses, and where they would live within the grasp
of an alien – and lethal – divinity. And finally, as if the consuls
were not satisfied with killing off some of their fellow-citizens
by famine and exposing others to plague, they must also plunge
the Roman people into a war of their own making: indeed, it
would seem that they were determined that the city should
suffer every possible misfortune merely because it refused to
remain enslaved to the rich. These speeches aroused such feelings of indignation among the people that they refused to obey
the consuls' orders to enlist and were filled with suspicion
against the proposed colony.

The senate was at a loss what to do, but in the meantime
Marcius had come to feel that he was a man of importance. He
cherished lofty ambitions, and since he knew that he had earned
the admiration of some of the most influential men in the state,
he openly took the initiative in opposing the popular leaders.
Accordingly, the colony was sent out, and the men who were
chosen by lot to occupy it were forced to go on pain of severe
penalties. Finally, when the people flatly refused to take part in
the campaign against the Volscians, Marcius organized a force
made up of his own clients[50] and as many other men as he
could persuade to join him, and launched a raid on the territory of Antium. There he found large stocks of grain and

captured great numbers of prisoners and of cattle. He kept
none of these spoils for himself, but marched his troops back to
Rome laden with booty of every kind. This success quickly produced a change of heart among the rest of the people. They
envied their more fortunate fellow-citizens – and they were
filled with anger against Marcius. They deeply resented the
rapid growth of his power and reputation, because they
believed that it would be used against the interests of the
people.

14. Not long afterwards, however, Marcius stood for the consulship. The people then relented and reflected what a shame it
would be to insult and humiliate a man who had no superior
either in the nobility of his birth or in his courage, and who had
rendered so many notable services to the state. Now it was the
custom at Rome that the candidates for office should address
their fellow-citizens and appeal to them personally for their
votes, and they would walk about in the forum dressed in a
toga, but without a tunic underneath it.[51] They did this in some
cases to emphasize their humility by the simplicity of their
dress, or else, if they had wounds to show, to display the evidence of their courage. Certainly the people's insistence that
their candidates should present themselves ungirt and without
a tunic had nothing to do with any suspicion of bribery, for it
was not until long afterwards that the abuse of buying and selling votes crept in and money began to play an important part
in determining the election. Later on, however, this process of
corruption spread to the law courts and to the army, and finally,
when even the sword became enslaved by the power of gold,
the republic was converted into an autocracy. For it has rightly
been said that the man who first offers banquets and bribes to
the people is the first to destroy their liberties. In Rome this evil
seems to have crept in stealthily and gradually, and it was many
years before it became apparent. We do not know, for example,
who was the first Roman to bribe the people or the courts of
law, whereas at Athens Anytus,[52] the son of Anthemion, has
been named as the first man to give money to jurymen. He did
this when he was tried on a charge of treason for his failure to

relieve Pylos. However, this was at a time when the golden age
still prevailed at Rome and the forum was dominated by men
of uncorrupted virtue.

15. So when Marcius displayed the scars he bore from the
many battles in which for seventeen successive years he had
covered himself with glory in defence of Rome, the people were
put to shame by these proofs of his valour and agreed among
themselves that they would elect him consul. But when the
polling day arrived and Marcius made an ostentatious entry
into the forum, escorted with great ceremony by the entire
senate, while the patricians who surrounded him were clearly
more determined than ever to secure a victory, the people's
momentary feelings of goodwill towards him quickly subsided
and their mood changed to one of envy and resentment. These
sentiments were strengthened still further by the fear that if a
man who wielded so much influence among the patricians and
was so intensely aristocratic in his sympathies should ever hold
the chief office of state, he might deprive the people of every
liberty that they possessed.

For these reasons the people did not vote for Marcius. When
the other candidates had been declared elected, the senators
were bitterly indignant and felt that it was they rather than
Marcius who had been humiliated, while he revealed that he
was quite incapable of patience or self-control when faced with
a reverse. He had always given free rein to the impulses of spirit
and contentiousness in his nature, as if there were some inher-
ent grandeur and nobility in these qualities, and had never
allowed himself to be ruled by reason and discipline so as to
develop the combination of gravity and restraint which is so
indispensable a virtue for a statesman. He failed to understand
that a man who aspires to play a part in public affairs must
avoid above all things that tendency to obstinacy which is, in
Plato's phrase, the companion of solitude,[53] but rather must
mingle with men, and even cultivate the capacity to submit to
injury which some people so contemptuously deride. Marcius,
on the other hand, was always a simple man as well as an
obstinate one, and believed that it is under all circumstances

a brave man's duty to bear down and overwhelm all opposition: it never occurred to him that it might be a symptom of effeminate weakness to be unable to restrain the anger which bursts out like an abscess from the wounded and suffering spirit, and so he went away full of indignation and rancour towards the people. The younger patricians, that section of the community which was most conscious of the nobility of its birth and most ostentatious in flaunting it, had always been fanatically devoted to Marcius and they now rallied to his support, although in a manner that did him no good, since their expressions of sympathy and indignation served only to make his resentment more bitter. They had long regarded him as their leader, and while on active service they found him a most congenial instructor in the art of war, since he inspired them to vie with one another in acts of courage, and to rejoice in their successes without envying those of others.

16. Meanwhile, a large consignment of grain arrived in Rome. Much of this had been purchased in Italy, but an equal amount had been sent as a gift by Gelon, the tyrant of Syracuse.[54] The people were greatly encouraged as they hoped that this windfall would put an end not only to the scarcity of food, but also to political strife. The senate was promptly assembled, and the people waited eagerly outside the doors to hear the result of the debate. They expected that the price of grain would now fall to a reasonable figure and that the gift to the state would be distributed free of charge, and indeed this was the course recommended by a number of the senators.

But when Marcius rose to speak, he violently attacked those who upheld the people's interests and denounced them as demagogues and traitors to the aristocracy. He argued that they were fostering to their own ultimate peril the pernicious seeds of insolence and insubordination which had been sown among the masses. They should never have allowed these to take root in the first place, and above all they should never have conceded to the people such a powerful magistracy as the tribunate. As it was, the masses had now become formidable. Every demand which they put forward was granted, and no decision was ever imposed upon them against their will: they defied the authority of the consuls and were governed only by their own champions of misrule, whom they dignified by the title of rulers. So for the senate to sit there and decree bounties and free distributions of grain for the whole population, exactly what is done by the most extreme exponents of democracy among the Greeks,[55] would amount to nothing less than supporting them in their defiance of the constitution and would bring about the ruin of the whole state. 'The people will not regard these concessions', Marcius went on, 'as a reward for the campaigns in which they refused to serve, nor for the secessions whereby they betrayed their country, nor for the slanders against the senate which they have been so ready to believe. The conclusion they will certainly draw is that you are handing out these doles and gratuities because you are afraid of them and want to flatter them, and you will then find that there will be no limits to their disobedience nor to the disputes and agitations they will stir up. In short, to take the step which you propose would be sheer madness. What we should do, if we have any sense, is to abolish the office of tribune outright, since its only effect is to undermine the authority of the consuls and cause dissension in the city. The truth is that Rome is no longer a single commonwealth as once it was. It has been broken in two, and I do not believe that the two parts will ever again be joined, or become of one mind, or cease to inflame and torment one another.'

17. These arguments and others in the same strain had a powerful effect upon the younger senators, so that Marcius succeeded to an extraordinary degree in inspiring them with his own passionate convictions. He also had most of the richest men on his side, and finally his supporters all cried out that he was the only man in Rome who would never be influenced either by the threat of force or the desire to flatter. In spite of this, however, some of the older senators opposed him, because they could foresee where his policy might lead them. And it led, in fact, straight to disaster. For the tribunes had been present at the debate, and as soon as they saw that Marcius' motion was

likely to be carried, they rushed out and joined the crowd, shouting out loudly and calling upon the people to rally to their aid. There followed a stormy meeting of the assembly, and when Marcius' words were repeated in public the people were so carried away with fury that their first impulse was to break into the senate-house. However, the tribunes concentrated their attack on Marcius by laying a formal accusation against him, and he was then summoned by messenger to appear before the people and defend himself. When he contemptuously dismissed the officials who served this summons, the tribunes themselves went, accompanied by the aediles,[56] to bring him by force, and began to lay hands on his person. Thereupon the patricians crowded round him, forced back the tribunes and actually struck the aediles.

By this time nightfall put an end to the general tumult, but as soon as it was day the angry populace began to hurry in from all directions and gather in the forum. When the consuls[57] saw this they became seriously alarmed for the city's safety. They summoned a meeting of the senate and urged them to consider what sympathetic proposals and conciliatory resolutions they could put forward to appease and pacify the people. They appealed to the house to remember that this was no time for standing on their dignity or for a jealous assertion of their rights, but that they were facing a moment of great crisis in the affairs of Rome, which demanded a policy of moderation and humanity. The majority of the senators accepted this advice, whereupon the consuls went out and did their best to reason with the people and calm their indignation, answering dispassionately the charges which had been brought against the senate and rebuking the people for their own violence only in the mildest terms. On the question of the price of grain and the way in which it should be supplied, they declared that there would no longer be any cause for dispute.

18. At this news the majority of the people allowed their anger to subside, and to judge from the serious and orderly attention with which they listened, they were well on the way to being won over. The tribunes then rose and announced that since the

senate was now acting with such moderation, the people were
prepared in their turn to make any reasonable concessions.
They insisted, however, that Marcius should answer the following charges: Could he deny that he incited the senate to set
aside the constitution and abolish the privileges of the people?
Had he not refused to obey the people's order that he should
appear before them? And, finally, had he not insulted and
beaten the aediles in the forum, and thereby done everything in
his power to bring about a civil war by provoking his fellow-
citizens to resort to arms? In making this demand they had two
objects in mind. If Marcius were to curb his haughty temper,
which would be quite contrary to his nature, and throw himself
upon the people's mercy, he would be publicly humiliated; if on
the other hand he followed his normal instincts, he would do
something which would make the breach irreparable. It was
the second eventuality which they hoped for, and it turned out
that they had correctly judged their opponent's character.

Marcius came and stood before the people as if he intended
to offer a defence of his conduct, and his hearers listened to
him in dead silence. But instead of the apologetic language
which they had expected, he began to speak with an offensive
bluntness, which soon developed into an outright attack upon
the common people. At the same time both the tone of his voice
and the expression on his face conveyed a fearlessness which
betokened a total disdain and contempt for his audience, and
at this the people lost all patience and began to show their
mounting indignation and anger at his words. Thereupon
Sicinius, the most outspoken of the tribunes, after conferring
for a few moments with his colleagues, formally proclaimed
that the tribunes of the people had condemned Marcius to
death, and he ordered the aediles to take him immediately to
the top of the Tarpeian Rock[58] and throw him over the precipice. But when the aediles came to lay hands on him, many
people even among the plebeians felt that this was a terrible
and outrageous act, while the patricians, who were beside
themselves with grief and horror, hurried to the rescue, crying
out loudly as they ran. Some of them thrust away the officers
who were arresting Marcius and got him into their midst;

others stretched out their hands, since words or cries were lost amid the general tumult, to implore the people to show mercy. Before long the friends and relatives of the tribunes saw that it would be impossible to carry out his punishment, unless they were prepared to kill large numbers of patricians. They therefore persuaded the tribunes to revoke the cruel and unprecedented penalty which their sentence carried and not to use violence or put Marcius to death without a trial, but to hand him over and let his case by decided by the vote of the people. After this Sicinius, adopting a calmer tone, asked the patricians what they meant by snatching Marcius away from the people when a resolution had been passed to punish him. The patricians countered by asking, 'What do you mean by dragging away one of the foremost men in Rome without a trial, to execute a barbarous and illegal sentence?' 'Well, on that score at least you will have no cause for complaint or grievance against the people,' retorted Sicinius; 'they agree to your request that the man should have his trial. As for you, Marcius, you are summoned to appear on the third market day from now to satisfy the citizens of your innocence, if you can, and they will then judge your case by vote.'

19. The patricians were content to accept this solution for the moment and returned to their homes with a feeling of satisfaction, taking Marcius with them. But during the period which elapsed before the third market day – which the Romans hold every ninth day and so call *nundinae* – an expedition was sent against the city of Antium, and this encouraged them to hope that the trial might never take place after all. They calculated that the campaign might last long enough for the people to become amenable, and that their anger might be appeased or subside altogether once their minds were taken up by the war. However, a settlement was soon reached with the people of Antium and the citizens returned home. The patricians were now filled with alarm and held frequent meetings to discuss how they could avoid surrendering Marcius without at the same time giving the popular leaders the excuse to stir up new disorders. Appius Claudius,[59] who was generally regarded as

one of the bitterest opponents of the popular cause in Rome, solemnly declared that the senate would not only destroy itself but would utterly betray its duty to the state if it allowed the people to use their voting powers to pass judgement on patricians. On the other hand, the older senators and those most sympathetic to the claims of the people contended that they would not use this power harshly or severely, but would show their moderation and humanity once it was granted them. They considered that it was not a question of the people's despising the senate, but of believing that they were despised by it, and hence that they would feel themselves so much honoured and compensated by the privilege of being able to try a senator that they would lay aside their resentment as soon as this prerogative came into their hands.

20. Accordingly, when Marcius saw that the senate was torn between its regard for himself and its fear of the people, he asked the tribunes what were the terms of the accusation against him, and on what charge he would be tried if they brought him before the people. They told him that he was to be charged with aiming at tyranny, and that they would prove him guilty of attempting to set himself up as an absolute ruler. At this he rose to his feet and declared that he would immediately appear before the people to defend himself on that score, that he offered himself freely to any form of trial, and that if convicted he would submit to any form of punishment. 'But', he went on, 'be sure that you confine yourselves to the charge you have mentioned, and do not go back on your word to the senate.' The tribunes agreed and it was upon these conditions that the trial took place.

But when the people assembled, the tribunes' first move was to insist that the votes should be cast not by centuries but by tribes.[60] By this manoeuvre they ensured that the well-to-do and reputable citizens who served the state in its wars would be outnumbered by the poorest classes, who cared nothing for considerations of honour but liked to meddle in politics. Secondly, they ignored the charge of aiming at tyranny, which was impossible to prove, and repeated their attack upon the speech which Marcius had made in the senate, when he had opposed the reduction of the price of grain and urged that the tribunate should be abolished. But they also introduced a new charge into the indictment, which concerned the distribution of the spoils captured at Antium. They alleged that Marcius had not paid into the public treasury the money raised from the sale of the plunder, but had divided it among the volunteers who had taken part in the operation with him. It was this accusation which disconcerted Marcius more than any other. He had never expected it, and for the moment was completely at a loss for a reply which would convince the people. Instead, he began to praise the soldiers who had fought in the campaign, but this served only to provoke an uproar among those citizens who had not, and who were far more numerous. Finally, when the people came to vote he was condemned by a majority of three tribes and was sentenced to perpetual banishment.

The news of Marcius' condemnation was greeted with an outburst of public rejoicing such as had never been witnessed even for a victory over a foreign enemy, and the people departed to their homes in a mood of triumph, while the senators were correspondingly downcast and despondent. They bitterly regretted that they had not done everything in their power to oppose the trial, whatever the consequences, rather than allow the people to assume such authority and then abuse it so outrageously. At this moment there was no need for any of the privileges of dress or other signs of rank to distinguish the two classes: it was clear at once that the exultant look belonged to the plebeians and the downcast to the patricians.

21. The only exception was Marcius himself, who was neither dismayed nor humbled by the news. In his outward appearance, demeanour and expression he appeared to be the only man among all the patricians upon whom his misfortunes made no impression. But this apparent composure was based neither upon logic, equanimity, nor any intention of enduring his fate meekly. It was the product of a concentrated fury and indignation, which, although this is not generally understood, is really an expression of intense pain. For when grief turns to anger, it

is devoured, so to speak, by the flame which it generates, and any notion of humility or passive acceptance is utterly cast out. And so, just as a sick man seems to burn with fever, so the angry man seems to be full of energy, because he is suffering from a kind of inflammation, a swelling and a throbbing of the spirit. This was Marcius' state of mind, as was soon made apparent by his behaviour.

His first action was to go home, where his mother and his wife greeted him with tears and lamentations. He took them in his arms, told them that they must bear this blow of fate with patience, and, without any further delay, set off for the city gates. Although the entire body of patricians turned out to escort him, Marcius took no possessions with him into exile, nor did he utter a single request, but merely walked out of the city, accompanied by three or four of his clients. For a few days he stayed alone at a country estate, while a host of conflicting impulses crowded his brain, urged on by his anger: none of these was inspired by any praiseworthy or constructive purpose, but simply by the desire to revenge himself on the Roman people. Finally, he decided to incite one of the neighbouring countries to wage a destructive war against them, and the people whom he chose to approach first were the Volscians. He knew that they had great resources both in money and in fighting men, and he was confident that the recent defeats that they had suffered had not so much weakened their power as increased their hostility, and made them long to renew their quarrel with the Romans.

22. There was at Antium a man named Tullus Aufidius,[61] who, because of his wealth, his courage and his noble birth, enjoyed the position and respect almost of a king among the Volscian people. Marcius knew that this man hated him more bitterly than any other Roman. They had often hurled threats and challenges at one another in the battles they had fought, and out of the rivalry and boasting which ambition often provokes among young warriors, a private and personal animosity had grown up between them which went far beyond the hostility that prevailed between their respective peoples. At the same time,

Marcius sensed that Tullus possessed a certain magnanimity, and also that there was no other Volscian who was so passionately determined to revenge himself on the Romans. In short, Marcius acted as a living illustration of that famous saying: 'It is hard to fight with anger, for whatever it wants, it will pay the price, even at the cost of life itself.'[62] So Marcius dressed himself in clothes which completely transformed his normal appearance, and like Odysseus, 'Into the enemy's city he stole disguised . . .'[63]

23. It was evening when he arrived in the town, and although many people passed him in the streets, none of them recognized him. When he had found his way to Tullus' house, he quickly entered, took his place by the hearth in silence and, covering his head, seated himself there without uttering a word. The people of the house were astonished at his behaviour but did not venture to disturb him – for there was an air almost of majesty about his bearing and his silence – but they told Tullus, who was at supper, of this mysterious event. Tullus rose from the table, walked over to the stranger and asked who he was and why he had come. At this Marcius uncovered his face and after a moment's pause said: 'If you do not recognize me even now, Tullus, or if you cannot believe your own eyes, then I must act as my own accuser. I am Gaius Marcius, the man who has done you and the Volscian people more harm than any other, and the name of Coriolanus which I bear makes it impossible to deny the fact. This title is the one and only reward I have received for all the toils and perils I have endured, and it is a badge of my enmity to your country. This at least can never be taken away, but everything else has been stripped from me by the jealousy and insolence of the people, and the cowardice and treachery of the magistrates and the members of my own class. I have been driven out of Rome as an exile, and now I sit as a suppliant at your hearth. But I have not come to ask for safety or protection – for why should I have come here if I were afraid to die – but to take revenge on the men who have banished me, and already I have made a beginning by putting myself in your hands. Noble Tullus, if you are eager to fight

your enemies again, take advantage of my disgrace and make my misfortune the Volscian people's good fortune. I shall fight even better for you than I have fought against you, because the most dangerous opponents of all are those who know their enemies' secrets. But if you are tired of war, I have no desire to live, nor will there be any advantage in saving the life of a man who has for so long been your implacable enemy, but who now, when he offers you his services, turns out to be useless to you.'

When Tullus heard these words he was overjoyed, and giving him his right hand he said: 'Rise up, Marcius, and take courage. In offering yourself to us, you have brought us a great gift, in return for which you may expect a still greater one from the Volscian people.' Then he entertained Marcius at his table with every mark of kindness, and they spent the next few days discussing plans for the coming war.

24. Meanwhile, Rome was in a state of turmoil. Marcius' banishment had done much to arouse a feeling of hatred for the people among the patricians, and at the same time soothsayers, priests and private individuals all reported a succession of prodigies which were too significant to ignore. One of them was as follows. There was a certain Titus Latinus, not a prominent citizen but a quiet and sensible man, who was by no means addicted to superstition nor to pretentious exaggeration of his experiences. He had a dream in which Jupiter appeared to him and commanded him to tell the senate that the dancer whom they had chosen to lead the god's procession was a bad performer and thoroughly displeasing to him. Titus reported that the first time he saw this vision he paid little attention to it. Since then it had appeared to him a second and third time, and still he had taken no action. But not long after, he had seen his son – a boy of great promise – sicken and die, and he himself had lost the use of his limbs. He related these events to the senate after he had been brought there in a litter, and no sooner had he spoken, it is said, than he felt the strength returning to his body, and he rose to his feet and walked away without any help.[64]

The senators were astonished at his story and made an inquiry into the circumstances. They discovered that a certain householder had handed over one of his servants to his fellow-slaves with orders that he should be flogged through the market-place and then put to death. While they were carrying out this punishment and torturing the wretched man, whose pain made him writhe and twist his body into all kinds of hideous contortions, it so happened that the sacred procession in honour of Jupiter[65] came up behind. Many of those who took part in it were roused to indignation by this inhuman spectacle and the agonized movements of the victim, but nobody came to his rescue: all they did was to utter reproaches and abuse against a master who could inflict such a cruel punishment. In those days the Romans in general treated their slaves with great kindness; the masters worked and even took their meals side by side with them, and because they knew them so well were more considerate towards them. For example, if a slave had committed a fault, it was considered a severe punishment for him to be made to take up the piece of wood which supports the pole of a wagon and carry it round the neighbourhood. Any slave who was seen undergoing this punishment was disgraced and was no longer trusted either in his own or the neighbouring households. Henceforward he was known as a *furcifer*,[66] for what the Greeks call a prop or support is rendered in Latin by the word *furca*.

25. So when Latinus described his dream to the senators, and they were completely at a loss to identify this bad or unpleasing dancer who had headed the procession, some of them, because of the unusual nature of the punishment, remembered the slave who had been flogged through the forum and afterwards executed. Accordingly, after the agreement of the priests had been obtained, the slave's master was punished, and the procession and the public ceremonies in honour of the god were enacted a second time.[67]

This incident illustrates the foresight of Numa,[68] who in general showed the greatest wisdom in specifying the correct procedure for religious ceremonies, and who very properly laid down the following regulation to ensure the people's reverent attention. Whenever the magistrates or priests perform any religious function, a herald goes before them crying out in a loud voice, '*Hoc age*'. The phrase means 'mind this', and it is intended to remind the people to give their whole attention to the sacred rites and not to allow any pressure of business or worldly preoccupations to disturb them, the implication being that men's attention is seldom fixed, and most of their duties are, in a sense, extorted from them and effected under constraint. The Romans are also well accustomed to repeating sacrifices and processions, not only for the kind of reason I have described, but on far more trivial grounds. For example, if one of the horses which pull the sacred vehicles (which are known as *tensae*[69]) should become exhausted and stumble, or if the charioteer should take hold of the reins with his left hand, they decree that the procession must begin again. And at later periods of their history they have been known to perform a single sacrifice thirty times over, because some omission or mistake was believed to have taken place. Such is the piety and reverence of the Roman people in religious matters.

26. All this while Marcius and Tullus were secretly conferring with the leading men of Antium, and urging them to go to war with Rome while the city was still torn by party strife. At first the Volscians' sense of honour restrained them from seizing this advantage, because they had only recently concluded a truce and accepted a cessation of hostilities for two years. But then the Romans themselves provided a pretext by issuing at the public games a proclamation – prompted apparently by some suspicion or slanderous report – to the effect that all Volscians must leave the city before sunset. Some authorities maintain that Marcius himself tricked the Romans into this action by sending a man to the consuls in Rome to plant the false rumour that the Volscians had laid a plot to attack the Romans during the public games and set fire to the city.[70] At any rate, this proclamation made the Volscian people more hostile than ever towards the Romans. Tullus did his utmost to magnify the incident and stir up the people's anger, and finally he persuaded

them to send ambassadors to Rome with the demand that the territory and the cities annexed from the Volscians in the late war should be restored to them. When they heard these proposals the Romans became angry in their turn, and retorted that the Volscians might be the first to take up arms, but the Romans would be the last to lay them down. Thereupon Tullus summoned a general assembly, and after the people had voted for war he advised them to call in the help of Marcius. He urged them not to bear him any grudge for the harm he had done them, but to rest assured that he would be even more valuable as an ally than he had been deadly as an enemy.

27. Accordingly, Marcius was summoned and proceeded to address the people. His speech demonstrated that he was just as formidable an orator as his exploits had already proved him to be a soldier, and he convinced them that in the art of war his intelligence was no less remarkable than his courage. They therefore appointed him joint commander with Tullus and gave him full powers to conduct the campaign. But as he feared that the Volscians would take so long to mobilize and equip themselves that he would lose the most favourable moment to attack, he left instructions for the magistrates and other principal citizens to raise troops and collect supplies. Meanwhile, without waiting for the formalities of enlistment, he recruited a band of volunteers from among the most adventurous spirits and made a sudden raid upon Roman territory. He achieved complete surprise and secured so much plunder that the Volscians could neither use it up in their camp nor carry it away with them.

However, to Coriolanus the quantity of supplies which he captured and the damage or destruction which he inflicted upon the enemy's territory were the least important results of the expedition: its principal consequence, and indeed his main purpose in undertaking it, was to blacken the reputation of the patricians in the eyes of the Roman people. For while he despoiled and devastated all other properties, he took the strictest precautions to guard the estates of the patricians, and would allow no damage to be done nor anything to be carried away from them. This led to bitter recriminations and clashes between the rival factions in the capital: the patricians accused the people of having unjustly banished a man of great ability, while the people retorted with the charge that their opponents were trying to get their revenge by encouraging Marcius to attack his own country, and were now revelling in the spectacle of others being made to suffer from the enemy's depredations, while their own properties and sources of wealth outside the city were left completely untouched. After Marcius had achieved his purpose of sowing fresh dissensions among the Romans, and at the same time greatly increased the confidence of the Volscians and taught them to despise their enemies, he brought his troops safely back to their base.

28. Meanwhile, the Volscians had mobilized their entire strength with great speed and enthusiasm. The army they had raised turned out to be so large that they decided to leave some of the troops to garrison their cities, while the main body marched against the Romans. Marcius now left Tullus to decide which of these armies he wished to command. Tullus' reply was that as Marcius was clearly as brave a man as himself, and had always enjoyed better fortune in his battles, he should lead the army that was to take the field, while Tullus remained behind to guard the Volscian cities and provide the supplies for the fighting troops. So Marcius, this time with a larger force under his command, opened his campaign by attacking Circeii,[71] a town which was a colony of Rome. Here the people surrendered without resistance and he did them no harm. He then proceeded to ravage the region of Latium, as he expected that the Romans would risk a battle to defend the Latins, who were their allies and had dispatched a succession of envoys imploring their help. But at Rome the people showed no desire to fight, the consuls were reluctant to risk a campaign during the few weeks which remained of their term of office, and so the Latins' appeal was dismissed. Marcius then led his troops against the various Latin cities. Those which offered resistance, namely Tolerium, Lavicum, Pedum and, later on, Bola,[72] he captured by assault, enslaved their inhabitants and plundered

their property. But he showed great consideration for the cities which came over to his side of their own accord, and to make sure that his troops inflicted no damage upon them against his orders, he pitched his camp at a distance from them and kept away from their territory.

29. When he finally captured the town of Bovillae,[73] which is no more than 100 stades[74] from Rome, great quantities of treasure fell into his hands, and he put almost the whole adult population to the sword. After this success, even the Volscians who had been detailed to garrison their own cities refused to remain any longer at their posts, seized their arms and flocked to join Marcius, declaring that he was their only general and that they would recognize no other commander. His name and fame spread throughout the whole of Italy, and people asked one another with amazement how the valour of a single man could, by the mere act of changing sides, bring about such an extraordinary transformation in the fortunes of two peoples.

Meanwhile, in Rome, affairs were in utter disorder. The people refused to fight and spent all their time in devising party intrigues, making seditious speeches and blaming one another, until the news came that the enemy had besieged Lavinium.[75] It was here that the sacred relics of the ancestral gods of the Romans were stored, and it was indeed the birthplace of the Roman nation, being the first city ever founded by Aeneas. The news produced a complete and astonishing change of heart among the people, and an equally remarkable and unexpected one among the patricians. The people were now anxious to revoke the sentence of banishment against Marcius and invite him to return, but the senate, after they had met and debated this proposal, decided to reject it. It is possible that they were determined out of sheer spite to oppose any measure which the people put forward, or that they did not wish Marcius to owe his recall to the people's favour. Or it may have been that their anger had turned against Marcius himself, because he had now proved that he was the enemy of every class, in spite of the fact that he had been injured only by one, and was well aware that the most powerful and influential men in Rome sympathized and had suffered with him. When this resolution was made known to the people, they were helpless to proceed further, since they had no power to enact a law without a previous decree by the senate.[76]

30. The news of the senate's actions served only to make Marcius more resentful than ever. In his anger he immediately raised the siege of Lavinium, marched upon Rome and pitched his camp at the so-called Fossae Cluiliae,[77] which are only 40 stades[78] outside the city. Although the sight of his army spread dismay and panic among the citizens, it at least put an end to their quarrels, since nobody, whether consul or senator, dared to oppose the people's desire to recall Marcius. On the contrary, when the Romans saw their womenfolk running distractedly through the streets and the old men prostrating themselves as they wept and prayed before the shines of the gods, and knew that there was not a man in the city who was capable of inspiring them with courage or devising a plan of defence, then everybody agreed that the people had been right to attempt a reconciliation with Marcius, and the senate utterly wrong to give vent to its anger and its memories of past wrongs at the very moment when it would have been wise to put such emotions aside. Accordingly, it was unanimously resolved to send a delegation to Marcius to offer him the right to return to his country and implore him to put an end to the war.

The men whom the senate chose to make this appeal were all connected with Marcius either as friends or as kinsmen, and they expected at their first interview to be warmly welcomed by a man whom they knew well or who at least was a relative. Nothing of the kind happened. After being led through the enemy's camp, they were brought before him as he was seated in high state surrounded by the leading men of the Volscians, where he greeted them with an intolerably stern and arrogant expression. He then ordered them to explain the purpose of their visit, which they did in courteous and reasonable language and in a suitably conciliatory manner. When they had finished, he answered them harshly. He began by pouring out his bitter resentment at the injustices he had suffered; then, in his capacity as commander of the Volscians, he demanded that the Romans should restore the cities and the territory which they had annexed in the recent war, and at the same time pass a decree granting the Volscians the same civil rights as had recently been conceded to the Latins.[79] Finally, he told them that there could be no lasting peace between the two nations unless it were based upon just and equal rights. He gave them thirty days to consider these terms, and as soon as the envoys had departed he withdrew his troops from Roman territory.

31. There were a number of the Volscians who had for some time envied his success and felt uneasy at the influence he had acquired, and this action provided them with their first opportunity to attack him. Among these were Tullus, not because he had been personally wronged in any way by Marcius, but because, being only human, he was angry to find his reputation totally eclipsed and himself ignored by the Volscians, who now felt that Marcius was everything to them, and that the other leaders ought to be thankful for whatever measure of power and authority he allowed them to share. It was in this way that the first seeds of complaint and denunciation were scattered in secret, and Marcius' opponents began to meet and compare their grievances. They called his withdrawal from Roman territory an act of treachery, not because he had betrayed cities or armies, but because he had thrown away a critical and favourable opportunity, which is the deciding factor as to whether these or any other prizes are won or lost. The fact was that he had given the Romans a breathing space of thirty days, and in war it is always possible for a decisive change to take place in a far shorter time.

However, during this month of suspense Marcius was anything but idle. He attacked the Romans' allies, raided and devastated their territories and captured seven of their largest and more populous cities. All this while the Romans never ventured to send help to their friends. Their spirits were cowed, and they showed so little inclination for the war that you might have thought their limbs were paralysed or benumbed. When the thirty days had expired and Marcius appeared for the second time before Rome with his whole army, they sent another delegation to implore him to relent, to withdraw the Volscian troops from their territory and then put forward whatever terms he thought best for both parties. The Romans would not give way out of fear, but if he considered that certain concessions ought to be made to the Volscians, all these would be granted if they laid down their arms. Marcius' reply was that as commander of the Volscians he could not discuss this offer, but that as a man who was still a citizen of Rome, he strongly advised them to put themselves into a humbler frame of mind, reconsider what justice required of them and come back in three days' time with a ratification of his original demands. If they should decide otherwise, they must know that it would not be safe for them to enter his camp again with nothing but empty phrases.

32. When this delegation had returned to Rome and made its report to the senate, it was plain to all that the ship of state was being tossed on the billows of a fearful tempest, and since the waves seemed about to overwhelm it, it was decided to let go the sheet anchor. A decree was passed that the whole order of priests, the celebrants or custodians of the sacred mysteries, and those who practised the ancient and ancestral art of divination[80] from the flight of birds, should go in procession to Marcius, all of them dressed in the vestments used for the performance of their various functions, and should solemnly entreat him in the same manner as before to declare a truce and then discuss with his own countrymen what terms should be offered to the Volscians. Marcius went so far as to admit this deputation to his camp, but that was the limit of his tolerance. He spoke and behaved with them as harshly as before and curtly reminded them that the Romans must either offer a settlement which complied with his original terms, or else resign themselves to war.

When the priests returned, the Romans decided that they would remain quietly inside their city, doing no more than guarding the walls and repelling the enemy if they attempted an assault. Above all, they resolved to put their trust in the passing of time and accidents of fortune, since they could see no means of saving themselves by their own efforts. The city was full of confusion, terror and rumours of disaster, until at last something happened which resembled one of those incidents such as Homer often describes, although people are usually unwilling to believe them. When some great and unusual action is about to take place, the poet declares in his lofty manner:

> Then in his mind the grey-eyed Athena planted
> this notion,[81]

or again,

> Then some immortal changed his resolve by making
> him ponder
> The thought of what men might say,[82]

or again,

> Either because he suspected, or the god enjoined
> him to act.[83]

People are apt to despise Homer, and to think that by introducing miraculous exploits and fantastic tales he makes it impossible to believe in the power of men to decide their course of action. But the truth is that Homer does nothing of the kind, for whenever an action is natural, normal and the result of deliberation, he attributes this to our own powers, as we see in the phrase which he often uses:

> Then I took counsel within my stout heart . . .[84]

or again,

> Such were his words, and Peleus' son was sorely
> afflicted,
> So that within his rough breast two counsels strove
> for decision,[85]

or again,

> ... but she could never
> Lure the noble Bellerophon out of his upright
> resolve.[86]

On the other hand, when he wishes to describe some prodigious or extraordinary exploit, whose accomplishment demands an element of supernatural possession or a sudden rush of heroic courage, Homer does not represent the god as depriving a man of his choice of action, but rather as guiding it, or, on other occasions, not as implanting the impulse itself but rather the idea which inspires the impulse. Thus he does not suggest that the deed is involuntary, but rather that the hero's will is set in motion, while courage and hope are added to strengthen it. And indeed, unless we are to rule out completely the idea that the gods can initiate or influence our actions, in what other way can they give us their help or support? They certainly do not manipulate our bodies or control the movements of our hands or feet. Instead, they make us aware of motives, or present images to the imagination, or thoughts to the mind, and in this way they either arouse the powers of decision and action in our natures, or else restrain or divert them.

33. During these days of crisis in Rome various groups of women went to all the temples in the city, but the greatest number and the most nobly born offered up their prayers at the altar of Jupiter Capitolinus.[87] One of these was Valeria, a sister of the great Publicola,[88] who had rendered the state such immense services, both in war and in political life. Publicola had died some years before, as I have recorded in my biography of the man, but Valeria was still living and enjoyed great honour and respect in Rome, since her life was seen to be in every way worthy of her noble birth. This woman, then, suddenly experienced one of those intuitions such as I have described, and, recognizing with an insight which must surely have been divinely inspired what would be the best course, rose from her knees and called upon the other women to accompany her to

the house of Marcius' mother, Volumnia. She entered, and when she saw Volumnia sitting with her daughter-in-law Vergilia, holding Marcius' children on her lap, she called her companions round her and said: 'Volumnia and Vergilia, we have come to you as women to women, not because we have been ordered here by the senate or the consuls, but because our god, as I believe, has listened to our prayers and put into our hearts the inspiration that we should turn to you. We are here to implore you to attempt something which will not only be the salvation of ourselves and the whole Roman people, but which will bring you, if you agree, a greater glory than was earned even by the daughters of the Sabines, when they converted their fathers and their husbands from mortal enmity to friendship and peace.[89] Come now, and go along with us to Marcius; join us in entreating him to show compassion, and help us to bear this true and just testimony for your country, that although she has suffered great wrongs from him, she has never, even in her anger, done or thought of doing harm to you, but restores you safe into his hands, even though he may grant her no better terms on that account.'

When Valeria had finished speaking, the other women added their voices to hers in appealing to Volumnia, who then answered as follows: 'My friends, we share with you the misfortune which has come upon the whole Roman people, but we have another of our own. We have lost the glory and the virtue which Marcius once possessed, and we are forced to see him as a man who is imprisoned rather than protected by the arms of our enemies. And yet the greatest misfortune of all is that Rome has grown so weak that she must rest her hopes of safety upon us. I do not know whether Marcius will show any regard for us, since he has none for his country, which he once loved better than his mother, his wife and his children. But in any case take us, make what use of us you can and lead us to him. If we can do nothing else, we can die offering up our prayers for our country.'

34. With this she took Marcius' children and Vergilia, and set out with the other women for the Volscian camp. They were a pitiful sight, and even the enemy greeted them with a respectful

silence. It so happened that at that moment Marcius was seated
on a tribunal with his chief officers around him. When he first
caught sight of the procession of women approaching, he was
filled with amazement. Then he recognized his mother walking
at their head, and although he struggled hard to maintain his
remorseless and inflexible resolve, he found himself overcome
by his feelings. He could not bear to receive the women while
he was seated and so jumped down from the tribunal and ran
to meet them. He greeted his mother first and clasped her for a
long while in his arms, and then when he had embraced his
wife and children he could no longer hold back either his tears
or his affection, but allowed himself to be swept away by a
flood of emotion.

35. When he had thus relieved his pent-up feelings and understood that his mother wished to tell him something, he called
together the Volscian leaders and they heard Volumnia speak
as follows: 'My son, even if we were to say nothing, the wretch-
edness of our dress and our appearance should make you
understand in what misery we have lived at home ever since
you were banished. But now you must know that we who have
come to you here are the unhappiest women alive, for fate has
made that sight which should have been the most joyful into
the most terrible of all, when Volumnia is compelled to see her
son, and Vergilia her husband, turning his arms against the
walls of his native city. And even to pray to the gods, which
others may find a comfort in their misfortunes, has become
impossible for us, since we cannot ask them in the same breath
to make our country victorious and to keep you safe. When we
pray for you, we are calling down a curse upon Rome, such as
the bitterest of her enemies could desire, and your wife and
children are compelled to sacrifice either their native land or
you. As for me, I shall not wait for the war to decide this issue
for me. If I cannot prevail upon you to prefer friendship and
harmony to enmity and strife, and thus become the benefactor
of both countries rather than the scourge of one of them, then
you must know – and let there be no doubt of his – that you
shall never attack Rome unless you trample first upon the dead

body of the mother who bore you. I do not choose to wait for
the day when I shall be forced to watch my son led in triumph
by his fellow-citizens or triumphing over them. If I were to ask
you to save your country by ruining the Volscians, then I admit,
my son, that you would be faced with a cruel choice, since it is
neither honourable for a man to destroy his fellow-citizens, nor
just to betray those who have trusted him. But as it is, all we
ask is to be delivered from the disaster that threatens us. If this
is done, it will prove the salvation of both nations, but it will
bring more honour and glory to the Volscians. They have
shown themselves the superior in arms, and this fact puts them
in the position of being the givers of the two greatest blessings,
peace and friendship, while they themselves will receive no less.
If this happy issue comes to pass, you will have done more than
any man to bring it about; if not, you alone will bear the blame
from both sides. And although the chances of war are always
uncertain, this much is sure: if you conquer Rome, you will be
the evil genius of your country, but if you are defeated, the
world will say that to satisfy your revenge you did not hesitate
to bring disaster upon your friends and benefactors.'

36. While Volumnia was speaking, Marcius listened without
uttering a word, and after she had finished he stood for a long
while in silence, until she asked him: 'Why have you nothing to
say, my son? Is it right to sacrifice everything to anger and
resentment, but wrong to give way to your mother when she
pleads with you in such a cause as this? A great man has no
need to remember every wrong he has suffered, but a man who
is both good and great should remember the benefits that children receive from their parents, and he should repay these by
honouring and respecting them. Surely no man ought to value
gratitude more highly than yourself, since you are so relentless
in punishing ingratitude? And yet, although you have done
much to punish your country, you have shown no gratitude to
your mother. So it would have been an act of reverence on your
part to grant what I asked without any pressure, when I came
to plead in such a just and honourable cause; but since I cannot
persuade you, I must use my last resource.' As she spoke, she

and his wife and children threw themselves at his feet. At this Marcius cried out: 'Mother, mother, what have you done?' Then he raised her up and tenderly pressed her hand. 'You have won your victory,' he told her, 'you have saved Rome, but you have destroyed your son. This is my defeat, even though none but you could have defeated me.' He spoke privately for a few moments more to his mother and his wife, then sent them back to Rome as they wished. The next morning he marched the Volscian army out of Roman territory.

The Volscians themselves were variously affected by what had happened. Some of them now found fault with the man himself and with what he had done, others, who were in favour of a peaceful solution to the quarrel with Rome, approved of both, while others again, although they were angry at his action, could not regard him as a traitor, and thought it excusable to have yielded to such irresistible pressure. At any rate none refused to accept his orders and they all followed him obediently, although they did this rather because they admired his courage than because they any longer accepted his authority.

37. As for the Roman people, the end of the war revealed even more clearly the full extent of the terror and the sense of danger which had oppressed them while it lasted. As soon as they observed from the walls that the Volscian army was withdrawing, every temple in Rome was thrown open and the citizens decked themselves with garlands and offered up sacrifices, as if they were celebrating a victory. But the senate and the whole people showed their joy most of all in the honours and marks of affection which they paid to the women, who, they declared, had proved themselves beyond any doubt to be the saviours of the city. However, when the senate passed a decree to the effect that any honour or privilege which they asked for themselves should be granted by the magistrates, their only request was that a temple should be erected to the Fortune of Women.[90] They offered to pay the costs of building it, provided that the state would undertake to carry out at public expense all the sacrifices and other honours which are due to the gods. The

senate praised their public spirit, but nevertheless ordered the
temple and its statue to be built at the expense of the state. In
spite of this, the women raised money themselves and set up a
second image of the goddess, and the Romans say that as this
statue was placed in the temple, it was heard to utter the words,
'Women, your gift of me is pleasing to the gods.'[91]

38. According to the tradition that has come down to us, these
words were not merely uttered but repeated, but to say this is
to ask us to accept what is almost incredible and probably
never happened. It is not difficult to credit that statues may
have appeared to ooze with sweat, shed tears or exude something which resembles drops of blood, since wood and stone
often gather a mould which produces moisture, and not only
display various colours themselves, but take on other tints from
the atmosphere. And there is nothing to prevent us from believing that the gods sometimes communicate with us by means of
such phenomena. It is also possible that statues may give out a
sound which resembles a groan or a sigh, which is caused by a
fracture or splitting of the particles of which they may be composed, and produces a louder noise if it takes place inside.[92] But
the notion that articulate speech, so clear and abundant and
precise, could proceed from a lifeless object goes beyond the
bounds of possibility, since neither the human soul, nor even a
god, has ever spoken or conversed without possessing a body
which is organically constructed and fitted with the various
vocal members. Still, in a case where history compels our assent
by providing a large number of convincing witnesses, we are
forced to conclude that the imaginative faculty of the soul
underwent an experience which was not really a sensation, but
persuaded the people that it was one, just as, for example,
when we are asleep we believe that we see and hear, although
in reality we do neither. However, those who possess a deep
sense of reverence for the divine, and cherish religion so
strongly that they cannot disbelieve or reject phenomena of this
sort, find a powerful support for their faith in the miraculous
nature of the divine power, and the fact that its ways are not as
ours. Yet the divine bears no resemblance to the human either

in its nature or the scope of its activity or the skill or strength of its operations, nor is there anything incompatible with reason in the fact that it should achieve what is beyond our power, or execute what is impracticable for us; on the contrary, since it differs from us in every respect, it is in its works above all that it is unlike and remote from us. However, as Heracleitus remarks, most of the attributes of the divine escape our understanding owing to their incredibility.[93]

39. Now, when Marcius returned to Antium from his expedition, Tullus, who had long hated and felt jealous of him, began to make plans to remove his rival immediately, for he was afraid that if Marcius escaped him now, he was never likely to give him another such advantage. He therefore gathered together a large body of supporters to oppose Marcius, and then summoned him to lay down his command and render to the Volscians an account of his conduct as their general. Marcius was alarmed at the prospect of returning to private life while Tullus remained in authority and continued to exercise a powerful influence upon his countrymen, and so he answered that as he had received his command from the whole Volscian people, it was to them that he should surrender it, if this was their will; meanwhile, he was ready to give an account of his generalship to the people of Antium, if they desired it. So an assembly was summoned, and the popular orators, as had been arranged, did their utmost to rouse the people against him. But when Marcius rose to reply, even the rowdiest elements in his audience fell silent and allowed him to speak freely, while the best of the men of Antium, and those who were content with the peace, made it clear that they were well disposed towards him and would judge his case fairly. Tullus now began to be afraid of the effect of his opponent's defence, for he was an orator of great power, and the services he had originally rendered to the Volscians won him gratitude that far excelled the effect of his recent offence. Indeed, the whole indictment against him was really a proof of how much they owed him, for they would never have become conscious of a grievance at not capturing

Rome if Marcius' efforts had not brought them so close to success.

So the conspirators decided that there must be no delay and that they could not afford to wait to discover the feelings of the people. The boldest of them raised the cry that the Volscians must not listen to this traitor, nor allow him to keep his command and play the tyrant among them. Then they rushed upon him in a body and cut him down, and not a man stepped forward to defend him. But it soon became apparent that the conspirators did not carry the people with them. From every one of their cities crowds flocked to Antium to see Marcius' dead body, and he was buried with full honours, and his tomb hung with arms and trophies as the monument of a hero and a successful general.

When the Romans heard of his death, they took no action either to honour his memory or to condemn it, but simply gave their permission to the women of his family to wear mourning for him for ten months, as was the custom when any of them lost a father, a son or a brother. This was the longest period that was allowed for mourning and it was fixed by Numa Pompilius as I have mentioned in his Life.[94]

It was not long before the Volscians had cause to regret Marcius' death. First of all they had a dispute with the Aequians,[95] who were their allies and friends, over which of the two nations should command their armies, and carried the quarrel to the point of bloodshed. Next, they were defeated by the Romans, and in this battle Tullus was killed and the flower of the Volscian army perished. After this disaster they were content to accept the most humiliating terms, become the subjects of Rome and pledge themselves to obey her commands.[96]

CAMILLUS

INTRODUCTION TO CAMILLUS

Birth of a Legend

The Romans' conquest of Veii constituted a turning-point in their early history – or at least that is how the event was remembered. Rome's nearest rival, Veii (modern Isola Farnese), lay only 10 miles to the north and had by the fifth century BC become a flourishing and formidable competitor. Rome's ultimate victory, traditionally dated to 396 BC, brought the Romans such gains in land and manpower that they were able not merely to survive the Gallic invasion of 390 BC, but even to thrive in the years immediately following this catastrophe. The importance of the fall of Veii was never forgotten and over time was elaborated into an epic event recalling the grandeur of the Trojan War. Thus the siege of Veii was extended to ten years, and its resolution entailed a full apparatus of divine support and religious justification, all of which underscored the episode's momentousness. Furthermore, the annexation of Veii came to be viewed as the stimulus for an early and profound struggle over the preservation of the Romans' cultural identity. After the Gallic sack, the devastated site of Rome was very nearly abandoned in favour of resettlement in Veii. In the end, of course, the Romans elected to rebuild their city, and this escape from cultural annihilation was neatly credited to the wisdom of the very general who had conquered Veii in the first place, Marcus Furius Camillus, who thereby became a second founder of Rome.[1]

Naturally, his achievements were expanded by an admiring historiographical tradition.[2] It is the indispensable Camillus who defeats the Gauls, not once but twice (chs. 24–30, 40–41). He stymies the tyrannical aspirations of Marcus Manlius Capitolinus (ch. 36), and, after bringing to an end the political strife between patricians and plebeians, he dedicates a temple to Concord (ch. 42). Camillus accumulates offices and triumphs on an extraordinary scale and over a lengthy career: he was censor, consular tribune six times and dictator five times.

Now most of this record is fictitious, though as always in the case of early Rome, controversy is unavoidable. There is no obvious reason to doubt Camillus' victory at Veii, nor can it be excluded that he held more than one successful command during his lifetime, even if the particulars of his career have by now been obscured by the shadow of his legend. His heroic actions during the Gallic invasion, however, are later fabrications designed to mitigate the Romans' shame over their disgrace at the Allia. The same can be said for his second triumph over the same foe. And there are other components of his story that are demonstrably untrue, such as his temple of Concord.[3] Nevertheless, by the end of the republic Camillus' stature as Rome's saviour had been well established.[4] Plutarch's biography drew on a rich and celebratory record of a truly larger-than-life Roman hero.[5]

Gauls and the Gallic Sack of Rome

Around 390 BC a host of Gauls, a tribe known as the Senones, crossed the Apennines, routing the Romans at Allia and ultimately penetrating into southern Italy. Their purpose can only remain a matter of speculation.[6] The Romans believed that this horde sacked their city and spared the remnant guarding the Capitol only when bought off by gold. According to Polybius (2.18.1–4, 2.22.4–5), the Gauls came, saw and conquered – and returned to their own country undefeated by the Romans. Later tradition removed this intolerable disgrace by putting forward various avengers of Roman honour, but, in the end, it came to be widely accepted that it was Camillus who recovered the Romans' gold and expelled the Gauls from Roman territory.[7]

The Gallic sack became a fundamental and defining moment in the Romans' conception of themselves and their place in history. Throughout the republic, the Romans confessed their fear of Gauls, as if they remained an existential threat to the city, and this idea persisted into imperial times.[8] But the cultural memory was not exclusively a dark one. For Polybius (1.6.3–4), the sack of Rome was the starting point of Rome's rise to empire, and Roman writers routinely saw it as the second foundation of their city. Owing to the sheer destruction said to have been wrought by the Gauls, the Romans believed that their earlier history was, if not entirely lost, certainly never so accessible as Roman history *after* Allia. Only the Roman temples on the Capitoline Hill offered continuity with that distant past, and so the Capitol came, more and more, to symbolize Rome's eternal power.[9] This amplification of the consequences of Allia is also of a piece with the accretion of legends, not all of them consistent with one another, surrounding the sack of Rome, the most important of which for Plutarch's Life was the emergence of the figure of Camillus as Rome's saviour: it was a late development, unknown to Aristotle, who believed that he knew a different name for the man who saved Rome (ch. 22), or to Polybius, writing in the second century BC.[10]

The Gauls play an important if stereotypical role in this Life. Greeks and Romans alike tended to accumulate the peoples of northern Europe under the rubric of *Gauls* or *Celts* (Plutarch, like most Greek writers, tends to use these terms interchangeably), with little in the way of further discrimination, although it was known that so-called Gallic peoples differed in customs and in language. Like Scythians or Ethiopians or Indians, Gauls represented a basic barbarian type, whose natural habitat lay in the extreme regions of the world. Consequently, Gauls were rarely the subject of anthropological investigation, but instead remained useful as stereotypes that could be deployed in order to develop a stark and defining contrast with civilized peoples.

Gauls dwelt in cold climates – which made Italy or Greece an unnatural setting for them. They were big, brave and belligerent. They were also simple-minded and undisciplined, and here resided their only vulnerability. Romans and Greeks deemed themselves superior to Gauls because they were, in a word, *cultured*: smarter by nature and better educated. Therefore Gallic invasions of Italy and Greece had to fail in the end because Gauls lacked the temperament and training to sustain their advantages or master the material luxuries acquired by their martial successes. Put differently, Gauls were not merely uncivilized: they were unfit for civilization. Naturally there were exceptions to this depiction of the Gauls, especially as Gallic peoples became part of the Roman empire. But this hostile and negative characterization persisted, and it was typically put, as it is in this Life, to moralizing purposes: in his *Camillus* – and here Plutarch is following his sources – the Romans are defeated by the Gauls on account of their own moral failures (chs. 17–18).[11]

The Life of Camillus, *its Sources and Structure*

Camillus is paired with Themistocles (c. 524–459 BC), the dynamic hero of the Second Persian War (480–479 BC). It is almost certain that the beginning of the *Themistocles and Camillus* has been lost, and this pairing is also one of the very few lacking a closing comparison.[12] Nor is it possible to be entirely certain about Plutarch's specific sources for his *Camillus*. None is identified, apart from a solitary reference to Livy at chapter 6, a rare alternative version which inaccurately reports what Livy in fact wrote. Still, there is no reason to disbelieve Plutarch when he claims to have read Livy, and there are other traces, large and small, of Livy in this Life (see, especially, ch. 5).

It is not at all obvious, however, that Livy was Plutarch's sole or principal source. Another likely candidate is Dionysius of Halicarnassus, on whom Plutarch relied for his *Coriolanus* (see Introduction to that Life). He had similar incentives to do so here. In this instance, however, the assertion is impossible to prove because Dionysius' *Roman Antiquities* breaks down at this point in his narrative of early Roman history; instead we have only a smattering of Byzantine excerpts, in varying degrees of paraphrase. Still, even in this condition, Dionysius' influence is unmistakable.[13] And of course Plutarch will have turned to additional historical and antiquarian sources as well.

What Plutarch lacked was personal and anecdotal material suitable to a biography, and it is obvious how extensively he had to rely on purely historical narratives in his sources. As a consequence of this, Camillus actually disappears from his own Life in chapters 15–23, which rehearse in detail the origins of the Gauls, their incursion into Italy, the reasons for their hostility to Rome, the disaster at Allia and the Gauls' capture of the city itself, all of which elaborate the crisis for which Camillus was Rome's only solution. We learn little of Camillus' youth and are allowed only a solitary glimpse into his private life, when we are told of his debilitating grief at the death of his son (ch. 11). This biography is thus conspicuously unadorned by anecdotes or confidential moments – or flashes of wit or charm on the part of its subject. Instead, whenever Camillus is on stage, he is every inch the formal Roman magistrate: dignified and serious, and permitted to speak only by way of commands, orations and prayers to the gods, none of which opens the door to much in the way of personal characterization.

The contrast with *Themistocles* is striking. There Plutarch condenses or even eschews historical narrative (he assumes his readers' familiarity with the events of the Persian Wars), preferring to record a vast assortment of anecdotes and bon mots. Themistocles is accordingly both an impressive historical figure as well as a personality who is witty, abrasive, eloquent or envious. Whereas Camillus rarely appears outside his official capacities, much of *Themistocles* recounts private moments and especially the adventures of its subject's exile. It is stunning to find, within a single pairing, such different approaches to structure and presentation. Camillus, inscribed in Rome's larger historical narrative, is, for all his grandeur, less an actual historical agent than a model of Roman perfection: he is the recurring and mostly conservative answer to Rome's recurring problems. Even when he plays a part in the transformation of Roman society, by presiding over the decision to admit plebeians to the

consulship (ch. 42), his true role lies in preventing social conflict and breakdown, not in securing any particular reform.
Themistocles, less a paradigm and more human in his depiction, is unmistakably an agent of historical change, a man who
did not simply preserve but gave new shape to the destiny of
Athens (*Themistocles* 4).

Plutarch's Camillus

Camillus' character is made clear from the start: 'His readiness
to cooperate with others stemmed from his moderation
[*metriotēs*], which let him exercise command without reproach,
and it was his intelligence [*phronēsis*] that gave him the undisputed first place' (ch. 1). The political application of these same
qualities, Plutarch points out, is reflected in the fact that, for all
his many magistracies and commands, Camillus never held the
office of consul, because his career was played out during the
Conflict of the Orders, during which the consulship was itself
a contentious matter (ch. 1). Glorious and unexcelled in war,
Camillus sought to be a conciliatory statesman, and it is in
resolving the struggle of the orders over plebeian admission
to the consulship that Camillus concludes his brilliant career
(ch. 42).[14]

In Plutarch's telling, however, in the opening chapters of
the Life Camillus comes very near to failure. His gentler qualities are clearly innate and disclose themselves early in his
biography – he treats the Falerians mercifully (ch. 10) and he is
overwrought with grief at the death of his child ('for he was by
nature a gentle and kind man', ch. 11). Nevertheless, he was
also prey to corrosive and aristocratic passions. In celebrating
his first triumph, Camillus succumbed to conceit and presumption, inner states illustrated to everyone in his decision to ride
in a chariot drawn by four white horses (ch. 7), and during
the initial political debates over the possibility of dividing
the populace between Rome and Veii, 'it was Camillus who, more
than anyone else, took a stand against the preferences of the
multitude, for he was in no way inclined to evade public hatred
by surrendering his freedom of speech' (ch. 11). His uncom-

promising opposition to this measure overwhelmed the Roman public – but left it resentful. When he was subsequently indicted before the people, Camillus refused to endure the indignity and, like Achilles, angrily withdrew into exile (ch. 12). But when disaster struck and Rome was sacked by the Gauls, Camillus, unlike Achilles, was not distracted by his anger. Thereafter, in this Life, he carefully avoids inciting envy in others, and endeavours to keep clear of open conflict (e.g. chs. 24 and 37), preferring cooperation to strife, conduct that culminates in his vow to build a temple to Concord (ch. 42). Which is not to say that Camillus becomes a political weakling: it is he who is responsible for the ultimate suppression of Manlius' sedition (ch. 36). Political harmony is here represented as a source of strength and stability. Plutarch's Camillus is thus a very different Camillus from Livy's, who remains stern and formidable – even frightening – in his authoritarian dealings with the common people.[15]

Camillus ages before our eyes in his continual offices. He is uniformly, perhaps monotonously, successful in battle, less so in managing domestic conflicts. Still, throughout the latter chapters of his Life, he remains the constant champion of social harmony. He is not always master of the situation when events turn critical (chs. 39 and 42), nor is he often the agent who finally delivers the resolution. Instead, his presence, his stature and his imperturbability signify to his contemporaries and to the reader the necessity – and the grandeur – of cooperation and compromise in the face of extremism. Camillus dies full of years and achievements, and his passing is mourned by the Romans (ch. 43), although it must be admitted that his obituary is singular in Plutarch for its brevity.[16]

Camillus and Themistocles

Plutarch had not yet written his Coriolanus and Alcibiades when he began this pairing.[17] But he was plainly uninterested in exploiting the correspondence traditionally drawn by Romans between Coriolanus and Themistocles, preferring instead to match the saviour of Greece with Camillus, a far greater hero.

Themistocles, the champion of Panhellenism, he paired with
the Roman embodiment of *concordia*, political harmony (for
which the Greek word is *homonoia*): for Plutarch Panhellenism
and political harmony were twin virtues, precious and essential
to preserving Hellenic culture in imperial Rome.[18] There were
also unmistakable similarities between the lives of Themistocles and Camillus: each man rescued his city from a barbarian
invader, and did so after his city had been sacked; each suffered, in the aftermath of a great victory, the envy of others
(chs. 7–8 and 11, after the capture of Veii; *Themistocles* 19–23,
after the battle of Salamis); and each retired into exile. And one
can detect further if perhaps less striking parallels: each is said
to spring from a modest family (ch. 2; *Themistocles* 1), each is
connected with various goddesses (chs. 5–6 and 36; *Themisto-*
cles 22 and 30), each was tried *in absentia* (ch. 13; *Themistocles*
23), and each played a part in the rebuilding of his city (ch. 31;
Themistocles 19).

At the same time, however, striking differences obtrude.
Like Camillus, Themistocles was highly intelligent, but instead
of *phronēsis* he was endowed with *synēsis*, a keen and quick
capacity for grasping the best course of action (*Themistocles*
2). It was this quality that gave him his profound foresight and
his crucial powers of persuasion – and rendered him adaptive,
cunning and witty. And it was owing to these traits that
Themistocles became influential enough to preserve the freedom of the Greeks.

Questions of cultural identity were to the fore in the elite
Graeco-Roman society of the Roman empire,[19] and it is obvious
how this pairing interrogates the essential conditions for Roman
and Greek culture. The conflict over removing the Romans to
Veii is a struggle over Roman identity. Although the Romans
began as a nation of immigrants, their religion – the favour
of the gods that makes Rome the centre of a great empire
(ch. 31) – is shown to be wedded to the physical situation of
their city (again, the Capitol is a significant marker of Roman
power). In the end, it is by way of divine communication that
the senate and people are persuaded to rebuild and not to abandon Rome (ch. 32). By contrast, the autochthonous Athenians,

under Themistocles' leadership, constitute a city of their own wherever they travel (*Themistocles* 11). Even the gods, prodded a bit by Themistocles, grant the Athenians permission to withdraw from the site of Athens (*Themistocles* 10), and the Athenians will remain Athenians even if they resettle in the west, in Italy (*Themistocles* 11). In the end, of course, the Athenians, like the Romans, rebuild their city on its original site. Nevertheless, it is obvious how the Athenians' identity, in its versatility, is unlike the Romans'.

Nor is Themistocles' cultural identity fastened to a particular place: for all the travels and adaptations entailed by his exile, he remains ever the true Athenian. He leaves his native city, and shows himself adept, by virtue of his *synēsis*, at mastering local customs and languages in Persia (*Themistocles* 27–31). But neither different dress nor different speech can suffice to obliterate his essential Hellenic qualities. When the Persian king calls on Themistocles to fight against the Greeks, he takes his own life 'in a manner that was worthy of it', an action that earns admiration from Greeks and Persians alike (*Themistocles* 31). His legacy in Greece abides, and Plutarch closes his Life with a compliment to the great man's descendant, 'Themistocles the Athenian, who was a friend and fellow-student of mine' (*Themistocles* 32). It does not seem a hard thing to recognize which culture, in this pairing, is deemed the more robust and vital, for all the greater majesty and success of its Roman hero.

LIFE OF CAMILLUS

[d. 365 BC]

1. Let us turn now to Furius Camillus. Many extraordinary things are reported about him, the most singular and astonishing of which is that, although he achieved great successes when holding high military command – he held the office of dictator five times, he celebrated four triumphs and he is commemorated as a second founder of Rome – he never once held the office of consul. This was owing to the political conditions of the time, for the people were in conflict with the senate and as a result refused to elect consuls, preferring instead to elect military tribunes with consular powers.[1] The men who held this office acted with the same authority and power as consuls, but inasmuch as their regime was divided among several, it was deemed less oppressive, and the fact that six men instead of two[2] were entrusted with managing public affairs went some way towards appeasing those who were hostile to oligarchy. It was during this time that Camillus reached the height of his achievements and glory, and, since the temper of the people was against it, he refused to become consul – although the government did in fact revert to consular elections many times during the course of his career. Still, he held many different offices,[3] and when in office he so conducted himself that, even when he was the one in sole command, he exercised his authority in cooperation with others, and when in reality the authority was not exclusively his but was shared with others, the resulting glory was always his and his alone. His readiness to cooperate with others stemmed from his moderation, which let him exercise command without reproach, and it was his intelligence that gave him the undisputed first place.

2. At a time when the house of the Furii was not very distinguished, Camillus, through his own actions, was the first of his line to win fame,[4] which he did by serving under the dictator Postumius Tubertus[5] in a great battle against the Aequians and the Volscians. Riding out ahead of the army, he continued his charge even after he was wounded in the thigh; with the missile still hanging from his wound, he went on to attack the bravest of the enemy and put them to flight. For this deed he received many honours, the most notable of which was his appointment as censor,[6] in those days a highly prestigious office. It is still remembered, as one of the finest accomplishments of his censorship, that he constrained unmarried men, in some instances by way of persuasion, in others through the threat of fines, to marry the many women whom the wars had left widows. Another act of his, an unavoidable one under the circumstances, obliged orphans, who previously had been exempted, to pay taxes. This step was made necessary by Rome's continuous wars, which entailed great expense.

The most exacting campaign at that time was the siege of Veii, whose population, according to some, are called Veientani. This was by far the most splendid city in Etruria, in no way inferior to Rome either in the quantity of her arms or in the multitude of her soldiers. Proud of her wealth and also of the luxury, refinement and sumptuousness of her citizens' way of life, she had waged many noble contests with the Romans for glory and power. By this time, however, worn down by severe reversals, the people of Veii had abandoned their past ambitions. Fortified behind high and strong walls, they had filled their city with arms, missiles, grain and all manner of provisions, which made them confident they could endure a siege that, though protracted, would be no less strenuous and wearisome for their besiegers. This was because the Romans had become accustomed to making short campaigns at the start of the summer, while spending their winters at home. Now, however, for the first time, the consular tribunes had ordered them to build forts and fortify their camp, spending winter and summer alike in enemy country – and this had gone on for nearly seven years. For this reason, the Roman people

began to criticize their commanders for conducting this siege
too timidly, and so they removed them and chose fresh generals. Camillus, who was elected consular tribune for the
second time,[7] was one of these, but he did not yet play a part at
the siege of Veii. Instead, he was put in charge of the war
against the Falerians[8] and Capenates,[9] who had taken advantage of the Romans' complete preoccupation with their war
against the Etruscans to make raids into Roman territory,
thereby causing severe disturbances. These enemies were now
overwhelmed by Camillus and, after they had suffered severe
losses, shut up within their own walls.

3. As the siege persisted, a calamity occurred at the Alban lake[10]
that, because it exhibited no obvious cause, nor could it be
explained by any natural phenomenon, seemed a marvellous
prodigy and occasioned great alarm. The season was autumn,[11]
and during the previous summer nothing in the way of excessive rainfall had been observed, nor any remarkable weather
caused by southerly winds. Of the lakes, rivers and various
streams that abound in Italy, some were entirely dry, others
reduced to a trickle and even the biggest rivers ran low between
high banks – which was usual during the summer. The Alban
lake, by contrast, which is fed only by its own waters and is
surrounded by fertile mountains, began to rise – visibly but
inexplicably, unless some divinity caused it – and it continued
to swell, gently, without any surge or waves, until it first
reached the base of the mountains and then, little by little, rose
to reach their peaks. At first this was an object of wonder only
for shepherds and herdsmen. But when the volume and sheer
weight of the water broke down the barrier which, like an isthmus, separated the lake from the region lying below it, resulting
in an enormous flood that poured down through the fields and
vineyards and discharged into the sea, then not only were the
Romans shocked by this but all the inhabitants of Italy came to
the conclusion that what had happened was deeply ominous.
Nowhere was this event talked about more than in the army
besieging Veii, as a result of which even the besieged came to
hear of the calamity at the lake.

4. Now, it is routinely the case that a long siege entails frequent meetings and conferences between the opposing parties, and thus it happened that a certain Roman became so familiar with a citizen of Veii that they were soon speaking freely with one another. This man from Veii was deeply versed in ancient oracles and was reputed to be highly skilled in divination. When the Roman observed how, after hearing the story of the lake, the men became overjoyed and took to ridiculing the siege, he went on to tell him that this was not the only marvel that had lately occurred and that other signs, stranger even than this one, had befallen the Romans. He added that he was willing to tell him all about these portents, just in case this might help him, even in the midst of these public misfortunes, to improve his personal circumstances. For his part, the man from Veii gave this proposal an eager hearing and consented to a meeting in which he hoped to learn some forbidden secrets. So the Roman led him along, conversing with him as they walked, until little by little they had gone a good way beyond the city gate. At that moment, the Roman, who was the stronger man, seized him, and, with the assistance of others who came running from the camp, delivered him to the generals. The man from Veii, utterly helpless and all too aware that his own destiny was now inescapable, revealed the forbidden secrets of his native city: that it was not possible for Veii to be captured until the Alban lake had first burst forth and made fresh channels to the sea, and thereafter the enemy had driven back the waters, diverted their course and prevented them from mingling with the sea any longer.

When the senate learned of these things, it was at a complete loss as to what to do. So it decreed that an embassy be sent to Delphi to consult the god. The envoys,[12] Cossius Licinius, Valerius Potitus and Fabius Ambustus, were very distinguished men who made their voyage, consulted with the god, and returned with more than one response, several of which informed the Romans that some of their ancestral rites in the Latin festivals[13] had been neglected. As for the Alban water, the oracle commanded them to keep it away from the sea and, if it were possible, to force it back into its ancient pool, or, failing that, by digging ditches and trenches, to divert it into the plain, thereby exhausting it. When these responses were reported, the priests performed the necessary sacrifices[14] while the people went to work diverting the course of the water.

5. In the tenth year of the war, the senate abolished all other magistracies and appointed Camillus dictator.[15] He in turn chose Cornelius Scipio[16] as his master of the horse. His first act was to make solemn vows to the gods that, if they should grant a glorious conclusion to the war, he would celebrate splendid games and dedicate a temple to the goddess whom the Romans call Mater Matuta.[17] This goddess, on the basis of the sacred rites employed in worshipping her, could reasonably be identified with Leucothea. Women bring a slave girl into the sanctuary, where they beat her with rods; they then drive her out; after this, they embrace the children of their brothers instead of their own; and as they perform the goddess's sacrifices, their actions resemble what is involved in performing 'the nursing of Dionysus' and 'the sufferings experienced by Ino at the hands of her husband's concubine'.[18] Be that as it may, after making vows, Camillus invaded the land of the Faliscans and defeated them in a great battle along with the Capenates who had come to their aid. He then turned to the siege of Veii.

He recognized that any attempt to take the city by a direct assault would be difficult and dangerous, and so he proceeded to dig tunnels under the earth, since the earth around the city was suitable for excavation and allowed shafts to be dug at such depths that they went undetected by the enemy. Soon his hopes were well on their way to being realized, at which time he launched a frontal assault on the city that forced the enemy to man their walls. Meanwhile, others, tunnelling unnoticed beneath the earth, reached the interior of the citadel, below the temple of Juno, which was the largest and most honoured temple in the city. It is recorded in our sources that the commander of the Etruscans happened to be sacrificing in that very temple at that very moment. When his seer looked into the entrails of the sacrificial victim, he cried out in a loud voice, announcing that the god would grant victory to whoever completed these rituals. The Romans who were in the tunnels underneath, as soon as they heard this pronouncement, immediately tore through the pavement and rushed up from the shaft below, uttering their battle cry and clashing their weapons, at which the enemy were terrified and ran away. The Roman soldiers then seized the entrails and carried them back to Camillus. To some readers, perhaps, this will seem too much like a fable.[19]

In any event, the city was taken by storm, and while the soldiers were pillaging and heaping up a boundless supply of plunder, Camillus gazed down on them from the citadel. As he stood there, he first burst into tears,[20] and then, after he had been congratulated by those who were with him, he lifted his hands to the gods and said this in prayer: 'O greatest Jupiter, and gods who judge righteous and wicked actions, you know well that we Romans have not acted unjustly but instead have been compelled to defend ourselves and to exact vengeance from this city of hostile and lawless men. But', he continued, 'if the price for our success is some kind of reversal, then I pray that, for the sake of the city and the army of the Romans, it may fall upon me, though with as little harm as possible.' With these words, he turned himself to the right, which is the Romans' custom after offering the gods prayer or adoration,[21] but in doing so he stumbled and fell. Those with him were astonished, but after he had picked himself up from his fall he said that this little disaster,[22] in retribution for so great a good fortune, was in answer to his prayer.

6. After sacking the city, he decided to remove the image of Juno to Rome, just as he had vowed,[23] and he assembled workmen for this very purpose. But first he offered the goddess sacrifice and prayed that she would accept this devotion and kindly consent to dwell in Rome with the other gods of the city.[24] And the statue, they say, answered in a low voice, saying that she was willing and agreed. Livy, however, says that, although Camillus did indeed offer up this prayer, touching the goddess and inviting her to come to Rome, it was actually the bystanders who gave the answer that she was willing and that she eagerly agreed to come along with him.[25]

Those who believe in this miracle and try to defend it have, as the strongest advocate for their position, the good fortune of Rome, which from its insignificant and contemptible origins could never have attained invincible glory and an empire without from time to time experiencing many notable manifestations of the god who was its present help. Furthermore, they call attention to similar phenomena, such as statues dripping with sweat or uttering audible groans or turning themselves to the side or closing their eyes, occurrences which many historians of the past have recorded.[26] And I could mention many marvellous things reported by men of my own day that should not be dismissed lightly. In matters of this nature, however, excessive credulity and excessive cynicism are equally dangerous. This is because human nature, owing to its weakness, cannot restrain itself and lacks all self-control, and as a consequence it inclines one moment towards vain superstition, another towards a disdainful neglect of the gods. Discreet piety is best, as is the avoidance of all extremes.[27]

7. Whether it was on account of the brilliance of his achievement, for he had captured a city that had rivalled Rome in a siege lasting ten years, or it was owing to the adoration of others, Camillus now became conceited and embraced a degree of presumption that was importunate in a lawful civil magistrate. This showed itself in the display of pride with which he celebrated his triumph, when he mounted a chariot drawn by four white horses[28] and drove it through Rome, a thing which no general had ever done before or has ever done since, for the Romans believe that such a vehicle is sacred and is devoted to the king and father of the gods. In doing this he became hateful to his fellow-citizens, who were not accustomed to such extravagant exhibitions.

He incurred their resentment for a second reason as well, by opposing a law that would divide the city, for the tribunes of the people had proposed a measure separating the people and the senate into two equal parts, one of which would remain in Rome, while the other one, to be selected by lot, would move to the city they had just conquered. The grounds for making this proposal were that, if it were carried out, they would all of them enjoy far greater resources, and, with two large and attractive cities in their possession, could better preserve their territory and their overall prosperity. Which is why the people, who were numerous and poor, joyously welcomed this measure and constantly crowded around the rostra demanding that it be put to a vote. But the senate and the most powerful of the citizens outside the senate saw in the tribunes' proposal not simply the division of Rome, but instead her destruction, and, being averse to its passage, they turned to Camillus for assistance. Because he was wary of an open political contest, Camillus introduced, again and again, various pretexts that kept the people busy with other matters, and in this way he staved off the bill's ratification. And this added to his unpopularity.

Still, the chief and most conspicuous reason for animosity against him stemmed from the controversy over tithing the spoils from Veii, and on this point the people had a reasonable, if not an entirely just, basis for their hostility. For it appears that, when Camillus set out on the campaign against Veii, he made a vow that should he take the city he would dedicate a tenth of the spoil to the god at Delphi. But when the city had been taken and as it was being sacked, either because he was averse to giving offence to his soldiers or because, in the midst of so many responsibilities, he simply forgot his vow, let his troops take possession of all their plunder without imposing any restriction for the tithe. At a later time, however, after he had relinquished his command, he referred this matter to the senate, and the priests announced that their sacrifices yielded revelations of a divine anger that demanded Camillus' thank-offerings as propitiation.

8. The senate, however, decreed that a new distribution of spoils would not take place, for that would have been difficult. Instead, anyone who had received any share of the plunder should, under oath, restore to the public one tenth of it. This resulted in a good deal of rancour as well as real hardship among the soldiers, who were poor men who had worked hard, and yet were now forced to return a rather large portion of

what they had gained and had already spent. Camillus, when he was assaulted by popular protests over this, had no better excuse to offer than an embarrassing admission that he had forgotten his vow. For their part, the soldiers complained bitterly that although Camillus had once made a vow to tithe his enemy's goods, he was now paying the tithe out of the property of his fellow-citizens.

Each man nevertheless brought in his due portion, and it was decreed that a massive golden bowl should be made and sent to Delphi. Gold, however, was scarce in the city, and this left the magistrates with the problem of coming up with a way of acquiring it. Then the women of the city, after due deliberation, contributed their golden jewellery for use in making the offering, and all told this amounted to 8 talents of gold.[29] In order to honour these women appropriately, the senate decreed that, whenever a woman died, a funeral oration should be pronounced for her, just as is done in the case of men. For until that time it was not the custom, when a woman died, to deliver a public encomium.[30] The senate then chose three of the noblest men[31] of the city as ambassadors to the oracle and sent them off in a war ship, well manned and sumptuously adorned in the array of a religious festival.

Now storm and calm alike are dangers at sea, and it so happened that everyone on this voyage came close to destruction, when suddenly, outside of all expectation, they escaped from their peril. For as they were passing near the Aeolian islands, and the wind died down, the people of Lipara launched several triremes against them, fearing they were pirates.[32] The Romans pleaded with them and lifted their hands in supplication, and on account of this the Liparians did not ram their ship but instead took it in tow and brought it into their harbour, where they announced that the Romans' goods and persons were to be sold on the grounds they were pirates. In the end the Liparians agreed to release the Romans, but persuading them took a great deal of effort, and this was credited to the courage and influence of a single man, Timesitheus, the Liparians general. Afterwards, he launched his own ships, accompanied the Romans on their voyage and assisted them in their dedication[33] of the bowl. For all these favours he was rightly honoured by the Romans.[34]

9. Now, when the tribunes of the people began once more to press for the law dividing the city, at that very juncture war broke out against the Faliscans and this event allowed the leading men to hold assemblies to deal with the new crisis. Because the Romans were facing circumstances that required a general whose authority and reputation had been proven by experience,[35] they elected Camillus, along with five others, as consular tribunes. After the elections, Camillus took command of the army and invaded the territory of the Faliscans. There he laid siege to Falerii, a well-fortified city amply equipped with all that was needed for waging war. He was fully aware that capturing this city would require a good deal of effort and time. In truth, however, it was his desire to keep the Romans occupied and, by so doing, distract them. In this way he could prevent them from remaining idle at home or becoming adherents of the tribunes of the people and thus lapsing into factional strife. Indeed, this was a remedy that the Romans were experts in applying, as if they were physicians, in order to discharge upsetting humours from the state.[36]

10. The Falerians took little account of the siege, so confident were they in the strength of their city, which was fortified on all sides. As a result, apart from the men who defended the walls, everyone strolled the streets of the city in ordinary clothes, and their sons continued to attend school and were routinely led along by their teacher outside the walls, where they walked about and took their exercise. Now, it was the custom of the Falerians, like the Greeks, to employ a single teacher for many pupils, for they wished their sons, from the very start, to associate with one another and be brought up in one another's company. But this teacher came up with a scheme to betray the Falerians by exploiting his pupils. Every day he led them out beyond the city wall, at first only a little, and, after they had exercised, he led them back inside. Then, little by little, he led them farther and farther out, until the practice became so

familiar that the boys grew fearless, as if there were no danger. Finally, he led them to the Romans' outposts, where he handed them over to the enemy and demanded that he be led to Camillus. This was done and, when he was standing before the general, he told him that, although he was the teacher and supervisor of these children, he preferred gaining Camillus' favour to fulfilling his legitimate responsibilities: this is why he had come, in order to deliver the city by surrendering its sons. As Camillus listened, however, this deed struck him as vile. Turning to his companions, he said, 'War is harsh, and it is waged with grievous injustice and violence. But there exist certain laws that, even in war, good men will not violate, and we must not pursue victory so eagerly that we fail to flee any obligations incurred through wicked and impious actions.' The truly great general, Camillus went on to say, wages war in the confidence of his native valour: he does not rely on another man's baseness. He then ordered his slaves to tear off the teacher's clothing, bind his hands behind his back and give rods and whips to the boys, so that they might punish this traitor as they drove him back into the city.

Meanwhile, the Falerians had become aware of the teacher's treachery and, as one would expect, because of this terrible disaster the city was filled with lamentations. Men and women alike rushed madly to the walls and gates, but, just as they did so, the boys came into view; they were beating their teacher, who was naked and bound, and they were invoking Camillus as their saviour and father and god. As they beheld this marvellous sight, the parents of the boys, along with the rest of the citizenry, were seized with admiration for Camillus' justice. They quickly held an assembly, after which they dispatched envoys who turned the entire city over to Camillus. Camillus sent them on to Rome, where, standing in the senate, they declared that the Romans, by holding justice in greater honour than victory, had taught them to love defeat more than freedom, not because they believed themselves inferior in might, but rather because they confessed themselves surpassed in virtue. The senate in its turn entrusted Camillus with the authority to make any decisions or arrangements that were required to settle affairs with the Falerians. He took from them a sum of money, established friendship with all the Faliscans, and withdrew from their territory.

11. The Roman soldiers, however, had been expecting to pillage Falerii, and so, when they returned to Rome empty-handed, began to speak ill of Camillus to their fellow-citizens, denouncing him for his hostility towards the poor and because he begrudged them the spoils of war. In addition, the tribunes of the people once again proposed dividing the city and summoned the people to cast their votes on the matter, and this time it was Camillus who, more than anyone else, took a stand against the preferences of the multitude, for he was in no way inclined to evade public hatred by surrendering his freedom of speech. Because of his resistance, the people voted the law down, but they did so against their will and were so very angry with Camillus that their hostility was not a bit softened by pity when he suffered a grave personal misfortune, for he lost one of his two sons to sickness. He suffered this loss with immoderate grief, for he was by nature a gentle and kind man, and even when a formal indictment was lodged against him, his sorrow kept him at home, where he secluded himself with the women of his household.

12. Now Camillus' prosecutor was Lucius Apuleius[37] and the charge against him was the theft of Etruscan plunder. And to be sure, certain bronze doors that had been a part of the spoil of Veii were said to have been seen in his house. But in reality the people were exasperated with Camillus and it was obvious they would seize upon any pretext for condemning him. For this reason he assembled his friends and former comrades in arms, of whom there was a considerable number, and he pleaded with them not to allow him to be unjustly condemned on base accusations and mocked by his enemies. After his friends had conferred and deliberated among themselves, they replied that, although they did not think they could aid him during the trial itself, they would nonetheless help him to pay whatever fine was imposed. This he deemed intolerable and resolved in his

anger to leave the city and go into exile. So, after embracing his wife and son, he walked silently from his house to the city gate. There he stopped and turned around. Stretching out his hands to the Capitol, he prayed to the gods that, if his banishment was unjust and he was being abused by the insolence and envy of the people, then might the Romans soon repent of it and show to all mankind how much they missed and needed Camillus.

13. Thus, like Achilles, he laid curses on his fellow-citizens, and then he left the city.[38] He was condemned in his absence and fined 15,000 asses, a sum which, when converted into silver, is 1,500 drachmas. For the *as* was the currency of that time, and a coin worth 10 copper pieces was for this reason called a *denarius*.[39]

Now there is no Roman who does not believe that the prayers of Camillus were followed by an immediate judgement and that he exacted vengeance for the wrong that had been done to him. But this was far from gratifying to him. On the contrary, it was a source of grief. Still, what happened next was memorable and came to be widely known. For retribution struck Rome on a grand scale, when devastation and danger – and disgrace – fell upon the city. Either it was fortune that caused events to turn out this way, or it was the action of one of the gods, who refused to overlook it when virtue was treated so ungratefully.

14. The first sign of a great evil to come was the death of the censor Julius,[40] for the Romans have a special reverence for the office of censor and they think of it as something sacred. The second sign occurred before the exile of Camillus. Marcus Caedicius[41] was a man of no great distinction, but, although he was not a member of the senatorial order, he nonetheless enjoyed a reputation for being fair and kind. He came before the consular tribunes to report a matter he believed worthy of their consideration. He said that, during the previous night, as he was walking along the street called New Way, someone called out to him in a loud voice, yet when he turned he saw no one.

However, he then heard a voice that was louder than a mortal's voice speaking these words: 'Go, Marcus Caedicius, early in the morning and tell the magistrates that in a short time they should expect the Gauls.' When they heard this story, however, the consular tribunes treated it like a joke and a source of amusement. It was not long afterwards that Camillus was indicted and withdrew from the city.

15. The Gauls are a Celtic people,[42] and they are said to have abandoned their own country because their numbers were so great that it could no longer sustain them all, which led them to go in search of a new one. They comprised tens of thousands of young warriors, who took with them an even greater number of women and children. Some of them passed over the Rhipaean mountains,[43] moving towards the northern ocean, and occupied the remotest parts of Europe, whereas others settled between the Pyrenees and the Alps, near the Senones and the Bituriges,[44] and for a long time they lived there. But eventually they discovered a taste for wine,[45] when it was first brought to them from Italy. They so marvelled at this drink, and were all of them so transported by the novel pleasure it gave, that they seized their weapons, took along their families and rushed to the Alps, seeking out the land which yielded this extraordinary fruit, as if the rest of the world were barren and savage.

The man who first brought wine to the Gauls, and so more than anyone else spurred them to invade Italy, is said to have been Arruns, an Etruscan. He was a distinguished man, and not at all of a bad character, but he had experienced the following misfortune. He was guardian to an orphan, who was heir to the richest estate in the city and who was much admired for his beauty. His name was Lucumo. From his youth, Lucumo had lived in Arruns' household, and when he became a young man he did not leave even then but still pretended to enjoy living with him. In reality, he had corrupted Arruns' wife, and had been corrupted by her, though they had kept the matter hidden for a long time. When, however, their passion for one another reached such a pitch that they could neither restrain nor conceal their desires, the young man seized the woman, carried her away and openly kept her as his wife. Her husband took this case to court, but he was defeated by Lucumo's extensive network of friends and by his extravagant outlays of money, and so Arruns left his native city. He then learned about the Gauls, travelled to meet them and led their expedition into Italy.[46]

16. The Gauls made their invasion and quickly subdued all the lands which the Etruscans had in ancient times occupied. This territory extended from the Alps down to both seas, the names of which are themselves evidence of Etruscan occupation, for the northern sea, the Adriatic, takes its name from the Etruscan city of Adria,[47] while the one in the south is called simply the Etruscan Sea.[48] This entire region is rich in trees, enjoys excellent pastures and is well watered by rivers. Within it lay eighteen large and beautiful cities,[49] each of them handsomely equipped for profitable industry and luxurious lifestyles. The Gauls took these cities away from the Etruscans and kept them for themselves. But those events took place long ago.[50]

17. It was not long after Camillus' exile that the Gauls began campaigning against the Etruscan city of Clusium[51] and put it under siege. The Clusians then appealed to the Romans for assistance, asking them to send ambassadors and letters on their behalf to the barbarians. Three men of the Fabii[52] were sent, each of whom enjoyed high rank and distinction. The Gauls received these men courteously, in deference to the name of Rome, and suspended their assault against the city's walls while they conferred with them. The Gauls were asked what injury they had suffered at the hands of the Clusians that led them to attack their city, at which Brennus, the king of the Gauls, laughed and said, 'The Clusians wrong us in this: though they are able to farm only a small parcel of land, they nevertheless insist on possessing a great deal of it and they refuse to share any of it with us, although we are strangers, many in number and poor. You too, Romans, have suffered similar wrongs, formerly at the hands of the Albans, the Fidenates[53] and the Ardeates,[54] and more recently from the Veientines, Capenates and many of the Faliscans and Volscians: if they

refuse to share their goods with you, you wage war against them, enslave them, pillage their cities and raze them to the ground. Not that you do anything cruel or unjust acting in this way. On the contrary, you are obeying the most ancient of all laws, which awards to the strong the possessions of the weak, a principle that begins with the divine and extends to the beasts of the field, for it is in the nature even of these creatures for the strong to dominate the weak.[55] Therefore do not pity the Clusians, whom we are besieging, lest you teach the Gauls to become kind and compassionate to those who are oppressed by you.'

This speech made it clear to the Romans that there was no coming to terms with Brennus, and so they went into Clusium, where they encouraged the soldiers and roused them to join in a sally against the barbarians. They did this because they wished either to test the valour of the Clusian soldiers or to exhibit their own. The Clusians then erupted from their city and fighting was soon raging just outside the city walls. At that moment one of the Fabii, Quintus Ambustus, charged his horse against a Gaul, a man of great and noble stature, who was riding far in front of the others. Ambustus was not recognized at first, owing to the quickness of the fight and his shining armour, which hid his face. But when he had prevailed in combat, throwing the Gaul from his horse, and was stripping the man of his armour, Brennus recognized him and called upon the gods to be witnesses how, contrary to the common laws and practices of all mankind, which are holy and just, this man had come to him as an ambassador and yet was now engaged in making war. He stopped fighting immediately and let the Clusians alone, leading his army against Rome instead. Because he did not wish it to appear that the Gauls actually welcomed this injury and were simply looking for a pretext for war, Brennus sent ahead a demand that Quintus Ambustus be handed over for punishment. In the meantime he continued his advance, though he moved slowly.

18. When the senate met in Rome, many denounced Fabius,[56] especially the priests called Fetiales, who invoked religious

scruples as they urged the senate to lay the guilt for what had been done on the one man who was responsible, thereby freeing everyone else from the stain of his sacrilege. These Fetiales were established by Numa Pompilius, the most mild and just of kings, as the protectors of peace: it was their role to render judgements and decisions as to the grounds on which the Romans could justly make war.[57] The senate referred this matter to the people, before whom the priests unanimously condemned Fabius for what he had done. But the multitude regarded religion with such scorn and contempt that they elected this same Fabius consular tribune – along with his brothers. When the Gauls learned of this, they were furious. They allowed nothing to slow them down as they advanced against Rome with all possible speed. The sheer numbers of the Gauls, their dazzling equipment, their fierce violence, all inspired terror wherever they came, and because of this everyone in their path believed that their lands were already as good as lost and that their cities would soon be captured. Contrary to all expectation, however, the Gauls did them no harm. They did not even take anything from their fields. As they passed near the cities on their way, they proclaimed that they were marching against Rome and that the Romans were their only enemies: all others they regarded as friends.

Against this barbarian onslaught, the consular tribunes led the Romans forth to battle. In so far as numbers were concerned, they were not inferior, for there were no fewer than 40,000 soldiers on the Roman side. Most of them, however, were untrained and were handling arms for the first time. Moreover, they had neglected their religious practices, for they did not offer sacrifices in order to find good omens, nor did they consult the diviners, as was fitting before the perils of battle.[58] Still, what most of all upset their actions was having too many men in command. Before this time, when confronted with less critical struggles, they had often chosen a single leader, called a dictator, because they realized how it is a real advantage, in the midst of a dangerous crisis, for everyone to obey the judgement of one man possessing absolute authority and jurisdiction. And the unfair treatment that Camillus had received did just as much harm, for it was now felt to be dangerous to exercise command unless one curried the favour of the public.

The Romans advanced about 90 stades from the city and pitched camp beside the River Allia,[59] not far from where it flows into the Tiber. There the barbarians fell on them unexpectedly, and, after a disgraceful and confused struggle, the Romans were routed. The Gauls drove the Romans' left wing straight into the river and destroyed it. The right wing suffered fewer losses, but only because it escaped the Gauls' onslaught by retreating from the plain into the hills, and from there most of the Romans fled back to the city. As for the rest, those who escaped from the enemy, who had become wearied by the slaughter, fled by night to Veii, for they believed that Rome must by now be destroyed and all her citizens dead.

19. This battle was fought just after the summer solstice, around the time of a full moon, on the very day on which the Fabian disaster, in which 300 of the Fabii were once annihilated by the Etruscans, had taken place.[60] This second defeat, however, was so much worse than its predecessor that, even now, this day is called the Day of Allia,[61] from the name of the river.

Now on the topic of unspeakable days – whether we must consider some days truly unlucky, or whether Heracleitus was correct when he reproached Hesiod for designating some days good and others bad, insisting that the poet did not understand that the nature of every day is the same – this is a matter I have examined elsewhere.[62] Still, it is perhaps appropriate, even in this account, to mention a few examples. The Boeotians,[63] on the fifth day of their month Hippodromius, which the Athenians call Hecatombaeon,[64] won two glorious victories which secured the freedom of the Greeks: one at Leuctra and the other, more than 200 years earlier, at Ceressus, when they defeated Lattamyas and the Thessalians.[65] Then again, on the sixth day of the month of Boedromion, the Persians were defeated by the Greeks at Marathon,[66] and on the third day of the same month they were defeated by the Greeks at both

Plataea and Mycale,[67] and they were also defeated at Arbela[68] by the Greeks on the twenty-sixth day of this month. Furthermore, the Athenians won a battle at sea off Naxos,[69] under the command of Chabrias,[70] during Boedromion, around the time of the full moon, and on the twentieth day of that month were victorious at Salamis,[71] as I have shown in my essay *On Days*.

Clearly the month of Thargelion[72] has been unfortunate for the barbarians, for it was during this month that Alexander defeated the generals of the Great King at Granicus,[73] and on the twenty-fourth day of this month the Carthaginians were beaten by Timoleon in Sicily.[74] And it seems that it was on this same day in the month of Thargelion that Troy fell, according to Ephorus, Callisthenes, Damastes and Malacas.[75] By contrast, the month of Metageitnion,[76] which the Boeotians call Panemus, has not been auspicious for the Greeks. On the seventh day of this month they lost the battle of Crannon to Antipater[77] and were ruined. Before this, on the same day, they had fought against Philip[78] at Chaeronea and lost. And in the same year, and on this same day in the month of Metageitnion, Archidamus[79] and his army, which had invaded Italy, were destroyed by the barbarians there. The Chalcedonians[80] observe the twenty-second day of this month because it has consistently brought them the majority – and the most severe – of their misfortunes.

I am all too aware that about the time of the Mysteries, Thebes was razed to the ground for the second time, by Alexander, and that, subsequently, the Athenians received a garrison of Macedonians, on the twentieth of Boedromion, the very day on which they lead forth the mystic Iacchus.[81] Similarly, the Romans once lost to the Cimbrians an army under the command of Caepio, but at a later time, on the same day, with Lucullus as general, defeated Tigranes[82] and the Armenians. King Attalus and Pompey the Great each died on his own birthday.[83] Put simply, it is possible to point out many men who, on the same days of the calendar, have had entirely contrary experiences. Nevertheless, for the Romans, the Day of Allia is one of the unluckiest, and because of it two additional days in each month are also regarded as unlucky. This is what routinely happens in the aftermath of some chance event: piety and superstition excel all limits. But these matters have been treated more carefully in my *Roman Questions*.[84]

20. In the aftermath of this battle, had the Gauls raced in hot pursuit after those who fled, nothing could have prevented Rome's destruction and the deaths of all who remained there. So much terror did the fugitives inspire when they reached the city that everyone in it was entirely given over to confusion and bewilderment. But at the time the barbarians did not grasp the extent of their victory; in their elation, they instead turned to celebrating and dividing the spoils they had taken from the Romans' camp, all of which afforded ample time for the multitudes in Rome who were deserting the city to make their escape. As for those who had decided to remain, the Gauls' delay afforded them time to regain their hope and make preparations to defend themselves. They abandoned all the rest of the city except the Capitol, which they fortified with ramparts, and they supplied themselves with missiles. Their central concern was the safety of the sacred objects of the city, many of which they carried to the Capitol, while the Vestal Virgins[85] hastily gathered up the fire of Vesta, along with the other sacred objects in their care, and took them away as they fled.

According to some sources, however, the Vestals protect only the imperishable fire, the veneration of which was instituted by King Numa on the grounds that it is the fundamental element in all things. For in nature fire is the thing most characterized by motion, and all generation is either a kind of motion or happens in combination with motion. Now all other parts of matter, whenever heat is absent, lie inert, as if dead, and these inert parts of matter desire the force of fire, as if it were a soul, and as soon as this force is present, they become capable of acting and being acted upon. It is Numa who was so learned that he is reputed to have enjoyed conversations with the Muses, who is said to have consecrated the Vestals' fire, ordaining that it should be kept burning as a symbol of the eternal force that orders and activates all things.[86] Other writers, however, claim that this fire is kept burning in front of sacred objects for the purpose of their purification, as is the custom among the Greeks, and that everything apart from the fire is kept hidden[87] within the temple and is seen by no one except the Vestal Virgins. It is commonly believed that the Trojan Palladium,[88] which was carried to Italy by Aeneas, is hidden there. But others say that the Samothracian images are kept there, and they relate how Dardanus brought these with him to Troy and, after he had founded the city, celebrated their rites and their consecration, and how Aeneas, when Troy fell, stole these images away, preserving them until he came to Italy.[89] Those who profess to have the most knowledge of these matters insist that two small jars are stored there, one of which is open and empty, the other is full and sealed, and that both of these can be viewed only by the Vestals. Others, however, believe that these authorities have been misled by the fact that, when they were fleeing Rome, the Vestals stored most of the sacred objects in two jars and hid them underground beneath the temple of Quirinus,[90] and to this day that spot bears the name Jars.[91]

21. In any case, the Vestals took the most precious and important of the sacred objects with them as they fled beside the river. There, among the other fugitives, was Lucius Albinius, a common citizen, who was carrying in a wagon his small children, his wife and their essential possessions. When he saw the Vestals bearing in their arms the sacred objects of the gods, making their way unassisted and with great difficulty, he immediately removed his children, his wife and his possessions from his wagon so that he could hand it over to the Vestals for making their escape to a Greek city.[92] The piety of Albinius, and the respect he showed the gods in this moment of extreme danger, could not rightly go unremarked.

The priests of the other gods, as well as the senior men who had been consuls and had celebrated triumphs, could not bear to forsake the city, and so, donning their sacred and official attire, offered prayers, led by Fabius[93] the chief priest, in which they devoted themselves to the gods as a sacrifice on behalf of their country. They then seated themselves in the forum on ivory chairs, and, so arrayed, awaited their fates.

22. On the third day after the battle, Brennus brought his army up to the city. There he found its gates open and its walls undefended, which led him at first to suspect an ambush, because he could not imagine so total a collapse on the part of the Romans. But, once he recognized the truth, he entered by the Colline Gate and captured Rome. This took place a little more than 360 years after the foundation of the city, if one can believe that anything in the way of an exact chronology has been preserved in this matter, especially when confusion associated with this very episode has led to controversies in the chronology of later events. It seems, however, that faint rumours of this disaster, and of the capture of the city, quickly made their way to Greece. For Heracleides of Pontus, who lived soon after these events, records, in his essay *On the Soul*, a story from the west claiming that an army of Hyperboreans had come from far away and captured a Greek city called Rome, settled somewhere on the Great Sea. Now I am hardly surprised that Heracleides, a writer inclined towards fable and invention, should embellish the true story of Rome's fall with fictitious items like Hyperboreans and the Great Sea.[94] By contrast, it is obvious that the philosopher Aristotle had heard an accurate report of the city's capture by the Gauls, although he calls the saviour of the city Lucius, when in fact Camillus' name was not Lucius but Marcus.[95] Details such as this, however, were arrived at by conjecture.

After Brennus took possession of the city, he set a guard around the Capitol while he went down to the forum. There he was astonished to see men sitting silently in state, who did not rise to meet their enemies, nor did they alter their expressions or their colour. Instead, they sat calmly and fearlessly, each of them leaning on the staff he held, as they gazed into one another's faces. This strange sight surprised and perplexed the Gauls, and for some time they hesitated, uncertain whether they should approach or touch these men whom they mistook for higher beings. Finally one of them made so bold as to come near Manius Papirius,[96] and, putting forward his hand, gently touched his chin and stroked his long beard. Papirius at once took his staff and struck the barbarian hard upon his head, at which the barbarian drew his sword and killed him. After that, the Gauls fell upon the others and slew them all, and they went on cutting down anyone else who came in their way. For many days they pillaged and plundered the private homes of the city, at length setting them on fire and burning them to the ground, so angry were they at the men who were holding the Capitol. For these men would not yield, although the Gauls summoned them to surrender. Moreover, when attacked, they fought back and drove the enemy from the ramparts. For this reason, the Gauls inflicted every cruel abuse on the city, and they slaughtered everyone they captured, men and women, young and old alike.

23. The siege continued for a long time and the Gauls began to run out of supplies. So they divided their forces, some remaining with their king in order to guard the Capitol, while the rest ravaged the countryside, falling on villages and pillaging them. They did not do this as a single army. Instead, they ranged about in different companies under different commanders, and their successes rendered them so supremely confident that they were soon conducting raids without any fear whatsoever. The largest and best disciplined of these forces advanced towards the city of Ardea, where Camillus had been living since his exile, uninvolved in public business and immersed in private life. He was not, however, the sort of man whose hopes and designs were centred on avoiding the notice of his enemies. On the contrary, he actively looked for an opportunity to punish them. Consequently, when he concluded that the Ardeans had sufficient numbers of men to defend themselves, but lacked courage owing to the inexperience and timidity of their generals, he began to urge the younger men not to attribute the Romans' calamity to the valour of the Celts: the Romans suffered on account of their own rashness, he insisted, and no one should credit what had happened to the deeds of the Celts, for they did not deserve their victory, which should instead be

seen as the work of fortune. It was a noble thing, he said, even if it was also dangerous, to repel the attack of a foreign and barbarian invader, whose purpose in conquering was the same as that of fire: to destroy whatever it could. If, moreover, they were courageous and resolute, he would provide them with a victory that was safe and sure.

When Camillus was assured that the young men embraced his arguments, he went to the magistrates and council of Ardea and persuaded them as well. Everyone of military age he then armed, but kept them inside the city's walls to prevent the enemy, who were near, from becoming aware of them. At that time, in fact, the Gauls were raiding the nearby countryside, and, when they found themselves burdened by a surfeit of plunder, decided to pitch camp on the plain, unworried and unconcerned about defences. Soon night fell on their drunken carousing and their entire camp was silent. After Camillus learned this from his scouts, he led the Ardeans out of their city. Crossing silently to the camp, at around midnight they attacked with a roar of loud cries and trumpet blasts. This completely confused the Gauls, who were drunk and so were scarcely awakened even by this clamour. A few of them, sobered by their fear, equipped themselves and fought back against Camillus and his men, and so fell in combat. Most of them, however, remained drunk and were barely awake. They were unarmed when the attack occurred and were easily cut down. Only a few escaped the camp under cover of darkness, but in the morning the cavalry found them wandering in small groups through the countryside. They chased them down and finished them off.

24. News of this exploit quickly spread throughout other cities and inspired many men of military age to join Camillus, especially those Romans who had fled from the battle of Allia and were now in Veii, lamenting their condition with sentiments like this: 'What a great leader has been stolen from Rome by a divinity who now adorns Ardea with the achievements of Camillus! The city that gave birth to this splendid man and equipped him for life is now dead and gone, while we, for want of a general, forsake Italy and sit cooped up behind foreign

walls. Come, let us send to Ardea and demand back our general, or let us take up our weapons and go to him! For he is no longer an exile, nor are we any longer citizens, since our country no longer exists but has been vanquished by our enemies.' On this they all agreed and invited Camillus to take command. He refused to do so, however, unless the citizens still on the Capitol elected him in accordance with the law, for, in his view, it was they who preserved what remained of the legitimate state of Rome. Their commands he would eagerly obey, but he would never involve himself in Roman affairs against their wishes. Camillus' deference exhibited his nobility and was admired, but it was far from obvious how any of this could be communicated to the Capitol. In fact, it looked impossible for a messenger to make his way to the citadel so long as the enemy occupied the city.

25. Now there was a young man named Pontius Cominius,[97] a citizen of ordinary birth who possessed a deep passion for glory and honour. He volunteered for this difficult task. He did not carry a letter for the men on the Capitol lest, should he be captured, the enemy learn Camillus' intentions from it, and he wore cheap garments, beneath which he carried corks. He was fearless and managed to make most of his journey in a single day. As he approached Rome, it was beginning to grow dark. The bridge over the river was closed to him because it was being guarded by the barbarians, and so he wrapped his garments around his head (they did not weigh very much), attached the corks to his body and, buoyed up by them, got across and made his way to the city. By taking notice of the Gauls' campfires and by listening for whatever noise they made, he succeeded in avoiding any of the enemy who were awake, until eventually he came to the Carmental Gate,[98] where it was very quiet. This is also the place, more than any other, where the Capitoline Hill is steep and sheer, on every approach a huge jagged cliff. Unnoticed by the enemy, Cominius climbed, straining and struggling, along the hollow of the escarpment until at last he reached the Romans who were guarding the wall. He called out, identified himself and was pulled up. He was then led in

front of the men in charge. Before a quickly convened senate, Cominius announced Camillus' victory, which none of them had yet learned about, and he explained the decisions taken by the soldiers at Veii. He went on to urge them to confirm Camillus in his command because he was the only man the citizens outside the city would obey. After the senators had listened and deliberated, they appointed Camillus dictator[99] and sent Cominius back again. He returned by the same route he had come, with just as much good luck as before, once again escaping the enemy's notice. He announced the senate's decision to the Romans at Veii.

26. These soldiers welcomed the news enthusiastically, and by the time Camillus arrived he found 20,000 men already in arms. He collected even more from the allies and began making preparations for an attack. [So it was that Camillus was appointed dictator for the second time. He proceeded to Veii, where he took command of the soldiers there, and he collected even more troops from the allies, all for the purpose of making an attack on the enemy.][100]

Meanwhile, in Rome, some of the barbarians just happened to pass near the spot where Pontius had climbed to the Capitol by night and noticed the many places where his hands and his feet had left marks as he was clambering his way up – as well as other places where plants had been torn from the rocks on which they had been growing and where the earth had slipped. This they reported to their king, who came along and made an inspection, but at the time did nothing more. That evening, however, he selected those Celts who were most agile and most talented at climbing mountains, to whom he said: 'The enemy have revealed to us an unknown route against them and have shown us that this approach is neither impenetrable nor impassable. It would be a great disgrace, when we have begun so well, if in the end we should fail and abandon this place, supposing it to be impregnable, when the enemy themselves are teaching us how to take it. For where it was easy for one man to climb, it will not be difficult for many, one after the other, to do the same. Quite the contrary, in fact, for they will be able to offer one another stout support. Every man who undertakes this hazardous mission will receive gifts and honours befitting his bravery.'

27. When the king finished speaking, the Gauls were eager to volunteer. Around midnight a large party began to climb, staying silent and clinging tightly to the cliff as they made their ascent past places that were precipitous and difficult. In the end, the climb proved less arduous than expected. Consequently, when the men in the lead had attained the summit and had armed themselves for battle, they very nearly captured the outer fortifications by falling upon its sleeping watchmen, for neither man nor dog was aware of their presence. But near the temple of Juno the Romans kept sacred geese, which in ordinary circumstances were fed generously, but at this time, because supplies were meagre and there was barely enough grain for the soldiers, were neglected and had lapsed into a miserable condition. Now by their very nature geese have keen hearing and are frightened by every sound, and, owing to their hunger, these geese were more than normally wakeful and restless. So, when they perceived the approach of the Gauls, they darted at them with a honking so loud that it awakened the garrison. Detected, the barbarians launched a loud and vigorous attack, but the Romans fought back at once, quickly snatching up whatever weapon was nearest. Manlius, a former consul,[101] a strong man renowned for his fearlessness, was first into the fray, confronting two of the enemy at the same time. With his sword he lopped off the right hand of one, as the Gaul was lifting his axe, and by striking the other in the face with his shield he knocked him backwards and down the cliff. Taking his stand on the city wall with men who rushed to join him, Manlius drove back the rest of the enemy, few of whom had managed to reach the top and none of whom was now doing anything to match the audacity of their climb. Thus the Romans escaped this danger, and, as soon as it was morning, they flung the captain of the night-watch off the cliff, hurling him down to the enemy below. They voted to mark Manlius' heroic victory with a reward that brought him greater honour than actual

profit: everyone brought him his day's allowance of food and
drink, which was 'half a pound', as the Romans put it, of the
local grain and an eighth of a pint of wine.[102]

28. After this failure, the Gauls began to lose heart. Fear of
Camillus kept them from foraging, but this left them in need
of provisions, and because they were dwelling amid heaps of
unburied corpses, they were gradually afflicted by disease. All
about them was ruin, the deep ashes of which were blown
about by hot winds, fouling the air and making it parched and
stinging. Breathing itself became difficult and painful, but what
affected them most of all was the shock to their system caused
by their change of climate, for they had come from a place
where shade offered easy respite from the heat of the summer
into a low-lying land whose temperatures remained warm even
in autumn. On top of all this was the long and tedious siege of
the Capitol, which had now gone on for seven months. For all
these reasons, mortality in the camp was high, and the number
of the dead was so great that they could no longer be buried.

None of this, however, improved matters for the besieged.
Their hunger increased, as did their despair when they had
heard nothing further of Camillus, whose messengers were
unable to reach them because the city was now very closely
guarded by the barbarians. Inasmuch, then, as each side was
experiencing hardship, so both began to look for some means
of arranging a truce, a possibility which in the first instance
was explored by the sentries who stood guard nearest one
another. Soon it was decided by the leaders on the Roman side
that the consular tribune Sulpicius[103] should hold a parley
with Brennus. It was agreed that, if the Romans furnished
1,000 pounds of gold, the Gauls would take it and straightaway leave the city and the country. Oaths were sworn to
confirm the terms of this agreement, and the gold was duly
delivered. As the gold was being measured out, however, the
Gauls tampered with the weights, secretly at first, but soon
they were blatantly pulling at the balance of the scale and
wildly distorting its accuracy. This was enough to anger the
Romans, when Brennus, with an insolent laugh, removed his

sword and belt and tossed both on the scale. Suplicius then asked, 'What is this?' 'What else', replied Brennus, 'but woe to the conquered!' This has since become a proverbial saying.[104] Some of the Romans became enraged by this and wanted to reclaim their gold and go back to enduring the siege. But others recommended giving in to these trivial injustices, urging their comrades not to think that it was in paying more that they disgraced themselves but rather in paying at all, and reminding them how in this crisis they had no choice but to put aside their honour and submit to such things.

29. As the Romans continued to bicker among themselves – and with the Celts – Camillus led his army to the gates of the city. When he was apprised of the situation within, he ordered the rest of his soldiers to put themselves in battle formation and to advance slowly, while he, along with his best men, hastened onwards until they reached the quarrelling Romans, who stood aside for him, since he was dictator, and received him with a courteous silence. Camillus then lifted the gold from the scales and gave it to his attendants, after which he ordered the Celts to take their scales and weights and depart, warning them that it was the Romans' custom to rescue their city with iron, not with gold. In reaction to this, Brennus flew into a rage, claiming that he had been cheated by this breach of the Romans' agreement. Camillus, however, replied that the terms of that agreement had not been arrived at legitimately and therefore were invalid. Because he had been chosen dictator, no other Roman magistrate was legally authorized to arrange a truce, and therefore Brennus had come to terms with men who were not empowered to negotiate on Rome's behalf. Now, however, was the proper time for the Gauls to express their wishes, for they were in the presence of the magistrate who possessed the full legal competence to grant pardon to those who asked for it – and to punish the rest, unless they repented. This made Brennus cry out in fury, and a skirmish ensued, each side going so far as to draw their swords and struggle with one another in a confused melee, which was unsurprising since they were fighting amid houses and narrow lanes and other places where

it was impossible to line up in battle array. Brennus soon recovered his senses, however, and led the Celts back to their camp, with the loss of only a few men. That night he broke camp, left the city and, after proceeding 60 stades, pitched a new camp along the road to Gabii.[105] But at daybreak Camillus attacked them. He was splendid in his arms, and the soldiers under his command were once again Romans in full possession of their old courage. For a long time a fierce battle raged, but in the end the enemy were struck down in a terrible slaughter and their camp was seized. Some of the Gauls who fled were chased down and killed immediately, but most of them dispersed, only to be set upon and killed by men in the surrounding villages and cities.

30. Thus was Rome captured unexpectedly, and even more unexpectedly rescued, after seven full months of barbarian occupation, for the Gauls entered the city a few days after the Ides of Quintilis and were driven out around the Ides of February.[106] Camillus celebrated a triumph, as was only right for a man who had saved his country when it was lost and who now restored its citizens to their own city. The Romans who had been outside the city during the occupation, joined by their wives and children, followed Camillus as he entered Rome, while those who had been besieged on the Capitol and had come very close to starving to death, came out to meet them amid much embracing and weeping for joy in this moment of happiness. The priests and their attendants bore the sacred objects they had either buried in the city before they fled or had carried off as they escaped. In this way everyone could see that these had all been preserved, a most welcome sight that was greeted with jubilation, for it now seemed that the gods, too, were returning to Rome. After Camillus had made sacrifices and had ritually purified the city, in strict obedience to the instructions of men learned in these matters, he restored the existing temples and erected a new one, to Rumour and Voice,[107] once he had located the very spot where, during the night, a divine voice had warned Marcus Caedicius about the barbarian army.

31. Uncovering the sites of the temples that had been destroyed
was extremely difficult and demanded the most extraordinary
exertions, but it was managed owing to Camillus' zeal and the
hard work of the priests. As for rebuilding the rest of the city,
which was still in a state of utter ruin, the sheer enormity of the
task left the people in complete despair. They kept putting off
the work, complaining that they had no materials and that they
needed rest and relief from their misfortunes instead of toil and
exhaustion in an undertaking they had neither the resources
nor the strength to carry out. Accordingly, their thoughts
recurred, little by little, to Veii, for that city remained intact
and was already furnished with everything. This was a situation ripe for demagogy, and soon politicians keen to curry
public favour began venting seditious speeches that lashed out
against Camillus. It was only for the sake of his personal ambition and glory, they claimed, that he was depriving the people
of a city that was perfectly equipped for them to live in, forcing
them instead to dwell amid ruins and erect what was in essence
a massive funeral pyre – all in order that he be called, not
simply the first citizen and general of Rome, but, replacing
Romulus, its very founder.

The senate, because it was fearful of these complaints, kept
Camillus in office for a full year, contrary to his preferences and
in spite of the fact that no one had ever been dictator longer
than six months. In addition to this, the senate endeavoured to
temper the public's mood by means of friendly persuasion and
by exhibiting a spirit of reconciliation. The senators pointed to
the city's ancestral tombs and sepulchres, and they recalled its
shrines and holy places, consecrated and bequeathed to the
people by Romulus or Numa or one of the other kings. They
also rehearsed religious reasons for remaining in Rome, emphasizing in particular how the freshly severed head discovered
when the foundations of the Capitol were dug signified that
Rome was destined to be the head of all Italy.[108] Furthermore,
they drew the people's attention to the sacred fire of Vesta,
which, now that the war was over, had just been rekindled by
the Vestal Virgins. They advised them that if, by deserting the
city, they should lose or extinguish this flame, they would be

greatly disgraced, whether the city was left to immigrants and foreigners or abandoned to flocks and herds. Again and again, the senators pressed individual Romans privately, as well as the community at large, employing arguments like these. But they also listened patiently as the people complained about their wretched condition and when they pleaded that they not be forced to repair the fragments of their ruined city – for they were like men who had escaped death at sea, alive, yes, but naked and destitute – when there was another city at their disposal.

32. Camillus finally decided to put the matter before the senate. He opened the proceedings by delivering a long speech strongly in favour of remaining in Rome, but he allowed anyone else who wished to address the subject to speak freely. He then called on Lucius Lucretius,[109] who was usually the first in the senate to express his view whenever an issue came to a vote, and asked him to deliver his opinion, after which he would call on the remaining senators in their turn. Silence fell, and, just as Lucretius was about to begin speaking, it so happened that a centurion, who was leading the watch of the day and was passing outside, shouted to his standard-bearer to halt and fix his standard on the spot, for, he said, this was the best place for them to take up their position and to remain. When this utterance was overheard, at so critical a moment of uncertainty about the future, Lucretius, in a spirit of religious deference, said simply that he agreed with the god,[110] and each of the senators followed his example. Astonishingly, even the multitude then repented of its previous anger, and they cheered and encouraged one another in their labours. They set to work restoring the city, not by any orderly plan, but instead everyone began to build wherever he pleased or happened to find a spot. This explains Rome's confusing and narrow streets as well as the haphazard placement of its houses. They certainly worked very rapidly, for we are told that within a year the city was completely rebuilt, not just its houses but its city walls as well.

Camillus had assigned certain men the job of locating and marking out the boundaries of Rome's sacred places, for they were all in complete disorder. Now these men, as they were inspecting the Palatine Hill, discovered that the shrine of Mars,[111] like all the other sacred buildings, had been wrecked and burnt to the ground by the barbarians. And yet, while clearing and cleaning the place, they happened to find, buried deep beneath a large pile of ashes, the augural staff of Romulus. This kind of staff, curled at one end, is called a *lituus* and it is employed by the Romans in marking out the precincts of the sky whenever they engage in divination from the flight of birds, just as Romulus, who was skilled in augury, had done with this one.[112] When Romulus vanished[113] and no longer appeared among mortals, the priests watched over his staff, like any other sacred object, and kept it inviolate, and so now, when it was discovered intact and undamaged, although everything else had been destroyed, they rejoiced in their confidence for the future of Rome, for they believed this was a sure sign of her eternal invincibility.

33. The Romans were still involved in rebuilding their city when war broke out. The Aequians, Volscians and Latins invaded their territory, while the Etruscans laid siege to Sutrium,[114] a city allied to Rome. During this war, the consular tribunes in command of the army that was encamped near Mount Maecius found themselves surrounded by the Latins and at risk of being overwhelmed, and so they sent to Rome for help. It was on this occasion that Camillus was appointed dictator for the third time.[115]

There are two accounts of this war, and I shall begin with the fabulous version,[116] according to which the Latins, either as a pretext or because they honestly wished to revive the ancient relationship between their two nations, asked the Romans to supply them with freeborn virgins whom they might take as wives. The Romans did not know what to do, for on the one hand they dreaded the prospect of war while their circumstances remained disturbed and unsettled, yet, on the other, they suspected that the Latins' request for wives was in reality a demand for hostages, even if, for the sake of appearances, they spoke about the matter in terms of marriage ties. At this very moment, a slave girl named Tutula, or, in some versions, Philotis, advised the magistrates to send her to the enemy, along with other slave girls who were in the bloom of youth and possessed the looks of freeborn Romans. They should be dressed, she proposed, as brides from the nobility. The rest, she told them, they could leave to her. The magistrates liked her idea, and so they selected as many slave girls as she thought suitable, adorned them in fine clothing and gold and handed them over to the Latins, who were encamped not far from the city. During the night, while the other women stole away with the swords of the enemy, Tutula, or Philotis, climbed to the top of a wild fig tree, spread her cloak behind her and lifted a torch towards Rome. She had agreed on this signal with the magistrates, but the other citizens knew nothing about it, which explains why the Roman soldiers rushed from the city in so much confusion, urged on by their officers and calling out to one another by name, and why they only just managed to put themselves in battle array before storming the camp of the enemy, whom they found asleep and completely unaware. Most of them were killed and their camp was captured. This took place on the Nones of July (which in those days was called Quintilis), and the festival the Romans celebrate on that day commemorates this event. They begin by running out of the city gate in crowds, loudly shouting many ordinary and familiar names, like Gaius, Marcus, Lucius and so forth, in imitation of the way the soldiers cried out to one another on that occasion as they rushed forth so hurriedly. Then the slave girls, brightly dressed, run about, playfully teasing the men they meet, and among themselves they conduct a mock battle, which recalls how they once played a part in the struggle against the Latins. And as they enjoy their feast, they sit beneath shade provided by the branches of a fig tree. They call this day the Capratine Nones,[117] for they believe that it was from a wild fig tree that the slave lifted her torch and the Romans call a wild fig tree a *caprificus*.

There are others, however, who explain this festival as a commemoration of the fate of Romulus, for it was on this same day that he vanished, outside the city gate, in sudden darkness and storm, or, as many think, during an eclipse of the sun. They claim that the day is called the Capratine Nones on account of the place where he disappeared, for a she-goat is called a *capra*, and Romulus vanished as he was addressing the people at a place known as the Goat's Marsh, an event which is recorded in his Life.[118]

34. It is the other version of this war that most authorities prefer. In it, Camillus, when he was appointed dictator for the third time, was forced to enlist men of the city who were in fact too old for military service. This was because the army commanded by the consular tribunes had been trapped by the Latins and Volscians. Camillus began by making a lengthy circuit around Mount Maecius, which let him elude detection by the enemy and position his army securely in their rear. Then, by lighting numerous torches, he signalled his arrival to the Romans who were besieged in their camp. Taking courage from this, they began making preparations to march forth and join battle, which prompted the Latins and Volscians to withdraw to their own camp and barricade themselves on all sides with a strong wooden palisade, for they were now exposed to the enemy from both the front and the rear, and awaiting reinforcements from home as well as additional assistance from the Etruscans. When Camillus recognized their design, he became worried that, just as he had surrounded his enemy, he might himself soon be surrounded by them. And so he wasted no time in seizing the advantage of the moment.

Now the enemy's defences were made of wood, and he observed how each morning at daybreak a strong wind blew down from the mountains. So he equipped himself with a supply of flammable arrows, and, around sunrise, led his army forward. He ordered some of his soldiers to make a loud din and, from a different quarter, to launch a missile attack, while he, along with the men he had assigned to shoot the burning arrows, took their position on the side of the enemy's camp where the wind usually blew with its greatest force. There he awaited his opportunity. When the fighting had begun and the sun rose and a strong wind began to set in, he gave the signal to commence, and the Romans launched countless firebrands against the enemy's fortifications. Flames spread quickly in all directions as the fire was fed by the crowded timbers of the wooden barricade, nor did the Latins have any means at their disposal for warding off the flames or extinguishing them. Soon their camp was burning everywhere, and the Latins were forced into a small crowded space, until finally they had no choice but to make a charge against an enemy that was drawn up in battle formation immediately outside their camp. Few of the Latins or Volscians escaped, and fire continued to take the lives of those who were left behind in the camp, until it was put out by the Romans so they could set to plundering.

35. After defeating the Latins, Camillus left his son, Lucius, in charge of the camp to keep guard over the prisoners and the spoil while he invaded the enemy's territory. He captured the city of the Aequians, reduced the Volscians, then immediately led his army towards Sutrium, unaware of what had already happened there. Because he believed the Sutrians were still in danger and under siege by the Etruscans, he was rushing to their rescue. But the Sutrians had already surrendered their city to the enemy and been driven out, completely destitute, possessing nothing but the clothes they wore. When Camillus met them, they were dragging along their wives and children and bewailing their misfortune. At the sight of this Camillus was struck with compassion, and he noticed how his soldiers, as the Sutrians reached out and clung to them, wept and expressed anger at what had taken place. He decided not to delay the Etruscans' punishment and so marched directly to Sutrium on that very day, reasoning that men who had just captured a rich and prosperous city and expelled the vanquished, and who did not expect any enemies to launch an attack, would be utterly undisciplined and unprotected when he arrived. And he was right. Not only did he pass through the city's territory undetected, he actually appeared at the gates and took possession of the city's walls before his enemy realized what had happened. Not a single guard had been posted, since they had all instead occupied houses throughout the city and begun feasting and drinking.

When finally they perceived that the city now belonged to the Romans, they were so gorged with food and drink that most of them did not even try to flee. Instead, they simply sat where they were, awaiting a base and disgraceful end, or surrendered themselves to the Romans. In this way the city of Sutrium was captured twice in a single day, and it happened that those who had seized it then lost it, and those who had lost it regained it, all owing to the actions of Camillus.

36. For these victories he was awarded a triumph, which brought him no less favour and credit than his two previous ones, for even those who were disposed to envy him and attribute his successes to good fortune instead of valour now had no choice but to ascribe his glorious reputation to his ability and energy. Of all his rivals and detractors, none was more distinguished than Marcus Manlius, the man who had been first to repel the Gauls from Rome's citadel when they launched their night attack on the Capitol, and who for this reason was called Capitolinus.[119] This man deemed himself the foremost citizen in Rome, yet he was unable to surpass Camillus' brilliant reputation. As a result, he turned to the tried and true course of anyone seeking to establish a tyranny: he began to curry the favour of the multitude, especially of men who were in debt, whom he sometimes aided by pleading their cases against creditors, but at other times went so far as to rescue by force, thereby preventing their coming to trial at all. In a short time he had acquired a massive following among the poor, whose audacity and violence in the forum so frightened the best citizens that Quintus Capitolinus was appointed dictator[120] in order to restore order. He threw Manlius into prison, but in reaction the people put on the garb of mourners, a thing which is done by the Romans only in times of serious public calamities. The senate, fearing an insurrection, ordered Manlius' release, but afterwards he was no better for his ordeal. In fact, he incited the multitude even more violently than before and filled the city with sedition. It was at this moment that Camillus was again elected consular tribune.[121]

Now when Manlius was brought to trial, the physical

situation of the court proved detrimental to his prosecutors,[122] for the very spot on the Capitol where Manlius had stood his ground on that night when fighting off the Gauls overlooked the forum, and the very sight of this place inspired pity. Manlius, too, stretched out his hands in this direction and wept as he recalled his contest there, all of which confounded his judges, who more than once adjourned his trial because, although they were unwilling to acquit him when the evidence of his guilt was unmistakable, at the same time they could not execute the law when, owing to the location of the court, the proof of his great deed was in plain view. Camillus recognized this and consequently moved the court outside the gate of the city to the Peteline Grove,[123] a place with no view of the Capitol. There the prosecution made its case, and the memory of Manlius' past heroism could no longer diminish the judges' righteous anger against his current misdeeds. Manlius was consequently convicted, taken to the top of the Capitol and flung from the cliff, so that one and the same place became a memorial to his glory and disgrace. The Romans also razed his house and built in its place a temple to the goddess they call Moneta.[124] They further decreed that thereafter no patrician should ever dwell on the Capitol.[125]

37. For a sixth time Camillus was nominated as consular tribune,[126] but he tried to decline the office on the grounds that he was advanced in years. Perhaps, too, he feared how, in the aftermath of anyone's glorious success, other men often grow resentful and the gods often inflict retribution. His most obvious reason for refusing was his physical infirmity, for, at the time, he happened to be a sick man. The people, however, would not excuse him, crying out that their need was not for him actually to lead the cavalry or the legions into combat but rather for his counsel and instruction. Thus he was constrained to assume military command and immediately, in cooperation with another consular tribune, Lucius Furius,[127] lead the army against the Praenestines[128] and Volscians, who, with a large force, were ravaging the territory of Rome's allies.

Camillus led the army forth and made camp near the enemy,

whom he thought it best to exhaust over an extended period of
time, so that if a pitched battle should eventuate he could join
in the fighting after he had recovered his health and strength.
His colleague Lucius, however, was carried away by his passion
for glory and so was impatient for combat, and in all the officers he excited the same fervour. Camillus, worried that it
might appear that jealousy motivated him to deprive the young
men of a glorious victory, reluctantly agreed that Lucius should
take command, while he remained in camp, on account of his
sickness, with only a few soldiers. But Lucius was reckless in
command and quickly routed. When he learned that the
Romans were in retreat, Camillus could not restrain himself
but leapt from his sickbed and rushed with his soldiers to the
gate of the camp. He forced his way through the fleeing Romans
until he reached their pursuers. This inspired the men who had
rushed past him to turn around and follow, while those still
hurrying towards him from the battlefield halted and put themselves once more into battle formation, crying out to one
another that they must not desert Camillus. In this way, the
enemy's pursuit was turned back.

On the next day, Camillus led out the army, joined battle
and won a complete victory, taking the enemy camp by charging into it at the same time as the enemy fled into it and killing
most of them. After this, when he was informed that the city
of Satricum[129] had been captured by the Etruscans, and its
inhabitants – all of them now Romans – had been put to the
sword, he sent the main body of the army, which comprised the
heavy-infantry, back to Rome, while he led the youngest and
most zealous of his men against the Etruscans who were still
holding the city. He defeated them. Some he drove away, the
rest he slew.

38. In returning to Rome with an abundance of plunder, Camillus demonstrated how very wise the people had been when they
had been unafraid of a general who, though old and unwell,
nevertheless possessed experience and bravery, and when they
had preferred him, despite his unwillingness and illness, to
younger and more robust men who ardently sought the com-

mand. Consequently, when it was reported that the Tusculans[130] were in revolt, Camillus was instructed to march out against them after he had chosen another of the consular tribunes as his colleague. Although each of them wanted the appointment and openly asked for it, Camillus selected Lucius Furius – to the surprise of everyone, for he was the man who had recently been so eager for combat, against the advice of Camillus, and had nearly lost the battle. But Camillus, it seems, wanted to obscure this man's misfortune and to make an end to his shame, which is why he preferred him to all the others.

The Tusculans made an ingenious attempt to rectify their transgression once they learned that Camillus was advancing against them. They filled their lands with farmers and shepherds, as if it were a time of peace, they kept open the gates of their city and their children continued studying their lessons. As for the urban populace, craftsmen made a show of plying their trades in the shops while the wealthier citizens strolled about in the forum, clad in their ordinary garments, and the magistrates busied themselves in assigning quarters for the Romans, all as if no one expected any danger or was conscious of having done anything wrong. None of these exertions on the part of the Tusculans induced Camillus to doubt that they had in fact acted treasonably. Still, they earned his compassion because, although guilty of treason, they had repented of it. So he ordered them to go to the senate to try to persuade that body to put aside its anger. He even helped them to win the senate's forgiveness, with the result that the city was entirely absolved of its guilt and admitted to Roman citizenship. These were Camillus' most illustrious achievements when he was consular tribune for the sixth time.

39. After these events, the city was disturbed by a radical controversy,[131] incited by Licinius Stolo, that put the senate at odds with the people, who were demanding that in the coming consular elections one of the two consuls must be a plebeian instead of both being patrician. Tribunes of the people were then elected, but consular elections were thwarted by the multitude.[132] Because there were no magistrates, public business became increasingly

confused and disorderly, which led the senate, very much against
the wishes of the people, to appoint Camillus dictator for the
fourth time.[133] Nor was Camillus eager to hold this office, for he
did not want to find himself opposing men whose extensive military service entitled them to point out how, serving side by side
with them in war, he had accomplished far greater things than he
had in politics when cooperating with the patricians. Furthermore, they claimed, the patricians were motivated by nothing
other than envy when they selected him as dictator, for they
expected that he would crush the people, should he prevail, or, if
he failed, be crushed by them. Camillus nevertheless made an
attempt to ward off present evils. When he learned the day on
which the tribunes intended to put their legislation to a vote, he
issued a proclamation for a general mustering of the army and
ordered the people, under threat of heavy fines should anyone
disobey, to leave the forum and to assemble on the Campus Martius. In retaliation, the tribunes resisted his threats by making a
solemn oath to fine him 50,000 silver drachmas unless he stopped
trying to steal the people's right to vote for this law. As a consequence of this – whether it was because he feared a second
banishment and condemnation, thinking such a thing wholly
unsuitable for a man of his age and accomplishments, or because
he was powerless, even if he wished it, to overcome the might of
the people, which had become so strong as to be invincible –
Camillus withdrew to his house, and, after pretending for some
days to be ill, resigned his office.

The senate then appointed another dictator,[134] who, after
selecting as his master of the horse the very Stolo who was
leading the sedition, allowed the enactment of a law that was
most unwelcome to the patricians, for it forbade anyone's possessing more than 500 *iugera* of land.[135] At that time Stolo was
highly esteemed on account of this legislative success, but,
somewhat later, he was found to have in his possession more
land than he had permitted others to have, and so had to pay
the penalty fixed by his own law.

40. Strife over the election of consuls persisted, which remained
the main difficulty – indeed, the fundamental and most troub-

ling controversy in the senate's disagreements with the people
at this time. Then news reached the city, by reliable reports,
that the Celts had again advanced from the Adriatic Sea and
were descending on Rome in vast numbers. The realities of this
invasion came hard on the heels of its report, for the countryside was ravaged and those who could not easily escape to
Rome fled into the mountains. This terror brought an end to
faction: the rich in cooperation with the poor, and the senate in
concert with the people, all unanimously agreed that Camillus
be appointed dictator for the fifth time.[136] He was by now very
old – he was nearly eighty – but because he recognized the crisis
and the danger facing Rome, he neither asked to be excused, as
before, nor did he offer any pretexts. Instead, he immediately
accepted the command and began levying troops.

Camillus perceived that the barbarians' effectiveness in combat depended chiefly on their use of swords, which, like all
barbarians, they wielded without any skill. Instead, they hacked
away at the shoulders and heads of their opponents. Consequently, he had helmets cast for his soldiers made entirely of
iron and smooth on their surface, so that when the enemy's
swords struck them they would either glance off or be shattered. He also had his men's shields fitted with bronze rims,
because, being made of wood, they could not resist the enemy's
blows. Besides this, he trained his soldiers to fight by holding
their long javelins in their hands, and, by thrusting them under
the enemy's swords, to parry their downward strokes.

41. When the Gauls drew near Rome, they were laden with an
abundance of spoil. They pitched their camp beside the River
Anio.[137] Camillus then led out his forces, but he posted them on
a gently sloping hill marked by many hollows in which he concealed the bulk of his army. As for the troops the Gauls could
see, they appeared to have positioned themselves at the top of
the hill because they were frightened. Camillus wanted to
reinforce this impression, and so he allowed the Gauls to go on
plundering in the areas below his position, while he remained
inactive behind his fortifications. This went on until he observed
that some of the Gauls had gone out into the countryside to

forage, while the rest stayed in their camp, spending their time in feasting and drinking. During the night, Camillus sent his light-armed troops forward, where they could hinder the barbarians as they tried to put themselves into battle formation and harass them as soon as they issued from their camp. At daybreak he led forth his infantry, whom he drew up into position on the plain below where the enemy could see that they were numerous and bold, not few and timid as the barbarians had supposed.

This was the first blow to the confidence of the Celts, for they believed it was disgraceful if anyone other than themselves was first to launch an attack. Then the assault of the light-armed troops prevented the Gauls from getting into their usual array or finding their places in their regular platoons. Instead, they had to fight in complete chaos and disorder. Finally, when Camillus advanced with the infantry, the barbarians raised their swords and rushed into battle, but the Romans fought back with their javelins, while their iron armour withstood the blows of the enemy, actually bending back the edges of their weapons, which were made of soft and poorly tempered metal. Soon the Gauls' swords were twisted and doubled, and their shields were pierced and weighed down by the javelins that were stuck in them. Therefore they tossed away their own weapons and tried to get hold of the Romans' by grabbing their javelins in an attempt to snatch them away. The Romans, however, as soon as they saw that the enemy was defenceless, began to use their own swords, with the result that there was great slaughter in the front ranks of the Gauls, while the remainder scattered throughout the plain, for Camillus had already occupied the hilltops and highlands, and the Gauls knew that their camp could easily be taken because in their arrogance they had failed to fortify it.

This battle is said to have been fought thirteen years after Rome was sacked,[138] and for the Romans it ushered in genuine confidence where the Celts were concerned. Before this campaign, the Romans had been afraid of the barbarians, believing that their previous victory had been owing, not to their own prowess, but to the Gauls' illness at the time as well as their surprising bad luck. So great had been the Romans' fear that when they passed a law exempting priests from military service they excluded any war against the Gauls.[139]

42. This was the last of Camillus' military contests, for his capture of Velitrae[140] was a mere pendant to this battle inasmuch as that city surrendered without a fight. The greatest of his political struggles, however, lay before him, and it was made all the more difficult by the assurance the people felt in the aftermath of their victory, for they now insisted on electing a consul from the ranks of the plebeians, contrary to the established law. This the senators opposed, and they would not allow Camillus to resign his dictatorship, hoping that, by dint of his authority and supreme power, he might prove better able to defend the aristocracy. While he was seated in the forum and conducting public business, however, an officer sent by the tribunes of the people commanded him to follow, and he actually put his hands on Camillus, as if he were going to drag him away. A hue and cry then filled the forum, like never before, as Camillus' associates shoved the plebeian officer from the tribunal and the multitude below shouted for him to arrest the dictator. Camillus was at a loss what to do, but he did not abdicate his office. Instead, he led the senators into the senate-house, and, before entering, turned towards the Capitol and prayed that the gods might bring these present troubles to their happiest conclusion, vowing to build a temple to Concord when this disturbance had ended.

In the senate, although there was a fierce clash of opposing opinions, in the end the more moderate view, which was for yielding to the people, prevailed. Thus it was granted that one of the consuls should be chosen from the plebeians. When the dictator announced this decree of the senate to the people, they were of course very happy to be reconciled with the patricians, and they escorted Camillus to his house with cheers and applause. On the following day the people assembled and voted to build a temple of Concord, just as Camillus had vowed, and, in commemoration of what had taken place, they decided it should face the forum and the place of assembly.[141] They also voted to add a day to the feast called the Latin Festival[142] and thereafter to celebrate it for four days, during which all Romans should perform sacrifices with garlands on their heads. At the elections subsequently conducted by Camillus, Marcus Aemilius was elected consul from the patrician order, while Lucius Sextius became the first plebeian consul.[143] This was the last of Camillus' public actions.

43. In the very next year[144] a terrible epidemic afflicted Rome, taking the lives of countless numbers of the common people and most of the magistrates. Camillus, too, died at this time. His end was hardly untimely, in view of his many years and his great attainments, yet his death inspired more grief among the Romans than did the deaths of all the others who perished of the plague during this time.

FABIUS MAXIMUS

INTRODUCTION TO
FABIUS MAXIMUS

The Fabius of History

Quintus Fabius Maximus was a leading statesman and general during the Hannibalic, or Second Punic, War (218–201 BC) who remained a venerated figure in subsequent Roman tradition. He derived from the most distinguished family of the time. Although his father died too young to have reached the consulship, his grandfather, great-grandfather and great-great-grandfather each held multiple consulships and enjoyed the prestige of being designated the leading man in the senate (*princeps senatus*).[1] Fabius was probably born around 275 BC, was chosen to be an augur during his boyhood (in 265) and was consul for the first time in 233. Thereafter he was censor in 230, consul for the second time in 228 and dictator around 221, although it is unclear for what purpose, and in any case he resigned almost immediately on religious grounds (*Marcellus* 5). It is unknown what Fabius achieved while holding these magistracies, so sparse is our historical record of them. Nevertheless, it is obvious that he was a senior and notable personage even before the Second Punic War began.

For Rome, no war could match in significance its desperate struggle with Hannibal (247–183 or 182 BC). No sooner had the Romans made themselves masters of Italy than they came into conflict with the north African state of Carthage, long the leading power in the western Mediterranean. The two cities fought a long war over Sicily, the First Punic War (264–241 BC), during which Rome for the first time campaigned outside Italy.[2] After losing Sicily to Rome, Carthage built a new empire in Spain – and it was out of Spain that Hannibal marched when he invaded Italy in 218 BC. The Second Punic War was fought on many fronts, Spain, Sicily and Italy itself, where in the early years of the war Hannibal seemed certain to prevail. But the leadership of Romans like Fabius Maximus and Claudius Marcellus gave Rome the time and resolution eventually to gain an advantage in every theatre. When Publius Scipio invaded Africa, Hannibal rushed to his city's defence, but was decisively defeated at the battle of Zama in 202 BC. Publius was hailed as Scipio Africanus, and Carthage was reduced to a second-rate power. Few, however, in the first years of the war, could have foreseen such a victory.[3]

Hannibal's startling invasion of Italy and the crushing defeats he inflicted on Rome at the Trebia and Lake Trasimene in 218 and 217 BC led to Fabius' emergency appointment as dictator (for the second time). It was at this moment that he imposed his strategy of attrition: Fabius was convinced that Hannibal could not long sustain an offensive posture with his relatively small army – unless further victories inspired defections among the allies. Consequently, Fabius pursued a policy of harassment and, ultimately, containment, allowing Hannibal to ravage the wealthy and fertile region of Campania yet blocking the plain's exits. But Hannibal outfoxed Fabius, and in escaping from Campania discredited Fabius' policy. In reaction, Rome fielded a massive army in 216 BC, which was devastatingly defeated by Hannibal at Cannae.

Thereafter Rome recurred to Fabian tactics, which proved effective in blunting Hannibal's menace and allowed Rome to exploit its vast superiority in manpower.[4] Fabius was consul in 215 and again in 214 BC, and he served as an officer under the command of his son, who was consul in 213. In later traditions he was hailed as the Delayer (*Cunctator*), and the epic poet Ennius praised him as *unus homo nobis cunctando restituit rem* (the one man who, by delaying, preserved for us our nation': Ennius, *Annals* 363, see Skutsch, p. 102). Fabius did not hold office again until 209 BC, when he was consul for his fifth and final time. In that year he captured Tarentum, brutally sacked the city and celebrated a triumph for the deed.

Fabius was abundantly honoured in his own lifetime. In 215 BC he dedicated to Venus Erycina a temple that he had vowed during his second dictatorship. And in the census of 209 BC he was designated the leading man of the senate (*princeps senatus*), a position to which he was reappointed in 204 BC. And in 203 BC, when Hannibal at last forsook Italy, the senate and people of Rome awarded Fabius a 'crown of grass' (*corona graminea*), a distinction granted to a general who has rescued a besieged city, because Fabius had, in effect, saved Rome from its Hannibalic siege.[5] In the very final phase of his career, however, Fabius found himself on the wrong side of history, when he bitterly opposed Scipio's proposal to invade North Africa. Fabius died in 203 BC, before the final victory won by Scipio's success at the battle of Zama in the next year.

Plutarch's Fabius

In this pairing, Fabius is matched with Pericles, the famous Athenian statesman who dominated his city's politics from 444 until his death in 429 BC. Plutarch's admiration for each man is indicated by the lengthy and formal prologue that precedes their paired biographies (*Pericles* 1–2). There he concludes his prologue by observing:

> These two men possessed many virtues in common, but above all, through their moderation, their uprightness, and their ability to endure the follies of their peoples and their colleagues in office, they rendered the very greatest service to their countries.
>
> (*Pericles* 2)

It is on these individual qualities that Plutarch's *Fabius Maximus* concentrates, even in moments when its protagonist fails to exhibit them. Uprightness and honesty (*dikaiosyne*) and especially mildness and moderation (*praotes*) are stressed

throughout this Life.[6] Fabius is incorruptible and committed
to honouring his obligations, even to Hannibal: for instance,
at chapter 7 he sacrifices his own estates to fulfil his agreement
to ransom hostages because he 'could not tolerate the idea of
cheating Hannibal or of abandoning the Roman prisoners to
their fate'.[7]

Praotes is Fabius' chief virtue. For the Greeks, the man
who was moderate and gentle was a man who, although he
experienced genuine and even deep feelings, nonetheless managed to keep them under control (Aristotle, *Nicomachean Ethics*
1125b26), and Plutarch uses the word to describe an admirable
self-restraint in all matters.[8] It is because Fabius is moderate
that he is able to endure the follies of others and remains indifferent to public opinion.[9] This is clearest when, in chapter 5,
his friends urge him to attack Hannibal in order to wipe out
aspersions against his courage. He answers:

> In that case I should be an even greater coward than they say I
> am, if I were to abandon the plans I believe to be right because of
> a few sneers and words of abuse.

In chapter 10, when the Romans have shown their preference
for Minucius' more aggressive approach to dealing with Hannibal and, in essence, have demoted Fabius, he continues
unbowed:

> Fabius endured these vexations calmly and without stress, in so
> far as they concerned him personally, thus confirming the truth of
> the philosophical maxim that a truly good man can neither be
> insulted nor disgraced.

Related to Fabius' moderation is his caution – his *asphaleia*.[10]
This is not the same as timidity: the word implies security and
safeness, and Fabius is an opponent who remains so steady that
he cannot be overthrown. Plutarch underscores this quality by
using the imagery of wrestling (chs. 5, 19, 23). Fabius and
Hannibal are competing athletes – and throughout this Life,
fascinatingly, it is Hannibal who best understands the merits of

his Roman adversary (chs. 5, 7, 12, 19, 23). In the end, when Fabius outwits Hannibal to recapture Tarentum,

> The Romans saw that he was dealing with Hannibal like an experienced wrestler, and had mastered the technique of frustrating his opponent's moves, now that his grips and holds had lost their original force.

> (ch. 23)

Yet it is in this moment of triumph that Fabius unexpectedly betrays his natural virtues, and a moral decline sets in.

In order to recover Tarentum, Fabius relied on the disloyalty of a Bruttian officer, a member of Hannibal's garrison within the city (chs. 21–2). However, when the city was finally taken through treachery, Fabius, frightened of any disgrace this tactic might incur, buried the evidence of his intrigue:

> At this point, however, Fabius' ambition seems to have proved stronger than his principles, for he ordered his men to put the Bruttian contingent to the sword before anyone else, so as to conceal the fact that he had captured the city by treachery.

Fabius failed, however, to mislead anyone, and, consequently, 'incurred the charge of bad faith and inhumanity'. He goes on to sack the city, in an excess of brutality that leads Plutarch to emphasize his hero's inferiority to the Roman general Marcellus, since Fabius' actions at Tarentum 'proved by the contrast between them that Marcellus was a man of extraordinary mildness [*praotes*] and humanity [*philanthropia*], as I have indicated in his Life' (ch. 22). In this episode, according to Plutarch, Fabius' cardinal virtues were withered in the glare of his ambition (*philotimia*).

Another moral failure was Fabius' contentious reaction to Scipio's proposal to invade Africa. Plutarch insists that his hero was honestly motivated by his native caution and moderation, but concedes that, when his efforts to block Scipio were unsuccessful, Fabius turned violent and extreme, and once more gave in to ambition as well as contentiousness:

the effort to check his opponent's rising influence made his attitude more violent and extreme and introduced an element of ambition and personal rivalry into the conflict.

(ch. 25)

There are few vices of which Plutarch disapproves more strongly than unrestrained ambition and rivalry, which renders this assessment nothing short of damning.[11] Fabius even went so far as to try to persuade Crassus, Scipio's colleague in the consulship, to replace Scipio as commander of the forces destined for Africa, but Crassus refused 'because by nature he was a gentle man [*praos*] and had no inclination to quarrel with his colleague' (ch. 25), an explanation that confronts the reader with the reality that, in this section of his Life, Fabius has again become untrue to his central virtue. The Roman public come to the conclusion that Fabius is desperately jealous of Scipio (ch. 25), and whereas, in the early days of the war against Hannibal, Fabius' moderation more than once gave the people courage, now, at the very moment the Carthaginian retreats from Italy, Fabius suffuses the Romans with dismay (ch. 26).

Between the fall of Tarentum and Scipio's return, Plutarch discusses the consulship of Fabius' son, which took place in 213 BC, but has been postponed by the biographer until this final phase of Fabius' career (ch. 24). The episode is deemed notable – and admirable – on account of Fabius' studied deference to his son's consular authority. It furthermore inspires Plutarch to recall the conduct of Fabius' great-grandfather, the first Fabius Maximus, who served his consular son as a lieutenant and, later, dutifully followed in the procession of his son's triumph:

he took pride in the fact that while he had authority over his son as a private individual and was himself in both name and in reality the greatest man of the state, yet he was ready to submit himself to the law and the chief magistrate.

(ch. 24)

This is, Plutarch clearly believes, the correct attitude for any Roman. It is quite striking, then, that in the immediately following episode Plutarch lurches forward to 205 BC, when Scipio returns to Rome, is elected consul and is confronted by Fabius' efforts to subvert his command, clearly an unseemly move by Fabian standards.

Fabius' transformation at Tarentum is perplexing, and the harsh portrayal of the last phase of his career is surprising. And, unless the biographer is relying for this section of the Life on a source now lost to us, Fabius' moral collapse in his final days is Plutarch's own innovation.[12] Now the conflict between Scipio and Fabius was a historical fact, and enough evidence subsists to make it clear that ancient writers elaborated their rivalry, yet this competition did not routinely come at the expense of Fabius' dignity or rectitude.[13] Quite the contrary. In Livy, it is Scipio, not Fabius, whose conduct is troubling when the two men clash,[14] and in Cicero's *On Old Age*, a piece known to Plutarch, Fabius is the paradigm of a man whose virtuous life carried him to a satisfying old age.[15] Fabius' moral meltdown in this Life, then, is plainly at odds with what Plutarch knew to be a prevailing version of his hero's maturity.

Plutarch does not offer an explanation for his hero's forceful and foolish – and in certain respects unethical – opposition to the strategy of Scipio, the indispensable victor in the Second Punic War. Nevertheless, the reader can only experience unease when watching a man who has heretofore been a paradigm of old age's wise counsel degrade into something of a caricature. Still, Plutarch stresses, Fabius' motives were not wholly disreputable, and in any case this ultimate lapse does not vitiate the whole of his career. Although his hostility to Scipio incurs unpopularity in Rome, these feelings vanish at the moment of his death, when the whole of the city remembers him as a father, so that 'in his death he received the honour and regard which he had earned by the conduct of his life' (ch. 27).

Fabius and Pericles

Although, as critics of Plutarch have observed, the careers of Pericles and Fabius ostensibly share little in common, Plutarch infuses his pairing with an abundance of similarities, significant and superficial alike. Each man has the heart of a lion, and each bears a physical peculiarity. Both (in very different ways) experience almost monarchical power. Fabius and Pericles alike eschew superstition, exhibit fortitude in the face of personal misfortune, employ oratory effectively – and each embodies moderation and honesty, qualities which they put to work for the greater good of their respective nations.[16]

And yet Pericles, unlike Fabius, remained steadfast and unalterable throughout his life, even in the teeth of hostile public opinion. Plutarch, in an extended simile, represents him as the skilful helmsman of the ship of state, who trusts his own expertise and remains indifferent to the fears of his passengers (*Pericles* 34). This image recurs near the end of *Fabius Maximus*, but there it is the victorious Scipio, not the jealous and carping Fabius, who is the captain (ch. 27). Pericles dies before his city falls, Fabius before his city triumphs. Although he was an agent – perhaps, according to Plutarch, the key agent – of Rome's salvation, Fabius nevertheless ended his life in a role unworthy of the statesmanship and moral excellence exhibited in all but its final chapters.

Sources

In this Life, Plutarch cites none of his sources explicitly, apart from his passing reference to Poseidonius' report that Fabius was known as the shield, Marcellus the sword, of Rome (ch. 19). Most of what we know about Fabius' career we find in Livy's and Polybius' narratives of the Second Punic War, and there is no reason to doubt that Plutarch consulted these writers.[17]

There are moments in *Fabius Maximus*, however, when Plutarch diverges from both Polybius and Livy. In some instances, these differences probably reflect carelessness or error. In others, they result from Plutarch's own amplification and artistry. Still, some critics prefer to explain these variations by invoking other, now lost, sources for the Second Punic War, which is certainly possible if not really demonstrable or necessary.[18] Because Plutarch explicitly names Poseidonius, the distinguished philosopher and polymath who flourished in the first century BC, it is sometimes suggested that he was a significant source for this Life. This seems unlikely, however: Poseidonius is mentioned only by way of a single, striking phrase, also cited in Plutarch's earlier *Marcellus*, and there is no good evidence that, even for that Life, Poseidonius was an important source.[19]

Hannibal plays a significant role in *Fabius Maximus*. Not only is he Fabius' adversary, his is often the gaze through which we are allowed to see the Roman's true military talents. During the Second Punic War, Hannibal was accompanied by two Greek historians, Silenus of Caleacte and Sosylus of Sparta, each of whom composed accounts (now lost) of the war, and their works made their way into the Romans' accounts.[20] Polybius, for instance, consulted Silenus, and he read (and criticized) Sosylus. They were also available to Plutarch, though it is unclear whether he went so far as to consult them for himself.

Which is not to say that Plutarch did not read widely. He found pertinent information in Cicero's *On Old Age*. He also exploited collections of the sayings of famous men (chs. 8, 20, 23, 24) as well as authors of exemplary literature, such as Valerius Maximus, whom he possibly exploits in this Life (and whom he cites elsewhere).[21] It is possible, even likely, that Cornelius Nepos wrote a (now lost) biography of Fabius, and, even if Plutarch never mentions them, there were family studies at his disposal – Pomponius Atticus, Cicero's great friend, composed a history of the Fabii Maximi,[22] although it is perhaps significant that Plutarch tells us almost nothing of Fabius' career before the Hannibalic War.

LIFE OF FABIUS MAXIMUS

[*c.* 275–203 BC]

1. Such was the man Pericles proved himself to be in his most memorable actions as they have come down to us.[1] Now let us turn our narrative to Fabius.

It was a nymph, according to one legend, or a woman of the country according to another, who lay with Hercules by the River Tiber and bore him Fabius. This man was the founder of the family of the Fabii, which was to become one of the greatest and most distinguished in Rome. Another tradition has it that the original members of the family were called Fodii in ancient times, because of their practice of trapping wild beasts in pits – and even up to the present day ditches are known in Latin as *fossae*, and *fodere* is the Latin verb meaning *to dig*. Then, in the course of time and through the change of two letters, according to this theory, they became known as Fabii.[2] At any rate, this family produced a large number of eminent men, the greatest of whom was Rullus, who for this reason was given the surname of Maximus.[3] The fourth in descent from him was the Fabius who is the subject of this Life.[4]

He was nicknamed Verrucosus because of a physical peculiarity, a small wart[5] which grew on his upper lip, and while he was still a child people called him Ovicula[6] or *lambkin*, because of his grave and gentle nature. He grew up with a quiet and placid disposition, showed an extraordinary caution even when he was indulging in childish pleasures, and learned his lessons slowly and laboriously; and these characteristics, combined with his docile, almost submissive, behaviour towards his companions, led those who did not know him thoroughly to suppose that he was dull and stupid. It was only a few who could see beyond these superficial qualities and discern the greatness of spirit, the lion-like temper and the unshakeable resolution which lay in the depths of his soul. But as time went on and his mind was stirred by the demands of the life of action, he soon proved to all alike that this apparent lack of energy was really due to his freedom from over-mastering passions, and that his caution proceeded from a soundly based judgement, while the fact that he never acted on impulse and was not easily persuaded meant that he was steadfast and resolute in all circumstances.[7]

He took note early in life both of the greatness of Rome's power and of the numerous wars that threatened it, and so he trained his body for fighting, since he considered its fitness to be his natural armour. At the same time, he practised public speaking as an instrument with which to sway the people, and created a style which was the perfect expression of his way of life. His oratory carried no superfluous ornaments or empty mannerisms, but it was full of the solid sense which characterized the man, and was reinforced by an abundance of maxims and generalizations which recalled the weighty judgements of Thucydides. One of his speeches has actually been preserved: he delivered it as a funeral oration over his son, who died after he had held the office of consul.[8]

2. In the first of his five consulships Fabius won a triumph over the Ligurians.[9] He won a pitched battle, inflicting heavy losses on them, whereupon they withdrew into the Alps and ceased to ravage and plunder the Italian provinces that lay on their frontier. Then Hannibal broke into Italy, won his first victory at the battle of the River Trebia[10] and pressed on through Etruria, ravaging the countryside as he went. The inhabitants of Rome were filled with terror and dismay at the news of his advance and a number of portents were observed, some of them commonplace enough, such as peals of thunder, but others were as inexplicable as they were unfamiliar. Thus it was reported that shields began to sweat blood, that at Antium[11] the ripe grain bled when cut by reapers, that blazing red-hot stones rained down from the sky, and that at Falerii[12] the heavens were seen

to open and many tablets to fall, one of which was inscribed with the words *Mars is brandishing his weapons*.

However, none of these prodigies could daunt the consul Gaius Flaminius, who, besides being an ambitious and hot-tempered man, had been encouraged by the victories which he had won against all expectation only a few years before.[13] On that occasion, although the senate had disagreed with his plan, and his colleague had vehemently opposed it, he had engaged the Gauls in a pitched battle and defeated them. Fabius himself was not much disturbed by those portents which alarmed so many of his countrymen, because he considered them incoherent and lacking in meaning. He was much more impressed by the reports of the small size of Hannibal's force and of how poorly it was supplied, and he urged the Romans to have patience and on no account to engage a commander who led an army that had been hardened in many contests for the very purpose of forcing a decisive battle. Instead, they should send help to their allies, keep their subject cities under control and allow Hannibal's strength, which must now be at its peak, to waste away like a flame that flares up brightly but has little fuel to sustain it.

3. But Flaminius refused to listen to these arguments. He declared that he would not allow the campaign to be conducted near Rome, nor would he, like Camillus of old, fight a battle for a city within her very walls,[14] and he therefore gave orders to the military tribunes to lead out the army. But as he leapt on his horse, the animal, for no apparent reason, was seized with a fit of trembling and shied violently, so that Flaminius was unseated and thrown to the ground on his head.[15] Even this did nothing to divert him from his purpose: he proceeded to march out to meet Hannibal according to his original plan, and drew up his army near Lake Trasimene in Etruria.[16]

When the two armies were locked in battle, at the critical moment in the action, an earthquake took place which destroyed several cities, diverted rivers from their channels and split off great fragments of cliffs, and yet in spite of the violence of the catastrophe none of those who were engaged in the battle noticed it at all. Flaminius himself fought with heroic strength and courage, but was cut down at last, and around him perished the flower of his army. The rest were routed and a tremendous carnage followed. Fifteen thousand Romans were killed and as many more taken prisoner. Hannibal was anxious to bury Flaminius' body with military honours as a tribute to his valour, but it could not be found, and it was never discovered how it had disappeared.

Now, when the Romans had been defeated in the first action of the campaign at the River Trebia, neither the general who wrote the dispatch nor the messenger who carried it gave a straightforward account of the battle: it was represented as being a disputed and uncertain victory. But as soon as Pomponius[17] the praetor learned of this second defeat, he summoned an assembly of the people, faced them and gave them the news in plain words, without any attempt to evade or disguise it. 'Men of Rome,' he said, 'we have been defeated in a great battle, our army has been destroyed and the consul Flaminius is dead. You must consider now what we are to do to save ourselves.' His speech fell upon the great expanse of faces turned towards him like a sudden storm-blast on the surface of the sea. The whole city was thrown into an uproar, and in such a mood of panic no man could take a grip on his thoughts and reflect calmly. But at length the people found themselves driven to the same conclusion, namely, that the situation demanded the absolute authority of a single man (or, as the Romans call it, a dictatorship), who would wield this power with the utmost energy and without fear, and that Fabius Maximus was the only man fitted for this task. He alone, they believed, possessed a spirit and a dignity of character which were equal to the greatness of the office, and besides this, he was of an age at which the strength of the body is fully capable of executing the decisions of the mind, while boldness is tempered with discretion.

4. Accordingly, the people passed a decree to this effect and Fabius was declared dictator. He in turn appointed Marcus Minucius[18] to be his master of the horse, and then at once asked

the senate's permission to use a horse[19] while he himself was on active service. I should explain that according to an ancient law the dictator was forbidden this privilege. The reason may have been that since the army had always been organized so that its main strength lay in the infantry, the Romans believed that their commander should always station himself with the phalanx and never leave it, or possibly that since the dictator's power is in other respects as great as a tyrant's, they considered that in this detail at least he should be shown to be dependent on the people. At any rate, Fabius was anxious to impress the people immediately with the importance and grandeur of his office, so as to make them more docile and obedient to his orders. He therefore appeared in public attended by the full body of twenty-four lictors[20] carrying their fasces. And when the surviving consul came to meet him, he sent an officer with orders that he should dismiss his lictors, lay down the insignia of his office and meet the dictator as a private citizen.[21]

After this he made the best of beginnings, that is by turning his attention to religious matters, and he left the people in no doubt that their defeat had not been brought about by any cowardice on the part of their soldiers, but by their general's neglectful and contemptuous attitude towards religious observances. By this means he persuaded them that instead of becoming frightened of their enemies they should give their minds to honouring and propitiating the gods. He did not attempt to implant a spirit of superstition, but he invoked the people's piety to strengthen their courage, and he sought to dispel their fear of the enemy by instilling the faith that the gods were on the side of Rome. At the same time many of the so-called Sibylline Books,[22] which contain secret advice of great importance to the state, were brought out to be consulted, and it is said that some of the oracular pronouncements they contained actually corresponded to the chance happenings and events of the time.

What was discovered in this way could not be made public, but the dictator came before the people and made a vow in their presence to sacrifice to the gods a whole year's increase, that is, all the young produced in the coming spring by the goats, pigs, sheep and cattle from every mountain, plain, river and meadow within the bounds of Italy.[23] He also pledged himself to celebrate a musical and dramatic festival,[24] and spend on it the sum of 333 sestertia, 333 denarii and a third of a denarius exactly. This sum in Greek money amounts to 83,583 drachmas and two obols.[25] It is difficult to discover the reason why this precise amount was specified, unless it was perhaps to honour the spiritual nature of the number three: this is a perfect number by nature, and is also the first of odd numbers, the beginning of quantity, and contains within itself the first differences and the elements of every number.[26]

5. By encouraging the people in this way to fix their thoughts upon religious matters, Fabius contrived to strengthen their confidence in the future. For his part, however, he trusted entirely to his own efforts to win the victory, since he believed that the gods grant men success according to the courage and wisdom that they display, and in this frame of mind he turned his attention to Hannibal. He was determined not to fight a pitched battle, and since he had time and manpower and money on his side, his plan was to exhaust his opponent's strength, and gradually to wear down his small army and meagre resources. With this object in view he always bivouacked in mountainous country, where he was out of reach of the enemy's cavalry, and at the same time hung menacingly over the Carthaginian camp. If the enemy stayed still, he did the same. If they moved, he would make a detour, descend a little distance from the heights and show himself just far enough away to prevent himself from being forced into an action against his will, yet near enough to create the suspicion, from the very slowness of his movements, that he might be about to attack.

But the Romans soon became contemptuous of these time-killing tactics and Fabius began to be despised in his own camp, while the enemy – with one exception – were convinced that he was a nonentity who was utterly devoid of warlike spirit. The exception was Hannibal. He, and he alone, perceived his opponent's shrewdness and understood the strategy which Fabius had laid down for the war. He therefore made up his

mind that he must use every trick to lure or force the enemy
into battle, or else the Carthaginian cause was lost, since his
men were being prevented from exploiting their superiority in
training, while their manpower and resources, in which they
were inferior to the Romans, were being steadily exhausted to
no purpose. And so he brought into play all the arts and stratagems of war and tried every one in turn, like a skilful wrestler
who watches for his first opportunity to secure a hold on his
adversary. First he would attack Fabius' army directly, then try
and throw it into confusion, then draw him from one place to
another, all in the effort to lure him away from the safety of his
defensive tactics.

Fabius, however, had complete faith in his plan, followed it
consistently and refused to be drawn. But he was provoked by
his master of the horse, Minucius, a headstrong officer who
longed for action regardless of the circumstances, and who
tried to increase his popularity by raising empty hopes and
working up his men's spirits to a state of wild enthusiasm. The
soldiers mocked at Fabius and contemptuously called him
Hannibal's pedagogue,[27] but they thought Minucius a great
man and a general worthy of Rome. This encouraged the master of the horse to indulge his boastful tactics more than ever
and to make fun of Fabius' tactics of encamping on high
ground, where, as he put it, the dictator took great trouble to
provide them with splendid seats to witness the spectacle of
Italy being laid waste with fire and sword. He was also fond of
asking Fabius' friends whether he thought he was leading the
troops up to heaven, since he had evidently ceased to take any
interest in events on earth, or whether he was enveloping them
in clouds and mist simply to escape from the enemy. Fabius'
friends reported these remarks, and urged him to wipe out such
aspersions on his courage by risking a battle. His answer was:
'In that case I should be an even greater coward than they say I
am, if I were to abandon the plans I believe to be right because
of a few sneers and words of abuse. There is nothing shameful
in experiencing fear for your country's sake. But the man who
allows himself to be frightened by the opinions of others, or by
their slanders or abuse, proves that he is unworthy of such

a high office as this, since he makes himself the slave of the very men whom it is his duty to restrain and overrule when they go astray and their judgement deserts them.'

6. Not long after this Hannibal committed a serious blunder. He wished to put some distance between Fabius' army and his own, and to occupy a stretch of open country where he could find good pasturage. He therefore gave orders to his guides that, immediately after the evening meal, they should lead the army into the district of Casinum.[28] But they did not take the name correctly because of his foreign pronunciation, with the result that they hurried on his troops to the outskirts of Campania and into the neighbourhood of Casilinum,[29] through the midst of which flows the River Olthornus, which the Romans call Vulturnus.[30] The whole region is surrounded by mountains, but there is a narrow defile which leads down to the sea. Here the river overflows so as to form marshes and high sand dunes, and finally discharges itself into the sea on a beach, where there is no anchorage because of the heavy breakers. While Hannibal was marching down into this valley, Fabius took advantage of his knowledge of the roads to send his troops round and block the pass with a detachment of 4,000 infantry. He posted the rest of his army in a strong position on the neighbouring heights, and then with the lightest and most active of his troops attacked the Carthaginian rearguard, killed about 800 of them and threw the whole army into disorder. Hannibal quickly recognized his mistake and the danger of his position and crucified the guides who had led him there, but he could see no means of forcing his way out or dislodging the enemy from the mountain passes which they held so securely. At last, when his men were beginning to lose heart and sink into despair because they believed they were surrounded on all sides by dangers from which there was no escape, he hit upon a trick to deceive the enemy. This is what he did.

He gave orders for his troops to take some 2,000 of the oxen which they had captured, and to fasten to each of their horns a torch consisting of a bundle of twigs or dry faggots. Then, after nightfall, at a given signal his men were to light the torches and

drive the cattle along the defiles and towards the passes where
the Romans were posted. As soon as these orders had been carried out, by which time it was already dark, he had the rest of
his army ready to move, and proceeded to advance at a slow
pace. At first, so long as the flames were low and only burning
the wood, the cattle moved on steadily towards the mountains
as they were being driven up the slopes, while the shepherds
and herdsmen who looked down from the neighbouring heights
stared with amazement at the flames which streamed from
their horns and imagined that this must be a whole army
marching in close column and carrying innumerable torches.
But when the horns had been burned down to the quick and
the flames reached the raw flesh, the cattle began to shake and
toss their heads in agony and covered one another with show-
ers of sparks and embers. Soon they began to stampede, and
then, mad with pain and fear, galloped off on a wild career
down the slopes, with their foreheads and tails ablaze and setting fire to a great part of the forest as they passed. All this was
a terrifying sight to the Romans guarding the passes. The flames
appeared to come from numbers of men running to and fro and
brandishing torches in their hands, and the Romans were
thrown into the utmost confusion and alarm, since they
believed that they were completely surrounded and that the
enemy were about to attack from all directions at once. Their
courage deserted them and they fled from their posts, fell back
on the main body of the army, which was stationed on the
heights, and abandoned the defiles. In a moment Hannibal's
light troops came up and seized the passes, and the rest of the
Carthaginian army marched safely through, heavily loaded
with plunder.

7. Fabius discovered the trick which had been played on him
before the night was over, for some of the cattle had been
caught by the Romans during their stampede. But he was afraid
of falling into an ambush in the dark, and so kept his men
under arms but did not allow them to move. As soon as it was
light, however, he pursued the enemy and harried their rearguard. There were many hand-to-hand encounters over difficult

ground and much confused fighting. At last Hannibal detached from his advance guard a body of his Spanish light infantry, fast-moving troops who were agile and practised mountaineers. They fell upon the heavily armoured Roman infantry, killed many of them and forced Fabius to retreat. This episode brought down more abuse and contempt upon Fabius than anything that had happened before. He had refused the challenge of an outright trial of strength in his hope of overcoming Hannibal through superior judgement and foresight, but it was in these very qualities that the Carthaginian had manifestly out-generalled and defeated him.

Hannibal was anxious to increase the general resentment against Fabius still further. Accordingly, when he arrived at Fabius' country estates, he gave orders that these should be spared while all the surrounding property should be ravaged and burned, and even had a guard put on them to make sure that nothing should be removed and no damage done.[31] When the news reached Rome it provoked a fresh wave of indignation against Fabius. The tribunes of the people kept up a stream of denunciation against him, most of which was instigated and encouraged by Metilius.[32] He did this not out of any personal animosity towards Fabius, but because he was a relative of Minucius, the master of the horse, and believed that if he could lower Fabius' reputation, he would be raising his subordinate's.

The senate was also displeased with the dictator, and censured him in particular for the terms he had made with Hannibal about the exchange of prisoners of war. The two commanders had agreed to exchange prisoners man for man, and if either side held more than the other, the surplus prisoners were to be redeemed at a ransom of 250 drachmas each. When the exchange had been carried out man for man, it was found that Hannibal still had 240 Romans left. The senate decided that it would not provide the ransom for these and blamed Fabius for having acted improperly and against the interests of the state in attempting to rescue men who had fallen into captivity only because of their own cowardice.[33] When Fabius heard this news, he did not allow his countrymen's anger to disturb him, but since he had no ready money of his own and could not tolerate the idea of cheating Hannibal or of abandoning the Roman prisoners to their fate, he sent his son to Rome with instructions to sell his estates[34] and bring him the money immediately at the camp. The young man carried out the sale and returned without delay, whereupon Fabius dispatched the ransom to Hannibal and recovered the prisoners. Many of these men later offered to repay him, but he would accept nothing and insisted that the debt should be cancelled for every one of them.

8. After this he was recalled to Rome by the priests to be present at various sacrifices as the duties of his office demanded, and he then handed over the command to Minucius with orders not to become involved in a battle nor to engage the enemy in any way. Fabius not only issued these orders as dictator, but he repeated them to his deputy as his personal advice and request. Minucius paid little attention to any of these warnings, and immediately began to test the enemy's strength. One day he noticed that Hannibal had dispatched the greater part of his army on a foraging expedition. He promptly attacked the remainder, driving them back into their entrenchments with heavy losses, and spread panic among the rest who were afraid that he would now lay siege to their camp; then, when Hannibal concentrated his forces again inside the camp, Minucius succeeded in withdrawing his troops without loss. This engagement vastly increased Minucius' own arrogance and high opinion of himself and filled his soldiers with a rash confidence. An inflated report of the action quickly reached Rome, and Fabius' comment when he heard it was that he feared the consequences of Minucius' *success* much more than his failure.[35] Nevertheless, the people were delighted at the news and hurried exultantly to a meeting in the forum. There the tribune Metilius mounted the rostra and delivered a rabble-rousing speech, in which he glorified Minucius and denounced his superior. He attacked Fabius not merely as an effete and spiritless leader but also as a traitor, and he included in the same accusation many of the ablest and most distinguished men in

the state. First of all they had led Rome into the war, he said, to destroy the power of the people, and then they had promptly delivered the city into the hands of a single dictator who was answerable to no man, and who by his dilatory tactics would allow Hannibal ample time to establish himself and summon another army from Libya, since he could now claim that he held Italy in his power.

9. When Fabius addressed the people, he wasted no time in defending himself against the tribune's charges. He merely said that the sacrifices and other religious rites must be carried out as quickly as possible, to enable him to return to the army and punish Minucius for having attacked the enemy against his orders. These words produced a great commotion among the people, since they now understood the danger in which Minucius stood. The dictator has the power to imprison and even to inflict capital punishment without trial, and they believed that Fabius, who was normally the mildest of men, had at last been provoked to an extent which would render him harsh and implacable. This thought alarmed them so much that nobody dared to speak except for Metilius, who could rely upon his personal immunity as a tribune of the people, for this is the only office which is not deprived of its prerogatives by the appointment of a dictator, but survives intact when all the rest have their functions suspended.[36] So he now made an impassioned appeal to the people. He implored them not to abandon Minucius, nor to allow him to suffer the penalty which Manlius Torquatus had inflicted on his son,[37] whom he had beheaded after he had been awarded the laurel crown for an act of the utmost gallantry, and urged instead that they should deprive Fabius of his dictatorial powers and entrust the control of affairs to one who was able and willing to save his country.

The people were moved by these words, and yet, in spite of Fabius' unpopularity, they lacked the courage to compel him to lay down the dictatorship. Instead, they voted that Minucius should be given an equal share in the command and should carry on the war with the same powers as the dictator,[38] a division of authority for which there was no precedent in Roman history. A little later, it is true, a similar situation arose after the disaster at Cannae.[39] On that occasion Marcus Junius, the dictator, was in command of the army, and it became necessary that the vacant places in the senate should be filled, since so many senators had lost their lives in the battle, and so the people elected Fabius Buteo as a second dictator.[40] But when he had taken up his office and discharged his task of selecting the men to fill the senate, he immediately dismissed his lictors and the rest of his retinue, slipped into the crowd and mingled with the people in the forum, where he proceeded to occupy himself with his private concerns and transact business like any ordinary citizen.

10. When the people had conferred upon Minucius the same powers as the dictator's, they expected that Fabius would feel he had been shorn of his authority and humiliated, but here they completely misjudged their man. The truth was he did not regard their folly as being in any way a misfortune for himself. His attitude was like that of Diogenes the philosopher,[41] who, when he was once told 'the people are mocking you', retorted 'but I am not mocked', meaning that the only people who really suffer ridicule are those who allow it to influence them and are put out by it. So Fabius endured these vexations calmly and without stress, in so far as they concerned him personally, thus confirming the truth of the philosophical maxim that a truly good man can neither be insulted nor disgraced.[42] And yet for his country's sake he could not but be distressed at the people's folly, since they had placed such opportunities in the hands of a man who was ruled by an insane ambition for military success. He feared that Minucius with his infatuated craving for empty glory and prestige might cause some irreparable disaster before he could be stopped, and Fabius therefore left the city in great secrecy.

When he arrived at the camp he found that Minucius' behaviour had become intolerable. He was overbearing and puffed up with conceit, and at once demanded to be given supreme command of the army on alternate days. Fabius refused his request, since he preferred to command a part of the army permanently rather than the whole of it by turns.[43] He therefore took charge of the first and fourth legions himself and gave the second and third to Minucius, while the allied troops[44] were equally divided between them. When Minucius put on haughty airs and boasted of the fact that the most powerful office of the state had been humbled and its authority reduced on his account, Fabius quietly reminded him that his real opponent, if he stopped to consider the matter, was not Fabius but Hannibal. But, he went on, if he must persist in treating his colleague as a rival, let their rivalry concern itself with ensuring the safety of Rome. Minucius should take care that he, the man who had been honoured and proclaimed the victor by the people, should not be found to have served the Romans worse than the man who had been subdued and humiliated by them.

11. Minucius regarded this as an old man's disingenuous talk, and when he had taken command of the troops allotted to him, he moved into a separate camp. Meanwhile Hannibal, who had kept himself informed of these events, watched his opponent's movements closely. There was a hill between the Romans and the Carthaginians which could be occupied without difficulty, and which, once secured, offered a strong position for the camp and was well supplied in every way. The plain which surrounded it appeared to be perfectly smooth and level, when seen from a distance, but in reality the ground was broken by many small ditches and hollows. For this reason, although it would have been easy to make a surprise advance and occupy the hill, Hannibal had preferred to leave it untouched in the hope of enticing the enemy into battle. As soon as he saw Minucius detach his forces from those of Fabius, he sent out scattered bodies of troops during the night with orders to hide themselves among the ditches and depressions in the ground. Then, at first light, he dispatched a few men to occupy the hill without any attempt at concealment, a tactic designed to lure Minucius into fighting for it.

His plan worked. First of all Minucius sent forward his light-armed troops, then his cavalry, and finally, when he saw that Hannibal was coming to the rescue of his men on the hill,

he drew up his whole army and marched down into the plain.
His men attacked courageously, advancing in the face of a hail
of missiles from the hill, coming to close quarters there and
holding their ground. Then Hannibal, seeing that his enemy
was well and truly in the trap and had exposed his unguarded
rear to the troops who were waiting in ambush, raised the signal. Thereupon his men sprang up from their hiding-places on
all sides and attacked with loud shouts, cutting down the rear
ranks of the enemy. An indescribable confusion and panic
spread through the Roman army. Minucius himself felt his confidence gone and began to glance anxiously at his commanders
in turn. None of them had the courage to stand their ground,
and before long they broke and fled; but this proved a disastrous move, for the Numidian cavalry,[45] who were now the
masters of the field, galloped round the plain and cut down the
fugitives as they vainly attempted to scatter.

12. None of this had escaped Fabius, who by now was well
aware of the terrible danger that threatened the Romans. He
had foreseen the consequences of Minucius' rashness, drawn
up his own troops under arms and kept himself informed of the
progress of the battle, not through the reports of scouts but
from his own observations from a point of vantage in front
of his camp. When he saw Minucius' army surrounded and
thrown into confusion, and when the sound of their cries told
him that the Romans were no longer holding their ground but
had given way to panic and were in full retreat, he struck his
thigh,[46] and with a deep sigh exclaimed to those around him,
'By Hercules, Minucius has destroyed himself more quickly
than I expected, and yet he was lucky that it did not happen
sooner.' He then gave orders for the standards to advance with
all speed and for the rest of the army to follow, and called out
in a loud voice, 'My soldiers, every one of you must hurry forward. There is no time to lose. Think of Marcus Minucius. He
is a valiant man and loves his country. And if he has made a
mistake in his eagerness to drive back the enemy, we will blame
him for that another time.'

As soon as he appeared on the scene, he routed and scattered the Numidian cavalry who were galloping about the plain. Then he turned against the troops who were attacking the Roman rear, and killed all whom he met. The remainder gave way, before they were cut off and surrounded as the Romans had been, and made their escape. When Hannibal saw Fabius showing a vigour far beyond his years, as he forced his way through the thick of the battle up the hill towards Minucius, he knew that the battle had turned against him. He therefore broke off the action, signalled a retreat and led the Carthaginians back to their camp, and for their part the Romans were equally grateful for a respite. It is said that as Hannibal marched back, he spoke jokingly to his friends about Fabius in some such words as these: 'Haven't I kept telling you that the cloud we have seen hovering over the mountain tops would one day burst into a furious storm?'[47]

13. When the battle was over and Fabius' men had stripped the spoils from the enemy's troops they had killed, the dictator retired to his camp without uttering a single overbearing or reproachful word in criticism of his colleague. Minucius, however, paraded his men and addressed them as follows: 'Fellow-soldiers, it is beyond the powers of mortal man to be placed in command of great enterprises and never to make a mistake, but it is a mark of courage and good sense to be able to profit from one's errors and to treat a reverse as a lesson for the future. Let me confess then that although I have some slight excuse for blaming Fortune, I have far more reason to praise her. In the short space of a single day I have been taught what it has taken me all my life to learn. I can now see that I am not capable of commanding others, but need a commander myself, and that for all these years I have been cherishing the ambition to rise above men whom I ought to have felt honoured to acknowledge as my superiors. Now, in all other matters the dictator shall be your leader, but in expressing our thanks to him I shall take the lead, and set an example by showing that I am ready to follow his advice and obey his orders.'

After these words he ordered the eagles to be raised aloft and all his men to follow them, and led the way to Fabius' camp. As soon as he arrived he went to the general's tent, while the whole army looked on in astonishment and wonder. When Fabius came outside, Minucius had the standards of the legions planted in front of him and addressed him in a loud voice as 'Father', while his soldiers greeted Fabius' men as 'Patrons', which is the title that freedmen use towards those who have given them their liberty.[48] When silence had been restored, Minucius said: 'Dictator, on this day you have won two victories, one over Hannibal through your bravery, and the other over your colleague through your generalship and your generosity. With the first you saved our lives, and with the second you taught us a lesson, and just as Hannibal's superiority disgraced us, so yours has given us back not only our safety but our honour. I call you by the name of Father, because it is the most honourable that I can use, and yet even a father's kindness is not so great as the kindness I have received from you. My father gave me my life, but you have saved not only this life but the lives of all the men under me.' As he ended, he embraced Fabius and kissed him, and the soldiers on both sides followed his example, so that the whole camp was filled with rejoicing and tears of happiness.

14. After this Fabius laid down his office of dictator and consuls were once more elected.[49] The first to be chosen carried on the defensive tactics which Fabius had created, avoiding pitched battles but giving support to the allies and preventing them from going over to the enemy. But then came the year in which Terentius Varro was elected to the consulship.[50] He was a man of humble birth, who was remarkable chiefly for his obsequious flattery of the people, combined with his liking for impetuous action, and since his utter lack of experience was equalled only by his self-confidence, it soon became clear that he was prepared to risk everything on a single throw. He liked to thunder at people in the assembly that the war would make no progress so long as the Romans continued to employ men such as Fabius for their generals, but that he would defeat the enemy on the first day he set eyes on them. He did not confine himself to making these speeches, but he enlisted and assem-

bled a larger force than Rome had ever put into the field against any enemy. He mobilized 88,000 men[51] for his campaign and this caused the greatest alarm to Fabius and all the more thoughtful Romans, for they believed that if the city were to lose so many men in the prime of life, she would never recover from the blow.

Terentius' colleague was Aemilius Paullus,[52] a man who, despite his great experience of war, was unpopular with the people and was afraid of them because of a fine which they had once imposed on him. Accordingly, Fabius did his utmost to exhort and encourage him to resist his colleague's impetuosity, explaining that, if he wished to serve his country, he would find himself contending just as much with Terentius as with Hannibal. The former, he said, was eager to fight because he did not know where his own strength lay, and Hannibal was eager because he was too well aware of his own weakness. 'But you must believe me, Paullus,' he went on, 'when I say that I understand Hannibal's situation far better than Terentius does, and I am certain that, if no battle takes place with him for a year, he will either perish in Italy, if he chooses to remain, or else be forced to depart. Remember that even now, when he is supposed to be supreme and to have gained complete control of the country, not one of his enemies has come over to his side, and he does not now possess even a third part of the army that set out from Carthage.' To this Paullus is said to have replied: 'If I had only myself to consider, I would rather fall by the spears of the enemy than be condemned again by the votes of my fellow-countrymen. But if our country is now in such danger, I will try to make sure that my conduct as a general satisfies Fabius rather than all the men who are pressing me to take the opposite course.' Having taken this resolve, Paullus set out for the campaign.

15. Varro insisted on observing the practice whereby each consul took command of the army on alternate days. He then pitched his camp opposite Hannibal's on the banks of the River Aufidus[53] near the town named Cannae,[54] and at daybreak hoisted the signal for battle, which is a scarlet tunic hung out

over the general's tent. At first even the Carthaginians were dismayed, not only by the Roman commander's apparent boldness, but also by the strength of his army, which was more than double their own. Hannibal ordered his troops to prepare for action, while he himself with a few companions rode out to the crest of a gently rising slope, from which he could look down on the enemy as they formed their order of battle. When one of his companions, an officer of equal rank named Gisco, remarked that the numbers of the enemy seemed amazingly large, Hannibal looked grave for a moment, and said: 'There is another thing which you have not noticed, Gisco, which is even more amazing,' and when Gisco asked what this was, he replied, 'The fact that in all this enormous host there isn't a single man called Gisco.' The joke caught the whole party off guard and they all began to laugh; then, as they rode down from the high ground, they repeated it to everyone they met, so that their high spirits quickly spread among the troops, and the officers of Hannibal's staff were completely overcome with laughter. The Carthaginians took heart when they saw this, for they thought that their general must have great contempt for the Romans if he could laugh and joke like this in the face of danger.

16. In the battle itself Hannibal made use of a number of stratagems. First he took advantage of the ground to post his men with the wind behind them. It was a scorching wind which swept across the bare and sandy plains like a hurricane, whipping up choking clouds of dust that blew over the Carthaginian lines, straight into the faces of the Romans, who were thrown into confusion as they turned away to avoid the blast. His second ruse lay in his order of battle. His best and most warlike troops were stationed on the wings, while the weakest were concentrated in the centre, which he intended to use as a wedge projecting far ahead of the rest of the line. The orders given to the crack formations were as follows. The Romans would cut the Carthaginian centre to pieces, and as they pressed forward in pursuit, the centre would fall back forming a hollow, until the Romans had penetrated deep into their enemies' line of

battle. At this moment the Carthaginian wings would wheel sharply inwards, attack the Romans from the flanks and envelop them by closing in upon the rear. It was this manoeuvre, it seems, which brought about the fearful carnage that followed. When the Carthaginian centre gave ground and the Romans surged forward in pursuit, Hannibal's line was transformed into a crescent; thereupon the commanders of the picked troops on the wings wheeled them swiftly to right and left and attacked the enemy on their unguarded flanks, so that the Romans were overwhelmed and slaughtered to a man, except for the few who escaped before their encirclement was complete.

It is said that the Roman cavalry also suffered an unexpected misfortune. Paullus' horse, it appears, was wounded and threw its rider, whereupon one man after another of his staff dismounted and came on foot to help the consul. When the main body of the cavalry saw this, they assumed it was a general order, with the result that every man dismounted and engaged the enemy on foot. Hannibal saw this and remarked, 'This is better than having them all delivered over to me in chains.' However, for episodes of this kind I may refer the reader to those historians who have reported the war in detail.[55]

As for the two consuls, Varro galloped off with a few followers to the city of Venusia,[56] but Paullus, caught in the surging torrent of the rout, covered with the barbs which still hung in his wounds, and overwhelmed in both body and spirit by the weight of his misfortune, sat with his back against a stone and waited for the enemy to dispatch him. His head and face were so streaked and disfigured with blood that scarcely anyone could recognize him; even his friends and attendants passed him by, unaware that this was their general. At last Cornelius Lentulus,[57] a young patrician, caught sight of him and knew who he was. He jumped from his horse, led it up to Paullus, and besought the consul to take it and save himself for the sake of his fellow-citizens, who had never needed a brave commander so much as at that moment. But nothing could persuade Paullus to give way to his entreaty, and he compelled the young man, in spite of his tears, to mount his horse again. Then he rose to his feet, clasped Lentulus' hand and said to him, 'Tell Fabius Maximus, and you yourself bear witness, that Aemilius Paullus followed his friend's advice to the end and stood by every one of the undertakings he had given, but he was vanquished first by Varro and then by Hannibal.' When he had given Lentulus this message, he sent him away, and, plunging into the midst of the slaughter, he met his death. It is said that 50,000 Romans were killed in this battle and 4,000 captured alive, while after the fighting no fewer than 10,000 were captured[58] in the camps of the two consuls.

17. After this overwhelming success, Hannibal's friends urged him to follow up his good fortune and force his way into Rome on the heels of the retreating enemy, and they assured him that, if he pressed on, he would be dining on the Capitol on the fifth day after his victory. It is not easy to say what consideration could have held him back. It almost seems as if his evil genius or some divine power intervened at this moment to fill him with the timidity and irresolution which he now showed. This is why Barca the Carthaginian[59] is reported to have said to him angrily, 'You know how to win a victory, Hannibal, but you have no idea how to exploit it.' In spite of this, his victory brought about a tremendous change in his situation. Before it he had not controlled a single city, trading station or seaport in Italy, and had found great difficulty in obtaining even a bare supply of provisions by foraging; he had not possessed any secure base of operations, but had been obliged to roam about the countryside with his army, as if it were a whole troop of brigands. But after Cannae he brought almost the whole of Italy under his control. Most of its peoples, and the most significant of them, came over to him of their own accord, and Capua,[60] which was the most important city after Rome, gave him her complete support.

'It is no small evil', Euripides tells us, 'to put friends to the test,'[61] and the same, it would seem, applies to prudent generals. The very strategy, which before the battle had been condemned as passive and cowardly, now came to be regarded as the product of a superhuman power of reasoning and almost miraculous intelligence capable of penetrating the future and of prophesying a disaster which could scarcely be believed by those who experienced it. So it was upon Fabius that the Romans centred their last hopes. His wisdom was the sanctuary to which men fled for refuge, as they might to a temple or an altar, and they believed that it was his practical capacity above all which had preserved the unity of Rome at this moment, and had prevented her citizens from deserting the city and dispersing, as had happened during the disasters of the Gallic invasion.[62] For before, when the people had felt secure, it was Fabius who had appeared to be cautious and timid, but now, when all others were giving way to boundless grief and helpless bewilderment, he was the only man to walk the streets with a resolute step, a serene expression and a kindly voice. It was he who checked all womanish lamentations, and prevented those who wished to bewail their sorrows from assembling in public. On the other hand, he persuaded the senate to continue to hold its meetings, stiffened the resolution of the magistrates and made himself the strength and the moving spirit of all the offices of state, since every man looked to him for guidance.

18. He placed guards at the gates of Rome to prevent the frightened crowds from abandoning the city, and he regulated the times and the places at which it was permissible to lament the dead.[63] Those who wished to go into mourning were ordered to do so in their homes for a period of thirty days, at the end of which all mourning was to cease and the city was to be purified of such rites. Since the festival of Ceres[64] happened to fall within these dates, it was thought better to cancel both the sacrifices and the procession, since the small numbers and the dejection of those taking part could only bear a painful witness to the magnitude of the disaster; for it is the honours they receive from the fortunate which give most pleasure to the gods. However, all the rites which the augurs recommended to appease the anger of the gods or to avert inauspicious omens were duly performed.[65] Besides this, Pictor,[66] a relative of Fabius Maximus, was sent to consult the oracle at Delphi, and when two of the Vestal Virgins[67] were found to have been seduced,

one of them was buried alive, according to the traditional custom, and the other took her own life.

But perhaps what may impress us most of all today was the spirit of calm composure which the city displayed when Varro, the surviving consul, returned after his flight from the battlefield. He arrived in a state of the deepest dejection and humiliation, as a man who had brought a most terrible and disgraceful calamity upon his country, to find himself met by the senate and the whole populace, who welcomed him at the gates. As soon as calm had been restored, the magistrates and senior members of the senate – of whom Fabius was one – praised him because even in the midst of such a disaster he had never abandoned hope for the city, but had presented himself to take up the duties of government and to invoke the aid of the laws and of his fellow-citizens, confident that their salvation lay in their own hands.

19. When at length the citizens learned that Hannibal had turned aside after the battle and set off for the other parts of Italy, their courage revived and they once more sent armies and generals into the field. The most remarkable of these were Fabius Maximus and Claudius Marcellus, both of whom earned high praise, although for qualities which were almost diametrically opposed. Marcellus, as I have related in his Life, was a brilliant leader who possessed a dynamic energy and audacity, a doughty fighting-man of the same breed as those noble warriors whom Homer calls 'mighty in combat' and 'lovers of battle'.[68] Accordingly, he conducted his first operations against Hannibal in a spirit of enterprise and daring which matched Hannibal's own. Fabius, on the other hand, clung to his original ideas and placed his faith in the principle that if nobody fought with Hannibal, or even harassed him, his army would wear itself out and its fighting qualities would swiftly decline, like an athlete whose physique has been overtaxed and exhausted. This was the reason, so Poseidonius tells us, why their countrymen called Fabius the shield and Marcellus the sword of Rome,[69] because the combination of the steadiness and caution of the one with the warlike ardour of the other

proved the salvation of their country. In his frequent encounters with Marcellus, it was as though Hannibal had to face a
raging torrent, which battered and swept away his forces, while
against Fabius, whose tactics were slow, silent and yet relentless in their steady pressure, his strength was gradually and
imperceptibly undermined and drained away. In the end, he
was reduced to a situation in which he was exhausted with
fighting Marcellus, and afraid of Fabius because he could not
fight him.

These men were Hannibal's opponents almost continuously,
either as praetor, consul or proconsul, for each of them was
elected consul five times.[70] However, while Marcellus was serving his fifth term as consul, Hannibal contrived to lure him into
an ambush in which Marcellus was killed,[71] but although he
tried every kind of ruse and stratagem against Fabius, he never
gained an advantage over him. Once, it is true, he was able to
deceive him and very nearly inflicted a crushing defeat. He
forged a number of letters which were supposed to have come
from the leading citizens of Metapontum[72] and sent them to
Fabius. They offered to surrender the city if he would present
himself there, and indicated that the conspirators were only
waiting for him to come and show himself in their neighbourhood. Fabius was impressed by their letters, and resolved to
detach a part of his army and set out for Metapontum by night.
But when he found out that the auspices were unfavourable, he
decided to cancel his plan, and soon afterwards he discovered
that the letters had been cleverly forged by Hannibal, who was
waiting in ambush for him near the city,[73] and we may perhaps
attribute this escape to the favour of the gods.

20. When several of the Italian cities attempted to revolt and
there were uprisings among the allies, Fabius believed that the
best policy was to reason with them sympathetically and to dissuade and restrain them by lenient measures, without inquiring
too closely into every case of doubtful loyalty or treating every
suspected person harshly. It is said, for example, that when a
certain Marsian soldier,[74] a man of note among the allies both
for the nobility of his birth and his courage, was found to be

discussing with some of the soldiers the prospects of deserting to the enemy, Fabius showed no sign of anger, but admitted that the man had been unjustly passed over. This much, he said, was the fault of his commanders, who were apt to show favouritism rather than give courage its due when they awarded honours, but in future it would be the man's own fault if he did not come directly to Fabius whenever he wished to make a request. Having said this, he presented him with a charger and other rewards for valour, and from that time onwards there was no more faithful or devoted man in the army. Fabius thought it a shame that trainers of horses and dogs should be able to soften the obstinacy, discontent and savage spirit of their charges by means of care, intimate knowledge and a regular diet, rather than by the use of whips or heavy collars, and yet that an officer who has the command of men should not base his discipline mainly upon kindness and gentleness, but should treat them with more harshness and violence than even farmers do with wild figs, olives or pear trees, whose nature they can domesticate by careful cultivation, until they bear excellent olives and pears and figs.

In the same way, when his officers reported to him that another soldier, this time a Lucanian,[75] was repeatedly deserting his post and absenting himself from the camp, Fabius asked them their opinion of him in other respects. All of them testified that it would be difficult to find a better soldier, and quoted several of his exploits in which he had shown extraordinary courage. When the general had inquired further into the cause of the man's disobedience, he found that the soldier was in love with a girl and frequently took the risk of making long journeys from the camp to meet her. Accordingly, Fabius sent some of his men to arrest the girl without her lover's knowledge, and hid her in his own tent. Then he summoned the Lucanian to a private interview and told him, 'I know that you have many times spent the night outside the camp contrary to the customs and regulations of the Roman army. I also know that you have done good service in the past. In consideration of this, I propose to overlook your present offence, but for the future I shall hand you over to the charge of someone who will be answerable for you.' Then, to the soldier's amazement, Fabius produced the girl and put her into his hands, saying: 'This is the person who has given her word that you will stay in the camp with us. Now you can prove by your conduct that you had no other discreditable motive, but that this girl and your love for her was the only reason that made you desert your post.' Such is the account that we have of this episode.[76]

21. Fabius succeeded in recapturing the city of Tarentum,[77] which the Romans had originally lost by treachery,[78] and here another love affair played its part. There was a young Tarentine in the Roman army whose sister was particularly devoted to him. The commander of the garrison stationed by Hannibal to defend the city, who was a Bruttian,[79] had fallen deeply in love with this girl, and this fact encouraged her brother to hope that he might turn it to the advantage of the Romans. Fabius gave his consent to the scheme, and the young man made his way into the city under the pretence of having deserted the army to visit his sister. For the first few days of his stay the Bruttian remained at home, since the girl supposed that her brother knew nothing of their love affair. Then her brother said to her: 'When I was in the Roman army, there were rumours that one of the commanders of the garrison has been paying court to you. Who is he? If he is a man of high reputation who is well known for his courage – as I have been told – it makes little difference what country he belongs to, since war throws all our affairs into confusion and mixes all the nations together. It is no disgrace to yield to necessity. On the contrary, in these days when right has so little power, we must think ourselves lucky if might, supposing we are obliged to surrender to it, turns out not to be too disagreeable.' After this the girl sent for the Bruttian and introduced him to her brother, who quickly won the barbarian's confidence. Not only did he encourage the love affair, but it was clear that he persuaded his sister to show more tenderness and compliance to her lover than before. From here it was a simple step, since the Bruttian was not only a lover but a mercenary, to persuade him to transfer his allegiance to the Romans by the promise of a large reward which he would receive from Fabius.

This is the commonest version of the story.[80] But some writers say that the woman who seduced the Bruttian from his allegiance was not a Tarentine but was herself a Bruttian, and that she had previously been Fabius' concubine. When she discovered that a fellow-countryman and acquaintance of hers was in command of the garrison, she informed Fabius, met and spoke with the man beneath the city walls and gradually won him over to the Roman cause.

22. While this plot was being hatched, Fabius wished to devise a scheme to draw Hannibal away from the neighbourhood, and he therefore gave orders to the garrison of Rhegium[81] to overrun and ravage the territory of the Bruttians and take Caulonia[82] by storm. This body of troops at Rhegium was 8,000 strong. Many of them were deserters, and they included the worse elements of the force which Marcellus had sent home from Sicily in disgrace;[83] in fact they were men who were considered expendable and whose loss would cause the least possible harm or distress to Rome. Fabius hoped that by throwing out this force as bait before Hannibal he would lure him away from Tarentum, and this was exactly what happened. Hannibal immediately hurried with his army to Bruttium to pursue them, and meanwhile Fabius moved in to besiege Tarentum.

On the sixth day of the siege, the young man, whose sister had helped him to concert his plan with the Bruttian commander, came to visit Fabius at night. He had seen and inspected the place where the Bruttian would be keeping watch to let in the besiegers and hand over the city. But Fabius was not prepared to make his plans entirely dependent on this act of treachery. Accordingly, he himself led a body of troops to the appointed place, while the rest of the army launched a general attack on the walls by land and sea. Their assault was accompanied by a tremendous clamour and commotion, until most of the Tarentines had rushed to the support of the defenders. Then the Bruttian gave Fabius the signal, whereupon he and his men scaled the walls and took possession of the city.

At this point, however, Fabius' ambition seems to have

proved stronger than his principles, for he ordered his men to put the Bruttian contingent to the sword before anyone else, so as to conceal the fact that he had captured the city by treachery. However, he completely failed to win the glory he sought and instead he incurred the charge of bad faith and inhumanity. Besides the Bruttians many of the Tarentines were killed, 30,000 of them were sold into slavery, their city was sacked by the Roman army and the public treasury was enriched by the sum of 3,000 talents. While everything else was being carried off as plunder, it is said that the officer who was drawing up a schedule of public property asked Fabius what were his orders concerning the gods, by which he meant the paintings and statues, and that Fabius replied, 'Let us leave the Tarentines their angry gods.' However, he removed the giant statue of Hercules[84] and had it placed on the Capitol, and close by he erected an equestrian statue of himself in bronze. Fabius showed himself to be far more arbitrary in dealing with these matters than Marcellus, or rather he proved by the contrast between them that Marcellus was a man of extraordinary mildness and humanity, as I have indicated in his Life.[85]

23. It is said that Hannibal arrived within 40 stades[86] of Tarentum when the city fell, and that in public he merely remarked, 'It seems that the Romans have found another Hannibal, for we have lost Tarentum in the same way that we took it.' But in private he admitted to his friends that he had long recognized that it was very difficult for them to conquer Italy with their present forces, and that he now believed it was impossible.

For this success Fabius celebrated a second triumph, which was even more magnificent than his first.[87] The Romans saw that he was dealing with Hannibal like an experienced wrestler, and had mastered the technique of frustrating his opponent's moves, now that his grips and holds had lost their original force. The truth was that some of Hannibal's troops had become enervated by luxury and plunder,[88] while others had had their fighting qualities blunted and worn down by incessant campaigning.

Now, there was a certain Marcus Livius,[89] who had been in command of the garrison at Tarentum when Hannibal had persuaded the city to revolt. He had seized the citadel, however, and had never been dislodged from this position, but continued to hold out until the town was recaptured by the Romans. Livius was annoyed at the honours which were conferred on Fabius, and on this occasion he was so far carried away by his jealousy and ambition as to declare that it was not Fabius but *he* who was responsible for the capture of Tarentum. At this Fabius burst out laughing and retorted: 'You are quite right, Livius. If you had not lost the city, I could never have recaptured it.'[90]

24. One of the many marks of honour which the people bestowed upon Fabius was to elect his son as consul.[91] After he had taken up his office and was dealing with some business concerning the conduct of the war, his father, either because of his age and weakness, or perhaps because he was putting his son to the test, mounted his horse and rode towards him through the crowd of bystanders. The young man caught sight of him at a distance and refused to allow this affront to his office. He sent a lictor to order him to dismount and approach on foot if he had any business with the consul. Those who were present were offended at this command and turned their eyes towards Fabius in silence, while their looks expressed their indignation at such officious treatment of a man of his reputation. But Fabius himself leapt from his horse, and with open arms almost ran to his son and embraced him affectionately, saying, 'You are right, my son, both in your thought and your action. You understand the nature of the people who have chosen you to govern and the grandeur of the office you have received from them. This was the way in which we and our forefathers made Rome great, by putting the honour and the service of our country before those of our own parents and children.'[92]

And indeed, there is a similar story concerning the great-grandfather of our Fabius.[93] Even though he possessed the greatest reputation and influence of any man in Rome, had served five times as consul and had celebrated the most magnificent triumphs after the greatest wars of his time, nevertheless, when his son became consul and set out for the war, he himself served as his subordinate.[94] Then, in the triumph that followed,[95] while the son entered the city in a four-horse chariot, the father followed on horseback with the rest of the procession, and he took pride in the fact that while he had authority over his son as a private individual[96] and was himself in both name and in reality the greatest man of the state, yet he was ready to submit himself to the law and the chief magistrate. This, of course, was not the only admirable thing about him.

Fabius had the misfortune to lose his son, but he bore this blow patiently like a wise man and a good father. It is the custom at Rome, whenever a famous man dies, for one of his relatives to pronounce a funeral oration. Fabius delivered this from his place in the forum, and later wrote out his speech and distributed it among his friends.[97]

25. Meanwhile, Cornelius Scipio[98] had been sent to Spain, where he not only defeated the Carthaginians in a series of battles and drove them out of the country, but also brought a great many tribes over to his side, captured great cities and achieved glorious deeds for Rome. When he returned to the capital, he was acclaimed and idolized as no Roman had ever been before, and was promptly elected consul.[99] But since he recognized that the people expected and demanded some achievement from him, he came to the conclusion that the strategy of containing Hannibal in Italy was now out of date and had become an old man's task. His plan was that the Romans should pour troops into Libya, attack and ravage the territory of Carthage itself and transfer the scene of the war from Italy to Libya, and so he threw himself heart and soul into the task of arousing the people to support this policy.

But now Fabius did his utmost to spread doubts and misgivings of every kind against the proposal. He argued that they were rushing into grave and unknown perils under the leadership of a hot-headed young man, and he did not hesitate to say or do anything which he thought might dissuade his fellow-countrymen from adopting his opponent's policy. He succeeded in convincing the senate, but the people believed that he was attacking Scipio out of jealousy of his exploits, and also because he was afraid that if Scipio achieved some brilliant and decisive success and either finished off the war or removed it from Italy, then he himself might be condemned as a lazy and cowardly general for having allowed the fighting to drag on for so many years.

It seems likely that Fabius' opposition originally sprang from his instinctive caution and prudence and that he was genuinely alarmed by the risks involved in Scipio's strategy, which indeed were great, but that in the course of time the effort to check his opponent's rising influence made his attitude more violent and extreme and introduced an element of ambition and personal rivalry into the conflict. He even tried to persuade Crassus,[100] Scipio's fellow-consul, not to hand over the command of the army to his colleague but to lead it to Carthage himself, if the decision to invade Africa were adopted, and he also prevented the voting of any funds for the campaign. Scipio was left in the position of having to find the money himself, and he therefore collected it on his private account from the cities of Etruria, which were devotedly loyal to him.[101] As for Crassus, he remained at home,[102] partly because by nature he was a gentle man and had no inclination to quarrel with his colleague, and partly on account of his religiosity, since he held the office of high priest.[103]

26. After this Fabius adopted a different set of tactics. He tried to prevent the young men who were anxious to serve under Scipio from taking part in the campaign. He complained at meetings of the senate and assembly that it was not merely a question of Scipio's running away from Hannibal: he was proposing to sail off with the whole reserve of Italy's manpower, and he was deluding these young men with false hopes and persuading them to abandon their parents, their wives and their city, while a conquering and still undefeated enemy threatened the very gates of Rome. He succeeded in alarming the Romans to such an extent with these arguments that they decreed Scipio should take with him only the troops that were already in Sicily,[104] together with a detachment of 300 picked men who had served him loyally in Spain. In insisting on this

policy, Fabius was clearly dominated by the dictates of his own cautious nature.

However, no sooner had Scipio arrived in Africa than almost immediately news began to arrive in Rome of extraordinary achievements, brilliant exploits and decisive victories.[105] The reports were quickly substantiated by the immense spoils which followed these successes. The king of Numidia was captured, two of the enemy's camps were burned and destroyed, together with great quantities of men, horses and arms, and envoys were sent to Hannibal[106] with urgent instructions that he must abandon his fruitless hopes in Italy and hasten home to the rescue of his native city. And yet when every tongue in Rome was applauding Scipio's victories, this was the moment which Fabius chose to demand that he should be recalled[107] and a successor sent out. He did not attempt to justify this request, but merely repeated the familiar proverb to the effect that it was dangerous to entrust such immense operations to the fortune of one man, since it was difficult for any single man to enjoy good fortune at all times.

This proposal offended most of Fabius' fellow-citizens, who felt that he was now acting out of mere peevishness and malice, or else that in his old age he had lost all his courage and confidence and was obsessed by an exaggerated fear of Hannibal. For even when Hannibal and his army had sailed away from Italy,[108] Fabius still could not refrain from casting gloom over the general rejoicings and dashing his fellow-countrymen's spirits. The city, he prophesied, was now facing her final and most terrible ordeal, for they would find Hannibal a far more formidable enemy under the walls of Carthage than he had ever been in Italy, and Scipio would have to meet an army which was still reeking with the blood of many generals, dictators and consuls. By means of such speeches he again succeeded in filling the city with dismay, and although the war had been transferred to Africa, yet its terrors seemed to have moved closer than ever to Rome.

27. But not long afterwards Scipio defeated Hannibal himself[109] in a pitched battle and crushed the pride of Carthage

underfoot. He gave his countrymen a joy that went far beyond all their hopes, and in restoring their supremacy, 'righted the ship that storms so long had tossed'.[110] Fabius Maximus, however, did not live to see the end of the war, nor did he ever hear of Hannibal's overthrow, nor witness the glorious and lasting prosperity of his country, for at about the time when Hannibal sailed from Italy, he fell sick and died.

Epaminondas was buried by the Thebans at public expense, because when he died, so the story goes, he was so poor that nothing was found in his house but a single iron spit.[111] The Romans did not bury Fabius at the expense of the state, but every citizen contributed the smallest coin in his possession towards the funeral.[112] This was not because he was so poor as to need their help, but rather because they felt that they were burying the father of the people. Thus, in his death he received the honour and regard which he had earned by the conduct of his life.

COMPARISON OF PERICLES
AND FABIUS MAXIMUS

1 (28). Such, then, is the story of these men's lives. Now, since each of them left behind many noble proofs of his excellence both in civic and military affairs, let us begin with their accomplishments in war. Pericles had at his disposal a people who were at the height of their prosperity, were great in their own right and at the peak of their imperial power.[1] One could, therefore, attribute it to the good fortune and might of his city that Pericles never experienced a reversal or a defeat, whereas Fabius, because he took charge of Rome's affairs when its circumstances were disgraceful and disastrous, did not merely preserve intact a city that was flourishing but instead restored his from the brink of total catastrophe. Furthermore, the glorious deeds of Cimon,[2] the victorious trophies set up by Myronides[3] and Leocrates[4] and the many triumphs of Tolmides[5] made it possible for Pericles, when he held the office of general, to enrich his city with holidays and festivals[6] rather than wage war for the sake of recovering Athens' possessions or protecting her from her enemies. But Fabius, who witnessed so many routs and defeats, saw so many consuls and praetors slain and slaughtered, and beheld lakes and plains and forests filled with the bodies of soldiers and rivers flowing with blood and gore as far as the sea, took Rome into his own hands, reviving and steadying his city, which he would not allow to collapse into utter ruin owing to the failures of other men. Mind you, managing a city that has been humbled by misfortunes, and has little choice but to hearken to a man of good

sense, might be deemed less difficult than reining in the insolence and audacity of a people[7] rendered conceited and arrogant
by their success, and it was by way of this very achievement
that Pericles most clearly showed himself to be master in Athens. Still, the severity and the magnitude of the evils afflicting
the Romans revealed the steadfast resolution and greatness of
Fabius, who never allowed himself to become confused and
who never abandoned his carefully reasoned plans.

2 (29). Pericles' conquest of Samos[8] can be set beside Fabius'
capture of Tarentum,[9] and so too, by Zeus! his taking of
Euboea[10] with Fabius' seizing the cities of Campania,[11] although
the reduction of Capua was the work of the consuls Fulvius
and Appius.[12] In so far as set battles are concerned, Fabius seems
to have won only one, the victory for which he celebrated his
first triumph,[13] whereas Pericles erected nine trophies[14] for
defeating enemies on land and at sea. However, one can find no
record of any action by Pericles that is comparable to Fabius'
when he snatched Minucius away from Hannibal and saved an
entire Roman army.[15] That was a truly noble deed, demonstrat-
ing in a single moment Fabius' valour, his intelligence and his
kindness. Then again, we have no evidence that Pericles ever
suffered a defeat on the order of Fabius' when Hannibal out-
generalled him through his cunning stratagem employing
oxen.[16] Fabius had actually trapped his enemy within a narrow
defile, which, by a stroke of good fortune for the Romans,
Hannibal had entered of his own accord, but he let him escape
unnoticed in the night, and when day came Hannibal advanced
forcefully, defeating his erstwhile captor.

Furthermore, if it is essential that a good general not only
take full advantage of present circumstances but also be a
sound judge of things to come, then we must certainly notice
that Pericles foresaw and foretold how the Athenians' war
would come to an end, for they tried to accomplish too much
and lost their empire.[17] But it was only by rejecting Fabius'
advice that the Romans decided to send Scipio against the
Carthaginians[18] and consequently won a complete victory —
not through good luck but rather on account of the wisdom

and valour of their general, who utterly vanquished the enemy. Therefore, the very disasters suffered by his country attest to Pericles' keen intellect, while the Romans' victory is proof that Fabius got it wrong. Indeed, it is no worse for a general to stumble into misfortune because he lacks perspicacity than it is for him to miss an opportunity because he lacks confidence. Inexperience, in my opinion, is the common cause of each failure, for it both engenders rashness in a man and robs him of his courage.[19] So much, then, for their achievements in war.

3 (30). Let us now turn to civic affairs. Pericles is the object of harsh criticism on account of his role in the Peloponnesian War, the complaint being that he caused it by refusing to make any concessions to the Spartans when he was at odds with them.[20] But I am confident that Fabius Maximus would never have conceded anything to the Carthaginians and would nobly have endured any danger for the sake of Rome's empire. Nevertheless, the decency and mildness that Fabius displayed towards Minucius count as reproaches against Pericles' factious subversion of Cimon[21] and Thucydides,[22] worthy and aristocratic men whom he subjected to ostracism and banishment. Still, Pericles had more power and influence than did Fabius. For this reason, he was able to prevent any other general's faulty strategy from doing his city harm. The sole exception was Tolmides, who was alienated from Pericles and opposed him violently: this man ultimately met with defeat when he attacked the Boeotians.[23] All the others, however, took Pericles' part and deferred to his judgement, so great was his authority. Fabius, by contrast, though sure and unerring in his own commands, was inferior to Pericles in that he was unable to restrain his fellow Romans, who would not have suffered so many great disasters had Fabius possessed the same influence with them that Pericles had over the Athenians.

Both men exhibited the same high-mindedness in so far as money was concerned, one of them by accepting none of the gifts offered him, the other through his generosity to men in need, when at his own expense he ransomed the prisoners of war.[24] Admittedly, the sum he paid was not a steep one but only around 6 talents.[25] As for Pericles, one should observe how, although he could easily have enriched himself at the expense of the allies and kings who, on account of his extraordinary stature, endeavoured to cultivate his friendship, he nevertheless kept himself honest and incorruptible.[26]

At last we come to Pericles' grand public works,[27] his construction of the temples and other monuments with which he adorned Athens. These so far excel all of Rome's proud edifices, everything built before the time of the Caesars, that no comparison is even possible, so pre-eminent are they in their sheer magnificence and splendour.

MARCELLUS

INTRODUCTION TO
MARCELLUS

Warrior and Philhellene

Marcus Claudius Marcellus was one of Rome's paramount military leaders during the late third century BC. His victory at Clastidium in 222 became legendary, and in Roman accounts of the Second Punic War (218–201 BC) he is routinely paired with Fabius Maximus, the one acting as the shield of Rome, the other its sword, in the formulation recorded by the Greek writer Poseidonius (ch. 9). He famously captured – and sacked – the wealthy Greek city of Syracuse. And he fell in combat against Hannibal. A thoroughly Roman hero, then, though one whose subsequent reputation was sometimes sullied by complaints about his violence, ruthlessness and recklessness. Not so in Plutarch's Life, however, where Marcellus, for all his martial disposition, exhibits the first signs of Rome's true promise as a mighty nation imbued with Greek values and ideals. For Plutarch, he is Rome's first practical philhellene.

History

Marcellus was born around 270 BC into a family of plebeian nobility: the Claudii Marcelli attained their first consulship in 331 BC, and the son of the consul of 331 was himself consul in 287 BC. Presumably these are the grandfather and great-grandfather of our Marcellus. Nothing is known of his childhood. His youth is similarly obscure: after serving in the

First Punic War (264–241 BC), Marcellus was inducted into the college of augurs and elected aedile and praetor, all at dates unknown to us.

Marcellus bursts into history as consul in 222 BC, at a time when the Romans were at war with the Gauls of northern Italy.[1] Marcellus won a major victory near the town of Clastidium, where he killed a Gallic king in single combat, a deed unparalleled in Rome since the fifth century BC. After a second decisive battle, he was awarded a triumph (chs. 7–8). Marcellus' triumph was an extraordinary affair. Because he had slain the Gallic chief in personal combat, he could lay claim to the *spolia opima* – the best of trophies – the despoiled armour of his opponent destined for consecration to Jupiter Feretrius, a ritual established in the mythical past by Romulus when he struck down Acron of Caenina (ch. 8). In the intervening centuries, only the elusive Aulus Cornelius Cossus had equalled Romulus' feat, when, as consul, he cut down Lars Tolumnius, king of Veii. By putting himself forward as the third Roman warrior to win the *spolia opima*, Marcellus revived – to some degree, perhaps, invented – and in any case exploited an ancient custom that marked him out as the embodiment of pristine Roman valour.[2]

The outbreak of the Second Punic War brought Marcellus to prominence once again.[3] In the aftermath of Hannibal's early victories in Italy, Marcellus offered a stout resistance, gaining some notable if not spectacular successes. In 215 he saved the city of Nola from falling into enemy hands (chs. 10–11), and in the following year, in cooperation with Fabius Maximus, regained some of Rome's losses to the Carthaginians. Marcellus' energetic response to Hannibal's menace, even if it fell short of decisive victory, was nonetheless instrumental in stymieing Hannibal's strategy in Italy – and it marked him out as the right man for securing Sicily from a renewed and vigorous Carthaginian offensive there.[4]

Although Marcellus' Syracusan campaign consumes a large portion of this Life (chs. 13–21), Plutarch presents his reader with an almost confusingly abridged account of its background and prosecution. Sicily had been the prize of the First Punic War, when Rome wrested control of the island from Carthage.

Its territories, apart from the kingdom of Syracuse, an independent but subordinate ally, served as sources of revenue and grain whose value only increased amid the scarcities entrained by Hannibal's invasion. It was natural, then, that Carthage should attempt to recover the island. At the start of the war, however, Roman interests in Sicily were tenaciously guarded by her ally, Hiero II, the king of Syracuse, a rich and mighty city. But he died in 215 BC, leaving his fifteen-year-old grandson, Hieronymus, as heir.

Political convulsions supervened. The new king's advisers took the view that Carthage was in the ascendant and urged a reconsideration of the city's Roman alliance. Hoping to exploit this fresh opportunity, Hannibal sent two brothers – Hippocrates and Epicydes, who were half-Carthaginian and half-Syracusan – to persuade the new king to side with him. It was under these circumstances that the senate, late in 214 BC, sent Marcellus to take over affairs in Sicily.

Syracuse was ridden with intrigue, and Hieronymus, out of his depth, was soon assassinated, an event which led to widespread civil disruption, marked by a failed coup and the execution of the residue of the royal family. The city then reverted to a republican-style government. Nonetheless, this new regime remained open to negotiations with Rome, and Marcellus was soon involved in diplomatic exertions to restore the old alliance.

All attempts at a peaceful settlement collapsed, however, when Hippocrates and Epicydes took control of Leontini, a large city that was Syracuse's most important dependency. Leontini then revolted against Syracuse and, at the same time, declared its hostility to Rome. In reaction, Marcellus stormed the place. This turned to the advantage of Hippocrates and Epicydes, however, who made their way back to Syracuse and inflamed anti-Roman feelings by claiming that Marcellus was committing atrocities against the Leontines. They then seized control of Syracuse, plunging the city into a war against Rome.

After a siege lasting two years, Marcellus captured Syracuse. He then handed the city over to his soldiers, who looted the place. Marcellus himself took little by way of personal plunder – only, we are told, a single sphere that had once belonged to Archimedes (Cicero, *The Republic* 1.21) – but he arranged for the dispossession of an astonishing quantity of fine artwork, which he transferred to Rome. He quickly dealt with what little Carthaginian resistance remained in Sicily, and soon the island was almost entirely pacified. The recovery of Sicily was a major victory and an important turning-point in the war, but when Marcellus returned to Rome in 211 BC, his opponents in the senate refused him a triumph, for reasons both technical and invidious.

No degree of political sharp practice, however, could deny Marcellus all recognition, and the senate was forced to concur in his demand for an *ovatio*, a lesser triumph. Marcellus' skill in self-advertisement did not forsake him. On the day before his ovation, he celebrated a private triumph on the Alban Mount, an allegedly ancient ceremony that had in fact only recently been invented, in 231 BC, by the consul Gaius Papirius Maso.[5] The combination of these pageants, unprecedented and never repeated, was designed to thrill the public and foil the envy of Marcellus' rivals, and it was a spectacular success. In his ovation, Marcellus paraded the splendid Greek art he had plundered in Syracuse, spoil that was now the property of the Roman people. He furthermore advertised his glory in the Greek world as well as in Rome, setting up dedications in Sicily, in Samothrace, in Rhodes and in Delphi.[6]

Despite opposition against him in the senate, Marcellus was swept into the consulship for 210 BC. He campaigned in Italy against Hannibal, not without effect, but in 208, when he was again consul, Marcellus was ambushed and fell in the fighting, an inglorious ending that is the focus of Plutarch's criticism of the man in this Life.

Reputation

Marcellus' remorseless valour became legendary at Rome.[7] His heroic stature reached its zenith during the reign of Augustus: as the ancestor nonpareil of the emperor's nephew, son-in-law and likely heir (ch. 30), the victor at Syracuse constituted indisputable proof of the young Marcellus' native brilliance, and of Rome's irreplaceable loss in the tragedy of the young man's early death.[8] When Augustus pronounced his funeral oration, he naturally rehearsed the history of the Claudii Marcelli – including the career of their greatest general – and the emperor's praise secured Marcellus' imperial reputation.

The historian Polybius, by contrast, was unimpressed, even hostile. Of *spolia opima* or Marcellus' triumph he makes no mention (2.34). Marcellus' removal of Syracuse's artwork he deems a blunder: Polybius does not object to plundering the city's wealth – that, after all, is the fuel of empire – but in taking their art the Romans gained no real profit and incurred only resentment and envy (9.10). He is nothing short of severe in his condemnation of Marcellus' final and fatal campaign against Hannibal: 'He stumbled into this destructive misfortune because he conducted himself with childlike simplicity and not as a general ought to act' (10.32–3).

Livy's treatment of Marcellus, although mostly favourable, nevertheless preserves Polybius' reproaches – and adds others. Livy does not disguise Marcellus' harsh treatment of the vanquished (23.42–3, 24.37–8; cf. Cassius Dio 15.31), and he acknowledges claims asserted by other writers that Marcellus' early victories against Hannibal were exaggerated (23.16). Like Polybius, Livy (25.40.2) disapproves of Marcellus' removal of Syracuse's art, but on the very different grounds that such luxuries were morally corrupting.[9] Livy will not attribute Marcellus' death to incompetence, but he objects to his unnatural obsession with defeating Hannibal, which was unsuitable to his age and attainments (27.27.11).[10]

Plutarch's Marcellus

Plutarch does not ignore these controversies, but in this Life they are either repudiated or dismissed – apart from the charge of rashness that resulted in Marcellus' unfortunate death. Plutarch's Marcellus exhibits valour and industry, and combines his spirited passion for battle with high-mindedness (*Pelopidas* 2; *Comparison Pelopidas–Marcellus* 1). At the same time, his merits are not confined to combat. Marcellus possesses the prized quality of *philanthropia* (ch. 10), the exquisite humanity which Plutarch bundles with kindness and generosity – and which he esteems as the essential virtue of Greek civilization.[11] Consequently, and despite a tradition inclined to emphasize his ruthlessness and severity, Plutarch's Marcellus exhibits moderation and compassion, and it is Marcellus, first of all the Romans, as Plutarch claims explicitly, who stands as proof to the Greeks that Rome is capable of more than brute violence (chs. 19–20). On this point Plutarch is so insistent that he repeats it in his *Fabius Maximus* (ch. 22), where he contrasts Marcellus' humanity with the injustice of Fabius' violence at Tarentum.

This moral superiority cannot derive from philosophical instruction: such a thing did not yet exist in a Rome that Plutarch likens to the primitive world of the Homeric epics (ch. 1). Marcellus was, nevertheless, deeply affected by a temperamental fondness for the Greek learning he could never obtain:

> He had enough regard for Greek culture and literature to make him honour and admire those who excelled in them, but he himself never found the leisure to master or even study these subjects to the extent that he would have wished.
>
> (ch. 1)

This is a Marcellan instinct that is entirely his biographer's invention, but it constitutes the crucial element of Marcellus' true excellence, which Plutarch manages to detect even in the sacking of Syracuse.

This is why Plutarch commends, where others censure, Marcellus' controversial ovation, when he flooded Rome with Greek works of art. Although Livy connects Marcellus' imports with the Romans' tradition of a moral decline – and Plutarch is honest enough to include this brand of criticism in his Life – for Plutarch this occasion marks nothing less than a transformation in the cultural fabric of Rome, which he emphasizes by way of an unrealistically exaggerated contrast between Roman conditions before and after the ovation (ch. 21).[12] The older generation in Rome disapproves, but Marcellus remains confident that he is inculcating in the Roman public a salutary admiration for Greek art (ch. 21), an attitude which, like his own nascent Hellenism, is a crucial step forward in Rome's cultural evolution.

Marcellus and Pelopidas

Plutarch's Marcellus is nearly flawless – nearly. His failure lay, as Polybius recognized (10.32), in the recklessness of his death, an end not merely inglorious but positively dangerous, because so many lives and designs depend on the safety of a leader. In throwing away his life, Marcellus threw away all his gifts and qualities (*Comparison Pelopidas–Marcellus* 3), and it is around this poignant tragedy that Plutarch constructs both this Life and its pairing with the Greek Pelopidas.

Plutarch matches Marcellus with a Boeotian hero, the Theban general Pelopidas (*c.* 410–364 BC), who, with the brilliant Epaminondas, was a leading figure in the struggle to liberate Thebes from Spartan control. Pelopidas won a victory over the Spartans at the battle of Tegyra (375 BC), and, in command of the Theban Sacred Band, helped Epaminondas to defeat the Spartans decisively at Leuctra (371 BC).[13] Pelopidas ended his life in battle against Alexander of Pherae, a tyrant whom he endeavoured to slay in hand-to-hand combat. In spite of Pelopidas' death, however, Pherae was defeated, and Pelopidas was honoured with a statue erected at Delphi.[14]

The prologue to this pairing is an exposition of the principle, also enunciated by Polybius, that a general must not act with the impetuosity of a subaltern (*Pelopidas* 1–2), and Plutarch returns to the same point in his conclusion to the work. In this respect, both Pelopidas and Marcellus behaved unreasonably. How different, Plutarch observes, as Polybius (10.33) had done before him, was Hannibal, who, for all his many battles, remained unwounded and in command (*Comparison Pelopidas–Marcellus* 3).

The diagnosis of their common failure is straightforward: each was a man of bold spirits and passion (*thumeidēs*: see

Comparison Pelopidas–Marcellus 1), a martial advantage but
one requiring temperance. Plutarch routinely criticizes commanders who fall in battle because they are unable to restrain
their passions, always a debacle owed to want of reason.[15] As
Plutarch makes clear in *Coriolanus*, in order to put even noble
passions to their best purposes, one requires education (*paideia*).[16] Now, although he was a Greek, Pelopidas remained
uninterested in philosophical pursuits (*Pelopidas* 4), whereas
Marcellus, for all his philhellenic tendencies, was raised in a
Rome where a proper education was impossible (ch. 1). Nevertheless, Plutarch's treatment of both Pelopidas and Marcellus is
encomiastic: their sole deficiency, he insists, should not vitiate
their life's work (*Comparison Pelopidas–Marcellus* 3). At the
same time, because each man's nearness to perfection underlines
the disaster of his fall, this pairing reveals how even the best of
men can fall prey to their passions if insufficiently educated.

It is easy to forget, when reading this pairing, that Pelopidas
lived more than a century and a half *before* Marcellus, so
primitive is the atmosphere of the Roman's Life: he and his generation are, from the beginning, described in Homeric terms
(ch. 1), they resort to human sacrifice (ch. 3) and they dwell in
a city 'filled with bloodstained arms and the spoils of barbarian
tribes' (ch. 21).[17] But Marcellus began to change all that, and
this is unmistakably illustrated in the last sentence of his Life,
when Plutarch describes how Rome memorialized Marcellus'
descendant, Augustus' nephew and son-in-law: 'It was in his
honour and to his memory that Octavia dedicated a library and
Caesar a theatre, both of which bear his name to this day' (ch.
30). The ultimate expression of Marcellus' natural philhellenism is imperial Rome, shaped by the quintessentially Greek
institutions of libraries and theatres.

Sources

An abundance of potential sources was at Plutarch's disposal,
and he cites by name several authorities: the first-century BC
polymath Poseidonius (chs. 1, 9, 20, 30), Livy (chs. 11, 24, 30),
the emperor Augustus (ch. 30 and *Comparison Pelopidas–*

Marcellus 1), the biographer Cornelius Nepos (ch. 30 and *Comparison Pelopidas–Marcellus* 1), Polybius (*Comparison Pelopidas–Marcellus* 1), Valerius Maximus (ch. 30) and Juba, the learned king of Mauretania and friend of Augustus (*Comparison Pelopidas–Marcellus* 1), who composed, among many works, a history of Rome (in Greek) which is now lost (*FGrH* 275). In more than one instance in this Life, Plutarch cites his sources inaccurately or even entirely erroneously (these are indicated in the notes to the translation), evidence of haste or carelessness in composition that must qualify any attempt to arrive at his main sources. Still, there can be no doubt that Plutarch studied Polybius closely, and there is no reason to doubt his claim that he consulted Livy.[18] The belief that Plutarch relied heavily on the lost histories of Coelius Antipater[19] or Valerius Antias[20] is long-standing, though it is not entirely compelling. There is, however, no reason why he could not at least have looked at them.

It would be especially helpful to know the source of Plutarch's Poseidonian information. Poseidonius' lost *History*, a continuation of Polybius, covered world history – by then mostly Roman history – from 146 down to sometime in the 80s BC. Although the work apparently teemed with digressions, it is difficult to see how Marcellus could have crept into it in any important way. It has been suggested that Poseidonius composed a monograph of some sort that was devoted to Marcellus, and one can well imagine the Claudii Marcelli of the late republic commissioning such a work. After all, Cicero's distinguished friend, Atticus, at the behest of the same family, penned a detailed history of the Claudii Marcelli (Nepos, *Letters to Atticus* 18.3). But this can never be more than a surmise, and any item of the Poseidonian material in Plutarch, even the famous metaphor of the shield and the sword, could originate in a digression or a passing remark in another work.[21]

LIFE OF MARCELLUS

[c. 270–208 BC]

1. Marcus Claudius, who five times held the office of consul of the Roman people, was the son of Marcus, and according to Poseidonius[1] was the first of his family to be given the name of Marcellus, which means warlike.[2] Much of his experience was concerned with the art of war and he possessed a powerful arm and a vigorous body. By his very nature he was a 'lover of battle', a daring soldier who, in every conflict, proved himself 'mighty in combat'[3] – and yet, in other respects, he was modest and humane. He had enough regard for Greek culture and literature to make him honour and admire those who excelled in them, but he himself never found the leisure to master or even study these subjects to the extent that he would have wished. For if ever there were men for whom Zeus, as Homer says,

> Decreed that from youth till ripe old age must labour
> Fighting in arduous wars . . .[4]

they were the foremost Romans of his generation. In their youth they campaigned against the Carthaginians for the possession of Sicily, in their prime they fought the Gauls for the defence of Italy itself and as veterans they found themselves matched once more against the Carthaginians, this time under Hannibal.[5] In this way they never enjoyed the relief from active service which old age brings to most men, but because of their noble birth and their prowess in war they were constantly summoned to take up new commands.

2. Marcellus was a trained and expert soldier in every branch of fighting, but it was above all in single combat that he excelled: he never declined a challenge and he killed every opponent who challenged him. In Sicily he saved the life of his brother Otacilius,[6] when he was in mortal danger, by covering him with his shield and killing his attackers. For these exploits he was awarded crowns and other decorations by the commanders, although he was still only a young man, and as his reputation increased, the people elected him to the office of curule aedile,[7] and the priests chose him to be an augur. This is the priesthood to which the law assigns as one of its most important functions the observation and study of signs and significations arising from the flight of birds.[8]

While he was aedile he was obliged to bring a disagreeable accusation before the senate. He had a son, also named Marcus, who was just then in the flower of his youthful beauty, and who was admired by his fellow-countrymen as much for his modesty and his exemplary upbringing as for his good looks. Marcellus' colleague, Capitolinus,[9] a dissolute man whose passions were as shameless as they were uncontrolled, tried to seduce him. The boy at first repelled his advances by himself, but when they were repeated, he confided in his father. Marcellus was furious and denounced the man before the senate. Capitolinus tried by various shifts and evasions to quibble his way out of the charge, then appealed to the tribunes of the people and finally, when they rejected his plea, flatly denied the accusation. As there had been no witnesses of his behaviour, the senate decided to send for the boy. When he appeared before them and they saw how he blushed and wept, and how his feelings of shame were mingled with an unquenchable indignation, they decided that no further proof was necessary, but immediately condemned Capitolinus and fined him. Marcellus used the money from the fine to commission some silver libation bowls and dedicated these to the gods.

3. After the First Punic War had ended in its twenty-second year, Rome once more found herself engaged in a struggle with the Gauls.[10] The Insubrians were a Celtic people inhabiting the

part of Italy which lies at the foot of the Alps, and although they were strong in numbers, they not only mobilized their own forces, but called in the help of the Gallic mercenaries known as the Gaesati.[11]

It seemed to be a piece of miraculously good fortune for Rome that this Gallic war did not break out while the struggle with Carthage was still in progress, but that the Gauls, like a third competitor, sat on one side awaiting their turn and remained scrupulously inactive while the other two nations fought each other, and only then stripped for action when the victors were ready to receive their challenge. But even so the prospect of the war aroused the deepest fears among the Romans, partly because they would be engaging an enemy who lived so near their own frontiers and homes, and partly because of the traditional renown of the Gauls, whom the Romans seem to have feared more than any other enemy. The Romans never forgot that it was this people who had once captured their city, and afterwards they had passed a law that their priests should normally be exempt from military service, the exception being in the event of a fresh invasion by the Gauls.[12] They gave further proof of their fears in their exceptional preparations for the war, for it is said that never before nor since were so many thousands of Romans called upon to bear arms at once, and also in the extraordinary sacrifices which they offered to the gods.

The Romans do not practise any barbarous or outlandish rites, and in the humane sentiments which they cherish towards their divinities they come nearer than any other people to the Greeks. Nevertheless, at the outbreak of this war they felt obliged to carry out certain oracular instructions laid down in the Sibylline Books,[13] and to bury alive two Greeks – a man and a woman – and likewise two Gauls in the place known as the Cattle-market;[14] and in accordance with these oracles they still to this day in the month of November perform certain ceremonies, which may not be spoken of or witnessed by either Greeks or Gauls.[15]

4. The opening battles of this war brought great victories and also great disasters to the Romans, but none of these proved

decisive, until the two consuls Flaminius and Furius[16] led a strong army against the Insubrians. Just as they set out, however, the river which flows through Picenum[17] was seen to be running with blood; it was reported that three moons had been seen at the city of Ariminum,[18] and at the same time the augurs, whose duty it was to observe the flight of birds during the consular elections, insisted that the omens had been inauspicious and hostile at the moment when the victorious candidates' names had been announced. Thereupon, the senate immediately had letters dispatched to the camp in which they summoned the consuls to return to the city as quickly as possible to lay down their office,[19] and forbade them to undertake any action against the enemy so long as they remained in authority.

When these letters were delivered, Flaminius refused to open them until he had first engaged the barbarians, routed them in battle and overrun their territory. For this reason, when he returned to Rome laden with great quantities of booty, the people would not go out to meet him. Instead, because he had not immediately complied with the order recalling him, but had disobeyed the letters and treated them with insolent contempt, the people came near to denying him the honour of a triumph, and as soon as he had celebrated it, they compelled both him and his colleague to lay down the consulship and they reduced him to the rank of private citizen.[20] Such were the scruples of the Romans in referring all their affairs to the will of the gods, nor would they tolerate the smallest oversight in the observation of omens and traditional rites, even if the omission were followed by the most brilliant successes. In short, they regarded it as more important for the safety of the state that their magistrates should honour religious observances than that they should defeat their enemies.

5. An example of their belief is the case of Tiberius Sempronius,[21] a man whose reputation for courage and upright conduct was second to none in Rome, and who announced the names of Scipio Nasica and Gaius Marcius[22] as his successors in the consulship. After these two men had arrived in their provinces and taken up command of their armies, Sempronius came by chance

upon a book which specified the various religious ceremonials, and discovered in it an instruction of which he had never even heard before. It was this. Whenever a consul has hired a house or a tent outside the city walls for the purpose of sitting there and taking the auspices by observing the flight of birds, and he is obliged for any reason to return to the city before sure signs have appeared, he must give up the house which he originally hired and take another, and must begin all his observations afresh.[23] Tiberius had apparently been unaware of this instruction and had twice used the same house before proclaiming as consuls the men whose names I have mentioned. When he discovered his error he reported the matter to the senate. The senate decided that they could not treat even such a minor act of negligence lightly, but sent out letters to the consuls, who in turn immediately left their provinces, returned to Rome with all speed and resigned their appointments.

This took place at a later date. But, at about the same time as the episode of Flaminius, there are the examples of two priests of the noblest families who were deprived of their offices: Cornelius Cethegus,[24] because he failed to observe the proper procedure in presenting the entrails of a victim, and Quintus Sulpicius,[25] because, while he was sacrificing, the peaked cap, which is worn by the priests who are known as *flamines*,[26] had fallen off his head. Again, because the squeak of a shrew-mouse (which the Romans call a *sorex*) was heard at the moment when Minucius the dictator[27] was appointing Gaius Flaminius[28] as his master of the horse, the people thereupon deprived both men of their positions and put others in their places. Yet although they were so scrupulous in observing these minute details, they did not indulge in any kind of superstition, because they never permitted any change or departure from their ancient rites.

6. To return to our narrative. When Flaminius and his colleague Furius had resigned their offices, Marcellus was chosen as consul by the so-called *interreges*,[29] and after taking up the office he nominated Gnaeus Cornelius as his colleague.[30] Now we read that, although the Gauls put forward a number of con-

ciliatory proposals and although the senate was in favour of concluding peace, Marcellus stirred up the people's indignation so as to persuade them to continue the war.[31] In spite of this it appears that a peace was made, and that the Gaesati broke it when they crossed the Alps and stirred up the Insubrians.[32] The Gaesati mustered 30,000 men, while the Insubrians' numbers were even larger, and since they were now full of confidence in their strength, they immediately marched against Acerrae,[33] a town which was situated to the north of the River Po. Having arrived in this region, their king Britomartus[34] detached a force of 10,000 Gaesati and proceeded to ravage the country in the neighbourhood of the Po.

When this news reached Marcellus, he left his colleague at Acerrae in command of all the heavy-infantry and a third of the cavalry. Then, taking with him the rest of the cavalry and 600 of the most agile of his light infantry, he marched day and night without a halt until he came up with the 10,000 Gaesati near Clastidium,[35] a Gallic village which had submitted to Roman rule not long before. There was no time for him to rest or refresh his troops, since his arrival was quickly discovered by the barbarians. They felt nothing but contempt for his tiny force of infantry, and, since they were Gauls, had no great opinion of the Roman cavalry. The Gauls are particularly formidable at fighting on horseback, and in fact they have the reputation of excelling in this arm above any other, while on this occasion they also greatly outnumbered Marcellus. Headed by their king and shouting blood-curdling threats at the tops of their voices, they immediately launched a furious charge, expecting to sweep the Romans away.

But Marcellus was determined to prevent them from outflanking and encircling his small force; as he led his cavalry forward he made them fan out, and so extended his wings into a thin line until he was almost in contact with the enemy. Then, just as he was turning to launch a charge, his horse, startled by the enemy's ferocious shouts, suddenly wheeled about and carried him to the rear. Marcellus was alarmed that this sight might be taken as a bad omen and create confusion among the Romans, so he at once reined his horse to the left and forced the animal to face the enemy. At the same time he went through the movements of praying to the sun, as if it was for this purpose that he had wheeled around his horse, for the Romans always turn in this way when they offer worship to the gods.[36] Then just before he closed with the enemy, he is said to have vowed that he would consecrate to Jupiter Feretrius[37] the finest suit of armour to be found among the Gauls.

7. It was now that the king of the Gauls first saw Marcellus. He guessed from his badges of rank that this was the Roman commander, and, riding far out in front of his men, he made directly for him, shouting out a challenge and brandishing his lance. He stood out among the rest of the Gauls, not only for his size but for his complete suit of armour, which was embossed with gold and silver and decorated with brilliant colours and elaborate designs, so that it glittered like lightning. As Marcellus glanced along the enemy's ranks, he thought that this was the finest armour of all, and concluded that it must be the offering which he had vowed to the god. So he charged the Gaul and pierced his breastplate with his lance; the impetus of his horse hurled his opponent to the ground still living, and a second and a third blow immediately dispatched him. Thereupon, Marcellus leapt from his horse and, laying his hands on the dead man's armour, he gazed up to heaven and cried aloud: 'Jupiter Feretrius, you who judge the great deeds of generals and captains in war and on the battlefield, I call upon you to witness that I, a Roman general and a consul, have killed with my own hand a general and a king, that I am the third Roman commander to do this,[38] and that I dedicate to you the first and the finest of the spoils. I pray that you will grant us no less good fortune as we fight out the rest of the war.'

As he ended his prayer, the Roman cavalry charged and found themselves engaging not only the Gallic horsemen but also their supporting infantry, who attacked them at the same time. But in the end they won a victory which was as unparalleled as it was unexpected. Never before nor since, so we are told, had so few mounted troops overcome such a large combined force of cavalry and infantry. The Gauls lost the greater part of their army, and their weapons and baggage were captured, after which Marcellus returned to join his colleague, who was holding out with difficulty against another Gallic army in the neighbourhood of their largest and most populous city. This was Mediolanum,[39] which the Cisalpine Gauls regard as the capital of their country, and they defended it with such spirit that Cornelius found his army had become the besieged rather than the besiegers. However, when Marcellus arrived and the Gaesati learned that their king had been defeated and killed, they retired to their own territory. Mediolanum was captured and the Gauls surrendered the rest of their cities of their own accord and offered their submission to the Romans. They were granted peace on equitable terms.

8. The senate decreed that only Marcellus should be granted a triumph. His procession produced a superb spectacle such as has seldom been seen in Rome, both for the splendour and riches of the spoils of war and for the gigantic size of the prisoners. But the most unusual and impressive sight of all was that of the general himself, when he appeared to carry the barbarian king's armour as an offering to the god. He had cut the tall, straight trunk of a young oak tree, trimmed it into the shape of a trophy, and upon this he had fastened and hung the spoils, with each part of the armour arranged in its proper position. When the procession began to move, he took up the tree himself, mounted his four-horse chariot and in this way an image of victory, the finest and most glorious ever seen in his day, was borne in state through the city. His troops followed, clad in their most brilliant armour, and as they marched they sang odes composed for the occasion and paeans of victory in honour of the god and their general. In this way Marcellus traversed the city until he reached the temple of Jupiter Feretrius, where he dismounted and dedicated his offering.

He was the third, and, up to our day, the last Roman to achieve this feat. The first was Romulus, who offered up the spoils of Acron of Caenina;[40] the second was Cornelius Cossus with the spoils of Tolumnius[41] the Etruscan; after them Marcellus with the spoils of Britomartus, king of the Gauls; and since

Marcellus there has been no one. The god to whom the spoils
were dedicated is called Jupiter Feretrius. Some people say that
this surname is derived from *pheretron*, referring to the *car* in
which the trophy was carried. The word is Greek, like many
others which had at that time been absorbed into Latin.[42]
Others say that the epithet refers to Jupiter as the wielder of the
thunderbolt, since *ferire* is the Latin word which means *to
strike*. Another explanation is that the word is derived from a
blow given to the enemy, because even down to the present day,
when the Romans are pursuing their enemies, they encourage
one another by shouting the word *feri*, meaning *strike!* The
word for spoils in general is *spolia*, but these particular spoils
are known as *spolia opima*.[43] It has been pointed out, however,
that Numa Pompilius in his commentaries[44] mentions three categories of *opima*. He lays it down that those of the first degree
are to be consecrated to Jupiter Feretrius, those of the second
to Mars, and those of the third to Quirinus, and also that the
reward for the first is to be 300 asses,[45] for the second 200, and
for the third 100. However, the most generally accepted account
is that the only spoils which rank as *opima* are those which are
captured in a pitched battle before the fighting begins, when
the general kills the opposing commander with his own hand.
So much then for this subject.

The Roman people were so overjoyed at this victory and at
the ending of the war that they sent the Pythian Apollo at Delphi a golden bowl as a thank-offering.[46] They also presented a
generous share of the spoils to the allied cities, and sent many
gifts to Hiero[47] the ruler of Syracuse, who was their friend
and ally.

9. After Hannibal had invaded Italy,[48] Marcellus was sent to
Sicily in command of a fleet.[49] Then came the disastrous defeat
at Cannae,[50] in which thousands of Romans were killed and
only a few saved their lives by fleeing to Canusium.[51] Everyone
expected that Hannibal would immediately march on the capital, now that he had destroyed the flower of the Roman army.
At this point Marcellus dispatched 1,500 men from his fleet to
help to defend Rome, and then, under orders from the senate,

he went to Canusium, collected the soldiers who had taken refuge there and made a sortie from their fortified camp to show Hannibal that he had no intention of abandoning the surrounding countryside.

By this time the Romans had lost the greater number of their generals and prominent men in battle, while Fabius Maximus,[52] who had earned the highest reputation for his reliability and shrewdness of judgement, was blamed for his excessive caution, and his anxiety to avoid losses at any cost was attacked as mere cowardly passivity. The people regarded him as a general who was perfectly qualified to carry on a defensive campaign, but who could never move over to the offensive. They therefore turned to Marcellus, and, in the hope of combining his boldness and energy with Fabius' caution and foresight, they sometimes elected both as consuls together[53] and sometimes sent out one as consul and the other as proconsul. Poseidonius says that Fabius was called the shield and Marcellus the sword of Rome. And indeed, Hannibal himself declared that he feared Fabius as a pedagogue[54] and Marcellus as an opponent. The first prevented him from inflicting losses on the Romans; the second inflicted them on him.[55]

10. One of the first consequences of Hannibal's victory at Cannae was that his troops became over-confident and careless of their discipline. Scattered groups of men would leave their camp and roam the countryside in search of plunder, whereupon Marcellus would swoop down and cut off these stragglers, and in this way he gradually weakened the Carthaginian army. Secondly, he did much to relieve the situation of Neapolis and of Nola.[56] In Neapolis he strengthened the resolution of the citizens, who were already staunch allies of Rome by their own choice. Nola, on the other hand, he found in a far more unsettled state, since the senate[57] was unable either to control or to win over the people, who wished to ally themselves with Hannibal.

One of Nola's leading citizens, who was prominent not only for his aristocratic birth but also for his bravery in the field, was a man named Bandius.[58] He had shown the greatest courage in fighting for the Romans at Cannae, where he had killed many Carthaginians, and when he was at last found among the heaps of the dead with his body riddled with barbs, Hannibal felt so much admiration for his gallantry that he not only released him without a ransom, but presented him with gifts of his own accord and entertained him as a personal friend. In return for this generous treatment, Bandius became one of Hannibal's more ardent supporters, and proceeded to use all his influence to make the people revolt against Rome.

Marcellus felt that it would be a crime to put to death a man of such brilliant achievements, who had fought side by side with the Romans in their greatest battles; and in addition to his natural kindliness of manner he possessed the knack of winning the confidence of men who are dedicated to the pursuit of honour. So, one day when Bandius greeted him, he asked him who he was. Of course Marcellus knew this perfectly well, but he wanted an excuse to strike up a conversation with him. Then, when the man answered 'Lucius Bandius', Marcellus, pretending to be surprised and delighted, exclaimed: 'What, are you the same Lucius Bandius who is more talked of in Rome than any other man who fought at Cannae – the only soldier, so they say, who did not abandon Aemilius Paullus,[59] the consul, but received in your own body most of the spears and arrows that were aimed at him?' When Bandius answered that he *was* the man and showed Marcellus some of his scars, the general went on: 'Well then, since you carry with you all these marks of your devotion to Rome, why did you not come to us at once? Do you think that we are slow to reward such courage in our friends, when even our enemies go out of their way to honour it?' After paying Bandius these compliments he embraced him, and soon afterwards presented him with a war horse and 500 silver drachmas.

11. After this Bandius became a staunch supporter and ally of Marcellus, and played an important part in tracking down and denouncing the activities of Hannibal's partisans. These were very numerous, and they organized a plot to seize the Roman baggage-train as soon as the army marched out against the

enemy. Marcellus therefore marshalled his troops inside the city, had the baggage placed near the various gates and then issued a proclamation forbidding the citizens of Nola to approach the walls. In this way he made sure that there were no armed men to be seen, and Hannibal was tricked into leading his troops up to the walls without first putting them into battle order, as he supposed that fighting was going on inside the city.

At this moment Marcellus ordered the gate behind which he was waiting to be thrown open. He had his best cavalry formations with him, and immediately launched them against the enemy. Soon after, his infantry sallied forth from another gate, and with loud shouts bore down upon the Carthaginians at the run. Finally, while Hannibal was regrouping his forces to meet these attacks, a third gate was flung open, and through this the remainder of the Roman army poured out and attacked the enemy on all sides. This unexpected onslaught threw the Carthaginians into confusion, and they put up only a weak resistance against the first attack, because of the troops they could see in the distance bearing down upon them. Hannibal's troops were driven back to their camp with heavy losses both in killed and wounded, the first occasion on which they had ever been put to flight by the Romans. It is said that more than 5,000 of them lost their lives against a bare 500 on the Roman side; Livy, however, does not consider that the Carthaginians suffered a major defeat in this battle, nor does he say that they lost so many men, but he confirms that the victory brought great prestige to Marcellus, and had a wonderful effect in raising the spirits of the Romans after the disasters they had suffered.[60] They could now feel that they were faced not by an invincible and irresistible enemy, but by one who was just as liable to suffer a defeat as themselves.

12. It was for this reason that when one of the consuls was killed,[61] the people called upon Marcellus to take his place. They did this even though he was absent from Rome at the time, and, in spite of the wishes of the magistrates, they postponed the election until he could return from the army. When

he arrived, he was elected consul by a unanimous vote. But it so happened that a peal of thunder was heard at that moment, and the augurs regarded this as an inauspicious omen. However, their fear of the people was such that they did not dare to oppose his election openly, and so Marcellus himself voluntarily resigned his office.[62] But this did not mean that he laid down his military command; instead, he was created proconsul, returned to Nola and began to take action there against the party which had sided with the Carthaginians.

When Hannibal hurried to Nola to rescue his supporters and tried to bring about a pitched battle, Marcellus refused to be drawn; but as soon as Hannibal had allowed the greater part of his force to disperse on various plundering raids, and was no longer expecting a battle, the Romans made a sortie and attacked him. Marcellus had armed his infantry with the long spears which are used in naval fighting, and had taught them to watch for their opportunity and hurl their weapons at the enemy from long range, as the Carthaginians were not trained in throwing the javelin and carried only short spears for hand-to-hand fighting. These tactics seem to have produced remarkable results. All the Carthaginians who were engaged in this battle with the Romans turned tail and fled at once. They lost 5,000 dead and 6,000 prisoners, while four of their elephants were killed and two captured alive. But the most significant event of all was that on the third day after the battle more than 300 Spanish and Numidian horsemen deserted to the Romans. This was the first time that Hannibal had ever experienced such a disaster, for although he commanded a barbarian army composed of many separate and diverse nationalities, he had succeeded year after year in preserving a spirit which united all the troops serving under him. Nevertheless, the men who deserted to the Romans remained completely loyal for the rest of the war both to Marcellus and to the generals who succeeded him.

13. In the following year,[63] after Marcellus had been elected consul for the third time, he sailed to Sicily. Hannibal's successes in Italy had encouraged the Carthaginians to make another attempt to recover the island, especially as the affairs

of Syracuse had been thrown into confusion after the death of the tyrant Hieronymus.[64] Indeed, the situation there had already compelled the Romans to dispatch an army under the praetor Appius Claudius.[65]

As soon as Marcellus had taken over the command of this force, great numbers of Romans, whose predicament I shall now describe, presented themselves at his camp to petition him. Of the Roman army which had faced Hannibal at Cannae, some had fled from the battlefield, while so many had been taken prisoner that it was believed that the Romans did not have enough men left to defend the walls of the capital. Yet in spite of this, the citizens' resolve remained so firm and their spirit so unconquerable that although Hannibal offered to release his prisoners of war for a small ransom, the people voted against their return. Instead, they allowed some to be put to death and others to be sold into slavery outside Italy. As for the large numbers of survivors who had saved themselves by running away, they sent them to Sicily and forbade them to set foot again in Italy so long as the war against Hannibal lasted. These were the men who crowded around Marcellus as soon as he arrived, threw themselves at his feet and implored him with tears and lamentations to admit them once more to honourable military service: they swore they would prove by their actions that the defeat they had suffered had been caused by misfortune not by cowardice. Marcellus took pity on them and wrote to the senate asking for permission to enlist these men so as to make up the losses in his own army as they occurred. A lengthy debate followed, at the end of which the senate's verdict was that the Romans did not need the services of cowards, but that if Marcellus nevertheless wished to employ them, they must not be awarded any of the usual honours or prizes for valour. This decree angered Marcellus, and when he returned to Rome after the end of the war in Sicily, he reproached the senate because they had not allowed him in consideration of his many great services to rescue this large body of citizens from their wretched situation.

14. But to return to the campaign in Sicily. Marcellus was first of all confronted with an outrage committed by Hippocrates,

a general of the Syracusans.[66] This man, in order to secure the support of the Carthaginians and make himself tyrant, slaughtered many of the Romans living in Leontini, whereupon Marcellus stormed and captured the city.[67] He did no harm to the native inhabitants, but ordered all the deserters whom he captured to be flogged and put to death.[68] At this Hippocrates first sent a report to Syracuse that Marcellus was massacring all the men of Leontini, and when this rumour had created a panic in the city, he suddenly attacked and captured it. Marcellus responded by moving his whole army up to Syracuse. He encamped close by and sent envoys into the city to give the people the true account of what had happened at Leontini, but this manoeuvre proved ineffective and the Syracusans refused to listen, because Hippocrates and his supporters were now in control.

Marcellus' next action was to attack the city by land and sea simultaneously, the land forces being commanded by Appius, while Marcellus directed a fleet of sixty quinquiremes, which were equipped with many different kinds of weapons and missiles. In addition, he had built a siege-engine, which was mounted on a huge platform supported by eight galleys lashed together,[69] and with this he sailed up to the city walls, confident that the size and the imposing spectacle of his armament, together with his personal prestige, would combine to overawe the Syracusans.

But he had reckoned without Archimedes, and the Roman machines turned out to be insignificant not only in the philosopher's estimation, but also by comparison with those which he had constructed himself. Archimedes did not regard his military inventions as an achievement of any importance, but merely as a by-product – which he occasionally pursued for his own amusement – of his serious work, namely, the study of geometry. He had done this in the past because Hiero, the former ruler of Syracuse, had often pressed and finally persuaded him to divert his studies from the pursuit of abstract principles to the solution of practical problems, and to make his theories more intelligible to the majority of mankind by applying them through the medium of the senses to the needs of everyday life.

It was Eudoxus and Archytas[70] who were the originators of the now celebrated and highly prized art of mechanics. They used it with great ingenuity to illustrate geometrical theorems, and to support propositions too intricate for proof by word or diagram by means of mechanical demonstrations easily grasped by the senses. For example, to solve the problem of finding two mean proportional lines, which are necessary for the construction of many other geometrical figures,[71] both mathematicians resorted to mechanical means,[72] and adapted to their purposes certain instruments that are essentially rulers that slide and bend and are thus able to construct conic sections. Plato was indignant at these developments, and attacked both men for having corrupted and destroyed the ideal purity of geometry.[73] He complained that they had caused her to forsake the realm of disembodied and abstract thought for that of material objects, and to employ instruments which required much base and manual labour. For this reason mechanics came to be separated from geometry, and as the subject was for a long time disregarded by philosophers, it took its place among the military arts.

However this may be, Archimedes in writing to Hiero, who was both a relative[74] and a friend of his, asserted that with any given force it was possible to move any given weight, and then, carried away with enthusiasm at the power of his demonstration, so we are told, went on to enlarge his claim, and declared that if he were given another world to stand on, he could move the earth. Hiero was amazed, and invited him to put his theorem into practice and show him some great weight moved by a tiny force. Archimedes chose for his demonstration a three-masted merchantman of the royal fleet, which had been hauled ashore with immense labour by a large gang of men, and he proceeded to have the ship loaded with her usual freight and embarked a large number of passengers. He then seated himself at some distance away and without using any noticeable force, but merely exerting traction with his hand through a complex system of pulleys, he drew the vessel towards him with as smooth and even a motion as if she were gliding through the water. The king was deeply impressed, and recognizing the

potentialities of his skill, he persuaded Archimedes to construct
for him a number of engines designed both for attack and
defence, which could be employed in any kind of siege-warfare.
Hiero himself never had occasion to use these, since most of his
life was spent at peace amid festivals and public ceremonies,
but when the present war broke out, the apparatus was ready
for the Syracusans to use and its inventor was at hand to direct
its employment.

15. When the Romans first attacked by sea and land, the Syracusans were struck dumb with terror and believed that nothing
could resist the onslaught of such powerful forces. But presently Archimedes brought his engines to bear and launched a
tremendous barrage against the Roman army. This consisted of
a variety of missiles, including a great volley of stones which
descended upon their target with an incredible noise and velocity. There was no protection against this artillery, and the
soldiers were knocked down in swathes and their ranks thrown
into confusion. At the same time huge beams were run out
from the walls so as to project over the Roman ships; some of
them were then sunk by great weights dropped from above,
while others were seized at the bows by iron claws or by beaks
like those of cranes, hauled into the air by means of counter-
weights until they stood upright upon their sterns, and then
allowed to plunge to the bottom – or else they were spun round
by means of windlasses situated inside the city and dashed
against the steep cliffs and rocks which jutted out under the
walls, with great loss of life to the crews. Often there would be
seen the terrifying spectacle of a ship being lifted clean out of
the water into the air and whirled about as it hung there, until
every man had been shaken out of the hull and thrown in different directions, after which it would be dashed down empty
upon the walls. As for the enormous siege-engine which Marcellus brought up, mounted on eight galleys as I have described,
and known as a *sambuca* because of its resemblance to the
musical instrument of that name,[75] a stone weighing 10 talents[76] was discharged while it was still approaching the city
wall, immediately followed by a second and a third. These

descended on their target with a thunderous crash and a great surge of water shattered the platform on which the machine was mounted, loosened the bolts which held it together and dislodged the whole framework from the hulks that supported it. Marcellus, finding his plan of attack thus brought to a standstill, drew off his ships as quickly as possible and ordered his land forces to retire.

After this he held a council of war and formed a new plan to move up as closely as possible to the walls under cover of darkness. The Romans calculated that the cables which Archimedes used for his siege-engines imparted such a tremendous velocity to the missiles they discharged that these would go flying over their heads, but that at close quarters, where a low trajectory was required, they would be ineffective. However, Archimedes, it seems, had long ago foreseen such a possibility and had designed engines which were suitable for any distance and missiles to match them. He had had a large number of loopholes made in the walls, and in these he placed short-range weapons known as *scorpions*,[77] which were invisible to the attacker, but could be discharged as soon as he arrived at close quarters.

16. So when the Romans crept up to the walls expecting to surprise the enemy, they were again greeted by a hail of missiles. Huge stones were dropped on them almost perpendicularly, and it seemed as if they were faced by a curtain of darts along the whole length of the wall, so that the attackers soon fell back. But here, too, even while they were hurrying, as they hoped, out of danger, they came under fire from the medium-range catapults which caused heavy losses among them; at the same time, many of their ships were dashed against one another, and all this while they were helpless to retaliate. Archimedes had mounted most of his weapons under the cover of the city walls, and the Romans began to believe that they were fighting against a supernatural enemy, as they found themselves constantly struck down by opponents whom they could never see.

17. Marcellus, however, escaped unhurt from this assault and afterwards made fun of his own siege experts and engineers.

'We may as well give up fighting this geometrical Briareus',[78] he said, 'who uses our ships like cups to ladle water out of the sea, who has whipped our *sambuca* and driven her off in disgrace,[79] and who can outdo the hundred-handed giants of mythology in hurling so many different missiles at us at once.' For the truth was that all the rest of the Syracusans merely provided the manpower to operate Archimedes' inventions, and it was his mind which directed and controlled every manoeuvre. All other weapons were discarded, and it was upon his alone that the city relied both for attack and defence. At last, the Romans were reduced to such a state of alarm that if they saw so much as a length of rope or a piece of timber appear over the top of the wall, it was enough to make them cry out, 'Look, Archimedes is aiming one of his machines at us!' and they would turn their backs and run. When Marcellus saw this, he abandoned all attempts to capture the city by assault, and settled down to reduce it by blockade.

As for Archimedes, he was a man who possessed such exalted ideals, such profound spiritual vision and such a wealth of scientific knowledge that, although his inventions had earned him a reputation for almost superhuman intellectual power, he would not deign to leave behind him any writings on his mechanical discoveries.[80] He regarded the business of engineering, and indeed of every art which ministers to the material needs of life, as an ignoble and sordid activity, and he concentrated his ambition exclusively upon those speculations whose beauty and subtlety are untainted by the claims of necessity. These studies, he believed, are incomparably superior to any others, since here the grandeur and beauty of the subject matter vie for our admiration with the cogency and precision of the methods of proof.

Certainly, in the whole science of geometry, it is impossible to find more difficult and intricate problems handled in simpler and purer terms than in his works. Some writers attribute this to his natural genius. Others maintain that a phenomenal industry lay behind the apparently effortless ease with which he obtained his results. The fact is that no amount of mental effort of his own would enable a man to hit upon the proof of one of Archimedes' theorems, and yet as soon as it is explained to him, he feels that he might have discovered it himself, so smooth and rapid is the path by which Archimedes leads us to the required conclusion. So it is not at all difficult to credit some of the stories which have been told about him: of how, for example, he often seemed so bewitched by the song of some inner and familiar Siren that he would forget to eat his food or take care of his person; or how, when he was carried by force, as he often was, to the bath for his body to be washed and anointed, he would trace geometrical figures in the ashes and draw diagrams with his finger in the oil which had been rubbed over his skin. Such was the rapture which his work inspired in him, so as to make him truly the captive of the Muses. And although he was responsible for many discoveries of great value, he is said to have asked his friends and relatives to place on his tomb after his death nothing more than the shape of a cylinder enclosing a sphere, with an inscription explaining the ratio by which the containing solid exceeds the contained.[81]

18. Such was Archimedes' character, and in so far as it rested with him, he kept himself and his city unconquered. But while Syracuse was being blockaded, Marcellus did not remain idle. He captured Megara,[82] one of the most ancient of the Greek settlements in Sicily, and he also stormed Hippocrates' camp at Acrillae,[83] and killed more than 8,000 of his men, launching his attacks while the enemy were still digging their entrenchments. Besides this, he overran a large part of Sicily, persuaded a number of cities to revolt from the Carthaginians and defeated his opponents wherever he encountered resistance.

Some while afterwards[84] he captured a man named Damippus,[85] a Spartan who had attempted to escape from Syracuse by ship. The Syracusans were anxious to ransom him, and during the numerous meetings and negotiations that followed, Marcellus noticed a particular tower which was carelessly guarded and into which he could infiltrate men unobserved, since the wall in its immediate vicinity was easy to climb. During his visits to parley with the Syracusans he had the height to the tower carefully measured and scaling ladders prepared.

Marcellus chose a moment when the Syracusans were celebrating a feast-day in honour of Artemis and had given themselves up to drinking and other festivities. Before they knew what he was about, he had not only seized the tower but also occupied the Hexapyla.[86] When the citizens discovered what had happened, and while they were running to and fro in confusion and attempting to muster their forces, Marcellus ordered his trumpets to be sounded from all sides at once. The Syracusans fled from the sound in terror and imagined that the whole city had already been captured. But in fact they still held Achradina, which is the largest, most handsome and most strongly defended quarter, because it had been fortified on the landward side, where it adjoins the other districts of the city, one part of which is known as Neapolis and the other as Tyche.[87]

19. When these districts had been captured, Marcellus made his entry at daybreak through the Hexapyla amid the congratulations of his officers. It is said that as he looked down from the heights upon the great and magnificent city below, he wept[88] as he thought of its impending fate, and of how its appearance would be transformed in a few hours' time when his army had sacked it. For his troops had demanded their plunder and not one of his officers dared to resist them. Indeed, many of them had urged that they should set fire to the city and raze it to the ground. Marcellus refused to tolerate this suggestion, but, much against his will, he allowed his men to carry off property and slaves. However, he gave strict orders that they must not lay a hand on free citizens, nor kill, outrage or enslave any Syracusan.

And yet, in spite of having shown such moderation, he felt that the city had been subjected to a pitiable fate, and even in the moment of triumph he was filled with sorrow and compassion as he saw the brilliant prosperity of so many generations being swept away in a few short hours. It is said that as much wealth was carried away from Syracuse as was taken at a later date from Carthage. Not long afterwards, the rest of the city was captured by treachery and given over to plunder, except for the royal property, which was handed over to the Roman treasury.[89]

But what distressed Marcellus most of all was the death of Archimedes. As fate would have it, the philosopher was by himself, engrossed in working out some calculation by means of a diagram, and his eyes and his thoughts were so intent upon the problem that he was completely unaware that the Romans had broken through the defences, or that the city had been captured. Suddenly, a soldier came upon him and ordered him to accompany him to Marcellus. Archimedes refused to move until he had worked out his problem and established his demonstration, whereupon the soldier flew into a rage, drew his sword and killed him. According to another account, the Roman came up with a drawn sword and threatened to kill him there and then; when Archimedes saw him, he begged him to stay his hand for a moment, so that he should not leave his theorem imperfect and without its demonstration, but the soldier paid no attention and dispatched him at once. There is yet a third story to the effect that Archimedes was on his way to Marcellus bringing some of his instruments, such as sundials and spheres and quadrants, with the help of which the magnitude of the sun could be perceived by the naked eye, when some soldiers met him, and, believing that he was carrying gold in the box, promptly killed him. At any rate, it is generally agreed that Marcellus was deeply affected by his death, that he abhorred the man who had killed him as if he had committed an act of sacrilege and that he sought out Archimedes' relatives and treated them with honour.

20. The Romans were regarded by other peoples as masters of the art of war and formidable adversaries on the battlefield, but they had so far given little indication that they could show kindness or humanity or the civil virtues in general, and Marcellus seems to have been the first to demonstrate to the Greeks that the Romans possessed a stronger sense of justice than they themselves. He behaved with such fairness to all who came into contact with him, and conferred so many benefits upon cities and private individuals that, if the peoples of Enna[90] or Megara or Syracuse were subjected to any harsh treatment, it was generally believed that the fault for this lay with the vanquished rather than the victors.

Here I will quote one example out of many. There is a Sicilian town named Engyium, which is of no great size, but is very ancient and is celebrated because of the appearance there of the goddesses who are known as the Mothers.[91] Tradition had it that the local temple was built by Cretans, and the people used to keep on show there a number of spears and bronze helmets, some of them inscribed with the name of Meriones,[92] and others with that of Ulysses (which is to say, Odysseus), who are reputed to have dedicated these to the goddesses. The people were ardent supporters of the Carthaginians, but their most prominent citizen, whose name was Nicias, did his utmost to persuade them to go over to the Romans, arguing his case in bold and outspoken language in the public assembly, and attacking his opponents' policy as unsound. His enemies became alarmed at his growing influence and prestige, and planned to kidnap him and hand him over to the Carthaginians.

Nicias soon became aware of their plot and of the fact that he was being secretly watched, and so he purposely let fall in public a number of irreverent references to the Mothers, and went out of his way to show that he could neither believe in the generally accepted legend about their appearances nor even respect it. This action delighted his enemies, since he seemed to be providing them with excellent grounds for the punishment they had in store for him. But just as they had completed their preparations to seize him, a public assembly was held, and during the debate, while Nicias was actually offering some advice to the people, he suddenly threw himself to the ground. Then, after waiting for a few moments amid the silence and astonishment which naturally followed this action, he raised his head, turned it about and began to speak in a low and trembling tone, which little by little he made shriller and more intense. Finally, when he saw that the whole assembly had been struck dumb with horror, he threw off his cloak, tore open his tunic and, leaping up half-naked, rushed towards the exit of the theatre, crying out that he was pursued by the Mothers. So strong was his fellow-citizens' awe of the gods that not one of them dared to lay a hand on him or stand in his path. Instead, everyone made way for him as he dashed to the city gates, imitating as he ran the shrieks and gestures that might be expected of a man who was possessed and out of his wits. At the same time his wife, who had been let into the secret and was helping him play his part, took her children with her and prostrated herself as a suppliant before the shrines of the goddesses. Then, under pretence of looking for her husband as he wandered about the countryside, she made her way safely out of the city without any hindrance, and in this way they all escaped to Marcellus' camp at Syracuse.

The leading men of Engyium went on to insult the Romans and commit various acts of hostility against them, and at length Marcellus captured the town, had the people put in chains and was about to execute them. At this point Nicias, who was standing by, burst into tears and clasping Marcellus' hands and knees pleaded with him to spare the lives of his fellow-countrymen, beginning with his enemies. Marcellus relented, set them all free and refrained from punishing their city, while he also presented Nicias with a large estate and a number of gifts. At least this is the story which we have from Poseidonius[93] the philosopher.

21. When the Romans recalled Marcellus to carry on the war against Hannibal[94] in Italy, he took back with him most of the statues and other offerings which the Syracusans had dedicated to the gods, including their finest works of art, for he intended that these should not only decorate his triumph but also adorn the capital. Before this date Rome neither possessed nor, indeed, was even aware of such elegant and exquisite creations, nor was there any taste for a graceful and delicate art of this kind. Instead, the city was filled with the bloodstained arms and spoils of barbarian tribes, and crowned with the monuments and trophies of victorious campaigns, so that to the unwarlike visitor or the aesthete she offered almost nothing to gladden or reassure the eye. Indeed, just as Epaminondas[95] speaks of the Boeotian plain as 'a dancing-floor of Ares',[96] and Xenophon refers to Ephesus as 'an arsenal of war',[97] so it seems to me that one might have summed up the Rome of those days in Pindar's phrase as 'a sanctuary of Ares who revels in war'.[98]

At any rate, Marcellus greatly pleased the common people, because he adorned the capital with works of art which possessed the Hellenic grace and charm and truth to nature. On the other hand, it was Fabius Maximus who earned the approval of the older generation, because after he had captured Tarentum he neither disturbed nor removed a single monument of this kind. He carried off all the money and valuables which had belonged to the city, but allowed all the statues to remain in their places, and on this occasion made the remark which has since become famous: 'Let us leave the Tarentines these angry gods of theirs!'[99] Such people blamed Marcellus in the first place for bringing discredit upon the name of Rome, because he paraded not only men but gods[100] like captives in his triumphal procession; and secondly, because hitherto the people had been accustomed to spend their time either in fighting or in agriculture and had never tasted luxury or leisure, so that their character had been as Euripides describes that of Heracles, 'rough, unpolished, but on great occasions noble'.[101] Now, on the contrary, he was teaching them to become lazy and glib connoisseurs of art and artists, so that they idled away the greater part of the day in clever and trivial chatter about aesthetics. In spite of such criticisms, Marcellus spoke with pride of what he had done and he liked to claim even to Greeks that he had taught the ignorant Romans to admire and honour the glories of Greek art.[102]

22. Marcellus' enemies opposed the granting of a triumph to him, on the grounds that the campaign in Sicily was not yet finished, and that a third triumph[103] would arouse undue envy. The general therefore gave way of his own free will and agreed to lead the main procession to the Alban Mount, and to enter the city only with the minor ceremony, which the Greeks call an *eua* and the Romans an *ovatio*.[104] The general who leads this does not ride in a four-horse chariot heralded by trumpets and wearing a crown of laurel, as happens in a major triumph, but walks in the procession in shoes, escorted by a large company of flute-players and wearing a crown of myrtle, so that his appearance is peaceable and friendly rather than menacing.

This is a clear proof, it seems to me, that in ancient times it was not so much the importance of a general's achievement as the manner in which he had accomplished it which decided whether a major triumph or an ovatio was granted him. Those who had conquered by fighting a battle and killing their enemies entered the city with the martial and awe-inspiring pomp of the formal triumph, after crowning their men and their weapons with abundant wreaths of laurel, as was also the custom whenever they purified the army with lustral rites. On the other hand the generals who had had no occasion to appeal to arms, but had brought everything to a successful issue by means of diplomacy, persuasion and negotiation were granted by the law the honour of conducting this peaceful and festive procession in the manner of a paean of thanksgiving. For the flute is an instrument of peace and the myrtle is beloved of Aphrodite, who of all the gods and goddesses is the most averse to violence and war.[105] The name of ovatio for this minor triumph is not derived from the Greek euasmos, as is generally supposed (for the major triumph is also accompanied by songs and cries of euae!), but the word has been twisted by the Greeks into a form that bears a meaning in their language, because they are convinced that the ceremony is also partly intended to honour Dionysus, among whose names are those of Euius and Thriambos. The true explanation, however, is a different one, namely, that it was customary for the general if taking part in the major triumph to sacrifice an ox, and if in the minor a sheep. Now the Latin for sheep is ovis and this is why the minor triumph is called ovatio.[106] It is also worth mentioning here that the instructions laid down by the lawgiver of Sparta are exactly the opposite of those observed by the Romans. In Sparta the returning general, if he had overcome the enemy by deception or persuasion, sacrificed an ox, and if by force of arms a cock.[107] For although the Spartans were the most warlike of peoples, they believed that an exploit achieved by means of argument and intelligence[108] was greater and more worthy of a human being than one effected by mere force and courage. As to which of these opinions is to be preferred, I leave it to the reader to decide.

23. While Marcellus was serving his fourth term as consul,[109] his enemies[110] persuaded the Syracusans to come to Rome, lay accusations against him and denounce him before the senate for having perpetrated terrible injustices contrary to the terms of their surrender. It so happened that when they arrived, Marcellus was engaged in performing a sacrifice on the Capitol, but as the senate was still sitting, the Syracusans immediately presented themselves before it and begged that their grievances might be heard and justice granted them. Marcellus' fellow-consul[111] was indignant that his colleague should be accused in his absence and tried to have them ejected from the chamber, but as soon as Marcellus heard of their arrival, he hurried to the senate-house. Then, seating himself as consul in his curule chair, he began to dispatch the regular business of the day. When this was finished, he came down from his chair, and taking his stand as a private citizen in the place where those who had been put on trial customarily offered their defence, he called upon the Syracusans to press their charges.[112]

The dignity and assurance of his manner thoroughly disconcerted them, and they were abashed to find that the man who had been irresistible in the field was still more formidable and unassailable in his consular robe of purple. But at length, with the encouragement of Marcellus' opponents, they began their impeachment and urged their plea for justice, in the course of which they indulged in much lamentation for the fate of their city. The substance of their complaint was that, in spite of their being friends and allies of the Roman people, they had suffered harsher treatment at Marcellus' hands than that which other generals had meted out even to conquered enemies. Marcellus retorted that they had committed many hostile acts against the Romans, for which they had received no punishment whatsoever, except for the kind of damage from which it is impossible to protect a population when a city is taken by storm. The fact that their city had been captured, he added, was due to their own wilful refusal of his repeated offers of terms. They certainly could not plead that they had been forced into war by tyrannical rulers, for they had themselves elected these very rulers with the object of going to war.

After both sides had been heard and the Syracusans, according to the usual custom, had withdrawn, Marcellus handed over the presidency of the senate to his colleague, left the chamber with his accusers and stood outside the doors. His appearance remained perfectly normal and showed not a trace of apprehension for the verdict nor of anger against the Syracusans: he simply waited with the utmost serenity and self-control to hear the outcome of the case. When the votes had been cast and he was declared not guilty, the Syracusans threw themselves at his feet. They implored him with tears in their eyes to put away his anger against the delegates before him and to take pity on the rest of the city, which never forgets a kindness and would henceforth be eternally grateful to him. Marcellus was moved by this appeal: he pardoned the envoys, and thereafter became a constant benefactor[113] to their city. He had already restored to them their freedom, the right to be governed by their own laws and what remained of their property, and these concessions were confirmed by the senate. In return, the people conferred many of their highest honours upon him, and in particular they passed a law that whenever Marcellus or any of his descendants should land in Sicily, the Syracusans should wear garlands and offer sacrifices to the gods.[114]

24. Soon after this he again took the field against Hannibal. Ever since the defeat at Cannae, the other consuls and generals had relied almost without exception upon the strategy of avoiding an engagement at all costs, and certainly none had had the courage to risk a pitched battle with the enemy. Marcellus, however, chose precisely the opposite course, because he was convinced that, long before the period allowed for wearing down Hannibal's strength had elapsed, Italy herself would have bled to death. He believed too that Fabius, by constantly insisting upon safety at all costs, was pursuing the wrong method to heal his country's affliction: the danger was that Rome was already drooping under her burdens, and that if they continued to wait as he proposed, the end of the war might well coincide with her total collapse. Fabius, as he saw it, was like one of those timid physicians who shrink from applying drastic

remedies and imagine that a disease has subsided, when it is really the patient's powers of resistance which have been exhausted.

Accordingly, his first move was to regain control of the principal Samnite cities[115] which had revolted. There he found large sums of money and stocks of grain, and he also captured the Carthaginian detachments amounting to 3,000 soldiers whom Hannibal had stationed to defend them. Next, after Hannibal had defeated and killed the proconsul Gnaeus Fulvius[116] in Apulia, together with eleven military tribunes, and had cut to pieces the greater part of his army, Marcellus sent letters to Rome telling the citizens to take heart, since he was already on the march and would see to it that Hannibal's triumph was short lived. Livy remarks that when these letters were read they did not do much to reassure the Romans, but rather increased their alarm.[117] They reflected that the risk which lay ahead of them was even greater than the defeat they had just suffered, in proportion as Marcellus was a better general than Fulvius.

However, Marcellus, according to his promise, at once marched after Hannibal and made contact with him in Lucania. There he found him entrenched in a strong position on high ground near the city of Numistro,[118] and so he encamped in the plain. On the following day, Marcellus was the first to draw up his troops in battle order, and a great battle ensued which, although desperately contested, remained indecisive. The fighting began at nine o'clock in the morning and was only broken off with difficulty after nightfall. But at daybreak Marcellus once more led out his army, formed up his men amid the heaps of dead and challenged Hannibal to fight again to decide the victory. This time Hannibal declined battle, whereupon Marcellus, after stripping the enemy's dead and burying his own, continued to pursue the Carthaginians.

He won the highest admiration for his skill in this campaign, because although Hannibal repeatedly set ambushes for him, Marcellus escaped every one and had the better of their skirmishing encounters. For this reason, when the time for the consular elections approached, the senate decided that it was advisable to summon the other consul from Sicily rather than to recall Marcellus at the moment when he was grappling with Hannibal. When the consul arrived, the senate instructed him to declare Quintus Fulvius dictator.[119] The reason for this procedure was that a dictator cannot be chosen either by the people or by the senate. Instead, one of the consuls or praetors appears before the assembled people and nominates the man whom he himself has selected. This is the derivation of the word *dictator*, for the verb *dicere* in Latin signifies *to name or declare*.[120] Some writers, however, maintain that the dictator is so called because he does not put any question to the vote or to a show of hands, but issues his decrees and pronouncements on his own authority and according to his own judgement, and it is noteworthy that the orders of magistrates, which the Greeks call *ordinances*, are called by the Romans *edicta*.[121]

25. However, when Marcellus' colleague arrived from Sicily, he wished to nominate a candidate other than Fulvius as dictator, and in order to avoid being forced to act against his own judgement he sailed back to Sicily by night. In this situation Quintus Fulvius was nominated as dictator by the people, and the senate wrote to Marcellus requesting him to support this measure. He did so, proclaimed Quintus Fulvius dictator, and in this way confirmed the people's choice, while he himself was appointed proconsul for the following year.[122] Then, after conferring with Fabius Maximus,[123] it was agreed that while Fabius should besiege Tarentum, Marcellus should follow Hannibal closely, divert his attention and prevent him from making any move to relieve the city. Accordingly, he set out and came up with the Carthaginians at Canusium.

Although Hannibal constantly shifted his camp and avoided a battle, Marcellus never lost contact with him, and at last attacked him when he had encamped, and by harassing him with skirmishers succeeded in drawing him out of his entrenchments. Hannibal advanced and Marcellus received his attack, but nightfall put an end to the fighting. The next morning Marcellus again took to the field, and formed up his troops in battle order. At this, Hannibal, in great anxiety, called the Carthaginians together and appealed to them to fight as they had never done before. 'You see', he told them, 'that even after all the great victories we have won, we shall not be able to breathe in peace, or enjoy the leisure we have earned by our superiority in arms, until we have driven this fellow away.'

After this the two armies met, and during the fighting Marcellus seems to have made an ill-judged manoeuvre which cost him the battle. He found his right wing hard pressed and ordered one of his legions to advance to the front to support it, but this change of formation threw his ranks into confusion and allowed the enemy to carry off the victory, the Romans losing 2,700 men. Marcellus then withdrew his troops into his fortified camp, called them together and reprimanded them, telling them that he could see many Roman weapons and bodies, but not a single Roman worthy of the name. They asked his pardon, whereupon he said that he could not give this when they had been driven off the field, but only after they had made themselves masters of it. However, he assured them that he would fight again on the next day, so that the first news to reach Rome would be of their victory, not of their rout. As he dismissed the troops, he gave orders that the cohorts which had been defeated should be issued with rations of barley instead of wheat. His words made so deep an impression that, although many of his soldiers had suffered painful and dangerous wounds in the fighting, it is said that every man in the army felt Marcellus' reproaches more keenly than his own hurts.

26. At daybreak Marcellus had the scarlet tunic hung out, which is the usual signal for offering battle. At their own request, the disgraced units were posted in the front of the line, and the military tribunes led out the rest of the army and deployed it in battle order. When Hannibal learned this, he exclaimed, 'Hercules, what do we do with a man who refuses to accept either good fortune or bad? This is the only general who gives his enemy no rest when he is victorious, nor takes any himself when he is defeated. We shall never have done with fighting him, it seems, because he attacks out of confidence when he is winning, and out of shame when he is beaten.' Then the two armies engaged, and when Hannibal saw that the issue

was evenly balanced, he gave orders for his elephants to be brought up to the front and launched against the Roman line. The shock of their charge broke up the formation of the front ranks and caused great disorder, but one of the military tribunes snatched up a standard, and, facing the elephants, struck the leading beast with the iron spike and forced it to wheel about. The elephant collided with the animal immediately behind, and threw it and the rest of the column into confusion.

Marcellus saw this and at once ordered his cavalry to charge at full speed into the struggling mass, so as to increase the enemy's disorder. The cavalry made a brilliant charge and pursued the retreating Carthaginians, cutting them down until they reached their own camp, but it was the plunging of their dying and wounded elephants which caused the greatest slaughter among the enemy. More than 8,000 Carthaginians are said to have lost their lives, while of the Roman force 3,000 were killed, and almost all the survivors wounded. It was this fact which allowed Hannibal to break camp during the night and put a long distance between himself and the Romans. Marcellus was unable to pursue him because of the large numbers of his own wounded, and he later withdrew at a leisurely pace into Campania and spent the summer at Sinuessa,[124] allowing his soldiers to regain their strength.

27. Hannibal, on the other hand, now that he had disengaged himself from Marcellus, felt confident enough to let his troops roam as freely as if they were disbanded, and he sent them raiding, plundering and burning throughout the length and breadth of Italy. Meanwhile, Marcellus had fallen into disfavour at Rome, and his enemies persuaded Publicius Bibulus,[125] one of the tribunes of the people – a clever speaker and a violent party politician – to bring an accusation against him. This man frequently harangued the assembly, and tried to persuade them to hand over the command of Marcellus' army to another general. 'Marcellus', he said, 'exchanged a few passes with the enemy, but now he has left the wrestling school and retired to the hot baths to refresh himself.'

When he heard of this, Marcellus put his legates in charge of the army and travelled to Rome to answer the slanders brought against him and defend his good name. There he found that an indictment based on these calumnies had already been drawn up.[126] A day was appointed for the trial, and after the people had assembled in the Circus Flaminius, Bibulus rose and delivered his impeachment. Marcellus' own defence was short and simple, but a number of the most prominent and distinguished Romans paid glowing tributes to his generalship and upheld his actions in the most outspoken terms. They reminded the people that if they condemned Marcellus for cowardice, they would prove themselves to be far worse judges of character than Hannibal, for Marcellus was the one general whom the Carthaginian always sought to avoid, in fact he employed every trick he knew to elude him – so as to engage the others. These speeches had such an effect that Bibulus' hopes were completely frustrated, and in the end Marcellus was not only acquitted of the charges against him, but was actually elected consul for the fifth time.[127]

28. As soon as he had taken up his office, he succeeded in bringing under control a dangerous situation in Etruria, where the people were on the verge of revolt, and he then visited and pacified the cities of the region. After this he wished to dedicate to Honour and to Valour[128] a temple which he had built out of the spoils he had captured in Sicily, but this scheme was frustrated by the priests, who refused to agree to a single temple's being occupied by two deities. Accordingly, Marcellus began to build another temple adjoining the first. Although vexed by the priests' opposition, he also regarded it as an ominous sign. And indeed, that year was filled with prodigies[129] which caused him anxiety. Several temples were struck by lightning and the gold offerings in the shrine of Jupiter were gnawed by mice. There were also reports that an ox had uttered human speech, and that a boy had been born with an elephant's head; and, worse still, when various rites and sacrifices were performed to expiate these prodigies, the seers encountered unfavourable omens and therefore kept him in Rome, although he chafed at inaction and was fretting to be gone.

For no man was ever so consumed by a single passion – to

match himself against Hannibal in a decisive battle. His one dream by night, his single topic of discussion with his friends and colleagues and his sole prayer to the gods was that he might meet Hannibal fairly in the field. I truly believe that his heart's desire would have been to have the two armies surrounded by a wall or a rampart where they would fight out the issue. And, but for the fact that he was already loaded with honours, and had given ample proof that in respect of good sense and maturity of judgement he could stand comparison with any general in history, I should have said that he had fallen a victim to a callow obsession for honour which was quite out of keeping with his years, for by the time that he entered upon his fifth consulship he had already passed the age of sixty.

29. However, when at last the sacrifices and rites of purification recommended by the soothsayers had been performed, he took to the field with his colleague[130] and set himself to harass Hannibal's army in its camp between Bantia and Venusia,[131] trying by every possible means to bring his opponent to battle. Hannibal refused to be drawn, but when he learned that the Romans had detached a force to attack the Epizephyrian Locrians,[132] he laid an ambush in the hills near Petelia[133] and killed 2,500 of their men. This action filled Marcellus with an overwhelming passion to get to grips with the enemy and he moved his forces still closer to Hannibal.

Between the two camps there was a hill which appeared to offer a useful vantage point, and was thickly covered with trees and shrubs. Its slopes provided lookout posts which commanded a view of both camps, and streams could be seen flowing down the sides. The Romans were astonished that Hannibal, who had had the first choice of such a strong natural position, had not occupied it but had left it for the enemy. It appears that in fact he did consider it a good site for a camp, but an even better one for ambush, and it was for this purpose that he chose to use it. He concealed a force of javelin-throwers and spearmen among the woods and hollows, as he felt certain that the Romans would be allured to the place because of its obvious natural advantages, and in the event his calculations were exactly fulfilled. In their camp the Romans immediately began to talk about the necessity of occupying the place, and they enlarged on the advantages they would gain over their enemies by encamping on it, or at the very least by fortifying it.

Accordingly, Marcellus decided to ride forward with a few horsemen and reconnoitre the site. But before doing this he sent for his soothsayer and offered up a sacrifice, and when the first victim had been killed, the soothsayer showed him that its liver had no head. When he sacrificed for the second time, the head of the liver turned out to be unusually large, while all the other indications appeared exceptionally auspicious, and this seemed to dispel the misgivings aroused by the first offering. However, the soothsayers declared that this sequence of events disturbed them even more, because when unusually forbidding or threatening omens are immediately followed by others which are exceptionally favourable, the unexpectedness of the change is in itself a matter for suspicion. But since, in Pindar's words, 'not fire, not walls of iron, can hinder fate',[134] Marcellus rode out, taking with him his colleague Crispinus, his son,[135] who was a military tribune, and 220 horsemen in all. None of these, as it happened, was a Roman: they were all Etruscans, with the exception of forty men of Fregellae,[136] who had given Marcellus many proofs of their loyalty and courage.

On the crest of the hill, which was thickly wooded, the enemy had posted a lookout. He could not be seen by the Romans, but could observe every movement in their camp. This man signalled the approach of the reconnoitring party to the troops who were hiding in ambush, and they allowed Marcellus to ride close to them. Then all of a sudden they sprang to their feet, surrounded his party, flung their javelins, stabbed with their spears, pursued those who ran away and fell upon those who stood their ground. These were the forty men of Fregellae, who, after the Etruscans had galloped off at the first onslaught, rallied round the two consuls and fought to defend them. Finally Crispinus, who had been hit by two javelins, wheeled his horse and fled, while Marcellus was run through the side with a broad-bladed spear, the Latin name for which is *lancea*. Then the few survivors among the Fregellans left

Marcellus lying where he had fallen, rescued his son who had been wounded and made their escape back to the camp. In this skirmish there were hardly more than forty men killed, but five lictors and eighteen horsemen were taken prisoner and Crispinus died of his wounds a few days later. To have lost both their consuls in a single action was a disaster that had never before struck the Romans.

30. Hannibal took little interest in the fate of the other soldiers, but when he heard that Marcellus had been killed, he immediately hurried to the spot and stood for a long time by the dead body, admiring its strength and beauty. He uttered not a single boastful word, nor did he show any sign of exultation, such as might be expected of a man who had just rid himself of a bitter and formidable enemy. But after he had expressed his wonder at the unexpectedness of Marcellus' death, he removed his signet ring,[137] but gave orders that his body should be treated with honour, wrapped in a fine robe, adorned and burned. After this he collected the ashes in a silver urn, crowned it with a gilded wreath and sent it to Marcellus' son. But on the way a party of Numidians fell in with the men who were escorting the urn. They tried to seize it by force, and when the others resisted, they fought and in the struggle the ashes were scattered far and wide. When Hannibal heard this, he remarked, 'Nothing can be done against the will of the gods.' He ordered the Numidians to be punished, but made no further effort to collect or return the remains, since he evidently felt that the strange manner in which Marcellus had met his death and been denied a proper burial indicated that some divine purpose was at work. This, at any rate, is the account which we find in Cornelius Nepos and Valerius Maximus, but according to Livy and Augustus Caesar the urn was returned to Marcellus' son and buried with splendid ceremony.[138]

Besides the monuments which Marcellus dedicated in Rome there was a gymnasium at Catana in Sicily which bore his name, and statues and votive tablets from among the plunder of Syracuse were set up in the temple of the gods named the Cabiri in Samothrace,[139] and in the temple of Athena at

Lindus.[140] On the statue there, according to Poseidonius, the following epigram was inscribed:

> Stranger, this man you behold was the guiding star of his
> country.
> Claudius Marcellus by name, born of a glorious line;
> Seven times consul, he led the armies of Rome into battle,
> Death and destruction he dealt to all who invaded his land.

The author of these verses has counted his two appointments as proconsul as well as his five consulships. His descendants continued to distinguish themselves down to the time of that Marcellus,[141] the nephew of Caesar, whose parents were Caesar's sister Octavia and Gaius Marcellus. He died while he was holding the office of aedile at Rome, soon after he had married Caesar's daughter. It was in his honour and to his memory that Octavia dedicated a library and Caesar a theatre,[142] both of which bear his name to this day.

COMPARISON OF PELOPIDAS
AND MARCELLUS

1 (31). These are the matters that I thought worthy of record from all that historians have written about Marcellus and Pelopidas. In nature and in character they were very alike, as if in these respects they were rivals, for each was valorous, tireless, bold and high-minded. Between them this appears to be their sole difference: whereas Marcellus, in many of the cities he conquered, massacred their populations,[1] Epaminondas and Pelopidas executed no one in the aftermath of their victories, nor did they sell any cities into slavery. And, it is widely agreed, had they been present at the time, that the Thebans would not have treated the Orchomenians as they did.[2]

As for their exploits, those performed by Marcellus in his war against the Celts were extraordinary and admirable, for he routed a great force of cavalry and infantry with only a small detachment of mounted troops at his disposal. It is difficult to find in any historical account a comparable achievement by any other general, and he slew the enemy's king. By contrast, Pelopidas failed when attempting the same deed, for he was struck down and slain by the tyrant[3] before he could do the striking. Nevertheless, with the successes of Marcellus we may compare the battles of Leuctra and Tegyra,[4] the most glorious and grand of all conflicts. Furthermore, Marcellus accomplished nothing by means of stealth or ambuscade that bears comparison with Pelopidas' feat when he returned from exile and put an end to the tyrants of Thebes.[5] Indeed, of all actions ever committed through concealment and cunning, this one seems the most notable.

Hannibal was indeed a terrible and formidable enemy for the Romans, but so, too, were the Lacedaemonians for the Thebans, and it is a well-established fact that they were vanquished by Pelopidas at Tegyra and Leuctra, whereas, at least according to Polybius, Hannibal was never defeated by Marcellus but instead remained unbeaten until he confronted Scipio.[6] Still, I prefer the evidence of Livy, Caesar, Nepos and, among historians writing in Greek, King Juba:[7] they insist that, in several conflicts, Marcellus routed Hannibal's forces, even if these events had no great bearing on the outcome of the war and even if, as seems likely, some of this fighting took place when the Carthaginian was executing a ruse.

What rightly and reasonably inspires admiration, however, is that after defeat had been inflicted on so many armies, after so many generals had perished in battle, and after the whole of their empire had been thrown into utter confusion, the Romans still had the courage to face their foes. For there was one man who restored the army's ardour and its desire to come to blows with the enemy instead of remaining overcome by fear and dread. He re-called Rome's soldiers to their valour and confidence, so that not only were they unwilling to yield victory but they actually fought for it with all their heart and might. This man was Marcellus. Indeed, when their devastating losses had accustomed the Romans to be grateful whenever they managed to escape Hannibal by flight, Marcellus taught them to feel disgraced if they survived defeat, to be ashamed if they even came close to surrendering and anguished if they were not victorious.

2 (32). Now Pelopidas never experienced defeat when he was in command, and Marcellus won more victories than any other Roman of his time. Perhaps, then, it seems fair to make no distinction between the one general, who achieved so many successes and was so difficult to overcome, and the other, who was unbeatable. Marcellus, to be sure, took Syracuse, whereas Pelopidas failed to take Sparta. But in my opinion it was a

greater triumph to march to Sparta and be the first man to lead an army over the River Eurotas[8] than it was to conquer Sicily – unless, by Zeus! anyone should maintain that this exploit, like the victory at Leuctra, ought to be credited to Epaminondas[9] instead of Pelopidas, while no one but Marcellus had any share in the glory of capturing Syracuse. For it was Marcellus alone who took Syracuse, and he routed the Celts without a colleague. And in the contest against Hannibal, when no one would assist him and everyone discouraged him, it was Marcellus who took the field and changed the nature of the war through being the first general to exhibit boldness.

3 (33). I do not praise the death of either man. Indeed, I am distressed and annoyed at the sheer thoughtlessness that brought disaster upon each of them. And I admire Hannibal because – although he fought so many battles it would weary one to count them all – he received not even a single wound. I also hold in high esteem the character of Chrysantes in *The Education of Cyrus*,[10] who, at the very moment when his blade was raised and he was about to strike down his enemy, heard the trumpet sound retreat and therefore let the man go, while he retired from battle calmly and decorously.

Still, this much is undeniable: Pelopidas' actions can be excused because, in addition to the violent passion that stirred him during combat, he was impelled by a noble anger to seek vengeance.[11] For the best thing is that a general should be victorious and remain alive. However, 'if he must die, let him give up his life valorously',[12] as Euripides puts it, for then he does not merely suffer death but rather his death is a deed that he executes himself. Apart from the anger that animated him, Pelopidas recognized how the true realization of his victory lay in the death of the tyrant, and this motive was certainly a reasonable one. Indeed, it would be difficult to find another act of valour whose promise was so noble or so glorious.

Marcellus, by contrast, although he was not hard pressed by circumstances and was not swept up by the passion that, in moments of great danger, dislodges our prudence, nonetheless stupidly put himself at risk and died – not, however, the death of a general but of a skirmisher or a scout. His five consulates, his three triumphs, the spoils and trophies he had taken from kings, all these he simply cast beneath the feet of Iberians and Numidians who were no more than battle fodder for the Carthaginians. Thus was each man his own nemesis, bringing retribution on his own success, when that Roman who excelled all others in valour, in power and in glory threw his life away among the scouts of Fregellae.

This should not be taken as a condemnation of these men but rather as an indignant and frank complaint on their behalf against themselves and their courage, to which quality they sacrificed their other virtues because each was heedless of his life and soul, as if their deaths affected only themselves and not their country, their friends and their allies.

After his death, Pelopidas was buried by his allies,[13] on whose behalf he had fallen. Marcellus was buried by his enemies, against whom he had fallen. The end of the former was enviable and blessed, to be sure, but there is something finer and better than the affection inspired by favours one has received and this is when one's hatred is overcome by admiration for the very virtue that has brought one grief in the past. For in this case it is nobility itself which is honoured, whereas in the other it is more a matter of esteeming utility and advantage than virtue.

ARATUS

INTRODUCTION
TO ARATUS

Aratus and the Rise of the Achaean League

In the period between the death of Alexander the Great in
323 BC and the battle of Pydna in 168 BC, when, in Polybius'
words, 'the Romans succeeded in subjecting nearly the whole
of the inhabited world to their sole authority' (1.1.5), the cities
of Greece found themselves in an uneven competition with
powerful kingdoms governed by Macedonian dynasties. The
most important of these Hellenistic monarchies were the Antigonids in Macedon, the Ptolemies in Egypt and, possessing
dominions that reached from Syria throughout the near
east, the Seleucids – each regal house energetically striving
for primacy in the Greek world. Sometimes they gained
influence through royal benefactions, at other times through
less welcome impositions, like the installation of obedient
tyrants or even military garrisons serving under royal commanders. In this geopolitical arena, individual cities were at an
obvious disadvantage, and as a consequence many endeavoured to improve their odds by forming themselves into
leagues.[1] Such leagues became sovereign federal states, and
through their unity acquired wealth and manpower sufficient
to resist, if not in the end to overcome, the encroachments of
the kings.

The two chief leagues of the third and second centuries BC
were the Achaeans and the Aetolians. Aetolia was a rough and
mountainous region of northwest central Greece, lying along

the northern coast of the Gulf of Corinth. Most Aetolian cities were small, apart from Naupactus and Heraclea, and the austere economic conditions of the region stimulated raiding parties and brigandage.[2] On the other side of the Gulf of Corinth lay Achaea, which stretched across the northeast of the Peloponnese. Aegium, modern Aigio, located on the Gulf of Corinth, was its capital city. Achaea was more developed and generally more prosperous than Aetolia, but far less formidable. The Achaean League had fallen into disuse early in the third century BC and was reconstituted only in 280 BC, a time when the Aetolians had already become a redoubtable military power. Put differently, the Achaean League was second rate, and it was Aratus who changed all that.[3]

In 271 BC Aratus was born into an aristocratic family in Sicyon. His father Cleinias was assassinated in a political coup in 264 BC. Aratus, who was only seven at the time, was smuggled out of the city and sent to Argos, where he grew up in dignified exile (chs. 2–3). In 251 BC, at the age of twenty, Aratus assembled a force of Sicyonian exiles and sympathizers and with it liberated his native city from tyranny (chs. 5–9), although it appears that, afterwards, Aratus remained more or less in sole charge of Sicyonian affairs, by what constitutional mechanism is unknown.[4]

It was at this time that Sicyon joined the Achaean League (ch. 9). The league was governed by annually elected magistrates, the chief of whom was the general (*strategos*). He was assisted by a cavalry commander (*hipparch*), by a league secretary and by numerous other elected civic officers. Basic authority, however, lay with an assembly of all male citizens, the men of military age, who ordinarily met four times each year in order to elect magistrates and make final decisions about matters of national importance.[5]

In the aftermath of its liberation, Sicyon was threatened by social revolution (chs. 12–14). At first, Aratus looked for help to Antigonus Gonatas, the king of Macedon, from whom he received a payment of 25 talents (ch. 11). In exchange, Aratus directed Sicyonian attacks against the king's new enemy in Corinth (ch. 18).[6] This strategically situated city had long been

garrisoned by the Macedonians, but, around 249 BC, its commander, Alexander, a nephew of the king, declared himself an
independent dynast. Hence Antigonus' hostility and Aratus'
assaults. But the nimble Alexander quickly joined the Achaean
League, thus neutralizing Sicyon's usefulness to Macedon, since
Aratus could hardly attack another member of the league.
Consequently, Aratus turned to Antigonus' rival, Ptolemy II,
for financial assistance, and it was Egyptian aid that led to the
final resolution of Sicyon's domestic troubles.

In 245 BC, at the age of twenty-six, Aratus was elected
general of the Achaean League. So commanding a presence in
Achaean politics was he that he went on to win election every
other year (an interval between offices was constitutionally
mandated) for almost the rest of his life. As general he was
relentlessly hostile to the Aetolians, and he vigorously resisted
Macedonian influence in the Peloponnese. In 243 BC, in the
most significant military exploit of his career, he captured Corinth, which by then had been regained by Antigonus and for
whom its fresh loss was a major blow (chs. 16–24). At this
point, the Achaean League declared Ptolemy III its leader
(*hegemon*), which was in reality no more than an honorific
designation for the king but a clear statement of the league's
hostility towards Macedon. Antigonus reacted by forming an
alliance between himself and Aetolia against the Achaeans,
who in turn allied themselves with Sparta. Under Aratus' leadership, the territorial expansion of the Achaean League found
expression as a policy of liberation, whereby Greek cities were
first freed from tyrants or garrisons and thereafter coerced into
joining the league of their liberators (chs. 25–35). This policy
was effective in increasing the league's strength largely at the
expense of Antigonus and his allies.

The death of Antigonus in 239 BC resulted in further Macedonian setbacks. The Aetolians, turning against their erstwhile
ally, signed a peace treaty with the Achaeans, who continued to
expand in the Peloponnese until, by 229 BC, the Achaean
League was bigger and richer than ever before. Now, however,
many of its new members, cities like Argos and Megalopolis,
were traditionally hostile to Sparta, and they managed to drag

the league into a fresh conflict with this city, despite its alliance with the league.

Perhaps this was inevitable, as Sparta, too, was a resurgent power. Under its young king, Cleomenes III,[7] who came to his throne around 235 BC, Sparta had extended its sway into Arcadia and into territories controlled by the Achaean League. These encroachments led the Achaeans to declare war in 228 BC, although Aratus was reluctant to do so. At the end of 227 BC, however, Cleomenes violently seized absolute power in Sparta and introduced a series of radical reforms, all designed to restore the city's traditional military might. The immediate result was a significant increase in Sparta's military manpower, and this enlarged army, under Cleomenes' leadership, allowed the Spartans to gain the upper hand in their war with the Achaeans (chs. 35–8). One effect of Sparta's success was a rash of seditious behaviour throughout the league, including in Sicyon and Corinth, by groups who were weary of war and willing to accommodate an ascendant Cleomenes (chs. 39–40). Soon, the Spartan king demanded that the Achaeans name him their *hegemon*, a condition for peace that appealed to many in the league. Not, however, to Aratus, who managed to persuade the league to continue the war by allying itself with Macedon, now ruled by Antigonus Doson (chs. 38 and 42). This was a drastic and startling volte-face, for which Aratus was harshly criticized, both by contemporaries and later writers, including Plutarch (ch. 38). This was because the king demanded a steep price for his alliance: he insisted that *he* be named the *hegemon* of the league and Corinth be restored to Macedonian control (chs. 41–2).

Aratus' Macedonian policy transformed Greek politics in a lasting way. In 224 BC Antigonus, now the league's *hegemon*, entered the war. Cleomenes collapsed quickly, and, after his defeat at the battle of Sellasia in 222 BC, fled to Egypt. Of far greater consequence for the Achaeans was a new alliance contrived by Antigonus during the course of the war: the Hellenic League, itself a league of leagues ostensibly organized for mutual defence though in reality a diplomatic device for consolidating Macedonian supremacy in Greece. The existence of Antigonus' very extensive Hellenic League, however, helped to establish a common peace in the Peloponnese. Even the Aetolians, who as enemies of Macedon were not included in the new alliance, were for the moment quiet.

During the war against Cleomenes, Aratus found himself gradually reduced to the condition of a royal courtier. He remained a powerful figure, to be sure, but balancing Achaean and Macedonian interests proved to be a recurring challenge, and Aratus was always aware that many competing constituencies, not all of them well intentioned where Achaea was concerned, hankered after the king's favour. Aratus prospered under Antigonus, but, under his successor, Philip V, who came to the throne in 221 BC, matters ultimately proved less satisfactory, and, near the end of his life, Aratus was no longer a royal favourite. But that was later. In 219 BC Aratus managed to persuade Philip to launch the Hellenic League into a war against the Aetolians, the so-called Social War of 219 to 217 BC. When, however, Philip learned that Hannibal had inflicted a major defeat on the Romans at Lake Trasimene, he preferred to campaign in Illyria, where he hoped, by taking advantage of Carthaginian pressure on Rome, to make himself master of the region and, perhaps, to cross into Italy.[8] Consequently, he hastily imposed peace on all the combatants.

In 214 BC Aratus refused the king's offer to accompany him on his ill-fated campaign in Illyria. Still, Achaea could not avoid its entanglement in Macedonian affairs. In 215 BC, as the *hegemon* of the Hellenic League, Philip made an alliance with Hannibal, and this treaty led to the First Macedonian War (214–205 BC), of which the disaster in Illyria was only the beginning.[9] The Aetolians entered this war on the Roman side, while the Achaeans, as they were in duty bound to do owing to Aratus' previous diplomacy, fought for Philip. But Aratus saw none of this. He died in 213 BC, the revered architect of the Achaean League.

Plutarch's Aratus

Aratus is distinct from the other biographies in this volume in that it is not one in a pair of Greek and Roman Lives set in parallel.[10] Here, then, Plutarch is able to write for a Greek audience, to whom Macedonians are foreigners (chs. 38 and 47), about a Greek hero who distinguishes himself in a world in which Romans are hardly on the scene. Plutarch covers this same period elsewhere, in his *Agis & Cleomenes*, and it is clear enough that he viewed this time as an important one in the history of Greece. It is, unfortunately, impossible to determine just when Plutarch wrote *Aratus*, though it is a fair surmise that it preceded his composition of the *Parallel Lives*.

The work is dedicated to Polycrates of Sicyon, a descendant of Aratus, and to his two young sons, in the hope that they will find in their distant ancestor a model for emulation (ch. 1).[11] Naturally, Plutarch did not expect the boys to grow up to capture citadels or command armies, and elsewhere he cautions his readers against learning the wrong lessons from the martial glory of the Greek past.[12] Valour and love of honour were nevertheless enduring virtues, and the vicissitudes of Aratus' career exhibited the importance of moral excellence in often difficult circumstances. Aratus' devotion to public life (ch. 10), furthermore, in the view of a man like Plutarch, ought to inspire all Greeks. And Polycrates' sons had before their eyes living proof of the right way to imitate Aratus, for their father, Plutarch emphasizes throughout the opening chapter, has succeeded in uniting his own excellence with the virtues of his forebear.[13] Indeed, this Life is designed to aid Polycrates' sons in emulating their father by way of their common devotion to the memory of Aratus.

The focus, then, is on Aratus, his deeds and his choices, and Plutarch assumes his readers possess a basic familiarity with the history of the Achaean League. This is why, once he comes to the end of the Cleomenean War, he offers little in the way of historical contextualization, to the extent that a reader will learn little of the Social War and nothing of its resolution. The rise of the Achaeans, covered in the Life's first thirty-five chapters, and not their subsequent subordination to Macedon, is after all a more inspiring topic for young readers. In the later chapters, more important than any sequence of campaigns is Aratus' struggle – despite Philip's moral decline – to preserve his and the league's independence and integrity, when he alone of Philip's counsellors will dare to give him wise instead of opportunistic advice (chs. 48 and 50). Here, too – perhaps here especially – there was much for Polycrates' sons to learn.

This Life, then, is primarily pedagogical, which accounts for its frequently didactic tone.[14] At chapter 19, to take a single example, the author presses his young readers to see the contemporary relevance (and share in the excitement) of Aratus' devotion to honour:

> Who would not admire, or even now join in striving to match, the magnanimity of such a hero, who purchased great peril at so high a price, who pledged what were considered the finest of his possessions so that by night he might make his way among his enemies and struggle for his very life, who received no security except the expectation of winning honour?

Similar schoolmasterly moments recur throughout the biography.

But it would be a mistake to conclude that *Aratus* lacks sophisticated touches. For Aratus, role model that he is, was nonetheless a complex character, as Polybius famously pointed out (4.8):

> He had nearly all the qualities that make for a perfect man of affairs. He was forceful in speaking, penetrating in thought and resolute in keeping his own counsel. He was second to none in his capacity for dealing civilly with his political rivals, for making friends and for forming fresh alliances. Furthermore, he was pre-eminent in the art of intrigue, in contriving schemes and in forming plots against an enemy, and he had the endurance and boldness to execute them successfully ... But this very same man, whenever he attempted a campaign in the field, was slow in conception, timid in action and wanting in daring. Consequently, the Peloponnese was filled with trophies marking his defeats ...

In Plutarch, too, Aratus is an unsimple figure, but his description rewrites Polybius' in important ways: he is cautious rather than cowardly, more a high-minded statesman than simply a soldier or politician (ch. 10). Yet Plutarch's Aratus, like Polybius', is still an imperfect man, and whereas Polybius attributes his deficiencies to the nature of things, Plutarch finds the fault in Aratus' lack of a properly philosophical education, a recurring theme in his assessments of virtue and vice.[15] Even a man, even a man who is a Greek, possessing Aratus' natural capacities – his intelligence (*deinotēs*) and quick wit (*synēsis*) – requires a proper education.[16]

For Plutarch, Aratus' most significant failure lay in his decision to make Antigonus *hegemon* of the Achaean League instead of Cleomenes (ch. 38). The basis for his complaint is plain enough: whatever his faults, Cleomenes was a Greek, whereas Antigonus was a foreigner, and this violation of Panhellenic unity cannot, in Plutarch's view, be excused entirely by Aratus' claim that 'he was not the master of state affairs but was instead mastered by them' (ch. 41; surely extracted from Aratus' *Memoirs*).[17] Prior to this decision, Aratus' excesses are attributed to his hatred of tyranny or passion for freedom (chs. 25, 28, 32), but thereafter he is implicated in Macedonian enormities like the massacre and enslavement of the Mantineans (ch. 45) and the cruel death of Aristomachus (ch. 44).

Aratus was ultimately destroyed, and his household corrupted, by his decision to appeal to the Macedonians, a reality he did not fail to recognize (ch. 52). But this end did nothing to vitiate the man's greatness or his eternal glory, and the grateful Achaeans elevated Aratus to divine status. Later generations, however, proved less appreciative, perhaps because they failed to grasp the right way to learn from the past. Most of Aratus' honours, Plutarch complains, 'have lapsed, owing to the passage of time and changing circumstances' (ch. 53). And yet the true and enduring legacy of this great man, Plutarch makes clear, can be guaranteed by emulation on the part of the present generation – if, that is, they profit by the instruction of this Life.

Sources

Even in his lifetime, Aratus was a celebrated man, and his policies inspired strong feelings of admiration or dislike (ch. 45).[18] He composed *Memoirs*[19] that dealt with his life down to

220 BC, and this work is Plutarch's principal source for the years leading to the Cleomenean War. Plutarch also read Polybius (who had also read Aratus). Polybius was an authoritative historian in any case, but, because he had himself been a distinguished leader in the Achaean League,[20] he had access to local information and traditions inaccessible to other writers. He, too, and predictably, was an admirer of Aratus.[21] Polybius' *History* and Aratus' *Memoirs* are Plutarch's most important sources for this Life.

A hostile view was available in the *History* of Phylarchus, who narrated, in twenty-eight books, the events in the Peloponnese that occurred between 272 BC and the death of Cleomenes. Phylarchus was a contemporary of the events he described and no neutral observer: he disliked both the Macedonian monarchy and the policies of the Achaean League but commended Cleomenes highly – too highly in Plutarch's opinion (ch. 38). His account of this period, a sensationalist piece of writing according to his critics, was nonetheless influential, as is evidenced by Polybius' lengthy rebuttal of it (2.56–63). Plutarch mined Phylarchus when he composed his *Agis & Cleomenes* and *Pyrrhus*, and here he is the likely source for most of the criticisms of Aratus that Plutarch reports.[22]

Plutarch also consulted the historian Deinias of Argos (ch. 29), a little-known figure who may have played a role in assassinating the Sicyonian tyrant Abantidas (ch. 3), in which case he would be a slightly older contemporary of Aratus.[23] He composed a history of Argos down to his own times, and this work probably informs much of what Plutarch has to say about events at Argos.

LIFE OF ARATUS

[271–213 BC]

1. There is an ancient proverb, Polycrates,[1] which the philosopher Chrysippus[2] cites, not in its correct formulation (because, I think, he was anxious not to say anything inauspicious), but rather as he thought it better: 'Who will praise a father if not his fortunate sons?' But he is contradicted by Dionysodorus of Troezen,[3] who restores this saying to its true wording: 'Who will praise a father if not his unfortunate sons?'[4]

The purpose of this maxim, according to Dionysodorus, is to silence those men who, lacking any fine qualities of their own, endeavour to cover themselves in the virtue of their ancestors by praising them extravagantly.

But for anyone who, as Pindar puts it, 'exhibits in his nature the nobility of his forefathers',[5] and who patterns his life after the finest examples in his family's history – and you are such a man – how could he do better than to recollect the best of his ancestors both by listening, again and again, to their stories and by telling them himself? This is hardly because men of this kind lack virtues of their own or because their renown depends on the glories of others, but rather because they prefer to connect their own achievements with the deeds of their forebears as a means of praising them not only as the founders of their lines but also as guides of their own lives.

This is why, now that I have composed a *Life of Aratus*, your fellow-citizen and forefather, a figure to whom you do great credit both in your reputation and in your influence, I am sending it to you – not because you have failed to strive from your earliest days to learn as much as possible about the deeds of your distinguished ancestor, but in order that your own sons,

Polycrates and Pythocles, may grow up listening to and reading
about noble examples from their own family's past, examples
which they will be quite right to imitate. For it is the mark of a
man in love with himself, and not of a man who loves what is
noble, to believe that he is always superior to everyone else.[6]

2. With the dissolution of Sicyon's pure Doric aristocratic
constitution – like a harmony ruined by dissonance – the city
collapsed into factional strife marked by struggles between
ambitious demagogues.[7] Nor did this malady and perturbation
cease, as one tyrant was exchanged for another, until, after the
murder of Cleon,[8] Timocleides and Cleinias were elected to be
the chief magistrates.[9] Now, these were men of high renown
and profound influence among their fellow-citizens, but no
sooner did a degree of political stability appear to have been
restored than Timocleides died and Abantidas, the son of
Paseas, tried to make himself tyrant. He murdered Cleinias,[10]
and of his friends and family, some he exiled, others he put to
death. He even tried to kill Cleinias' son, Aratus, who at the
age of seven was left fatherless, but the boy, taking advantage
of the disorder in his house, managed to escape with the others
who fled. He wandered about in the city, frightened and helpless, until by sheer chance he passed unnoticed into the house
of a woman who, although she was a sister of Abantidas, was
married to Prophantus, a brother of Cleinias. Her name was
Soso. This woman was of a noble disposition, and she believed
that it was owing to divine favour that the boy had taken
refuge with her. Consequently, she hid him in her house until
by night she could send him secretly to Argos.[11]

3. In this way, Aratus was rescued and succeeded in escaping
his peril, and it was from this time on that his character was
marked by a fierce and ardent hatred of tyrants[12] which grew
greater as he did. At Argos he received a liberal education from
his hosts and from the friends of his father, and, when he saw
how big and strong he was growing, devoted himself to athletic
training with such success that he competed in the pentathlon,[13] winning wreaths of victory. Even in his statues one can

detect his athletic appearance, nor does his intelligent face or his majestic bearing disguise entirely the effects of his hearty appetite or of his exercise with a mattock.[14] This perhaps explains why his application to the study of oratory was insufficiently diligent for anyone entering into political affairs,[15] although he was probably a more capable speaker than he appears to those writers who base their judgement on the *Memoirs*[16] which he left behind. This work was little more than a pastime, which he hastily composed in the midst of his serious political and military struggles, relying on whatever words happened to come to him at the time.

Abantidas was later assassinated[17] by Deinias[18] and Aristotle the dialectician.[19] He was in the habit of attending their philosophical discussions in the market-place, where he routinely took part in their disputations, and the two men encouraged this practice in order to lay a plot against him and take his life. Paseas, the father of Abantidas, then seized power, but he was treacherously slain by Nicocles, who then proclaimed himself tyrant. It was observed at the time how this Nicocles bore a strong likeness to Periander,[20] the son of Cypselus, just as the Persian Orontes[21] resembled Alcmaeon, the son of Amphiaraus,[22] and just as, according to Myrsilus,[23] there was a Spartan youth who looked like Hector and was trampled beneath the feet of a multitude of onlookers, once they perceived the resemblance.

4. Nicocles was tyrant for four months, during which time he did the city great harm, nearly losing it to the Aetolians when they were laying plans against it.[24] By this time Aratus had become a young man who was highly esteemed on account of his noble birth and intelligence, which was clearly neither trivial nor idle, but marked rather by a strikingly mature seriousness and prudence. This is why the exiles from Sicyon took great notice of him, as did Nicocles, who maintained a keen interest in his activities, keeping a secret surveillance on everything the young man undertook. This was not because he feared any enterprise so bold or daring as the one Aratus finally carried out. Instead, he suspected that Aratus was in negotiations with the kings who had been his father's friends and hosts.[25] And in

truth Aratus had taken steps along that very path, but when Antigonus[26] kept neglecting him and since Egypt and Ptolemy[27] were too far away to offer any reasonable expectations of assistance, Aratus resolved to overthrow Nicocles on his own.

5. The first men to whom Aratus conveyed his intentions were Aristomachus[28] and Ecdelus.[29] The former was an exile from Sicyon, the latter an Arcadian[30] from Megalopolis,[31] alike a philosopher and man of action, who at Athens had been a close friend of Arcesilaus the Academic.[32] These men were enthusiastic in their support, but when he discussed this matter with the other exiles, although some took part because they were ashamed to disappoint the hope he placed in them, most actually tried to dissuade Aratus on the grounds that his inexperience was making him reckless.

His plan was to occupy a site in the territory of Sicyon and, with that as his base, launch attacks against the tyrant. But then there arrived in Argos a man from Sicyon who had broken out of its prison, a brother of Xenocles, himself one of the exiles.[33] When he was brought to Aratus by Xenocles, he described how narrow was the section of the city's wall he had climbed over when making his escape: on the inside, it was almost level with the ground, because it was attached to rocky heights, and on the outside it was not too tall to be surmounted by means of ladders. When Aratus heard this, he sent Xenocles, along with two of his own slaves, Seuthas and Technon, to examine the wall, for he had now made up his mind to risk everything on a single attempt, secret and swift, should it prove possible, instead of struggling in a long war or in open combat – a private individual matched against a tyrant. After they had taken measurements of the wall, Xenocles and his companions returned. They reported that the place in question was neither inaccessible nor even very difficult to manage so far as its natural features were concerned, but it was hard to approach without detection on account of some dogs belonging to a certain gardener: they were small but extremely fierce, and impossible to calm down. Aratus immediately set to work to execute this new plan.

6. Now in procuring weapons for themselves they did nothing to attract anyone's notice, since in those days nearly everybody was occupied in brigandage or in raiding their neighbours. As for ladders, the craftsman Euphranor could assemble them out in the open, because his trade shielded him from any suspicion, and he, too, was one of the exiles. Each of Aratus' friends in Argos supplied him with ten men, although they possessed only a few slaves, and Aratus himself armed thirty of his own slaves. He also hired a few mercenaries, through the agency of Protos and Xenophilus, who were leaders of a gang of robbers, letting them believe that he was planning a raid on the territory of Sicyon in order to steal the king's horses.[34] He sent most of these men ahead, in small bands, with instructions to wait at the tower of Polygnotus.[35] Caphisias was also sent on in advance, along with four others, none of them equipped for combat. Their mission was to come by night to the gardener's house, pretending to be travellers, so that, after he had taken them in, they could lock up both the gardener and his dogs inside his house, for there was no other way to get past them. The ladders could be dismantled, and so they packed them into boxes, thus concealing them, and sent them ahead in wagons.

During this time there arrived in Argos some spies of Nicocles, and it was reported that they were going about in secret and keeping a close watch on Aratus. Therefore, early one morning, Aratus went outdoors and showed himself in the market-place, where he spent some time with his friends. After that, he exercised in the gymnasium and then led home from the wrestling school a few of the young men with whom he was accustomed to drink and enjoy himself. Later, one of his slaves was seen carrying garlands through the market-place, another purchasing torches, and still another conversing with the women routinely employed to play the harp and flute at drinking parties. Now when the spies saw this, they were fooled completely, and with a laugh said to one another, 'Truly there is nothing more craven than a tyrant, since Nicocles, although master of a great city and a powerful army, is afraid of a mere boy who squanders on entertainments and carousing what money is left to him in his exile.'

7. The spies, then, were duped and departed. Aratus, however, as soon as he had finished his meal, left the city, joined the men who awaited him at the tower of Polygnotus and led them to Nemea, where he disclosed his plan. Most of his men had not yet been informed of it, and so his address to them was replete with promises and exhortations. He gave as the watchword 'Victorious Apollo', and led them towards Sicyon, regulating his march by the movement of the moon, quickening or slowing his pace accordingly, so that he could profit from its light while on his way and arrive at the garden near the wall just as the moon was setting. There he was met by Caphisias, who had failed to restrain the dogs (they had run off too quickly) but had succeeded in locking up the gardener. Discouraged by this, most of his men pressed Aratus to withdraw, but he reassured them, promising that he would lead them back if the dogs caused too great a disturbance.

At this time, he sent ahead the men who carried the ladders under the command of Ecdelus[36] and Mnasitheus. He followed slowly. Almost immediately the dogs began barking wildly as they ran alongside Ecdelus' men. Nonetheless, they managed to reach the wall and plant their ladders securely against it. But just as the first of the men were beginning their climb, the officer responsible for changing the guard for the morning watch began making his rounds. He was ringing a bell and was followed by soldiers carrying numerous torches and making a great deal of noise. The men on the ladders crouched down where they were and easily escaped any notice. But then more guards came along, in the opposite direction, and this put Aratus' men in grave danger. These men too, however, passed by without discovering anything. At once Mnasitheus and Ecdelus mounted the wall, and, after they had posted sentries inside the city on the streets along the wall, sent Technon[37] to Aratus with instructions to hurry forward.

8. The distance between the garden and the wall was not great, nor between the garden and a tower in which a large hunting dog was on watch. This dog, however, did not notice the approach of Aratus' men, perhaps because he was by nature

a lazy dog or perhaps because he was exhausted by the exertions of the previous day. But he was stirred by the barking of the gardener's little dogs and so began to growl, quietly and indistinctly at first, but when they came closer his growling turned loud and fierce. Soon he was barking ferociously, and a nearby sentinel cried out to the dog's master asking whether his dog would bark so savagely unless there was something amiss. From the tower he answered that there was nothing to fear and that his dog had been excited by the lights carried by the guards and by the noise of the bell. More than anything else, this gave courage to Aratus' men, for they believed the dog's master was aware of their plot but was concealing them and there must be many others in the city who would likewise take their part.

When the rest of the men came to the wall, however, they found themselves in great danger because their ascent was taking so long. This was the fault of the ladders, which trembled and threatened to give way unless they climbed one at a time, and slowly. The hour was pressing, moreover, when the roosters would begin to crow and farmers would begin to arrive from the countryside, bringing their produce to the market-place. Consequently, Aratus climbed hurriedly to the top, although only forty men had preceded him, and he waited just long enough for a few others to join him before he set off for the tyrant's house and the barracks where the mercenaries passed the night. These he fell upon suddenly, capturing all of them without killing anyone. He then sent messages to his friends,[38] urgently summoning each of them out of their houses. And from everywhere they rushed to him. Soon it was daybreak and the theatre was crowded with anxious men who had only rumours to go on and knew nothing of what had just taken place. Then the herald stepped forward and proclaimed that Aratus, son of Cleinias, invited his fellow-citizens to reclaim their freedom.

9. Persuaded that the event they had so long anticipated had indeed arrived, they rushed in a body to the tyrant's residence and set it on fire. A great flame arose from the burning house which could be seen as far away as Corinth,[39] and in fact the astonished Corinthians very nearly set out to offer their assist-

ance. As for Nicocles, he slipped out unnoticed by way of an underground passage and fled the city, while Aratus' men joined with the Sicyonians in putting out the blaze and subsequently plundering the residence. Not only did Aratus do nothing to stop this, he handed over to the citizenry what remained of the tyrant's wealth. In all of this, not a single person was slain or injured, neither among the assailants nor among their enemies: Fortune protected this enterprise, keeping it pure and unsullied by civil bloodshed.[40]

Aratus restored everyone who had been banished by Nicocles, and the number of these came to eighty. He also recalled those who had been expelled by previous tyrants, and of these there were not fewer than 500, some of whom had been in exile for as long as fifty years. Most of these returned impoverished and so tried to recover the properties that had once been theirs. But when these men returned to their former farms and houses, they put Aratus in a very difficult situation, for he could see how Antigonus threatened the city from the outside and was envious of the freedom it had regained,[41] while at the same time the city was shaken within by strife and faction.[42]

With this in mind, Aratus decided that matters would be best if Sicyon joined the Achaean League,[43] and so, although they were Dorians, the Sicyonians willingly adopted the name and constitution of the Achaeans, who, at that time, enjoyed neither fame nor great power.[44] Most of them in fact dwelt in small cities, whose territories were neither bountiful nor extensive, located along a coast that offered nothing in the way of good harbours, and where the sea washed against a steep and craggy shore. But they, more than any other people, demonstrated the invincibility of Greek valour whenever it is well regulated, consolidated by unity of purpose and under the direction of an intelligent leader. For although they had almost no share in the ancient glories of the Greeks, and although at this time they did not possess collectively the influence of even a single city of any standing, nevertheless, owing to their prudence and harmony, and because instead of suffering envy they preferred to follow and obey that man among them who was foremost in virtue, they not only preserved their freedom when

confronted by many formidable cities, principalities and tyrannies, but also saved and liberated much of the rest of Greece.

10. In his very nature Aratus was a statesman: he was magnani-
mous, more concerned with the management of civic affairs
than his personal ones, a man who hated tyrants bitterly and
yet always regulated his enmities and friendships on the basis
of what was best for the public good. For this reason, he did
not so much appear a firm friend as a conciliatory and mild
enemy, reacting to political circumstances so as to adjust his
position for the good of the state. His real passion lay in preserving harmony among different peoples, cooperation and
community among cities, and unanimity in assemblies and
meetings in theatres. Indeed, nothing was more attractive to
him than these things. In warfare and in open contests, he was
timid and diffident, but when it came to stealing an advantage
or secretly manipulating cities and tyrants, he was masterful.
For this reason, although he earned many unexpected successes
on account of his boldness, it seems that his caution caused him
to miss just as many opportunities.[45] Indeed, one may conclude
that, just as there are certain animals that can see well at night
but are blinded by day, because the moisture in their eyes is too
rarefied and delicate to endure any exposure to sunlight, so
there exists a kind of man whose cleverness and intelligence are
readily broken down, almost by nature, when events take place
out in the open and are proclaimed by heralds,[46] and yet, in
affairs that are secret and covert, his capacities recover. This is
a peculiarity that arises when one lacks a sound philosophical
education, and it can afflict even a man of the finest natural
qualities, whose virtue develops in the absence of any correct
understanding of moral philosophy, just like a fruit that grows
spontaneously and without cultivation. This is a truth that can
be demonstrated by numerous examples.[47]

11. When Aratus had joined himself and his city to the Achaeans, he served in the league's cavalry, where his ready obedience
won him the affection of his commanders, for although he had
already made great contributions to the league by adding to it

his own renown, as well as the might of his own city, he never-theless subordinated himself, like any other soldier, to the authority of whoever of the Achaeans was acting as general, whether he was from Dyme or Tritaea[48] or from a city even smaller than either of these. Furthermore, when he received from the king[49] a gift of money to the amount of 25 talents, Aratus accepted it but at once handed it over to his fellow-citizens, who were greatly in need of money, not least to pay for ransoming men who had been taken prisoner.

12. At Sicyon, however, the restored exiles could not be per-suaded to stop harassing those who had come into possession of their former properties, and the city was coming danger-ously close to breaking out in violent turmoil. Aratus recognized that the only hope of peace lay in the generosity of Ptolemy and so decided to set sail in order to ask the king to furnish him with enough money to resolve the crisis. He embarked from Methone,[50] above Malea, intending to take advantage of favour-able winds along the regular passage, but once at sea strong gales and rough waves forced his captain off course and they barely managed to reach Hydria.[51] Yet this place lay in enemy territory, for it belonged to Antigonus, who had installed a gar-rison there.[52] Aratus was aware of this, and so went ashore, abandoned his ship and withdrew inland, well away from the sea, accompanied by one of his friends, Timanthes.[53] They hid themselves in a dense wood, where they passed a very difficult night. It was not long before the commander of the garrison came to the ship and demanded Aratus, but he was tricked by Aratus' slaves, who said that he had fled as soon as he had arrived, sailing off to Euboea. Aratus' ship, however, and all its cargo, including his slaves, were claimed as contraband and seized by the commander.

For several days Aratus remained in this helpless condition, when a stroke of good fortune occurred. A Roman ship[54] put in at the place he was staying, where at times he came out himself in order to inspect the sea, although for the most part he kept himself concealed. This vessel was bound for Syria, but Aratus went on board and persuaded the captain to carry him as far as

Caria.[55] This voyage entailed as many perils as his previous one. After a long time, he made his way from Caria to Egypt. There he was immediately received by the king, who was very kindly disposed towards him, both for his own sake and on account of the drawings and paintings Aratus had furnished him from Greece.[56] Aratus was himself a consummate connoisseur, never ceasing to collect the works of the most skilled artists, especially pieces by Pamphilus and Melanthus,[57] which he would then send to the king.

13. The fame of Sicyon's exquisite and excellent paintings[58] was still well and truly flourishing in those days, so much so that it was generally accepted that they and they alone possessed a beauty that was incorruptible. It was for this reason that the famous Apelles,[59] who was already much admired, came to Sicyon and paid a talent to be enrolled among the city's artists, keener to share in their reputation than in their actual technique. Consequently, although when Aratus liberated the city he immediately destroyed all the other portraits of tyrants, he deliberated at great length over the portrait of Aristratus,[60] who had held power during the time of Philip.[61] This painting was the product of the school of Melanthus: in it, Aristratus was depicted standing alongside a chariot bearing Victory. Apelles, too, had had a hand in making this picture, according to the geographer Polemon.[62] This piece was so captivating in appearance that Aratus was deeply affected by its execution. Nonetheless, owing to his hatred of tyrants, he ordered its removal and destruction. At this, we are told, the painter Neacles,[63] who was a friend of Aratus, beseeched him with tears to spare the work, and, when he could not persuade him, declared that war should be waged against tyrants, not the portraits of tyrants. 'Let us, then, leave the chariot and Victory, and for you I shall expunge from the painting the image of Aristratus himself.' Aratus gave his consent. Neacles erased Aristratus. In his place he painted a single palm, for he did not dare add anything more. They say, however, that the feet of the effaced Aristratus, beneath the chariot, escaped his notice.

Now the king was already fond of Aratus on account of the gifts of artwork he had received, and his esteem for the man grew as he became better acquainted with him. And so he made him a present of 150 talents. Aratus took 40 talents with him at once and returned to the Peloponnese. The remainder the king divided into smaller sums which he later sent in instalments.[64]

14. Now, it was a truly great deed to acquire so large a sum of money for his fellow-citizens. Other men, who were generals or demagogues, had, in exchange for much less money, wronged or enslaved or betrayed their cities, which is why it was a far nobler thing when Aratus employed this wealth to resolve differences between the rich and the poor and bring them into concord, an action which brought security and stability to the whole of the populace. Furthermore, when he was entrusted with an extraordinary authority, Aratus exhibited admirable moderation, for when he was appointed arbiter over the administration of the restored exiles' affairs, with full and absolute jurisdiction, he refused to exercise this office alone. Instead, he enlisted the aid of fifteen of his fellow-citizens, in cooperation with whom, after much effort and extended negotiations, he succeeded in restoring amity and harmony to the city.[65] In recognition of these services, not only did the whole of the citizen body bestow fitting honours on him, but the restored exiles, on their own, erected a bronze statue of him on which they inscribed these verses:

> The wisdom of this man, his contests and his valour in
>> defence of Greece
>> Are famed as far away as the Pillars of Heracles.[66]
> Still, Aratus, we who have returned to our city, erected this
>> statue of you,
>> In honour of your virtue and your justice,
> A statue of our saviour dedicated to the Saviour Gods,[67]
>> because to your city
>> You brought equity and a divine observance of the
>>> rule of law.

15. The gratitude earned by Aratus for performing these services put him beyond the envy of any of his fellow-citizens, but

Antigonus, the king, was not at all pleased by Aratus' success and so decided he must either completely win the man over, making him his friend, or in any case detach him from Ptolemy. For this reason, he behaved with great generosity and kindness towards Aratus, who for his part did not at all welcome the king's attentions. The most notable instance of this occurred when the king was sacrificing to the gods at Corinth and sent portions of the offering to Aratus at Sicyon. Then, during the banquet, he said in a loud voice to the many who were present, 'My opinion of this young Sicyonian had not extended beyond deeming him liberal in character and a patriot, but he also appears to be a competent judge of the lifestyles and practices of kings. For in the past he was inclined to overlook me and place his hopes farther afield, admiring instead Egyptian wealth, no doubt because he had heard of its elephants and fleets and fine palaces. Now, however, he has looked behind the scenes and learned how everything there is mere theatricality and stagecraft, and as a consequence has attached himself entirely to me. As for me, I welcome this young man and intend to make every possible use of his services, and I ask you to think of him as a friend.'[68] The king's remarks were exploited by others who, motivated by jealousy and malevolence, vied with one another in writing letters to Ptolemy[69] denouncing Aratus, and so effective were they that Ptolemy sent a representative to Aratus conveying his reproaches. Thus one observes how much envy and ill-will are entailed by friendship with a king or tyrant, for these connections are highly desired and sought after with an ardent passion.

16. When Aratus was elected general of the Achaean League for the first time,[70] he laid waste the territories of Locris and Calydon,[71] each of which lies opposite Achaea. He then proceeded, in command of an army of 10,000 soldiers, to go to the aid of the Boeotians, but he arrived too late and they were defeated[72] by the Aetolians in a battle at Chaeronea[73] in which their boeotarch,[74] Aboeocritus, fell along with 1,000 of his men.

A year later, when he was once again general,[75] Aratus undertook the recovery of the Acrocorinth[76] – not merely to advance the interests of Sicyon and the Achaeans but, by expelling the Macedonian garrison that held the place, to free all of Greece from its tyrannical influence. Chares[77] the Athenian, after he had defeated in battle the generals of the Great King,[78] wrote to the Athenian people that his victory was a sister to the battle of Marathon. One would not err in describing Aratus' achievement as a sister to the deeds of the Theban Pelopidas or Thrasybulus the Athenian, each of whom was a slayer of tyrants,[79] except that Aratus' success surpassed theirs in that he acted, not against fellow-Greeks, but against a foreign and alien power. For the Isthmus,[80] by separating the seas, attaches and unites the Greek mainland with the Peloponnese. But whenever the Acrocorinth, a steep height rising up in the middle of Greece, is occupied by a garrison, everything south of the Isthmus is cut off and it is impossible for exchanges with the mainland or journeys to and fro to take place, nor military expeditions by land or sea. Thus whoever garrisons the Acrocorinth becomes the region's sole lord and master, which is why the younger Philip[81] appeared to be stating a truth and not making a joke when he called the city of Corinth the fetters of Greece.

17. Naturally, then, this place has always been an object of contention for every king and ruler. Antigonus' desire to possess it, however, was animated by a yearning that came very close to being an insane passion, and so he schemed to steal it away through trickery, since there was no hope of seizing it openly and by force. At that time, the Acrocorinth belonged to Alexander,[82] but when he died – poisoned, or so it was rumoured, on Antigonus' orders – his wife, Nicaea,[83] succeeded him and so came into possession of the citadel. At once Antigonus secretly sent her his son, Demetrius,[84] who instilled in her sweet expectations of a royal marriage and a life joined with a handsome young man, although she was already a woman past her prime. In this way, the king snared her, using his son as a bit of bait.

But Nicaea did not hand over the Acrocorinth. On the contrary, she continued to guard it closely. Antigonus, however, pretended not to care about this and proceeded to celebrate the wedding in Corinth, supplying shows and feasts every day, like a man overcome by pleasure and gaiety and therefore wholly given over to amusement and recreation. Then his opportunity arrived. Amoebeus[85] was to sing in the theatre, and Antigonus himself escorted Nicaea to the spectacle. She was borne in a litter fitted out with regal ornaments, luxuriating in her new honour and not in the least expecting what was about to happen. When they came to the road that led up to the citadel, Antigonus gave orders that Nicaea should be carried on to the theatre, while he said his farewells to Amoebeus. He said farewell to the wedding as well, and instead rushed to the Acrocorinth, which demanded some exertion for a man of his years. He found the gate locked, but knocked with his staff and ordered it to be opened. The men inside, who were confused by this unexpected event, did as they were told. And now that he was master of the place, Antigonus could not contain himself. He revelled with delight, drinking in the streets and frolicking in the market-place; he wore garlands on his head and kept the company of flute-girls. Although he was an old man who had experienced profound changes of fortune in the course of his life, he nonetheless celebrated wildly, greeting and saluting everyone he met. Thus one observes how joy, unless tempered by reason, disturbs and unsettles the soul even more than grief or fear.

18. Now once Antigonus had gained possession of the Acrocorinth, as I have just explained, he guarded it closely, employing men in whom he reposed great trust, and in charge of these he set Persaeus[86] the philosopher. As for Aratus, he had actually begun plotting to seize the Acrocorinth while Alexander was still alive, but, after Alexander made an alliance with the Achaeans, had desisted.[87] These new circumstances, however, offered him an opportunity to renew his scheming.

In Corinth there were four brothers, of Syrian origin, one of whom, Diocles by name, was a mercenary who served in the garrison. The other three, after they had stolen some gold belonging to the king, made their way to Sicyon to see Aegias, a banker with whom Aratus also did business.[88] On this occasion, with Aegias' assistance, they disposed of a part of the gold, but the remainder was exchanged little by little, as Erginus, another of the brothers, travelled again and again to Sicyon. He soon became quite friendly with Aegias, and one day, when he had been led in conversation to the topic of the garrison, mentioned how, while going up to see his brother, he had observed a gap in the cliff's escarpment: it was sloped and led to a place where the wall of the citadel was very low. Aegias then began to joke with him and said, 'My dear fellow, do you steal the king's gold in bits and pieces when you could sell an hour of your time for a great sum of money? Don't you know that burglars and traitors alike,[89] if they are caught, must expect the same death as their punishment?' Erginus then laughed aloud, and he agreed to sound out Diocles: as for his remaining brothers, he did not trust them at all. A few days later he returned and arranged to lead Aratus to the place where the wall of the citadel was not more than 15 feet high. Furthermore, he and Diocles would cooperate in all that should follow.

19. Aratus agreed to give the brothers 60 talents if he was successful, and, if he failed, so long as he and they survived the attempt, to give each of them a house and a single talent. The 60 talents for Erginus and his brother had to be deposited with Aegias, but Aratus had nothing like that amount of money to hand nor was he willing to risk suspicion by borrowing, so he collected most of his drinking vessels and his wife's gold jewellery and deposited them with Aegias as security for the full sum. For Aratus was so exalted in spirit and so passionate in seeking after noble ends that, since he knew Phocion and Epaminondas[90] were regarded as the best and most just of the Greeks because they turned down great gifts and refused to sacrifice their honour for money, so he decided to expend his private wealth secretly and to advance the funds needed for this enterprise – despite the danger he risked, he and he alone, for the sake of all his fellow-citizens, who were not even aware of this adventure. Who would not admire, or not even now join in

striving to match, the magnanimity of such a hero, who purchased great peril at so high a price, who pledged what were considered the finest of his possessions so that by night he might make his way among his enemies and struggle for his very life, who received no security except the expectation of winning honour?

20. Now this scheme to take the citadel was dangerous enough, but it was made more dangerous still owing to a mistake, attributable to ignorance, made at the very beginning of the enterprise. Aratus' slave, Technon, had been sent by his master to inspect the wall with Diocles, but he had not previously met Diocles in person. Nevertheless, he believed he could recognize him because Erginus had described his appearance: he was a man with curly hair and dark complexion and was cleanshaven. It had been agreed that Technon would await Erginus and Diocles at a place just outside the city called Ornis.[91] While he was waiting, the eldest brother of Erginus and Diocles happened by. His name was Dionysius and he had no part in their plan nor was he even aware of it. He bore a strong resemblance to Diocles, and Technon, misled by their similarity, asked him if he had any connection with Erginus. When Dionysius responded that they were brothers, Technon was convinced that he was speaking with Diocles and, without demanding his name or looking for any further sign of his identity, grasped his hand and began to chat with him, inquiring after the arrangements he had made with Erginus. Dionysius did not correct Technon's mistake but instead guilefully agreed with everything he said. He began to walk back towards the city, and Technon followed, suspecting nothing and simply carrying on their conversation. They were very near the city, and Dionysius was on the point of arresting Technon, when by a sudden reversal of fortune Erginus approached. Perceiving the error and the danger, he signalled to Technon that he should flee, and they both ran off, making their escape to Aratus. He, however, was unwilling to give up hope. Instead, he immediately sent Erginus to Dionysius with gold to purchase his silence. Erginus did this, and brought Dionysius back with him to meet Aratus. As soon

as he was there, they would not let him go. They bound him and kept him under guard, locked away inside Aratus' house, while they prepared themselves for action.

21. When everything was in readiness, Aratus ordered the rest of his troops to pass the night under arms, while he selected 400 men – few of whom knew what their real mission was to be – and led them towards the gates of Corinth that lie near the sanctuary of Hera.[92] It was the middle of the summer and the moon was full, the night sky was clear and cloudless, and this raised a fear that the gleam of the weapons in the moonlight might attract the notice of the guards. But just as the first soldiers were arriving at the gate, clouds rose from the sea, shrouding the city and the places nearby in darkness. Then they all sat down and removed their shoes, for little noise is made, nor is there much slipping, when men climb ladders in their bare feet. Meanwhile, Erginus selected seven young men who disguised themselves as travellers and followed him to the gate, which they reached without attracting attention. There they killed the gatekeeper, along with the sentries posted with him. At the same time as this was happening, the ladders were raised. Aratus got a hundred men over the wall very quickly, then, ordering the rest to follow as rapidly as possible, pulled up the ladders. As he marched his men through the city towards the citadel, Aratus was filled with joy that they had escaped detection and was confident of their success.

At that moment there appeared in the distance four men, who were on patrol and coming towards them carrying torches. Aratus' men were still in the shadows and remained unseen, but they could see the watchmen moving closer. Drawing back beneath the walls and buildings, they took shelter – and lay in ambush. They fell upon the men and killed three of them, but the fourth escaped, although a sword had inflicted a wound to his head, and he let out a cry that the enemy were within the gates. Soon the trumpets sounded and the city was alerted, the streets were filled with people rushing about, and everywhere there were many lights, some in the city below, others in the citadel above. A confusing clamour arose on all sides.

22. Meanwhile, Aratus was struggling to make his way up along the cliff, but the going was slow and laborious because, since the path lay mostly amid crags that overshadowed it and there were many twists and turns as it neared the wall of the citadel, he kept straying from it. But then, we are told, something marvellous occurred. The moon parted the clouds, and in shining forth it illuminated the most difficult stretch of the path, so that Aratus was able to reach the wall at the desired location. The clouds then came together again, plunging everything into darkness.

As for the 300 soldiers whom Aratus had left outside the gate near the temple of Hera, when they entered the city they were unable, amid so much commotion and so many searching lights, to find the same path as Aratus or follow his traces. So they huddled closely and hid themselves in the darkness of a hollow in the cliff, where they waited in great distress and unbearable anxiety. For Aratus and his men had already begun to fight and the sentries on the wall were flinging spears down at them. The combatants' shouts rang everywhere, and their cries echoed down the sides of the cliff so that no one knew whence they originated. While the 300 remained confused about where to turn, Archelaus,[93] the commander of the king's soldiers, passed by, leading a large force towards the citadel with shouts and trumpet blasts. They were on their way to attack Aratus' party, so the 300, just as if they had been lying in ambush, sprang forward and killed the first of the soldiers they fell upon, sowing panic among Archelaus and the rest, whom they put to flight and pursued until they were dispersed and scattered throughout the city.

At the very moment this victory was complete, Erginus came down from the fighting above to announce that Aratus had engaged the enemy, who were defending themselves stoutly, and that along the wall a great struggle was taking place, at which their aid was needed at once. They ordered him to lead them there straightaway. As they climbed, they announced their approach with shouts that reassured their friends. The full moon made their arms gleam and, spread along the length of the path, they appeared to the enemy more numerous than they actually were. Similarly, the echoing of their voices as they cried out in the night gave a false impression of a larger force. Finally, they rejoined their comrades, repulsed the enemy, seized possession of the citadel and captured its garrison just as the day was dawning. As the sun shone down upon their success, the rest of Aratus' army arrived from Sicyon.[94] The Corinthians gladly welcomed them at the gates and helped them to round up the king's soldiers.

23. When everything appeared secure, Aratus descended from the citadel into the theatre, which was filled with an immense crowd who had come to see him and to hear whatever he had to say to the Corinthians. Aratus stationed his Achaean soldiers at each of the side entrances, then came forward from behind the stage to its centre, still wearing his breastplate. His face was plainly affected by weariness and loss of sleep, and the exhilaration and joy felt by his spirit were overcome by his sheer physical exhaustion. As soon as he appeared, his audience erupted in all manner of expressions of goodwill, and, since he was still holding his spear in his right hand, he bent his knee a little and inclined his body slightly so he could rest himself on his weapon.[95] He stood silently in this pose for a long time as he received their applause and cheers, their praises for his valour and congratulations on his good fortune. When they stopped and became quiet, he collected himself and delivered a speech on behalf of the Achaeans that was suitable to the deed he had just performed, and he persuaded the Corinthians to join the Achaean League. He also restored the keys to the city gates, handing them over to the Corinthians for the first time since the days of Philip.[96]

As for Antigonus' officers, Aratus released Archelaus, whom he had captured, but slew Theophrastus[97] because he refused to quit his post. Persaeus, as soon as the citadel was taken, had escaped to Cenchreae.[98] The story is told that, at a later time, when Persaeus was enjoying a leisurely conversation, someone remarked that in his opinion only the wise man could be a good general. 'Ah, by the gods!' he responded, 'there was a time when this doctrine of Zeno's was very attractive to me as well, but I have since changed my mind, having learned my lesson from a young Sicyonian.'[99] This anecdote about Persaeus is related by numerous authors.[100]

24. Aratus at once seized control of the temple of Hera and of Lechaeum[101] and took possession of twenty-five of the king's ships. He sold 500 horses and 400 Syrians. The Achaeans installed a garrison of 400 men on the Acrocorinth, along with fifty guard dogs and their keepers.

Now the Romans, in their admiration of Philopoemen, call him 'the last of the Greeks',[102] in the sense that after him no great man appeared among the Greeks. But I would call this success of Aratus the last and latest of the Greeks' achievements, a match for the greatest in its daring and in its fortunate outcome, as later events revealed. For Megara[103] deserted Antigonus in order to attach itself to Aratus, and Troezen and Epidaurus[104] both joined the Achaean League. Aratus, extending himself for the first time beyond the environs of Sicyon, invaded Attica and, crossing over to Salamis, plundered the island, employing the Achaeans' forces just as he wished, as if they were men released from prison. Any free men he captured he returned without ransom to the Athenians, in order to give them a reason to rise in revolt.[105] He made Ptolemy[106] an ally of the Achaeans, and appointed him their leader in war by land or by sea. Such was his influence among the Achaeans that, inasmuch as he could not legally be elected general every year, he was instead chosen every other year, and in any case, by dint of his actions and counsel, he was always in authority. For they saw how he put nothing – not wealth, not glory, not friendship with kings, not even the advantage of his native city – before the increase of the Achaean League.[107] For he recognized that the Greek cities, because they were weak individually, could preserve themselves only through mutual support, bound together – as it were – to their common advantage. For just as the parts of a body live and breathe on account of their integration into a single being, but decay and putrefy whenever they become separated and disjoined, so likewise are cities ruined by those who rupture their unity, whereas they are increased by one another whenever they become parts of a greater whole and share in a collective design.

25. Aratus was indignant when he observed how, although the best of the surrounding cities had gained their freedom, the Argives remained enslaved. And so he decided to kill their tyrant, Aristomachus,[108] for he wanted to give this city the gift of liberty, to discharge his debt for its generosity in rearing him and to attach Argos to the Achaean League. Bold men were found, resolute enough to carry out this deed, of whom Aeschylus and Charimenes[109] the soothsayer were the leaders. But they lacked swords: it was forbidden to possess them, and the tyrant inflicted grave punishments on anyone who had them. Consequently, Aratus had small daggers made for them in Corinth, which he had sewn into packsaddles, and these were put on beasts of burden transporting other merchandise to Argos. Charimenes the soothsayer, however, added a new man to the conspiracy, a fellow who was unworthy to play a part in it, and for this reason Aeschylus and his followers were offended and decided to act on their own, excluding Charimenes. When he learned of this, Charimenes was incensed and denounced the conspirators just as they were about to move against the tyrant. Even so, most of them managed to make their escape from the market-place and flee to Corinth.

Not long afterwards, however, Aristomachus was murdered by his slaves. Then Aristippus[110] seized power, and he was an even worse tyrant than his predecessor. Aratus called up all the Achaeans of military age and at once led them to the aid of the city, counting on the enthusiastic support of the Argives themselves.[111] Most of them, however, had become habituated to their servitude and not a single man came over to his side.[112] He withdrew, but he had already implicated the Achaeans in a charge of inciting war during a time of peace. Indeed, they were accused of this very action and their case was heard by the Mantineans.[113] Perhaps because Aratus did not take part in these proceedings, Aristippus, who acted as plaintiff, won his case, and the Achaeans were fined 30 minas.[114]

Aratus himself remained simultaneously hated and feared by

the tyrant, who constantly plotted his death, scheming in which
he found an ally in King Antigonus. And from nearly everywhere there appeared men who were ready to perpetrate this
deed on their behalf, keeping themselves ever alert for an
opportunity. There is, however, no better protection for a man
in power than sincere and constant affection, for, whenever the
multitude and aristocracy alike become frightened, not *of* their
leader but *on his behalf*, he sees with many eyes and hears with
many ears, and therefore learns of everything in advance. This
observation prompts me to interrupt my narrative at this point,
in order to offer an account of the sort of life led by Aristippus,
for his is an illustration of the true condition of a tyrant, an
office that men envy, and of anyone who possesses the majesty
of absolute power, which men regard as a felicitous state
worthy of celebration.

26. For although he had Antigonus as his ally and maintained
a large bodyguard for his personal security, and had left not a
single one of his enemies alive in the city, nonetheless Aristippus ordered his soldiers and guards to stand in formation in the
peristyle outside his residence. As for his slaves, as soon as he
had taken his meal, he dismissed them at once, locking himself
inside an interior room. He would then retreat with his concubine into a small upstairs bedroom, which was closed by a
trapdoor on which he placed his bed. There he slept as a man
in his state might be expected to sleep: troubledly and anxiously. The ladder to this room was removed by his concubine's
mother, who then locked it away in another room. In the
morning she would put it back in its place and call out to this
awe-inspiring tyrant, who would then crawl down from his lair
like a serpent.[115]

Aratus, by contrast, came to possess perpetual authority, not
violently by force of arms but in accordance with the law and
owing to his virtue. He dressed simply, in an ordinary tunic and
cloak, declared himself the common enemy of all tyrants everywhere and left behind a posterity whose glory continues among
the Greeks to this present day.[116] As for these men who seize
citadels, surround themselves with bodyguards and resort to

weapons and gates and trapdoors for their personal safety, only a few, like hares, have escaped a violent death. And not one of them has left behind a house or a family or a tomb to honour his memory.

27. Aratus, then, made many attempts against Aristippus, sometimes covertly and sometimes openly, as he endeavoured to take Argos. Once he deployed ladders and managed, with a few men and at great peril, to climb the city wall, where he cut down the guards who rushed to its defence. When day came, the tyrant attacked him from all sides, while the Argives, as if this combat were not for the sake of their freedom but merely a contest in the Nemean Games[117] which they were judging, sat as impartial and unprejudiced spectators, keeping absolutely still. Aratus fought stoutly, but was struck by a spear that pierced his thigh. Still, he held his ground and, although hard pressed by his enemies, could not be dislodged until nightfall.[118] And if he had kept up his struggle through the night as well, he would not have failed, for the tyrant was already making preparations for flight and had sent a great part of his property down to the sea. But no one informed Aratus of this. Meanwhile, he was running out of water and his strength was failing him on account of his wound. Consequently, he led his soldiers away.

28. When he decided to abandon this approach, he openly invaded Argive territory at the head of his army and began to ravage the countryside. Along the River Chares[119] a fierce battle against Aristippus ensued, after which Aratus was reproached for deserting the contest and tossing away victory. For it happened that the rest of his forces unquestionably got the advantage and advanced a long way in pursuit of the enemy, whereas he, without being driven from his position by the adversary but simply because his nerve failed him and he was gripped by fear, made a disorderly retreat to the camp. When the other soldiers returned from the chase, they were angry because, although they had routed the enemy and slain far more of them than had been lost on their side, nonetheless they

had allowed the vanquished to erect a trophy in victory over themselves. In his shame, Aratus decided to fight a second battle over the trophy, and so, after waiting a day, he again arrayed his army for battle. But when he saw how much more numerous than before the tyrant's forces had grown, and when he perceived how much more boldly they readied themselves for battle, his daring forsook him and he departed, satisfying himself with a truce that allowed him to collect his dead.

Nevertheless, owing to his experience in diplomacy and political affairs, and on account of his personal influence, Aratus was able to retrieve this failure by bringing Cleonae[120] into the Achaean League – and by celebrating the Nemean Games in Cleonae, which he justified on the grounds that this city had a superior ancestral claim to host the games. But the Argives also celebrated the games, and it was then for the very first time that the asylum and safe passage granted to contestants in the games was violated, for the Achaeans regarded anyone who competed in the games at Argos as enemies, and, if they caught them passing through their territories, sold them into slavery – so extreme and so implacable was Aratus in his hatred of tyrants!

29. Not long after this,[121] when Aratus learned that Aristippus was looking for an opportunity to attack Cleonae but was restrained by his fear of the forces installed in Corinth, he issued a proclamation for the army to assemble. He ordered his soldiers to take along provisions for several days and then marched to Cenchreae, hoping thereby to incite Aristippus to move against Cleonae, if he believed Aratus was no longer at hand. And this is exactly what happened: Aristippus immediately left Argos at the head of his forces. When it was dark, however, Aratus returned to Corinth, posted guards along the road and led the Achaeans to Cleonae. His men followed him in such good order and with such speed and enthusiasm that not only did they escape discovery on the march but they also managed to enter Cleonae on that same night and put themselves in battle array without Aristippus ever becoming aware of their presence. At daybreak, the gates were thrown open and the trumpet sounded. Uttering war cries, Aratus rushed against

the enemy and routed them instantly, carrying on his pursuit in the direction he believed Aristippus was most likely to flee, for the terrain offered many routes of escape. He chased him as far as Mycenae,[122] where, as Deinias[123] informs us, the tyrant was overtaken and slaughtered by a certain Cretan named Tragiscus. Although more than 1,500 of the enemy fell in battle and although Aratus had gained such a glorious success, in which he did not lose even a single soldier, he nonetheless failed to capture or liberate Argos, because Agias[124] and the younger Aristomachus[125] entered the city with the king's troops and seized control of its affairs.

This event did much to silence the calumnies, the mockery and the vulgar jests made at Aratus' expense by those who, hoping to flatter and win favour with tyrants, told stories about how the general of the Achaeans, just before battle, would have troubles with his bowels, or how drowsiness and vertigo[126] would grip him as soon as it was time for the trumpet to sound, or how, after he had arrayed his forces for battle and given the watchword, he would ask his officers and commanders whether his further presence was required – inasmuch as the die was already cast – and would proceed to await the outcome far from the actual combat. Indeed, remarks like these were so prevalent that even philosophers, in their lectures, when they are investigating whether palpitations of the heart and alterations in colour and runny bowels in the presence of danger are signs of cowardice or are instead indications of a faulty physical constitution and a frigid temperament, always cite Aratus as an example of a brave general who nonetheless always suffered these maladies before combat.

30. After Aratus had destroyed Aristippus, he began immediately to plot against Lydiades[127] of Megalopolis, who was tyrant in his native city. Now this man possessed a noble nature, which expressed itself in his strong desire to win honour. Unlike most autocrats, then, he had not usurped power because he was dissolute or greedy but rather because, fired in his youth by a desire for glory, he had naively applied to his grand aspirations the false and empty claims made for tyranny, how it is

something felicitous and wonderful. Now that he had established himself as tyrant, however, he found himself burdened by the weight of absolute power. Jealous of Aratus' successes, and fearful of his schemes, Lydiades experienced a change of heart which led him to devise the most noble design, first, to liberate himself from hatred and fear and from soldiers and bodyguards, and, second, to become his city's benefactor. Consequently, he sent for Aratus, surrendered his office and enrolled his city in the Achaean League.[128] For this reason, the Achaeans honoured him greatly and elected him general.[129]

Urged on by his ambitious nature, Lydiades at once endeavoured to surpass Aratus in glory, and this led him to decree many needless undertakings, including an expedition against the Lacedaemonians.[130] When Aratus opposed him, he was viewed by others as acting out of envy, and so Lydiades was elected general for a second time,[131] even though Aratus was openly hostile to his candidature and worked hard to secure the office for someone else. Now Aratus, as I mentioned before, was general every other year. Lydiades, too, enjoyed popular favour and held the office every other year in alternation with Aratus – until he was elected for the third time.[132] It was then that he declared before the Achaeans his open enmity with Aratus and made many accusations against him, after which he found himself rejected and disregarded by a public who believed Lydiades was contending against a man of authentic and unalloyed virtue, whereas his own character was artificial.[133] For just as in the fable of Aesop, when the cuckoo asks the little birds why they flee from him, they tell him it is because one day he will be a hawk,[134] so in the case of Lydiades, because he had once been a tyrant, he was always stalked by the suspicion that his repudiation of tyranny had been insincere.

31. Aratus won fame for his dealings with the Aetolians at a time when the Achaeans were keen to do battle with them at the edge of Megarian territory[135] and Agis,[136] the king of the Lacedaemonians, had come with his army and was urging the Achaeans to fight.[137] Aratus was opposed to this, and for that reason was widely vilified and greatly mocked and jeered at for

effeminacy and cowardice, but he would not abandon what he deemed an advantageous policy[138] for fear of appearing dishonourable. Consequently, he allowed the enemy uncontested passage across the Geranian mountains[139] and into the Peloponnese. When, however, the Aetolians, during the progress of their march, suddenly captured Pellene,[140] Aratus became an altogether different man, nor did he waste time gathering and assembling an army from the whole of Achaea. Instead, he set at once to attack the enemy with the forces at his disposal.

As it was, the Aetolians, flush from their success, had become undisciplined and sure of themselves, and this rendered them vulnerable. For no sooner had they entered the city than the soldiers were dispersed throughout the private houses, where they jostled one another and brawled over the plunder, while their officers and commanders went around seizing the wives and daughters of the Pellenians. Taking off their helmets, they set them on the heads of the women they grabbed, so that no one else would take them, inasmuch as it would be clear from the helmet who was each woman's master. Now the Aetolians had given themselves up entirely to these activities, when suddenly they learned that Aratus was attacking them. They were stricken with panic – as one would expect of soldiers in such a state of disorder – and even before all of them had become aware of the danger, those Aetolians who were the first to engage the Achaeans, at the city gates and in the suburbs, had already been defeated and put to flight. The very sight of these men fleeing in retreat disheartened the others who were rallying to come to their aid.

32. In the midst of this tumult, the following incident occurred. One of the prisoners was a daughter of Epigethes, a distinguished man, and she was a magnificent woman, beautiful and statuesque. Now she happened to be sitting in the sanctuary of Artemis, because a captain of one of the elite corps had left her there, having seized her and put his triple-crested helmet on her head. All of a sudden, she rushed out to view the uproar taking place in the streets, and as she stood in front of the gates of the sanctuary and gazed down upon the combatants below, still

wearing the triple-crested helmet, the citizens saw in her a prodigy of superhuman majesty, whereas the enemy, believing they beheld a divine apparition, were so overcome with terror and astonishment that not a single man continued to defend himself.

The Pellenians themselves, however, tell a different story. According to them, the wooden image of the goddess is ordinarily stored away and left untouched, and on those occasions when the priestess removes it and carries it outside, no one looks directly at it but instead everyone turns away, for the sight of it is terrifying and dangerous for human beings and even trees, if this image is carried past them, become sterile and abort their fruit. During this conflict, they claim, the priestess carried the image out of the sanctuary and by constantly turning it in the faces of the Aetolians, deprived them of their senses and their reason.[141]

In his *Memoirs*, however, Aratus mentions nothing like any of this.[142] He reports only that he routed the Aetolians, chasing them first into the city but finally driving them out by force, killing 700 of them. This exploit has been celebrated as one of the greatest ever, and the painter Timanthes[143] depicted the battle in a painting of the most vivid composition.

33. Even after this victory, however, because so many nations and dynasts were joined by their common hostility against the Achaeans, Aratus immediately endeavoured to create bonds of friendship with the Aetolians, and in this matter he enjoyed the support of Pantaleon,[144] their most influential figure. He succeeded not only in making peace but also in establishing an alliance between the two leagues.[145]

In his zeal to liberate Athens,[146] Aratus came in for severe criticism on the part of the Achaeans and suffered damage to his reputation. This was because, although they had concluded a truce with the Macedonians and suspended hostilities, Aratus nonetheless made an attempt to capture the Piraeus.[147] He denies this in the *Memoirs* that he left behind, instead blaming Erginus, his collaborator in the attack on the Acrocorinth.[148] He maintains that Erginus attacked the Piraeus on his own initiative, and, when his ladder broke and he was being pursued, kept crying out for Aratus by name, as if Aratus were actually present, and by doing this tricked the enemy and effected his escape. But this defence is unconvincing. For it is unlikely that Erginus, who was merely a private individual and a Syrian, would have conceived of an undertaking this bold unless Aratus were in charge, and unless Aratus had supplied him with the soldiers and the opportunity to make his attack. Aratus' own actions prove this point, for he attempted to seize the Piraeus not twice or even three times but multiple times, nor, in spite of his failures, did he let it go, but each time, like an unrequited lover, regained his confidence – because he always came so close to success even when his hopes were dashed. Once he actually wrenched his leg as he was fleeing across the Thriasian plain,[149] and his treatment for this injury[150] required numerous incisions. Consequently, for a long time he conducted his campaigns while being carried in a litter.

34. When Antigonus died[151] and was succeeded as king by Demetrius, Aratus' struggle for Athens increased in intensity, and he regarded the Macedonians with total contempt. And so, after he was defeated in battle at Phylacia by Bithys,[152] a general of Demetrius – and there were many stories abroad that claimed he had been captured, and others alleging that he had died – Diogenes,[153] who was the commander of the garrison in the Piraeus, sent a letter to Corinth ordering the Achaeans to withdraw from the city, since Aratus was dead. It so happened, however, that when the letter arrived Aratus was actually in Corinth, and Diogenes' emissaries, after furnishing a good deal of entertainment and laughter, went away. Furthermore, the king himself sent a ship from Macedon: its mission was to bring Aratus to him in chains. And the Athenians leapt beyond the limits of frivolity in their flattery of the Macedonians when they put on garlands at the first report of Aratus' death. At this Aratus was furious and at once marched out against them, advancing as far as the Academy.[154] There he was persuaded to do them no harm.

Thereafter the Athenians recognized his virtue, and when,

after the death of Demetrius,[155] they decided it was time to win back their freedom, they appealed to Aratus for help. Although at the time another man[156] was acting as the general of the Achaeans, while Aratus remained bedridden with a long illness, he nevertheless had himself carried to the city in a litter so he could be of service, and succeeded in persuading Diogenes, the commander of the garrison, to give the Piraeus, Munychia, Salamis and Sunium[157] to the Athenians in exchange for 150 talents, to which sum Aratus himself contributed 20 talents. Aegina and Hermione[158] then immediately joined the Achaean League, as did the greater part of Arcadia, and because at this time the Macedonians were busied with struggles along their frontiers against neighbouring enemies,[159] whereas the Aetolians were Achaean allies, the power of the Achaean League was greatly magnified.

35. Now Aratus returned to his long-standing pursuit,[160] for he could no longer bear the presence of tyranny in nearby Argos, and so he sent representatives to Aristomachus in an attempt to persuade him to lay down his power and attach his city to the Achaean League, indeed, to emulate Lydiades[161] by preferring to become the distinguished and honoured general of a great nation instead of remaining hated and in constant danger as the tyrant of a single city. Aristomachus consented, and instructed Aratus to send him 50 talents so that he could settle with the soldiers who served him and dismiss them. This sum was furnished.

At this time,[162] however, it was Lydiades who was general, and his ambition led him to try to make it appear to the Achaeans that this agreement was his own achievement. Consequently, he disparaged Aratus to Aristomachus, pointing out that he was a man who was unrelenting in his hatred for tyrants. And when Lydiades had persuaded Aristomachus to entrust the whole matter to himself, it was he who introduced Aristomachus to the Achaeans. But on this occasion the Achaean assembly made absolutely clear its goodwill towards Aratus and its confidence in him, for when he angrily opposed the proposals regarding Aristomachus, the assembly rejected them.

Later, when Aratus was persuaded to adopt his previous position and appeared in person before the assembly to argue in support of these proposals, the assembly quickly and enthusiastically ratified them. Argos and Phlius[163] were admitted into the league, and in the following year Aristomachus was elected general.[164]

Aristomachus enjoyed high prestige among the Achaeans, and, wanting to invade Laconia,[165] he summoned Aratus to come to him from Athens.[166] Aratus instead wrote him a letter in which he discouraged this expedition, for he did not want the Achaeans to find themselves in a struggle against Cleomenes,[167] a bold figure who was growing increasingly, and dangerously, powerful. But when Aristomachus set out anyway, Aratus obeyed unconditionally and joined the campaign in person. Still, it was during this invasion that, when Cleomenes came upon them at Pallantium,[168] Aratus prevented Aristomachus from engaging him in battle.[169] For this he was denounced by Lydiades, when the two of them were contending for the office of general, but the vote was favourable to Aratus and for the twelfth time[170] he was elected general.

36. During his year in office, Aratus was defeated by Cleomenes in a battle near the Lycaeum[171] and took to flight. Because he was separated from the others during the night, everyone believed that he had been killed, and once again a report of his death circulated widely among the Greeks, but in fact he was safe. And instead of being satisfied with escaping alive, he rallied his troops and seized this opportunity, when no one was expecting it or even giving any thought to its possibility, for a sudden assault on Mantinea, a city that was allied to Cleomenes. He captured the city, installed a garrison and made all its resident aliens into full citizens.[172] All on his own, then, Aratus gained for the defeated Achaeans what they could not easily have acquired had they been victorious.[173]

The Lacedaemonians then undertook a new expedition, this time against Megalopolis. Aratus went to the city's aid, but was hesitant about giving Cleomenes an opportunity of using skirmishers to draw the Achaeans into a pitched battle, and for this reason resisted the Megalopolitans in their demands for action. Aratus had never been naturally well disposed to fighting pitched battles, and on this occasion his army was inferior in numbers. And he was up against a man who was daring and young, whereas his own courage was past its prime and his ambition had dimmed. He also thought that the reputation Cleomenes did not yet possess, but was trying to gain by his daring, he had already and must preserve by way of his caution.

37. Nevertheless, his light-armed troops did make a sally against the Spartans and drove them back as far as their camp, where Aratus' men became dispersed among the tents. Even then Aratus would not advance his infantry. Instead, he stationed them before a ravine separating the two forces and ordered them not to cross it. This inaction outraged Lydiades, who hurled abuse at Aratus and then summoned the cavalry, bidding them go to the help of the pursuers and not let victory slip away. He furthermore pleaded with them not to forsake him as he went into combat for the sake of his native city. He was soon joined by many brave men, and taking courage in their numbers he attacked the enemy's right wing, which he routed and put to flight. His ardour and his desire for glory, however, combined to make him reckless, and he let himself be drawn into terrain that was very complex, heavily planted with trees and lined with broad ditches. Here he was ambushed by Cleomenes and fell,[174] after fighting brilliantly and nobly before the gates of his native city. The rest of the cavalry fled back to the main line of the infantry, throwing the soldiers into confusion and thus spreading their experience of defeat over the whole of the army. Aratus was severely blamed for this, because he appeared to have abandoned Lydiades. The Achaeans left the field in anger and Aratus was compelled to follow them to Aegium.[175] There an assembly was held which voted to deny him funds and to stop providing him with mercenaries: if he wished to continue this war, he must provide his own means for doing so.[176]

38. Indignant at this treatment, Aratus resolved at once to surrender the public seal and resign his office, but, after giving the matter some thought, he continued as general for the rest of his term. Leading the Achaeans to Orchomenus,[177] he fought a battle with Megistonous,[178] Cleomenes' stepfather, in which he gained a victory,[179] killing 300 of the enemy and capturing Megistonous alive. Now, it had become customary for Aratus to be general every other year, but when next his turn came round, although he was nominated, he refused to accept the office, and Timoxenus was elected general.[180] The excuse that is usually given for his refusal is that he was angry with the Achaean public, but this is unconvincing. His actual reason was the state of affairs in which the Achaean League found itself.

For no longer did the power of Cleomenes advance quietly and gradually, nor were his designs any longer hindered by civic authorities. Indeed, after he had murdered the ephors,[181] redistributed the land and made many resident aliens into full citizens, he possessed complete control of Sparta.[182] At once he began to menace the Achaeans and demand that he be granted hegemony over the league.[183] Indeed, this is why Aratus is regarded by many as blameworthy, because, at a time when affairs of state were beset by surge and storm, he was like a ship's pilot who deserts his post and leaves the rudder to someone else[184] – when the right thing for him to do was to take command of the Achaean League, whether or not it was willing, and save it.

Or if he despaired of Achaean affairs and the might of the Achaean League, it was better that he should yield to Cleomenes than reduce the Peloponnese to a condition of barbarism by allowing Macedonian garrisons to be installed[185] and by filling the Acrocorinth with troops of Illyrians and Gauls.[186] Nor, in the case of men he had overcome militarily and politically – and whom he constantly abuses in the pages of his *Memoirs* – should he have turned them into despots in their own cities while diplomatically describing them as allies. For if Cleomenes was lawless and tyrannical – and it must be conceded that he was – he was nevertheless descended from the

Heracleidae[187] and a native of Sparta, and even the most obscure citizen of that city was more worthy than the greatest of the Macedonians to be made their leader by men who have even the least regard for the noble character of Greek birth. Furthermore, Cleomenes, when he sought this office from the Achaeans, promised the cities many good things in exchange for the honour and title they were bestowing,[188] whereas Antigonus,[189] although he was proclaimed their leader with absolute authority on land and at sea, would not accept the office until the Achaeans agreed to offer him the Acrocorinth as payment[190] for his leadership. In this he copied the hunter in Aesop's fable, for he would not mount the Achaeans, however much they begged him to do so and submitted themselves through their embassies and decrees, until they accepted garrisons and offered him hostages, just as if they were consenting to wear bridles.[191]

And yet Aratus employs all his eloquence in justifying his decision as one dictated by necessity. Polybius, however, says that Aratus had long been suspicious of Cleomenes' boldness, and, well before there was any necessity of doing so, had begun secret negotiations with Antigonus.[192] He also induced the Megalopolitans to ask the Achaeans to make an appeal to Antigonus,[193] for these were the people suffering the most in this war, since Cleomenes was constantly invading and plundering their territory. Phylarchus[194] gives a similar account of these events, although one would be loath to accord him complete credence without Polybius' corroboration, for he is so fond of Cleomenes that, whenever he mentions him, he is carried away by his enthusiasm for the man, and he writes his *History* as if he were making a case in court, always accusing Aratus and defending Cleomenes.

39. The Achaeans, then, lost Mantinea when Cleomenes recaptured it,[195] and, after they were defeated by him in a pitched battle near Hecatombaeum,[196] became so panic-stricken that they immediately invited Cleomenes to come to Argos and there accept leadership of the league.[197] However, when Aratus learned that Cleomenes was on his way and had reached Lerna[198] with his army, he became frightened and sent repre-

sentatives to ask Cleomenes to come with 300 men only, inasmuch as he was joining friends and allies: if, however, he did not trust the Achaeans, he could accept hostages. Cleomenes responded that he was insulted and mocked by these demands, and so departed. First, however, he wrote a letter to the Achaeans filled with accusations and invective directed against Aratus. Aratus responded with letters denouncing Cleomenes. They went so far in abusing and defaming one another that they even maligned each other's marriages and wives.

After this, Cleomenes sent a herald to the Achaeans to declare war. He came very close, with the help of traitors, to capturing the city of Sicyon,[199] then turned aside to assault Pellene, which he took after the Achaean commander[200] fled. Shortly thereafter he captured Pheneus and Penteleium.[201] Then Argos went over to his side, and Phlius accepted a Spartan garrison. In short, not one of the cities that had recently been added to the Achaean League remained safe or reliable. Indeed, Aratus found himself surrounded by great turmoil, for he saw how agitation was spreading throughout the Peloponnese as all its cities were being disrupted by revolutionaries.[202]

40. Indeed, no place remained undisturbed, nor was anyone satisfied with the current condition of political affairs, but even at Sicyon and Corinth there were many who were known to be in negotiations with Cleomenes, men who, owing to their passion for personal power, had long held the Achaean League in secret disaffection. In order to check these parties, Aratus was invested with absolute power.[203] In Sicyon he executed any who were disloyal, but in Corinth, when he tried to discover and punish traitors there, he angered the multitude, who, in their simmering hostility against the government of the Achaean League, had begun to feel oppressed by it.[204] Therefore the Corinthians hastily assembled in the temple of Apollo and summoned Aratus, having resolved either to kill or arrest him, after which they would rise up against the league. He came, leading his horse behind him, like a man without any distrust or suspicion, when suddenly many in the assembly leapt to their feet, hurling abuse and accusations. Aratus, however, kept

his composure, and with a mild voice asked them to sit down
and not to stand all at once, shouting in an unruly fashion, but
instead to allow inside those who were waiting at the door. As
he was saying these things, Aratus gradually retired, as if he
were intending to hand over his horse to someone, and in this
way he slipped out. As he made his way through the city, he
spoke calmly with any Corinthians he met and advised them to
go to the temple of Apollo, and he carried on like this without
attracting attention until he had reached the citadel. There he
leapt on his horse and ordered Cleopater, the commander of
the garrison, to guard the place closely. He then rode to Sicyon,
followed by only thirty of his soldiers, for the rest had deserted
him and dispersed. The Corinthians soon learned of his escape,
and, although they pursued him, failed to capture him. They
then summoned Cleomenes and handed their city over to him.
For his part, the king believed that what he received from the
Corinthians was less than what he had lost when they let
Aratus get away. When all the inhabitants of the region known
as Acte[205] came over to Cleomenes and put their cities under his
control, he began to build a wall and a palisade around the
Acrocorinth.

41. A majority of the Achaeans joined Aratus at Sicyon, and, at
an assembly convened there, he was elected general with absolute authority. He then surrounded himself with a bodyguard
recruited entirely from his fellow-citizens. For thirty-three
years[206] he had directed the political affairs of the Achaeans
and had been of all the Greeks pre-eminent both in power and
reputation. But now he found himself isolated and helpless,
like a man adrift in the shipwreck of his native city, amid great
surge and peril. For the Aetolians, when he sought their aid,
refused him,[207] and although the Athenians were grateful and
well disposed to him, they were prevented from helping him by
Eurycleides and Micion.[208]

Now, Aratus possessed a house and property in Corinth,
which Cleomenes did not touch, nor would he allow anyone
else to do so. Instead, summoning Aratus' friends and stew-
ards, he instructed them to manage and protect everything as if

they were to render an account to Aratus himself. Privately, the king sent Tripylus[209] to Aratus, as well as, later, Megistonous, Cleomenes' stepfather, with promises of many things, including an annual pension of 12 talents, which would double the pension sent by Ptolemy, who each year paid Aratus 6 talents.[210] In exchange, Cleomenes demanded that he be declared the leader of the Achaeans and enjoy an equal share with them in safeguarding the Acrocorinth. Aratus responded that he was not the master of state affairs but was instead mastered by them. Cleomenes decided that Aratus was mocking him and at once invaded the territory of Sicyon, ravaging and plundering it. For three months he encamped before the city, but Aratus held out steadfastly. During this time, he pondered whether he should accept Antigonus as an ally on the condition of handing over the Acrocorinth to him, for the king was unwilling to help on any other terms.

42. The Achaeans then held an assembly at Aegium and summoned Aratus to attend.[211] But it was dangerous for him to travel, since Cleomenes was encamped before the city. Furthermore, his fellow-citizens wanted to keep him in Sicyon and begged him not to expose himself to harm while the enemy were near, and even the women and children clung to him, weeping and crowding round him as if he were their common father and saviour. Nevertheless, after reassuring and comforting them, he rode out of the city and down to the sea in the company of ten friends and his son, who was now a young man.[212] There they found ships lying at anchor, and, embarking on these, were conveyed to the assembly in Aegium. At this assembly the Achaeans resolved to summon Antigonus and hand over the Acrocorinth to him. Aratus even sent his son to the king, along with the other hostages. Angered by these actions, the Corinthians plundered Aratus' property and made a present of his house to Cleomenes.

43. As Antigonus drew near with his army – he led a force of 20,000 Macedonian infantrymen and 1,300 cavalrymen – Aratus, along with the federal magistrates[213] of the Achaean

League, travelled by sea to meet him at Pegae.[214] He had to elude Cleomenes to get there, and yet, at the same time, he was dubious about Antigonus and absolutely distrusted the Macedonians. This was because he knew how his own rise to eminence had been predicated on the harm he had done Macedonian interests and that the first and most important of his political principles had been his hatred of the previous Antigonus. Nevertheless, because he recognized that he had been brought to this juncture by the inexorable force of his circumstances, to which even those who appear masters are really slaves, he did not flinch from this dreadful encounter. As for Antigonus, when he was informed that Aratus was coming to meet him, whereas he greeted the other Achaeans politely but with due restraint, Aratus he at once welcomed with exceptional honour. And because in all his subsequent dealings with Aratus the king found him to be a man of courage and intelligence, he drew him into his inner circle.

It was not only that Aratus was valuable in important affairs. More than anyone else, he was a charming companion when the king was at leisure. Therefore, although Antigonus was still young,[215] as soon as he observed how Aratus was by nature exceptionally well suited to be a king's friend, he consistently preferred his intimacy to anyone else's, either of the Achaeans or of the Macedonians who had accompanied him. In this way an omen which a god had revealed to Aratus through a sacrificial victim came to be proved true. For we are told that, not long before these events took place, Aratus was offering a sacrifice in which two gall-bladders were found wrapped within a single layer of fat inside the victim's liver, which the seer interpreted as meaning that very soon Aratus would enter into an intimate friendship with what he most hated and opposed. At the time Aratus put little stock in this prediction, since it was his habit to distrust sacrificial signs or oracles and to prefer relying on his own calculations. Later, however, at a time when the war was going well, Antigonus gave a feast at Corinth to which he invited many guests. One of them was Aratus, whom the king allowed to recline near himself in a position of honour.

It was not long before the king demanded that a cover be brought and asked Aratus whether it seemed cold to him as well. When Aratus answered that he was indeed shivering from the chill, the king directed him to draw nearer so that the slaves could cover both of them with the blanket they brought. At that moment Aratus remembered the sacrifice and burst out laughing. He then told the king about the omen and the prediction it inspired. But this happened at a later time.

44. After Antigonus and the Achaeans had exchanged oaths at Pegae, they turned directly to their campaign against the enemy. But inasmuch as Cleomenes had fortified Corinth, and its citizens defended themselves energetically, their struggle to take the city was a difficult one.[216] In the meantime, Aristotle of Argos,[217] a friend of Aratus, contacted him in secret, promising the defection of his city from Cleomenes if Aratus would bring forces there. After consulting with Antigonus, Aratus took 1,500 soldiers[218] and boarded ships that sailed swiftly from the Isthmus to Epidaurus. But the Argives staged their revolt before Aratus arrived, falling upon Cleomenes' men and locking them up in the citadel. When Cleomenes learned of this, he was afraid that, if his enemies seized control of Argos, they could cut him off from returning safely to Sparta. Consequently, he abandoned the Acrocorinth during the night and rushed to the aid of his forces in Argos.[219] He reached the city ahead of Aratus and once there quashed the Argive insurrection. Not long after this Aratus drew near, and when Antigonus, too, came into view with his army, Cleomenes withdrew to Mantinea.[220]

On account of this, all the cities that had defected again joined the Achaeans, and Antigonus took possession of the Acrocorinth. Aratus was elected general by the Argives,[221] and he persuaded them to make a present to Antigonus of all the properties of the tyrant[222] and those who had betrayed the city to Cleomenes. As for Aristomachus, he was tortured and drowned in the sea at Cenchreae. This episode did great damage to Aratus' reputation, since a man who was by no means wicked, who had often cooperated with Aratus and who on his advice had surrendered his power and brought his city into the Achaean League, was nonetheless put to death in so lawless a fashion.[223]

45. By this time, Aratus was held to blame for other matters of Achaean policy as well. For instance, it was deemed his fault that they had made a present to Antigonus of the city of Corinth, as if it were simply some small village; that they had permitted him to sack Orchomenus[224] and install a Macedonian garrison there; that they had decreed that they would neither write nor send an embassy to any other king without Antigonus' permission;[225] that they were obliged to furnish supplies and salaries for Macedonian soldiers;[226] and that there were sacrifices, processions and games in Antigonus' honour, which were initiated by Aratus' fellow-citizens, who welcomed Antigonus into their city,[227] where he lived in Aratus' house as his guest. But his critics were unaware that, since he had given the reins to Antigonus, he was being dragged along in the train of the king's authority and was no longer master of anything except his own voice, and even then it was dangerous for him to speak freely. For many of the king's actions clearly upset Aratus, especially his treatment of statues. The statues of the tyrants in Argos, which had been removed from view,[228] Antigonus restored, yet at the same time he removed the statues of the men who had captured the Acrocorinth,[229] with the exception of Aratus'. Aratus made numerous appeals to the king regarding these matters, but could not persuade him.

The behaviour of the Achaeans towards Mantinea[230] has also been condemned as contrary to the values of the Greeks. For after they had conquered the Mantineans, with the assistance of Antigonus, they put to death the most illustrious or eminent of its citizens. Of the rest of the population, some they sold into slavery, others they sent to Macedon in chains, and they enslaved their children and wives. They divided among themselves a third of the money thus acquired, and the other two thirds they handed over to the Macedonians. Admittedly, these actions conform to the law of reprisal, for although it is an odious thing to treat men of the same race and blood in this way out of anger, nevertheless 'in the midst of necessity even cruelty becomes sweet',[231] as Semonides puts it, applying, as it were, healing and restoration to an anguished and festering soul. Where the subsequent treatment of this city is concerned, however, Aratus can hardly be excused by appealing either to honour or necessity. After the Achaeans received this city as a gift from Antigonus, they decided to resettle it and chose Aratus as its founder. He was also general at the time and secured a decree abolishing the name of Mantinea and instead naming the city Antigonea, which it is called even today.[232] And so, because of Aratus, the name of 'lovely Mantinea'[233] appears to have been altogether blotted out, while its current name preserves the honour of those who exterminated and killed its citizens.

46. Later Cleomenes was defeated in a decisive battle[234] near Sellasia. He then quit Sparta and sailed for Egypt.[235] Antigonus, after he had shown Aratus every just and friendly consideration, led his forces back to Macedon. There he fell ill, and so he sent the successor to his throne, Philip, who was still quite a young man,[236] to the Peloponnese. He urged Philip to attach himself very closely to Aratus, and through him to be introduced to the cities and become known to the Achaeans. And indeed, Philip was so warmly welcomed by Aratus that, when he returned to Macedon, he was teeming with goodwill towards the man and charged with ambition and zeal for the affairs of the Greeks.

47. After the death of Antigonus,[237] the Aetolians began to despise the Achaeans for their laxity, since, now that they had got into the habit of letting themselves be rescued by foreign hands and shielding themselves behind Macedonian arms, they had fallen into sloth and indiscipline. Accordingly, the Aetolians thrust themselves into the affairs of the Peloponnese. Pillaging the territories of Patrae and Dyme[238] along the way, the Aetolians invaded Messenia and ravaged it.[239] Aratus was enraged by this, but he perceived that Timoxenus, who was general at the time, was hesitating and temporizing because his term of

office was nearly at its end. Aratus had been elected to succeed him, and so took office five days early in order to go to the aid of the Messenians. He assembled a force of Achaeans, but, because they were unfit and untrained, they met with defeat at Caphyae.[240] Aratus was criticized for conducting this operation impetuously, and so, checked yet again, gave his plans up for lost and abandoned his hopes. Thereafter, even though the Aetolians gave him many openings, he ignored them, letting them romp wantonly and insolently through the Peloponnese as if they were revellers at a party. So once more the Achaeans stretched out their hands towards Macedon and sought to bring Philip into Greek affairs, not least because, owing to the king's goodwill and loyalty to Aratus,[241] they expected to find him disposed to be both helpful and compliant in all matters.

48. It was then,[242] for the first time, that the king let himself be persuaded by the calumnies against Aratus voiced by Apelles and Megaleas[243] and certain other courtiers. As a consequence, he associated himself with the Achaean faction opposing Aratus and encouraged the Achaeans to elect Eperatus[244] as their general. This man, however, was thoroughly despised by the Achaeans, and, so long as Aratus remained uninvolved, Achaean affairs failed to prosper. Philip then perceived the magnitude of his error[245] and reverted to his former association with Aratus, entrusting himself entirely to his advice. By and by, as their common endeavours tended to enhance his own power and reputation, Philip attached himself even more closely to Aratus, for he was convinced that it was due to this man that he was increasing in both glory and grandeur. And everyone agreed that Aratus was a sound tutor, not only for a democracy but also for a monarchy. For his conduct and his character were reflected, like splashes of colour, in the deeds of the king. Indeed, instances of this include the young king's moderation towards the Lacedaemonians when they had wronged him,[246] his negotiations with the Cretans, through which he brought the whole island over to his side in only a few days[247] and his marvellously energetic campaign against the Aetolians. All of these achievements added to Philip's reputation for taking good

advice and to Aratus' for having good advice to give. These
successes only inflamed the jealousy of the king's courtiers,
who, having failed to do Aratus any harm by way of their
secret calumnies, now began to insult him openly at their banquets, abusing him with great vulgarity and insolence. Once
they went so far as to pursue him and throw stones at him as
he was returning to his tent after dinner. Philip was incensed by
this and at once fined them 20 talents.[248] Later, however,
because these men continued to appear detrimental to his
affairs and a source of trouble, he put them to death.[249]

49. But soon the king, elevated by his successes and his steady
flow of good fortune, began to develop many grand passions,
and his native perversity, proving too strong for his artificial
pretence to virtue, stripped it away, little by little laying bare
and revealing his true character. He began by committing a private transgression against the younger Aratus, when he seduced
his wife,[250] a misdeed that went undetected for a long time
because he was a guest in their home. Then he started treating
the Greek cities harshly, and it soon became clear that he no
longer intended to be guided by his association with Aratus. It
was at Messene that Philip first exhibited suspicious behaviour.[251] The city was beset by factional strife and Aratus was
late in coming to its aid, whereas Philip arrived a day before
him and had no sooner entered the city than, like a gadfly,
began to excite the factions one against the other. In private, he
asked the generals of the Messenians if they had laws they
could enforce against the multitude, and, again in private, he
asked the leaders of the multitude if they had hands they could
raise against the tyrants. Encouraged by this, the magistrates
tried to arrest the demagogues, but they, advancing at the head
of the multitude, killed the magistrates as well as nearly
200 other citizens.

50. After Philip had brought about this dreadful massacre and
while he continued to aggravate the mutual hostilities of the
Messenians, Aratus arrived. He did not hide his indignation
at what had taken place, nor did he curb his son when he

reproached Philip bitterly and insulted him. Now the young man, so it seems, was a lover of Philip, and during his speech on that occasion said to Philip that there was no longer anything beautiful in his appearance, after committing a deed so foul, but he had instead become the ugliest of all men. Philip did not respond to this, although everyone expected him to do so, since more than once during the young Aratus' speech he had burst out in anger. Instead, he acted as if he bore these strictures meekly, like a man whose nature was moderate and civil, and, taking the senior Aratus by his right hand, he guided him from the theatre.

He led him to the Ithomatas[252] in order to make a sacrifice to Zeus and to inspect the place, for it is no less well fortified than the Acrocorinth and, should a garrison be installed there, it would be a formidable stronghold very difficult for its neighbours to take by force. Philip went up and sacrificed, and, when the seer presented him with the entrails of the ox, he took them in both hands and showed them to Aratus and Demetrius[253] of Pharus. He leaned towards each of them in turn, asking what it was they detected in the sacrifice: should he become master of the citadel or restore it to the Messenians? Demetrius laughed and answered, 'If you have the soul of a seer, you will release the place, but, if you have the soul of a king, you will seize the bull by both horns.' He was speaking metaphorically, indicating that, if Philip added the Ithomatas to the Acrocorinth, then the whole of the Peloponnese would be tamed and subjected to his will. Aratus for a long time said nothing, but, when Philip pressed him to give his opinion, said, 'There are, Philip, many tall mountains in Crete, and many citadels exist in Boeotia and Phocis; and throughout Acarnania,[254] both inland and on its shores, there are many admirably well fortified places, not one of which you occupy, and yet all these peoples willingly obey you.[255] Brigands cling to cliffs and dwell on precipices, whereas for a king there is no stronger or surer protection than loyalty and gratitude. It is owing to these that the Cretan sea and the Peloponnese lie open to you. And it is owing to these that you, at your young age, are already leader here, and master there.'[256]

As he was speaking, Philip handed the entrails to the seer. He then took Aratus by the hand and said, 'Come, then, let us take the same road,' indicating he had been dislodged from his position by Aratus and would give up the city.

51. Soon, however, Aratus began to withdraw from the court and gradually retired from his intimate association with Philip. When the king was crossing into Epirus and asked Aratus to join him in this expedition,[257] he refused and stayed behind, for he was afraid of tainting himself with the dark reputation Philip was earning. After Philip, hard pressed by the Romans, disgracefully destroyed his fleet and his entire enterprise collapsed in failure,[258] he returned to the Peloponnese, where he again tried to cheat the Messenians. When he was found out, he injured them openly by ravaging their lands.[259] After this, Aratus shunned the king in every way, nor did he trust him in the least, for he had become aware of the scandalous affair taking place in the women's quarters of his household.[260] He was sorely grieved by this matter, but hid it from his son, who, should he learn of the outrage, could do nothing to avenge himself. Indeed, Philip seemed to have undergone a profound and inexplicable transformation, from a gentle king and a sober youth into a lecherous man and an odious tyrant. But in fact there was no alteration in Philip's nature. Instead, once he believed he could act with impunity, he at last revealed his perversity,[261] which he had long disguised out of fear.

52. From the very beginning, Philip had been accustomed to regard Aratus with a mixture of shame and fear, and this became clear from the way he treated Aratus now. For he was eager to see him dead, thinking that he could never enjoy the independence of a free man, much less the licence of a tyrant or a king, so long as Aratus lived. But he did not want Aratus killed by force. Instead, he ordered Taurion,[262] one of his officers and friends, to carry this out in some secret way, preferably by poisoning him at a time when the king was not present. So Taurion became a regular associate of Aratus and administered

poison to him – not one that works violently and quickly but
one that starts by causing gentle fevers and a weak cough and
only gradually brings about death. None of this went unnoticed
by Aratus, but, since there was nothing to be gained by making
accusations, he endured his suffering silently and in a mild
spirit, as if he had an illness of a common and familiar kind.
Only once did he deviate from this. When one of his friends,
who happened to be with him in his room, saw him spit blood
and was surprised, Aratus said, 'These, Cephalon, are the
wages of royal friendship.'

53. This is how he died, at Aegium, while general for the
seventeenth time.[263] The Achaeans strongly desired that he be
buried there and that he receive a memorial worthy of the life
he had led, but the Sicyonians felt it would be a misfortune if
he were not interred in their city, and they persuaded the
Achaeans to hand over his body. But there was an ancient law
that no one could be buried within the city's walls, and this law
was scrupulously and superstitiously observed,[264] so they sent
to Delphi to consult the Pythia[265] about this matter and she
answered them with this oracle:

Do you wish, Sicyon, to honour Aratus eternally for the lives he saved,
With sacred celebrations in the name of your departed lord?
Whatever place is distressed by this man or distresses him
Is unholy, be it made of earth or sky or sea.[266]

When this response was reported, all the Achaeans rejoiced,
especially the Sicyonians, who, changing at once from grief to
festivity, donned garlands and white garments in order to bring
the body of Aratus from Aegium into their city amid paeans and
choruses. They chose a commanding site and buried him there,
hailing him as the founder and saviour of their city. Even today
this place is called the Arateium and there they offer him sacrifices.[267] One is performed on the day when he freed the city
from tyranny, which is the fifth day of the month Daesius, which
the Athenians call Anthesterion.[268] They call this sacrifice the

Soteria.[269] The other one takes place on the anniversary of his birth. The first of these sacrifices is performed by the priest of Zeus the Saviour, the second by the priest of Aratus, who wears a headband which is not entirely white but white and purple. Hymns are sung to the accompaniment of the lyre by members of the Artists of Dionysus.[270] The gymnasiarch[271] also takes part in the procession, leading the boys and young men of military age, and he is followed by the city's council and all other citizens who wish to take part. These sacred rites, performed on their prescribed days, are still observed, but only a few traces of the ancient ceremonies remain. Most of these honours have lapsed, owing to the passage of time and changing circumstances.

54. Such, according to historians, was the life and character of the senior Aratus. As for his son, he was robbed of his reason by Philip, who was by nature an abominable man, marked by insolence and cruelty alike. He gave him poisons that, although they did not kill him, nonetheless left him crazed. Indeed, Philip reduced him to a creature possessed of frantic desires – at once frightening and strange – for bizarre adventures and for experiences that were both shameful and destructive. Consequently, his death, although it came when he was still a young man and in the full bloom of life, was not a misfortune but rather a deliverance from evil, and his salvation.

For his unholy crime, however, Philip never ceased, so long as he lived, paying just penalties to Zeus, protector of hospitality and friendship. For when he was vanquished in war by the Romans and submitted himself to their dominion, he was deprived of most of his empire, surrendered all his navy except five ships, promised to pay an indemnity of 1,000 talents and sent his son to Rome as a hostage.[272] Owing only to the Romans' pity did he keep Macedon and its tributaries. He was continually executing the noblest of his subjects as well as his closest kinsmen, as a result of which his entire kingdom feared and hated him. Amid so many evils, he enjoyed only one spot of good fortune, a son[273] who excelled in virtue. But he killed him too, out of envy and jealousy of the honour paid him by the

Romans. His kingdom, then, he left to his other son, Perseus, who, we learn, was not his legitimate son but spurious, the offspring of a seamstress named Gnathaenion.[274] It is Perseus whom Aemilius led in triumph, and in him the royal line of the Antigonids came to its end.[275] By contrast, the line of Aratus continues in Sicyon and Pellene down to my own time.

PHILOPOEMEN

INTRODUCTION TO
PHILOPOEMEN

Last of the Greeks

Only in his pairing of Philopoemen and Flamininus does Plutarch set two contemporaries in parallel, men who, although allies, were, at times at least, rivals as well. In a sense, then, although *Philopoemen* and *Flamininus* were relatively early entries to the *Parallel Lives*,[1] in their composition and themes they reflect many of the concerns of Plutarch's entire literary project. Which is to say that here Plutarch finds space to comment on the cultural situation of Greece in a world increasingly dominated by Rome – while focusing most closely on the timeless moral condition of two gifted men who, even if they do not entirely overcome the deficiencies in their character, remain great men nonetheless.

Philopoemen was remembered as 'the last of the Greeks', a description that in Plutarch underscores his importance as a representative of Greek national character.[2] Although a controversial figure in his own time, he was idolized by the historian Polybius, who knew and admired him and who, like his father Lycortas, shared his political orientation. Polybius composed an encomium of Philopoemen in three books, though that work is now lost, and he is a central figure in the historian's account of the politics of the Achaean League. Polybius' Philopoemen is every inch the Greek hero: strong and valorous, hard working and honest, and a patriot under whose leadership Achaea at last brings unity to the Peloponnese. Plutarch's treatment of Philopoemen, by contrast, although it relies heavily on Polybius and shares his favourable view of the man, eschews hagiography.[3]

Philopoemen and the Achaean League

Despite his fame, Philopoemen's career was unevenly recorded. He was born at Megalopolis around 253 BC and was a young man during the Cleomenean War of 228–222 BC, the event which attached the Achaean League to Macedon.[4] When, in 223 BC, Sparta's king, Cleomenes, captured Megalopolis, Philopoemen played a leading role in rallying the city's populace and aiding its escape to Messene. In the next year, at the battle of Sellasia, he led a bold cavalry charge wrongly represented in later sources as decisive to its outcome. Still, this feat certainly brought him to the attention of Antigonus Doson, the king of Macedon and the leader, or *hegemon*, of the Hellenic League (to which the Achaean League by then belonged). For the next ten years of Philopoemen's life he campaigned in Crete on behalf of the city of Gortyn. We know almost nothing of that period – plainly it did not interest Polybius – but it has plausibly been argued that in Crete Philopoemen worked in the interests of Macedon and against those of Sparta. While he was away, Philip V succeeded Antigonus on the Macedonian throne, and the leading figure in the Achaean League, Aratus, died. When Philopoemen returned from Crete, in 211 or 210 BC, he was immediately elected the league's *hipparch*, the commander of its cavalry, for 210/9, proof that his time in Crete had added to his reputation and influence at home.[5]

During his term as *hipparch*, Philopoemen laboured to improve the Achaean League's military proficiency, a slow development that gradually enhanced its capacity for asserting a degree of independence in its international relationships at a time when the league was increasingly dependent on, and subordinate to, its *hegemon* Philip V.[6] Nonetheless, true to its obligations, the Achaeans fought alongside Philip against Rome in the First Macedonian War (214–205 BC), during which Philopoemen held the office of general (*strategos*) three

times. For the most part, however, the Achaeans concentrated
their hostilities against Sparta, at that time a Roman ally. Sparta
was in the hands of Machanidas, yet another in a sequence of
absolute rulers in a city suffering from continual social unrest
and faction.[7] Philopoemen defeated him at the battle of Mantinea in 207 BC, a success that for ever secured his reputation
for valour and generalship in Greece (chs. 10–11).

The battle of Mantinea also occasioned the beginning of the
Achaean League's drift away from Macedon. At the same time,
Machanidas' successor in Sparta, Nabis, began to work mira-
cles there.[8] Soon, in combination with Cnossus on Crete, Sparta
was once more an international power and a threat to the
Achaean League. By 204 BC Achaea and Sparta were intermit-
tently at war, until, sometime in 202/1 BC, Nabis seized control
of Messene. At this provocation, Philopoemen, though a private
citizen, raised a force sufficient to drive Nabis out (ch. 12), a
bold achievement that won him acclaim and a fresh term as
general. Achaea soon declared war on Nabis, while Philopoemen once more departed for Crete.

But before he removed himself to Crete, Philopoemen presided
over the first of Rome's overtures to the Achaean League.[9] It was
obvious that Rome and Macedon would again come to blows,
only this time the stakes were to be much higher than in the First
Macedonian War and the Romans hoped to persuade the Greeks
to side with them against Philip.[10] Naturally, the Achaean League
preferred to find a middle path between such powerful belliger-
ents. As for Philopoemen, because he did not remain on the scene
but departed in 200 or 199 BC, he was not an obvious influence
in subsequent Achaean deliberations, which went Rome's way. It
has been suggested that Philopoemen's second visit to Crete, as
mysterious to modern scholars as his first, was at least in part
intended to blunt Nabis' influence there.[11]

In his absence, there were drastic transformations in the
political situation of Greece and of the Achaean League. War
broke out between Philip and Rome, the Second Macedonian
War (200–197 BC), and in 199/8 BC, the league, dissolving its
connection with Philip, sided with the Romans (Livy 32.19–23).
In the following year, Nabis followed his Achaean enemies into

the Roman fold, although he was not above double-dealing with Philip when it suited his interests. In the year after that, Philip was defeated – a victory followed up by the Romans' decreeing the freedom of the Greeks. Philopoemen missed it all, however, and did not return from Crete until sometime in 194/3 BC.[12]

His time in Crete had done little to diminish his standing in the league. He was again general in 193/2 BC, when he continued to oppose Nabis, despite the Romans' unwillingness to tolerate further warfare between their two allies. For his part, Philopoemen insisted that the Achaeans' alliance with the Romans did not deprive them of an independent foreign policy, and this position led to serious conflicts between the Achaean general and the Roman Flamininus, who, after his victory over Philip, was the main representative of Roman policy in Greece. In 192 BC Nabis was assassinated, and Philopoemen forcibly united Sparta with the Achaean League.[13]

From 191 to 188 BC, Rome was at war with Antiochus the Great and his Aetolian allies. During this contest the Achaeans remained loyal to Rome.[14] Meanwhile, the condition of Sparta remained a source of controversy within and without the Achaean League. The effects of social upheaval over so long a time had left the city in a shattered state, and internal political rivalries had dispersed a multitude of Spartan exiles throughout Greece. It was Philopoemen's desire to resolve Sparta's difficulties – but only in ways that helped to ensure Achaean domination, interference that provoked Spartan resistance and led to a prolonged cycle of conflicts. In the end, Philopoemen imposed order through mass execution, the destruction of the city's defences and the eradication of the traditional Lycurgan constitution (ch. 16).[15]

Spartan appeals to Rome were answered by further Roman efforts to persuade the Achaean League to moderate its treatment of the city. Rome sent a series of distinguished embassies, including, in 183 BC, a commission of three former consuls headed by Flamininus, in an attempt to improve Sparta's situation. All were rebuffed by Philopoemen and his supporters, including Lycortas. These diplomatic exchanges about Sparta took place within a larger Achaean debate over how far the league should go in accommodating Roman demands. In every case, Philopoemen insisted on the Romans' observing the letter of their alliance, a position that led to personal friction between himself and Flamininus and made the Greek leader unpopular with the Roman senate.[16] Before the matter could be satisfactorily resolved, Messene rebelled against the Achaean League in 182 BC. Philopoemen, who was then general for the eighth time, responded militarily, was captured by the Messenians and put to death by them (chs. 18–20).[17] The Achaeans, led by Lycortas, quickly reasserted control in Messene and honoured Philopoemen with a public funeral (ch. 21: Polybius 23.16).

Plutarch's Philopoemen

Plutarch's treatment of Philopoemen, although favourable, is more textured and qualified than Polybius'. In this Life, as well as in *Titus Flamininus*, Plutarch emphasizes the themes of Greek freedom, of Roman influence, of Greek independence in the presence of Roman power – and of Greek contentiousness. These were all matters of contemporary relevance for Plutarch's readers. Elsewhere, Plutarch is at pains to remind Greek leaders how their powers are exercised in a universe dominated by Rome: 'As you enter into office . . . you must say to yourself, "You rule as a subject: the city is subject to proconsuls, the procurators of Caesar"' (*Moralia* 813e). Greek politicians had an absolute duty, in Plutarch's view, to deal with Roman government in a dignified yet sensibly subordinate manner – and especially to avoid domestic faction. These were the keys to their enjoying in the best way the freedom that the Romans permitted them to have (*Moralia* 814b–816a, 824c). And it was, to return to Plutarch's representation of things in this pairing, the Greeks' historic failure to rid themselves of contentiousness that ultimately frustrated their desire for independence. In *Titus Flamininus* (ch. 11), after the proclamation of Greek freedom in 196 BC, Plutarch provides an account of Greek reflections on the significance of the event:

At this moment of celebration, it was all the more natural that
they should talk and reflect on the fate of Greece. They thought
of all the wars she had fought for freedom; but freedom had
never come more firmly or delightfully than now, and it had come
almost without blood and without grief, championed by another
people . . . If one discounted [the wars against Persia], all Greece's
wars had been fought internally for slavery, every one of her trophies had been also a disaster and reproach for Greece, which
had generally been overthrown by its leaders' evil ways and
contentiousness.

Contentiousness, which by Plutarch's day appears to have con-
joined the ideas of 'love of victory' (*philonikia*) with 'love of
strife' (*philoneikia*), is here depicted as something like a congenital failure on the part of the Greeks' heroes, valiant though
they were.[18] The last of the Greeks, Plutarch insists, shared this
debilitating quality.[19]

Plutarch's Philopoemen is a man possessed of a great nature,
the kind of character Plutarch later analysed in strongly Platonic terms when he turned to Coriolanus and Alcibiades.[20]
Here Plutarch underscores Philopoemen's *phronēma*, his pride
or spirit, which, especially when activated by anger, induces
him to perform bold but sometimes inappropriate deeds.[21] For
example (ch. 16), when Flamininus and the Achaean general
Diophanes, marched on Sparta:

That stirred Philopoemen's anger, and he did something which
was not precedented nor strictly justifiable, but was certainly the
great deed of a great-hearted man [i.e. a man with 'a great spirit',
a *megalon phronēma*]. He went to Sparta himself, and barred the
entry of the Achaean general and the Roman consul, private citizen though he was.

Or, again (ch. 17), when Philopoemen opposes Flamininus'
attempt to restore the Spartan exiles, only to secure their restoration in the following year so that the credit could be his,
Plutarch observes: 'That was the sort of combative and conten-

tious approach to authority that his proud spirit [*phronēma*] inspired.' In each passage we see Philopoemen so roused that he cannot resist a startling confrontation. Still, it is so-far-so-good at this stage of his Life, inasmuch as in each of these instances Philopoemen scored a success, with no real harm done.

According to Plutarch, a nature like Philopoemen's demands a philosophical education to moderate it,[22] and although Philopoemen had the benefit of excellent teachers (ch. 1), his approach to the higher forms of Greek culture was narrow and selective (ch. 4). He was more interested in warfare, the enterprise which consumed his attention, something marked from the beginning by Plutarch's initial likening of the young Philopoemen to Achilles under the tutelage of Phoenix (ch. 1). Consequently, his great nature fell prey to contentiousness, the result of which, in this Life, is his indecently harsh treatment of Sparta and his abolition of its ancient constitution, by which action he mistreated his fellow-Greeks 'in the most savage and unprecedented way imaginable' (ch. 16). It is also Philopoemen's contentiousness that, in the end, brings about his own humiliation and death. The point is made explicitly in the final *Comparison*, which insists that Philopoemen 'was also thought to have thrown away his life in his anger and contentiousness, for his hastening to Messene was not timely, but quicker than it should have been' (*Comparison Philopoemen–Flamininus* 1).

For Plutarch, however, none of this diminishes Philopoemen's undisputed virtue. Contentious he may have been, but Philopoemen was also a champion of Greek freedom. Victor at Mantinea, where he struck down the tyrant Machanidas, Philopoemen was celebrated at the Nemean festival, and rightly so according to Plutarch. Philopoemen also liberated Messene from the tyrant Nabis and defeated him in battle, deeds that inspired Greek adulation even as they stimulated Flamininus' jealousy (chs. 14–15). And it was Philopoemen who brought Sparta into the Achaean League, thereby unifying the Peloponnese under a single government free from autocracy. Even Philopoemen's resistance to Roman interference in Greece,

Plutarch makes clear, was in pursuit of freedom (*Comparison Philopoemen–Flamininus* 3). He struggled to preserve Greece's dignity as well as its liberty, which is why, although Plutarch esteems Flamininus' benefactions towards Greece as 'noble', Philopoemen's dignified independence in the face of Roman power was 'nobler still' (*Comparison Philopoemen–Flamininus* 3).

In a sense, Philopoemen, like the Plutarchan heroes of the late republic such as the Younger Cato or Brutus, was a man who found himself pitted against the inevitable: the rise of Rome, like the end of the republic in favour of imperial rule, was divinely propelled.[23] Plutarch openly concedes the Greeks' – and Philopoemen's – failure to overcome their principal deficiency, but he quite naturally mourns Greece's loss of independence, even if it was unavoidable. All of this is inscribed in the conclusion of this Life, when Plutarch observes how Philopoemen's excellence was recognized by the Romans, when, after the Achaean War of 146 BC, they refused to remove Philopoemen's statues. In this, Plutarch observes, the Romans did the correct thing: 'Rewards and gratitude are owed to benefactors from those they benefit, but good men deserve honour from all those like themselves' (ch. 21). But this gesture, he hardly need elaborate, came only after the destruction of Corinth, the very city in which Flamininus had proclaimed the freedom of the Greeks fifty years before. Now, however, although Greece was not formally annexed, the days of its independence were truly at an end.[24] Philopoemen's fight, however futile, had been for something worth fighting for.

Sources

Plutarch's most important source for this Life was Polybius, both his *Histories*, which cover the period of Philopoemen's life in Books 10–24 (not all of which are preserved for us in their entirety) and his (now lost) encomium of Philopoemen. Livy narrates this same period in Books 24–39 (Philopoemen's death is recorded at Livy 39.50), but it is unlikely that Plutarch felt any need to consult him when he had Polybius at his disposal.

For the early chapters of this Life, Plutarch also turned to
Phylarchus, as he did for his *Aratus* and his *Agis & Cleomenes*.[25]
Finally, at chapter 16 Plutarch cites Aristocrates (*FGrH* 591), a
Spartan historian of the early imperial period who composed a
history of Sparta from the time of Lycurgus down at least to the
time of Nabis.

PHILOPOEMEN

[c. 253–182 BC]

1. There was once a Mantinean called Cleander,[1] an aristocrat and one of the most powerful men in the city. He fell upon hard times, was driven into exile, and came to Megalopolis.[2] It was mainly because of Philopoemen's father, Craugis,[3] a man distinguished in every respect and Cleander's personal friend, that he chose the city; and as long as Craugis was alive he did everything he could for Cleander, and when he died Cleander repaid his generosity by acting as guardian to his orphaned son. It was like Homer's tale of Phoenix bringing up Achilles.[4] In just the same way, Philopoemen's character from the very beginning was moulded and grew in a noble and kingly way.

When Philopoemen reached adolescence, the Megalopolitans Ecdelus and Demophanes[5] took over his guardianship. Both men had been disciples of Arcesilaus[6] in the Academy, and stood out among their contemporaries for their application of philosophy to the realities of politics. They liberated their own city from tyranny by secretly organizing the group which was to kill Aristodemus;[7] they helped Aratus in expelling Nicocles, tyrant of Sicyon;[8] and when the men of Cyrene[9] asked them for help when their city had collapsed into political chaos, they sailed out and imposed a most splendid settlement which restored order and legality. They themselves counted Philopoemen's education among their achievements, claiming that through their philosophy they had moulded the boy into a blessing for all Greece. Indeed, it was as if Greece had borne him in her old age as a late-born brother to those great leaders of old, and Greece consequently loved him greatly, bestowing power on him which grew along with his glory. A Roman once praised him as 'the last of the Greeks':[10] never again (that was the implication) did Greece bear a man who was truly great, and worthy of her past.

2. Some people think he was ugly, but that is not true, as we can see from a surviving statue at Delphi.[11] There is a story of a woman of Megara[12] who failed to recognize him when he was her guest, but that was because of a certain easy-going unpretentiousness in his manner. She had heard that the general of the Achaeans was coming, and, very flustered, was preparing dinner: it happened that her husband was away. Then Philopoemen arrived, wearing a cheap soldier's cloak. She thought he was one of the servants who had been sent on ahead, and told him to help with the preparations. He immediately threw off his cloak and began to cut the wood. Then the husband came in, Philopoemen's old guest-friend,[13] and saw what was happening. 'What's this, Philopoemen?' he asked. 'It can only be one thing,' replied Philopoemen in broad Doric:[14] 'I'm paying the punishment for my wretched appearance.' As for the rest of his body, Titus Flamininus once said jokingly that 'you have fine hands and legs, Philopoemen, but no belly', for he was rather slender in the middle. But the joke was really aimed at his military power, for he had fine infantry and cavalry but was often short of money. These, then, are the stories they tell about Philopoemen in the schools.[15]

3. As for his character, his ambition was not altogether free of contentiousness nor devoid of irascibility. He particularly wanted to model himself on Epaminondas,[16] and he certainly reproduced a powerful version of Epaminondas' energy, his insight and his incorruptibility. But he could not retain his mildness or gravity or humanity towards political opponents, for his anger and contentiousness were simply too strong. He consequently seemed more attuned to military than to political excellence: even in childhood he was already fond of soldierly things, and threw himself enthusiastically into the lessons which were helpful for this – practice in armed fighting, for instance, or riding.

He was naturally good at wrestling, too, but when some of his friends and tutors encouraged him to train systematically, he first asked them whether athletics would compromise his military training. They replied by telling him the truth: that an athlete's body and lifestyle are totally different from a soldier's, and in particular their training and diet diverge widely[17]— athletes need lots of sleep, they have regular meals and eat until they are full, and they follow a carefully ordered regimen with prescribed periods of activity and rest; that is what develops and keeps them in peak condition, and the slightest disturbance or change in their routine quickly changes them for the worse. But a soldier needs to be experienced in every sort of irregularity and fluctuation, and in particular he must be able to bear privation and sleeplessness with ease. When Philopoemen was told this, he not only kept well away from athletics himself and ridiculed the activity: later, when he was general, he also did everything he could to discourage the practice by penalizing and humiliating anyone who took part in any kind of athletic competition. They were making the most useful bodies quite useless, he said, for the contests for which they were really needed.

4. His training was not finished when he reached the end of his formal education. In the regular thieving and plundering raids which his countrymen made into Laconia,[18] he disciplined himself to be the first to march out and the last to return; and he spent his spare time developing his agility and strength through hunting or farming on his fine estate. This was some 2½ miles away from Megalopolis, and he would walk out to it every day after dinner or supper, then throw himself down on any mat he found and take his sleep just like any of the workmen. Next morning he would get up early and help with pruning the vines and herding the cattle, then go back to the city and join his friends and the magistrates in managing the business of public affairs.[19] When money came in from his campaigns he would spend it on horses and weapons and ransoming prisoners, not on his own household or property: that, he thought, was to be maintained and improved from his farming, the most virtuous

way of making money. And, indeed, farming was no sideline, for Philopoemen thought it entirely right for a man to have wealth of his own if he was going to keep his hands off other people's.

He listened to philosophers' lectures and read their books, but he was selective, choosing only those he thought would help him in developing virtue and courage; and he had similar tastes in Homer, favouring those passages which would encourage bravery and stimulate the imagination. Apart from Homer, his favourite reading matter was the *Tactics* of Evangelus,[20] and he knew the histories of Alexander's campaigns;[21] he thought that literature was conducive to action, provided it was not read just to pass the time or to provide topics for idle conversation.

When it came to tactical problems, he did not bother with the maps or diagrams in notebooks: he examined the topographical questions and tried things out on the battlefields themselves. He would examine how slopes would meet one another, or where a plain suddenly fell away, and as he walked around he would think questions over and put them to his companions: what would happen to the shape of a phalanx[22] when it met a stream or a ditch or a narrow pass, and was drawn out and then compressed back in upon itself? It really does seem that this man spent more of his energy and ambition on military matters than he should have done, welcoming warfare as the most challenging and varied sphere in which excellence shows itself, and despising as idlers anyone who fell short of his standards.

5. He was already thirty when King Cleomenes[23] of Sparta suddenly attacked Megalopolis by night, overcame the guards and burst in and took control of the central square. Philopoemen rushed to the rescue, but was unable to force the enemy out, despite fighting vigorously and boldly. Still, in a way he managed to steal his countrymen away from the city by fighting against their pursuers and drawing Cleomenes' attack on to himself; he staggered back last of all, wounded and without his horse.

They got away to Messene,[24] and Cleomenes sent a messenger to them offering to restore the city with all its possessions and its territory.[25] The Megalopolitans were delighted by this, and eager to return; but when Philopoemen saw how keen they were he spoke against accepting the offer. Cleomenes was not giving back the city, he explained, he was simply acquiring its citizens as well, so that the city would be even more firmly within his power:[26] for he would hardly be able to sit idly guarding empty walls and houses, but would have to abandon the city if it were deserted. These arguments[27] convinced the citizens and they rejected the offer, but Philopoemen thus gave Cleomenes the excuse to destroy and dismantle most of the city, and return to Sparta loaded with its wealth.

6. Soon King Antigonus[28] arrived and marched with the Achaeans against Cleomenes, who occupied the heights and passes around Sellasia.[29] Antigonus drew up his army nearby, intending to attack Cleomenes and force a passage. Philopoemen was stationed among the cavalry[30] with his fellow-countrymen, and next to them were the Illyrians,[31] who had been given the flank to defend as they were so numerous and such fierce fighters. Their[32] orders were to remain stationary in reserve until the king raised a signal – a purple cloak on a spear – from the other wing.

The commanders tried to force the Spartans back by launching the Illyrians against them, and as this was happening the Achaeans kept to their orders and waited in their ranks. Cleomenes' brother Eucleidas[33] realized that this was creating a gap in the enemy line of battle, and quickly sent his lightest troops around the rear; they were told to attack the Illyrians from behind, and, now that they were separated from the cavalry, to draw them away completely. That is exactly what happened, and the light troops were beginning to detach the Illyrians and throw them into disorder. But Philopoemen saw that it was not difficult to attack these light troops, and that this was the right moment to strike. First of all he told the king's officers, but they ignored his advice – indeed, they thought he must be mad, for he did not yet have the sort of great reputation which would have lent credibility to such an ambitious stratagem. So he led his countrymen into action himself. First of all there was confusion, then some of the enemy light troops fled and many were killed.

At this point Philopoemen wanted to give Antigonus' men even more encouragement, and bring them swiftly into action while the enemy were in such disorder. So he leapt from his horse and went on foot to some rough, winding terrain, full of streams and gullies. As he was still wearing his cavalryman's breastplate and heavy armour, it was a difficult and exhausting struggle. Then he was wounded, with both his thighs pierced through by a single javelin. The wound was not mortal, but it was certainly grave: the point was even sticking out on the other side. To start with he was completely immobilized by it, and he could not think what to do, for the javelin's thong made it difficult to pull the point back through the wound. No one even dared to touch it. But the battle was reaching its critical point, and Philopoemen was chafing with eagerness to return to the fight. By moving his legs backwards and forwards he managed to break the javelin in the middle, and he immediately gave orders to pull each half outwards.[34] Once he was freed, he grabbed his sword and rushed through the front line against the enemy, an encouraging and inspiring sight to his fellow-soldiers.

Antigonus went on to win the battle,[35] and later he asked the Macedonians why they had moved the cavalry forward without his orders. They explained, rather defensively, that it was not their fault: they had no option but to join battle with the enemy, because a young Megalopolitan lad[36] had started the attack. Antigonus laughed aloud: 'That lad', he said, 'has done the job of a great general.'[37]

7. Philopoemen predictably became famous for this exploit, and Antigonus was eager for him to join his own staff, offering him a command and a rich reward. But Philopoemen politely declined. He would always find it hard to take orders meekly, and he knew it. But he did not want to be inactive or to have time on his hands, so to continue his military training and exercise he went to fight in Crete. There he spent a long time[38]

practising his skills among men whose fighting ability was as formidable and varied as their lifestyle was restrained and disciplined, and on his return to Achaea his reputation was such that he was immediately appointed *hipparch*.[39]

He took over a cavalry force which was deplorable. When it came to a campaign, they would grab whatever wretched horse they could find; they avoided most of the campaigns themselves, sending substitutes instead; they were totally and dreadfully inexperienced and cowardly; and yet the commanders turned a blind eye to all this, because the cavalry was made up of the most powerful men in Achaea, and could exercise particular authority[40] over rewards and punishments.

Undeterred, Philopoemen put a stop to all this. He even went around every city himself, speaking individually to all the young men, stirring them up with ambition and punishing any who needed it; he instituted exercises and parades and competitions with the maximum number of spectators; and in a short time he instilled an extraordinary vigour and enthusiasm into everyone. Most important of all, in tactical terms, he made them nimble and agile in turning and wheeling, both by squadron and by single horseman. After this training, the whole formation would change its position with such natural ease that it seemed just like an individual moving his body at will.[41]

When the fierce battle was fought at the River Larissus[42] against the Aetolians and Eleians, the Eleian *hipparch* Damophantus[43] rode straight for him, but Philopoemen responded to the attack by getting in his spear-thrust first and cutting him down. As soon as he had fallen the enemy fled, and Philopoemen's reputation rose even further. The young could not rival his bravery nor the old his insight, and, in fighting as in leadership, he was peerless.

8. It was Aratus who first brought power and prestige to the Achaean League.[44] Previously it had been unimportant and fragmented, but Aratus gave it unity – a peculiarly humane political achievement, indeed, and one which was worthy of Greece. When land forms in the middle of rivers, the process tends to start from just a few small particles which solidify, and

then more material flows in and is captured, so that eventually everything combines to become firm, stable and hard.[45] In just the same way, Greece had at that time been weak and drifting, often fragmenting into its individual cities, but the Achaeans had begun the process of consolidation. First they themselves united, then they added some of their surrounding cities by helping them to liberate themselves from their tyrants;[46] they added others to the alliance by diplomacy, building on a communion of interests; and they aspired to bring the whole Peloponnese together as a single body and a single power.[47]

While Aratus was still alive,[48] most of their acquisitions were gained with the help of Macedonian arms, as they paid court first to Ptolemy and then to Antigonus and Philip, kings who were playing a central role in Greek affairs.[49] But when Philopoemen's primacy began the Achaeans were generally strong enough to fight powerful enemies on their own, and the days of imported champions were over. Aratus himself had a reputation for ineffectuality in warfare, and owed most of his successes to his charm, his gentle tact and his friendships with the kings, as I have explained in his own Life.[50] Philopoemen was different. He was a fine warrior, effective in arms, and with a record of good fortune and success which had begun with his very first encounters. He raised the Achaeans' confidence along with their power, and with him they grew used to victory and triumph in most of their conflicts.

9. First he reformed the Achaean tactics and weaponry,[51] which were in a sorry state. They used light shields which were easy to wield but too slender to protect the body, and spears which were much smaller than the Macedonian pikes: all this certainly made them mobile, and they were effective and formidable at long range, but the enemy held the advantage in close exchanges. The Achaeans were not used to forming up in companies, either, and in the phalanx they neither couched their pikes nor linked their shields in the Macedonian fashion,[52] so that they could readily be pressed together or dragged apart. Philopoemen pointed out the problems, and persuaded them to switch from light shield and spear to heavy shield and

pike. They adopted helmets, breastplates and greaves, and practised a standing and stationary rather than mobile and light-armed style of combat.

Once he had persuaded the young men to take up arms, the next thing was to inspire a confident belief in their own invincibility, then shrewdly to redirect their tastes for luxury and extravagance in a new direction. It was not possible to remove their empty and shallow vanity completely – it was too ingrained, with their taste for fancy clothing and dyed coverlets, and their preoccupation with outdoing one another in their smart dinner parties and fine tableware. But Philopoemen began to divert this dandyism from inessentials to things which were vital and honourable, and swiftly persuaded everyone to cut back on their everyday consumption: they now competed instead in the conspicuous splendour of their military outfits. Soon the workshops could be seen full of men breaking up goblets and Thericlean cups,[53] and using the gold and silver to plate cuirasses, shields and bridles; every stadium was packed with colts being trained and young men practising at fighting with their arms; the women had their hands full dyeing helmets and crests and embroidering horsemen's tunics and soldiers' cloaks.

The sight spurred the Achaeans' confidence, and inspired a bold eagerness to take risks and face dangers. For conspicuous extravagance on anything else makes people soft and effeminate: it is as if the tingles of sensation break down the power of the mind. But expenditure that is directed in this way makes the spirit strong and grand. When Achilles' new arms were laid beside him, Homer made him swell with vigour at the sight, inflamed by the thought of using them.[54] Philopoemen's young men were similarly inspired. Next he trained and exercised them in tactical movements, and they responded eagerly and ambitiously; they were also extraordinarily enthusiastic about the close order in which he drew them up, for it seemed to give a firm solid barrier which could withstand anything; and their body armour came to feel light and manageable, as in sheer delight at its splendour and beauty they fondled it and made a habit of wearing it. They could not wait to use their weapons in action and fight it out with the enemy.

10. This was the time when the Achaeans were fighting their war against Machanidas,[55] tyrant of Sparta, a man who had designs on the whole Peloponnese, and the resources and power to carry them through. News arrived that Machanidas had invaded Mantinea,[56] and Philopoemen led the army out against him. The generals drew up their armies close to the city: each deployed great numbers of mercenaries, as well as virtually all their citizen forces. The two armies closed with one another, and Machanidas' mercenaries routed the Achaean advanced detachment (this consisted of javelin-throwers and light cavalry[57]); but then, instead of moving straight on the main fighting force and breaking up their position, they fell away in pursuit and rushed straight past the Achaean phalanx, which steadfastly kept its ranks.

This was certainly a considerable reverse for Philopoemen, coming as it did right at the start of the battle – indeed, it appeared that the day was entirely lost. But Philopoemen made a show of disregarding it, pretending it was nothing serious. He realized too that the enemy were making a grave mistake in breaking off in pursuit in this way, for it detached them from their main phalanx and left a gap in their lines. So he made no move to prevent their attack on the section which was in flight, but let them go past until the gap became vast; then, when he saw that the Spartan phalanx was left exposed, he immediately led a charge against their hoplites,[58] swiftly moving out to launch a flank attack. The Spartans had been left leaderless, and they had not the slightest expectation that they would be engaged; indeed, they had an impression of total victory once they saw that Machanidas was off in pursuit. Philopoemen drove them back, with dreadful carnage – more than 4,000 are said to have died; then he charged against Machanidas himself as he returned with the mercenaries from his pursuit.

There was a broad, deep ditch separating the generals, and the two men rode along it opposite one another; the one was anxious to cross it and escape, the other equally determined to stop him. They hardly seemed like commanders in battle, but more like a wild beast at bay and a skilful hunter confronting him. Then the tyrant's horse – a strong, fierce animal, bloodstained on both flanks by his spurs – tried to leap across, but his forequarters caught on the bank, and he tried to struggle out with his front legs. Philopoemen's closest fighting companions in any battle were always Simmias and Polyaenus,[59] and now these two both charged at Machanidas, levelling their spears to strike – but Philopoemen reached him first. He saw that the struggling horse was raising his head in such a way as to protect Machanidas, and so turned his own horse a little to one side; then he grasped his spear firmly in the centre, thrust Machanidas to the ground and pressed the point home with all his weight. There is a bronze statue[60] of Philopoemen at Delphi showing him in exactly that attitude, set up by the Achaeans to show their admiration both for his heroism and for his tactical brilliance.

11. There is a story, too, which is told about the Nemean festival.[61] It was not long after the victory at Mantinea, and Philopoemen was general for the second time.[62] He was at leisure, for fighting had stopped for the festival. But first he put his phalanx on parade before the assembled Greeks, arrayed in their finery and moving through the exercises with their usual rapidity and vigour. Then he entered the theatre just as the musical competition was taking place, accompanied by his young men in their military cloaks and their purple tunics; all were in the peak of physical condition, all of the same age, and their demeanour conveyed their respect for the leader and their fierce youthful confidence, born of many glorious contests. They had just arrived when it chanced that the lyre-player Pylades,[63] performing Timotheus' *Persians*,[64] sang the opening line: 'He wrought Greece her freedom, her grand and glorious crown.'

His voice had an amplitude which went perfectly with the resonance of the verse. The whole theatre turned its eyes on Philopoemen, and applauded in jubilation: they thought of Greece's ancient glory, and began to hope for it once more. Their belief in themselves now recaptured something of that spirit of old.

12. When a young horse misses its usual master and is ridden by a stranger, it often shies and bridles and behaves unnaturally.

The Achaean League was rather like that when it came to battles or dangers. When anyone else was in command, its morale was low, and it turned its gaze longingly to Philopoemen; but the moment he was seen, it sprang up again and was immediately full of confidence and vigour. One reason for this was that they could see that he had a corresponding effect on the enemy. He was the one general whom they could not bear to face, so great was their fear of his reputation and his name. Their actions made that very plain.

One example[65] was King Philip of Macedon sending secret assassins to Argos to kill Philopoemen, thinking that the Achaeans would once again become submissive if he were out of the way; but news of the plot leaked out, and that did grave damage to Philip's popularity and reputation among the Greeks.[66]

Then there was the instance when the Boeotians were besieging Megara, and expecting to take it quickly.[67] Suddenly, a report reached them that Philopoemen was on his way to help the besieged, and was already nearing the city. That was quite untrue – but the Boeotians still abandoned their ladders, though they were already in position against the walls, and turned tail in flight.

A further example came when Nabis, the successor of Machanidas as tyrant of Sparta, had suddenly captured Messene.[68] As it happened, Philopoemen held no public office at the time, and had no forces under his command. First he tried to persuade the Achaean general Lysippus[69] to march to the Messenians' assistance, but Lysippus refused, claiming that the city was already lost now that the enemy was inside the walls. Philopoemen went anyway to the city's aid, and with him went his own fellow-citizens, without waiting for any legal enactment or formal election, following their superior as if he were their natural leader at all times. When news reached Nabis that Philopoemen was already near, he did not stay his ground, even though he was encamped in the city itself; instead, he stole out of some other gate and quickly led his army away, counting it good fortune enough if he made good his escape. And escape he did, but Messene was liberated.[70]

13. Those are deeds which tell to Philopoemen's credit. On the other side, there was his second spell in Crete.[71] He was responding to an appeal from the people of Gortyn,[72] who asked him to serve as general for their war. But many held it against him, for it took him away when his own country was under attack from Nabis; some said he was shunning danger, some that it was a badly timed piece of ambition among foreigners. Yet at the time the Megalopolitans were under such constant attack that they were forced to live within the walls and sow their crops in the streets, with their fields ravaged and the enemy encamped almost at the gates; and meanwhile, Philopoemen was away fighting Cretans, an overseas commander, so that his enemies naturally attacked him for running away from the war at home.

There were some, however, who argued differently. The Achaeans had picked other men to be their generals,[73] and Philopoemen was a private citizen: he had simply put his own leisure at the disposal of the Gortynians when they wanted him as their leader. For Philopoemen was no friend of leisure. It was as if he wanted to treat his skills as a general and soldier just like any other accomplishment, and keep them in constant action and use. He made that clear by the remark he once made about Ptolemy.[74] Some people were praising the king for giving his army superb training every single day, and submitting his own body to an excellent, tough regime of exercise under arms. 'And who', asked Philopoemen, 'can respect a king of that age who is training rather than achieving?'

The Megalopolitans were indignant at Philopoemen's absence, which they thought an act of betrayal, and they tried to exile him. But the Achaeans prevented this by sending their general Aristaenus[75] to Megalopolis, a man who was Philopoemen's political opponent, but who now prevented the condemnation from going through. The whole episode led Philopoemen's fellow-citizens to ignore him pointedly when he returned, and so he incited many of the neighbouring villages to revolt, encouraging them to argue that they had not originally made any contribution to Megalopolis nor lived under its power; and he himself openly supported such arguments, and played a part in raising a faction to oppose Megalopolis in the assembly of the Achaeans.[76]

But that was all later. For the moment he was busy helping the Gortynians in Crete. He did not behave like a traditional Peloponnesian and Arcadian and fight a simple, honourable war; instead, he adopted the Cretan style and used their type of clever trickery in developing a style of combat which was full of furtiveness and traps. He soon showed the Cretans up as mere boys at this sort of trade, and their tricks seemed silly and shallow when measured against the products of authentic experience.

14. People admired him for this, and he returned to the Peloponnese with a brilliant reputation from these Cretan exploits. He found that Philip had been crushed by Titus,[77] and that Nabis was at war with the Achaeans and with Rome.[78]

He was immediately elected to a command[79] in that campaign, and took the risk of engaging Nabis in a sea battle;[80] but here his experience turned out to match that of Epaminondas,[81] with his performance in naval contests falling far short of his own military excellence and reputation. But there was one difference. Some people say that Epaminondas was chary of allowing his countrymen any contact with the rewards of the sea, fearing lest (in Plato's phrase[82]) they might change from steadfast hoplites into degenerate mariners; for that reason, so they say, Epaminondas deliberately returned from Asia and the islands without achieving anything. Philopoemen, on the other hand, was quite convinced[83] that his infantry skills would stand him in good stead for naval contests as well, but he found out to his cost what a massive part of military excellence consists in training, and how much additional effectiveness it always gives to those who have experience.

Philopoemen consequently lost the naval battle because of his lack of expertise, but that was not all. There was a particular ship, an old but famous one, which had not sailed for forty years.[84] Philopoemen filled it with men and launched it, but it soon began to take on water, and the men on board were in great danger. His enemy thought little of him after that episode, and they formed the impression that he had totally given up the sea; Philopoemen himself was perfectly aware of this, and he also saw the arrogant confidence with which they were now prosecuting the siege of Gytheum.[85] So he immediately sailed against them, taking them quite by surprise as they carelessly relaxed after their victory; and he disembarked his men by night, attacked the enemy and set fire to the tents, burning down the camp and killing many of their men.

A few days later, Nabis suddenly appeared before him as he was marching through some difficult terrain. The Achaeans were alarmed, for it seemed inconceivable that they could fight their way to safety in such a tough position, with the enemy appearing to have them trapped. But Philopoemen waited for a short time and examined the terrain closely, and then gave a demonstration that tactical skill is the prince of all military arts. Thus he slightly altered the disposition of his own battle-line and adapted it to meet the danger, and calmly and easily overcame the difficulties which had seemed so hopeless; then he attacked the enemy and routed them thoroughly. He noticed that they had not made their escape to the city, but had scattered in different directions through the countryside. This was heavily wooded, with hills all around, and hard going for horses because of the numerous channels and ravines. Philopoemen halted the pursuit and pitched camp, even though it was still daylight. He realized that the enemy would try to steal back in ones and twos to the city under cover of darkness, and so he stationed a large force of the Achaeans in ambush on the streams and hills near the city, armed with short swords. That was where most of Nabis' men met their deaths. Each of them was making his way back as best he could, and there was no concerted retreat: they were just like birds flying down into a trap, as one after another fell into their enemy's hands near the city.[86]

15. After this he was the darling of the Greeks, who piled honours upon him in their theatres; and Titus, fond as he was of honour, began to feel a little irritation.[87] He was a Roman consul:[88] did he not deserve more of the Achaeans' admiration

than this Arcadian fellow? And he thought his services were far greater than Philopoemen's, given that by a single decree[89] he had liberated all those parts of Greece which had been enslaved to Philip and the Macedonians. And so Titus made terms with Nabis and brought the war to an end;[90] Nabis met his death, assassinated by the Aetolians;[91] and Sparta was in turmoil. Philopoemen grasped his moment. He attacked in force,[92] and by a mixture of compulsion and persuasion he brought the city over to join the Achaeans. That won him extraordinary admiration among the Achaeans, such was the fame and power of the mighty city he had acquired; and indeed, it was no small achievement to make Sparta part of Achaea. He had also encouraged and strengthened the Spartan nobility, and they hoped to find in him the guardian of their freedom.

They therefore voted to give him the proceeds of the sale of Nabis' house and property, which amounted to 120 talents, and sent him an embassy to inform him.[93] That was the moment when the man revealed himself in the purest light as possessing the reality of virtue, not just the semblance.[94] In the first place, none of the Spartiates[95] was willing to discuss bribery with a man like this, and in their nervousness and embarrassment they asked his guest-friend Timolaus[96] to approach him. Timolaus duly went to Megalopolis. When he was entertained by Philopoemen, he saw at close quarters the gravity of his manner, the simplicity of his lifestyle and a character which was utterly impervious to corruption; so he said nothing about the gift, made up some other excuse for his visit and went away. He was sent a second time, and the same thing happened. On his third visit, he finally brought himself to reveal what the city wanted. Philopoemen listened with pleasure. Then he travelled to Sparta himself, and advised them not to waste their bribes on friends and men of quality, for they could enjoy their virtue free of charge. It was the evil men whom they should buy up and corrupt, and those who were opposing the city in the congress:[97] that way the gifts might purchase silence and save the city trouble. It was wiser, he said, to deflect their enemies from plain speaking, not their friends. That is the measure of the man's splendid attitude towards money.

16. Then came news that more agitation was afoot in Sparta.[98] Diophanes[99] was now the general of the Achaeans, and when he heard this he determined to punish them; the Spartans too prepared for war, and this disturbed the whole Peloponnese. At this, Philopoemen tried to calm and restrain Diophanes. He pointed out the nature of the situation. They lay under the shadow of King Antiochus[100] and of the Romans – both with their massive armies – and a good commander should turn his thoughts in that direction; he ought not to stir up trouble at home, but should turn a blind eye and a deaf ear to such misdemeanours. But Diophanes would not listen. Instead, he joined Titus in invading Laconia, and marched directly on Sparta itself.[101] That stirred Philopoemen's anger, and he did something which was not precedented nor strictly justifiable, but was certainly the great deed of a great-hearted man. He went to Sparta himself, and barred the entry of the Achaean general and the Roman consul,[102] private citizen though he was;[103] and he calmed down the internal agitation and brought the Spartans back into the league, just as they had been at the outset.

Time passed, and Philopoemen himself had some grievance against the Spartans.[104] He was general at the time,[105] and he restored their exiles and killed a number of Spartiates, 80 according to Polybius, 350 according to Aristocrates.[106] He took down the walls; he cut off a large part of their territory and gave it to the Megalopolitans; he took all those who had been given Spartan citizenship[107] by the tyrant, and transported them to Achaea and settled them there, except for 3,000 who were unwilling to leave Sparta. These he sold into slavery, then used the money to build a portico in Megalopolis:[108] that seemed to add insult to the injury.

He had by now had enough of the Spartans. Their suffering had already outstripped their misdeeds, but Philopoemen continued to trample on them, and he treated the constitution in the most savage and unprecedented way imaginable: he dismantled and destroyed the Spartan system of education,[109] and forced their children and young men to undergo the traditional Achaean education rather than that of their own country. The assumption was that they would never be cowed as long as they followed the laws of Lycurgus. This then was the time when their series of great disasters had forced them to offer their sinews to Philopoemen to cut, and they became submissive and humble. Years later they received permission from the Romans to abandon the Achaean political system, and they restored and re-established their traditional one,[110] at least as far as was possible after such sufferings and destruction.

17. When war broke out in Greece between the Romans and Antiochus,[111] Philopoemen was a private citizen,[112] but there were various sights which made him most irritated not to be in command: Antiochus himself was sitting in Chalcis,[113] idling away his days in marriages and love-affairs with girls far too young for him, while the Syrians[114] were wandering undisciplined and unsupervised around the cities and wallowing in luxury. 'I envy the Romans their victory,' Philopoemen would say. 'If I had been general, I would have cut them all to pieces in their taverns.'

After their victory,[115] the Romans grew more and more involved in Greek affairs,[116] and they began to bring the Achaeans under their power. The demagogues were not prepared to stand up to them; Roman strength, with Heaven's help, grew steadily greater and more extensive; matters were approaching the end which the cycle of Fortune needed to reach.[117] Now Philopoemen behaved like a good helmsman struggling against the tide. He accepted that he needed to make some concessions to circumstances, but carried on the struggle on most of the issues, and endeavoured to draw the most powerful speakers and statesmen in the direction of liberty.

The most influential man among the Achaeans was now Aristaenus of Megalopolis,[118] and he consistently cultivated the Romans, arguing that the Achaeans should do nothing to oppose or offend them. Philopoemen, they say, listened to him in the congress and said nothing, until finally his anger and indignation proved too much for him: 'My dear man,' he burst out, 'why are you so eager to see the day of Greece's destiny?'[119] There was also an occasion when the Roman consul Manius[120] had defeated Antiochus, and presented the Achaeans with a demand that they should allow the Spartan exiles to return.[121] Titus supported Manius' demand. Philopoemen refused to allow the Achaeans to agree: it was not that he was hostile to the exiles, but he wanted their return to be the work of himself and the Achaeans, and not to come about thanks to Titus and the Romans. When he was general the following year, he restored the exiles himself.[122] That was the sort of combative and contentious approach to authority that his proud spirit inspired.

18. He was already in his seventieth year when he was general of the Achaeans for the eighth time.[123] By then he hoped not merely to escape warfare during his time in office, but also that events would allow him to spend the rest of his life in peace; rather as diseases become less acute as the human body loses its strength, so the Greek cities were becoming less contentious as they grew feebler. Yet a sort of nemesis[124] overtook him as his life approached its conclusion, rather like an athlete who is running well near the end of his race.

There is a story of a gathering when people were praising some man with a reputation for generalship: 'How can one respect a man', said Philopoemen, 'who was taken alive by the enemy?' And then a few days later Deinocrates[125] of Messene, a man who was a personal enemy of Philopoemen and was generally disliked for his evil and immoral behaviour, led Messene in a rebellion from the Achaean League,[126] and news arrived that he was on the point of taking a certain village called Colonides.[127] At the time Philopoemen lay sick with a fever in Argos, but on hearing this he hurried to Megalopolis,[128] covering more than 400 stades in a single day.[129] From there he went straight on to the aid of Colonides. He had with him a cavalry force which consisted of the most prestigious of the citizens; but they were men who were still young, following Philopoemen as volunteers because of the goodwill and enthusiasm he inspired.

They rode to Messene, Deinocrates came to meet them and the two forces engaged near the hill of Evander.[130] The Megalopolitans turned Deinocrates himself to flight, but then there suddenly appeared a force of 500 men who were guarding the Messenian borders. The first army was already as good as defeated, but at the sight of this second force they gathered once again on the hills, and Philopoemen was nervous that he might be surrounded. He was also keen to spare the horsemen. So he retreated through difficult terrain, stationing himself at the rear and frequently making sallies against the enemy so as to draw them all against his own person. The Messenians did not dare to return his attacks, but circled around and cried out noisily in the distance. Philopoemen had to keep stopping because of the young men under his command, and sent one after another off to safety, till he suddenly found himself cut off in the middle of the enemy.

Still no one dared to fight him at close quarters, but the missiles rained in on him from a distance, and he was forced back onto some steep and rocky ground. It was hard to handle his horse, and he kept tearing him with his spurs. Philopoemen bore his old age lightly thanks to his continual hard training, and there was no impediment there to his escape. But his recent illness had made him weak, and he was weary from the march; he grew sluggish and immobile, and was finally thrown to the ground when his horse slipped. It was a hard fall, and he suffered a blow to the head. He lay silent for a long time, so that the enemy thought he was dead and tried to move and despoil the body. At that point he raised his head and opened his eyes. They all fell on him, twisted his hands behind his back, bound him and led him away. As they did so they piled insults and abuse upon him, a man who would never have dreamed that he could suffer such a thing at the hands of Deinocrates.

19. Back in the city[131] everyone was extraordinarily excited by the news, and they crowded to the gates. But when they saw Philopoemen dragged along as a prisoner, it seemed so unworthy of his glory and his achievements and triumphs of old that most were moved to pity and sympathy: the tears welled as they reflected on the fragility and transience and emptiness of human greatness. Then, gradually a mood of generosity spread

among the ordinary people.[132] Should they not recall the blessings he had brought them in the past, and the freedom he had restored by expelling the tyrant Nabis?[133] There were only a few who played for Deinocrates' favour and urged that the man be tortured and killed as a stern and implacable foe – and one who would be all the more dangerous to Deinocrates if he were to escape death after being captured and humiliated at his hands. So, despite the opposition, they took him to the so-called Treasury. This was an underground cavern without light and air; it was not blocked off by a door, but by a great rock which was rolled up to it. They imprisoned him there, placed the rock in position and stationed an armed guard all around.

Meanwhile, the Achaean cavalry had regrouped after their flight, and Philopoemen was nowhere to be seen. They assumed he must be dead. For a long time they remained where they were, calling aloud on Philopoemen and telling one another how dishonourable and unfair was their escape: here they were after abandoning their commander to the enemy, a man who had risked his own life for their sake. Then they went forward and made inquiries, and heard how he had been captured. They immediately spread the news around the cities of Achaea, and everywhere it was regarded as a great calamity. The cities decided to send an embassy to the Messenians to demand the man's return, and meanwhile they made preparations for a military invasion.

20. While they were engaged on this, Deinocrates was afraid of delay. Time, he thought, was the one thing most likely to save Philopoemen, and he wanted to strike before the Achaeans could intervene.[134] It grew dark, and the Messenian crowd dispersed. Deinocrates opened the prison and sent in a public slave with some poison; his orders were to take it to Philopoemen and not to leave him until he had drunk it down. The slave found him lying on the floor in his soldier's cloak. He was not asleep, but deep in grief and anxiety. When he saw the light and the man standing by him with the poisoned cup, he managed to gather himself in his weak state and sit up; he took the cup and asked if the slave had any news about the cavalry, and par-

ticularly about Lycortas.[135] The man told him that most had escaped. Philopoemen inclined his head, and looked calmly at him: 'That is good,' he said, 'if not everything has gone badly.' That was all he said or uttered; he drained the cup, and lay back down again. The poison met with little resistance, and he died quickly in his weakened state.

21. When news of his death reached the Achaeans, the cities felt a common sense of shame and grief. The men of military age collected with the councillors at Megalopolis, and there was no delay at all in exacting vengeance; they elected Lycortas as their general,[136] invaded Messenia and ravaged the country, until the Messenians reached agreement and allowed the Achaean force to enter the city.[137] Deinocrates forestalled them by taking his own life. As for the others, those who had voted for Philopoemen's death were killed by them;[138] those who had voted to torture him were rounded up by Lycortas to suffer mutilation before they died.

They burnt Philopoemen's body and placed his ashes in an urn. It was all done in an ordered and careful way, and the homeward procession was triumphal as well as funerary: it was a sight to see – some people wearing crowns, the same persons weeping, the enemies led in chains. The urn itself, barely visible under all its garlands and crowns, was carried by Polybius,[139] the son of the Achaean general, and he was surrounded by the most prominent of the Achaeans. The soldiers followed in full armour, riding elaborately decorated horses and giving an impression neither of being downcast by their great grief nor of exultation at their victory.

People poured out to meet them from the cities and villages on the way, and it was as if they were congratulating the man himself on his return from campaign, touching the urn and escorting it back to Megalopolis. Then the elder men joined the gathering along with the women and children, and now the sound of mourning spread among the army until they reached the city. They were thinking with sadness of how much they would miss him; his death seemed to bring with it the end of the city's supremacy among the Achaeans. The urn was buried with all the honours one would expect; the Messenian prisoners were stoned to death next to the tomb.

There were many statues erected to Philopoemen, and many honours voted by the cities.[140] Later, at the time when Greece was suffering the troubles which culminated in the destruction of Corinth,[141] a certain Roman tried to remove them all: Philopoemen was Rome's bitter enemy, he needed to be driven out – it was all just as if he were still alive. Speeches were made, Polybius opposed the man's slanderous charges[142] and neither Mummius nor the commissioners[143] would allow the destruction of the honours of so famous a man, even though he had mounted considerable opposition to Titus and Manius. They were able to distinguish between human excellence and the needs of the time, and between honour and advantage. This was the correct and proper view. Rewards and gratitude are owed to benefactors from those whom they benefit, but good men deserve honour from all those like themselves. That is the story of Philopoemen.

TITUS FLAMININUS

INTRODUCTION TO TITUS FLAMININUS

The Freedom of the Greeks

It was unlikely in the extreme that Plutarch would have overlooked Flamininus, who vanquished Philip V and liberated Greece from Macedonian domination. Indeed, although a Roman, Flamininus was an honoured hero in Greece, a supreme benefactor – and Plutarch believed strongly in gratitude. But it could also not go unobserved that Flamininus' proclamation of the freedom of the Greeks in Corinth in 196 BC did not in fact usher in a new age of Greek independence. Instead, and not very gradually, Macedonian suzerainty was replaced by Roman authority. Admittedly, in Plutarch's view, this transition was part of a divine plan,[1] but its end was undeniable:

People did not only receive Roman commanders into their towns, they even sent and called for them and put themselves in their hands; and it was not merely peoples and cities which did this, but even kings who were wronged by other kings and fled to the Romans' arms. The result was that in a short time, perhaps with God's assistance, everything was within their power.

(ch. 12)

In pairing Philopoemen, 'the last of the Greeks', with the contemporary Roman who was their liberator, Plutarch rendered unmistakable the disturbing incompatibility of Greek freedom with the rise of Rome, and thus emphasized for his

readers the unavoidable challenge, for the Greeks, of finding
the right response to this uncomfortable circumstance. The
problem pervades each Life.[2] At the same time, however, Plutarch will not allow this weighty and, even in his own day,
disquieting issue – elsewhere Plutarch underscores the potentially uneasy situation of elite Greeks who are nonetheless
subordinate to Roman power[3] – to blunt his admiration for the
individual excellence of his hero, whose meteoric rise was, Plutarch makes the point clearly, a stroke of luck for the Romans:

> if the Greeks could not be detached from Philip, the war would
> certainly not be a question of a single battle. At the time Greece
> had little experience of Rome, and this was their first practical
> exposure. What would have happened if the commander had not
> been naturally a fine man, one who turned more readily to words
> than to war, one who carried conviction as he met people, one
> who was unaggressive to those he met, one who strained for just-
> ice? Greece would certainly not have been so ready to accept the
> rule of foreigners instead of those they knew.
>
> (ch. 2)

Titus Quinctius Flamininus

Almost no aspect of Flamininus' career is uncontroversial,
which is perhaps not surprising for a man so deeply involved in
the politics and diplomacy of his time. He was born in 229 or
228 BC, to an ancient patrician family but one which had in
recent generations missed out on holding the consulship. In
208 BC he served in the Second Punic War as a tribune of the
soldiers under Marcellus, during the year in which the consul
fell to Hannibal, and, soon afterwards, but still at an unknown
date, was elected quaestor.[4] In 205 BC he was part of the
Roman garrison at Tarentum, serving, possibly as quaestor,
under Quintus Claudius, the praetor of 208 BC.[5] Upon
Claudius' death, Flamininus was put in command and granted
the military authority of a praetor, a remarkable appointment
for a man so young, and a clear token of the esteem in which he
was already held by the senate. He remained in this post for two

or three years, and it is usually accepted that it was during this period, while negotiating Roman military governance in a Greek city, that Flamininus developed the easy facility with Greek culture and politics that would prove the hallmark of his career.

Flamininus performed so well at Tarentum that he was thereafter awarded two plum assignments: first, in 201 BC, he was placed on a commission whose duty was to provide land for veterans of the Second Punic War, and, in the next year, he joined the board responsible for establishing a Roman colony at Venusia. However mundane such posts may sound, they were in fact important positions, and each presented its holder with a chance to acquire extensive gratitude and influence among likely voters. It was an opportunity Flamininus did not bungle. He quickly amassed a strong political following and, as a consequence, put himself forward for the consulship of 198 BC, an unconventional decision inasmuch as he was too young even to stand for the office of praetor, the magistracy that normally preceded the consulship.[6] But it is clear that Flamininus enjoyed considerable establishment support: when his candidature was challenged by two tribunes, the senate instructed them to leave the matter to the Roman people. Flamininus was then duly elected. His was a breathtakingly swift rise.

Nor did it take Flamininus long to win glory on the battlefield. After Carthage had been defeated, in 201 BC, the senate turned its attention to Philip V of Macedon, whom Rome continued to regard as an enemy even after the conclusion of the First Macedonian War (214–205 BC).[7] In 200 BC, hostilities were resumed, with the Aetolian League again serving as a Roman ally.[8] But the early years of this war favoured Philip, and, by the time of Flamininus' election, the Roman war effort had largely stalled. That soon changed.

Flamininus brought renewed vigour and diplomatic acumen. In negotiations with Philip, the consul demanded his total evacuation from Greece, designating Rome a champion of Greek freedom, itself a posture long familiar in Hellenistic diplomacy.[9] Naturally Philip refused, but he was soon defeated by Flamininus at the battle of Aoüs Gorge (chs. 3–5), a success that was instrumental in rallying most of Greece to the Roman side. Having gained this advantage, Flamininus went on, in 197 BC, to win a decisive victory at the battle of Cynoscephalae (ch. 8). After his defeat, Philip's kingdom was restricted mostly to Macedon, an indemnity was imposed and he was compelled to become an ally of Rome. The Romans then turned to the business of restoring the affairs of all the Greek communities that had been captured during the course of the war (ch. 12), a settlement in which the Aetolians found Flamininus ungenerous (chs. 9–10).[10] Their disaffection would soon lead to another war for Greek freedom.

In the rest of Greece, however, Flamininus was idolized when, in 196 BC, he proclaimed the freedom of the Greeks, in both Europe and Asia Minor (chs. 10–11). Now by this decree the Romans meant to convey that Greek cities would no longer be subject to Hellenistic kings, not that thereafter they would be immune from receiving Roman advice they were expected to heed. Still, this policy represented a significant attempt on the part of Rome to secure Greek loyalty, to win their 'hearts and minds'. For their part, the Greeks filled their country with tokens of honour, including divine honours, for Flamininus (chs. 12 and 16–17). His final project was a war against Nabis, the tyrant of Sparta (ch. 13), the purpose of which, from the Romans' perspective, was to dislodge him from Argos, although Rome's Achaean allies had different aims in mind (*Philopoemen* 15). In 194 BC, Flamininus – and all the Romans in Greece – returned to Italy, where he celebrated an unprecedented three-day triumph (chs. 13–14). By this time his political clout in Rome was so formidable that he easily propelled his brother Lucius into the consulship of 192 BC, despite the opposition of Scipio Africanus, who was supporting rival candidates (Livy 35.10).

The Romans' guarantee of Greek freedom, including the freedom of Greek cities in Asia Minor, was intended at least in part to put diplomatic pressure on Antiochus the Great, the king of the Seleucid empire and a rival to Rome for influence in the Greek east.[11] At the same time, Antiochus was being cultivated by the dissatisfied Aetolians, who ultimately persuaded the king to enter Greece to defend its freedom against what was portrayed to him by the Aetolians as Roman domination (ch. 15).

The two liberating powers soon came to blows. Flamininus played an important role in the diplomatic negotiations that preceded the outbreak of this war, first in 193 BC when he met with Antiochus' ambassadors in Rome (Livy 34.57-9), and thereafter in Greece, where he tried to keep the Aetolians from pursuing their aggressive line and where his influence was instrumental in preserving the loyalty of Rome's remaining allies (ch. 15).[12] When the Syrian War broke out in 191 BC, Flamininus was still in Greece, endeavouring to preserve the spirit of his original settlement, not least through his continuing efforts to resolve hostilities between Rome and the Aetolian League (chs. 15-17). He returned to Rome in 190 BC and in the following year was elected censor, at an age when other men were only just preparing to stand for the consulship.

The year 183 BC marked Flamininus' last incursion into Greek affairs, when, as part of a commission of former consuls, he tried in vain to persuade the Achaean League to moderate its treatment of Sparta (*Philopoemen* 17).[13] This embassy then went on to Bithynia, where it resolved hostilities between its king, Prusias I, and Eumenes II, the king of Pergamum. While there, however, Flamininus insisted on the extradition of Hannibal, who had become a refugee in the court of Prusias, in reaction to which Hannibal committed suicide (chs. 20-21). Back in Rome, Flamininus initiated communications with Demetrius, the pro-Roman son of Philip V, perhaps as his supporter in palace intrigue, but the affair remains obscure, and in any case Demetrius was executed in 180 BC.[14] Flamininus then vanishes from our sources, an absence which is extraordinary in view of his distinguished standing and has yet to be satisfactorily explained. His death is recorded in Livy (41.28.11) by way of an account of the splendid gladiatorial games given in his honour by his son.

Plutarch's Titus Flamininus

Plutarch's *Flamininus* is explicit, perhaps to the extent of becoming unsubtle, in drawing the character of its subject. We are told immediately that, although easily angered, he was quick to relent, and that he was motivated by a keen desire to act as a benefactor to others (ch. 1). A delicate balance for anyone in a position of power, but Flamininus, Plutarch hastens to add in the following chapter, was a man brimming with charm and who 'strained for justice'. It is not until chapter 5, after Flamininus has defeated Philip in the battle of Aoüs Gorge, that Plutarch discloses the Greeks' reaction to the Roman consul:

> They had heard from the Macedonians that a man was approaching in command of a barbarian army, conquering and enslaving everything in arms; then they met a person who was young in years, welcoming in appearance, speaking Greek like a native and a lover of true honour. They were wholly enchanted, and they went off and filled the cities with goodwill for him: they had, they thought, their champion of freedom.
>
> (ch. 5)

Flamininus, then, was one of them, almost, and was fired by his passion for 'true honour'.

Just as Philopoemen was affected by contentiousness (*philoneikia*), so in this Life Flamininus is driven by ambition, literally by his 'love of honour' (*philotimia*). This trait, for Plutarch, was an ambiguous and dangerous one.[15] A desire for renown was a healthy urge, if rightly pursued, but it was all too easy for *philotimia* to degrade into *philoneikia* or worse, and the career of Coriolanus, in this volume, exhibits the grave peril of ambition in a man of imperfect character.[16] If *philotimia* is to thrive and prove beneficial in a man's life, it must, according to Plutarch, be tempered by a suitably philosophical education,[17] and for a Roman of Flamininus' time this kind of instruction was unavailable. Nor does Plutarch suggest that Flamininus ever received such an education, however good his Greek was. Thus, for a reader of Plutarch, Flamininus' *philotimia* is something of a red flag, and it activates apprehension.

But, as the Life unfolds, Flamininus wins honour after honour, in Rome and especially in Greece, when, as the agent of their liberation, he is honoured by the Greeks as a god. In this way, Plutarch presents his reader with a Flamininus who, by virtue of his natural gifts, seems to escape the hazard of his *philotimia*. Or did he? The final act in Flamininus' Life is his hounding to death of Hannibal (ch. 20), which, Plutarch states, was motivated by ambition and resulted in the first stain on Flamininus' reputation:

> Titus' natural ambition brought him credit, as long as he had sufficient material to exercise it in the wars which I have described. He even served a further term as tribune after his consulship, though no one was pressing him to do so. But he grew older, his commands were over and the rest of his life offered no sphere of action; and at this stage it became clearer that he could not restrain his lust for glory and the youthfulness of his emotions. This seems to be the key to the vigour with which he hounded Hannibal, something which made him very unpopular.

In depicting Hannibal's death, Plutarch reprises Philopoemen's in a drama that casts Flamininus in the role of Deinocrates, a highly unflattering portrayal.[18] And so, it would seem, in the end Flamininus' ambition overwhelmed his finer qualities, not least his commitment to justice (emphasized in chs. 1–2) and his natural inclination towards mercy (ch. 1). Flamininus' failure is put into sharper relief when Plutarch introduces an internal comparison with Scipio Africanus: *he* treated Hannibal with 'clemency and magnanimity' (ch. 21).

Yet Plutarch does not end there. He goes on to put the case for those who approved of Flamininus' deed, and the argument is a strong one. It is not, however, an entirely unproblematic one in a pairing concerned with the nature of Roman power. For this argument focuses on the reality of Roman imperialism and its relevance for Flamininus' persecution of Hannibal, whose abiding menace is demonstrated by adducing instances from the Romans' later history in which their eastern empire was threatened. Here Plutarch refers to the revolt of Aristonicus (133–129 BC) and the wars with Mithridates (88–85, 83–81 and 73–63 BC), violent episodes in Rome's conquest of Asia Minor. What is disturbing about this defence is that, on its own terms, Flamininus ceases to be the liberator of anything, but instead becomes the grim instrument of Roman power. 'That is why', Plutarch concludes, 'some people say that Titus was not acting on his own initiative, but was sent with Lucius Scipio on an embassy whose sole purpose was Hannibal's death' (ch. 21). This, too, is a dark note, even if it is no longer a matter of Flamininus' personal ambition.

Still, it signals a significant alteration in Flamininus' behaviour. Let us recur to chapter 12. There, as we have seen, Plutarch describes the expansion of Rome's power throughout Greece in the aftermath of Philip's defeat. He also emphasizes that Flamininus did not see himself as an agent of Roman encroachment: 'The result was that in a short time, perhaps with God's assistance, everything was within their power. But Titus himself took most pride of all in the freeing of Greece.' And so he remains their advocate, during and after the war with Antiochus, even in the case of the disloyal Aetolians and Chalcidians (chs. 15–16).[19] By the end of his Life, however, he has either failed in his devotion to 'true honour', sacrificing Hannibal on the altar of his ambition, or he has lost his former individuality and commitment to freedom, caught up in the inexorable advance of Roman imperialism.

Perhaps this is less than fully surprising. After all, for all his fluency in Greek and his advocacy of Greek freedom, Flamininus was a Roman and not a Greek. It is often observed how successfully Plutarch, in composing his two Lives dealing with contemporaries who were active in the same theatre, avoids covering the same topics or events twice. There is in fact only one episode common to both Lives: Flamininus' decision to terminate the war against Nabis, an intertextual moment that is signalled by its repetition of Flamininus' jealousy of Philopoemen. In each Life, an exasperated and puzzled Flamininus wonders why a Roman consul and a champion of Greek freedom did not deserve greater praise than 'this Arcadian fellow' (*Philopoemen* 15, *Flamininus* 13). Flamininus is perplexed, however, because he does not understand what is at stake for the Greeks in their liberation by Rome. When he declares the freedom of the Greeks (chs. 10–11), the jubilant response of the audience is accompanied by an account of the Greeks' reflections on their own history and on their present circumstances, a Plutarchan innovation that diverges from his sources: both Polybius and Livy, in their versions of the proclamation, dilate on Roman virtue and Roman power, not on the feelings of the people they liberated.[20] In Plutarch, by contrast, although the Greeks are truly grateful to the Romans, they also clearly regret their missed opportunities, the failures of their past and their current condition, which requires the goodwill of a foreign power. This atmosphere is important in both Lives, and it helps to explain Flamininus' incomprehension. It is true that he brought the Greeks their liberation from Macedon, but Philopoemen is a champion of Greek *independence* – on account of whom the Greeks 'thought of Greece's ancient glory, and began to hope for it once more. Their belief in themselves now recaptured something of that spirit of old' (*Philopoemen* 11).[21] For all his Hellenism, Flamininus simply cannot see his role in Greece from the Greeks' perspective. He remains a foreigner.

Sources

Plutarch's most important sources for this Life were Polybius (Books 18–23) and Livy (Books 32–40). He also relies on Cicero, especially Cicero's essay *On Old Age*. Plutarch cites the first-century BC annalist Valerius Antias (see Introduction to *Romulus*) at chapter 18 and refers to his version of Hannibal's death at chapter 21, but probably did not consult him directly (in each case Valerius' account is reported by Livy). More difficult to assess is Plutarch's use of Gaius Sempronius Tuditanus, who was consul in 129 BC and celebrated a triumph: he wrote a work on the Roman magistracies as well as a history, the scope and scale of which are irrecoverable.[22] Plutarch cites him in chapter 14. Other sources seem to lie behind Plutarch's text, which includes material that cannot certainly be traced back to any of the sources listed so far. But these sources are beyond recognition.

LIFE OF TITUS FLAMININUS

[c. 229–174 BC]

1. The man we are setting beside Philopoemen is Titus Quinctius Flamininus. Anyone who wishes can gauge his appearance from the bronze statue in Rome, which is positioned next to the great Apollo from Carthage, opposite the Circus,[1] and is identified by a Greek inscription. As for his character, he is said to have been swift and sharp in his responses to people, and this came out both in the way he showed anger and in his granting of favours; but the quality took different forms in each case. When it was a question of punishment, his decisions were light ones, and he readily abandoned them; when it came to acts of favour, he would carry them through, and kept up his goodwill to the people he had helped, just as if they had been the ones to do the helping and he the one to benefit; when he had given people favours, he was eager to continue attending to their interests and safety, treating them just as if they were his most prized possessions.

His ambition for honour and glory was unsurpassed, he aspired to perform the noblest and greatest of deeds by his own efforts, and so he took more pleasure in those who wanted help than in those who could do him favours. The one group he regarded as the material on which his virtue could work, the other as if they were his rivals for glory.

His education was one in practical soldiering, for Rome at the time was fighting many great contests, and her young men were taught from the outset to command by serving on campaign. First he served as military tribune under the consul Marcellus in the Hannibalic War.[2] Marcellus was ambushed

and killed,[3] but Titus was appointed to govern the territory of
Tarentum and the city itself after it had been captured for the
second time.[4] Here he won as good a reputation for his justice
as he had for his military record, and for this reason, when
colonies were being dispatched to the two cities of Narnia and
Cosa,[5] he was chosen to be their leader and founder.

2. It was this success in particular which inspired him to miss
out the intermediate offices which young men usually held –
the tribunate, praetorship and aedileship[6] – and to think himself
ready for the consulship itself; and he came down to the forum
as a candidate, supported by his followers from the colonies.
The tribunes Fulvius and Manius[7] objected. It was a monstrous
thing, they said, for a young man to elbow his way into the
highest office against all laws and precedents;[8] it was as if he
was still uninitiated in the first rites and mysteries of the state.
The senate left it to the people's vote, and the people elected
him consul together with Sextus Aelius.[9] He was not yet thirty
years old.[10]

The lot brought him the war against Philip and the Macedonians,[11] and it was a stroke of luck for the Romans that this
issue and this people fell to him. They did not call for a commander whose hallmark was always war and violence, but were
more susceptible to persuasion and to charm. The Macedonian
realm gave Philip an adequate spearhead for battle; but if the war
dragged on, the whole fighting force depended on Greece. Greece
was their strength, their supplier, their refuge, their entire machine:
if the Greeks could not be detached from Philip, the war would
certainly not be a question of a single battle. At the time Greece
had little experience of Rome, and this was their first practical
exposure.[12] What would have happened if the commander had
not been naturally a fine man, one who turned more readily to
words than to war, one who carried conviction as he met people,
one who was unaggressive to those he met, one who strained for
justice? Greece would certainly not have been so ready to accept
the rule of foreigners[13] instead of those they knew. That emerges
clearly if we look at the man's achievements.

3. Titus saw that his predecessors in command, first Sulpicius[14] and then Publius Villius,[15] had invaded Macedon late in the season, and their slow start to the war had forced them to exhaust their efforts in skirmishing for positions and sparring with Philip over routes and provisions. This, he decided, was a mistake. Those men had spent their year at home with their honours and their politics, and had only come out to campaign at the end; but he was not going to try to gain an additional year in office, one of the consulship and one of warfare: his ambition was to combine the two and provide a term of office which contributed actively to the war. Thus he abandoned those honours of the city and his presidential functions; he asked the senate to let him have the services of his brother Lucius[16] as naval commander, and they agreed; he took as his spearhead those of Scipio's army who were still fit and willing, the conquerors of Hasdrubal in Spain and Hannibal himself in Africa,[17] 3,000 in number,[18] and he crossed safely to Epirus.[19]

There he found Publius with his army encamped against Philip, who was defending the approaches around the River Apsus[20] and the Narrows.[21] Philip had occupied this position for some considerable time, and Publius was making no progress, such was the strength of the enemy position. Titus took over the army, sent Publius away and examined the terrain. The position is as naturally strong as the Narrows at Tempe,[22] though it does not have such beautiful trees, such green foliage or such pleasant haunts and meadows. There are massive, towering mountains which converge to produce one vast deep ravine: through this the Apsus runs, and it comes to resemble the Peneius in its appearance and the speed of its current, in that its waters cover the rest of the valley but leave a precipitous cutting and narrow path next to the river's flow. In normal circumstances it would be difficult for an army to negotiate; once guarded, it would become utterly impossible.

4. There were some who tried to take Titus on a circuitous route through Dassaretis by Lyncus, where there was an easy and straightforward road.[23] But Titus was nervous of moving too far away from the sea, into terrain which was difficult and

poor in crops. With Philip avoiding battle, there was a danger
that the Romans would run into difficulties of provisioning,
and Titus would be forced to retreat to the sea, as unsuccessful
as his predecessor. So he decided to launch an attack with all
his power, and try to force an entry through the gorge.[24] Philip
was occupying the mountains with his phalanx. Javelins and
arrows rained down on the Romans from everywhere on both
flanks. There were clashes and the fighting was fierce. Men
were falling on both sides. No end of the war was in sight.

Then some local herdsmen[25] came up. They told Titus of a
path which the enemy had overlooked, and they undertook to
guide the army along it and to bring it to the tops of the mountains in two days' time. They provided someone to vouch for
their identity and good faith, Charops son of Machatas,[26] a
prominent man of Epirus and a good friend of the Romans,
even though his fear of Philip had led him to keep his collaboration quiet. That persuaded Titus, and he sent one military
tribune with 4,000 infantry and 300 cavalry. The shepherds led
the way in chains.[27] During the daytime they rested, concealing
themselves in caves or woods; at night they marched on, by the
light of the moon, which was then at its fullest.[28]

Once Titus had sent them off, he rested the army for the
intervening days, except for drawing the enemy off with some
skirmishing; but when the day came on which the turning party
was due to appear on the mountain tops, Titus moved his
whole force at dawn,[29] both heavy- and light-armed. He divided
his army into three. He himself led his cohorts in columns into
the narrowest part of the gorge, along by the river itself. The
Macedonian missiles came down; he grappled with the enemy
which met him on the difficult terrain; meanwhile the other
two divisions tried to join the attack on either side, and eagerly
pressed on to the rough ground.

The sun came up, and a gentle spiral of smoke could be seen:
nothing very obvious, rather like a mountain mist rising up in
the distance and gently becoming apparent. The enemy did not
see it – it was to their rear, where the heights had already been
taken; the Romans were uncertain about it, as amid such hard
fighting they were so eager to interpret it according to their

wishes. But it grew stronger and stronger, and gradually became
a black cloud; now it was big enough to be clearly a beacon of
good news. The Romans raised a cry, pressed on powerfully
and forced the enemy back into the roughest places; the others
answered their cry from the enemy rear, on the heights.

5. All the enemy turned immediately to headlong flight,[30]
though no more than 2,000 were killed, for the rough nature of
the land ruled out any pursuit. But the Romans plundered the
money, tents and slaves of the beaten army and took possession
of the Narrows, then marched through Epirus, but with extraordinary discipline and restraint. They were far from their
ships and the sea. They had not received their monthly ration
of grain and had no facilities for buying any. Yet they still
refrained from ravaging the territory, despite all the abundance
of booty which it offered.

This was because Titus had heard what Philip was doing. He
was going through Thessaly like a man in retreat, driving the
inhabitants out of the cities into the mountains, burning the
cities, offering to his men as plunder what was too heavy or
plentiful for the inhabitants to remove: it was as if he was
already ceding the country to the Romans.[31] That stirred Titus'
ambition, and he told his men to take care of the country on
their march as if it had been handed over to them as their own.
The results of that discipline were quickly visible: as soon as
they reached Thessaly the cities came over to him,[32] the Greeks
south of Thermopylae were eager to see him and full of excited
enthusiasm,[33] and the Achaeans renounced their alliance with
Philip and voted to join the Romans in making war;[34] the Opuntians[35] too, even though the Aetolians were then enthusiastic
allies of the Romans and were asking to take over their city and
guard it, refused the request, and sent for Titus and entrusted
themselves wholly to his good faith.

Pyrrhus' remark is still recalled, when from a lookout point
he first caught sight of the Roman army in battle array:[36] these
barbarians' line of battle, he said, does not look as barbarian
as all that. When people first met Titus they had to speak in
similar terms. They had heard from the Macedonians that a

man was approaching in command of a barbarian army, conquering and enslaving everything in arms; then they met a person who was young in years, welcoming in appearance, speaking Greek like a native and a lover of true honour. They were wholly enchanted, and they went off and filled the cities with goodwill for him: they had, they thought, their champion of freedom.[37] Then Philip seemed ready to come to terms, and Titus met him and offered him peace and alliance, on condition that he allowed the Greeks their independence and removed his garrisons; and Philip refused.[38] At that point even Philip's supporters came to the view that the Romans had not come to fight the Greeks, but to fight the Macedonians on the Greeks' behalf.

6. The rest of Greece came over to him without any trouble, with one exception.[39] He was making his way peaceably through Boeotia when he was met by the leading men of Thebes. They favoured the Macedonians because of Brachyllas,[40] but were also full of welcoming words and honour for Titus; the presumption was that they were allies of both sides. He responded to them in friendly terms and greeted them warmly; then he went slowly on his way, sometimes asking questions and gathering information, sometimes telling them things in return, distracting them deliberately until his soldiers could come up from their march.[41]

Then, at the head of his men, he went into the city along with the Thebans. They were anything but happy with this – but they did not like to stop him, given that he was followed by a considerable number of soldiers. Once Titus was inside, he spoke as if there were no question of the city being already in his power, and he tried to persuade them to come over to the Romans. King Attalus[42] was there too, and joined in the appeals and encouragement to the Thebans. It seems that Attalus was ambitious to play the enthusiastic speaker for Titus – too enthusiastic, indeed, for a man of his age. Some fit of giddiness or flux came over him while he was speaking, and he lost his senses and fell. Soon after he returned by ship to Asia, where he died. The Boeotians joined Rome.

7. Philip now dispatched ambassadors to Rome, and Titus too sent representatives of his own,[43] whose object was to get the senate to vote him an additional period in command, if the war was to continue; if not, to ensure that the peace came about through Titus' efforts.[44] For he was strongly ambitious, and his fear was that he might lose the glory if another general were sent to take over the war. His friends proved successful, ensuring both that Philip did not get what he wanted and that Titus retained command of the war.

When news of the decision arrived, Titus, agitated and hopeful, immediately moved into Thessaly to fight Philip. His force numbered more than 26,000 men, including an Aetolian detachment of 6,000 infantry and 400 cavalry. Philip's army was of a similar size.[45] The two armies closed on one another and came to Scotussa;[46] that was where they were to risk conflict. Yet the armies were not as fearful of meeting one another as one would expect. It was more that they were filled with vigour and ambition. The Romans relished the prospect of defeating the Macedonians, whom Alexander[47] had made such a byword among them for formidable strength and power; the Macedonians thought that the Romans were greater than the Persians, and so victory here would show Philip to be a more brilliant general than Alexander. Thus Titus encouraged his men to show themselves fine and vigorous warriors: here they would be fighting in the fairest of theatres, in Greece, against the best of adversaries.[48] And Philip? It may have been bad luck, it may have been negligence born of the urgency of the moment; anyway, there was a high burial mound outside his camp,[49] and he climbed onto this to make his speech. He began with the usual material which orators use to encourage troops before battle, but there was great dispirit everywhere because of the bad omen. Philip, disturbed, held off battle for that day.

8. The next day dawned. It had been a mild, damp night, and the clouds turned to mist: the whole plain was filled with a thick dark fog, with the dense air coming down from the heights to fill the space between the two armies. Thus day began with all the ground invisible. Both sides had sent out

parties to cover and observe the enemy, and very soon these stumbled on one another. Then the battle began, at the region called Cynoscephalae or 'Dog's Heads', so-called because many ridges lie close and in parallel, and their gently rising summits resemble that shape.[50] As one would expect of such hard terrain, there were many shifts of fortune, with flights here and pursuits there, and each side sending reinforcements from the camp to support those divisions which were in trouble and retreating. Then the air began to clear, they could see what was happening and they joined battle in full force.

Philip's right wing was successful; he was coming from higher sloping ground, and he threw the whole of his phalanx against the Romans. Even the best of the legionaries could not withstand the momentum of the Macedonian linked shields and the ferocity of their couched spears. But the Macedonian left wing was strung out across the ridges and skewed out of position, and Titus, deciding to write off the wing that was in difficulties, came up sharply to support this other wing. As he launched his attack, the unevenness and roughness of the land prevented the Macedonians from making ranks as a phalanx and strengthening their formation in depth; yet that is the strong point of their force, and their weaponry is too heavy and cumbersome to suit them for hand-to-hand combat. The phalanx is like a living creature of irresistible strength as long as it remains as one body and keeps its linked shields in a single order; immediately it breaks up, the individual soldier loses his effectiveness, both because of the nature of his weaponry and because his strength lies in the combination of the interlocking parts of the whole rather than in his individual power.[51] Once the first Macedonians turned to flight, some pursued the fugitives, others outflanked those who were still fighting and cut them down; before long even the victorious wing of the Macedonians was drawn off and forced to flee, throwing down its arms. The dead numbered no fewer than 8,000, and about 5,000 were captured.[52] Philip escaped safely and people blamed the Aetolians,[53] who turned to plundering and destroying the enemy camp while the Romans were still in pursuit, so that on their return they found nothing left.

9. At first it was a question of mutual recriminations and disagreements, then the Aetolians began to cause more and more
irritation to Titus[54] himself. They were claiming the victory for
themselves,[55] and the versions they spread were prejudicing the
Greeks to give them the credit; poets and even ordinary people
were singing and writing of them, and putting them in the first
place as they celebrated the achievement. Most popular of all
was this epigram:

> Unwept and unburied,[56] here, traveller, we lie, on this ridge of
>   Thessaly,
>   We who were 30,000 men.
> We fell to Aetolia's sword, and to those Latins
>   Whom Titus brought from broad Italy,
> A great pain to Emathia.[57] And that brash spirit of Philip?
>   It is gone, swifter than the swift deer.[58]

That was Alcaeus' work,[59] a deliberate insult to Philip, and an
exaggeration of the numbers who fell. But it was to be heard in
many places and on many lips, and it caused more pain to Titus
than to Philip. As for Philip, he simply responded in Alcaeus'
own mocking vein, with an elegiac couplet:

> Unbarked and unleafy, here, traveller, it stands,
>   On this ridge: a sheer bare stake of wood – for Alcaeus.[60]

But Titus, full of ambition before the Greeks, was immoder-
ately sensitive to all this. For this reason he began to conduct
affairs wholly on his own, with no attention whatever to the
Aetolians.[61] They were annoyed by this, and when Titus received
proposals and an embassy from the Macedonians about peace
terms, they went round the other cities full of complaint. The
same thing was happening again, they cried: he was selling
peace to Philip, when there was a chance to finish the war once
and for all, and to destroy the source of power from which the
slavery of Greece was born.

  That was what the Aetolians said, and it stirred up the allies;
but the suspicions were dispelled by Philip himself, when he came

to settle terms[62] and surrendered unconditionally to Titus and the Romans. Thus Titus ended the war. He restored to Philip the kingdom of Macedon, but ordered him to withdraw from Greece, fined him 1,000 talents, took away all his ships except ten and sent one of his sons, Demetrius, to be a hostage in Rome.[63]

This was a remarkably shrewd reading of events and feeling for what was to come. For Hannibal the African – Rome's greatest enemy and now in exile – was already at King Antiochus' court[64] and was urging him forward, now that fortune was smiling so much on his advancing power; and as for Antiochus himself, all those magnificent achievements which had earned him the name of 'the Great' were encouraging him to think of universal empire, and his particular target was Rome.[65] What would have happened if Titus had not foreseen this and wisely agreed to make peace? The war with Antiochus would have supervened in Greece on the war with Philip; their communion of concerns would have united the two greatest and mightiest kings of the day against Rome; there would have been new contests and dangers to match those of the war against Hannibal. As it was, Titus grasped the opportunity to interpose peace between the two wars, cutting short the last before the next could begin, and robbing one king of his last hope, the other of his first.

10. Then, however, the ten commissioners dispatched by the senate advised Titus[66] to give the other Greeks their freedom, but to keep garrisons at Corinth, Chalcis and Demetrias[67] to protect against Antiochus. There was no mistaking the torrent of recriminations which this produced from the Aetolians, nor the effect these had on the other cities in breaking out their resentment. Titus should loose the fetters of Greece, said the Aetolians (that was Philip's phrase[68] for the three cities I have mentioned); the Greeks had exchanged their old collar for a new one, smoother but heavier than before;[69] were they now content? Did they admire Titus as their benefactor, for loosing Greece's feet and binding her by the neck instead? Titus was pained and annoyed by this, and eventually his entreaties persuaded the commission to free these cities too from their garrisons,[70] so that his gift to the Greeks should be complete and unimpaired.

It was the time of the Isthmian Games.[71] The stadium was full of spectators watching the athletics: that was natural, now Greece was free of wars at last. They hoped for freedom, but they already had peace, and that was what they were celebrating at the festival.[72] Then the trumpeter signalled everyone to be silent. A herald came forward to the middle of the stadium and made the proclamation: the Roman senate and the consul[73] and general Titus Quinctius, having defeated Philip and the Macedonians, were now liberating Corinth, Phocis, Locris, Euboea, Phthiotic Achaea, Magnesia, Thessaly and Perrhaebia,[74] free of all garrisons and tribute, in possession of their ancestral constitutions. At first not everyone had heard, or at least heard clearly; there was a confused, disturbed movement in the stadium, with the astonished spectators asking each other what had been said: could the proclamation be repeated? Then silence fell again, the herald raised his voice and cried more vigorously so that all could hear, and the decree reached everyone: the delighted shout which greeted it was unbelievably loud, so loud that it even reached the sea. The theatre audience leapt to its feet. No one paid any attention to the athletes, for now all the spectators were eager to jump up and hail and shake by the hand the saviour and champion of Greece.

There were even some ravens flying overhead who fell down into the stadium:[75] people often say that by way of exaggerating the loudness of a sound, but on this occasion it actually happened. The reason for this is the fragmenting of the air. A vast and loud sound breaks up the air, which consequently is unable to support the creatures flying through it; that makes them slip down as if they were poised over a void. An alternative explanation might, I suppose, be that they are transfixed by a shock as if by a missile, and therefore fall dying. Perhaps it is also a whirling of the air, with the turbulence being great enough to bring on an effect of eddying and suction, just as on the sea.[76]

11. As for Titus himself, it was as well that he swiftly moved away now that the spectacle was ended, fearing the vigour and press of the crowd. There were vast numbers mobbing him on

every side, and his very life was in danger.[77] Nightfall came
before they finally tired of shouting around his tent, and as they
left they were still greeting and embracing all the friends and
fellow-citizens they saw, and then they turned to eating and
drinking together.

At this moment of celebration, it was all the more natural
that they should talk and reflect on the fate of Greece.[78] They
thought of all the wars she had fought for freedom; but freedom had never come more firmly or delightfully than now, and
it had come almost without blood and without grief, championed by another people, this finest and most enviable of prizes.
Bravery and wisdom were rare possessions among mortals, but
the man of justice was the rarest good of all. People like Agesilaus, Lysander, Nicias and Alcibiades[79] had known how to fight
their wars well, and how to lead their men to victories over
land and sea; but they had not known how to use their victories
for glorious ends or to bestow noble favours. If one discounted
Marathon, Salamis, Plataea and Thermopylae, and Cimon's
victories at the Eurymedon and in Cyprus,[80] all Greece's wars
had been fought internally for slavery, every one of her trophies
had also been a disaster and reproach for Greece, which had
generally been overthrown by its leaders' evil ways and contentiousness. Now these foreigners had come, people who seemed
to have only slight sparks and insignificant traces of an ancient
shared ancestry;[81] it was remarkable that they should even have
any helpful words or thoughts to spare for Greece. Yet it was
their perils and their labours that had now taken Greece away
from its harsh masters and tyrants, and set her free.

12. Those were the reflections of the Greeks; and the Romans'
behaviour lived up to the terms of the decrees. For Titus dispatched a number of men on simultaneous missions,[82] Lentulus
to Asia to free Bargylia,[83] Stertinius[84] to Thrace to release the
cities and islands there from Philip's garrisons, while Publius
Villius[85] sailed to confer with Antiochus about the freedom of
the Greeks under his control. Titus himself made his way to
Chalcis, then sailed from there to Magnesia, removing the
garrisons and restoring their ancestral constitutions to the

peoples.[86] In Argos he was made president of the Nemean Games, and celebrated the festival in the best possible way; there too he had a herald repeat the proclamation of freedom to the Greeks.[87] As he went from city to city he created a state of lawfulness and great justice and mutual harmony and affection,[88] putting an end to internal strife, restoring the exiles and basking as much in reconciling the Greeks by the arts of persuasion as he had in his victory over Macedon: indeed, by now freedom seemed only a minute part of the benefits they owed to him.

There is a story told of the philosopher Xenocrates.[89] The tax-collectors were hauling him off for failing to pay the metic tax, but he was rescued by the orator Lycurgus,[90] who not merely released him but also fined the tax-collectors for their presumption. Then they say that Xenocrates met Lycurgus' children. 'I am repaying your father very generously,' he said: 'all the world is praising him for what he did.' In the same way, Titus and the Romans were repaid with gratitude for their benefits to the Greeks, but in their case the gratitude generated not merely praise, but also a deserved confidence and authority among all mankind. People did not only receive Roman commanders into their towns, they even sent and called for them and put themselves in their hands; and it was not merely peoples and cities which did this, but even kings who were wronged by other kings and fled to the Romans' arms. The result was that in a short time, perhaps with God's assistance,[91] everything was within their power.

But Titus himself took most pride of all in the freeing of Greece: that can be seen from the silver bucklers and his own body shield which he dedicated at Delphi, with the inscription:

Hail you Sons of Zeus,[92] who revel in your swift horsemanship; hail you Tyndarids, kings of Sparta; Titus, descendant of Aeneas, has given you the highest gift of all, freedom for the children of the Greeks.

He also dedicated a gold crown to Apollo with the inscription:

This golden, radiant crown is to lie on the ambrosial locks of the son of Leto: it is the gift of the great captain of the Aeneadae.[93] Far-darting one, give the glory of might to the god-like Titus.

Corinth, it has so turned out, has now twice been the scene of the same experience for Greece: for it was in Corinth that first Titus, then again Nero[94] in our own lifetime, set the Greeks free and independent, and in each case similarly at the Isthmian Games. Titus used a herald, as I have said;[95] Nero made the speech himself, climbing on a rostrum in the central square to address the crowd. But that was later.

13. To return to Titus: at that time he had entered upon the fairest and most righteous of wars, that against Nabis,[96] the most pernicious and lawless tyrant of Sparta; but at the end Titus cheated Greece of her hopes, deciding not to conquer him when he had the opportunity to do so. Instead he came to terms, thereby abandoning Sparta to an undeserved slavery.[97] Perhaps he was afraid that the war might drag on, and another commander might come from Rome and take the glory; perhaps it was more a question of contentiousness and jealousy of the honours of Philopoemen. For that man was the most accomplished Greek of the day in every respect, and in particular he had performed remarkable feats of audacity and skill in this present war. The Achaeans responded by paying him honour and respect in the theatres; just as much, indeed, as they had paid to Titus, and this annoyed Titus intensely. Here he was, a Roman consul, fighting as Greece's champion: it could not be right for this Arcadian fellow,[98] a commander in these minor frontier wars, to win from them the same admiration. Still, Titus himself gave a different defence of his actions, saying that he had abandoned the war because he saw that the destruction of the tyrant would involve the other Spartiates in great suffering.[99]

The Achaeans passed many votes in his honour, but none seemed to match the benefits they had received, with one exception, which he valued more than all the others. This was the following. There were many Romans who had fallen on hard times in the Hannibalic War. Sold into slavery, they were now scattered all over the world: in Greece there were 1,200 of them.[100] Their change of fortune had been pitiful enough before, but now it was especially so: some were meeting their sons, others their brothers or their friends, slaves meeting free men and prisoners meeting conquerors. Titus was not prepared simply to deprive their masters of their property, despite all the pain which he felt on their behalf. But the Achaeans ransomed these men, paying 5 minas for each, and gathered them all together to give to Titus just as he was about to set sail. So he departed in the most delighted of spirits, given that his noble deeds had been nobly repaid, in a way which was fitting for a great man and a lover of his countrymen. It would appear that this was the most brilliant aspect of all in the triumph which he celebrated.[101] It is customary for slaves to shave their heads and wear the cap of freedom when they are manumitted, and now these men did the same, and that was how they escorted Titus in his triumphal procession.

14. The spoils carried in the procession also contributed to the glorious sight.[102] There were Greek helmets and Macedonian shields and pikes, and also a very considerable amount of money: Tuditanus[103] reports that the parade included 3,713 pounds of melted gold, 43,270 pounds of silver and 14,514 gold Philippics.[104] On top of that Philip owed his 1,000 talents,[105] though in this case the Romans were later persuaded to remit payment,[106] largely thanks to Titus' intervention; they also voted to make Philip an ally, and released his son[107] from being a hostage.

15. Then came Antiochus' arrival in Greece.[108] He crossed with a large fleet and army, and set about stirring up the cities to rebellion and to internal faction. His partners in this were the Aetolians, with their long-standing bitterness and hostility towards the Roman people.[109] Now the Aetolians gave Antiochus the programme and excuse for war of freeing the Greeks. Not that the Greeks wanted this; they were free already – but

for want of a more plausible pretext the Aetolians suggested to Antiochus the use of this fairest of names.

The extent and reputation of Antiochus' power made the Romans very apprehensive. They sent Manius Acilius as consul and commander in the war, but added Titus as his legate.[110] This was for the sake of the Greeks, and indeed, for some of them the simple sight of the man was enough to strengthen their loyalty. Others were beginning to be in a less healthy state, but their personal goodwill for Titus was like some timely medicine, and these too he rallied and led away from error. Only a few escaped his heartening influence, people who had already been treated in advance and totally corrupted by the Aetolians; and even these, despite all his anger and irritation, he kept safe after the battle.

For Antiochus was defeated at Thermopylae,[111] and immediately sailed away in flight to Asia:[112] then the consul Manius divided up the Aetolians, attacking and besieging some himself and allowing King Philip to destroy others.[113] That was how it came about that Dolopians and Magnesians were being plundered by the Macedonians, and Athamanians and Aperantians[114] too; Manius himself had destroyed Heraclea and was besieging Naupactus,[115] which was still in Aetolian possession. At this point Titus took pity on the Greeks, and sailed from the Peloponnese to intercede with the consul.[116]

At first he rebuked him: Manius had won the war, so why let Philip take its spoils? Here he was wasting his time with a single city, while the Macedonians were taking over many entire races and kingdoms. Then the besieged people of Naupactus caught sight of him, called to him from the walls and stretched out their hands to him imploringly. For the moment he said nothing, but turned around and went away in tears; but later he talked again with Manius and soothed his anger.[117] The result was that the Aetolians were granted a truce for a specified period, in which they could send an embassy to Rome and make their claim for moderate treatment.[118]

16. But what caused Titus the most argument and trouble of all was his intercession on behalf of Chalcis. Manius was infuriated

with the Chalcidians, because of the marriage which Antiochus had celebrated there when the war was already in progress:[119] it was an untimely and inappropriate marriage, with this elderly man falling in love with a young girl, the daughter of Cleoptolemus and, so they say, the most beautiful girl alive. This brought the Chalcidians over to support the king with the greatest enthusiasm, and they turned the city over to him to serve as his base for the war. After the battle, Antiochus came to Chalcis as quickly as he could, then took his girl, his money and his friends, and sailed away to Asia. The angry Manius immediately moved on Chalcis.[120] He was accompanied by Titus,[121] who tried to mollify him and pleaded with him until he was finally placated and won over, so effective were Titus' entreaties with him and the Roman officials.

That was the salvation of Chalcis, and they consecrated the biggest and most magnificent of their votive offerings to Titus.[122] Inscriptions are still visible such as 'the people dedicated this gymnasium to Titus and to Heracles', and again 'the people dedicated this Delphinium[123] to Titus and to Apollo'. Even in our own day there is a priest of Titus appointed by election, and when the Chalcidians sacrifice to Titus they sing a specially composed paean after making the libations. There is no room to quote the whole of the paean, but I give the song's ending:

> We revere the faith of the Romans,
> The object of so many great prayers,
> That it should offer protection through oaths;
> Girls, sing
> Of great Zeus, and Rome, and Titus too, and Roman faith.
> Cry Paean!
> Hail, saviour Titus!

17. The other Greeks too offered Titus suitable honours, and there was a further element as well, one which lent the honours truth and sincerity: that was a remarkable personal enthusiasm for his natural fairness and moderation. For even on those occasions when he clashed with individuals for reasons of

politics or ambition, as with Philopoemen, and again with Diophanes[124] when he was general of the Achaeans, Titus' anger was not deep-seated and he did not carry it through into action; there would be a few words delivered with the frankness of free public debate, and that would be the end of it. So no one thought him a bitter man, though many felt he was naturally irascible and changeable; but they also noticed that he was the most pleasant of all companions, with a gift for delightful and pointed remarks.[125]

There was an occasion, for instance, when the Achaeans were laying claim to the island of Zacynthus,[126] and Titus was trying to put them off: 'You'll be in danger,' he said, 'like the tortoise, if you poke your head out beyond the Peloponnese.'[127] On his first meeting with Philip to discuss terms for a truce and a peace,[128] Philip remarked that Titus had come with lots of companions, whereas he himself had no one: 'That's your own fault,' retorted Titus; 'you've killed all your friends and relations.' Then there was the time when Deinocrates[129] of Messene had come to Rome, got drunk at a party and danced wearing a woman's tunic. The next day he asked Titus to give him assistance, for he planned to lead Messene in a breakaway from the Achaeans. 'I'll think about that,' said Titus; 'but I'm amazed that, if you are set on plans as great as that, you can sing and dance at parties.' Then the Achaeans were receiving envoys from Antiochus,[130] who listed all the vast numbers of the king's army and enumerated them under their many different names. Titus told the Achaeans the story of a time when he was dining with a friend, and was taking him to task for the variety of the meat-dishes, and asking in amazement where he had got hold of such a varied diet. His friend told him that the dishes were all of pork, but had been served and spiced differently. 'So,' said Titus, 'you too, you men of Achaea, don't be amazed at the power of Antiochus, when you hear of these "spear-carriers" and "javelin-carriers" and "foot-companions". They're all Syrians, and only their silly little weapons are different.'

18. His achievements in Greece and the war with Antiochus now concluded, Titus was elected censor:[131] that is the highest

office, a sort of culmination of a political career. His colleague in office was Marcellus,[132] the son of the Marcellus who was five times consul. They expelled from the senate four men, none of them persons of particular note; they also accepted as citizens all those who enrolled, provided they were of free birth. They were forced to do this by the tribune Terentius Culleo,[133] who persuaded the people to vote this through in order to spite the aristocrats.

The two most distinguished and influential men of the day were now at odds with one another: these were Scipio Africanus and Marcus Cato.[134] The first of these Titus made leader of the senate as a mark of his excellence and pre-eminence,[135] but he came to be on very bad terms with Cato because of the following incident. Titus had a brother, Lucius Flamininus.[136] He was not at all like Titus in nature, and an aspect of this was a dreadful liberality in taking his pleasures and a total contempt for decency. Lucius had a young boyfriend, whom he took out with him when he was at the head of an army, and always had with him as a provincial governor.[137] There was a party once, and this boy put on a coy tone with Lucius: 'I love you so much', said the boy, 'that I left the gladiatorial show to come here, even though I've never yet seen a man killed: that's how much I've put your pleasure above my own.' Lucius was delighted. 'Don't worry,' he said: 'I'll make sure your desire is satisfied,' and he gave orders for one of the condemned prisoners to be brought there from the prison. He sent for the lictor,[138] and he gave orders for the prisoner's head to be cut off right there in the party.

Valerius Antias[139] says that this was a favour to a girlfriend rather than a boyfriend; Livy quotes a speech of Cato himself for the version that a Gallic deserter arrived with his wife and children[140] at the doors, and Lucius received him into the party and slew him with his own hand, all as a favour to his boyfriend.[141] It is reasonable to assume that this was said by Cato to aggravate his charge.[142] There are many authorities who say that the executed man was not a deserter but a condemned prisoner,[143] including Cicero, in his *On Old Age*, who puts the story in the mouth of Cato himself.

19. Then Cato became censor,[144] and in the course of his review of the senate he expelled Lucius; this was despite his consular status, and the fact that his brother seemed to share in his dishonour. Thus the two of them went together before the people, humble and in tears; and their request to their fellow-citizens seemed a reasonable one, for they asked that Cato should publicly set out the reasons for his charge, and give an explanation why he should have inflicted such dishonour on a distinguished house. Cato held nothing back; he came out, stood next to his fellow-censor, and asked Titus if he knew of the party. Titus denied all knowledge of it, and so Cato gave an account of what had happened; then he challenged Lucius to state if he denied the truth of anything that had been said.[145] Lucius said nothing. The people now acknowledged that the dishonour had been justified, and they escorted Cato from the rostrum with warm applause.

Titus was devastated by what had happened to his brother, and joined forces with Cato's old enemies.[146] He managed to carry the day in the senate and secure the annulment of all the public contracts which Cato had given, whether for sale, hire or purchase; he also set up many serious lawsuits against him.[147] I cannot describe this as conduct which was right or worthy of a public man, to take up an incurable enmity against a law-abiding magistrate and the finest of citizens, on behalf of a man who was certainly one of his family but was also unworthy of him and deserving of his punishment.[148] Still, there was one occasion when the Roman people were gathered in the theatre for a spectacle and the senate had assumed their front seats in their usual special dress;[149] then Lucius was seen sitting far away from the stage, humbled and dishonoured. They felt pity for him, and the ordinary people would not put up with the sad sight; they cried out for him to move, and he finally did so, with the consulars receiving him to sit with them.[150]

20. Titus' natural ambition brought him credit, as long as he had sufficient material to exercise it in the wars which I have described. He even served a further term as tribune[151] after his

consulship, though no one was pressing him to do so. But he grew older, his commands were over and the rest of his life offered no sphere of action; and at this stage it became clearer that he could not restrain his lust for glory and the youthfulness of his emotions. This seems to be the key to the vigour with which he hounded Hannibal,[152] something which made him very unpopular.

Hannibal had fled secretly from his home in Carthage,[153] and was for some time in Antiochus' company; but then Antiochus accepted with relief the peace terms after the battle in Phrygia,[154] and this drove Hannibal into exile once more. He wandered far and wide, and finally found a home in Bithynia, at the court of Prusias.[155] Everyone at Rome knew this perfectly well, but all turned a blind eye on this weak old man, and felt that he was a sort of victim of destiny. Titus now arrived at Prusias' court; he had been sent by the senate on an embassy concerning some other matter.[156] When he saw Hannibal living there, he was infuriated that he should still be alive, and despite all Prusias' pleas and entreaties on behalf of a suppliant and friend he would not relent.[157]

It appears that there was an ancient oracle about Hannibal's death: 'Libyssan earth will hide the body of Hannibal.' Hannibal himself took this as a reference to Libya and burial in Carthage, and inferred that he would end his days there. But there is in Bithynia a sandy place by the sea, and a small village nearby called Libyssa.[158] That was where Hannibal was living, in a state of continual fear of the Romans and distrust of Prusias' irresolution. He had consequently already made his preparations, digging seven underground tunnels out of his house; these ran in different directions, each of them coming to the surface under cover some way away. When he now heard the decision of Titus, Hannibal tried to escape through the tunnels, but was confronted by guards sent by the king. He decided to take his own life. Some say that he wound his tunic around his neck, and ordered his servant to get leverage from behind by pressing his knee against his master's hip, then to pull the neck back hard and squeeze and twist until it choked him, and that is how he killed himself; some prefer the version that he followed the model of Themistocles and Midas and drank bull's blood.[159] Livy says[160] that he had poison with him, mixed it, and said as he took the cup: 'Let us now take their great worry away from the Romans, who thought it too much of a burden and a delay to wait for the death of a hated old man. Still, Titus' victory will not be an enviable one, nor worthy of his ancestors, the men who sent secretly to Pyrrhus, their enemy and their victor, and warned him of the attempt to poison him.'[161]

21. That is how they say Hannibal met his death. When the news reached the senate, a fair number were appalled by what they saw as Titus' excessiveness and brutality. Hannibal had been like an old bird, wingless and docked, allowed to live as a tamed animal; now Titus had killed him. No one had been pressing him to do this; it was just for his own glory, to gain his place in history as Hannibal's killer. This put into relief the clemency and magnanimity shown by Scipio Africanus, whom they now came to admire all the more. Scipio had met the unconquered and formidable Hannibal, and had defeated him in Africa; yet he did not drive him into exile nor demand his surrender from his countrymen. When they met to negotiate before the battle he grasped his hand warmly, then when they made terms after the battle he did not add to the man's ill fortune with any further audacity or persecution. There is a story, too, of another meeting in Ephesus.[162] The first point was the way that they walked together. Hannibal took the place of honour, and Scipio made no objection, walking simply and unpretentiously. Then they fell to discussing generals. Hannibal claimed that Alexander had been the greatest general of all time, with Pyrrhus in second place and himself in third. Africanus[163] gently smiled. 'What if I had not beaten you?' he asked. 'In that case, Scipio,' replied Hannibal, 'I would not have put myself third among generals, but first.' Most people now admired Scipio for this, and reviled Titus for the way he had behaved; it was as if he had laid hands on a corpse which belonged to others.

But there was another view as well, and some praised him

for what he had done. They thought that, as long as Hannibal lived, he was a fire which needed only to be fanned. Even when he was in his prime, it was not his bodily power or the strength of his hand which the Romans had to fear, it was his brilliance and skill, coupled with his natural bitterness and hostility to Rome. Those qualities were not lessened by age; his nature was still there, deep in his character; fortune was not a constant, and as it changed it inspired hopes which elicited aggression from those whose hatred fed their hostility.

And later events perhaps offered even more justification for Titus. First there was Aristonicus, the lyre-player's boy, who filled all Asia with wars and rebellions thanks to the reputation of Eumenes;[164] then there was Mithridates, who after Sulla and Fimbria and the loss of so many great armies and generals could still rise against Lucullus with such power by land and sea.[165] Nor was Hannibal's low state any humbler than that of Gaius Marius. Hannibal had a king as his friend, he lived his usual life, he spent his days among ships and horses and soldiers; whereas the Romans regarded the fortunes of Marius, this wandering beggar in Libya, as a matter for derision, and then a little later they were being slaughtered and tortured and were worshipping at his feet in Rome.[166] Thus present circumstances are no guide at all to the future; life's changes end only with life itself. That is why some people say that Titus was not acting on his own initiative, but was sent with Lucius Scipio on an embassy whose sole purpose was Hannibal's death.[167]

We have discovered no further deed of Titus, either political or military, and he met a peaceful death:[168] so it is time to consider the comparison.

COMPARISON OF
PHILOPOEMEN AND
TITUS FLAMININUS

1 (22). If we consider the magnitude of their benefactions to the Greeks, it is not fitting to compare Philopoemen with Titus – nor, for that matter, with many others[1] who were better men than Philopoemen. For they were Greeks fighting their wars against other Greeks, while Titus was a non-Greek fighting on behalf of the Greeks; and, at a time when Philopoemen was unable to help his own beleaguered countrymen but had gone away to Crete,[2] at that very moment Titus defeated Philip in the heart of Greece and set her peoples and all her cities free.[3] If one were to examine the battles fought by each of them, Philopoemen killed more Greeks as commander of the Achaeans than Titus killed Macedonians[4] as helper of the Greeks.

As for their mistakes, the one man's arose from his love of honour, the other's[5] from his contentiousness; the one's anger was swift,[6] the other's was implacable. For Titus ensured that Philip retained the title and position of king, and was forgiving to the Aetolians;[7] Philopoemen was led by his anger to deprive his own country of the lands which lay around it and the contributions they paid.[8] Again, the one was steadfast in his support for those he had benefited, the other was swift to cancel any links of gratitude in his wrath: for he had once been a benefactor of the Spartans, then later tore down the city's walls and took away its territory, then finally changed and destroyed its constitution itself.[9] He was also thought to have thrown away his life in his anger and contentiousness,[10] for his hastening to Messene was not timely, but quicker than it should have been; he was not a man like Titus, whose campaigns were always guided by thoughtful calculation and an eye for safety.[11]

2 (23). If, however, we consider the numbers of wars fought and triumphs gained, then Philopoemen's skill and experience seem the more firmly based of the two. The one man's struggle with Philip was decided in two contests,[12] the other won countless battles, and left no room for anyone to contend that it was luck, rather than expertise, which carried him to success. Again, the one gained his glory by making use of Roman power when it was at its height, the other by making use of that of Greece when she was already waning and past her best, so that the one man's successes were his own, the other's those of his state: for the one man commanded good soldiers, the other as commander made his soldiers good.

Indeed, the fact that the one man's contests were against Greeks was certainly unfortunate, but it made his military excellence absolutely clear: for when other things are equal, the victors are those with the superior military excellence. Thus he fought his wars against the most warlike of the Greeks – the Cretans and the Spartans: the Cretans being the most accomplished in guile and the Spartans the most valiant in boldness – and he defeated both.[13]

Titus also won his victory with the forces which were already at hand, using the weapons and tactics which had come down to him; Philopoemen made his own innovations and changes in this sort of military organization,[14] so that the key to victory was freshly discovered by the one, already available to help the other. As for hand-to-hand combat, we can point to many great deeds of Philopoemen[15] but none of the other man; indeed, a certain Aetolian called Archedamus[16] mocked him for this, telling of a time when Archedamus was running with drawn sword towards those of the Macedonians who were fighting and keeping their formation, while Titus was standing with his hands upturned to Heaven, deep in prayer.[17]

3 (24). A further point: all Titus' noble achievements came when he was a commander or ambassador,[18] whereas Philopoemen ensured that he was no worse or less active for the Achaeans as a private citizen than as a commander. For it was as a private citizen that he expelled Nabis from Messene and liberated the Messenians, and as a private citizen that he barred Sparta to the commander Diophanes and Titus as they approached, and thus saved the city.[19] He was such a natural leader that he knew how to exercise power not merely according to the laws but even over the laws, when this was expedient; he did not need to be given authority by those over whom it was exercised, but he made use of these people themselves when it was necessary, for they regarded as their general the man who took thought for their welfare rather than the man whom they had chosen themselves. So Titus' generous and caring deeds towards the Greeks were noble, but Philopoemen's deeds towards the Romans, harsh and hard-headed as they were in their pursuit of freedom, were nobler still; for it is easier to give favours to those who want them than to resist and cause pain to those more powerful than oneself.

When we consider the men in this way, the differences become hard to evaluate. Consider whether, if we give the crown to the Greek for military skill and leadership and to the Roman for justice and generosity, we shall not seem to go wrong.[20]

ELDER CATO

INTRODUCTION TO
ELDER CATO

Cato and Roman Virtue

Cato was a self-made man who rose to the top – he was consul, triumphant general and censor – through personal valour, oratory and literary accomplishment. Indeed, he invented Latin historiography, was the first political figure in Rome to publish his orations and, by way of his treatises and essays, imposed on contemporaries and posterity his stern and uncompromising view of what it meant to be an authentic Roman aristocrat. So successful was he in fashioning an enduring model of senatorial probity, and in adducing himself as its finest exemplar, that he remained an icon of Roman virtue down to Plutarch's own day and beyond: 'For speech and for action his reputation excels all others' by far', as Fronto put it.[1]

Plutarch had at his disposal an abundance of flattering portraits of the man. He was idolized by Cicero,[2] and Livy offered his readers a copious and comprehensive celebration of Cato's talents and character, in a passage that was nonetheless honest enough to include notice of its subject's acerbity and contentiousness (39.40.4–12). And still Livy concludes:

> His reason could not be vanquished by his appetites; his integrity was uncompromising; influence and wealth he despised; in his frugality, his capacity for hard work and for danger, in the steely constitution of his body and mind, he remained unbroken, even in old age, which shatters everything.

Much, then, for Plutarch to admire, in a eulogistic tradition of long standing – originating, in fact, in Cato's own writings, their author being, as Livy described him, 'in no way whatsoever inclined to stint in self-praise' (34.15.9).

But if Plutarch could not deny Cato's greatness, this biography is far from uncritical, which is perhaps not surprising in the case of a Roman who 'pronounced with all the solemnity of a prophet that if ever the Romans became infected with the literature of Greece, they would lose their empire' (ch. 23).[3] Such a view was obviously unacceptable to Plutarch, not least from an orator and writer whose compositions, he insists, 'are often enriched by ideas and anecdotes borrowed from the Greek, and many of his maxims and proverbs are literally translated from it' (ch. 2). In Plutarch's account, this is only one of several inconsistencies that, in the end, raise profound questions about the authentic Cato and his real character.

The Historical Cato

Cato was born in 234 BC, a member of the local aristocracy in Tusculum. By this time, Roman political life was no longer riven by strife between patricians and plebeians, but was instead dominated by men called nobles – *nobiles* – who came from families whose ancestors had been consuls. Noble families possessed great wealth and enjoyed wide influence, and their natural superiority was largely conceded by the voters of Rome, who preferred to elect nobles to high office till the last days of the republic. This was a mentality that made it difficult for a newcomer in public life. For such a man, if he was rich enough and exhibited military or forensic talent, it was possible to reach the lower magistracies and find a seat in the senate, where he would be described, with some disdain, as a New Man (*novus homo*). Rising to the praetorship, however, was a different matter, and the consulship was nearly out of the question.[4] That rare New Man who succeeded in becoming consul ennobled his family thereafter. Cato was a New Man, and his rise to the consulship was as singular as it was spectacular.

He got there by way of military distinction and personal rectitude. When he was still seventeen years old, Cato enlisted as a cavalry officer and fought in the Second Punic War, serving under the most distinguished generals of the time, Claudius Marcellus and Fabius Maximus.[5] At the battle of the Metaurus in 207 BC, when the Romans destroyed the army of Hasdrubal as it attempted to relieve Hannibal, Cato displayed conspicuous valour for which he won high praise.[6] At home, he exhibited old-fashioned parsimony and hard work, always admirable values in republican Rome, and he was tireless in local public life. This brought him to the attention of the patrician Lucius Valerius Flaccus, with whose assistance Cato began a political career in Rome. He was quaestor in 204 BC, aedile in 199[7] and praetor in 198. It was a swift and successful rise, during which, by way of his conduct and published speeches, Cato fashioned himself, in the view of the public, as a New Man who brought, or perhaps brought *back*, to the senate the kind of moral fibre they associated with their ancestors. He was elected to the consulship of 195 BC, with his friend Valerius Flaccus as colleague.

Cato's province was Nearer Spain. There he campaigned against local tribes, not without successes but not truly decisively. In his dispatches to Rome, however, he represented his victories in grand, even hyperbolic, terms: 'Cato himself tells us that he captured more cities than he stayed days in Spain' (ch. 10). His true accomplishment lay elsewhere. Spain was rich in iron and silver, and Cato organized the province's mines on a highly profitable basis, a development as attractive to Roman businessmen as it was to his senatorial peers.[8] Furthermore, he did not stint in rewarding his soldiers, to whom he gave an extraordinarily large bounty (ch. 10). It is hardly surprising, then, that when Cato returned to Rome, there was no resistance to his application for a triumph. But Cato had not in fact subdued the tribes in his province, as he claimed.[9]

Cato's energies were not extinguished by his consulship and triumph. In 191 BC, he acted as a tribune of the soldiers during Acilius Glabrio's campaign against Antiochus the Great, during which he played an important role in the battle of

Thermopylae (chs. 12–14). Naturally, it was later written up by Cato as if it were *the* decisive role. He also carried on a series of intense political struggles, in the senate and especially in the courts, where he was a dominating speaker. He stood unsuccessfully for the censorship of 189 BC, but tried again in 184, when he was elected.[10] Cato's censorship was remembered and esteemed for its severity. At the time, however, it aroused a good deal of rancour among the nobility. Still, although some of its measures were invalidated by the senate, its enforcement of traditional standards was popular with the public at large. And Cato carried on. For the remainder of his life he remained a powerful political force. Even in his final months, he was giving speeches in his own defence and in the prosecution of others.

Cato's contribution to Latin literature cannot be overestimated. By publishing his speeches – over 150 were known to Cicero – he established the literary oration as a Roman genre.[11] Cato also composed didactic epistles (addressed to his elder son Marcus), a handbook on Roman medicine and introductions to Roman history suitable for the young. His principal monographs dealt with agriculture (his *On Agriculture* – the only work of Cato's that survives in its entirety) and with military affairs and civil law. Without question his most consequential work was the *Origins*, which covered the early history of Rome and of other Italian peoples, and then reviewed Roman history from the First Punic War down to Cato's own day. This was the first work of Roman history composed in Latin, and its influence was both profound and lasting. In Cicero's day, almost no one any longer read Cato's speeches (see Cicero, *Brutus* 65), and his essays had largely been superseded, but the style of the *Origins* inspired Sallust and through him Tacitus. And by Plutarch's day, Cato's literary star was again in the ascendant: Hadrian preferred his speeches to Cicero's, and he continued to be admired by imperial litterateurs, such as Favorinus and Sulpicius Apollinaris, and Cornelius Fronto and Aulus Gellius. Marcus Aurelius, too, studied him eagerly.[12]

Cato's attitude towards Greek culture remains a matter of dispute for modern scholars and is a part of the larger problem of the role of Greek culture in Roman society. Now, there is no question but that from its very beginnings Roman culture incorporated Hellenic elements, a reality that did not escape the Romans, for whom an important aspect of their cultural identity was the presence of things Greek in the midst of things quintessentially Roman.[13] It was not the adaptation of elements of Greek culture per se that was ever controversial in Rome. Instead, there was conflict over *which* Greek practices the Romans accepted, and the spirit in which they were received by the Romans. This was always an unfinished matter, and in the second century BC Cato, because his views were at once strident and influential, became a locus for subsequent Roman, and for modern, reflections on the nature of Hellenism in Rome.[14]

It is obvious that Cato's writings were influenced by Greek literature. Each of the genres in which he worked had Greek antecedents, and, as Plutarch observed, there were traces of his Greek reading in his Latin pronouncements. What is unclear, however, is the depth of Cato's erudition. Was it limited and cursory, or does his literary achievement reflect a more thorough engagement with Greek literature? In his *On Old Age* (3), for instance, Cicero gives us a Cato who is remarkably well versed in Greek literature and philosophy, but in this dialogue, Cicero points out explicitly, the extent of Cato's learning is exaggerated. Cato's Hellenism, and the degree of his genuine hostility towards Hellenism, continue to provoke debate, but implicit in that discussion is the question of whether the Roman's denunciation of Greek medicine or Greek philosophy or Greek literature constituted his honest opinion or was actually some kind of posture.[15] It is this aspect of Cato's career that Plutarch finds arresting.

Plutarch's Cato

Plutarch found much to admire in Cato: his valour (chs. 1–3, 10–11, 12–14), his rigorous moral standards (chs. 16–19), his energetic public service, even in old age (chs. 12, 24), his dutiful and kindly devotion to his family (ch. 20) and, especially, his old-fashioned austerity (chs. 1–4, 6, 10). These virtues are all registered and elaborated, and Plutarch concludes this Life in highly complimentary fashion with a coda describing Cato's progeny (ch. 27), here with its final emphasis on the Younger Cato, another great man and also the subject of a Plutarchan biography. This kind of tag is one of Plutarch's favoured means of indicating approval, also to be found in this volume at the conclusion of *Marcellus* and *Aratus*.[16] In sum, then, this is a positive biography of a distinguished Roman hero.

But naturally in Plutarch there are complications. Plutarch early on condemns Cato's inhumane treatment of his slaves (ch. 5) and, near the end of his Life, describes Cato's repeated calls for Carthage's destruction as 'excessively brutal' (ch. 27). Cato's unremitting controversies and remorseless quarrels, many of which are enumerated in this Life, could have been adduced as evidence of Cato's contentiousness, a theme that attracts Plutarch's attention in other Lives.[17] But here, interestingly, although Cato's failing is conspicuous and the issue therefore available to the biographer, it goes largely unhighlighted.[18] Instead, Plutarch is much more concerned with the question of Cato's consistency, itself an important aristocratic value among Romans.

At chapter 16, in the introduction to Cato's thorough and severe censorship, Plutarch describes the institution approvingly:

> The Romans did not think it proper that anyone should be left free to follow his personal preferences and appetites, whether in marriage, the begetting of children, the regulation of his daily life or the entertainment of his friends, without a large measure of surveillance and control. They believed that a man's true character was more clearly revealed in his private life than in his public or political career.

Cato puts these principles into action, even going so far as to expel from the senate a rising man named Manilius 'on the ground that he had kissed his wife passionately by daylight in the presence of his daughter' (ch. 17). Yet very soon Cato is sleeping with a slave girl under the same roof as his disapproving son and daughter-in-law, an awkward situation he resolves by marrying the extremely young daughter of a client (ch. 24). Cato justifies this action by appropriating the sentiments of the Athenian tyrant Peisistratus, which was perhaps not the best precedent to reach for, and the whole matter is so thoroughly objectionable to Plutarch that he closes his *Comparison* (ch. 6) in forceful animadversions on Cato's hypocrisy.

Less direct is Plutarch's examination of Cato's austerity. In the early chapters of the Life, Cato is the embodiment of Roman parsimony. Later, however, he gives grand dinner parties at which he holds his slaves to exacting standards in the preparation and presentation of each meal, any violation of which incurs a whipping (ch. 21). Cato's claims to be indifferent to wealth are also vitiated by his unrelenting capitalism (ch. 21). There begins to appear in this Life a very real gap between what Cato preaches and what he practises. This becomes even more obvious for anyone who comes to *Cato* after first reading its Greek parallel.

Plutarch pairs Cato with the Athenian statesman Aristeides (c. 530–468 BC), who was known as 'the Just'. Although the historical Aristeides was a wily politician, in Plutarch's Life he becomes a mild man of consistent principle. He shares with Cato, at least the Cato of the first half of his Life, an indifference to wealth (*Aristeides* 1 and 27). His simple lifestyle and lofty moral scruples form the basis for Plutarch's matching Aristeides with Cato, and these are the dominant themes in Aristeides' Life, along with his astonishing capacity for collaboration and cooperation, even with his rivals (e.g. chs. 3–4, 25 and *Comparison Aristeides–Elder Cato* 5). From boyhood, according to Plutarch, Aristeides possessed a steadfast character utterly lacking in falsehood or deceit (ch. 2), which is why he was admired and trusted on all sides. In the *Comparison*, Plutarch insists that Aristeides was free from contentiousness, and this is marked out as evidence of his mildness (*praotes*), a virtue prized by Plutarch as essential for moral perfection and civic excellence.[19] And Plutarch goes on to agree with Plato's judgement that Aristeides was superior to all his contemporaries because, even when engaged in statecraft, he led his city towards virtue (ch. 25, alluding to Plato's *Gorgias* 526b).

The closing of *Aristeides* (ch. 27) is novel. It, too, employs the progeny trope that concludes other Lives, but with a twist. Here it is the poverty of Aristeides' descendants that is emphasized, as is the willingness of the Athenians to honour the great man by way of kindness to his family. Such conduct, he concludes, was characteristic of the humanity and benevolence of Athens, virtuous behaviour, he adds, of the kind the city continues to exhibit even in Plutarch's own day, and for which it is rightly admired. In essence, it is Athens and its virtues that represent Aristeides' legacy in this Life. In this way, Plutarch brings a suitably Hellenic closure – Plato's praise and the symbolism of Athens – to Aristeides' flawless life, marked by its consistent and authentic principles.

A key inconsistency in *Elder Cato* lies in its subject's attitude towards Greek culture. Cato's hostility is pointed out more than once (chs. 12 and 22–3). At the same time, as Plutarch is at pains to observe, Cato's celebrated eloquence, like his wisdom, actually derives from his acquaintance with Greek literature. Even when Cato attacks Greek medicine, Plutarch suggests, he does so by way of an idea he has borrowed from a Greek source. Plutarch's exasperation with Cato reaches its pitch in his subject's prediction that Greek culture would spell doom for Rome, a belief that was patently untrue, as the evidence of Plutarch's own day made clear:

> he pronounced with all the solemnity of a prophet that if ever the Romans became infected with the literature of Greece, they would lose their empire. At any rate, time has exposed the emptiness of this ominous prophecy, for in the age when the city rose to the zenith of her greatness, her people had made themselves familiar with Greek learning and culture in all its forms.
>
> (ch. 23)

But did Cato, whose literary achievement was, in Plutarch's view, grounded in Greek literature, really believe this? In this matter as in others, the credibility gap opened by Plutarch's account renders the degree of Cato's true attitude towards Greek literature uncertain. Cato simply lacks the transparency and steadfastness of Aristeides.

Cato's lack of consistency recurs throughout the *Comparison*, most pointedly in Plutarch's complaint that Cato simultaneously praises the simple life and yet expounds and practices the best methods of accumulating wealth. In a sharp rhetorical turn, Plutarch does not simply ask the reader to make a judgement in this matter (a common Plutarchan device), but instead seeks the opinion of Cato himself:

> I would very much like to put this question to Cato himself: if wealth is something that should be enjoyed, why, after amassing so much, do you boast of being satisfied with little?
>
> (*Comparison* 4)

Plutarch leaves us with the problem of inferring Cato's answer, and our reflections can only underscore the difficulty of diagnosing the authentic Cato.

This Life concludes in fascinating ironies that stress its complexities. The culmination of Cato's legacy resides in the Younger Cato. But this man would never have existed were it not for Cato's scandalous second marriage, which excites so much disapproval from Plutarch. There is also Plutarch's final description of the Younger Cato, whom we meet in terms that could only shock his forebear, for in the end he is 'Cato the Philosopher' (ch. 27).

Sources

It is clear that Plutarch relied heavily on Cato's own writings. Many were readily available in his day, and inasmuch as their study was fashionable he could easily consult learned Roman friends. It is less obvious whether he used the biography of Cato by Cornelius Nepos (the extant *Cato* is merely an abbreviation of Nepos' more ambitious work *Cato* 3.5). It is true that there is information in Nepos which Plutarch omits, but this in and of itself does not prove Plutarch did not read him.

More important than Nepos, however, were Polybius (principally Books 3–40, though for most of the period of Cato's mature career these books are highly fragmentary) and Livy (Books 31–45). Plutarch also appropriated various aspects of the humane and affable Cato portrayed by Cicero in his *On Old Age*: that was the Cato who was certainly Plutarch's preference.[20]

LIFE OF ELDER CATO

[234–149 BC]

1. Marcus Cato's family is said to have originated from Tusculum,[1] although he himself was brought up and spent his life – before he devoted himself to politics and soldiering – on a family estate in a country of the Sabines.[2] None of his ancestors appears to have made any mark in Roman history, but Cato himself praises his father, Marcus, as a man of courage and a capable soldier. He also mentions that his grandfather Cato was several times decorated for valour in battle, and was awarded by the state treasury for his gallantry the price of the five horses which had been killed under him in battle.

The Romans were in the habit of describing as New Men all those whose ancestors had never risen to high office, but who were beginning to become prominent through their own efforts, and Cato soon acquired this title.[3] He himself used to say that he was certainly new to honours and positions of authority, but that as regards deeds of valour performed by his ancestors, his name was as old as any. Originally his third name was not Cato, but Priscus:[4] he earned the name Cato later in his life on account of his remarkable abilities, for the Romans apply to a man of skill and experience the epithet *catus*.[5]

In appearance he was red-haired and possessed piercing grey eyes, as we learn from the author of this rather malicious epigram:

> Red-haired, grey-eyed, snapping at all comers, even in Hades,
> Porcius, Queen Persephone will turn you away from the gate.[6]

Ever since his early youth he had trained himself to work with his own hands, serve as a soldier and follow a sober mode of living, and hence he possessed a tough constitution and a body which was as strong as it was healthy. He also developed his powers of speech, which he regarded almost as a second body, and, for the man who has no intention of leading an obscure or idle existence, as an indispensable instrument which serves not only the necessary but also the higher purposes of life. So he practised and perfected his oratory in the towns and villages near Rome, where he acted as an advocate for all who needed him, and he earned the reputation first of being a vigorous pleader and then an effective orator. As time went on, the gravity and dignity of his character revealed themselves unmistakably to those who had dealings with him, and marked him out as a man who was clearly qualified for employment in great affairs and a position of leadership in the state. Not only did he provide his services in lawsuits without demanding a fee of any kind,[7] but he did not seem to regard the prestige acquired in these contests as the principal object of his efforts. On the contrary, he was far more anxious to distinguish himself in battles and campaigns against Rome's enemies, and his body was covered with honourable wounds before he had even reached manhood.

He says himself that he served in his first campaign when he was seventeen years old, at the time when Hannibal, at the height of his success, was laying all Italy waste[8] with fire and sword. In battle he was a formidable fighter, who stood his ground resolutely and confronted his opponents with a ferocious expression. He would greet the enemy with a harsh and menacing war cry, for he rightly believed, and reminded others, that such an appearance often frightens the enemy even more than cold steel.[9] When he was on the march, he used to carry his own armour and weapons on foot, and would be followed by a single attendant who looked after his food and utensils. It is said that he never lost his temper with this man, nor found fault with him when he served up a meal; in fact he would often join in and share the task of preparing food, so long as he was free from his military duties. On active service he drank nothing but water, except that occasionally when he was parched with thirst he would ask for vinegar,[10] or when his strength was exhausted add a little wine.

2. Near his estate[11] was a cottage which had belonged to Manius Curius, a redoubtable soldier of the past who had celebrated three triumphs.[12] Cato often visited the place, and the small size of the farm and the house itself inspired him to meditate upon its owner, who although he had become the greatest Roman of his day, had conquered the most warlike tribes and driven Pyrrhus out of Italy, continued to till this little patch of land with his own hands and to live in this cottage, even after he had celebrated his three triumphs. It was here that the ambassadors of the Samnites had found him sitting in front of his hearth boiling turnips. They offered him large sums of gold, but he sent them away, telling them that a man who could be satisfied with such a meal did not need gold. He added that he believed it more honourable to conquer those who possessed gold than to possess it himself.[13] Cato would return home with his mind full of these reflections; then he would look afresh at his own house and slaves and review his mode of life, and would undertake still more work with his own hands and cut down any sign of extravagance.

When Fabius Maximus captured the city of Tarentum,[14] it happened that Cato, who was still quite a young man,[15] was serving under his command. Cato was billeted with a man named Nearchus,[16] who belonged to the sect of the Pythagoreans, and this made him curious to learn something of their theories. When he heard Nearchus expounding the doctrine, which Plato also upholds,[17] 'that pleasure is to be condemned as the greatest incentive to evil, that the body is the greatest hindrance to the development of the soul, and that the soul can only release and purify herself by employing reason to divorce and deliver her from physical sensations', he became more and more attracted to these ideals of simplicity and self-discipline. Beyond this, we are told, he did not study Greek until late in life, and he did not begin to read Greek books until he was an old man.[18] Then he improved his oratory to some extent from the study of Thucydides,[19] and still more from Demosthenes.[20] But in spite of his limited acquaintance with the language, his writings are often enriched by ideas and anecdotes borrowed from the Greek, and many of his maxims and proverbs are literally translated from it.[21]

3. There was at Rome at this time a certain Valerius Flaccus,[22] a member of one of the oldest patrician families and a man of great political influence, who combined a keen eye for excellence while it was in the bud with the generosity to foster it and bring it to full flower. He owned the estate next to Cato's, and learned from his slaves of his neighbour's frugal and self-sufficient way of living. They told him to his amazement that it was Cato's practice to set out early on foot to the market-place of the local town; there he would plead the causes of all who required his services and later in the day return to his farm. Then he would set to work among his own labourers, wearing a sleeveless smock in winter and stripped to the waist in summer, and would sit down with them to eat the same bread and drink the same wine.[23] After they had told him other stories of Cato's just dealings and his moderation, and quoted some of his shrewd sayings, Valerius invited his neighbour to dinner. He soon discovered when he came to know him that his nature was gentle and refined, and that like a plant it needed to be cultivated and given room to expand; accordingly, Valerius encouraged him and at length prevailed upon him to take part in public life at Rome. Once he had settled there, his performance as an advocate quickly attracted admirers and friends, while at the same time Valerius' patronage brought him both honour and influence, so that it was not long before he obtained the office of military tribune and later quaestor.[24] From this point he quickly rose to such heights of fame and distinction that his name came to be associated with Valerius' own in the highest offices of state, and he served as his colleague first as consul and later as censor.[25]

Among the elder statesmen he attached himself most closely to Fabius Maximus.[26] At the time Fabius enjoyed the highest reputation and wielded the greatest power of any man in Rome, yet it was not these distinctions but rather the man's character and his way of life which Cato chose as his ideal. And it was the same considerations which persuaded him to oppose the great Scipio, later known as Africanus.[27] This distinguished man, although at the time barely in his thirties, was already becoming a serious rival to Fabius, who was generally believed to be jealous of him.[28] When Cato was posted to Africa to serve as Scipio's quaestor for the invasion of Carthage, he saw that his commander was not only indulging in his usual lavish personal expenditure, but was also squandering extravagantly high pay upon his troops.[29] He protested to Scipio and told him bluntly that the most important issue was not the question of expense, but the fact that he was corrupting the native simplicity of his men, who, as soon as they had more money than they needed for their everyday wants, would spend it on luxuries and the pleasures of the senses. Scipio retorted that when his plan of campaign was proceeding as it were under full sail, he had no use for a niggling quaestor, and that he would be called upon to account to the Roman people not for the money he had spent but for the battles he had won. Cato therefore left Scipio's army,[30] which was then being assembled in Sicily. He proceeded at once to Rome and helped Fabius to denounce the general before the senate. They attacked Scipio's waste of immense sums of money and his childish fondness for wrestling schools and theatrical performances, as if he had been appointed the impresario of some festival, not a commander on active service.[31] As a result of these accusations, tribunes were sent out[32] with authority to recall Scipio to Rome, if the charges were proved to be true. However, Scipio was able to impress upon the tribunes that success in war depends upon the size of the preparations made for it, and furthermore that he would indulge in agreeable diversions with his friends during his hours of leisure without allowing his sociability to make him neglectful of his serious duties. At any rate, his defence convinced the tribunes, and he set sail for Africa.

4. All this while, Cato's speeches continued to add greatly to his reputation, so that he came to be known as the Roman

Demosthenes,[33] but what created an even more powerful impression than his eloquence was his manner of living. His powers of expression merely set a standard for young men, which many of them were already striving their utmost to attain. But a man who observed the ancestral custom of working his own land, who was content with a cold breakfast, a frugal dinner, the simplest clothing and a humble cottage to live in, and who actually thought it more admirable to renounce luxuries than to acquire them – such a person was conspicuous by his rarity.[34] The truth was that by this date the Roman republic had grown too large to preserve its original purity of spirit, and the very authority which is exercised over so many realms and peoples constantly brought it into contact with, and obliged it to adapt itself to, an extraordinary diversity of habits and modes of living. So it was natural enough that everybody should admire Cato when they saw others prostrated by their labours or enervated by their pleasures, while he remained unaffected by either. What was even more remarkable was that he followed the same habits, not merely while he was young and full of ambition, but even when he was old and grey-headed and had served as a consul and celebrated a triumph, and that he continued, like some champion athlete, to observe the rules of his training and maintain his self-discipline to the end.

He tells us[35] that he never wore a garment which cost more than 100 drachmas, that even when he was praetor or consul he drank the same wine as his rowers,[36] that he bought the fish or meat for his dinner in the public market and never paid more than 30 asses for it,[37] and that he allowed himself this indulgence for the public good in order to strengthen his body for military service. He also mentions that when he was bequeathed an embroidered Babylonian rug, he immediately sold it, that none of his villas had plastered walls,[38] that he never paid more than 1,500 drachmas for a slave, since he was not looking for the exquisite or handsome type of domestic servant, but for sturdy labourers such as grooms and herdsmen, and that when they became too old to work, he felt it his duty to sell them rather than feed so many useless mouths.[39] In general he considered that nothing is cheap if it is superfluous, that what a man does not need is dear even if it cost only an *as*,[40] and that one should buy land for tilling and grazing, not to make gardens, where the object is merely to sprinkle the lawns and sweep the paths.

5. Some people attributed these actions to sheer meanness of spirit on Cato's part, while others upheld them on the grounds that he practised this austere and close-fisted way of life so as to correct and restrain the extravagance of others. For my own part, I regard his conduct towards his slaves in treating them like beasts of burden, exploiting them to the limits of their strength, and then, when they were old, driving them off and selling them, as the mark of a thoroughly ungenerous nature, which cannot recognize any bond between man and man but that of necessity. And yet we see that kindness possesses a far wider sphere of action than justice, for it is in the nature of things that law and justice are confined to our dealings with our fellow-men, whereas kindness and charity, which often flow from a gentle nature, like water from an abundant spring, may be extended even to dumb animals. A kindly man will take good care of his horses even when they are worn out in his service, and will look after his dogs, not only when they are puppies, but when they need special attention in their old age.

When the people of Athens were building the Parthenon, they turned loose those mules which had worked the hardest, put them out to grass and declared them to be exempted from any further service.[41] One of these, so the story goes, came back to the site of its own accord, trotted by the side of its companions which were hauling wagons in harness up the Acropolis, and even led the way as though encouraging and urging them on, whereupon the Athenians passed a decree that the animal should be fed at the public expense for the rest of its life. The graves of Cimon's race-horses too – a set of mares with which he won three victories at Olympia[42] – can still be seen near the tombs of his family. There are many instances of dogs which have become the faithful companions and friends of their masters: perhaps the most famous of all was Xanthippus' dog, which swam by the side of his trireme to Salamis when the Athenians were abandoning Athens,[43] and was buried with honour on the promontory, which is to this day called the Dog's Mound.

We ought never to treat living creatures like shoes or kitchen utensils, to be thrown away when they are broken or worn out in our service, but rather cultivate the habit of behaving with tenderness and consideration towards animals, if only for the sake of gaining practice in humanity when we come to deal with our fellow-men. For my part, I would not sell even my draught ox simply because of his age, far less turn out an old man from the home and the way of life to which he has grown accustomed for the sake of a few paltry coins, especially since he would be of no more use to the buyer than he was to the seller. But Cato goes so far as to boast of such economies, and says that he left behind him in Spain even the charger which he rode during his campaigns as consul, so as to save the state the cost of its transportation. Now, whether these actions are to be judged as examples of greatness or of pettiness of spirit is a question which the reader must decide for himself.

6. However, in other respects Cato's self-restraint deserves the highest commendation. For example, when he commanded an army he never drew for himself and his staff more than three Attic bushels[44] of wheat a month, and for his horses less than a bushel and a half of barley a day. When he became governor of Sardinia,[45] whereas his predecessors had been in the habit of charging the cost of their tents, beds and clothing to the public funds, and extorting immense sums from the province to pay for large retinues of servants and friends, and for sumptuous banquets and entertainments, he substituted an unheard-of economy in his administration. He imposed no charges whatever on the public treasury and visited the various cities on foot, followed by a single public slave,[46] who carried his robe and his cup for pouring libations. But although in these matters he treated the people under his authority with tolerance and a strict regard for economy, in other respects he governed with an exemplary dignity and severity.[47] He was inexorable in the

administration of justice, and direct and peremptory in the execution of his orders, so that the authority of Rome was never
more feared nor more loved than during his term of office.

7. These are also the qualities which distinguish Cato's oratory.
It was at once elegant and forceful, agreeable and vehement,
playful and severe, epigrammatic and combative. In the same
way, Plato remarks of Socrates[48] that superficially he impressed
the people as an uncouth man with a face like a satyr, who was
rude to everyone he met, but that his inward nature was deeply
serious, and full of thoughts which touched his listeners' hearts
and moved them to tears. For this reason I find it hard to understand those who say that the closest parallel to Cato's oratory
is to be found in the speeches of Lysias.[49] However, this kind of
question must be decided by those who are better qualified
than myself at defining the characteristics of Roman oratory.[50]
I shall now relate a few of Cato's memorable sayings, since I
believe that it is often a man's words rather than his appearance which throw light on his character.[51]

8. On one occasion, when he wished to dissuade the Roman
people from raising what he considered to be a quite unjustifi-
able clamour for a free distribution of grain, he began his
speech with the words, 'It is difficult, my fellow-citizens, to
argue with the belly, since it has no ears.' Then, when he was
attacking the extravagance of the day, he remarked, 'How can
we expect to save a city, where people are prepared to pay more
for a fish than for an ox?'[52] On another occasion he declared,
'The Roman people are like sheep: you cannot budge one of
them on its own, but when they are in a flock, they all follow
their leaders as a single body. In the same way, when you come
together in the assembly, you allow yourselves to be led by men
whose advice you would never think of following in your private affairs.' On the subject of the influence of women, he said,
'All mankind rule their wives, we rule all mankind, and our
wives rule us.' However, this saying is borrowed from Themistocles,[53] who, when he found his son constantly giving him orders
but doing so by way of instructions from his wife, told her, 'My

dear, the Athenians rule the Greeks, I rule the Athenians, you rule me, and our son rules you. So he must be careful, even at his young age, not to abuse his power, because it is greater than anyone else's.'

'The Roman people', he pointed out on another occasion, 'fix the value not only of dyes and colours, but also of men's occupations. For just as dyers make most use of the colours which they see are most popular, so your young men study and apply themselves to the subjects which they think will earn credit with you.' He also put it to the people that if they had won their empire by means of virtue and self-restraint, they should not allow themselves to fall away from these qualities, but that if it was through self-indulgence and vice, they should try to bring about a change for the better, since these qualities had already made them great enough. Those who were perpetually ambitious to hold high office, he compared to men who did not know their way, and who expected to be attended all the time by lictors, in case they should go astray.[54] He also found fault with the people for constantly electing the same men[55] to the most important positions. 'It can only be supposed,' he said, 'either that you do not think the office itself is of much consequence, or else that you believe there are very few men capable of filling it.' Speaking of one of his enemies, who was notorious for his dissolute and disreputable life, Cato said, 'That man's mother thinks of it as a curse, not a blessing, if anyone prays that her son should survive her.' And on another occasion, he pointed to a man who had sold his ancestral estate, which was near the sea, and, pretending to admire him for possessing greater strength than the sea itself, he said, 'The sea could only wash away a small part of his fields, but this man had drunk up every one of them without any difficulty at all.'[56]

When King Eumenes of Pergamum[57] paid a state visit to Rome, the senate received him with extraordinary honours, and the most prominent citizens in Rome vied with one another in showing him attention, whereupon Cato made a point of treating him with suspicion and reserve. 'But surely', someone said to him, 'Eumenes is an excellent man and a friend of Rome.' 'That may be,' replied Cato, 'but nevertheless a king is an animal that lives on human flesh.' He maintained that none of the kings who had enjoyed so great a reputation could be compared with Epaminondas or Pericles[58] or Themistocles or Manius Curius[59] or Hamilcar Barca.[60]

His enemies, he used to say, hated him because he got up early every day and devoted himself to public affairs, but neglected his own. Another saying of his was that he would rather do what was right and go unrewarded than do wrong and go unpunished,[61] and that he was prepared to forgive everybody's mistakes except his own.[62]

9. The Romans once sent three ambassadors to Bithynia,[63] one of whom suffered from gout, another had had his skull trepanned and the third was generally regarded as a fool. Cato ridiculed these appointments, and said that the Romans were sending out a delegation which could not muster a pair of feet, nor a head, nor a heart.[64] Scipio Africanus once approached him at Polybius' request to enlist his support on behalf of the Greek exiles from Achaea.[65] The question was debated at great length in the senate, some speakers contending that the men should be allowed to return home, and others that they should continue to be detained in Italy. At last Cato rose and asked: 'Have we nothing better to do than to spend an entire day sitting here and discussing whether some poor old Greeks are to be buried by our grave-diggers or their own?'[66] The senate then decreed that the men should be allowed to return home, but a few days later Polybius tried to have another proposal laid before the senate, whereby the exiles would have the honours and positions which they had formerly held in Achaea restored to them, and he asked Cato's opinion as to whether this petition was likely to succeed. Cato smiled and told him that what he was suggesting was rather as though Odysseus had wanted to go back into the Cyclops' cave to fetch a cap and belt he had left behind.[67]

'Wise men', he used to say, 'profit far more from the example of fools than the other way round. They learn to avoid the fools' mistakes, whereas fools do not imitate the successes of the wise.' He said that he liked to see young men blush rather than turn pale,[68] and that he had no use for a soldier who used his hands on the march and his feet when it came to fighting,[69] or one who snored louder in his sleep than he shouted in battle. There was an excessively fat Roman of whom he made fun by saying: 'How can a body like this be of any service to the state, when everything in it from the gullet to the groin is devoted to the belly?'[70] When a certain epicure wished to enjoy his company and sent him an invitation, he excused himself by saying that he could not spend his time with a man whose palate was so much more highly developed than his heart.[71] He also remarked once that a lover's soul lives in the body of his beloved.[72] As for regrets, he said that there were only three actions in his life of which he repented. The first was to have entrusted a secret to a woman, the second to have paid for his sea passage to a place instead of walking there and the third to have remained intestate for a whole day.[73] Speaking to an old man who was leading a depraved life, he remarked, 'Old age is vile enough as it is: do not add to it the deformity of vice.'[74] To a tribune of the people who was reputed to be a poisoner, had introduced an iniquitous bill and was trying to force its passage, he said, 'Young man, I do not know which will do us more harm, to drink your potions or to enact your bills.' And when he himself was attacked by a man who led an infamous and dissolute life, he retorted: 'We can never fight on equal terms: you are so hardened to abuse that you can return it just as easily as you suffer it, whereas for me it is as unusual to hear as it is unpleasant to utter.' These are some examples of his memorable sayings.

10. After he had served as consul with his close friend Valerius Flaccus, he was allotted the province which is known as Nearer Spain.[75] While he was engaged in subduing some of the tribes by force and winning over others by diplomacy, he was attacked by a huge army of barbarians and was in danger of being driven ignominiously out of the province. In this situation he appealed to a neighbouring tribe, the Celtiberians,[76] to join forces with him. When they demanded 200 talents as the price for their assistance, Cato's Roman officers thought it an intolerable humiliation that Romans should actually pay barbarians to

come to their rescue.[77] But Cato took the view that there was nothing shocking in this. If the Romans won, they could pay their allies out of the spoils of the campaign, not out of public funds, and if they lost there would be nobody left either to ask for the reward or to pay it.[78] In the battle which followed he won an overwhelming victory, and the rest of the campaign was brilliantly successful.[79] Polybius records[80] that in the space of a single day, the walls of all the cities on the Roman side of the River Baetis[81] were razed to the ground on Cato's orders, and yet these were very numerous and full of excellent fighting men. Cato himself tells us that he captured more cities than he stayed days in Spain.[82] And this is no idle boast, if in fact the number taken amounted to 400.

His soldiers enriched themselves greatly during this campaign, and over and above their plunder he presented each of them with a pound of silver,[83] saying that it was better that many of the Romans should return home with silver in their pockets than a few with gold. As for himself, he states that he took no share whatever of the spoils of war, apart from what he ate and drank. 'I do not blame those who seek to make their fortune in this way,' he added, 'but I would rather compete for bravery with the bravest than for money with the richest, or for covetousness with the most greedy.'[84] At any rate, he not only kept his own hands clean, but insisted that his staff should also be free from any taint of profiteering. He had five personal slaves with him while he was on active service. One of these, whose name was Paccius,[85] bought three boys at a public sale of prisoners of war, but when he found that Cato had learned of this transaction, he went and hanged himself rather than face his master. Cato sold the boys and returned the money he received for them to the public treasury.

11. While Cato was still serving in Spain, Scipio Africanus, because he was an enemy to Cato and wished to check the sequence of his successes and take the administration of Spanish affairs out of his hands, contrived to have himself appointed to succeed Cato as governor of the province.[86] He therefore travelled to Spain as quickly as he could and cut short Cato's

term of office.[87] However, Cato took with him five cohorts of infantry and 500 horsemen as an escort for his return journey, and on his march to Rome subdued the tribe of the Lacetanians[88] and put to death 600 deserters, whom they surrendered to him. Scipio was furious at this action, whereupon Cato replied with mock humility that Rome would truly be at her greatest when men of noble birth refused to yield the prizes of valour to those of humbler position, and when plebeians such as himself dared to contend with their superiors in birth and distinction. But in spite of Scipio's disapproval, the senate decreed that none of Cato's measures should be revoked or altered, so that Scipio's term of office, which he had so eagerly sought, was conspicuous for its inactivity and lack of initiative, and it was his own rather than Cato's reputation which suffered.

Cato on the other hand was honoured with a triumph.[89] But he neither abandoned nor relaxed his efforts, as is so often the case with men whose ambition is directed towards fame rather than virtue, and who, as soon as they have attained the highest honours, served as consul and celebrated a triumph, promptly withdraw from public affairs and devote the rest of their careers to a life of ease and pleasure. Instead, Cato behaved like a man who is all athirst for glory and reputation on his first entry into public life, and in this spirit he once more sprang into action and offered his services to his friends and his fellow-countrymen, both in the courts of law and in the field.

12. This was how he came to serve as legate under Titus Sempronius the consul, and helped him to subdue the region of Thrace and the territories bordering the Danube.[90] Later he was a military tribune under Manius Acilius[91] during his campaign in Greece against Antiochus the Great,[92] who, next to Hannibal, was the most formidable opponent the Romans had ever encountered. Antiochus first reconquered almost all the territory in Asia which had previously been ruled by Seleucus Nicator,[93] and subdued many warlike barbarian tribes, and finally his elation at these conquests led him to attack the Romans, whom he regarded as the only nation worthy to cross

swords with him. He used the restoration of Greek liberties as a specious pretext for his invasion, although in fact the people had no need for this gift, since the Romans had only recently freed them from the domination of Philip of Macedon.[94] At any rate, Antiochus crossed with an army into Greece, which was at once thrown into a turmoil of hopes and fears, and corrupted by the prospects of royal favour held out by the demagogues whom Antiochus had won over. Accordingly, Manius dispatched envoys to the various cities. In most of these Titus Flamininus succeeded in quelling the efforts of the agitators and in restoring the people to their allegiance, as I have described in detail in his Life,[95] but Cato was responsible for bringing over Corinth, Patrae and Aegium to the side of Rome.[96]

He also stayed for a considerable time in Athens, and we are told that a certain speech of his has survived which he delivered to the Athenian people in Greek. In this he told them of his admiration for the virtues of the ancient Athenians, and of his delight at seeing a city as beautiful and as magnificent as theirs. All this is untrue, since Cato in fact spoke to the Athenians through an interpreter. He was quite capable of addressing them in their own language, but he clung to Roman forms[97] and made a point of ridiculing those who admired everything that was Greek. For example, he made fun of the Roman author Postumius Albinus, who wrote a history in Greek and asked his readers to make allowances for his ignorance of the language.[98] Cato remarked that they might have made allowances if he had been compelled to undertake the task by a decree of the Amphictyony.[99] Cato himself claims that the Athenians were greatly impressed by the speed and the conciseness of his address, for the interpreter took a long time and a great many words to communicate what he expressed briefly, and in general he concludes that the Greeks speak from the lips, but the Romans from the heart.[100]

13. Now Antiochus had blocked the narrow pass of Thermopylae with his army and strengthened the natural defences of the position by means of walls and trenches, and there he sat, confident that it was impossible to attack him in Greece.[101]

And in fact the Romans did give up hope of forcing the pass by a frontal assault. However, Cato – remembering the famous outflanking march whereby the Persians had turned Leonidas' defences[102] – took a large force and set off under a cover of darkness. They had climbed to a considerable height, when their guide, who was a prisoner of war, lost the way and wandered helplessly along tracks which either gave out or ended in sheer precipices, until the soldiers were thoroughly disheartened and on the verge of despair. At this point Cato, recognizing the danger of their position, ordered the troops to halt, while he himself with a single companion named Lucius Mallius,[103] who was an expert mountaineer, went forward to reconnoitre the path. This he did with great difficulty and danger, as it was a moonless pitch-dark night, and the rocks and trees hindered them by preventing them from seeing distinctly where they were going. At last they came upon a path which they believed led down to the enemy's camp. As they returned, they left marks upon some of the most conspicuous rocks on the heights of Mount Callidromus,[104] and at last found their way back to the main body. Then they led the troops forward up to the signs, and started on the downward path. But when they had gone only a little way, the track again gave out, and a yawning precipice stretched below their feet. Once more fear and bewilderment descended on the troops, since it was impossible for them to know or to see that they were almost upon the enemy whom they sought. But presently the darkness began to fade, they believed that they could hear voices close by and soon they actually caught sight of Greek entrenchments and an outpost near the foot of the cliffs. Cato then halted his troops and called up the men of Firmum[105] for a private conference: this was a contingent which he had always found to be especially daring and reliable.

When they had run up and gathered round him, he told them: 'I need to capture one of the enemy alive and find out who this advance guard consists of and what is its strength, the order of battle of the main body and what preparations they have made to resist us. But to get your prisoner you will have to move without a second's hesitation, as quickly and as boldly

as a lion leaping on a timid herd.' When they had listened to
Cato's orders, the Firmians set off at a rush, just as they were,
poured down the mountain-side and hurled themselves upon
the enemy's sentinels. The surprise was complete and the whole
outpost was thrown into confusion and scattered at once. The
Firmians seized one man, arms and all, and hurried him back
to Cato. He soon discovered from the prisoner that the enemy's
main body was encamped in the pass with the king himself,
while the detachment which held the approach from the heights
above consisted of 600 picked Aetolians. Now that he knew
the weakness of the advance guard and the carelessness of their
dispositions, Cato was filled with confidence. He drew his
sword, and with a battle cry and a great blast of trumpets led
his men into the attack. When the enemy saw the Romans
pouring down upon them from the cliffs, they immediately fled
and took refuge with the main body, filling it with confusion
and dismay.

14. Meanwhile, Manius on the lower ground flung his whole
army into the pass and stormed the enemy's fortifications.
Antiochus was struck in the mouth by a stone, which shattered
his teeth and made him wheel his horse in agony, and before the
shock of the Roman charge his troops gave way at every point.
There was little enough hope of escape, since the mountain
tracks were hard to follow and led over difficult ground, while
deep marshes on the one side and steep cliffs on the other
threatened any who slipped and fell; but in spite of everything
the routed troops tried to force their way through the narrow
pass towards these dangers, and trampling upon one another in
their terror of the Romans' swords, many of them perished
miserably.

It would seem that Cato never stinted his own praise,[106] and
could never resist following up a great achievement with a
correspondingly boastful description of it, so he gives a characteristically inflated account of this battle. He says that those
who saw him pursuing and cutting down the enemy felt that
Rome owed more to Cato than he to his city, and that the consul Manius himself, flushed with victory, threw his arms around

him in a long embrace and cried aloud in sheer joy that neither
he nor the whole Roman people could ever repay Cato for his
services to the state. Immediately after the battle he was dispatched to Rome[107] to carry the news of his own exploits. He
sailed with a favourable wind to Brundisium,[108] crossed the
peninsula in a single day and, after travelling four days more,
reached Rome on the fifth day after his landing. His arrival
filled the whole city with rejoicing and sacrifices, and inspired
the people with the proud belief that they could conquer every
land and every sea.

15. These actions which I have described were the most remarkable achievements of Cato's military career. In his political life
he seems to have concerned himself most of all with the
impeachment and trial of wrongdoers. He undertook many
prosecutions himself, gave his help to others in bringing theirs,
and in some instances incited his fellow-citizens to open proceedings, as in the case of Petillius' prosecution of Scipio.[109]
Scipio's response, as a member of one of the greatest families in
Rome and a man of lofty spirit, was to trample these accusations underfoot, and when Cato found that he could not obtain
a conviction on a capital charge, he dropped the case. But he
joined the accusers of Scipio's brother Lucius, and was active in
securing his condemnation to pay a heavy fine to the state.
Lucius was unable to meet this and therefore became liable to
imprisonment, and it was only with difficulty and after the
intervention of the tribunes[110] that he was set free.

There is also a story of a young man who had brought an
action against an enemy of his dead father and succeeded in
obtaining his disfranchisement. When the case was over and he
was leaving the forum, Cato greeted him and said: 'This is the
kind of sacrifice we should offer up to the spirits of our parents,
not lambs nor kids, but the condemnation and then the tears of
their enemies.' Yet Cato himself did not escape with impunity.
Whenever in his political career he gave his enemies the slightest ground to attack him, he was repeatedly prosecuted and
sometimes in danger of being condemned. It is said that nearly
fifty impeachments[111] were brought against him, the last when he

was eighty-six years of age. It was on this occasion that he uttered the famous remark, 'It is hard for a man who has lived through one generation to be called upon to defend himself before another,'[112] but even this action was not his last, for four years later at the age of ninety[113] he impeached Servius Galba,[114] and indeed one might say of him as of Nestor that his life spanned three generations,[115] and he was active in each one of them. He fought many political contests with Scipio Africanus, as I have described above, and he lived to continue them with the younger Scipio,[116] who was Africanus' grandson by adoption, his father being that Aemilius Paullus who conquered Perseus and the Macedonians.

16. Ten years after his consulship Cato became a candidate for the censorship.[117] The office was regarded as the crowning honour of Roman civic life, and in a sense the culminating achievement of a political career.[118] Its powers were very extensive and they included the right to inquire into the lives and manners of the citizens. The Romans did not think it proper that anyone should be left free to follow his personal preferences and appetites, whether in marriage, the begetting of children, the regulation of his daily life or the entertainment of his friends, without a large measure of surveillance and control. They believed that a man's true character was more clearly revealed in his private life than in his public or political career, and they therefore chose two officials, one from among the so-called patricians and the other a plebeian,[119] whose duty it was to watch, regulate and punish any tendency to indulge in licentious or voluptuous habits and to depart from the traditional and established way of living. These officers were known as censors, and they had authority to degrade a Roman knight[120] or to expel a senator who led a vicious or disorderly life.[121] They also carried out and maintained a general census of property, kept a register of all the citizens according to their social and political classification, and exercised various other important powers.

Accordingly, when Cato became a candidate,[122] almost all the most prominent and influential members of the senate joined forces to oppose him. Those of them who belonged to the most ancient families were motivated by jealousy, since they regarded it as an insult to the nobility that men of totally undistinguished origin should be raised to the highest positions of honour and power, while others, who were conscious of having committed shameful misdeeds or departed from traditional customs, dreaded the austerity of Cato's disposition and felt sure that he would prove harsh and inexorable in his use of power.

So after conferring together and drawing up their plans, they put up no fewer than seven candidates to oppose Cato, and these men at once set themselves to court the people's votes by promising that they would show great leniency while in office, imagining that the common people desired a lax and indulgent regime. Cato, on the other hand, did not deign to offer any concessions whatever. He openly threatened wrongdoers in his speeches from the rostra, proclaimed that what the city needed was a drastic purification and exhorted the people, if they had any sense, to choose a physician who would prescribe not the most painless but the most strenuous course of treatment. He himself was such a one, he told them, among the plebeians, and among the patricians they should elect Valerius Flaccus. Flaccus was the only colleague, he insisted, with whom he could make some progress in cutting away and cauterizing the hydra-like[123] desire for luxury and degeneracy of the age. As for the rest of the candidates, it was clear that the only object of their efforts was to force their way into the office and pervert its functions, since they were afraid of those who would administer them with justice. On this occasion the Roman people showed itself to be truly great, and hence worthy of great leaders. They did not allow themselves to be deterred by Cato's inflexibility nor even by his arrogance. On the other hand, they rejected his smooth-spoken opponents, who had promised to do everything to please them, and they elected Flaccus together with Cato. Indeed, they treated Cato not as if he were a candidate for office, but already installed in it, and exercising his authority.

17. As soon as he was elected,[124] Cato appointed his friend and colleague Lucius Valerius Flaccus to be the leading man in the senate,[125] and he also expelled several of its members, including a certain Lucius Quinctius.[126] This man had been consul seven years before and – a distinction which counted for more even than the consulship – was the brother of the Titus Flamininus who had overcome King Philip of Macedon. The reason for his expulsion was as follows. There was a youth who had been Lucius' favourite ever since his boyhood. He kept him constantly at his side, even taking him on his campaigns, and allowed him to enjoy more honour and influence than any of his closest friends and relatives. While Lucius was serving as governor of his consular province, he held a drinking party. On this occasion the youth was reclining, as he usually did, next to Lucius and serving up flattery to his patron, who was in any case all too easily led astray by drink. 'I am so devoted to you', the boy told him, 'that once, when there was to be a gladiatorial show in Rome, I missed it to hurry out here and join you, even though I have always longed to see a man killed.' Lucius, who was anxious to demonstrate his affection, answered, 'I am not going to have you lying there holding a grudge against me on that account. I will soon put the matter right.' At this he gave orders for a criminal who had been condemned to death to be brought into the banquet, and for a lictor to stand by him with an axe. Then he again asked his favourite whether he wanted to see a man struck dead, and when the boy said he did, he ordered the prisoner to be beheaded. This is the account which most writers give of the incident, and when Cicero in his *On Old Age* introduces Cato as telling the story, he gives the same details.[127] According to Livy, however, the man who was executed was a Gallic deserter, and Lucius did not have him beheaded by a lictor, but struck the blow with his own hand, and he also mentions that this version of the story is repeated in a speech of Cato's own.[128] When Lucius was expelled from the senate in this way, his brother Titus was indignant and appealed to the people, demanding that Cato should explain the reasons for his action. Cato then did so and told the whole

story of the drinking party. Lucius tried to deny the affair, but
when Cato challenged him to a formal inquiry and a judicial
wager[129] on the result, he declined. After this everybody recognized that he had been justly punished. But some time later,
when a public spectacle was put on in the theatre, Lucius
walked past the seats reserved for men of consular rank and
took his place as far away as possible, among the least distinguished members of the audience. This action made the people
take pity on him, and they began to raise a clamour until they
obliged him to change his seat, thus restoring his dignity so far
as they could and alleviating the humiliation he had suffered.

Cato also expelled another senator, Manilius – despite the
fact that public opinion had marked him out as a strong candidate for the consulship – on the ground that he had kissed his
wife passionately by daylight in the presence of his daughter.[130]
For his own part, Cato declared, he never embraced his wife
except when a loud peal of thunder occurred, and it was a
favourite joke of his that he was a happy man whenever Jove
took it into his head to thunder.

18. Cato also had Lucius Scipio[131] expelled from the equestrian
order, even though the man had enjoyed the honour of a triumph. But on this occasion he was sharply criticized since it
was believed that he had acted out of personal spite, and that
his principal object had been to insult the memory of Lucius'
brother, the great Africanus.[132]

But what annoyed people more than anything else were his
efforts to cut down extravagance and luxury. These habits could
not be abolished outright, since most of the people were already
to some extent infected by them, and so Cato attempted an
indirect approach. He had an assessment made of all clothing,
carriages, women's ornaments, furniture and plate: whatever
exceeded 1,500 drachmas in value was rated at ten times its
worth and taxed accordingly, as he wished to ensure that those
whose possessions were the most valuable should also pay the
highest taxes. He then imposed a tax of 3 asses for every
1,000 drachmas assessed in this way, so that when owners of
property found themselves burdened with these charges, and

saw that people who enjoyed the same income but led frugal and simple lives paid far less in taxes, they might give up their extravagant habits.[133] However, the result of these measures was to earn him the hatred not only of those who put up with the taxes to enjoy their luxuries, but also of those who sacrificed the luxuries to avoid the taxes. The truth is that most people feel that they are deprived of their wealth if they are prevented from displaying it, and it is the superfluities, not the necessities of life, which really afford the opportunity for such display. This is the phenomenon which so much astonished Ariston[134] the philosopher, as we are told: he could not understand why men should regard it as a happier state to possess what is superfluous rather than what is essential. We may remember the story of Scopas[135] the Thessalian, one of whose friends asked him for an object which was of no great use to him, and pointed out, to justify his request, that he was not asking for anything which was really necessary or useful; whereupon Scopas replied: 'But it is just these useless and superfluous things which make me enjoy my wealth.' From this we see that the craving for wealth is not a passion that comes naturally to us, but is imposed by the vulgar and irrelevant opinions of the outside world.

19. Cato paid not the slightest attention to the protests which his measures aroused, but proceeded to make them more rigorous than ever. He cut off the pipes by which people were in the habit of diverting some of the public water supply into their homes and gardens; he had any houses which encroached on public land demolished, reduced the contracts for public works to the lowest, and raised the rent for public lands to the highest possible figure. All these proceedings made him intensely unpopular. Titus[136] and his friends organized a party to oppose his programme, prevailed upon the senate to cancel the contracts which he had arranged for the building of temples and other public works, and encouraged the boldest of the tribunes to prosecute him before the people and fine him 2 talents.[137] He also met with vehement opposition from the senate when he had built in the forum at public expense a basilica below the senate-house, which came to be known as the Basilica Porcia.[138]

But for all his unpopularity with the rich, Cato's activities as censor seem to have been wholeheartedly admired by the Roman people. At any rate, when they erected a statue to his honour in the temple of Health,[139] what they chose to commemorate was not his military campaigns nor his triumph but, according to the inscription, the fact that 'when the Roman state was sinking into decay, he became censor and through his wise leadership, sober discipline and sound principles restored its strength'. And yet at one time Cato used to ridicule those who took pleasure in receiving honours of this kind. Such people could never understand, he said, that the effigies in which they took so much pride were nothing more than the work of sculptors and painters, whereas the finest image of himself, as he saw it, was the one which his fellow-citizens carried in their hearts.[140] And if anyone showed surprise that there were so many statues which commemorated men of no distinction, but none of himself, he would answer, 'I had far rather that people should ask why there is no statue of me than why there is one.'[141] In short he believed that a good citizen should not accept even the praise that he had earned, unless this could benefit the state.

On the other hand, we should recognize that no man ever did more to heap praises upon himself. Cato tells us, for example, that when men were reproved for misconduct of one kind or another, they would say: 'It is not fair to blame us: we are not all Catos.' And again that men who tried to imitate his habits but went about it clumsily were known as 'left-handed Catos'. He also mentions that the senate at moments of great crisis looked to him as sailors do to their pilot, and that they would often postpone their most important business, if he could not be present. These claims, it is true, are confirmed by other writers, for his whole course of life, his eloquence and his age all combined to invest him with immense authority among the Romans.

20. He was also a good father, a kind husband and a most capable manager of his own household, since he was far from regarding this side of his affairs as trivial or allowing it to suffer

from neglect. For this reason, I think I should give some examples of his conduct in his private life. He chose his wife[142] for her family rather than her fortune, for he believed that while people of great wealth or high position cherish their own pride and self-esteem, nevertheless women of noble birth are by nature more ashamed of any disgraceful action and so are more obedient to their husbands in everything that is honourable. He used to say that a man who beats his wife or child is laying sacrilegious hands on the most sacred thing in the world. He considered that it was more praiseworthy to be a good husband than a great senator, and was also of the opinion that there was nothing much else to admire in Socrates of old except for the fact that he was always gentle and considerate in his dealings with his wife, who was a scold, and his children, who were half-witted.[143]

When his son[144] was born, Cato thought that nothing but the most important business of state should prevent him from being present when his wife gave the baby its bath and wrapped it in swaddling clothes. His wife suckled the child herself[145] and often did the same for the slaves' children, so as to encourage brotherly feelings in them towards her own son. As soon as the boy was able to learn, his father took charge of his schooling and taught him to read, although he had in the household an educated slave called Chilo who was a schoolmaster and taught many older boys. However, Cato did not think it right, so he tells us, that his son should be scolded or have his ears pulled by a slave, if he were slow to learn, and still less that he should be indebted to his slave in such a vital matter as his education. So he took it upon himself to teach the boy, not only his letters, but also the principles of Roman law. He also trained him in athletics, and taught him how to throw the javelin, fight in armour, ride a horse, use his fists in boxing, endure the extremes of heat and cold and swim across the roughest and most swiftly flowing stretches of the river.[146] He tells us that he composed his historical books,[147] writing them out with his own hand and in large characters, so that his son should possess in his own home the means of acquainting himself with the ancient annals and traditions of his country. He also mentions that he was as careful not to use any indecent expression before his son as he would have been in the presence of the Vestal Virgins, and that he never bathed with him. This last seems to have been the general custom among the Romans, and even fathers-in-law avoided bathing with their son-in-law, because they were ashamed to show themselves naked.[148] In later times, however, the Romans adopted from the Greeks the practice of stripping in the presence of other men, and they in turn corrupted the Greeks by introducing this same practice even in the presence of women.[149]

Such was Cato's approach to the noble task of forming and moulding his son for the pursuit of virtue. The boy was an exemplary pupil in his readiness to learn, and his spirit was a match for his natural goodness of disposition. But since his body was not strong enough to endure extreme hardship, Cato was obliged to relax a little the extraordinary austerity and self-discipline of his own way of life. However, his son, in spite of a delicate physique, became an excellent soldier, and fought with great distinction under Aemilius Paullus at the battle of Pydna, when the Romans defeated King Perseus.[150] During the fighting, his sword was either struck out of his hand or else slipped from his grasp when it became moist with sweat. The young man felt deeply ashamed at losing it, and so he turned to some of his companions and, rallying them to his side, charged the enemy again. The fighting was fierce, but at length he succeeded in clearing a space, and there he came upon the weapon amid the heaps of arms and corpses, where the bodies of friends and enemies lay piled high upon one another. Paullus, his commander, was greatly impressed by the young Cato's courage, and a letter has come down to us[151] written by the father to his son, in which he praises him in the highest terms for his gallantry and for the sense of honour which he showed in recovering his sword. He afterwards married Tertia, a daughter of Paullus and hence the sister of the younger Scipio, as he afterwards became known, and the distinction of this alliance with so noble a family was quite as much due to his own achievements as to his father's. In this way Cato was justly rewarded for the care which he had devoted to his son's education.

21. Cato possessed a large number of slaves, whom he usually bought from among the prisoners captured in war, but it was his practice to choose those who, like puppies or colts, were young enough to be trained and taught their duties. None of them ever entered any house but his own, unless they were sent on an errand by Cato or his wife, and if they were asked what Cato was doing, the reply was always that they did not know. It was a rule of his establishment that a slave must either be doing something about the house, or else be asleep. He much preferred the slaves who slept well, because he believed that they were more even-tempered than the wakeful ones, and that those who had had enough sleep produced better results at any task than those who were short of it. And as he was convinced that slaves were led into mischief more often on account of love affairs than for any other reason, he made it a rule that the men could sleep with the women slaves of the establishment, for a fixed price, but must have nothing to do with any others.

At the beginning of his career, when he was a poor man and was frequently on active service, he never complained of anything that he ate, and he used to say that it was ignoble to find fault with a servant for the food that he prepared. But in later life, when he had become more prosperous,[152] he used to invite his friends and colleagues to dinner, and immediately after the meal he would beat with a leather thong any of the slaves who had been careless in preparing or serving it. He constantly contrived to provoke quarrels and dissensions among his slaves,[153] and if they ever arrived at an understanding with one another he became alarmed and suspicious. If ever any of his slaves was suspected of committing a capital offence, he gave the culprit a formal trial in the presence of the rest, and if he was found guilty he had him put to death.

When he began to devote himself more energetically to making money, he came to regard agriculture as a pastime rather than as a source of income,[154] and he invested his capital in solid enterprises which involved the minimum of risk. He bought up fisheries,[155] hot springs, fuller's establishments, workshops[156] and estates which were rich in pasture-land or forest. All these undertakings brought in large profits and could not, to use his own phrase, be ruined by the whims of Jupiter.[157] He also used to lend money in what is surely the most disreputable form of speculation,[158] that is, the underwriting of ships. Those who wished to borrow money from him were obliged to form a large association, and when this reached the number of fifty, representing as many ships, he would take one share in the company through the agency of Quintio, one of his freedmen,[159] who used to accompany Cato's clients on their voyage and transact their business. In this way he drew a handsome profit, while at the same time spreading his risk and never venturing more than a fraction of his capital.

He would also lend money to any of his slaves who wished it. They used these sums to buy young slaves, and after training them and teaching them a trade for a year at Cato's expense, they would sell them again. Often Cato would keep these boys for himself, and he would then credit to the slave the price offered by the highest bidder. He tried to encourage his son to imitate these methods, and told him that to diminish one's capital was something that might be expected of a widow, but not of a man.[160] But he certainly went too far when he ventured once to declare that the man who deserved the highest praise, indeed who should be honoured almost as a god, was the one who at the end of his life was found to have added to his property more than he had inherited.

22. Cato was an old man when Carneades[161] the Academic and Diogenes[162] the Stoic arrived in Rome as ambassadors from Athens.[163] They had been sent to plead that the Athenians should be released from a sentence which had imposed on them a fine of 500 talents. The people of Oropus had brought an action, the Athenians had allowed the case to go by default and the people of Sicyon had pronounced judgement against them.[164] When the philosophers arrived, all the young Romans who had any taste for literature hurried to frequent their com-

pany, and listened to them with delight and wonder. Above all, they were spellbound by the grace and charm with which Carneades expressed himself. He was the ablest of the Greeks and his performance did not belie his reputation. His discourses attracted large and admiring audiences, and before long the city was filled as if by a rushing, mighty wind with the sound of his praises. The report spread that a Greek of extraordinary talents had arrived, who could subdue all opposition beneath the spell of his eloquence, and who had so bewitched all the youth of the city that they seemed to have abandoned all their other pleasures and pursuits and to have become utterly possessed by philosophy.

Most of the Romans were gratified by this, and were well content to see their sons embrace Greek culture and frequent the society of such estimable men. But Cato, from the moment that this passion for discussion first showed itself in Rome, was deeply disturbed. He was afraid that the younger generation might allow their ambitions to be diverted in this direction, and might come to value most highly a reputation that was based upon feats of oratory rather than upon feats of arms. So when the prestige of the philosophers continued to rise still higher, and no less eminent a man than Gaius Acilius[165] volunteered to act as their interpreter for their first audience with the senate, Cato made up his mind to find some plausible excuse for clearing the whole tribe of philosophers out of the city. Accordingly, he rose in the senate and criticized the authorities for having kept in such long suspense a delegation composed of men whose powers of persuasion were so remarkable that they could obtain any verdict that they wished. 'We ought to come to a decision as soon as possible,' he declared, 'and take a vote on their proposal, so that these distinguished men may return to their seats of learning and lecture to the sons of Greece, but leave the youth of Rome to give their attention to the laws and the magistrates, as they have done in the past.'

23. Cato did not take this action, as some people believe, out of personal animosity towards Carneades, but rather because he was opposed on principle to the study of philosophy,[166] and

because his patriotic fervour made him regard the whole of Greek culture and its methods of education with contempt. He asserts, for example, that Socrates was a turbulent windbag, who did his best to act the tyrant in his country by undermining its established customs and seducing his fellow-citizens into holding opinions which were contrary to the laws. He made fun of Isocrates[167] as a teacher of rhetoric, saying that his disciples went on studying with him until they were old men,[168] so that they were only able to practise the tricks they had learned and plead their cases in the court where Minos sat in judgement in Hades.[169] And in an effort to turn his son against Greek culture, he allowed himself an utterance which was absurdly rash for an old man: he pronounced with all the solemnity of a prophet that if ever the Romans became infected with the literature of Greece, they would lose their empire.[170] At any rate, time has exposed the emptiness of this ominous prophecy, for in the age when the city rose to the zenith of her greatness, her people had made themselves familiar with Greek learning and culture in all its forms.

However, Cato's dislike of the Greeks was not confined to philosophers: he was also deeply suspicious of the Greek physicians who practised in Rome. It seems he had heard of Hippocrates' celebrated reply[171] when he was called upon to attend the king of Persia for a fee amounting to many talents, and declared that he would never give his services to barbarians who were enemies of Greece. Cato maintained that all Greek physicians had taken an oath of this kind, and urged his son not to trust a single one of them. He himself had compiled a book of recipes and used them for the diet or treatment of any member of his household who fell ill. He never made his patients fast, but allowed them to eat herbs and morsels of duck, pigeon or hare. He maintained that this diet was light and thoroughly suitable for sick people, apart from the fact that it often produced nightmares, and he claimed that by following it he kept both himself and his family in perfect health.[172]

24. However, his self-sufficiency in these matters seems to have met with divine retribution, for he lost both his wife and his

son by disease. He himself, so far as physical health and strength
were concerned, possessed an iron constitution, and was able
for many years to resist the onset of old age. Even when he was
far advanced in years he continued to indulge his sexual appetite, and he finally took a second wife long after he passed the
age to marry. This was how it came about. After the death of
his first wife, he arranged a marriage between his son and
Aemilius Paullus' daughter, who was also the sister of the
younger Scipio; but while he himself remained a widower, he
consoled himself with a young slave girl, who came to his room
secretly to sleep with him. This intrigue soon came to light, as
might be expected in a small household which contained a
young daughter-in-law, and on one occasion, when the slave
seemed to flaunt her presence altogether too impudently on her
way to Cato's room, the old man could not fail to notice that
his son kept silent, glanced at her with intense dislike and then
turned away in disgust.

As soon as Cato understood that his behaviour annoyed his
children, he did not blame or find fault with them at all. Instead,
as he was walking towards the forum with his clients in the
usual way,[173] he called out to one of them whose name was
Salonius.[174] This man had been one of his scribes and now
regularly escorted him, and Cato asked him in a loud voice
whether he had yet found a suitable husband for his young
daughter. The man said that he had not, and had no intention
of settling the matter without first consulting his patron. 'Very
well,' replied Cato; 'I have found a suitable son-in-law, unless
you happen to object to his age: there is nothing wrong with
him in other respects, but he is a very old man.' Salonius at
once urged him to take the matter into his own hands and
betroth the girl to whomever he thought best, since she was
under his patronage and would always depend upon his good
offices. Thereupon Cato, without further ceremony, told him
that he wished to marry the girl himself. At first Salonius,
naturally enough, was astounded at the proposal, since he
supposed that Cato was well past the age to marry, and also
that his own family was far too humble to be allied with a
house which had earned consular rank and triumphal honours;

but once he saw that Cato was in earnest he gladly accepted, and as soon as they arrived at the forum, the betrothal ceremony was carried out.

While the preparations for the marriage were being made, Cato's son collected some of his friends, went to visit his father and asked whether he had done anything to harm or annoy him, to have a stepmother foisted upon him in this way. 'Heaven forbid, my boy!' answered Cato, 'you have been a model son to me, and I have no fault of any kind to find with you. It is simply that I want to leave behind me more sons like you of my blood, and more citizens like you to serve my country.'[175] However, this remark is said to have been made many years earlier by Peisistratus,[176] the tyrant of Athens, whose sons were already grown men when he married Timonassa of Argolis, by whom we are told he had two more children, Iophon and Thessalus. Cato also had a son by his second marriage, whom he named Salonius after his father-in-law,[177] but his first-born son died during his praetorship.[178] Cato often mentions him in his books as having been a good and courageous man, and it is said that he endured his loss with all the calm of a philosopher, nor did he take any less keen an interest in public affairs than before.

Unlike Lucius Lucullus and Metellus Pius[179] at a later date, he never became so enfeebled by old age as to abandon public service or to regard political activity as an oppressive duty; still less did he follow the example of Scipio Africanus before him, who because of the attacks of those who envied the glory he had won, turned his back on the Roman people and determined to spend the rest of his life in untroubled retirement.[180] Somebody is said to have advised Dionysius,[181] the ruler of Syracuse, that absolute power is the best winding-sheet for a man to die in, and in the same way it was Cato's belief that the service of the state was still the most honourable employment for old age. But whenever he had leisure, his favourite recreations consisted of writing books and farming.

25. He wrote discourses on an immense number of subjects and also histories.[182] When he was a young man he applied himself seriously to farming because of his poverty – in fact he

remarks that at that time he knew only two ways of acquiring money, by farming and by saving – but in later life he regarded agriculture as a hobby and a subject to study in theory. He also wrote a treatise on farming, which includes recipes[183] for making cakes and preserving fruit, so anxious was he to show that he possessed a superior and independent knowledge of every subject. His table was never so abundantly stocked as when he was in the country. He always invited his friends and acquaintances from the neighbourhood, and showed himself a gay and spirited host. And indeed his company was so agreeable that it was greatly sought after, not only by his contemporaries but even by the younger generations, for his experience was wide and he had read and heard a great deal that was worth repeating. He believed that a good table was the best place for making friends, and at his own table the conversation often dwelt on the praises of brave and honourable men, but he also made it a rule to refrain from mentioning those who were worthless or disreputable. Such persons were taboo in Cato's company, either by way of praise or blame.[184]

26. Some people consider that the last of his political achievements was the destruction of Carthage.[185] In the military sense it was the younger Scipio who brought this about, but the fact that the Romans went to war at all was very largely the consequence of Cato's advice. This was how it happened. Cato was sent out on a diplomatic mission[186] to investigate the causes of a dispute between the Carthaginians and Masinissa,[187] the king of Numidia, who were at this time at war. Masinissa had been a friend of the Roman people from the first, whereas the Carthaginians had entered into treaty relations with Rome only after the defeat which they had suffered at the hands of Scipio Africanus,[188] and this settlement had stripped them of their empire and compelled them to pay a heavy tribute to Rome. Nevertheless, it was at once apparent to Cato that the city was by no means crushed nor impoverished, as the Romans imagined. He found it teeming with a new generation of fighting men, overflowing with wealth, amply stocked with weapons and military supplies of every kind and full of confidence at this

revival of its strength. He drew the conclusion that this was no time for the Romans to occupy themselves with regulating the affairs of Masinissa and the Numidians, but that unless they found the means to crush a city which had always borne them an undying hatred and had now recovered its power to an incredible extent, they would find themselves as gravely threatened as before. He therefore returned with all speed to Rome, and warned the senate that the overwhelming defeats and misfortunes which the Carthaginians had suffered had done much to diminish their recklessness and over-confidence, but little to impair their strength, and that they were likely to emerge not weaker but more experienced in war. He was convinced that this present dispute with the Numidians was merely the prelude to an attack upon Rome, and that the peace and the treaty which existed between them were a convenient fiction to cover a period of suspense, until a suitable moment should arrive to begin a war.

27. As he ended this speech, it is said that Cato shook the folds of his toga and contrived to drop some Libyan figs on the floor of the senate-house, and when the senators admired their size and beauty, he remarked that the country which produced them was only three days' sail from Rome. Afterwards, however, Cato adopted a method of driving home his point that was excessively brutal: whenever his opinion was called for on any subject, he invariably concluded with the words, 'And furthermore, it is my opinion that Carthage must be destroyed!'[189] On the other hand Publius Scipio Nasica[190] made a point of adding the phrase, 'And in my view Carthage must be spared!' Scipio had already observed, no doubt, that the Roman people were by this time indulging in many excesses, and that the insolence occasioned by its prosperity prompted it to cast aside the control of the senate and force the whole state to follow in whichever direction the impulses of the masses might lead. He was therefore in favour of keeping the fear of Carthage hanging over the people as a check upon their arrogance, and he evidently also believed that although Carthage was not strong enough to threaten the Romans, she was not so weak that they

could afford to despise her. But this was precisely the danger that Cato feared: namely, that at a time when the Romans were intoxicated and carried away by their new-found power, they should allow a city which had always been great and had now been sobered by calamity to continue to threaten them. He believed that it was best to free the Romans from any fear of outside danger, so that they could devote themselves whole-heartedly to reforming their own shortcomings and abuses at home.

This is the way in which Cato is said to have brought about the third and last war against Carthage. He died almost imme-diately after it had begun,[191] leaving a prophecy that it would be ended by a man who was still young,[192] but who had already as a military tribune given remarkable proofs of his intelligence and daring in his encounters with the enemy. When his exploits were reported in Rome, Cato is said to have quoted the line from Homer in which Circe speaks of the prophet Teiresias in the underworld: 'Only his wisdom abides; the rest glide around him like shadows.'[193]

This prophecy Scipio soon confirmed by his actions. Cato left one son by his second wife, whose surname I have men-tioned was Salonius, and one grandson, the child of his first son who was already dead.[194] Salonius died while he was in office as praetor,[195] but his son Marcus later became consul.[196] This Marcus was the grandfather of Cato the Philosopher,[197] who for his courage and uprightness of character and the fame which these qualities brought him was one of the most remark-able men of his time.

COMPARISON OF
ARISTEIDES AND
ELDER CATO

1 (28). Now that I have recorded the memorable deeds of each man, it will not be easy, in comparing the whole of one's life with the entirety of the other's, to detect the differences between them, for they are obscured by their numerous and significant similarities. If, however, we must make a fine analysis of each in this *Comparison*, as we would study a poem or a painting, we should observe that common to both was a rise to political eminence based on native virtue and talent, and not inherited privilege. However, Aristeides became an illustrious man at a time when Athens had not yet become great, and when the popular leaders and generals with whom he was involved possessed fortunes that were all fairly modest and more or less alike. For the highest census classification in those days was 500 bushels of grain, the second was 300, and the third and last, 200.[1] Cato, by contrast, although he came from a small town and a way of life that one could only call rustic, plunged headlong into Roman politics as if into a boundless sea, nor was this a time when Rome was governed by the likes of Curius or Fabricius or Atilius,[2] or welcomed as its magistrates and popular leaders the kind of poor men who mounted the rostra after working their fields with their own hands, busy with plough or mattock. Instead, the public had become accustomed to taking into consideration the splendour of a candidate's

family, as well as his wealth, largesse and blandishments, and, owing to its arrogance and sway, toyed with those who sought office. It was not the same thing to have as one's rival Themistocles, who did not come from an illustrious family and had only a moderate fortune (for our sources say that when he began his political career he had only 3 or perhaps 5 talents[3]), as it was to contend for supremacy with men like Scipio Africanus or Servius Galba or Quinctius Flamininus[4] when one had no other advantage than a voice that spoke boldly in defence of justice.

2 (29). Furthermore, at Marathon and later at Plataea,[5] Aristeides was only one of ten generals,[6] whereas Cato was elected one of two consuls against numerous competitors and later one of two censors ahead of seven distinguished and eminent rivals.[7] Nor was Aristeides the foremost man in any of his victories: at Marathon it was Miltiades[8] who won the prize of valour; at Salamis[9] it was Themistocles; and at Plataea, according to Herodotus, it was Pausanias who 'won the noblest of victories'.[10] As for Aristeides, he must dispute even the second place with Sophanes, Ameinias, Callimachus and Cynaegeirus,[11] men who distinguished themselves brilliantly in these battles. Yet Cato was foremost in combat and in counsel not only when he was consul during the war in Spain,[12] but also at Thermopylae, when he was a tribune of the soldiers and another man was consul, for the glory of that victory was his, after he threw the doors wide open for the Romans to attack Antiochus by attacking the king from behind when he was looking only to the front.[13] Clearly that victory was Cato's achievement, and by driving Asia out of Greece he paved the way for Scipio.[14]

Both men, then, were invincible in war, but in politics Aristeides suffered a fall when he was checked and then ostracized by the faction of Themistocles,[15] whereas Cato, whose adversaries included nearly all of Rome's most eminent and influential men, continued, like a wrestler, to grapple with them even when he was very old, and he was never thrown by any of them. He was very often involved in court cases, both as a defendant and as a plaintiff. As plaintiff he frequently won a conviction, and as defendant he was always acquitted – thanks to his eloquence, his life's shield and his most potent weapon. Indeed, it is to his abilities as a speaker, and not to fortune or any guardian spirit, that one must attribute the fact that he never suffered a disgrace in public life. One is reminded of Antipater's high praise for the philosopher Aristotle when he wrote about him, after his death, that in addition to his many other fine qualities, the man possessed a talent for persuasion.[16]

3 (30). It is generally agreed that man's highest virtue lies in his capacity to govern a state, and most believe that an important aspect of this is the management of a household.[17] For in reality a city is the aggregate of its households, and the vigour of a state depends on the prosperity of its citizens in their private lives. For when Lycurgus banished silver and gold from Sparta, replacing it with a currency of iron spoiled by fire,[18] he did not by doing so release his fellow-citizens from the responsibility of managing their domestic expenses. Instead, he got rid of the enervating, festering and feverish symptoms that riches can excite, making provision instead for every citizen to enjoy an abundance of the things in life that are necessary and useful. For, with greater foresight than any other legislator, he worried even more about how the state would be affected by citizens who were helpless, homeless and destitute than by those who were extremely rich.[19]

Now, it is clear that Cato was as capable in administering his personal affairs as he was the affairs of state, for not only did he increase his own property and wealth but also taught others about domestic economy and farming by compiling many useful precepts on these subjects. Aristeides, by contrast, through his own poverty brought discredit on his well-known justice, as if justice were to blame for ruining families and turning men into beggars, and was a source of profit to everyone but its possessor.[20] Yet[21] Hesiod, in numerous passages, exhorts us to combine justice with sound economic practices and abuses idleness as the origin of injustice.[22] Homer, too, puts it well when he says:

> . . . hard work was never my delight
> Nor the sound management of a household, which breeds fine
>   children;
> Instead I was pleased by ships well equipped with oars
> And battles and well-polished javelins and arrows.[23]

Thus the poet gives us to understand that the men who neglect their households and the men who live by injustice are one and the same.[24] So it is not the case, as physicians say of olive oil, how it is most beneficial when applied to the outside of the body but very harmful when taken internally, that the just man is inevitably helpful to others but neglectful of himself and his family.[25] Which makes it a severe blemish on Aristeides' political career if it is true, as most authorities say it is, that he made no provisions for leaving behind dowries for his daughters or funds to cover the costs of his own burial.[26] Cato's family furnished Rome with praetors and consuls down to the fourth generation,[27] since his grandsons and even great-grandsons held the highest offices, whereas the descendants of Aristeides, though he was the foremost of the Greeks, were so degraded by their abject poverty that one of them made his living by interpreting dreams, while others were compelled by their penury to stretch out their hands in solicitation of public grants.[28] None of them was in a condition even to contemplate any illustrious deed worthy of their great ancestor.

4 (31). But should we not first dispute this point? Poverty is never dishonourable in itself but only when it is a mark of indolence, intemperance, extravagance or foolishness.[29] When it visits a man who is temperate, industrious, just and courageous, who devotes himself entirely to public service, then it is a sign of magnanimity and a great nature.[30] For a man cannot perform great deeds when he is preoccupied by little worries, no can he aid the many who are in need when he is himself in need of many things. The most important resource for public service is not wealth but self-sufficiency, for, when a man does not require private luxury, there is nothing to distract him from

his service to the state.[31] God is entirely free from need, and among mortal virtues it is the one that does the most to reduce our needs that is the most perfect and god-like.[32] For just as a body which is nobly conditioned and healthy requires nothing in the way of superfluous food or clothing, so a sound lifestyle and family life can be managed quite well without unnecessary expenses. One's goods ought to match one's needs. A man who amasses much but uses little of it is not a man who is self-sufficient. If he does not need it, he is foolish for acquiring what he does not want, and yet if he does want it, owing to his parsimony he makes himself miserable by denying himself the pleasure of using it.

I would very much like to put this question to Cato himself: If wealth is something that should be enjoyed, why, after amassing so much, do you boast of being satisfied with little? If in fact it is a mark of distinction, and indeed it is, for a man to eat whatever bread is to hand, or drink the same wine as labourers and slaves drink, or to have no need for purple robes or houses with plastered walls,[33] then Aristeides and Epaminondas and Manius Curius and Gaius Fabricius were surely correct in spurning the acquisition of things the use of which they deprecated. For it was unnecessary for a man who claims that turnips are a fine dish and boils them himself,[34] while his wife is busy baking bread,[35] to prattle on about the value of a single *as*[36] or to write a treatise on what practices allow one to become rich most quickly.[37] A simple and self-sufficient life is a great one, because it delivers one from anxiety over superfluous matters. This is why, so we are told, Aristeides proclaimed, at the trial of Callias, that while it was fitting for men who could not avoid their poverty to be ashamed of it, men like himself, who choose their poverty, should glory in it.[38] It would certainly be ridiculous to suppose that Aristeides' poverty was due to indolence, since without doing anything disgraceful he could easily have enriched himself by despoiling a single barbarian or seizing a single tent.[39] That, then, is enough on this matter.

5 (32). Let us turn now to their military commands. Cato's successes added little to Rome's empire, which was already vast,

whereas Aristeides' were some of the most noble, most glorious and most important achievements of the Greeks, namely Marathon, Salamis and Plataea. And Antiochus is hardly worthy of comparison with Xerxes,[40] nor the destruction of city walls in Spain with the deaths of tens of thousands of barbarians on land and at sea. In each of these battles, Aristeides was second to none when it came to fighting, but the glory and the crowns of honour he left to those who desired them more than he did, just as was his habit when it came to riches and silver, because in these matters as well he was superior to all. Now for my own part, I do not reproach Cato for his incessant boasting and for always claiming to be superior to everyone else.[41] He, however, in one of his speeches, insists that glorifying oneself, like reviling oneself, is disgusting.[42] In my opinion, the man who praises himself has made less progress towards virtue than the man who does not even need to be praised by others. For a modest indifference to glory contributes greatly towards the attainment of a mild disposition in political life, whereas ambition works in an opposite manner, exciting harshness and envy.[43] Of ambition Aristeides was entirely free, but Cato was possessed by it. For Aristeides saved Athens through his cooperation with Themistocles in the midst of great affairs, standing guard over him, so to speak, when he was general.[44] Cato, by contrast, through his opposition to Scipio, came close to undermining and ruining his command against the Carthaginians, when he vanquished the invincible Hannibal, and ultimately, by way of intrigue and calumny, drove him from Rome and secured his brother's shameful condemnation on charges of embezzlement.[45]

6 (33). As for self-restraint,[46] a virtue Cato always celebrated in the loveliest of panegyrics, Aristeides actually practised it with unsullied purity, while Cato, owing to a marriage that was dishonourable and out of season, was heavily censured in this regard. Indeed, it was certainly ignoble for a man of his age to introduce as stepmother to his adult son and his son's wife a girl whose father was no more than a petty official who earned his salary from the state. Whether he did this out of a desire for carnal pleasure or anger, seeking to punish his son for objecting

to his mistress, both his action and its pretext were disgraceful. In explaining himself to his son, it is plain that he resorted to irony, not the truth. For if he had wished to father other sons as virtuous as his first, then from the start he would have endeavoured to marry a noble woman instead of enjoying, so long as he could get away with it, sexual relations with a woman who was a common slave, unfit for marriage. And once he was found out, he chose as his father-in-law a man he could easily bend to his will, instead of one whose alliance would bring him the most honour.[47]

AEMILIUS PAULLUS

INTRODUCTION TO
AEMILIUS PAULLUS

History Man

Aemilius Paullus was destiny's man. That, at least, was the view of Polybius. The distinctive feature of his *Histories*, Polybius claimed, was its explication of the workings of Fortune (Tyche) in shaping history (1.4.1):

> For what gives my work its unique quality and what is the most amazing thing of our present time is this: Tyche has guided almost all the affairs of the world in one direction and has compelled them to incline towards one and the same end.

That end came at the battle of Pydna in 168 BC, when Aemilius Paullus defeated King Perseus, after which the kingdom of Macedon was done away with and 'the Romans succeeded in subjecting nearly the whole of the inhabited world to their sole authority' (1.1.5). This geopolitical transformation Polybius attributes to a world historical *tyche* (1.4.1), and it constitutes the central subject of his entire inquiry, which he concluded with the events of 167 BC, when, for better or worse, the Romans' dominion began. It is true that Polybius later expanded his project to 145 BC – just to investigate whether it *was* better or worse. But the salient point is his assertion that Tyche's grandest accomplishment culminated in the career of Aemilius Paullus.[1]

In the character of Aemilius Paullus, Polybius accumulates

all the various concepts of *tyche* in his *Histories*. Macedon, Polybius accepts, rose to great power through the workings of chance, but fell in part owing to Nemesis (another manifestation of *tyche*) activated by the crimes of Philip V.[2] The agent of Macedon's punishment, and of Fortune's design for Rome, was Aemilius. And yet, after his victory at Pydna, Fortune, jealous of the Roman's success, deprived him of his sons, a catastrophe attributable to *tyche* that he meets with dignity and fortitude.[3]

The momentous presence of Aemilius Paullus in Polybius is perhaps unsurprising in view of the historian's close connection with the man and his family.[4] His almost paradigmatic role in Polybius' *Histories* makes him the natural precursor of his brilliant son, and Polybius' friend, Scipio Aemilianus, whose career dominates the final books of the work. Plutarch, however, betrays little interest in Polybius' personal motives for his undoubtedly biased depiction of Aemilius. Instead, he takes Polybius at his word, concentrating instead on Aemilius' crucial role in the rise of Rome over Greece, which he liberates, once and for all, from the menace of Macedon.

Aemilius Paullus

Plutarch's Life is focused almost entirely on the campaign at Pydna and subsequent events (chs. 7–34), by which time Aemilius was around sixty years old, a former consul and triumphant general. He was born around 228 BC, a scion of an ancient patrician family eminent as early as the fifth century BC. His father had twice been consul, and there should have been no impediment to his son's ultimate elevation to the same office. Of Aemilius' early career we know very little save that he was dutiful in military matters, rising routinely through the magistracies (with a brilliant success in the aedilician elections for 193: ch. 3) to become praetor in 191. Assigned the province of Farther Spain, he campaigned successfully enough to be hailed Conquering General (*imperator*) by his troops, and the senate decreed a thanksgiving to the gods (*supplicatio*) in his honour. These were often the antecedents to a triumph, but not in

Aemilius' case.[5] And Aemilius was strangely unsuccessful, for a man of his lineage and attainments, in reaching the consulship, suffering more than one defeat at the polls.[6] In 182 BC he finally got in, and, at last, earned a triumph (ch. 6). His second consulship came fourteen years later in 168 BC. His province was the war against Perseus, and this is the best-known phase of his career.

The origins of the Third Macedonian War (171–168 BC) remain obscure due to the heavily apologetic strain of our literary sources, which insist, in different ways, that Rome went to war against Perseus only as a last and a defensive resort.[7] Polybius explained the war by appealing to the disloyalty of Philip V, the effects of which persisted after his death. Philip, according to Polybius (22.18.10–11; a view accepted by Plutarch in ch. 8), intended to wage a second war against Rome and before his death had commenced massive preparations. In 179 BC Perseus inherited both Philip's kingdom and his anti-Roman designs. But the belief that Philip or Perseus was scheming against Rome is probably nonsense. Although there is no doubt that Philip endeavoured to restore the military health of his kingdom, or that Perseus followed this same policy, there is no likelihood whatsoever that either intended to challenge Rome. This, however, did not prevent Perseus' rivals in the east[8] from pretending otherwise, and eventually the Roman senate began to see in Macedon a glittering source of plunder and glory, the seizing of which it justified through diplomatic chicanery. Perseus' true posture is probably made clear by his conduct after his victory over Publius Licinius Crassus in 171 BC: he sued for peace on terms disadvantageous to himself (Polybius 27.8.1–10).

Many if not most in the Greek east sided in sentiment if not in action with Perseus, hopeful that Macedon, whose ultimate submission was inevitable, might at least sustain its unequal balance of power with Rome, thereby allowing Greece a degree of genuine freedom as it negotiated the political space separating the two powers, a reality that even the Elder Cato appreciated.[9] The Romans' striking incompetence in prosecuting this war, as well as Perseus' resourcefulness (ch. 9), did little to dash these hopes. Hence the significance of Aemilius' over-whelming victory in 168 BC, after which Aemilius and a senatorial commission presided over the dismantling of the kingdom of Macedon and subjected every Greek ally to a severe and distrustful scrutiny, involving arrests, deportations and mass executions. The harshest treatment was reserved for Epirus, where Aemilius sacked seventy cities and sold 150,000 people into slavery. Such were the lessons meted out by Rome on the foolishness of resisting its supreme power.[10]

After Aemilius returned to Rome, although his political enemies attempted to block his triumph, they were unsuccess-ful. The celebration, however, was marred by the untimely death of his young sons, a personal misfortune central to Plu-tarch's Life (chs. 35–6). Aemilius was subsequently elected censor for 164 BC, after which he seems largely to have retired from public life, perhaps owing to illness. He died in 160 BC.

Plutarch's Aemilius

By the time Plutarch came to this pairing he was well along in his project, and it shows in his artistry and confidence alike.[11] The work begins with a formal and programmatic prologue. Two admirably balanced and thematically linked Lives follow, the subjects of which are both of them virtuous in the best Graeco-Roman sense of the term: each is an incorruptible and victorious warrior, and each wages war against opponents who, though mighty, deserve to fail because they are immoral.[12] This is indeed one of the most elegant of all Plutarch's pairings.

Plutarch's introduction, in which he explains his reasons for carrying on with the writing of the *Parallel Lives*, naturally attracts attention:

> I first set to work writing these Lives for the sake of others, but
> their composition has proved so congenial that I now persist in it
> for my own improvement. I am using history as if it were a mir-
> ror, in the reflection of which I am trying to adorn my own life,
> so to speak, by making its virtues resemble the ones displayed in

my biographies. For me the experience is very much like actually
spending time with these figures from the past and enjoying their
companionship.

(ch. 1)

Here Plutarch fashions himself as the ideal reader of his own
biographies, and in so doing makes clear the importance of
their exemplarity in the reader's – every reader's – moral
improvement. Admittedly, this is unsurprising stuff, but it is
rendered arresting by its simile of the mirror and its fantasy of
actually meeting and taking the measure of great figures from
the past. The idea that ethical development can derive from
making sensitive observations, of one's self and of others,
appears elsewhere in Plutarch, as does the mirror, whose utility
for self-observation is obvious.[13] Here, importantly, it is Plutarch's Lives that constitute the mirror by means of which we
are enabled to see ourselves in the actions of others. Plutarch
goes on to stress his 'constant historical research' (ch. 1), the
foundation for his biographical writing, and a reminder that it
is Plutarch the reader of history whose discrimination and craft
are responsible for the moral effect of his *Parallel Lives*.

In this pairing Plutarch sets together Aemilius and Timoleon
of Corinth:

These men were alike not only in the excellence of their moral
principles but also in the good fortune each enjoyed when it came
to actual events, and they will make it hard for you to decide
whether the greatest of their achievements were owed to their
good luck [*tyche*] or their intelligence.

(ch. 1)

These Lives are perhaps the most laudatory of all Plutarch's
biographies: Plutarch includes these men among the 'splendid
paragons of the past' (ch. 1), and the reader's attention is
explicitly focused on observing the true measure of each hero's
unquestioned greatness in order to make an accurate evalu-
ation of the role of *tyche*, especially beneficent *tyche*, in his Life.
The Polybian resonance of *tyche*, inescapable when Aemilius is

the subject, is plainly at work here, and, as was the case for Polybius, Plutarch's *tyche* will manifest itself in multiple guises, ranging from Providence to Nemesis to caprice. Both heroes are buffeted and benefited by them all.[14]

Throughout his Life, Aemilius is less a figure from history than a confection of traditional Roman virtues.[15] He is incorruptible and unacquisitive, qualities elaborated in Plutarch's recurring emphasis on the honourable poverty of his son-in-law Aelius Tubero (chs. 5, 28).[16] Both as a statesman and a general he refuses to court popularity (chs. 2–3, 11, 38). In war, he is as prudent as he is masterful (chs. 13, 17–18), and in victory he is generous to the vanquished (chs. 6, 26, 28, 39). Devotion to traditional practices marks his scrupulous religiosity (chs. 3, 10, 17), and he puts the health of the republic ahead of his personal happiness (ch. 36). Most important of all, of course, is the discipline he exhibits when confronted by fortune, good or ill, wisdom he expounds in a series of speeches addressed first to Perseus (ch. 26), then to his sons and officers (ch. 27) and finally to the Roman people (ch. 36). Owing to his correct grasp of the workings of fortune, he is an inspiration to others and is able to steel himself against catastrophe.

He is also an admirable family man, whose family, in the end, is doomed (chs. 5–6, 10, 15, 22, 27, 35–6).[17] In the opening chapters of this Life, Plutarch dilates on Aemilius' sons and his fatherly devotion (e.g. ch. 7). He also presents the reader with Aemilius' extended family, his sons-in-law, who, with his own children, are his strength in politics and in the war against Perseus (chs. 10, 22, 27–8). The Macedonian king also loved his children (ch. 26), but his personal failings brought ruin on his house as well as his kingdom, whereas the death of Aemilius' own sons and the extinction at least of his line of the Aemilii Paulli are due simply to chance. And Aemilius bears this misfortune more nobly than Perseus does his, going so far as to identify his own loss as a guarantee for Rome's good fortune (ch. 36).

Throughout this Life Plutarch underlines Aemilius' virtue by way of its stark contrast with the character of Perseus. The king, although astoundingly rich, is stingy (chs. 12–13, 23) and, although leader of a mighty army, a coward (chs. 19, 23, 34). And in defeat he is so craven a poltroon that his cringing, Aemilius complains, threatens to undermine the glory of Rome's conquest (ch. 26). Still, and typically, Aemilius pities him, and does what he can to help the fallen king (ch. 37), and if Perseus was beyond redemption, his son grew up to be a good and honourable servant of Rome (ch. 37). Perseus' early successes in the war (ch. 9) are undeniably inconsistent with his behaviour after Aemilius appears on the scene, but that solecism was a long-established part of the Romans' hostile representation of this king.[18] And although Plutarch went to the trouble of reading an account of the war favourable to Perseus, he was not sufficiently persuaded by it to alter the standard Roman treatment of the man. Instead, Plutarch delicately balances Perseus' personal weaknesses with the glamour and power of the Macedonian monarchy (e.g. ch. 13: 'Perseus he [Aemilius] despised, but he was very impressed by his preparations and his army'). In this Life, Perseus is the bad guy, in nearly every sense of the phrase: his failings justify Rome's conquest of Macedon and bring into relief the superiority of the Roman general who led him in triumph.

Aemilius and Timoleon

It has not gone unnoticed that Plutarch's decision to pair Aemilius with Timoleon is an unexpected one.[19] Timoleon was a Corinthian aristocrat who, at some point in the 360s BC, assassinated his brother, who had made himself tyrant. In 344, he travelled to Sicily, where he defeated Hicetas, the tyrant of Leontini, deposed Dionysius II, the tyrant of Syracuse, and expelled Carthage from the Greek regions of the island. Thereafter, he completed the job of eliminating tyranny from Sicily and gave Syracuse a new constitution.[20] But Plutarch carefully integrates the two men's careers. For instance, both find their true glory in mature accomplishments, both oppose unsavoury autocrats and both can be represented as men devoted to protecting Greeks from oppression by foreign powers.[21]

From this perspective, it is remarkable how Plutarch exerts

himself to portray Aemilius as a man of Hellenic tendencies. To
some degree, this was true of Polybius' portrayal as well, but
from the very start Plutarch is at pains to associate Aemilius
with things Greek. His family, according to one view, could
trace itself back to the son of the Greek philosopher Pythagoras
(ch. 2). The education of Aemilius' sons, in its every particular,
is Greek (ch. 6). And, in the aftermath of Pydna, Aemilius is
not merely an admirer of Greek culture, he shows himself adept
at hosting symposia and dinner parties in the correct Greek
fashion (ch. 28). Elsewhere, Plutarch insists on the importance
of a sound Greek education, especially a philosophical education, in attaining a consistently virtuous character.[22] Even a
paragon like Timoleon exhibited deficiency in his philosophical
rigour (*Timoleon* 5). But Aemilius' perfection could hardly be
attributed to a fictitious Greek education: Plutarch's commitment to historical truth would not allow that. Instead, Aemilius'
Hellenic proclivities had to be inferred from his conspicuous
ethical superiority.

Aemilius' Hellenic credentials are also burnished by his parallelism with Timoleon. In the Greek's Life, Plutarch is keen to
celebrate the true liberation of Greeks by a Greek who also
defends Greek freedom from Carthaginian aggression.[23] By
contrast, no amount of special pleading could alter the reality
that Aemilius' victory at Pydna was the final step in Rome's
conquest of Greece, as Polybius had emphasized. The juxta-
position of the two biographies, however, lets Plutarch impose
an equivalence on their achievements that adds the right sort
of lustre to Aemilius' campaign, as well as to the current state
of Roman governance in the Greek east.

What, one may then ask, does Aemilius do for Timoleon?
We have seen how this pairing focuses on the role of fortune in
the life of each hero, an element of Aemilius' Life that can
only activate its Polybian antecedents. *Tyche* is many things in
Plutarch's *Aemilius Paullus*, but, always in the background
when it is not in the foreground, is Polybius' world-historical
force, driving Aemilius and the Romans to their glorious destiny. It is through this atmosphere of Tyche's dynamics that the
reader comes to *Timoleon*, who, according to Plutarch, was

likewise guided by a providential Tyche when he freed Sicily from tyranny. Timoleon's connection to fortune was something Plutarch found in his sources, which were largely favourable.[24] Interestingly, however, Polybius also had something to say about Timoleon, and it was far from flattering (12.23.4–6):

> Timaeus[25] honoured Timoleon, who appears not only never to have accomplished any great enterprise, but never even to have tried one. In his whole life he made only a single move, and that was not a very significant one when one compares the extent of the inhabited world: I speak of his voyage from his native city to Syracuse. In my opinion, Timaeus was convinced that if Timoleon, who sought fame in a mere saucer of a place such as Sicily, could be shown to be comparable to the most glorious heroes, then Timaeus himself, who had written only of the affairs of Italy and Sicily, would be worthy of comparison with those writers whose books had dealt with worldwide events and with universal history.

But in the environment of Plutarch's pairing, his Timoleon benefits from his association with Aemilius. The providential forces that so conspicuously propelled Timoleon's liberation of the Greeks of Sicily recall for the reader the world-historical impulse that brought Rome to greatness by way of the career of Aemilius Paullus. The freedom of the Greeks and the rise of Rome are thus borne by the same Providence.[26]

Sources

It is obvious that Plutarch depends upon Polybius in this Life. He was the obvious and authoritative source to consult. Unfortunately, for the events of 195 to 165 BC, which Polybius covered in Books 19–30, our text of Polybius is fragmentary, which often makes comparison impossible. Plutarch also used an account of the Pydna campaign written by Publius Cornelius Scipio Nasica, the son-in-law of Scipio Africanus and a future consul and censor, who at the time of this war was serving as a tribune of the soldiers (chs. 15–18, 21, 26). His account was valued by Plutarch because Nasica was an eyewitness of the campaign.[27] Plutarch also used the otherwise unknown historian Poseidonius, also a contemporary and a participant in the war. He was the author of a history favourable to Perseus (chs. 19–21).[28]

It is not at all clear whether Plutarch consulted Livy (whose account of this period is sometimes fragmentary) for this Life. Of the observable similarities and differences between the two writers, none is conclusive on the matter. Nothing, of course, prevented his reading Livy, and it is likely that he did so.

LIFE OF AEMILIUS PAULLUS[1]

[*c.* 228–160 BC]

1. I first set to work writing these Lives for the sake of others, but their composition has proved so congenial that I now persist in it for my own improvement. I am using history as if it were a mirror, in the reflection of which I am trying to adorn my own life, so to speak, by making its virtues resemble the ones displayed in my biographies. For me the experience is very much like actually spending time with these figures from the past and enjoying their companionship: whenever, by way of my historical research, I welcome into my home one of my biographical subjects, I scrutinize him carefully, in order to determine 'his god-like aspect and magnificent size'.[2] I then select from the events of his career what is noblest and most important to know. 'Ah! Ah! What joy greater than this can one obtain?'[3] Or more efficacious in improving our character?

Democritus insists that we must pray to be visited by auspicious apparitions, by which he means that we should desire that the images that appear to us out of our surroundings be wholesome and noble instead of base and unlucky.[4] But in making this claim, Democritus insinuates into philosophy an opinion that is not simply false but is also conducive to boundless superstition. I, on the other hand, am always welcoming into my thoughts the records of the noblest and most illustrious of men. This is on account of my constant historical research and the deep familiarity with men of the past that comes from writing their biographies, which has prepared me to reject and repulse anything base or wicked or disgraceful cast at me in the course of my unavoidable dealings with contemporaries. Instead, I calmly and composedly shift my attention away from such provocations towards splendid paragons of the past. Two of these I have selected for you[5] in writing this present work, which includes the *Life of Timoleon of Corinth* and the *Life of Aemilius Paullus*. These men were alike not only in the excellence of their moral principles but also in the good fortune each enjoyed when it came to actual events, and they will make it hard for you to decide whether the greatest of their achievements were owed to their good luck or their intelligence.

2. The house of the Aemilii, most authorities agree, was one of the ancient patrician families of Rome. Some of the writers who attribute the education of King Numa to Pythagoras claim that the first member of this house, the man who bequeathed to it the name Aemilius, was Mamercus, who was a son of the philosopher Pythagoras[6] and was called Aemilius on account of the winning nature of his conversation as well as his overall charm.[7] Now most of the men from this family who aspired after virtue – and gained greatness as a consequence of that – also enjoyed good fortune. Lucius Paullus[8] was an exception, but even his defeat at Cannae demonstrated his intelligence and courage. For when he was unable to convince his colleague to avoid a pitched battle with the enemy, he took his part in the fighting despite his own reluctance to do so. When his colleague ran away, however, he took no part in that. Instead, although he had been exposed to mortal danger by the very man who had put the Romans at risk in the first place, Lucius stood his ground and perished in the struggle. Lucius Paullus had a daughter, Aemilia, who was the wife of the great Scipio,[9] and a son, Aemilius Paullus, the subject of this biography.

When Aemilius Paullus was a young man, Rome was crowded with great men made famous by their glory and virtue. Nevertheless, he cut his own figure. He did not pursue the same studies as did the other distinguished young men of his day, nor did he orient his career along the same lines. He refused to practise forensic oratory, and as for winning mass popularity, which requires constant public salutations and handshaking and expressions of goodwill, all of which transform public figures into zealous servants of the multitude,

Aemilius took no part in that.[10] Which is not to say that he lacked the capacity for any of this, but rather that he deemed it a far greater thing to acquire a glorious reputation founded on courage and justice and trustworthiness. And in these qualities he quickly excelled his contemporaries.

3. This became apparent when he stood for the first of the curule magistracies, the aedileship, in an election in which he came ahead of twelve competitors[11] – each of whom, it is reported, was later consul. And, when he was made one of the augurs[12] (this is what the Romans call the priests who supervise and sustain the art of divination from the movements of birds and from signs in the sky), he so completely devoted himself to ancestral customs and so thoroughly comprehended the ancients' scrupulosity where religion was concerned that he elevated this priesthood, which had been reduced to an office sought mostly for its honour and as an embellishment to one's reputation, into an exalted art. In so doing he testified on behalf of those philosophers who define religion as the science of doing service to the gods.[13] For he carried out his augural duties with skill and care, and at no time did he allow any other business to distract him from performing them properly. He omitted nothing from traditional practice, nor did he allow a single innovation. Instead, he was constantly at odds with his priestly colleagues, even over the smallest of points. It was his doctrine that, however mild one believed the gods to be and however disinclined to blame mortals for religious negligence, it was nevertheless harmful to the state to allow any disregard of ritual propriety, for no one initiates the destruction of a constitution by committing crime on a grand scale, but instead it is when men are careless in small matters that they subvert the security of more serious affairs.

He was similarly strict when it came to supervising and preserving traditional military conventions. When he was in command, he did not play the demagogue, nor did he strive to win his second military appointment while holding his first by gratifying his soldiers and treating them mildly, something most of his contemporaries did. Instead, like a priest presiding over some dread rite, he offered an exegesis of every military custom, and because he terrified anyone who was disobedient or violated military discipline, he managed to elevate his country's morale. For in his view, conquering the enemy was almost incidental to the education of his fellow-citizens.

4. During the war with Antiochus the Great,[14] when Rome's leading generals were employed against him, a new war broke out in the west owing to serious disturbances in Spain. Aemilius, who was then a praetor, was put in charge of that war, but not with six sets of fasces[15] (the number appropriate to a praetor); instead, he was allowed an additional six, which raised the dignity of his command to the level of a consul's.[16] Twice he defeated the barbarians in pitched battle and his forces killed nearly 30,000 of the enemy. He owed his success to the brilliance of his tactics, for he enabled his troops to achieve an easy victory when he crossed a certain river in order to place his army in a favourable position. He also subjugated 250 cities, which willingly opened their gates to him. When he returned to Rome he left behind a pacified and loyal province, not least because he had not exploited his command in order to enrich himself by even a single drachma. As a matter of fact, Aemilius was in most respects not an acquisitive man. At the same time, he was liberal and generous with his wealth. His assets, however, were not extensive, and when it was necessary, after his death, to restore his wife's dowry, his remaining estate barely sufficed to do so.[17]

5. He married Papiria, the daughter of Maso,[18] a man who had held the consulship. After he had lived with her for a long time, Aemilius divorced her, although she had given him superlative sons, for it was she who bore him the famous Scipio and Fabius Maximus.[19] No reason for this divorce has been preserved for us in any document, but there is a story about divorce that has the ring of truth to it and may be pertinent here. A Roman once divorced his wife, which led his friends to reprove him with remarks like 'But she is prudent, is she not? She is beautiful, is she not? She is fertile, is she not?' In reply, he displayed to them

his sandal (the sort the Romans call a *calceus*) and observed, 'It
is well made, is it not? It is new, is it not? Yet not one of you
can know which bit of my foot it blisters.'[20] For in reality
women are rarely divorced by their husbands owing to serious
or obvious failings. Instead, petty, but frequent, annoyance,
stemming from some minor but irritating incompatibility, is
exacerbated as a couple lives together – and it results in complete alienation, for all that it may pass undetected by others.

In any case, Aemilius divorced Papiria and married another
woman. She bore him two sons whom he reared in his own
home. But the sons from his earlier marriage he gave in adoption to two of Rome's noblest and most illustrious families:[21]
the elder was adopted by Fabius Maximus,[22] who had been
consul five times; the younger by the son of Scipio Africanus[23]
(a man who was also his cousin), from whom he, too, took the
name Scipio. As for Aemilius' daughters, one married the son
of Cato,[24] the other Aelius Tubero.[25]

Now this Aelius was an excellent man, who, more than any
other Roman, was successful in maintaining his dignity even in
the face of poverty. For he was one of sixteen relations, all of
the family Aelius, who lived together in a modest house and
shared a small estate: this home they kept in common, they and
their many children and wives. One of these wives was the
daughter of Aemilius, who was twice consul and who celebrated two triumphs. However, far from feeling ashamed of
her husband's poverty, she admired the virtue that kept him
poor. Nowadays, however, brothers and relations never cease
their bickering unless they subdivide their common property
by means of escarpments, rivers and walls, and unless they
separate themselves from one another with conspicuous open
spaces. History, then, offers the contemplative reader an opportunity to profit from the evidence of the past.

6. When Aemilius was elected consul,[26] he campaigned against
the Ligurians, who are also known as the Ligustinians. These
people dwelt at the foot of the Alps, in the extreme northern
limits of Italy and in that part of the Alps that looks across the
Tyrrhenian Sea towards Africa. They shared this region with

Gauls and with those Iberians who lived along the coast. The
Ligurians were a people at once warlike and violent tempered,
and because they lived so near the Romans, with whom they
sometimes came into conflict, they continually gained in military competence. By this time, they had taken to the sea as
pirates and were robbing and plundering in expeditions that
went as far as the Pillars of Heracles.[27]

They met Aemilius' advance with a force of 40,000 men, five
times the number of his Roman forces, who numbered only
8,000. Nevertheless, Aemilius fell upon the Ligurians, routed
them and penned them up in their fortified cities. He then
offered them humane, even conciliatory, terms of surrender. He
did this because the annihilation of the Ligurians would have
been detrimental to Roman interests: the Ligurians served as a
defensive bulwark against the migrations and depredations of
the Gauls, who were a constant threat to Italy. The Ligurians
trusted Aemilius, and therefore surrendered to him their cities
and ships. The cities Aemilius returned, either undamaged or,
at the worst, suffering only the loss of their fortifications. Their
ships, however, he took away. He left them no craft larger than
a three-oared vessel. He also freed everyone they had captured
on land or at sea (of whom there were in fact many, both
foreigners and Romans). These, then, were the celebrated and
glorious achievements of Aemilius' first consulship.[28]

Often, afterwards, Aemilius made it clear that he wished
once again to be elected consul, and once he even went so far
as to announce his candidature.[29] When, however, he failed to
obtain the office, he withdrew from active politics, devoting
himself instead to his religious duties as augur and to the
education of his sons. Each was reared in accordance with
traditional Roman custom, just as he had been himself, to
which training Aemilius added, with keen enthusiasm, a Greek
education. Not only were the boys' instructors in grammar,
philosophy and rhetoric Greeks, but so too were the sculptors
and painters employed by the family, as well as the trainers of
their horses and dogs, and the men who taught the boys how to
hunt. Unless he was hindered by public business, their father
was always present at their studies and exercises. It was scarcely

an exaggeration to say that he had become Rome's fondest parent.

7. Public affairs, by contrast, had reached a difficult pass. The Romans were waging a war against Perseus,[30] the king of the Macedonians, but the generals[31] they had sent against him had, owing to inexperience or timidity, managed their campaigns both disgracefully and stupidly, with the result that they had all suffered greater losses than they had inflicted – and they had all earned the people's opprobrium for their failures. After all, it had not been so long ago that the Romans had forced Antiochus, who was also called 'the Great', out of Asia and driven him beyond the Taurus mountains, where they had confined him to Syria.[32] There he counted himself fortunate to settle matters with the Romans at a cost of 15,000 talents. Not long before that, the Romans had defeated Philip[33] in Thessaly, thereby liberating the Greeks from Macedonian domination. And they had crushed Hannibal,[34] who excelled every king in daring and might. Consequently, it was felt to be intolerable that they were reduced to struggling with Perseus as if he were a rival equal to Rome, not least because it was believed that all this time Perseus had been waging war with an army composed only of the survivors of his father's past failure. The Romans were unaware that Philip, after his defeat, had strengthened the Macedonian army so that it was a vastly more formidable force than it had been before. Let me offer a brief explanation of this from the beginning.

8. Antigonus,[35] the most powerful of Alexander's generals and successors, acquired the title of king for himself and for his line. He had a son, Demetrius,[36] whose own son was Antigonus surnamed Gonatas.[37] This man's son, Demetrius, reigned for only a brief time, and, when he died, he left behind a son named Philip,[38] who was still a child. Because the leading men of Macedon feared that matters could descend into anarchy, they summoned Antigonus, who was a cousin of the deceased king, and arranged for him to marry Philip's mother. At first he was designated regent and general. Subsequently, he exhibited such

moderation and such enthusiasm for the common good that, he, too, received the title king. And he acquired the surname Doson owing to his habit of making promises that he failed to fulfil.[39] Philip succeeded him, and, although still quite young, displayed in abundance all the finest qualities of a king. This led men to believe that he would restore Macedon to her former greatness – and that he was the man to check the power of the Romans, which by then extended everywhere.

But he was defeated by Titus Flamininus in a major battle near Scotussa,[40] after which, reduced to a state of cringing fright, he handed his affairs over to the Romans and showed himself thankful to get off so lightly. Later, however, his condition grieved him: in his view, being king only by the good graces of the Romans was too much like being a slave grateful just to be fed, hardly the right position for a man possessing courage and resolution. He therefore applied his mind to making preparations for war, plotting in secret. He allowed his cities situated along the roads or on the coast to become so weak and desolated that they were held in contempt. In the hinterland, meanwhile, he was assembling a mighty army; his interior towns, fortresses and cities he filled with arms, money and fighting men. In this way he was secretly making himself fit for war, so to speak, even as he concealed his preparations. For he had stock-piled enough in the way of weaponry to equip 30,000 men, hoarded within his walls 8 million bushels of grain and put aside enough money to employ 10,000 mercenaries in defence of his country for ten years.

Before he could put his plans into effect, however, Philip died of distress and grief when he realized that he had unjustly put to death one of his two sons, Demetrius,[41] on the basis of a false accusation made by the other, who was his clear inferior. This remaining son was Perseus, who inherited his father's hatred of the Romans along with his father's kingdom. But he was too weak a man to shoulder this burden, on account of his deficient and depraved character, in which avarice was the most conspicuous of its many untoward desires. It is alleged by some that he was not actually Philip's son but instead had been taken at birth by Philip's wife from his mother, an Argive seamstress named Gnathaenion.⁴² Hence his fear of Demetrius and his principal motive for killing him: to prevent his being exposed as a bastard, if the royal house should have a legitimate heir.

9. Remarkably, for all that he was ignoble and base, Perseus seized the advantage of Philip's preparations in order to prosecute the war with constancy and vigour, repulsing consuls in command of armies and large fleets and sometimes winning victories over them. Publius Licinius⁴³ was the first of the Roman commanders to invade Macedon. Perseus routed him in a cavalry battle in which he slew 2,500 good men and took 600 others as prisoners.⁴⁴ He then launched an unexpected naval attack on the Roman fleet lying at anchor near Oreus.⁴⁵ In this raid he captured twenty transport ships along with their cargoes and sank the rest, which were filled with grain. He also seized four quinqueremes. He fought a second battle, in which he checked the consul Hostilius when he was trying to force his way into Macedon at Elimiae.⁴⁶ Later, when Hostilius had made his way into Macedon undetected, by way of Thessaly, Perseus offered him battle, but the Roman was too afraid to fight.

In addition to waging this war, as if he were a man with time on his hands, Perseus led a campaign against the Dardanians,⁴⁷ an action intended to convey how much he despised the Romans. He slaughtered 10,000 barbarians and carried home much plunder. Furthermore, he secretly stirred up the Gauls who dwell along the Danube, a warlike tribe of horsemen called Basternae,⁴⁸ and he invited the Illyrians,⁴⁹ through their king, Genthius, to join him in the war. It was widely rumoured that he had suborned the barbarians to make their way through Cisalpine Gaul, along the coast of the Adriatic, in order to invade Italy.

10. When the Romans discovered these things, they decided that this was not a time for the ingratiating promises of candidates who merely desired to be generals. Instead, they summoned a man of intelligence, who already knew how to conduct great affairs, to take command of the war. This man

was Aemilius Paullus, who, although he was somewhat advanced in age (he was around sixty years old), was nonetheless in excellent physical condition. He was also bolstered by his sons-in-law, by his young sons and by an abundance of friends and influential relatives, all of whom endeavoured to persuade him to yield when the people summoned him to the consulship. At first he pretended to spurn the masses, averting their zealous solicitations on the grounds that he did not want the office. But when they returned to his house every day, insisting that he come to the forum[50] and urging him with their cries, he relented. He immediately presented himself as a candidate for the consulship. When he entered the Campus Martius,[51] however, he did not give the impression of being someone who hoped to win an election, but rather a man who, already in possession of military victory, was offering this prize to his fellow-citizens. Everyone welcomed him with hope and enthusiasm, and they elected him consul for the second time. Moreover, they forbade the drawing of lots, the customary practice for awarding provincial commands. Instead, they voted him the command[52] of the Macedonian War without delay.

It is reported that, after he had been proclaimed general in the war against Perseus, he was escorted home, in splendid fashion, by the whole of the people. There he found his daughter, Tertia, who was still a child, weeping. So he embraced her and asked her why she was distressed. She hugged him and kissed him and said, 'Don't you know, father, that our Perseus has died?' She was speaking of a pet puppy called by that name. To this Aemilius responded, 'This is good fortune! Daughter, I accept the omen.' This is what Cicero the orator records in his book *On Divination*.[53]

11. It was customary for men who were elected to the consulship to express their gratitude for the favour, as it were, in a friendly speech delivered to the people from the rostra. Aemilius, however, when he had assembled his fellow-citizens, told them that, whereas he had sought his first consulship owing to his own desire for high office, he had sought his second owing

to their need for a general:[54] consequently he owed them no gratitude. Nevertheless, he continued, if they believed the war could be conducted better by someone else, he would resign his command. If, however, they placed their trust in him, they should not endeavour to become his fellow-generals or even to give speeches about the war. Instead, they should quietly furnish the supplies needed for the campaign. For if they tried to command their commander, the conduct of the war would look even more foolish than it already did. With this speech, he instilled in his fellow-citizens a deep reverence for himself and great expectations for the future. They were all pleased that they had ignored the flatterers and instead elected a man who was candid and who knew the business of being a general. This was how the Roman people subjected themselves to virtue and goodness, so that they might gain power and become the greatest of all nations.

12. When Aemilius set out on his campaign, he met with good luck on his voyage and enjoyed an easy journey to the Roman camp, which he reached quickly and safely.[55] All of this I can attribute to divine favour. But when I observe how, under his command, the war was won by his bold courage, by his skilful planning, by the eager service of his friends and by his brave tactics in the face of danger, I cannot attribute this man's glorious and brilliant achievement to his celebrated good fortune (which is often the case with other generals). Unless, that is, someone should suggest that Perseus' avarice should be ascribed to Aemilius' good luck, for it was Perseus' cowardice – where money is concerned – that entirely ruined the Macedonians' grand and glorious prospects for the war, during which their hopes had run high.

Perseus was joined, at his own request, by a force of Basternae comprising 10,000 cavalry and 10,000 light troops, all of them mercenaries, men ignorant of farming or sailing or pasturing flocks, who instead were constantly practising their sole occupation and craft, which was fighting and defeating their adversaries. When these men camped in the territory of the Maedi,[56] they began mingling with soldiers of the king. The

size of these men, their astonishing military training, their arrogant boasts and their violent threats against the enemy, all
combined to inspire courage among the Macedonians, who
came to believe that the Romans could never withstand these
men but would instead be terrified at the sight of them and
their bizarre, horrifying gestures. It had been Perseus' intention
to raise the morale of his troops in just this way. But when he
was asked to pay each mercenary commander 1,000 pieces of
gold, the sheer quantity of the expense made his head swim and
he became insanely stingy. He refused to pay[57] and quit the alliance. It was as if he were keeping the Romans' accounts for
them instead of waging war against them, and was anxious
about giving them an accurate record of his expenses in the
conflict between them. He should have taken a lesson from the
Romans, who, in addition to their other preparations, had
mustered 100,000 men[58] who were ready to do whatever was
needed.

Instead, although he was contending with a foe so numerous –
in a war for which he held in reserve vast resources – Persius
nevertheless counted out his gold and sealed it himself, as timid
of touching it as if it were another's property. Yet he was not
the offspring of some Lydian or Phoenician,[59] but rather a descendant of Philip and Alexander, whose nobility he claimed to
share.[60] They were men who mastered their enemies because
they believed that success should come at the cost of money,
not money at the price of success. Indeed, it is commonly said
that the cities of Greece were not captured by Philip but by
Philip's gold.[61] And Alexander, when he noticed, at the start of
his expedition to India, that his Macedonians were encumbered
by their Persian spoils, which had become bulky and heavy,
first he set fire to his own royal wagons and then persuaded his
men to do the same thing with theirs. As a result, they marched
off to war unburdened, like men released from their bonds.[62]
Perseus, by contrast, although he had lavished his wealth on
himself, his children and his kingdom, was unwilling to spend
even a small sum in order to purchase deliverance. Instead, he
chose to become a rich captive, carried off with the rest of his

great wealth, and to show the Romans how much he had saved and looked after on their behalf.

13. Not only did Perseus deceive the Gauls and send them away, he also persuaded Genthius the Illyrian, for a price of 300 talents, to join him in the war. He exhibited the money, all counted out, to Genthius' representatives, whom he allowed to seal it for themselves. After he was convinced that he had what he wanted, however, Genthius committed an act of terrible sacrilege: he arrested and imprisoned ambassadors who had been sent to him from Rome. Perseus then came to think that his money was no longer needed, inasmuch as Genthius had already made war with the Romans inevitable on account of his hostile and unjust actions. And so he deprived the wretched man of his 300 talents,[63] and he did nothing but watch when Genthius was removed from his kingdom, along with his wife and children, like birds taken from their nest, by Lucius Anicius,[64] the Roman in command of the army sent against him.

It was against such an adversary that Aemilius was sent. Perseus he despised, but he was very impressed by his preparations and his army, which consisted of 4,000 cavalry and nearly 40,000 heavy-infantry. Perseus had occupied a secure position,[65] at the foot of Mount Olympus and with the sea behind him, which was unassailable by any approach and had on all sides been fortified by ramparts and wooden barricades. There he enjoyed complete confidence, certain that time and expense would exhaust Aemilius.

For his part, Aemilius applied his active intelligence to every conceivable plan and tactic. He realized, however, that his men were vexed by any delay. Emboldened by the weak discipline imposed by their previous generals, they pressed him to consider many impractical suggestions, as if they were now in command. Aemilius took a dim view of this, urging his soldiers instead to concentrate on their physical fitness and on the condition of their weapons, so that, when their general gave them the order, they could wield their swords like proper Romans. He also ordered the night-watchmen to stand guard without spears, believing that his men would be more attentive and do a better job of staying awake if they were unable to defend themselves from an enemy attack.

14. His men were extremely upset owing to a shortage of water fit for drinking. Only a few feeble streams formed pools at the edge of the sea, and their water was of a very poor quality. Aemilius observed that the heights of nearby Mount Olympus were covered with trees, and on the evidence of the forest's green foliage he concluded that there must be sources of water flowing deep beneath the earth. Consequently, he dug numerous wells along the foot of the mountain which allowed these waters to escape. The wells were immediately filled with pure, flowing water, as the sheer force of the water's pressure pumped it into the emptied spaces.

There are some, however, who deny that where springs can be observed flowing from the earth, their source is an unseen supply of existing water. They insist that the emergence of a spring has nothing to do with the discharge of released water, but instead results from the instantaneous creation of water when solid matter is liquefied. In their view, moist vapour becomes liquid and fluid when, in the depths of the earth, it is put under pressure and cooled. Just as a woman's breasts are not like vessels filled with a ready flow of milk but must first transform the nourishment they contain inside themselves into milk and then filter that through to their surface, in the same way places where the earth is cool and in which there are many springs do not rest upon hidden waters, nor are there reservoirs below, filled with water that already exists, from which streams and deep and mighty rivers issue forth. What actually happens, so they argue, is that in these places vapour and air are forcibly compressed and condensed, with the result that they turn into water. It is certainly the case, or so they maintain, that whenever digging is done in these places water gushes more freely, which is an effect of the physical manipulation entailed by the digging – just as a woman's breasts react to the physical manipulation entailed by nursing, which moistens and softens the vapour. On the other hand, ground that is densely packed but is not manipulated (say, by digging) remains choked and incapable of creating water owing to the absence of the physical motion that allows for the production of moisture.

Anyone who holds this opinion simply invites the sceptic to make the argument that blood does not actually exist inside living things; instead, it is created whenever a wound is suffered, because a transformation of air or of flesh takes place and it is this that generates the flow of liquid blood. In any case, this theory is entirely refuted by the experience of men who, when digging underground channels or excavating in mines, encounter underground rivers which do not form slowly (as one would reasonably expect if they were created instantly by this physical movement of the earth), but gush forth in a flood. Furthermore, we observe that, when a rock is split open, it shoots forth a violent stream of water, and then it stops.[66] But that is enough on this topic.

15. Aemilius remained inactive for several days, and they say that never before had there been such stillness when two armies of so great a size as these were situated so near to one another. Persisting in his efforts to probe and explore every possibility, he learned that there remained one, and only one, unguarded passage, the route through Perrhaebia past the Pythium and Petra.[67] His hopefulness, owing to the fact that the passage had been left unguarded, exceeded his concerns about the roughness and difficulty of the terrain (which was the reason why the place had been left unguarded). And so he held a council of war to discuss the matter. Among those present, Scipio, surnamed Nasica, who was Scipio Africanus' son-in-law and who would later become one of the most influential men in the senate,[68] was the first to volunteer to lead a force through the pass in order to surround the enemy. Fabius Maximus, Aemilius' eldest son, although at the time still a young man, was the next to put himself forward, and he did so eagerly.

Aemilius was delighted, and he assigned them a force of men – but it was a smaller force than Polybius reports.[69] The correct number is provided by Nasica himself, in a short letter[70] he wrote for one of the kings, in which he recounted his exploits: 3,000 Italian auxiliaries, and 5,000 men for the left wing. In addition to these, Nasica took 120 cavalrymen as well as 200 men from the mixed Thracian and Cretan contingent commanded by Harpalus.[71] He then set out on the road heading towards the sea and made camp at Heracleum, as if he planned to sail around the coast in order to attack the enemy from the rear. After his soldiers had eaten their supper and night had fallen, he revealed to his officers his true designs and then led his forces, under cover of darkness, in the opposite direction, away from the sea. He halted below the Pythium, where he rested his soldiers. From this point, Mount Olympus rises to a height of more than 10 stades, a fact commemorated on an inscription by the man who measured it:

> The sacred height of the summit of Olympus, at Apollo's Pythium,
> As measured by a plumb-line, is 10 full stades and a plethron
>   less 4 feet.
> Xenagoras the son of Eumulus made this measurement.[72]
> Hail, O lord![73] Please be generous.

Geometers, however, say that no mountain has a height, and no sea a depth, exceeding 10 stades.[74] Nevertheless, Xenagoras does not seem to have taken his measurement carelessly. On the contrary, he appears to have worked scientifically and with the appropriate instruments.

16. This is where Nasica spent the night.[75] As for Perseus, because he observed no change in Aemilius' position, he did not know what was going on until a Cretan deserter, who had run away when the army was on the march, came to him with news of the Romans' circuitous manoeuvre. Although vexed by this information, Perseus did not move his camp. Instead, he dispatched Milo[76] with 10,000 foreign mercenaries and 2,000 Macedonians, with orders to move quickly in order to occupy the passes. Polybius reports[77] that these men were still asleep when the Romans fell on them, whereas Nasica says that it was only after an intense and dangerous battle that the heights were secured. He also tells us how he killed a Thracian

mercenary by driving a javelin through his chest when the man rushed at him, and that, after the enemy had all been driven away and Milo had made a disgraceful escape, without arms or armour and wearing only his tunic, he followed after them in safety and brought his forces down into the plain.

Confronted by these adverse developments, Perseus hastily broke camp and withdrew. He was now frightened, and his hopes were shattered. Nevertheless, he had no choice but to make a stand in front of Pydna[78] and risk battle there, unless he wanted his troops to disperse here and there among his cities, where they still could not escape the coming of the war. For now that the war had penetrated his country, it would not be possible to drive it out without bloodshed and loss of life. As it was, he enjoyed superiority in numbers if he kept his men where they were, and, in defence of their wives and children, they could be expected to fight strenuously – especially with their king observing everything and hazarding his own life in the struggle. It was by resorting to these arguments that Perseus' friends tried to encourage him, with the result that the king pitched camp and deployed his forces for battle.

He surveyed the lie of the land and assigned commands to his officers. It was his plan to engage the Romans as soon as they made their approach. His position[79] was not without advantages: there was a plain for his heavy-infantry, which required level footing and a smooth terrain, and there was a sequence of hills with places to where his skirmishers and light-armed troops could retreat and from where they could launch attacks. There were also rivers running through the middle of the plain, the Aeson and the Leucus, which at that time of year (it was near the end of summer[80]) were not very deep but which nevertheless seemed likely to cause the Romans difficulties.[81]

17. Aemilius joined his army with Nasica's forces and came down in battle formation against the enemy. When he observed their array, however, as well as their sheer numbers, he was so impressed that he halted his advance in order to think matters over. His young officers, by contrast, were keen to fight; they rode up and begged him not to delay. This was especially true

of Nasica, whose success at Olympus had stimulated his boldness. But Aemilius smiled and said to him, 'Yes of course – if I
were so young as you! But my many victories have taught me
to avoid the blunders of those who fall in defeat, and they will
not allow me, immediately after a march, to do battle with
heavy-infantry who are already drawn up in battle formation.'[82] Thereupon he ordered his vanguard, which was visible
to the enemy, to form into cohorts, thereby giving the appearance of readying for battle, while the men in the rear wheeled
around, dug fortifications and constructed a camp. Then he
removed his forward troops, line by line, beginning with those
closest to the rear, so that before the enemy knew it he had
broken up his battle-line and had in an orderly fashion brought
all his men within their fortifications.[83]

During the night,[84] after the soldiers had eaten and were either
resting or preparing to sleep, the moon, which was full and high
in the sky, suddenly grew dark, taking on all sorts of colours as
it lost its light, until it disappeared from sight.[85] The Romans, in
accordance with their custom, tried to call the moon's light back
by clashing metal objects together and by holding up to the heavens the flames of many brands and torches.[86] The Macedonians
did nothing like this. Instead, horror and astonishment gripped
their camp, and a rumour quietly made its way among many of
them that this portent signified the eclipse of a king. Now Aemilius possessed some knowledge and experience of the astronomical
phenomenon of eclipses, which occur at fixed intervals, when
the moon is carried in its course into the shadow of the earth and
is hidden from sight until it passes out of the darkened region
and again reflects the light of the sun. However, because he was
devoted to religious observance, and was very given to sacrifice
and divination, as soon as he saw that the moon was restored, he
sacrificed eleven heifers to it.

As soon as the next day arrived, he sacrificed twenty oxen to
Heracles, none of which delivered favourable omens. The
twenty-first, however, brought signs indicating victory so long
as the Romans remained on the defensive. He then made a vow
to sacrifice a hecatomb to the god and to celebrate games in his
honour, after which he ordered his officers to draw up the

troops in battle formation. He was waiting, however, for the sun to pass through its circuit and to decline, so that its morning light would not shine in the faces of his soldiers as they were fighting.[87] He passed this time in his tent, which faced the plain and the enemy's camp.

18. Towards evening, according to some, Aemilius himself contrived a stratagem for inducing the enemy to attack: the Romans, as they were driving out an unbridled horse, came into contact with the enemy, so the pursuit of this horse caused the battle to begin.[88] Others, however, say that the Thracians under Alexander's command[89] fell upon some Roman pack animals that were carrying in fodder and in reaction a sharp counter-attack was launched by 700 Ligurians, whereupon each side added reinforcements until both sides were joined in a full battle. Then Aemilius, like the pilot of a ship, gauged the magnitude of the looming contest by observing the swell and motion of the two armies. Leaving his tent, he moved among the ranks of his soldiers and encouraged them.

Meanwhile, Nasica rode out to the skirmishers and saw that nearly all of the enemy were entering the fray. In the vanguard were the Thracians, whose appearance, Nasica says, was terrifying, for they were tall men clad in black tunics, over which they wore gleaming white armour, most notably their greaves and shields, and in their right hands they bore heavy iron broadswords at shoulder height. The Thracians were followed by the mercenaries, whose equipment varied, and the Paeonians[90] were mixed with them. Next came a third division, elite troops selected from the best of the Macedonians on account of their valour and youth, shining brightly in their gilded armour and new red cloaks. As these men were occupying their positions in the battle formation, the heavy-infantry ranks of the Bronze Shields[91] marched from the camp behind them, filling the plain with the gleam of iron and the flashing of bronze, while the hills resounded with their shouts and cheers. The Macedonian forces advanced with such daring and speed that the first of them to be slain fell only 2 stades from the Roman camp.

19. As the attack began, Aemilius found on his arrival that the Macedonians, keeping their formation, had already lodged the tips of their pikes in the Romans' shields, which made it impossible for the Romans to reach them with their short swords. He then saw how the rest of the Macedonian troops had removed their light shields from their shoulders and, by positioning their pikes at an angle, were withstanding his heavy-infantry. And when he observed the powerful battle-line formed by their interlocked shields and the ferocity of their attack, he was astounded and gripped by fear, for he had never before seen a sight so terrifying as this one. Often, in his later years, he used to recollect what he had seen and the emotions it aroused in him. In that moment, however, he put on a cheerful and pleasant expression for his men, and he rode past them wearing neither helmet nor breastplate.

The Macedonian king, by contrast, according to Polybius, became frightened as soon as the battle had begun and rode back to the city on the pretext of making a sacrifice to Heracles, a god who does not accept craven sacrifices offered up by cowards, nor does he answer their unrighteous prayers. For it is unnatural that a man should hit the target who makes no shot, or win a battle without standing his ground, or, to put it more generally, that a man should succeed who fails to try, or that a wicked man should prosper. The god heard the prayers of Aemilius, however, because he asked for strength and victory with his spear in his hand, and from the thick of battle he invited the god to fight alongside him.

However, a certain Poseidonius,[92] who claims to have been a contemporary and to have taken part in this war, and who has composed a history of Perseus in several books, insists that it was not owing to cowardice, nor was it under the pretext of making a sacrifice, that the king left the battlefield, but instead because he had been kicked on the leg by a horse on the day before the battle. He goes on to say that during the battle, in spite of his pain and against the advice of his friends, he ordered a pack horse to be brought to him, mounted it and, without the protection of a breastplate, joined his heavy-infantry in the line of battle. Missiles of every sort were flying about him on all sides, and he was struck by an iron javelin, not by its tip but by its shaft, which ran along his left side with such force that it ripped his tunic and left a dark red bruise on his skin, which remained for a long time. This, then, is how Poseidonius defends Perseus.

20. The Romans, although they withstood the Macedonian advance, were unable to break the line of the heavy-infantry, until Salvius, the commander of the Paelignians,[93] seized his own troops' standard and hurled it into the enemy's ranks. At this, the Paelignians, for whom, like all other Italian soldiers, abandoning a standard is an unnatural and sacrilegious act, launched themselves against the place it lay, which resulted in dreadful casualties being suffered on both sides. The Romans tried using their swords to deflect the Macedonians' pikes, then shoving them back with their shields, and they even resorted to using their bare hands to seize them and push them aside. Yet the Macedonians gripped their pikes with both hands and continued their advance, impaling their enemies, armour and all – for neither shield nor breastplate can offer any protection against the Macedonian pike – and they tossed over their heads the bodies of the Paelignians and Marrucinians,[94] who abandoned reason and with bestial rage hurled themselves towards the enemy's blows and a certain death. After the first line had been cut down in this way, the ranks behind them were beaten back by the Macedonians, and though they did not turn and flee, they nevertheless retreated towards a mountain called Olocrus. At the sight of this withdrawal, according to Poseidonius, Aemilius rent his tunic. For while these soldiers were retiring, the rest of the Romans were being turned aside by the formation of the Macedonians' heavy-infantry, which offered no means of attacking it but instead met any assault with what one might call a dense palisade of pikes, which was entirely unassailable.

But as the terrain became less even and the battle-line became too long for their shields to remain firmly locked together, Aemilius noticed that the lines of the Macedonians' heavy-infantry were beginning to break up and suffer openings, a natural development when armies are large and the conditions of combat vary, some parts of the line being hard pressed whereas others advance steadily. Thereupon he rushed to the front, regrouped his cohorts and ordered them to make their way through the gaps and openings in the enemy lines, so that they could come to close quarters in many separate battles instead of fighting a single battle against the whole of the enemy's army. Aemilius gave these orders to his officers, who passed them on to the soldiers, and as soon as his men had penetrated the ranks of the enemy, thereby breaking up their formation, they proceeded to attack some of them from the flank, where they were unprotected, or cut down others by falling upon them from the rear. The battle formation of the Macedonian heavy-infantry disintegrated and so too did the strength it possessed when all of its members worked together as a unit. Because they now fought on their own or in small groups, they could only stab with their short daggers at the long shields of the Romans, and they only had light wicker shields with which to defend themselves from the Romans' swords, which were wielded with such force that they sliced through the Macedonians' armour and into their bodies. Thus they put up a weak resistance and were defeated.

21. The struggle was intense, however. Marcus, the son of Cato and son-in-law of Aemilius,[95] who was fighting the enemy with might and main, lost his sword. Inasmuch as he was a young man who had been instructed in the noblest principles and owed his distinguished father proof of his own distinguished valour, Marcus decided that life was not worth living if he remained alive and yet abandoned his own sword to become spoil for the enemy, and so he raced through the battlefield telling every friend and companion he saw of his misfortune and begging them for help. A large number of brave men then pushed their way through the rest, put themselves under his leadership and attacked the enemy. A great struggle followed, with much slaughter and many casualties, until they drove their opponents from the field, and after they had taken possession of an uncontested space, bare of any hostile troops, they

began to look for Marcus' sword. When at last it was found, buried beneath piles of armour and corpses, they were joyous, and, crying out in triumph, they threw themselves with even stronger passion against such of the enemy as had not fled or fallen.

In the end, the 3,000 elite Macedonian troops, who remained in formation and persevered in the fighting, were cut down to a man, and, of the rest, all of whom fled, so many were slain that the plain and the foothills were littered with dead bodies and the waters of the River Leucus were still red with blood when the Romans crossed it on the day after the battle. Indeed, it is reported that over 25,000 of the enemy perished, while the Romans lost a hundred men, according to Poseidonius, or, according to Nasica, eighty.[96]

22. This greatest of all battles was decided very quickly, for the Romans began fighting at the ninth hour and were victorious before the tenth.[97] The remainder of the day they spent in pursuit, which they continued for 120 stades,[98] which meant that it was late in the evening when they returned. Everyone was met by slaves bearing torches and conducted amid joyful shouting to the tents, which were brightly lit and adorned with wreaths of ivy and laurel – apart from their general, Aemilius, who was consumed with sorrow. Two of his sons had joined him in this campaign, and the younger one was missing. Aemilius loved him most of all, for he recognized in him a nature more inclined to virtue than in any of his brothers. He also possessed a passionate and ambitious spirit, and he was still little more than a boy,[99] which led his father to conclude that, owing to his inexperience, he must have been caught up among the enemy during the fighting and in this way perished. The whole army soon learned of their general's anguish and despair, and so left their meals and ran about with torches, some going to Aemilius' tent, others searching outside the fortifications among the many dead bodies there. Sorrow filled the camp, and the plain was filled with the sound of men crying out the name of Scipio. For from the beginning he was beloved by everyone, because no one else, even in his own distinguished

family, possessed a character so well suited for military command and political leadership. It had grown late and he was very nearly given up for lost when he, along with two or three companions, returned from pursuing the enemy, covered in the blood and gore of the fallen, for, like a young hound of fine pedigree, he had been carried away by the sheer pleasure of victory. This is the Scipio who in later years destroyed Carthage and Numantia[100] and became by far the foremost Roman of his day in virtue and in influence. And so Fortune postponed for another time[101] her retribution for Aemilius' success, restoring to him, on this occasion, the full and unsullied pleasure of victory.

23. Perseus hastened in flight from Pydna to Pella,[102] accompanied by his cavalry, almost all of whom had survived the battle. But later, when the men of the infantry[103] caught up with the cavalry, they abused them for their cowardice and betrayal, pulled them off their horses and began to beat them, violence that frightened the king into turning his horse off the road, and, in order to avoid being conspicuous, removing his purple cloak, which he placed in front of him, as well as his diadem, which he carried in his hands. He also dismounted and led his horse behind him, so that he could converse with his companions as he walked. But of his companions, one pretended to fasten a shoe that become loose, another that he needed to water his horse, and still another that he wanted water for himself, until, little by little, they all fell behind him and ran away, less afraid of the enemy than of their own king's cruelty. For he was outraged by the misfortunes he had suffered and sought to divert the responsibility for his defeat away from himself and against everyone else.

Perseus entered Pella by night, and when he was met by Euctus and Eulaeus, his treasurers, who reproved him for what had happened and peppered him, at this inopportune moment, with tactlessly candid advice, he became enraged and killed both of them with his own sword. After this no one remained with him except Evander[104] of Crete, Archedamus[105] of Aetolia and Neon[106] of Boeotia. And, of his soldiers, only the Cretans continued to follow him, not out of loyalty but because they were as devoted to his wealth as bees are to their honeycomb. He was in fact keeping with him a vast amount of treasure, out of which he had already distributed among the Cretans drinking cups, mixing bowls and other gold and silver implements, in all worth about 50 talents.

He went first to Amphipolis and from there to Galepsus,[107] by which time he began to grow less afraid and so relapsed into his long-standing and congenital malady, stinginess. He complained to his friends that he had thoughtlessly spread some of the gold treasure of Alexander the Great among the Cretans, and with tearful entreaties he pleaded with those who had this treasure to exchange it for money. It was obvious to those who understood him well that he was playing the part of a Cretan[108] – to the Cretans themselves – whereas those who took him at his word and returned what they had were cheated, for he did not pay them their money. Instead, he managed to acquire 30 talents from his friends, funds which would very soon be seized by his enemies but which now he carried with him to Samothrace, where he took refuge as a suppliant in the sanctuary of the Cabiri.[109]

24. Now the Macedonians' devotion to their kings has always been renowned, but on this occasion, feeling as if their prop had been shattered and that everything had collapsed with it, they put themselves in Aemilius' hands and in two days made him master of all Macedon. And this does seem to be good evidence for those who attribute his achievements to his good fortune. So, too, was what occurred when he was making a sacrifice, which was clear proof of divine favour: as Aemilius was performing a sacrifice in Amphipolis and the sacred rituals had begun, a thunderbolt struck the altar, set it on fire and thus consumed the offering. But the episode concerning the rumour of his victory was the clearest token of his divine favour and good fortune. On the fourth day after Perseus' defeat at Pydna, at which time the people of Rome were watching horse races, a story suddenly arose, in the front seats of the Circus, that Aemilius had defeated Perseus in a great battle and had

conquered all of Macedon. From there the rumour spread quickly among the multitude, and great joy erupted, expressed in cheers and clapping, which prevailed in the city for the entire day. Then, because no definite source for this story could be identified – it seemed instead to be prevalent everywhere at once – the rumour dissipated and finally vanished. But when, a few days later, they became reliably informed of the victory,[110] they were astonished at the earlier report and how, in that fiction, there resided the truth.

25. It is also said that a report of the battle fought on the River Sagra against the Italian Greeks reached the Peloponnesus on the same day as the battle was fought,[111] just as the battle with the Medes at Mycale was reported on the same day to the Plataeans.[112] And when the Romans defeated the Tarquins, who had marched against them joined by their Latin allies, only a little later did two tall and handsome men appear at Rome with a report from the army of what they had seen. These men, it was inferred at the time, were the Dioscuri.[113] The first man who met them at the spring in the forum, where they were cooling their horses which were heavy with sweat, expressed astonishment at their news of the victory. Whereupon, so we are told, they smiled gently and touched his beard with their hands, the instant effect of which was that the colour of his beard changed from black to red, an event that enhanced the credibility of their report and gave the man the surname Ahenobarbus,[114] which means *Bronze-Beard*. All of this is made more plausible by an event that took place in my own lifetime. When Antonius rose in rebellion against Domitian, and a great war in Germany was feared and at Rome everything was in turmoil, suddenly and spontaneously the common people, acting independently, began to report a victory, and soon the rumour spread throughout Rome that Antonius had been killed and that no part of his army had survived its defeat.[115] Everyone became so certain of this that many of the magistrates offered sacrifices to the gods. But when no one could be found who was the original author of this report, and instead its telling and retelling hearkened back until it was lost in the limitless

throng of the city, as if in a vast sea, it was realized that the report had no reliable source and so the rumour quickly vanished from the city. Yet when Domitian set out with his army to fight this war, and was already on the march, he was met by messages and letters telling him about the victory. And the day of the victory was the same day on which the rumour occurred, although the distance between the two places is more than 20,000 stades.[116] There is no one of my generation who is unaware of this event.

26. Gnaeus Octavius,[117] who was in command of Aemilius' fleet, anchored off Samothrace. Owing to his reverence for the gods, he respected Perseus' right to asylum, but he also endeavoured to prevent him from sailing off and escaping. Somehow, however, Perseus secretly persuaded a certain Cretan named Oroandes, who owned a small boat, to take him and his treasures on board. Oroandes, true to his Cretan nature, took aboard the treasure on one night and instructed Perseus to come on the next night to the harbour by the temple of Demeter, along with his children and his essential servants. As soon as it was evening, however, he sailed away. Now, Perseus had suffered pitiably when he let himself down out of a narrow window and along the city wall, joined by his children and his wife, who were unaccustomed to hardship or exile. But far more pitiable was the groan that erupted from him when he was informed, as he was wandering along the shore, that Oroandes had already been seen hurrying out to sea. It was now daybreak, and so, bereft of every hope, he fled back towards the city wall, and although the Romans saw him, he managed to get inside first, along with his wife. His children,[118] however, were captured and handed over to the Romans by a man named Ion, who long ago had been Perseus' lover but had now become his betrayer by supplying the most compelling reason for Perseus to come to the Romans and to surrender himself to those who held his children in their power, as even a wild animal will do when its young have been taken. Of all the Romans it was Nasica whom Perseus most trusted, and so he asked for him, but, being informed that he was not there, Perseus first wept at

his misfortune and then reflected on the reality that he had no choice in the matter. In the end, he surrendered himself to Gnaeus.

It was now that Perseus made it clear that avarice was not his most ignoble vice but, rather, his cowardice in the face of death, which robbed him of the only thing that misfortune cannot take away from the fallen, namely pity. For when, at his own request, he was brought before Aemilius, the Roman regarded him as a great man brought low by divine retribution and an evil fortune; he stood and came forward to meet him, attended by his friends and with tears in his eyes.[119] But Perseus, in a most shameful display, threw himself to the ground before him and then, clasping his knees, burst out in disgraceful cries and entreaties, none of which Aemilius could endure or even listen to. Instead, looking at him with a pained and sorrowful expression on his face, he said, 'Why, wretch, are you acquitting Fortune of the strongest indictment you could lodge against her, through actions that will make you appear to merit your misfortune and will make it appear that it is not your current condition but your former good fortune that was undeserved? And why are you undermining my victory and making my achievement look small by revealing yourself to be neither a noble nor a suitable antagonist for the Romans? You should be aware that courage on the part of the unfortunate earns them great respect even from their enemies, whereas, so far as Romans are concerned, cowardice is the most dishonourable thing of all, even if cowardice brings one prosperity.'

27. Still, despite his objections to the man, he raised Perseus up, offered him his hand and entrusted him to Tubero,[120] after which he drew his sons, his sons-in-law and other officers, especially the younger men, into his tent, where for a long time he sat in silent reflection, which provoked wonder in everyone. He then began to offer a disquisition on the nature of fortune and of human affairs. 'Is it fitting', he asked, 'for a mortal man to become bold when he enjoys success, or proud because he has conquered a nation or a city or a kingdom? Or should he instead contemplate this reversal of fortune, which provides for

any man who wages war an instructive example of our common vulnerability and teaches us that nothing is stable and secure? What sort of moment is it for mortals to be confident, when their victory over other men obliges them to be most afraid of Fortune, and when a happy man can be reduced to dejection by his knowledge that destiny follows a circular course, coming to different men at different times? The legacy of Alexander, who reached the supreme heights of power and possessed the greatest dominion, has collapsed in a single hour[121] and has been crushed beneath your feet, and you behold kings who were only recently surrounded by thousands of cavalry and tens of thousands of infantry now receiving from the hands of their enemy a daily ration of food and drink. Can you then believe that our own affairs enjoy any lasting protection from the vicissitudes of fortune? Young men, will you not then abandon your hollow insolence and let go of your pride in this victory, and instead look towards the future with humility, always watchful for the moment when the divine will at last exact from each of you retribution for your present prosperity?' They say that Aemilius discoursed at great length along these lines, and, when he dismissed the young men, their boasting and insolence had been well and truly curbed by his trenchant speech, as if by a bridle.

28. After this, he allowed his army a rest and himself a sightseeing tour of Greece, during which he busied himself with actions that were at once distinguished and humane.[122] As he travelled the country, he restored democratic governments and established their political institutions; he also handed out gifts to the cities, grain from the royal stores to some, oil to others. Indeed, it is said that such an abundance of supplies was found in the king's stores that the number of petitioners and recipients was exhausted before the quantity of the provisions that had been discovered.

At Delphi, when he saw a tall square pillar made out of white stone, on which a golden statue of Perseus was meant to stand, he ordered a statue of himself[123] to be placed there instead, observing that it was fitting that the vanquished should give way to their conquerors. And at Olympia he is said to have uttered that oft-quoted line, that Pheidias had sculpted the Zeus of Homer.[124]

When the ten commissioners arrived from Rome,[125] he restored their own country to the Macedonians and he gave them free and independent cities in which to dwell; they were obliged to pay the Romans 100 talents, which was less than half of what they used to pay in tribute to their kings. He celebrated every sort of game and contest, and he offered sacrifices to the gods at which he gave feasts and banquets, for all of which he made generous payments from the royal treasury. As he was organizing and arranging these banquets, and as he greeted and seated his guests, he accorded everyone all due honour and consideration, and he did so with such thoughtfulness and correctness that the Greeks were amazed to see how a man involved in great affairs did not neglect their amusements but instead gave even trivial matters the appropriate attention. And he was delighted by the fact that, amid so many splendid entertainments, it was he that his guests most enjoyed and took the most pleasure in watching, and to those who marvelled at his attention to detail, he used to say that the same intelligence was needed in ordering a battle formation successfully as in arranging a good symposium, though in the case of one the object was to inspire the most terror in the enemy, whereas in the other it was to stimulate the most pleasure in one's companions.[126]

Most of all, men praised his liberality and magnanimity, for he would not condescend even to look at the great quantities of silver and gold which had been collected from the royal treasuries but instead simply handed it all over to his quaestors[127] for deposit in the public treasury. He allowed his sons, who were devoted to literature, to take only the king's books for themselves. When he was awarding prizes for valour in the battle, he gave Aelius Tubero, his son-in-law, a bowl weighing 5 pounds. This is the Tubero who, as I said earlier,[128] lived with sixteen relations, all of them supported by one modest farm. And they say that this is the first silver that ever entered the house of the Aelian family and it came into their house on account of valour and honour, whereas up to that time neither the men nor their wives had used either silver or gold.

29. After he had put affairs in good order, Aemilius said farewell to the Greeks, and he exhorted the Macedonians to remember that their freedom was the gift of the Romans, which they could preserve through lawfulness and concord. He then marched against Epirus,[129] for he had received a senatorial decree instructing him to enrich the soldiers who had fought with him in the battle against Perseus at the expense of the cities[130] in that region. He wished to attack all the cities at once, suddenly, when no one was expecting it, so he summoned from each city its ten leading men, whom he ordered to bring back to him, on a fixed day, all the silver and gold they had in their houses and temples. He sent along, with each of these men, a military guard under the command of an officer, whose ostensible mission was to search out and take possession of the money. But when the appointed day arrived, at one and the same time these men set about overrunning and pillaging the cities, and in a single hour 150,000 people were enslaved and seventy cities were sacked. And yet, out of all this devastation and ruin, each soldier received no more than 11 drachmas as his share, while all mankind shuddered in horror at the outcome of this war, in which an entire nation was carved to bits so that each Roman soldier could receive so meagre a profit.[131]

30. After he had executed the senate's decree, a duty which was entirely contrary to his mild and just nature, Aemilius went down to Oricum.[132] From there he crossed over to Italy, along with the army, and he sailed up the River Tiber in the royal galley, which had sixteen banks of oars and was richly adorned with captured arms as well as cloths of red and purple, which incited the Romans to go outside the city as if they were attending a festival and were enjoying in advance the spectacle of a triumphal procession, following along the banks while the splashing oars gently carried the ship upstream.

Aemilius' soldiers, however, gazed covetously at the royal treasures, on the grounds that they had not received as much as

they believed they deserved, and for this reason they were
secretly angry and felt bitter towards Aemilius, while openly
they accused him of having been oppressive and tyrannical
when commanding them. They were entirely hostile to his
desire for a triumph.[133] When this came to the attention of
Servius Galba,[134] who was an enemy of Aemilius, although he
had been one of his military tribunes, he was emboldened to
declare in public that Aemilius should not be awarded a triumph. He also spread among the soldiers many false accusations
against their general, which only exacerbated the anger they
already felt, and then asked the tribunes of the people for
another day in which to continue his recriminations, inasmuch
as the present one was insufficient because there remained only
four hours of daylight. The tribunes, however, ordered him to
speak, if he had anything he wanted to say, and so he began to
deliver a lengthy speech, full of invective, which used up the
remainder of the day. At nightfall, the tribunes adjourned the
assembly, but the soldiers, whose brazenness had now been
amplified, rushed to join Galba, formed themselves into a unit
and proceeded to occupy the Capitol[135] before dawn, for it was
there that the tribunes of the people were planning to hold the
assembly.[136]

31. As soon as it was daybreak, the voting commenced, and, as
the first tribe was voting against the triumph, the news of what
was happening was brought down to the rest of the people and
to the senate. The multitude, although sorely grieved at this
insult to Aemilius, could do nothing[137] but cry out helplessly,
whereas the leading men of the senate roared against this outrage, exhorting one another to attack the insolent licence of the
soldiers, which would soon descend to every form of lawless-
ness and violence – if nothing were done to prevent their
depriving Aemilius Paullus of the honours of his victory. And
so they pushed their way through the crowd and climbed the
Capitol in a body, where they instructed the tribunes of the
people to halt the voting until they had finished what they
wanted to say to the public.

When all voting ceased and there was silence, Marcus Servilius,[138] a man of consular rank, who had slain twenty-three opponents in single combat, came forward. He said that he now understood, better than ever before, how great a commander Aemilius Paullus was, when he saw how disobedient and wicked the army was which Aemilius had used in winning such great and glorious victories, and he was astonished that the people could delight in triumphs over Illyrians and Libyans[139] and yet deny themselves the spectacle of a living king of Macedon and of the glories of Alexander and Philip, which had now been despoiled by Roman arms. 'Is it not a strange thing', he said, 'how previously, when an unsubstantiated rumour of victory reached the city,[140] you offered sacrifices to the gods and prayed that you would soon see the proof of this report, whereas now that your general has returned bearing true victory, you deprive the gods of honour and yourselves of joy, as if you feared beholding the immense scale of his achievement, or felt pity for your enemy? And yet it would be a better thing to dispense with the triumph because you pity your enemy than because you envy your general. However,' he continued, 'you have allowed your malice to become so intense that a man,[141] whose body is not only unscarred but is kept sleek by his delicate and effeminate lifestyle, dares to speak about leadership and about triumphs – to those of us who have learned from our own wounds how to distinguish a brave general from a cowardly one.' And with these words he tore open his garment and exhibited on his chest an incredible number of scars. He then turned around to uncover certain parts of his body that are deemed inappropriate to expose in public, and confronting Galba he said, 'You may laugh at these scars, but I take pride in them in the presence of my fellow-citizens, in whose defence I got them by constant riding, day and night. But proceed! Take these men off to vote. I too shall come down and, following along beside them all, learn which of them are wicked and ungrateful men who, when waging war, prefer to be commanded by demagogues instead of real generals.'

32. This speech, they say, affected the soldiers so powerfully that they changed their minds and a triumph for Aemilius was

ratified by all the tribes. And, we are told, it was conducted as follows. The people erected seating for horse racing in the theatres (the Romans call these *circuses*); they also erected seating in the forum, and they occupied any other part of the city that afforded a view of the procession, which they watched while adorned in fresh garments. Every temple was opened and filled with wreaths and incense. Numerous lictors and their assistants restrained the crowds, which thronged into the middle of the procession's route and rushed here and there, as they tried to keep the streets open and clear. Three days were devoted to celebrating the triumph,[142] the first of which was barely long enough to exhibit all the captured statues, paintings and colossal figures, which were carried on 250 wagons. On the next day, the most beautiful and precious of the Macedonian arms were carried through the city on many carts. The freshly polished bronze and iron of these weapons shone brightly, and they were carefully and artfully arranged in such a way that they appeared to be piled into random heaps, helmets lying next to shields and breastplates on top of greaves, while Cretan light shields, Thracian wicker shields and quivers were all mixed together with bridles for horses, and unsheathed swords stuck out from the piles, along with pikes which had also been planted there. All the arms were packed lightly enough that, as they were carried along, they struck each other and gave out a harsh and frightening sound, and, even though they were the spoils of a conquered enemy, it was unnerving to look at them. After the carts filled with arms there came 3,000 men bearing coined silver in 750 containers, each of which held 3 talents and was carried by four men, while still other men carried silver mixing bowls, drinking horns, drinking bowls and cups, each of which was well exhibited and each of which was extraordinary both in its size and in the depth of its enchasing.

33. Early in the morning of the third day, trumpeters led the way, but, instead of music suitable for a solemn procession or a parade, it was the call used by the Romans to rouse themselves for battle. Next came 120 well-nourished oxen, each with gilded horns and arrayed with fillets and wreaths; these

were being led to their sacrifice by young men wearing aprons with purple borders, who were attended by boys carrying gold and silver libation cups. After these came men bearing the gold coinage, which, like the silver, was distributed into containers holding 3 talents: there were seventy-seven of these containers in number. Following these were the men who bore the sacred bowl, which Aemilius had ordered to be made of 10 talents of gold and decorated with precious gems, then men displaying the Antigonid, Seleucid and Thericlean bowls,[143] and all the golden tableware that had belonged to Perseus. These were followed by the chariot of Perseus, which carried his arms as well as his diadem, which lay upon his arms. Then, after a small interval, the children of the king were led along as slaves, and with them were a crowd of nurses, teachers and tutors, all in tears and all stretching forth their hand to the spectators, teaching the children how to beg and supplicate. There were two boys and one girl, and they were too young to appreciate the gravity of their misfortune, but, because one day their lack of awareness would cease, they evoked even stronger pity, and consequently Perseus was almost unnoticed as he walked along. In their pity, the Romans instead kept their eyes fixed upon the children, and many wept, and all of them felt a mixture of pleasure and pain at the spectacle, until the children had passed.

34. Behind the children and their attendants came Perseus himself, clad in a dark cloak and wearing Macedonian boots and appearing utterly confused and bewildered by the great disaster he had suffered. He, too, was accompanied by a retinue of friends and associates, whose faces were heavy with grief, but, because their tearful expressions were always fixed upon Perseus, this led the spectators to believe that it was his misfortune which they lamented and that they cared little about their own fates.

Perseus, by contrast, had sent a message to Aemilius in which he pleaded that he not be led in the procession but instead be excluded from the triumph. Aemilius, however, in apparent mockery of Perseus' cowardice and fear of death, said, 'But this is the one thing that was in his power before, and remains so now, should he wish it', indicating that the king might choose death in preference to disgrace. But the coward could not bring himself to do that, and instead, unmanned by uncertain hopes, was reduced to being a part of the plunder.

Next in order after Perseus came 400 golden wreaths, which various cities had sent, along with their embassies, to Aemilius as prizes for his victory. Then came Aemilius himself, mounted on a magnificently adorned chariot. Although he was a man worth seeing even without such elaborate trappings of power, he wore a purple robe sprinkled with gold and in his right hand he held a spray of laurel. His entire army also carried sprays of laurel, as they followed the chariot of their general in their units and companies, all the while singing, sometimes traditional songs mixed with jests, sometimes hymns of victory and in praise of the achievements of Aemilius, who was admired and esteemed by everyone, and was envied by no one who was good. Perhaps, however, there exists a divinity whose role it is to diminish our prosperity, whenever it becomes exceedingly great, and add complexity to a mortal's life, so that it is not unmixed with evils or left altogether free from misfortune, so that instead, as Homer says, they seem to fare best whose fortunes tip the scale now in one direction, now in the other.[144]

35. For Aemilius had four sons, two of whom had been adopted by other families, as I have already said,[145] namely Scipio and Fabius, and two who were still boys, the children of his second wife, whom he kept at home. One of these boys died five days before Aemilius celebrated his triumph (he was only fourteen years old), and the other (who was only twelve), died three days after the triumph, so there was no one in Rome who was not affected by their father's grief, but, quite the contrary, everyone shuddered in horror at the savagery of Fortune, which had, without compunction, brought such great sorrow into a house filled with pride and joy and thank-offerings, and had mixed lamentations and weeping with hymns of victory and triumphs.

36. Aemilius, however, because he correctly understood that men need bravery and courage not only in the face of arms and

pikes but also against every assault of Fortune, adjusted and
arranged the mixed circumstances of his life so that the bad
was obscured by the good and his private affairs by his public
responsibilities, and thus he neither debased the grandeur nor
sullied the dignity of his victory. The first to die of his sons he
buried and immediately thereafter celebrated his triumph, as I
have said. And when, after his triumph, his second son died, he
assembled the Roman people and addressed them,[146] not as a
man who sought comfort but rather as one who sought to comfort his fellow-citizens in their grief over his misfortune. He
said that he had never been afraid of anything mortal men
might do to him, but, in so far as the gods were concerned, he
had always feared Fortune, believing that she was completely
untrustworthy and variable; and inasmuch as, during this war,
she had attended his actions like a favourable wind, he had
expected a change and a reversal. 'For in only one day,' he said,
'I crossed the Ionian Sea from Brundisium and landed at Cor-
cyra; from there, in five days, I came to Delphi and made
sacrifice to the god; and again, in another five days, I took command of the army in Macedon; after completing the traditional
lustrations, I immediately commenced military operations and
in fifteen further days brought the war to its glorious conclusion.[147] Still, I distrusted Fortune, because my affairs were
moving so smoothly, and, when there was no longer anything
to fear because there was no longer any risk of an attack by the
enemy, I become even more afraid, during my voyage home, of
a reversal in divine favour on account of my good fortune, for
I was carrying back to Rome a large and victorious army,
spoils and royal prisoners. Indeed, even when I had reached
you in safety and saw the city filled with delight and pride and
thank-offerings, still I remained suspicious of Fortune, knowing that she never bestows on mortals blessings that are at once
great and unmixed – and unenvied by the gods. And my soul
remained in agony, owing to this fear and my anxiety for the
future of this city, until I was struck by this terrible misfortune
to my own house and, during days that were consecrated to the
gods, busied myself instead with the successive funerals of my
two noble sons, who were my sole heirs. Now, consequently,

I no longer feel threatened by the danger that I had regarded as the most serious one – and I am confident, for I believe that Fortune will hereafter remain your reliable and salutary ally, because she has taken me and my sufferings as sufficient retribution to the gods for our successes, and has made the man who celebrated a triumph no less conspicuous an illustration of human frailty than the man who was led in one – except that Perseus, though he was conquered, has his children, whereas Aemilius, his conqueror, has lost his.'

37. This, we are told, is how Aemilius addressed the people, with noble and high-minded words pouring forth from his sincere and honest spirit. As for Perseus, although Aemilius pitied him for his reversal in fortune and earnestly wanted to help him, he could obtain no concession for him except that he be removed from the prison which in Latin is called *carcer*[148] to a clean place where he could more easily live like a human being. Although he was guarded closely, he nonetheless starved himself to death, according to most writers. But a few report that he died in a peculiar and unexpected way. The soldiers responsible for guarding him disapproved of something he did and became angry with him, but, inasmuch as they were unable to harm him or to do him any injury, they did not allow him to sleep: they were very careful to interrupt him whenever he lay down to sleep and resorted to every means of keeping him awake, until he was worn out in this way and died.[149] Two of his children also died. But the third, Alexander,[150] is said to have become skilled in enchasing and fine metal-work; he also learned to write and speak the Roman language and became a secretary to the magistrates, in which office he proved himself to be accomplished and refined.

38. Writers ascribe Aemilius' enormous popularity with the people to his achievements in Macedon, because he brought so much money into the public treasury that the people no longer had to pay taxes,[151] until the time of Hirtius and Pansa, who were consuls during the first war between Antonius and Caesar.[152] A peculiar and extraordinary feature of Aemilius is this:

although he enjoyed popular support and was highly honoured by the people, he remained within the aristocratic party and never spoke or acted to win the favour of the masses. Instead, in political matters he always sided with the most distinguished and influential men of the senate.

Years later, Appius cast this fact in the teeth of Scipio Africanus.[153] At that time, these men were the leading men in the city and each was a candidate for the censorship. One of them had the senate and the nobles on his side, for this was the traditional political position of the Appii, while the other, who was a great man in his own right, nevertheless always took advantage of the extensive favour and support which the people offered him. And so, when Appius saw Scipio entering the forum accompanied by men who were low-born ex-slaves, men who busied themselves in the forum and had enough influence to gather a mob and force any issue by way of vigorous canvassing or demonstrations, he called out in a loud voice, 'O Aemilius Paullus, groan beneath the earth when you learn that your son is being conducted to his censorship by Aemilius the auctioneer and Licinius Philonicus.'[154] Scipio won the goodwill of the people because in most matters he supported them, whereas Aemilius, although he was a staunch aristocrat, was loved by the masses just as much as anyone who appeared to be a strident demagogue or who curried favour with the masses.

They made this clear when, after all his other honours, they elected him censor,[155] which is the most sacred of all the magistracies, and very influential, not least because it examines everyone's way of life. For it lies within the power of the censors to expel from the senate anyone leading a disgraceful life, and to appoint the leading man in the senate, and to dishonour any licentious young man by depriving him of his horse.[156] They also oversee the valuation of properties and the census rolls. And so, the number of citizens registered when Aemilius was in office was 337,452; he appointed, as the leading man in the senate, Marcus Aemilius Lepidus,[157] who had already held this privileged position four times, and he expelled only three senators, none of them men of any distinction; and, in the review of the knights, he and his colleague Marcius Philippus[158] exercised similar moderation.

39. After he had carried out most of the central responsibilities of his censorship, Aemilius fell ill of a disease which was, at first, very serious, and although in time its severity diminished, it remained troublesome and he simply could not recover completely. He was persuaded by his physicians to sail to Elea[159] in Italy, and there he spent a good deal of time enjoying the peaceful countryside along the sea. The Romans longed for him, however, and men often cried out for him in the theatre, as if offering prayers, so eager were they to see him again. When at last a sacred ritual required his presence,[160] and his health seemed to be sufficiently restored for him to conduct it, he returned to Rome. There, along with the other priests, he performed the sacrifice, while the people gathered around him with unmistakable delight, and on the following day he again made a sacrifice to the gods, in a private ritual, for his personal recovery. Now, when this sacrifice had been carried out in the prescribed manner, and he had returned to his house to lie down, before he knew what was happening or could begin to sense any change, he became delirious and demented, and within three days he died,[161] having been blessed with everything that is deemed conducive to happiness.

His funeral procession inspired wonder in others because it revealed everyone's desire to honour the man's virtue through the noblest and most blessed of obsequies, not by means of gold or ivory or other expensive or extravagant furnishings, but instead through goodwill and honour and gratitude, and not exclusively on the part of his fellow-citizens but also on the part of his enemies. For it was certainly the case that of all the Iberians and Ligurians and Macedonians[162] who happened to be present in the city, those who were young and strong took it in turns to carry his bier, while their seniors followed in the procession, calling on Aemilius as their benefactor and the saviour of their countries. For it had not been only on those occasions when he made conquests that he had treated them all mildly and humanely, but rather, for the rest of his life, he had always been busy doing something good for them and had cared for them as though they were his relations or members of his household.

His estate, so we are told, barely amounted to 370,000 drachmas,[163] which he left to his two sons[164] but the younger son, Scipio, because he had been given in adoption to the wealthier family of Africanus, allowed his brother to have it all. This, it is said, was the character and the life of Aemilius Paullus.

Maps

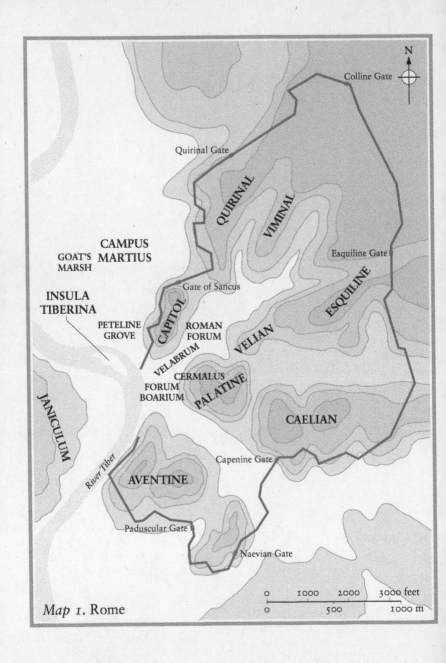

Map 1. Rome

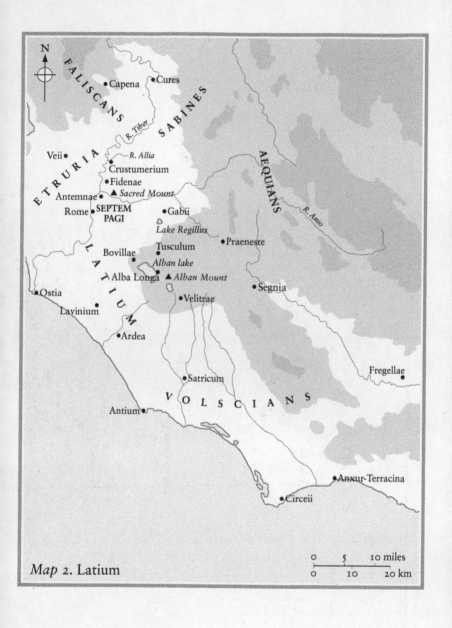

N

FALISCANS

• Capena   • Cures

SABINES

R. Tiber

ETRURIA

Veii •   R. Allia

• Crustumerium

• Fidenae

Antemnae •   ▲ Sacred Mount

AEQUIANS

Rome •   SEPTEM
PAGI

• Gabii

R. Anio

Lake Regillus

LATIUM   Tusculum •   • Praeneste

Bovillae •

Alban lake

Alba Longa   ▲ Alban Mount

• Ostia   • Segnia

Lavinium   • Velitrae

• Ardea

Fregellae •

• Satricum

VOLSCIANS

Antium •

• Anxur-Terracina

• Circeii

0   5   10 miles

Map 2. Latium   0   10   20 km

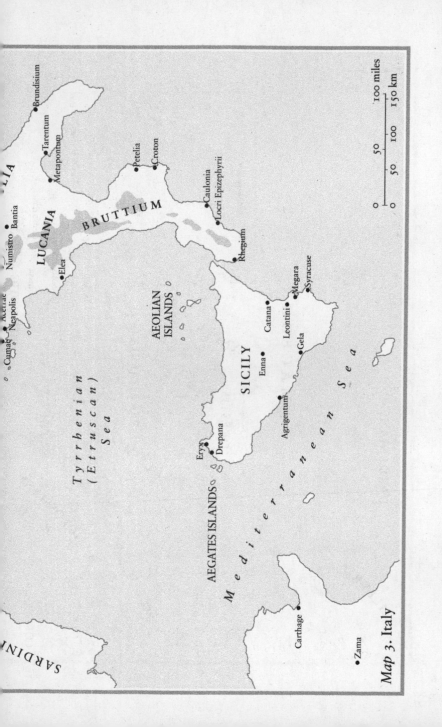

Map 3. Italy

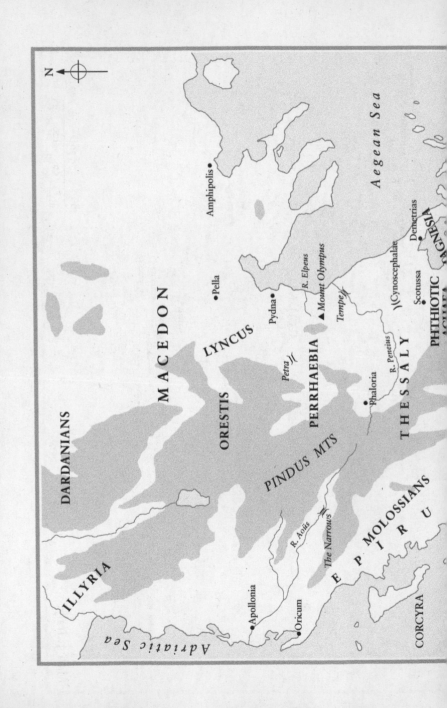

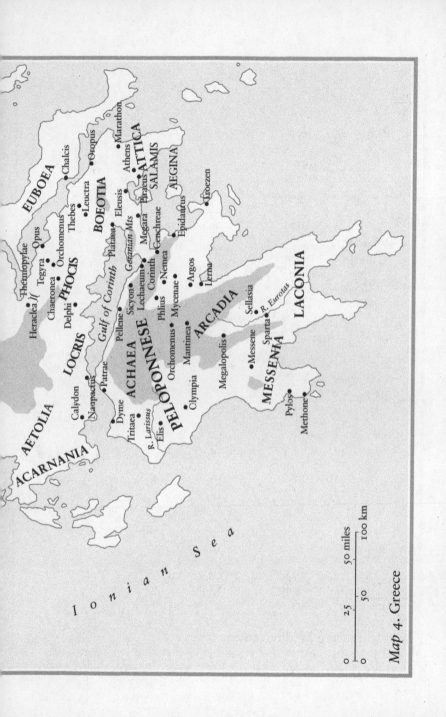

EUBOEA

Thermopylae
Heraclea
Opus
Tegyra
Chaeronea
Orchomenus
Delphi
PHOCIS
LOCRIS

Chalcis

Leuctra
Thebes
BOEOTIA

Oropus
Marathon
Athens
Piraeus
ATTICA
SALAMIS
AEGINA
Troezen

Plataea
Eleusis
Gerantian Mts
Megara
Cenchreae
Epidaurus

Gulf of Corinth
Sicyon
Lechaeum
Corinth
Pellene
Phlius
Nemea
Mycenae
Orchomenus
Mantinea
ARCADIA
Argos
Lerna

Patrae
ACHAEA
PELOPONNESE
Megalopolis
Sellasia
R. Eurotas
LACONIA

Calydon
Naupactus

AETOLIA

Dyme
Tritaea
R. Larissus
Elis
Olympia
Messene
MESSENIA
Sparta

ACARNANIA

Pylos
Methone

Ionian Sea

0   25   50 miles
0   50   100 km

Map 4. Greece

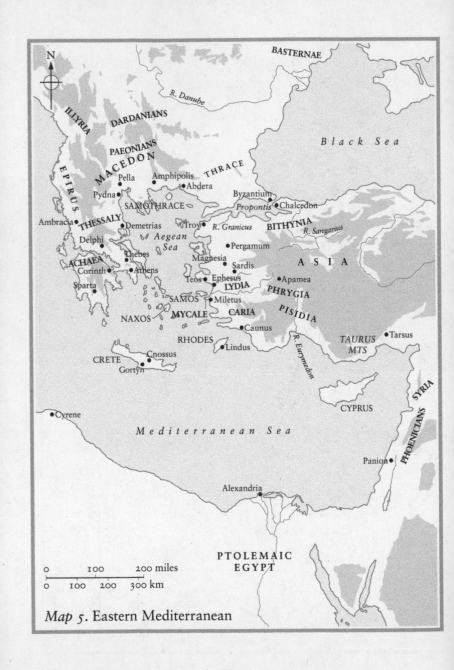

Map 5. Eastern Mediterranean

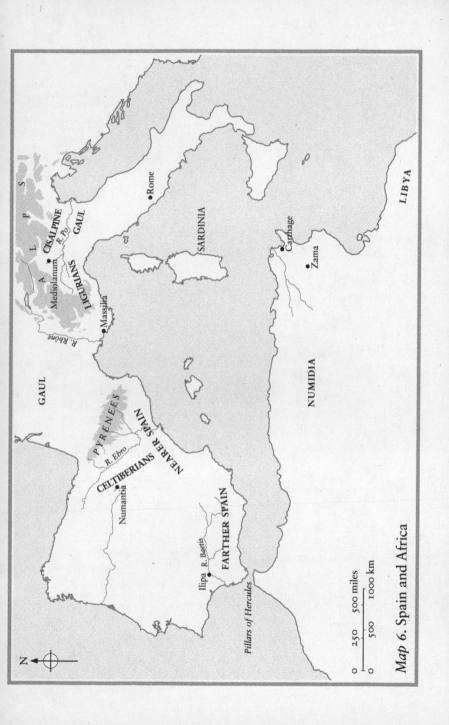

Map 6. Spain and Africa

Notes

All dates are BC unless stated otherwise. Dates expressed in the form 194/3 refer to the single administrative year favoured by the Greeks.

ROMULUS

Further Reading

There is no English commentary on the *Life of Romulus*. In Italian there is M. Bettalli and G. Vanotti (eds.), *Plutarco, Vite Parallele: Teseo e Romolo* (2003). Important interpretative contributions include: D. H. J. Larmour, 'Plutarch's Compositional Methods in the *Theseus and Romulus*', *TAPhA* 118 (1988), pp. 361–75, and Pelling, *P&H*, pp. 171–95. T. P. Wiseman, *Remus: A Roman Myth* (1995), provides a fascinating look at the complexity of the stories of Rome's origins, in both Greek and Roman writers, and the importance of kings to the Romans' conception of their own history is well discussed by C. Smith, 'Thinking about kings', *Bulletin of the Institute for Classical Studies* 54 (2011), pp. 21–42. M. Fox, *Roman Historical Myths: The Regal Period in Augustan Literature* (1996), is a useful discussion of how and to what purposes Livy and Dionysius deploy stories about early Rome.

A good introduction to the problems of the historiography of early Rome is Forsythe, *Early Rome*, pp. 59–77; see also General Introduction V. A more optimistic view of the reliability of early Roman traditions is maintained by Cornell, *Beginnings of Rome*, pp. 1–25, and S. P. Oakley, *A Commentary on Livy, Books 6–10*, vol. 1 (1997), pp. 21–108. A. Carandini, *Rome: Day One* (2011), is an attempt by an eminent archaeologist to validate the literary sources for early Rome by way of a tendentious interpretation of the city's material remains. In this Life, as well as in other Lives of early Romans (especially *Numa* and *Publicola*), Plutarch exhibits a strong interest in the historical topography of early Rome. This a subject that continues to generate controversy and, for scholarly appraisals of what we can know about Rome's topography and its history, the best resource is E. M. Steinby (ed.), *Lexicon Topographicum Urbis Romae*, 6 vols. (1993–2000).

Notes to the Introduction to Romulus

1. On the historical difficulties of early Rome, see General Introduction V (with further reading cited there).
2. On Caesar and Romulus, see S. Weinstock, *Divus Julius* (1971); on Augustus and Romulus, see K. Galinsky, *Augustan Culture* (1996), especially pp. 204–7.
3. Or so argues E. W. Haley, *Latomus* 64 (2005), pp. 969–80.
4. See C. Pelling, *Plutarch: Caesar* (2011), pp. 34–5.
5. See the discussion by Pelling, *P&H*, pp. 171–95.
6. Self-control (*sophrosyne*) was widely admired in Greek thought and is especially valued by Plutarch; see Duff, *Plutarch's Lives*, pp. 77–8. Plutarch also esteems military leaders who prefer to rely on their intelligence more than on their martial passions, a theme that emerges in nearly every Life in this volume: Camillus, for instance, as well as Aratus and Aemilius Paullus are characterized by their superior reasoning (Romulus' intelligence is stressed at ch. 6).
7. See Duff, *Plutarch's Lives*, pp. 89–94.
8. See General Introduction V.
9. On Fabius Pictor, see General Introduction. Wiseman, *Remus: A Roman Myth*, pp. 57–61, includes interesting speculations on Promathion's identity.
10. *HRR*, vol. 1, pp. cccv and 238.

Notes to the Life of Romulus

1. *Pelasgians ... Rome*: The Pelasgians were a mythical people, mentioned already in Homer (*Iliad* 2.840, 17.301) and deemed by Herodotus (1.57) to be a primordial Greek population. The Greek word *rhomē* means might, and this was also the Greek name for the city of Rome – hence this theory of Pelasgian origin.
2. *greet ... with kisses*: Plutarch also discusses this practice at *Moralia* 243f and 265b–e (where he cites Aristotle as his source).

3. *Italus and Leucaria*: Italus (the eponym for Italy) was a mythological king of the Oenotrians; Leucaria was the daughter of Latinus (Dion. Hal. 1.72.6).

4. *Rhomus . . . Diomedes*: See Dion. Hal. 1.72.6.

5. *Romis, a tyrant of the Latins*: Mentioned only here.

6. *Etruscans . . . Lydia to Italy*: According to Herodotus (1.94), the Etruscans came to Italy from Lydia. By contrast, Dion. Hal. (1.25–30) believed they were Italian natives, which appears more likely.

7. *Phorbas*: A Trojan mentioned at *Iliad* 14.490.

8. *Trojan woman I mentioned earlier*: Plutarch refers to Dexithea.

9. *Latinus, son of Telemachus*: In Hesiod (*Theogony* 1011–16), Latinus (eponym of the Latins) is the son of Circe and Odysseus, and king of the Etruscans.

10. *Aemilia . . . bore Romulus to Mars*: Many distinguished families in Rome, like the Aemilii or Julii, fabricated legendary genealogies for themselves.

11. *Lavinia*: Either the Delian-born wife of Aeneas (Dion. Hal. 1.59.3) or the daughter of Latinus, who also became Aeneas' wife.

12. *Tarchetius . . . Alba Longa*: Tarchetius is mentioned only here. But Alba Longa is routinely the city from whom Romulus and Remus derive, although in reality Alba Longa's antiquity was exaggerated by the Romans: see A. Grandazzi, *Alba Longa: histoire d'une legende* (2008).

13. *Tethys*: Daughter of Earth and Heaven, sister and consort of Ocean and by him the mother of all rivers and the Oceanids.

14. *Vesta*: The Roman goddess of the hearth.

15. *Promathion*: Not otherwise known, but see Introduction note 9.

16. *Diocles of Peparethus*: Greek historian of the third century BC (*FGrH* 840). Peparethus is the modern Skopelos Island.

17. *Fabius Pictor . . . follows*: See General Introduction V.

18. *Cermalus . . . brother*: The Cermalus was the western side of the Palatine Hill. Its derivation from *germanus* is found in Varro, *On the Latin Language* 5.54, probably Plutarch's source here.

19. *wild fig tree . . . libations of milk*: Traces of the Ruminal fig remained on the Palatine at the beginning of the imperial period (Livy 1.4, Ovid, *Fasti* 2.411), but there was also a tradition that this tree was removed to the Comitium by the augur Attus Navius (Pliny, *Natural History* 15.20.77; Tacitus, *Annals* 13.58). Rumina and her milky sacrifices are discussed by Varro, *On Agriculture* 2.11.5.

20. *Acca Larentia . . . Larentalia*: Acca Larentia is an elusive figure, for whom there remain two distinct mythical accounts (both recounted here by Plutarch). Her festival was celebrated in December. The ritual libation in April is mentioned only here and again at *Moralia* 272e–f.

21. *Velabrum*: Originally a marshy area between the Palatine, the Capitol and the Tiber, it eventually became a busy commercial district of the city. Varro, *On the Latin Language* 5.43, speculates on its etymology. Modern scholars favour its derivation from an Etruscan word for swamp, *vel*.

22. *Gabii*: A Latin city, approximately 12 miles (19 km) east of Rome. The twins' education at Gabii – in Greek – was an established part of the tradition well before Plutarch's day (see Dion. Hal. 1.84.5), but it is not in Livy.

23. *the Romans' seizure of the Sabine women*: The Rape of the Sabine Women is narrated in chs. 14–15.

24. *a sanctuary . . . Pythian*: The provision of an asylum under the protection of Apollo was a Greek institution. Rome had an asylum somewhere on the Capitoline, but only Plutarch mentions a god named Asylum or an oracle of Apollo ('the Pythian' refers to Apollo's oracle at Delphi) in association with the Roman asylum; see E. Dench, *Romulus' Asylum* (2005), pp. 2–5 and 20–25. Dion. Hal. (1.89 and 2.15.3–4) insists that Romans were not originally a mob of riff-raff and that Rome's asylum was open only to freeborn men fleeing injustice.

25. *site . . . in that place*: The exact site of Roma Quadrata, located somewhere on the Palatine, remains uncertain.

26. *Remorium . . . now called Rignarium*: Also Remus' burial place (ch. 11), though originally these were believed to be distinct places. Their identification and their location on the Aventine were well established by Cicero's day (Cicero, *On his Home* 136).

27. *Herodorus Ponticus*: Herodorus, from Heracleia on Pontus, was a mythographer who flourished around 400 (*FGrH* 31).

28. *'how could a bird . . . be pure?'*: Aeschylus, *Suppliant Women* 226.

29. *vultures . . . divine agency*: Plutarch revisits vultures at *Moralia* 286a–c.

30. *Quintus Metellus . . . Celer*: Plutarch refers to Quintus Caecilius Metellus Celer, tribune of the people in 90 BC. The Latin word *celer* simply means *fast* and has nothing to do with the figure of Celer who appears in some versions of the story of Romulus and Remus. See also ch. 26.

31. *the Remoria*: The same place as the Remorium mentioned in ch. 9.

32. *the Comitium*: Located between the senate-house and the Roman Forum, it was the earliest place of public assembly in Rome and throughout the republic remained an important site for public speaking and popular assemblies. But in this Life Romulus constructs his city on the Palatine (ch. 9), which suggests that Plutarch or his sources have confounded or conflated varying traditions.

33. *mundus*: Its location remains unknown. It was a vaulted pit that somehow connected Rome with the gods of the underworld (it was the object even of ancient antiquarian speculation). It is not clear if Plutarch has the same Mundus in mind here. The ritual Plutarch describes is a foundation ritual paralleled elsewhere, but without reference to the Mundus.

34. *pomerium ... city wall*: That is, *pomerium* derives from a contraction of *post murum*. This (false) etymology was commonly cited: see Varro, *On the Latin Language* 5.143; Livy 1.44.4–5.

35. *city gate ... unclean*: Plutarch attributes this information to Varro at *Moralia* 271a–b.

36. *eleventh day before the Calends of May*: This is 21 April.

37. *Parilia*: An agricultural festival, involving sacrifice, in honour of the mysterious divinity Pales. It is described in detail by Ovid at *Fasti* 4.721–82.

38. *thirtieth day of the month*: Plutarch refers to the last day of the lunar month (whatever day that happened to be in any Greek or in the Roman calendar).

39. *Antimachus*: Nothing further is known of him (he is also mentioned by Clement of Alexandria at *Miscellanies* 6.2.12).

40. *third year of the sixth Olympiad*: This is 753, which became the traditional foundation date. It was advanced by Varro, who relied on chronological research by Castor of Rhodes; see D. Feeney, *Caesar's Calendar: Ancient Times and the Beginnings of History* (2007), pp. 63–5.

41. *Varro the philosopher*: See Introduction.

42. *Tarutius*: Lucius Tarutius Firmanus, also a friend of Cicero (see Cicero, *On Divination* 2.47).

43. *twenty-third day ... of Choeac*: 24 June (772).

44. *twenty-third day ... of Thoth*: 24 March (771). By this calculation, Romulus was only eighteen when he founded Rome.

45. *ninth day ... of Pharmuthi*: 4 October.

46. *first act*: In the account given by Dion. Hal. (2.3), Romulus' first act is to ask the people to choose their new city's constitution.

47. *select . . . legion*: The Latin word for *select* is *legere*.

48. *patricians*: The Latin word for *father* is *pater*. The origin of the patrician order remains controversial: see C. J. Smith, *The Roman Clan* (2006), pp. 251–80.

49. *senate . . . elders*: The Latin word *senex* was used of men in their forties or older, senior figures in the demographic circumstances of antiquity. The Roman senate (*senatus*), while not restricted to men of this age, was nonetheless dominated by its most senior members.

50. *Evander*: An Arcadian hero, usually described as a son of Hermes, who eventually settled on the Palatine (long before the actual founding of Rome); see ch. 21.

51. *patronage . . . Patron*: *Patrocinium* denominates the relationship between a patron (*patronus*) and his client (*cliens*), which Plutarch describes below.

52. *conscript fathers*: The Latin expression Plutarch has in mind is *patres conscripti*. See also *Moralia* 278d.

53. *discussion of these matters*: The patron-client relationship is also described at length by Dion. Hal. (2.8–10).

54. *undertook this exploit in the following way*: In both Livy (1.9.1–6) and Dion. Hal. (2.30.1–2), the Rape of the Sabine Women is preceded by earnest diplomacy through which Romulus strives to gain the right of intermarriage with neighbouring cities.

55. *Consus*: The name probably derives from *condere* (meaning *to store away*) and Consus was a god of the granary. The festival of Consus, the Consualia, was celebrated on 21 August and 15 December. Plutarch refers below to the August celebration.

56. *god of horses*: The Greek divinity Poseidon was god both of the sea and of horses, for which reason he was often called *Poseidon Hippios* (Poseidon the god of horses). The Roman Neptune, by contrast, was not originally associated with horses. Horse races were a spectacular part of the Consualia, which prompted this Greek interpretation of Consus (hence, at Livy 1.9.6, *Neptunus Equester*, or Neptune the god of horses). Plutarch suggests this identification again at *Moralia* 276c. Dion. Hal. (2.31.2) associates Consus with Poseidon the Earth Shaker (in Greek religion Poseidon was responsible for earthquakes).

57. *curiae . . . named after them*: A *curia* was an early Roman neighbourhood. There were thirty *curiae*. Plutarch mentions this

claim again in ch. 20. On the origins of the *curiae*, see Smith, *The Roman Clan*, pp. 184–234.

58. *Valerius Antias . . . virgins*: On Valerius Antias and Juba, see Introduction. Plutarch revisits the number of Sabine women seized at *Comparison Theseus–Romulus* 6.

59. *Hostilius*: Hostus Hostilius was the grandfather of Tullus Hostilius, Rome's third king; see ch. 18. At Livy 1.12.2–3 he falls fighting bravely in the subsequent conflict with the Sabines.

60. *given to Romulus himself*: So Livy 1.11.2 – and Plutarch at *Comparison Theseus–Romulus* 6.

61. *Aollius . . . Avillius . . . Zenodotus*: Zenodotus (incorrectly) derived the Roman name Avillius from the Greek word *aollēs*, which means *in crowds*. Little is known of this Zenodotus, who may have lived in the second century BC. This is the only source that attributes children to Romulus.

62. *talasius . . . hymenaeus*: Romans shouted *talasio* at weddings but did not know why. Explanations proliferated (see e.g. Livy 1.9.12). Plutarch revisits the question at *Moralia* 271f, where he repeats this story. Romans also shouted *hymen hymenaee*.

63. *Sextius Sulla of Carthage*: A friend of Plutarch who is mentioned several times in his writings. When visiting Rome, Plutarch had been a guest in his home (*Moralia* 727b). See Jones *P&R*, p. 60.

64. *the cry is an exhortation . . . talasia*: The same view is expressed at *Numa* 8.

65. *it remains the custom . . . Roman Questions*: See *Moralia* 271d (lifting the bride), *Moralia* 284f (a wife's domestic duties) and *Moralia* 285b–d (the head of a spear). On *Roman Questions*, see General Introduction I.

66. *eighteenth day of the month . . . celebrated*: This is an error: the Consualia was celebrated on 21 August (see above, note 55).

67. *unwalled villages . . . fearless*: Lacedaemonian is another expression for Spartan, and the city of Sparta, during the classical period, did not have city walls. On the (false) tradition that the Sabines descended from Spartan colonists, see Dion. Hal. 2.49.4–5. Plutarch offers a different explanation for the Sabines' fondness for Spartan customs at *Numa* 1.

68. *Caenina*: A Latin, not a Sabine, city. Its location is uncertain and by Plutarch's day it no longer existed (Pliny, *Natural History* 3.68).

69. *Acron . . . punished*: Livy (1.10) offers very different motives for the belligerence of all the Sabines in their conflicts with Rome at this time.

70. *Rome always annexes ... the peoples whom she conquers*: A similar sentiment is offered (at greater length) at Dion. Hal. 2.16–17.

71. *trophy*: It was a Greek practice to dedicate a trophy (*tropaeon*), a suit of the enemy's armour set up on a stake, on the field of battle after a victory. Apart from the very rare ritual of *spolia opima* ('the first and finest of spoils'), trophies in Rome were mostly confined to triumphal art.

72. *a special garment*: Cf. the regal and much resented garment worn by Romulus at ch. 26.

73. *Roman triumphs*: On the triumph and on *spolia opima*, see Beard, *Roman Triumph*, especially pp. 72–4 (on Romulus' triumph), and Introduction to *Marcellus*.

74. *Jupiter Feretrius*: The temple of Jupiter Feretrius was located on the Capitoline. Plutarch offers further etymologies for Jupiter's epithet at *Marcellus* 8.

75. *Cossus*: Aulus Cornelius Cossus was probably consul in 428. He slew Lars Tolumnius, king of Veii (Livy 4.19).

76. *Marcellus ... vanquished Britomartus*: In 222 (*Marcellus* 6–8).

77. *Romulus employed a chariot*: See Dion. Hal. 2.34.2.

78. *Tarquinius*: Tarquinius Priscus, son of the Corinthian Demaratus, was the fifth king of Rome.

79. *triumph in a chariot*: Plutarch accepts this opinion at *Publicola* 9.

80. *Fidenae ... Antemnae*: Each was a Latin city and none was destroyed so early in Roman history as Plutarch here indicates (though only Antemnae existed into the first century BC). Fidenae is modern Castel Giubileo (on which see ch. 23), Crustumerium was located at modern Marcigliana Vecchia, and Antemnae was where the River Anio flows into the Tiber.

81. *Tatius*: This is Titus Tatius, who will share the Roman throne with Romulus.

82. *Antigonus*: It is not obvious which Antigonus Plutarch has in mind here. Antigonus Monophthalmus (382–301) and Antigonus Gonatas (277–239) are perhaps the likeliest candidates.

83. *Rhoemetalces*: A Thracian prince who in 31 BC betrayed Antony to support Octavian (the Caesar in this sentence); he was elevated to the Thracian throne in 22 BC.

84. *Galba*: The historian Gaius Sulpicius Galba (*HRR* 2.41) lived during the first century BC and was the grandfather of the emperor Galba.

85. *Antigonus*: Possibly Antigonus of Carystus, a writer and sculptor who flourished in the mid-second century BC. A collection of

anecdotes by him survives, but he was best known for his biographies of philosophers and for works on sculpture and painting.

86. *Simylus*: Not otherwise known.

87. *Celtic chief*: Plutarch uses the terms Gaul and Celt interchangeably (Introduction to *Camillus*).

88. *King Tarquinius*: The construction of the temple of Jupiter on the Capitoline was begun by Tarquinius Priscus and completed by Tarquinius Superbus (*Publicola* 14).

89. *Tarpeian Rock . . . evildoers*: This practice was discontinued in AD 43. Ancient sources disagree over the exact location of the Tarpeian Rock but it was probably on the southwest side of the Capitoline.

90. *Lake of Curtius*: The *lacus Curtius* (Plutarch here calls it by its Latin name) was a monument in the Roman Forum. There were several explanations of its origins, all of them fabulous (see Livy 1.12 and Dion. Hal. 2.42.2 for different versions of this tale).

91. *Hostilius . . . Numa*: See ch. 14.

92. *temple of Jupiter Stator*: Located at the foot of the Palatine near the Porta Mugonia.

93. *Regia . . . temple of Vesta*: The Regia was a small building, just outside the Roman Forum and near the temple of Vesta. The construction of each was attributed to King Numa (*Numa* 11 and 14).

94. *service . . . spinning wool*: See ch. 15.

95. *Quirites . . . Tatius*: Cures was Titus Tatius' native city and the birthplace of King Numa (*Numa* 3). It was located at modern Fosso Corese. The etymology of *Quirites* remains uncertain, though most scholars associate the word with *curiae* (note 57), seeing in the original Quirites the members of the *curiae*.

96. *Comitium*: See note 32. Plutarch found this etymology in Varro, *On the Latin Language* 5.155.

97. *a hundred . . . patricians*: According to Dion. Hal. (2.47.1–2), only fifty Sabines were added to the Roman senate, and at *Numa* 2 Plutarch states that, at the time of Romulus' death, there were 150 senators.

98. *three tribes . . . lucus*: Explanations of the three original tribes and their names proliferated in antiquity: see Cornell, *Beginnings of Rome*, pp. 114–18, and Smith, *The Roman Clan*, pp. 188–90.

99. *tribes*: The Latin word for tribe, *tribus*, derives from the same root as *tres*, the word for *three*; see Varro, *On the Latin Language* 5.55.

100. *phratries*: Here Plutarch uses the Greek word *phratry* – which refers to subdivisions of Greek tribes – to refer to the *curiae* (ch. 14 and note 57).

101. *courts that try homicide*: Standing courts were established in Rome only in the mid-second century BC, nor was there a single court assigned to deal with cases of homicide; see J. Harries, *Law and Crime in the Roman World* (2007).

102. *bulla*: An apotropaic amulet worn by boys; Plutarch has more to say about the bulla at *Moralia* 287f–288b.

103. *temple of Moneta*: The temple of Juno Moneta was on the Capitol (*Camillus* 36).

104. *made his beside the Steps of Cacus*: On the Palatine, at the top of the Steps of Cacus, was the Hut of Romulus (*Casa Romuli*); the bottom of the Steps are not preserved but they emerged into the Forum Boarium (Rome's earliest forum). Cacus was commonly portrayed as a monster slain by Hercules.

105. *Gaius Caesar*: The emperor Caligula (AD 12–41).

106. *Roman calendar . . . Life of Numa*: See *Numa* 9.

107. *Matronalia*: One of Rome's most popular festivals, it was celebrated on 1 March (*matrona* is the Latin word for a married woman).

108. *Carmentalia*: An ancient festival celebrated on 11 and 15 January. Even in antiquity there was considerable speculation about the origins of the festival and the identity of the deity honoured by it. The temple of Carmenta was located at the base of the Capitoline Hill near the Porta Carmentalis (*Moralia* 278b–c).

109. *Evander the Arcadian*: See ch. 13.

110. *carmina*: The Latin word *carmen* also refers to hymns and magical spells. It is linguistically cognate with the name Carmenta.

111. *Nicostrate*: Sometimes named as the wife, sometimes as the mother, of Evander.

112. *the Parilia*: In ch. 12.

113. *Lupercalia . . . purification*: The Lupercalia was celebrated on 15 February. *Februarius*, the Latin name for February, derived from *februa*, which referred to purification rituals. The origins and significance of the Lupercalia were debated in antiquity. See *Numa* 19 and *Moralia* 280b–c.

114. *Lycaea*: Livy (1.5.1), among others, (erroneously) linked the Lupercalia to the festival of Zeus Lycaeus (the Zeus of Mt Lycaea in Arcadia), itself associated with wolves (*lykos* is the Greek word for wolf).

115. *legendary she-wolf*: See ch. 4.
116. *Luperci*: The priests who celebrate the festival through the ritual actions Plutarch describes here.
117. *poems ... origins of Roman customs*: This is Boutas, fr. 234 in H. Lloyd Jones and P. Parsons, *Supplementum Hellenisticum* (1983). This Boutas is (for no good reason) sometimes identified with the freedman Boutas mentioned at *Younger Cato* 70.
118. *Gaius Acilius*: A senator who composed a history of Rome, in Greek, from its origins to his own day, which appeared around 142. He is also found in *Elder Cato* 22.
119. *Faunus*: A rustic divinity, one of whose roles was protector of flocks.
120. *puppies*: The Greek word for puppy is *skylax*. Plutarch also discusses puppy sacrifices in Rome at *Moralia* 280b–c.
121. *Vestals*: The six Vestal Virgins observed the rites of Vesta, the goddess of the hearth, who was essential to Rome's security; tending Vesta's fire, which was meant never to be extinguished, was the most conspicuous of their ritual tasks. At *Numa* 9 and *Camillus* 20 their introduction is attributed to Numa. In ch. 3 (above) Plutarch explains that, in Alba, the priestess of Vesta was expected to remain a virgin.
122. *divination from ... birds*: Plutarch refers to the Roman practice of augury (ch. 9), a crucial element in Roman religion and in the Roman constitution: see Lintott, *Constitution*, pp. 185–6, and *Moralia* 286a–c.
123. *This staff ... destroyed*: See *Camillus* 32.
124. *legislation ... parricide*: Festus (247) preserves an alleged law of Numa which stipulated that 'if someone knowingly and with malicious intention kills a free man, let him be a parricide'.
125. *after the war with Hannibal*: The Second Punic War ended in 201.
126. *Lucius Hostius*: Not mentioned elsewhere.
127. *Laurentum*: There was certainly a people known as Laurentes (e.g. Polybius 3.22.11) but there was no city of Laurentum. The Laurentes are routinely regarded as inhabitants of the town of Lavinium (modern Pratica di Mare).
128. *Armilustrium*: An open square on the Aventine where the festival called Armilustrium, marking the end of the campaigning season for the army, was celebrated on 19 October. Varro (*On the Latin Language* 6.22) and Festus (496) designate the Lauretum (or Loretum), also on the Aventine, Titus Tatius' burial place.

129. *Fidenae . . . near Rome*: See ch. 17.

130. *Ides of April*: This is 13 April. Different accounts of this campaign are provided by Livy 1.14 and Dion. Hal. 2.53.

131. *Ferentine Gate*: Rome had no Ferentine Gate. A neat and long-standing emendation proposes that an original *hylē (forest)* was corrupted into *pylē (gate)* and that Plutarch refers here to Silva Ferentina (the Ferentine forest) at the base of Mt Alba.

132. *Camerians*: People of Cameria (or Camerium), the location of which is unknown.

133. *temple of Vulcan*: The Vulcanal was located on the lower slopes of the Capitoline Hill overlooking the Roman Forum. According to Dion. Hal. (2.54.1–2), Romulus celebrated a triumph after this victory.

134. *Veii*: Modern Isola Farnese; see Introduction to *Camillus*.

135. *Aristomenes*: A Messenian hero of legendary proportions, usually assigned to the Second Messenian War against Sparta during the seventh century BC. See *Moralia* 159e and 660f, and Pausanias 4.19.2–3. In sacrificing each hecatomb Aristomenes signalled that he had slain a hundred Spartans (a hecatomb is the sacrifice of one hundred cattle).

136. *the Seven Districts*: A region located along the western bank of the Tiber.

137. *Ides of October*: 15 October. According to Dion. Hal. (2.55.3), this was Romulus' third triumph.

138. *Veientes*: The people of Veii.

139. *Sardis . . . Etruscan city*: Sardis was the capital of Lydia, and according to one ancient account of the Etruscans, they originated in Lydia (Herodotus 1.94). A similar account of this custom, linked to the Capitoline Games, appears at *Moralia* 277c–d. There was, however, a Roman proverb, 'Sardinians for sale, each worse than the other!', associated with the victories in Sardinia (*Sardi* is Latin for Sardinians) of Tiberius Sempronius Gracchus (consul 177): Plutarch's aetiology here may involve confusion with that saying. Still, Festus (428) preserves an antiquarian explanation of the practice at the Capitoline Games that is very similar to Plutarch's.

140. *apparel . . . purple*: At Livy 1.8 Romulus puts on majestic trappings in order to overawe the public and instil obedience to the laws.

141. *Celeres*: See ch. 10 and *Numa* 7. According to Dion. Hal. (2.13), the Celeres were established very early in Romulus' reign (and there is no suggestion that this action was offensive).

142. *Latin ... lictores*: Plutarch repeats this etymology at *Moralia* 280a–b; see also Gellius 12.3 and Festus 103.

143. *bacila*: Actually in Latin they are *bacula*.

144. *rods*: Plutarch here uses the word *rhabdos* for a *staff*, which was lighter than a *rod*, for which he uses the word *baktēria*, itself cognate with Latin *baculum* – all intended to explain the perhaps unexpected name for a lictor's staff.

145. *plausible explanation ... laos*: See also *Moralia* 280b. In Plutarch's day, the word *leitourgos* was pronounced *litourgos* and *leïton* was pronounced *liton*, so this (misleading) resemblance with *litor* was obvious enough.

146. *suspicion ... over the patricians*: Romulus' (alleged) assassination is often, as here, modelled on accounts of Caesar's assassination, which was motivated by senatorial indignation (see also Dion. Hal. 2.56.5, Valerius Maximus 5.3.1). Plutarch also describes the end of Romulus at *Numa* 2.

147. *Nones of July*: 7 July.

148. *Quintilis, as it was called then*: Until 153 the Roman year began in March and therefore *Quintilis* (meaning *fifth*) was the fifth month of the year. After Caesar's death, the month was re-named *Julius* (i.e. July) in his honour.

149. *ceremonies ... took place then*: See ch. 29; these festivals are the Flight of the People (*Poplifugia*) and the Capratine Nones (*Nonae Capratinae*), though in fact the former was celebrated on 5 July and not on 7 July (Plutarch conflates them here as well as at *Numa* 2 and *Camillus* 33).

150. *Scipio Africanus*: This is Scipio Aemilianus, the son of Aemilius Paullus whose Life is included in this volume (see Introduction to that Life). His death, in 129, remained controversial along the very lines put forth here by Plutarch.

151. *temple of Vulcan*: The Vulcanal (note 133).

152. *Goat's Marsh*: (*Caprae Palus*) In the Campus Martius, near the site of the Pantheon.

153. *Proculus ... forum*: More commonly, Julius Proculus is simply a farmer from Alba who happens to journey to Rome for the day (Cicero, *The Republic* 2.20; Dion. Hal. 2.63.3; Ovid, *Fasti* 2.499), but in this version (see also *Numa* 2) he is a representative of the patrician Julii, the ancestors of Caesar. In most accounts, however, the patrician Julii came to Rome from Alba during the reign of Tullius Hostilius (Livy 1.30.2).

154. *tell the Romans ... human power*: Plutarch's Romulus urges the Romans to practise self-restraint (*sophrosyne*), a key Greek

virtue. Similarly, at Dion. Hal. 2.18.1 it is stressed that Romulus strove to exhibit *sophrosyne* and in his account moderation was a hallmark of the reign (Dion. Hal. 2.53.3, 44.3 and 60.2). By contrast, Livy's Romulus tells Proculus simply to 'let the Romans cultivate the art of war' (1.15.7).

155. *Quirinus*: The origins of this god, who in his functions resembled Mars, remain vague. His presence in Rome was ancient, and his name is clearly associated with the collective designation Quirites (note 95) as well as with the Quirinal Hill (ch. 29). He was eventually (as here) assimilated to the deified Romulus.

156. *Aristaeus*: A legendary poet and wonder-worker from Proconnesus (the modern Turkish island of Marmara); his apparent death and several resurrections are rehearsed by Herodotus (4.13–14).

157. *Cleomedes*: An Olympic boxer who, after killing his opponent during a match, was denied the prize on account of his foul play; he then destroyed a school, killing many children, and took refuge in a temple of Athena, where he vanished (as Plutarch reports here). He was honoured as a hero by the Astypalaeans. See the more detailed account of Pausanias (6.9.6–8).

158. *oracle at Delphi*: Plutarch does not report the second line of the oracle, which was: 'Honour him with sacrifices, for he is no longer mortal.'

159. *Alcmene*: The mother of Heracles. In some versions of her story, after her death she is whisked to the Isle of the Dead to be the wife of Rhadamanthys, while a stone is substituted for her corpse. A stone said to be this very one was venerated in a shrine in Thebes according to Pherecydes (*FGrH* 3 F 84).

160. *'The body . . . from the gods'*: A fragment of a lost threnody (fr. 132 in W. H. Race, *Pindar*, vol. 2 (1997)), also quoted (at greater length and with slight variation) at *Moralia* 120c.

161. *'a dry soul is best'*: An excerpt from Heracleitus (fr. 118 DK), itself frequently and variously cited by ancient authors. C. H. Kahn, *The Art and Thought of Heraclitus* (1979), pp. 245–54, provides a full account of its context and philosophical significance.

162. *Enyalius*: Meaning *Warlike*, either an epithet of Ares or indicating a distinct Greek god of war. According to Dion. Hal. (2.50.3), Tatius established the worship of Enyalius at Rome. By the third century BC, Quirinus was identified with Enyalius (Polybius 3.25.6, cf. Dion. Hal. 2.48).

163. *curis*: The Sabine word for a spearhead. The derivation of Quirinus from *curis* originated with Varro (Dion. Hal. 2.48).

164. *Juno Curitis*: Her temple was in the Campus Martius. Her origins were perhaps Sabine (Festus 55).

165. *Regia . . . Mars*: On the Regia, see note 93. Within was a shrine to Mars that contained the Spear of Mars (*Hasta Martis*).

166. *Quirinalis*: The Romans believed, probably correctly, that there had been a temple to Quirinus on the Quirinal since very ancient times (Cicero, *The Republic* 2.20; *On the Laws* 1.3; Livy 4.21.9; Pliny, *Natural History* 15.120), but the earliest recorded temple was dedicated by the consul Lucius Papirius Cursor in 293 (Livy 10.46.7) and later rebuilt by Augustus into one of the largest temples in Rome.

167. *Flight of the People*: On 5 July the Flight of the People (*Poplifugia*) commemorated the day on which Romulus vanished or, by way of a muddle with the Capratine Nones (see below), a victory by the people of Rome over Fidenae in the aftermath of the Gallic sack (in another version preserved at Macrobius, *Saturnalia* 3.2.11, the invaders are Etruscans). The festival seems to have been largely forgotten by the first century BC (Varro, *On the Latin Language* 6.18).

168. *Capratine Nones*: Also called the Festival for Slave Women (*Ancillarum Feriae*), celebrated on 7 July.

169. *captured Rome*: Rome was sacked by the Gauls in 390.

170. *Philotis*: Plutarch recurs, at greater length, to the aetiological tale of Philotis at *Camillus* 33.

171. *commemoration . . . time*: Plutarch reveals his fascination with chronological coincidences of this kind at *Camillus* 19. In that same Life, at ch. 33, he dismisses the story of Philotis as 'fabulous'.

Notes to the Comparison of Theseus and Romulus

1. *Troezen*: A city near Argos (modern Trizina). Here Theseus was reared by his mother, Aethra, and her father, Pittheus, king of Troezen; see Plutarch, *Theseus* 3–6.

2. *'brave on account of his fear'*: Plutarch quotes (imprecisely and presumably from memory) Plato, *Phaedrus* 68d, which describes courage that is uninformed by philosophical reason.

3. *tyrant in Alba*: Plutarch refers to Acron (*Romulus* 16).

4. *Sciron . . . Corynetes*: *Theseus* 8 (Corynetes and Sinis), 10 (Sciron) and 11 (Procrustes); these were bandits slain by the young Theseus on his way from Troezen to Athens.

5. *Theseus . . . to Athens by sea*: As he was urged to do in *Theseus* 6.

6.   *Theseus' clash with the Centaurs and . . . Amazons*: *Theseus*
     26–8 (Amazons) and 30 (Centaurs).

7.   *Theseus' daring . . . cruel masters*: Each of these versions is
     told at *Theseus* 15–16 (Plutarch's account of Theseus' adventure
     in Crete extends to ch. 20). Although Plutarch introduces mul-
     tiple historicizing variations, he includes in his narrative the
     traditional myth: in order to free Athens from its tribute to
     Minos of Crete, Theseus included himself with the youths des-
     tined for sacrifice to the Minotaur, whom he slew; Minos'
     daughter, Ariadne, fell in love with him, and with her assistance
     he was able to find his way out of the labyrinth in which the
     Minotaur was confined. Ariadne left Crete with Theseus, but
     was deserted along the way back to Athens.

8.   *'a labour . . . salvation of the young'*: This was the view of
     Polemon of Athens, who was head of the Academy, 314–270.
     Plutarch cites it again at *Moralia* 780d; see also *Numa* 6.

9.   *worthy of a god's love . . . finest qualities*: In a common ver-
     sion of the story of Ariadne, she became the wife of Dionysus
     after she was deserted by Theseus; at *Theseus* 20 Plutarch
     reviews several accounts of Ariadne, but not this one (he omits
     'the more pleasing of these legends' because they are 'common
     knowledge').

10. *Theseus . . . his son*: Theseus' wife, Phaedra, developed an illicit
     passion for her stepson, Hippolytus, who rejected her advances.
     She then falsely accused Hippolytus to Theseus and took her
     own life, after which Hippolytus was cursed by his father and
     subsequently perished. The story was popular in ancient litera-
     ture, not least in tragedy (it is the subject of Euripides'
     Hippolytus). Plutarch passes over it lightly at *Theseus* 28, refer-
     ring the reader to the tragedians for details.

11. *eliminated . . . the names of . . . heroes*: This negative view of
     Theseus' centralization of Attica corresponds with the hostile
     complaints of the demagogue Menestheus at *Theseus* 32.

12. *He did not slay . . . criminals*: In contrast with Theseus (see above).

13. *death of Remus . . . attributed . . . not to Romulus*: *Romulus* 10.

14. *restored his grandfather . . . to the throne of Aeneas*: Romulus
     and Remus restore Numitor to his throne at *Romulus* 9.

15. *negligence regarding . . . the sail*: Theseus' father, Aegeus, gave
     his son a distinctive sail, which was to be hoisted on the return
     voyage from Crete if Theseus was safe. In the exuberance of the
     return journey, however, Theseus forgot to raise the correct sail
     and this led to his father's death (*Theseus* 17 and 22).

16. *the story . . . his death*: Relating the death of Aegeus at *Theseus* 22, Plutarch does not there mention this variation, which is not recorded elsewhere.

17. *Theseus' abductions . . . wedlock*: *Theseus* 19–20 (Ariadne), 26 (Antiope), 29 (Anaxo – and others) and 31–2 (Helen; Plutarch reports that Theseus was then fifty years old).

18. *Erechtheus . . . Cecrops*: Erechtheus was an early king of Athens (later identified with Poseidon and worshipped on the Acropolis). Cecrops was also an early king of Athens, often depicted as half-man, half-snake. These two were frequently viewed as the ancestors of all Athenians.

19. *carried off . . . 800 women*: *Romulus* 14.

20. *modesty . . . of Roman marriages*: Plutarch's comments on Romulus here may owe something to Dion. Hal. 2.24–6.1, where the king is depicted as a model legislator of marriage.

21. *In the course of . . . divorce his wife*: Plutarch makes the same point at *Comparison Lycurgus–Numa* 3, where he dates this first divorce more specifically to 230 years after the founding of Rome, which, for Plutarch, is 523. Spurius Carvilius, however, was the consul of 234, and so there is something amiss in Plutarch's chronology. Dion. Hal. (2.25.7) and Gellius (4.3) more plausibly date this divorce to 231, Valerius Maximus (2.1.4) to 234.

22. *the two kings*: Romulus and Titus Tatius.

23. *Aphidnae . . . Alexander*: Theseus installed the young Helen in Aphidnae, in Attica, where she was looked after by his mother, Aethra. Helen's brothers, Castor and Pollux, led the Spartans into Attica and after a battle captured Aphidnae, reclaiming their sister (*Theseus* 32–3). Alexander is another name for Paris, whose abduction of Helen led to the Trojan War.

24. *Hecuba*: The wife of Priam and often a central figure in accounts of the suffering of Trojan women enslaved after the fall of their city.

25. *mother of Theseus . . . tales told about Theseus*: At *Theseus* 34 Plutarch cites (without confidence) evidence that Aethra (Theseus' mother) was a slave in Troy. There were also legends that she was rescued, after the fall of Troy, by her grandchildren (Plutarch does not mention these).

26. *the oracle given to Aegeus*: Discussed at *Theseus* 3; in the *Comparison* Plutarch severely misrepresents its significance (the advice of the oracle was designed to ensure that Aegeus' heir was born legitimately and in Athens).

NUMA

Further Reading

There is no commentary on the *Life of Numa* in English. In Italian,
however, there is M. Manfredini and L. Piccirilli (eds.), *Plutarco, Vite
Parallele: Le vite di Licurgo e di Numa* (2nd edn, 1995). Important
for this Life's philosophical implications is L. de Blois and A. E. J.
Bons, 'Platonic Philosophy and Isocratean Virtues in Plutarch's *Numa*',
Ancient Society 23 (1992), pp. 159–88. For an insightful illustration
of how Numa's reputation could be exploited in Roman politics, see
E. Gabba, 'The *collegia* of Numa. Problems of method and political
ideas', *JRS* 74 (1984), pp. 81–6. On the regal period of Roman
history, see Introduction to *Romulus* and General Introduction V.

Notes to the Introduction to Numa

1. *Numa* 8 (see Plato, *Republic* 2.372e) and *Lycurgus* 5 (see Plato,
    Laws 691e).
2. See H. W. Bird, *Classical Journal* 81 (1986), pp. 243–481; and
    H. Brandt, *Museum Helveticum* 45 (1988), pp. 98–110.
3. See A. R. Birley, *Hadrian, the Restless Emperor* (1997), p. 42.
4. See A. Willi, *Museum Helveticum* 55 (1998), pp. 139–72.
5. de Blois and Bons, *Ancient Society* 23, pp. 159–88.
6. On *philanthropia*, see General Introduction III.
7. See H. Liebert, *History of Political Thought* 30 (2009), pp. 251–71;
    B. Boulet in L. de Blois, J. Bons, T. Kessels and D. M. Schenkeveld
    (eds.), *The Statesman in Plutarch's Lives*, vol. 2 (2004), pp.
    245–56.
8. *HRR*, vol. 1, pp. 120–38.

Notes to the Life of Numa

1. *There persists . . . Numa's own time*: On this opening sentence,
    see the discussion by M. H. Crawford, *Faventia* 20/1 (1998), pp.
    37–8.
2. *Clodius*: His identity is uncertain. He was possibly the first-
    century BC historian Quintus Claudius Quadrigarius, who began
    his history of Rome with the Gallic sack, but he is not associated
    with a work of the title specified here by Plutarch. Another pos-
    sibility is Gaius Clodius Licinus, who was suffect consul in AD 4

(*HRR* 2.77) and also a historian. The name Clodius, however, was extremely common.

3. *sacked by the Celts*: On the sack of Rome by the Gauls (or Celts, Plutarch uses these terms interchangeably), traditionally in 390, see Introduction to *Camillus*.

4. *records ... counterfeited ... illustrious houses*: This was a very real phenomenon in the later Roman republic: see T. P. Wiseman, *Roman Studies* (1987), pp. 201–18. Plutarch refers again to this problem at ch. 21.

5. *others ... insist ... Greek education*: This is the insistent view of Livy (1.18.1–4), who argues at length that Pythagoras (see following note) had nothing to do with Numa, nor did Numa receive instruction in foreign studies: his virtue derived from native Sabine discipline.

6. *Pythagoras*: A major philosopher of the sixth century BC. In addition to his lasting influence as a philosopher, he founded a secret, quasi-religious society that persisted into the empire and played a part in giving Neoplatonism its ultimate shape; see W. K. C. Guthrie, *A History of Philosophy*, vol. 1 (1962), pp. 146–319, and W. Burkert, *Lore and Science in Ancient Pythagoreanism* (1972).

7. *Pythagoras ... Numa's reign*: Dion. Hal. (2.58.3) cites this victory of Pythagoras, which took place in 713, in order to fix the year in which Numa was invited to become king of Rome.

8. *Sabines ... from Sparta*: See *Romulus* 16.

9. *Hippias of Elis*: A prominent sophist of the second half of the fifth century BC. He was expert in many subjects, including history, and his list of Olympian victors was influential (*FGrH* 6).

10. *a natural beginning ... life*: Plutarch begins his biography with Numa's ascension to the throne.

11. *Capratine Nones*: 7 July. For the events narrated in this paragraph, see *Romulus* 29 with the notes provided there.

12. *after the death ... selected from their number*: For these events, see *Romulus* 20 and 23.

13. *150 patricians*: At *Romulus* 20, however, Plutarch puts the membership of the combined Roman and Sabine senate at 200.

14. *for six hours each night ... private citizen*: Only Plutarch describes this arrangement. In other accounts, each senator holds office for five consecutive days (e.g. Cicero, *The Republic* 2.23; Livy 1.17.6; Dion. Hal. 2.57 and 62.1–3). On the interregnum, see Lintott, *Constitution*, pp. 28–9.

15. *Cures ... Quirites*: See *Romulus* 19.

16. *He was born ... April*: See *Romulus* 12. Plutarch means that this was Numa's birthday, not that he was born in the same year that Rome was founded. In ch. 2 above and at *Romulus* 29, he states that Romulus died in the thirty-eighth year of his reign, but Numa was forty when he became king (ch. 5).

17. *Tatius ... son-in-law*: Also reported by Zonaras 7.5, but unknown to Livy or Dion. Hal.

18. *Egeria*: A goddess associated with springs and routinely linked in Roman tradition with Numa.

19. *Attis*: The consort of the goddess Cybele.

20. *Rhodoetes*: An alternative name for Odius, a captain of the Bithynian Halizons during the Trojan War (*Iliad* 2.856–7, 5.38–42; see also Arrian *FGrH* 156 F 98). His association with a goddess is not otherwise attested.

21. *Endymion*: The consort of Selene, the moon-goddess. Only Plutarch describes this myth as Arcadian in origin.

22. *Phorbas*: The son variously of Lapithes or Triopas, he relieved the island of Rhodes from a plague of serpents and was consequently honoured as a hero.

23. *Hyacinthus*: A Doric hero beloved of Apollo and accidentally slain by him; from his blood sprang the hyacinth flower.

24. *Admetus*: A Thessalian hero who won Apollo's favour and is the central figure in Euripides' *Alcestis*. Apollo's passion for Admetus is mentioned at Callimachus, *Hymn to Zeus* 2.49.

25. *Hippolytus of Sicyon*: Pausanias (2.6.7) mentions a king of Sicyon named Hippolytus but says nothing about his being a favourite of Apollo.

26. *Cirrha*: A city in central Greece (modern Kirra).

27. *Pythia*: This was the priestess at Delphi who, while in a trance, received the oracle of Apollo, which was then reported to the priests at Delphi, who furnished it in verse form.

28. *Pindar and his poems*: See also *Moralia* 1103a and Pausanias 9.25.3.

29. *Archilochus ... Hesiod*: Both poets received cultic honours after their deaths; see further *Moralia* 162c, 560e and 969e.

30. *Sophocles ... his tomb*: On Sophocles' hospitality to Asclepius, see also *Moralia* 1103b. After his death, Sophocles received heroic honours under the name Dexion (*Etymologicum Magnum* s.v. Dexion).

31. *Zaleucus*: Seventh-century BC legislator from Locri in southern Italy; his historicity was doubted even in antiquity (Timaeus *FGrH* 566 F 130).

32. *Minos*: Legendary king of Crete who, after his death, became a judge in the underworld.

33. *Zoroaster*: The Greek form of Zarathustra, the founder of Zoroastrianism.

34. *'the road is broad'*: Bacchylides fr. 27 in D. A. Campbell, *Greek Lyric*, vol. 4 (1992).

35. *Numa . . . man of forty*: See note 16.

36. *Proculus*: Julius Proculus (ch. 2 and *Romulus* 28).

37. *Velesus*: This is Volusius Valerius, the ancestor of Publicola (*Publicola* 1 with note 3).

38. *Marcius*: Marcus Marcius, the (legendary) progenitor of the Marcian clan. His son married Numa's daughter Pompilia and was thus the father of the king Ancus Marcius (ch. 21).

39. *refusing . . . the kingship he was offered*: Livy's Numa does not resist his appointment as king (1.18.6), whereas Dion. Hal.'s, like Plutarch's, does (2.60.1).

40. *essential duty of a king . . . service to the gods*: This sentiment is repeated at *Moralia* 780d; see also *Comparison Theseus–Romulus* 1 with note 8.

41. *Spurius Vettius*: Mentioned only here.

42. *Tarpeian Hill*: See *Romulus* 18.

43. *the chief of the augurs . . . birds appeared from the right*: Plutarch's account of Numa's inauguration is simpler than Livy's (1.18.6–10). This ritual, crucial to Roman practice, is much discussed: see J. Linderski, *ANRW* 2.16.3 (1986), 2256–97.

44. *the swift men*: See *Romulus* 26. According to Dion. Hal. (2.64.3), Numa did not abolish the Celeres.

45. *flamines*: Special priests devoted to a single deity. There were three major *flamines* (the *flamen Dialis*, *flamen Martialis* and *flamen Quirinalis*, devoted to Jupiter, Mars and Quirinus respectively); there were also twelve minor *flamines*.

46. *pilamenes*: Plutarch here derives *flamines* or *pilamenes* from *pilos*, the Greek word for a felt hat; see also *Moralia* 274c and Dion. Hal. 2.64.2 (the distinctive headwear of the *flamines* was called an *apex* in Latin, and it was not simply a skull cap but had a point as well). Varro, *On the Latin Language* 5.84, offers a different etymology. Neither is correct.

47. *Juba*: See Introduction to *Romulus*.

48. *laena . . . chlaena*: Festus (104) offers a similar etymology.

49. *Cadmilus*: (or Casmilus) One of the Samothracian Cabiri (see *Marcellus* 30 with note 139 and *Aemilius* 23 with note 113), sometimes identified with Hermes. Varro (*On the Latin*

Language 7.3) draws the connection with the Latin word *camillus*.

50. *'city swollen with fiery phlegm'*: Plato, *Republic* 2.372e. Plutarch, borrowing an expression from Plato, *Laws* 691e, describes Sparta, when Lycurgus became king, as *feverish*.

51. *his golden thigh ... Olympic Games*: See also Porphyry, *Life of Plotinus* 25, 28; Iamblichus, *Life of Pythagoras* 62, 92, 135 and 140.

52. *Pythagoras ... solemn speech*: Timon of Phlius (*c.* 320–230) was a sceptic philosopher and poet. This passage, also quoted by Diogenes Laertius (8.36), comes from his *Lampoons*, a work that attacked all philosophers other than the sceptic Pyrrhus.

53. *as I mentioned before*: See ch. 4.

54. *Tacita ... speechless one*: The Silent Goddess (*Dea Muta*), a Roman goddess, is not routinely identified with one of the (Greek) Muses; see Ovid, *Fasti* 2.569–82.

55. *refused to make graven images ... intellect*: This dubious claim about early Roman religion was advanced by Varro (Augustine, *City of God* 4.32; Tertullian, *Apology* 25.12); see M. Beard, J. North and S. Price, *Religions of Rome*, vol. 1 (1998), pp. 10–11.

56. *Pythagorean ... practices ... shedding of blood*: See *Romulus* 12.

57. *Epicharmus*: A Sicilian writer of comedies active in the first quarter of the fifth century BC. The fragments of his verse make it clear that he engaged with philosophical ideas, and in antiquity philosophical works were also attributed to him. Although this is the earliest mention of his Pythagoreanism, he is included among the Pythagorean philosophers in his biography by Diogenes Laertius (8.78).

58. *Antenor*: Plutarch's reference here is uncertain. We know that one of Epicharmus' plays was titled *Antenor* (*Oxyrhynchus Papyri* 2659) and was presumably about the Trojan counsellor who in some accounts settled in Italy (e.g. Virgil, *Aeneid* 1.242); perhaps this was the source of a joke about Pythagoras and Rome and Plutarch's comment here reflects a garbled report of it.

59. *charm of his speech*: See *Aemilius* 2 with note 7. Numa's family is discussed further at ch. 21.

60. *monuments ... Pythagoras*: See also Pliny, *Natural History* 34.26.

61. *pontifices ... doing so*: This view also derives *pontifex* from *potens*, here in the sense of *being able* to do something.

62. *rituals ... on the bridge*: Plutarch refers here and below to the Sublician Bridge (*pons Sublicius*), Rome's oldest bridge. Its exact location remains uncertain. The first of these etymologies is mentioned only by Plutarch. The other two can be found at Varro, *On the Latin Language* 5.83.

63. *stone bridge ... Aemilius*: Rome's first stone bridge, routinely described as the Aemilian Bridge (*pons Aemilius*), was constructed in 179, when Marcus Fulvius Nobilior and Marcus Aemilius Lepidus were censors. It was wrecked by a storm in 156 and subsequently rebuilt, perhaps by a quaestor who was also an Aemilius, unless Plutarch meant to write *censor* (*tamēteuontos*) instead of *quaestor* (*tamieuontos*).

64. *interpreting ... correct ritual practice*: These duties of the *pontifex maximus* are also described at Dion. Hal. 2.73; see Beard, North and Price, *Religions of Rome*, vol. 1, pp. 55–8.

65. *Vestals ... eternal fire*: The six Vestal Virgins observed the rites of Vesta, the goddess of the hearth who was essential to Rome's security; tending Vesta's fire, which was meant never to be extinguished, was the most conspicuous of their ritual tasks. In other accounts, including *Romulus* 22, it is Romulus who establishes the Vestal Virgins.

66. *perpetual fire ... Athens*: Plutarch refers to the sacred fire in the temple of Apollo at Delphi (*Moralia* 385d; Aeschylus, *Libation Bearers* 1037; Pausanias 10.24.2) and in the Erechtheion in Athens (Strabo 9.396).

67. *Aristion*: Philosopher and tyrant in Athens from 88 to 86, when he was executed by Sulla. On his character and on this incident, see Plutarch, *Sulla* 13.

68. *Delphi its fire ... altar was destroyed*: Plutarch is our sole source for the extinction of the Delphian flame in these circumstances. Delphi was attacked but little damaged by the Persians in 480, and during the period 87–83 Sulla looted the treasuries of Delphi to help to pay for his campaign against Mithridates.

69. *concave mirrors ... fire*: See also *Moralia* 937a.

70. *recorded in my Life of Camillus ... these matters*: *Camillus* 20.

71. *Servius, two more were enrolled*: According to Dion. Hal. (2.67.1), it was Tarquinius Priscus, not Servius Tullius, who raised the number of Vestals to six.

72. *the right ... mothers of three children*: Plutarch explains this privilege by way of comparison with an imperial right, established by Augustus, for all women who were mothers of three

children. On the legal circumstances of Vestal Virgins, see Beard, North and Price, *Religions of Rome*, vol. 1, p. 51.

73. *lictors*: Official attendants who walked in front of magistrates carrying their fasces, which were bundles of rods capped with two-headed axes symbolizing a magistrate's *imperium* or power of command.

74. *alongside the ... rampart*: A portion of the Servian Wall along the Esquiline Hill was called the Agger (*the Rampart*); the Colline Gate is located at the northern end of the Agger.

75. *how the Romans punish ... vow of virginity*: See also *Moralia* 286e–f, Livy 28.11.6, Dion. Hal. 2.67.3, Valerius Maximus 1.1.6.

76. *temple of Vesta*: Located in the Roman Forum at the foot of the Palatine.

77. *Vesta ... identified with the earth*: This, however, is the view of Dion. Hal. (2.66.3) and Ovid (*Fasti* 6.267).

78. *Hestia ... Monad*: The Monad, or Unit, was a fundamental (if not now fully understood) principle in Pythagorean cosmology. Hestia, the Greek equivalent of Vesta (Plutarch in fact uses *Hestia* whenever he refers to *Vesta*), is here a reference to the cosmic hearth that constituted the centre of the Pythagorean universe. See e.g. Aristotle, *On the Heavens* 293a18, as well as Guthrie, *A History of Philosophy*, vol. 1, pp. 243–6, 292–3; and Burkert, *Lore and Science in Ancient Pythagoreanism*, pp. 36–8.

79. *Plato ... entity*: This is also reported at *Moralia* 1006c.

80. *the most important part of ourselves*: That is, the soul. For Plutarch, Numa's legislation recalls the sentiments of Plato, *Laws* 12.959b. The practicalities and sensibilities associated with Roman funerary practices are discussed by J. Bodel in V. Hope and E. Marshall (eds.), *Death and Disease in the Ancient City* (2000), pp. 128–51.

81. *Libitina*: A goddess associated with funerals and sometimes associated with Venus, see *Moralia* 269b; Varro, *On the Latin Language* 6.47; Dion. Hal. 4.15.5; and Festus 322.

82. *child of fewer than three years*: See also *Coriolanus* 39, but this matter remains unclear; see S. Treggiari, *Roman Marriage* (1991), pp. 493–4.

83. *Fetiales*: A Latin institution and not unique to Rome, although the Romans variously attributed their institution to Numa, Tullus Hostilius or Ancus Marcius. More detailed accounts of their origins and practices are provided by Livy (1.24.4–9 and 1.32. 5–13) and Dion. Hal. (2.72.1–9). Legend, ideology and historical

realities are usefully sorted out by F. Santangelo, *Bulletin of the Institute for Classical Studies* 51 (2008), pp. 63–93.

84. *Fetiales ... negotiation*: Plutarch accepts the derivation of the word *Fetiales* from Latin *fari* (*to speak*). A similar opinion lies behind Dion. Hal. 2.72.1. Other derivations were also current: e.g. Varro, *On the Latin Language* 5.86.

85. *Among the Greeks ... instead of violence*: Peace (*eirene*) is here derived from *eirein* (*to speak*). This is introduced in support of the etymology of Fetiales Plutarch has just endorsed (see notes above).

86. *Clusium*: Modern Chiusi.

87. *these are events ... Camillus*: *Camillus* 17–18.

88. *Salii*: Like the Fetiales, Salii were not unique to Rome. The priesthood was so ancient that many of its features were mysterious even to the Romans; see also Livy 1.20.3–4 and Dion. Hal. 2.10.

89. *spring*: This was the spring of the Camenae, divinities ultimately identified with the Muses, located on the Caelian Hill near the Capenine Gate.

90. *watch over these shields*: The original shield (the *ancile*) and its copies were housed in a shrine on the Palatine Hill (the Curia Saliorum).

91. *Salii*: The name of the priesthood derives from *salire* (*to leap*).

92. *Samothrace ... Mantinea*: This eponymous Salius is attributed to both cities (Festus 438).

93. *in the month of March*: In fact on 1 March.

94. *ancilia ... afflictions*: Plutarch adduces several (false) Greek etymologies for the word *ancile* in this order: *ancile* is derived from *angulos* (*curved*), from *angkon* (*elbow*), from *anekathen* (*from on high*), from *akesis* (*cure*), from *auchmon* (*of the drought*) and *anaschesis* (*cessation*).

95. *Anakes*: That is, *Kings*, a common way of addressing the Dioscuri in Athens and elsewhere in the Greek world.

96. *there are others who insist ... ancient memorial*: On this point, see Varro, *On the Latin Language* 6.49. The Salian Hymn (*Carmen Saliare*), excerpts from which survive, was unintelligible to the Romans by the first century BC.

97. *Regia ... royal dwelling*: See *Romulus* 18.

98. *Quirinal Hill ... location*: Numa added the Quirinal Hill to Rome (Dion. Hal. 2.62).

99. *with their minds concentrated*: So Porphyry, *Life of Plotinus* 38; Iamblichus, *Life of Pythagoras* 18.85.

100. *hoc age*: See also *Coriolanus* 25.

101. *Their teachings ... concealed except to a few*: For these and
other aphorisms, see *Moralia* 12e–f, 281a, 290e, 354e and 361a;
Plato, *Laws* 717a–b; Porphyry, *Life of Plotinus* 42. On
the secret doctrine of the Pythagoreans, see Burkert, *Lore and
Science in Ancient Pythagoreanism*.

102. *significance is hidden ... turn around when worshipping*: Cf.
Plutarch, *Camillus* 5, *Marcellus* 6 and *Moralia* 270d.

103. *Egyptian wheels*: See Clemens Alexandrinus, *Miscellanies*
5.8.45.

104. *He once invited ... rich furniture*: This is a simplified version of
a story told more fully and clearly by Dion. Hal. (2.60.5–7). Its
point is that, with the coming of the goddess, sumptuous foods
and furnishings were produced miraculously.

105. *Picus ... Faunus*: Picus was an early Latin king, later transformed into a woodpecker, or a prophet associated with Mars.
Faunus was a forest god, eventually identified with Pan. In some
accounts Picus is Faunus' father.

106. *Idaean Dactyls*: Magical beings associated with Mt Ida. Among
other things, they were viewed by some as the teachers of
Orpheus (an important figure in Pythagoreanism and therefore
another of Plutarch's associations of Numa with Pythagoras).

107. *Numa is said ... hair and sprats*: This story is also told by Ovid
(*Fasti* 3.291–346) and was reported in the now lost history
of Valerius Antias (*HRR* 1.239). The gods' transformations
may be Plutarch's own contribution to the tale, perhaps
inspired by the character of Proteus at Homer, *Odyssey*
4.414–59.

108. *Ilicium*: The altar of Jupiter Elicius – that is, Jupiter who was
'drawn down' or 'lured on' by Numa – was located on the Aventine Hill. The etymology of *Elicius* remain unclear, and Plutarch,
in describing Jupiter as 'kindly disposed' (*hileos*), hints at yet
another possibility.

109. *Faithfulness*: (*fides*) A crucial Roman value, its sense extending
from trustworthiness and loyalty to credit-worthiness in a financial sense. Although Numa is routinely put forward as the
founder of the first temple to Fides, Cicero (*On the Nature of the
Gods* 2.61) attributes that accomplishment to Aulus Atilius
Calatinus, the consul of 258 or 254.

110. *Terminus*: An ancient shrine established on the Capitoline. Terminus was the god of boundaries and landmarks. When, later,
the Romans began building their temple to Jupiter Best and

Greatest on the same spot, Terminus, naturally enough, would not give way, and so his shrine was incorporated into Jupiter's temple.

111. *remain pure . . . killing*: Plutarch also makes this point at *Moralia* 267d.

112. *pagi*: A *pagus* was, as Plutarch says, an administrative district in the countryside.

113. *Some he elevated . . . senses*: Dion. Hal. (2.76.1–3) discusses these same matters but adds that Numa's reforms also helped the Romans to avoid civil strife.

114. *division . . . trades and crafts*: An important feature of Roman society was its organization into associations called *collegia*: each *collegium* was at once a professional, regional and religious society, and the activities of *collegia* were central to the civic and social experiences of ordinary Romans. Both Plutarch and Pliny attribute the origin of *collegia* to Numa (Pliny, *Natural History* 34.1 and 35.159). Florus (1.6.3), however, attributes the *collegia* to Servius Tullius.

115. *I described earlier*: See ch. 2.

116. *his reform . . . living with a slave*: See Dion. Hal. 2.27.1–4 for a fuller discussion of this law and its background (which law, however, he does not connect with Numa).

117. *Mercedonius . . . calendar*: Plutarch gives Mercedonius as the intercalary month's name at *Caesar* 59 (see also Festus 115), where he discusses Caesar's calendrical reforms. In any case, this was an informal, not an official, designation. The intercalary month was not inserted at the end of February but at the point where February had five days remaining (consequently, the intercalary month included twenty-seven days). On the development of the Roman calendar, see D. Feeney, *Caesar's Calendar: Ancient Times and the Beginning of History* (2007).

118. *He changed the order . . . put first*: Plutarch repeats this at *Moralia* 289a–d, but in fact January became the first month of the Roman year only in 153.

119. *Arcadians have four*: Zonaras (7.5) agrees with Plutarch on the number of months in the Arcadian year, but other sources insist instead on three months (e.g. Pliny, *Natural History* 7.155; Macrobius, *Saturnalia* 1.12.2).

120. *the Tenth Month*: December is cognate with *decem* (*ten*), hence Plutarch's correct translation as *the Tenth Month*. On the months and their ancient etymologies, see Varro, *On the Latin Language* 6.33–4.

121. *fifth month after March*: This month was *Quintilis*, meaning *the fifth month* (*quintus* means *fifth*), later renamed *Julius* (i.e. July) after Julius Caesar.

122. *sixth month after March*: This month was *Sextilis*, meaning *the sixth month* (*sextus* means *sixth*), later renamed *August* after the emperor Augustus.

123. *March first . . . Aphrodite*: Romulus was the son of Mars and, by way of Aeneas, was also descended from Venus or Aphrodite. That April (*Aprilis*) derived from Aphrodite was a common though not universal opinion (see Ovid, *Fasti* 4.88; Macrobius, *Saturnalia* 1.12.12).

124. *Romans sacrifice . . . in April*: On the first day of April the Romans celebrated the Veneralia in honour of Venus.

125. *Aphril . . . April*: The pronunciation *Aphr*il, it was believed incorrectly, echoed the month's association with *Aphr*odite.

126. *name . . . opening in Latin*: Varro (*On the Latin Language* 6.33) preferred associating April with *aprire* (*to open*), another false etymology.

127. *stages of life . . . younger men*: So Varro, *On the Latin Language* 6.33.

128. *remaining months . . . tenth*: Apart from those mentioned already, Plutarch refers to September (the seventh month), October (the eighth month) and November (the ninth month).

129. *Domitian . . . seventh and eighth months*: Domitian renamed September *Germanicus* and October *Domitianus*, each name referring to himself (Suetonius, *Domitian* 13.3).

130. *February . . . resembles a purification*: On the derivation of *Februarius* and on the Lupercalia, see *Romulus* 21. During February the Romans observed several festivals of the dead: the Parentalia, the Feralia and the Caristia.

131. *Janus*: Originally the god of doors and gates (hence his two faces) and therefore of beginnings; he was eventually associated with safety, order and peace.

132. *the Gate of War*: This is the temple of Janus Geminus (or Janus Quirinus), located in the Roman Forum near the Curia. Building the temple of Janus is the first act of Numa's reign in Livy (1.19.2).

133. *victory over Antony*: At the battle of Actium in 31 BC. The gates were also closed by Augustus in 25 BC (Suetonius, *Life of Augustus* 22).

134. *consuls*: Titus Manlius Torquatus and Gaius Atilius Bulbus were consuls in 235.

135. *On shield handles ... sweet sleep*: Plutarch cites lines from a paean by Bacchylides (fr. 4 in Campbell, *Greek Lyric*, vol. 4).

136. *'For blessed is he ... from his mouth'*: Plutarch is quoting Plato, *Laws* 4.711e. This chapter of Numa also makes allusion to Plato, *Republic* 487e and 501e.

137. *According to some*: That was, according to Dion. Hal. (2.76.6), the opinion of Gnaeus Gellius, a historian of the second century BC.

138. *from Pinus ... kings*: The Pinarii were an ancient patrician family. The Marcii Reges (but see note 38 for a different account of their origins) and the Calpurnii were grand plebeian nobility. The Pomponii were not conspicuously distinguished during the republic (despite a consulship in the third century BC) but were very successful under the empire.

139. *to flatter these great families*: See note 4 above.

140. *Marcius ... the throne*: See ch. 5.

141. *Hostilius*: Tullus Hostilius, the third king of Rome (ch. 22).

142. *His death ... debilitating malady*: Numa dies a gentle death at Dion. Hal. 2.76.5. On Piso, see Introduction.

143. *the Janiculum*: A prominent ridge on the west bank of the Tiber and an early defensive outpost that was fortified by Ancus Martius (Livy 1.33.6, Dion. Hal. 3.45.1).

144. *Antias*: On Valerius Antias, see Introduction to *Romulus*.

145. *consuls*: Publius Cornelius Cethegus and Marcus Baebius Tamphilus were consuls in 181, so closer to 500 years later.

146. *Petilius*: Quintus Petilius Spurinus, later consul in 176. This episode is mentioned frequently: see e.g. Livy 40.29.9–14; Valerius Maximus 1.1.12; and Pliny, *Natural History* 13.84–7.

147. *the Comitium*: See *Romulus* 11.

148. *the last one ... exile*: Tarquinius Superbus (reigned 534–510), see *Publicola* 1.

149. *the remaining four*: These were Tullus Hostilius (reigned 673–642), who was struck by lightning; Ancus Marcius (reigned 642–617), although it is not elsewhere suggested that he came to a violent end; Tarquinius Priscus (reigned 616–579), who was assassinated by the sons of Ancus Marcius; and Servius Tullius (reigned 578–535), who was assassinated by Tarquinius Superbus.

Notes to the Comparison of Lycurgus and Numa

1. *divine source*: Lycurgus made use of the oracle of Apollo at Delphi (*Lycurgus* 6), Numa of the Muses (*Numa* 8).

2. *Numa ... a kingdom*: *Numa* 3–6. Lycurgus followed his brother

as king, but then discovered that his brother's widow was pregnant; although she was willing to abort her child for Lycurgus' sake, Lycurgus ultimately yielded the throne to his nephew (*Lycurgus* 3).

3. *whose pitch was too high*: This same Greek expression can describe actions that are impetuous or violent and so suggests Rome's warlike condition when Numa became king.

4. *Lycurgus suffered . . . to succeed*: *Lycurgus* 3 and 11.

5. *helots*: Descendants of the peoples conquered by the Spartans, they were somewhere between slave and free; their principal duty was to till the Spartans' lands.

6. *savage . . . practice*: At *Lycurgus* 28 Plutarch discusses Spartan brutality towards the helots but exonerates Lycurgus.

7. *age of Saturn*: The god Saturn was early on associated with the Greek Cronus and consequently came to be viewed as the divinity who presided over a golden age for mankind; his festival, the Saturnalia, was celebrated on 17 December. The Saturnalia goes unmentioned in Numa's Life.

8. *citizenry . . . shoemakers*: *Numa* 17.

9. *considered crafts . . . impure*: A common view on the part of elite Greeks but not one explicitly attributed to Lycurgus in Plutarch's Life.

10. *servants of Ares*: A frequent designation for warriors in Homer (e.g. *Iliad* 2.110) and in subsequent poetry; Ares was the Greek god of war.

11. *equality gained . . . constitution*: *Lycurgus* 8. By allocating equal portions of public land to his citizens, Lycurgus made them, in a sense, equals.

12. *land . . . allocated . . . city's land*: *Numa* 16.

13. *Roman husband . . . marry her once again*: This was not a Roman custom. Plutarch has in mind an event he narrates at *Younger Cato* 25, when Cato divorces his wife so that she can marry and bear children for Hortensius Hortalus, after which they divorce and she remarries Cato. Cato's behaviour was idiosyncratic, however, and its propriety was a recurring topic in debating exercises at Rome (e.g. Quintilian 3.5.11, 10.5.13).

14. *as I have already observed*: At *Lycurgus* 15.

15. *Numa was vigilant . . . young girls*: This goes unmentioned in Numa's Life.

16. *unsuitable to their sex . . . commentary from the poets*: Lycurgus' policies are favourably reviewed at *Lycurgus* 14.

17. *Ibycus ... 'thigh-flaunters'*: Ibycus of Rhegium was a sixth-century BC lyric poet. The context of this citation is unknown; see Ibycus, fr. 339, in D. A. Campbell, *Greek Lyric*, vol. 3 (1991).

18. *Never at home ... robes unfastened*: Cf. Euripides, *Andromache* 597–8 (slightly adapted).

19. *And that young girl ... Hermione*: A quotation from an otherwise unknown tragedy: fr. 872 in H. Lloyd-Jones, *Sophocles: Fragments* (2003).

20. *abduction*: Romulus 19.

21. *forbade ... meddling ... to keep silent*: None of this is mentioned in Numa's Life.

22. *a woman pleaded her own case in the forum*: Instances of women pleading in Roman courts are assembled at Valerius Maximus 8.3.

23. *first man to divorce ... after the founding of Rome*: There is something amiss in Plutarch's chronology: 230 years after the founding of Rome, for Plutarch, is 523. Spurius Carvilius, however, was the consul of 234. Dion. Hal. (2.25.7) and Gellius (4.3) more plausibly date this divorce to 231, Valerius Maximus (2.1.4) to 234. Plutarch also mentions this divorce at *Comparison Theseus–Romulus* 6.

24. *Thalaea ... mother-in-law*: This is the only reference to this episode. Although Pinarius and Gegania are good patrician names, Thalaea sounds Greek; whatever Plutarch's source, his information is spurious.

25. *marriageability ... natural to them*: Spartan marriage is described at *Lycurgus* 15.

26. *Romans give their daughters ... character*: Roman women routinely married for the first time in their teenage years, with twelve being the minimum age at which they could legally marry: see Treggiari, *Roman Marriage*, pp. 39–43.

27. *attention to boys ... games*: The Spartan regimen for boys and young men is described at *Lycurgus* 16–24.

28. *left it up to their fathers ... how best to raise their sons*: Numa 24.

29. *Spartans' oaths ... upbringing*: The Spartans' oath and Lycurgus' cunning exploitation of it are related at *Lycurgus* 29.

30. *After his death ... corpses*: Numa 20.

31. *Numa's institutions ... education of the young*: This criticism of Numa, that he did not establish a system of civic education, was a timely one for the Romans, who in Plutarch's day were becoming open to the matter of publicly supported education:

see P. Desideri in P. A. Stadter and L. Van der Stockt (eds.), *Sage and Emperor: Plutarch, Greek Intellectuals, and Roman Power in the Time of Trajan (98–117 AD)* (2002), pp. 315–27.

32. *riches ... justice*: These are among the fundamental qualities of Plato's ideal city (*Republic* 427e).

33. *Lacedaemonians ... destroyed*: At *Lycurgus* 29–30, Plutarch locates the subversion of Lycurgus' constitution during the reign of Agis II (*c.* 427–400). The Spartan hegemony of Greece was undone by the Thebans under Epaminondas at the battle of Leuctra in 371.

PUBLICOLA

Further Reading

There is no English commentary on the *Life of Publicola*, but there is a good one in Italian: E. Ruschenbush, G. Faranda, B. Scardigli, M. Affortunati and M. Manfredini (eds.), *Plutarco, Vite Parallele: Le vite di Solone e Publicola* (1994). This Life has not yet received much in the way of literary study, but there is an important chapter by M. Affortunati and B. Scardigli, 'Aspects of Plutarch's *Life of Publicola*', in P. A. Stadter (ed.), *Plutarch and the Historical Tradition* (1992), pp. 109–31.

On the fall of Rome's monarchy and the establishment of the republic, see Forsythe, *Early Rome*, pp. 147–200; Cornell, *Beginnings of Rome*, pp. 215–41; and General Introduction V. An illuminating introduction to legendary accretions affecting the story of early Rome is T. P. Wiseman, 'Roman Republic, Year One', *Greece & Rome* 45 (1998), pp. 19–26.

Notes to the Introduction to Publicola

1.   See A. Wallace-Hadrill, *JRS* 72 (1982), pp. 32–48, for a detailed introduction to the importance placed on these imperial qualities. More generally on Roman emperors, see F. Millar, *The Emperor in the Roman World* (1977).

2.   See A. M. Gowing, *Empire and Memory: The Representation of the Roman Republic in Imperial Culture* (2005), and A. B. Gallia, *Remembering the Roman Republic: Culture, Politics and History under the Principate* (2012).

3.   On the *lapis Satricum*, see Cornell, *Beginnings of Rome*, pp. 143–5.

4.   *HRR*, vol. 2, pp. 65–7.

Notes to the Life of Publicola

1. *Such a man ... was Solon*: This constitutes Plutarch's transition from his *Solon* to *Publicola*.
2. *received this name ... from the Roman people*: See ch. 10.
3. *Valerius ... differences*: Volusius Valerius was a Sabine who came to Rome with Titus Tatius and played a part in the peaceful settlement between Tatius and Romulus (Valerius Maximus 2.4.5, Dion. Hal. 4.67, 5.2). He does not, however, appear in Plutarch's account of this episode at *Romulus* 19. He was deemed a likely successor to Romulus before Numa was selected as monarch (*Numa* 17).
4. *wealth*: Publicola is again described as wealthy at *Comparison Solon–Publicola* 1, whereas it is his lack of wealth that is emphasized by Livy (2.17.7–8) and Dion. Hal. (5.48.3).
5. *Tarquinius Superbus*: Tarquin the Proud, see Introduction.
6. *Lucretia*: The daughter of Spurius Lucretius, and wife of Lucius Tarquinius Collatinus. Raped by Sextus Tarquinius, a son of Tarquinius Superbus, she took her own life.
7. *Lucius Brutus*: See Introduction.
8. *revolution*: The traditional leaders of the revolution, in addition to Brutus, were Spurius Lucretius, Collatinus and Publicola (e.g. Livy 1.58.6, 1.59.2; Dion. Hal. 4.67.3–4, 70.1–2 and 71.5).
9. *two men be elected*: It was decided that two men should be elected as consuls.
10. *opposition to the monarchy*: The death of his wife, it is here suggested, ensured his hostility to monarchy. In ch. 7, however, Plutarch indicates that Collatinus was distrusted by the public owing to his kinship with the Tarquins.
11. *oath*: See also Livy (2.1.9), Dion. Hal. (5.1.3) and Appian, *Civil Wars* (2.119), none of whom mentions Publicola's role.
12. *envoys*: Dion. Hal. (5.4–5) records one embassy instead of Plutarch's two (ch. 3); his Brutus opposes the proposals of the envoys and Publicola plays no role. Similarly, although Livy (2.3.5) records a debate in response to an embassy from Tarquinius, he does not mention Publicola.
13. *modest concessions*: The particulars of these modest proposals are provided by Dion. Hal. (5.4).
14. *who joined in ... proposal*: In Livy's account (2.2.7–11), Collatinus abdicates his consulship before this proposal is put before the Romans.

15. *first man ... Gaius Minucius*: According to Dion. Hal. (5.11.2), the first private citizen in Rome to address an assembly was Spurius Lucretius. In ch. 12, a different Minucius is one of the first two men to be elected quaestor.

16. *tyrants ... riches*: At Dion. Hal. 5.5.3–5.6.2 it is Collatinus who recommends the restoration of the Tarquins' property, and his proposal to the people narrowly passes.

17. *city's betrayal*: Accounts of this conspiracy (differing in various particulars) are provided by Livy (2.3–5) and Dion. Hal. (5.6.4–5.13.1).

18. *noblest families ... Collatinus*: Only the Aquillii, who were the sons of Collatinus' sister, are elsewhere attested as Collatinus' nephews (Dion. Hal, 5.6.4).

19. *Brutus ... one of their sisters*: Brutus' wife, Vitellia, is mentioned in Suetonius' biography of the emperor Vitellius (*Vitellius* 1.2).

20. *Two of Brutus' sons*: Titus Junius and Tiberius Junius.

21. *stupidity ... surname*: The Latin word *brutus* means *stupid*. Brutus' feigned stupidity is recounted by Livy (1.56.7–12) and Dion. Hal. (4.68–9).

22. *human sacrifice ... blood*: This gruesome ritual, appropriated from accounts of the Catilinarian conspiracy (e.g. Sallust, *Catilinarian Conspiracy* 22; Plutarch, *Cicero* 10), is not found in Livy or Dionysius.

23. *home of the Aquillii*: At Livy 2.4.4–6 the conspirators meet in the house of the Vitellii and Vindicius is their slave.

24. *a slave ... overhear their scheming*: By contrast, in both Livy (2.4.5–6) and Dion. Hal. (5.7) Vindicius becomes suspicious and sets out to uncover the plot against Rome.

25. *revealed everything to him*: At Livy 2.4.6 Vindicius reveals the plot to the two consuls, one of whom, in Livy's account, is Publicola.

26. *Marcus*: Marcus Valerius, consul in 505 (chs. 14 and 20). Roman tradition seems to have supplied Publicola with a second brother, not mentioned in this Life: Manius Valerius Maximus, dictator in 494.

27. *letters to Tarquinius*: Incriminating letters play a dramatic part in all versions of this conspiracy. Their importance reflects the influence of the Catilinarian conspiracy (e.g. Cicero, *Against Catiline* 3.10; Sallust, *Catilinarian Conspiracy* 44–5) on later historians of the early republic.

28. *Brutus ... did not remove his gaze ... punishment of his sons*: At Livy 2.5.8 Brutus evinces paternal feelings as he witnesses the punishment of his sons.

29. *enormity of his outrage*: At *Brutus* 1 Plutarch attributes Brutus' action to his anger.

30. *fitting ... judge of his own sons*: Brutus could order his sons' execution on the basis of his paternal authority (*patria potestas*), which granted fathers the power of life and death over their children.

31. *conspirators ... unanimously ... beheaded*: At Dion. Hal. 5.9–12 Collatinus attempts to save the conspirators by exercising his consular authority; Brutus then attempts to have Collatinus removed from office; finally Collatinus is persuaded to resign and retire honourably from Rome. After Publicola is elected consul to replace him, the conspirators are executed (Dion. Hal. 5.13.1).

32. *kinship with the royal family*: We are not told exactly how Tarquinius Collatinus was related to the royal family.

33. *curia*: On the *curiae*, see *Romulus* 14.

34. *Roman freedmen ... Appius*: Appius Claudius Caecus, during his censorship in 312, enhanced the electoral influence of freedmen by distributing them among all the Roman tribes (whereas they had previously been confined to the four urban tribes), a reform that was later reversed.

35. *manumission ... Vindicius*: The figure of Vindicius was invented in order to explain the manumission procedure known as *vindicta*, which the Romans believed was their original means of granting freedom and citizenship simultaneously; see S. Treggiari, *Roman Freedmen during the Late Republic* (1969), pp. 20–25.

36. *Campus Martius*: The Field of Mars, the area of Rome where today one finds (among other features) the Pantheon and the Piazza Navona.

37. *Between the Two Bridges*: In the first century BC this island, the *Insula Tiberina*, was connected to Rome by two bridges, the Pons Fabricius (the Fabrician Bridge) and the Pons Cestius (the Cestian Bridge), and hence was designated *Inter Duos Pontes* (*Between the Two Bridges*). The island was home to a temple of Aesculapius and several other divinities. Similar versions of this story are told by Livy (2.5.3–4) and Dion. Hal. (5.13.3–4).

38. *Some writers ... field*: See also Pliny, *Natural History* 34.25, and Gellius 7.7, where the Vestal is called Taracia. It has been suggested that this passage be emended to read *Taracia* instead of *Tarquinia* (see R. Flacelière and E. Chambry, *Plutarque, Vies*, vol. 2 (1968), pp. 66 and 214–15).

39. *Tarquinius ... turned to the Etruscans*: Tarquinius was assisted by the Etruscan cities of Veii and Tarquinii (Livy 2.6–7.4, Dion. Hal. 5.14–16).

40. *Horatian wood*: The uncertain reading of the manuscripts is easily emended to *Horatian* by way of comparison with Dion. Hal. 5.14.1. Livy, however, calls it the *Arsian* wood (2.7.2: *silva Arsia*), as does Valerius Maximus 1.8.5. By either name, the locality is unknown.

41. *Naevian meadow*: Otherwise unknown, but there was a Naevian wood on the Aventine outside the Naevian Gate.

42. *Aruns ... Brutus ... fell upon one another*: At Dion. Hal. 5.15.1–3 they fight a duel before the battle commences.

43. *voice of a god*: At Livy 2.7.2 the god is Silvanus; Dion. Hal. (5.16.1) is uncertain whether it is the hero Horatius or the god Faunus.

44. *Calends of March*: The Calends of any month is its first day, so this battle took place on 28 February.

45. *triumph ... chariot*: On the triumph generally and Publicola's triumph specifically, see Beard, *Roman Triumph*, pp. 258–9; on the early use of chariots in triumphs, see *Romulus* 16.

46. *Rome's great men ... oration*: Aristocratic funerals at Rome were admired and are described for us by Polybius (6.53–4). An excellent discussion of funerals and funeral orations is provided by H. Flower, *Ancestor Masks and Aristocratic Power in Roman Culture* (1996), pp. 91–158.

47. *Some believe ... Greek practice*: This is the view of Dion. Hal. (5.17.3–6).

48. *as ... Anaximenes reports*: Plutarch does not, however, mention this in the parallel Life. Anaximenes of Lampsacus (*c.* 380–320), whom Plutarch also mentions at *Demosthenes* 28 and *Cicero* 51, was a historian and rhetorician. *A Study of Rhetoric dedicated to Alexander*, the earliest surviving Greek rhetorical manual, is often attributed to him. Anaximenes' assertion about Solon does not come from the *Rhetoric*.

49. *the Velia*: The north side of the Palatine, overlooking the forum.

50. *he did not ... grow angry*: By contrast, at Livy 2.7.8–11 Publicola delivers a speech in which he registers his irritation with the public's unjust suspicions, after which he demolishes his house.

51. *razed it to the ground*: Plutarch relates this episode by way of the language of tragedy: Publicola's lifestyle is too theatrical (*tragikoteron*) and his incorrect behaviour is indicated with the word *hamartanein*, related to the critical term *hamartia*, the often fatal error of the tragic hero. Here, however, the untragic

result is the unfortunate destruction of a grand house, not a grand figure. On Plutarch's use of theatricality and of tragic diction, see the excellent treatment by J. M. Mossman in Scardigli, *Essays*, pp. 209–28.

52. *temple of Vica Pota*: The precise location of this temple is uncertain, but it was somewhere at the base of the Velia. The goddess Vica Pota was identified as a goddess of victory.

53. *whenever he came ... fasces*: This custom (lowering the fasces) is not otherwise attested. At Livy 2.7.7 it occurs only once. Fasces were bundles of rods with an axe which were carried by attendants called lictors and which symbolized the authority and power of the higher magistrates (i.e. consuls, praetors, dictators).

54. *Publicola ... biography*: *Publicola* is the most common form of this Valerian surname, variants of which include *Publicula* and *Poplicola* (this last being the form actually used by Plutarch in this Life). The Romans believed it derived from *populi colendi*, which means *favouring the people*.

55. *replenish the senate's membership*: At Livy 2.1.10 it is Brutus who adds new members to the senate; at Dion. Hal. 5.12.2 Brutus and Publicola carry this out jointly.

56. *the right to appeal ... the people*: The antiquity of a citizen's right to make an appeal to the people (known as *provocatio*) remains controversial: historians of early Rome may have modelled Publicola's measure on a law to the same purpose carried by Marcus Valerius Maximus Corvus in 300.

57. *abolished the taxes*: In ch. 12, however, new taxes are introduced by Publicola, along with the office of quaestor.

58. *punished disobedience ... two sheep*: This law is mentioned only here.

59. *obols*: The obol was an Athenian coin of little value; there were six obols to the drachma. Plutarch normally equates the Roman denarius with the Attic drachma (see General Introduction VI), so the total fine here is nearly 87 denarii – still rather steep for an ordinary Roman of any period.

60. *peculia ... pig*: *Peculium* refers to property that actually belongs to a head of household but whose use is entrusted to children or slaves. It is derived from *pecus* (*herd*), as is the Latin word for money (*pecunia*). Plutarch makes this same point at *Moralia* 274f–275a, where he names Fenestella, a first-century BC historian and antiquarian, as his source.

61. *Suillus ... porci*: Plutarch apparently expected his Greek readers to recognize the similarity between *Suillus* (*pork*) and Greek

suidion (*piglet*) and between *Bubulcus* (*ploughman* or *herdsman*) and Greek *boubotes* (*herdsman*). Suillus does not appear to be a very common name, but Suillius was the name of a distinguished imperial family and the Suillates were an Umbrian people (Pliny, *Natural History* 3.14.9).

62. *Publicola ... popular rights*: In other authors, Publicola receives his name in gratitude for his legislation: e.g. Cicero, *The Republic* 2.31; Livy 2.8; and Dion. Hal. 5.19.5.

63. *temple ... treasury*: See also *Moralia* 275a, where Publicola chooses this temple because it is conspicuous and defensible. The temple of Saturn was located in the forum at the base of the Capitoline.

64. *quaestors*: Ancient testimony regarding the origins of the quaestorship and the date at which it became an elective office is inconsistent. Tacitus (*Annals* 11.22) states that the first quaestorian elections took place in 447, but elsewhere elections are reported during the reign of Romulus: see Lintott, *Constitution*, pp. 133–7. Only Plutarch links Publicola to this institution.

65. *Publius Veturius ... Marcus Minucius*: Later, the first was consul in 499, the second in 497 and 491.

66. *not including ... orphans*: Camillus later removes the exemption from taxation enjoyed by orphans (*Camillus* 2).

67. *Lucretius*: Spurius Lucretius was one of the leaders of the revolution against Tarquinius Superbus; see also note 8.

68. *Marcus Horatius ... consul*: Marcus Horatius Pulvillus was again consul in 507 (ch. 14). Polybius (3.22.1) believed that he had been a consular colleague of Brutus.

69. *temple of Capitoline Jupiter*: This is the temple to Jupiter Best and Greatest, located on the Capitoline Hill and central to Roman civic religion.

70. *Veii*: Modern Isola Farnese. The Romans' conquest of Veii is a major episode in Plutarch's *Camillus* (chs. 2–6).

71. *Ratumena*: The location of this gate is uncertain. This story is also mentioned by Pliny, *Natural History* 8.161, and Festus 340–42.

72. *Tarquinius*: Tarquinius Priscus, son of the Corinthian Demaratus, was the fifth king of Rome.

73. *son or grandson*: Tarquinius Superbus was originally considered Priscus' son, but improved arithmetic on the part of the annalists led to the conclusion that he must be a grandson: see Livy 1.46.4, Dion. Hal. 4.7 (attributing this revision to the influential *Annals* of Lucius Calpurnius Piso Frugi, the consul of 133).

74. *drew lots ... dedication*: At Livy 2.8.6–8 the consuls draw lots and Publicola is allotted a war against Veii. At Dion. Hal. 5.35.3

he is away fighting marauding bandits. Dion. Hal., like Polybius (3.22.1) and Tacitus (*Histories* 3.73), dates this dedication to 507, when Publicola and Horatius were once again consuls.

75. *the Ides of September*: This is 13 September.

76. *Metageitnion*: This Athenian month began in August and ended in September.

77. *announcement ... untrue ... consecration*: Livy (2.8.6–8) records a similar attempt to subvert Horatius' dedication. Ordinarily a death in the family rendered its members ritually unable to perform certain religious acts (see e.g. Varro, *On the Latin Language* 5.23; Cicero, *On the Laws* 2.55; Gellius 4.6.8), but in this instance Horatius was clearly correct to proceed with his dedication.

78. *temple was destroyed during the civil wars*: This occurred in 83 BC, during the civil war fought when Sulla returned from fighting the Mithridatic War.

79. *second temple ... Catulus*: This temple was dedicated in 69 BC by Quintus Lutatius Catulus, consul in 78 BC.

80. *also destroyed ... reign of Vitellius*: During the year AD 69, after Nero's suicide in the previous year, civil war brought four emperors to power in succession: Galba, Otho, Vitellius and Vespasian. The temple was destroyed by Vitellius' soldiers during their struggle with forces loyal to Vespasian.

81. *he was luckier ... than Sulla*: Good fortune was a hallmark of Sulla's public image (he was known as *The Fortunate* (*Felix*); see e.g. Plutarch, *Sulla* 8, 34 and 38) and was also a quality emphasized in Vespasian's imperial propaganda.

82. *Vespasian's death ... consumed by fire*: Vespasian died in AD 79; his temple was burnt down in the great fire of AD 80. His son, Titus, began rebuilding but died in AD 81.

83. *dedicated by Domitian*: The date of this dedication is uncertain but was probably AD 82.

84. *Tarquinius ... his temple*: This was the assertion of Lucius Calpurnius Piso (note 73), which is reported by Livy (1.55.8–9) and rejected in favour of Fabius Pictor's figure of 40 talents. In measuring silver or gold, a single talent was reckoned as equivalent to 80 Roman pounds (Polybius 21.43, Livy 38.38.13). Piso's (and Plutarch's) figure of 40,000 pounds, then, is equivalent to 500 talents. On Greek and Roman money, see General Introduction VI.

85. *Pentelic marble*: Mt Pentelicon in Athens was famous for its fine marble.

86. *Epicharmus*: A Sicilian writer of comedies during the first quarter of the fifth century BC. Plutarch here quotes lines from a now lost work (G. Kaibel, *Comicorum Graecorum Fragmenta* (1899) fr. 274), lines he also cites at *Moralia* 510c.

87. *Midas*: A legendary Phrygian king who asked for and received, to his regret, a magical golden touch; see especially Ovid, *Metamorphoses* 11.90–193.

88. *great battle . . . with Brutus*: See ch. 9.

89. *Clusium*: Modern Chiusi.

90. *Porsenna . . . honour*: Although Porsenna is usually represented as he is here, a valiant king who comes to admire Roman heroism, in an alternative tradition he defeats Rome and imposes a humiliating treaty on them (Tacitus, *Histories* 3.72; Pliny, *Natural History* 34.139). This alternative tradition perhaps preserves the memory of a historical event.

91. *elected consul . . . colleague*: This is 508. Titus Lucretius is again consul in 504.

92. *Signuria*: The same city is mentioned at Dion. Hal. 5.20 but is otherwise unknown. It is perhaps a garbled reference to Segnia (modern Segni).

93. *fortified the place . . . war with Porsenna*: According to Dion. Hal. (5.20), the Romans garrisoned this city in 508, but the war with Porsenna did not occur until the next year (5.21.1). Livy (2.8.9–2.15.7), like Plutarch, sets the war in 508.

94. *the Janiculum*: See *Numa*, note 143.

95. *Publicola came to their aid*: At Livy 2.10.3 it is Horatius Cocles and not Publicola who rallies the men fleeing the Janiculum.

96. *wooden bridge over the Tiber*: This is the Sublician Bridge (*Pons Sublicius*), Rome's oldest bridge. It is described by Plutarch at *Numa* 9.

97. *Horatius Cocles*: The earliest extant account of the legendary defender of the Sublician Bridge is provided by Polybius 6.55.1–4, but that story, with variations, was often repeated; see Livy 2.10 and Dion. Hal. 5.23.2–5.25.4.

98. *Herminius . . . Larcius*: Titus Herminius Aquilinus and Spurius Larcius were (after this adventure) the consuls of 506.

99. *Cocles . . . lost an eye in combat*: *Cocles* means *one-eyed* (Varro, *On the Latin Language* 7.71).

100. *his nose was sunken . . . Cyclops*: Plutarch is our only source for the suggestion that Cocles was deformed in this way or that his name was derived from the Greek word *cyclops*.

101. *wounded . . . by an Etruscan spear*: According to Livy (2.10.11), Cocles was not wounded.

102. *food . . . they consume in a day*: Cf. the similar reward granted to Manlius Capitolinus at Plutarch, *Camillus* 27.

103. *temple of Vulcan . . . his wound*: The Vulcanal was located on the lower slopes of the Capitoline Hill overlooking the Roman Forum. Cocles' lameness helped to explain how a figure so valiant failed to reach the consulship (Dion. Hal. 5.25.3).

104. *another Etruscan army . . . Porsenna's*: Not an independent army according to Dion. Hal. (5.26.1) but a contingent commanded by Tarquinius' sons.

105. *Publicola . . . consul for the third time*: In 507 Publicola and Horatius were again consuls.

106. *being routed and losing 5,000 men*: A fuller account is provided at Livy 2.11.5–10.

107. *exploit of Mucius . . . various authors*: The story of Gaius Mucius Scaevola was as familiar to Roman readers as that of Cocles: see e.g. Livy 2.12–2.13.5 and Dion. Hal. 5.27–5.30.1.

108. *Porsenna believed . . . the courage of the Romans*: In Livy's version (2.13.2), by contrast, Porsenna is motivated principally by a concern for his own safety.

109. *Athenodorus*: A Stoic philosopher who was a friend of Cicero and later a protégé of the imperial family. Nothing further is known of his composition addressed to Octavia.

110. *Cordus*: Plutarch here writes *Opsigonos*, literally *born-afterwards*, and some translators prefer to render the name as *Postumus*, the Latin equivalent and a common cognomen (*Coriolanus* 11). But at Dion. Hal. 5.25.4 Dionysius gives Scaevola's original name as Gaius Mucius *Cordus*. The Latin word *cordus* means *late-born*, and Cordus is doubtless the name Plutarch (and Athenodorus) had in mind.

111. *turned against Tarquinius*: At Livy 2.13.2 Porsenna abandons Tarquinius' cause because he is impressed by the Romans' resolve; Publicola plays no specific part in his decision. Porsenna agrees to judge between Rome and Tarquinius at Dion. Hal. 5.32.4, but Publicola has no role.

112. *Cloelia . . . courageousness*: Cloelia's escape is another oft-told legend of the war with Porsenna and has many variations, e.g. Livy 2.13.6–11 and Dion. Hal. 5.32.3–5.35.2 (in neither of these accounts does Valeria play a role). Plutarch tells this same story at *Moralia* 250a–f.

113. *the Sacred Way*: (*Via Sacra*) The oldest of Rome's streets. It led from the vicinity of the temple of Jupiter the Stayer (*Romulus* 18) in the forum to the Capitoline. Cloelia's statue stood opposite Jupiter's temple (Pliny, *Natural History* 34.29).

114. *some insist . . . Valeria*: So Pliny (*Natural History* 34.29), attributing this claim to an otherwise unknown Annius Fetialis.

115. *sale of public goods . . . generosity*: The custom of proclaiming *bona Porsennae* (*the goods of Porsenna*) at the beginning of an auction perplexed the Romans, not least because it was a formality that ought to recall hostilities rather than friendship, as Livy observed. This aetiology was the means by which the Romans rendered it an expression of gratitude (Livy 2.14). Cf. the cry of 'Sardians for sale!' at *Romulus* 25.

116. *bronze statue*: Only Plutarch mentions this statue.

117. *Marcus Valerius . . . Postumius Tubero*: Consuls in 505.

118. *Publicola's . . . cooperation*: Publicola's role is mentioned only here.

119. *an inference . . . emerges*: Plutarch has in mind passages like Menander, *The Litigants* 554–5. Houses with doors opening outwards are mentioned as a distinct category at Pseudo-Aristotle, *Economics* 1347a1.

120. *following year . . . fourth consulship*: In 504 Publicola was again consul with Titus Lucretius (they had previously been consuls in 508).

121. *Sibylline Books*: The prophetic Sibyl of Cumae provided Tarquinius Priscus with secret books – a collection of oracles in Greek which were consulted by the Romans in times of crisis (Lactantius, *The Divine Institutes* 1.6). They were brought to Rome in the regal period. On instructions from the senate they were consulted during times of crisis by a special college of priests (most of whom were themselves senators).

122. *Dis*: Plutarch writes *Hades*, the Greek god of the underworld, but Valerius Maximus (2.4.5), in mentioning this same story, reports that Publicola sacrificed to Dis, also a god associated with the underworld (see also Zonaras 2.3.5) and doubtless the divinity Plutarch has in mind here.

123. *He also celebrated games . . . Delphic oracle*: This element is unique to Plutarch's account and is perhaps his own embellishment.

124. *two square plethra*: This is nearly half an acre (on plethra see General Introduction VI), the same amount of land that Romulus allocated to Rome's original settlers (Varro, *On Agriculture* 1.10.2).

125. *River Anio*: The modern Aniene.

126. *25 square plethra*: Not quite 6 acres.

127. *Clausus ... great influence*: Clausus was one of the consuls of 495.

128. *ancestor of the Claudian family ... Rome*: In a competing tradition, Appius Claudius came to Rome during the time of the
monarchy (Suetonius, *Tiberius* 1; Appian, *Kings* 12). During this
early period in Italy, aristocrats could easily remove themselves
from one city to another, what Tim Cornell has described as
'horizontal social mobility': see T. J. Cornell in D. Braund and C.
Gill (eds.), *Myth, History and Culture in Republican Rome:
Studies in Honour of T. P. Wiseman* (2003), p. 87.

129. *Fidenae*: Modern Castel Giubileo.

130. *son-in-law*: Mentioned only here.

131. *the Sabines set out ... taken prisoner*: Dion. Hal. (5.41–3) also
recounts this battle.

132. *consuls ... to succeed him*: The consuls of 503 were Agrippa
Menenius Lanatus and Publius Postumius Tubertus.

133. *buried at public expense*: In both Livy (2.16.7–8) and Dion. Hal.
(4.48.3–4), it was owing to Publicola's poverty as well as his
eminence that he was buried at public expense.

134. *quadrans*: A bronze coin of very low value, equivalent to a quarter of an as (see General Introduction VI).

135. *an enviable honour*: The same honour was paid to Brutus after
his death (Livy 2.16.7).

136. *his descendants ... in that place*: Burial within the city was forbidden except to descendants of Publicola and Gaius Fabricius
Luscinus, consul in 282 and 278 (Cicero, *On the Laws* 2.58; Plutarch, *Moralia* 282f–283a). Cf. the burial of Aratus (*Aratus* 53).

Notes to the Comparison of Solon and Publicola

1. *happiness ... Tellus*: Herodotus (1.30–33) tells the story of
Solon's visit to the sumptuous court of Croesus, king of Lydia.
When Croesus asked Solon whom he deemed the happiest of men,
Solon did not name Croesus (as the king expected) but instead
the obscure Tellus. Plutarch records his version of this episode at
Solon 27.

2. *most illustrious of our families ... Valerii*: The Publicolae and
Messalae were two branches of the patrician Valerii; bearers of
these names were still holding senatorial offices in Plutarch's day.

3. *Mimnermus*: Mimnermus of Smyrna, an elegiac poet of the
seventh century BC, whose poetry survives only as fragments.

In one, he hopes to die at sixty, unaffected by sickness or worry, whereas Solon preferred eighty; see Mimnermus, fr. 6, and Solon, fr. 20, in D. Gerber, *Greek Elegiac Poetry* (1999).

4. *Leave me not . . . to my friends*: Solon, fr. 21, in Gerber, *Greek Elegiac Poetry*.

5. *women of Rome . . . father*: *Publicola* 23.

6. *I want to have wealth . . . not desire*: Solon, fr. 13, lines 7–8, in Gerber, *Greek Elegiac Poetry*; Plutarch cites a fuller portion of this fragment and discusses it at *Solon* 2.

7. *wealth . . . to the poor*: *Publicola* 1 and 4. According to other accounts, however, Publicola was born poor (Livy 2.16.7, Dion. Hal. 5.48).

8. *he subtracted . . . acceptable . . . in Rome*: *Publicola* 10.

9. *right to elect . . . juries*: *Publicola* 11, *Solon* 18.

10. *senate . . . doubled the membership*: *Publicola* 11, *Solon* 19.

11. *consuls . . . public finances*: *Publicola* 12; Solon's legislation is discussed in Pseudo-Aristotle, *The Athenian Constitution* 7.3 and 8.1 – but not in Plutarch's Life.

12. *Solon's law . . . trial*: Solon's law is discussed in *The Athenian Constitution* 8.4 (not in Plutarch's Life); on Publicola's law, see *Publicola* 12.

13. *Solon . . . praises himself*: *Solon* 14 (citing Solon's own verses on the matter).

14. *no less noble . . . powers that he . . . possessed*: This refers to Publicola's brief tenure as sole consul (*Publicola* 10–12).

15. *They will be . . . oppressed*: Solon, fr. 6, in Gerber, *Greek Elegiac Poetry*.

16. *remission of debts . . . fellow-citizens*: *Solon* 15. Publicola instead introduced a tax reform in order to bring relief to the poor (*Publicola* 11).

17. *constitution . . . civil wars*: Solon saw his constitution subverted when Peisistratus seized power around 546 (*Solon* 30). The Romans' republican constitution, for all practical purposes, fell apart during the civil wars that began in 49 BC and came to an end with the supremacy of the first emperor, Augustus, in 31 BC.

18. *After he had enacted his laws . . . from Athens*: *Solon* 25; according to Plutarch, Solon left Athens in order to escape any odium excited by his legislation and to avoid the obligation of explaining its details.

19. *Solon knew in advance . . . tyranny they imposed*: Plutarch's account at *Solon* 30–31 puts Solon's response to Peisistratus in a much better light than here.

20. *Daimachus of Plataea*: A historian who lived in the first half of the fourth century BC (*FGrH* 65).
21. *I described earlier*: At *Solon* 8–9, where Solon plays the central role.
22. *Publicola ... as a warrior ... battles*: See especially *Publicola* 22–3.
23. *pretended to be mad ... recovering Salamis*: Solon had to find a ruse in order to circumvent an Athenian law against raising the issue of recovering Salamis (*Solon* 8).
24. *won over Porsenna ... friend of Rome*: *Publicola* 16–19.
25. *surrendered territories ... already conquered*: *Publicola* 18.
26. *renounced some foreign territory ... besieged them*: *Publicola* 19.

CORIOLANUS

Further Reading

There is no commentary in English on the *Life of Coriolanus*. In Italian there is F. Albini and C. B. R. Pelling, *Vita di Coriolano–Vita de Alcibiade* (1996), and in German B. Ahlrichs, *Prüfsten der Gemüter* (2005), offers so close a reading of the Life that it constitutes a commentary in its own right. Plutarch's methods and literary invention in composing *Coriolanus* are set out by D. A. Russell, 'Plutarch's Life of Coriolanus', in Scardigli, *Essays*, pp. 357–72. Duff, *Plutarch's Lives*, pp. 205–40, is an elegant unpacking of the complexities of this pairing, raising issues some of which are further explored by S. Verdegem in 'Parallels and contrasts: Plutarch's *Comparison of Coriolanus and Alcibiades*' in Humble, *Plutarch's Lives*, pp. 23–44. Strong passions and their political perils, in practice and in theory, are examined in essays by P. W. Ludwig and R. A. Kaster in R. K. Balot (eds.), *A Companion to Greek and Roman Political Thought* (2009). Shakespeare's adaptation of the *Life of Coriolanus* is discussed in the introduction to L. Bliss's edition of the play (2000). For a detailed study of the Coriolanus story as it passes from Dion. Hal. to Plutarch to Shakespeare, see Pelling, *P&H*, pp. 387–411.

Notes to the Introduction to Coriolanus

1. See Cicero, *Letters to Atticus* 9.10.3, *Brutus* 41–3, *On Friendship* 42.
2. Russell in Scardigli, *Essays*, pp. 357–72, examines in detail the implications of Plutarch's adaptations of Dion. Hal.

3. See Cornell, *Beginnings of Rome*, pp. 242–92, 327–44; K. A. Raaflaub, *Social Struggles in Archaic Rome: New Perspectives on the Conflict of the Orders* (2nd edn, 2005); and Forsythe, *Early Rome*, pp. 147–267.

4. See General Introduction V.

5. Volumnia and Vergilia are also plebeian names. Veturia, however, is a patrician name.

6. The relative dates of Plutarch's pairings are discussed by Jones, 'Chronology', pp. 106–14.

7. Alcibiades (451–404) was a flamboyant aristocrat who became a leading politician and general in Athens. During the Peloponnesian War he was exiled and joined the Spartans, whom he later deserted for the Persians, before returning to Athens as a dominant political and military figure. Exiled again, he remained involved in international politics until he was assassinated.

8. See the discussion by D. Gribble, *Alcibiades and Athens: A Study in Literary Presentation* (1999), p. 220.

9. See Duff, *Plutarch's Lives*, pp. 222–40.

10. The Roman Life precedes its Greek counterpart only in three pairings (*Aemilius Paullus–Timoleon*, *Sertorius–Eumenes* and *Coriolanus–Alcibiades*). That this represents Plutarch's design seems more probable than the conclusion that it results from editorial blundering, and the likeliest explanation in each case is that Plutarch preferred to put before his reader first the simpler then the more complex of the two Lives (Pelling, *P&H*, pp. 357–9).

11. What is missing here, in Plutarch's view, are the values of a sound Greek liberal education (*paideiea*), which he regards as essential to any healthy moral compass (General Introduction III). This is a routine concern in Plutarch's Roman Lives: see Pelling, 'Roman heroes', and Swain, 'Culture'. Another great nature in Plutarchan biography belongs to the king Demetrius, who is paired with Antony (*Demetrius* 1).

12. Contentiousness and a passion for honour – *philoneikia* and *philonikia* – are basic parts of Coriolanus' moral make-up (ch. 15). Their dangerous nexus is explored more fully and explicitly in Plutarch's *Philopoemen*.

13. Coriolanus' behaviour contrasts sharply with that of the exiled Camillus (*Camillus* 23).

14. A concise review of philosophical views on anger, including Plutarch's, can be found in W. V. Harris, *Restraining Rage: The Ideology of Anger Control in Classical Antiquity* (2001), pp. 88–128.

15. See the important discussion by T. Whitmarsh in S. Goldhill (ed.), *Being Greek Under Rome* (2001), pp. 269–305.

16. See Pelling, *P&H*, pp. 365–86.

17. See T. North and J. Mossman, *Plutarch: Selected Lives* (1998); H. Heuer, *Shakespeare Survey* 10 (1957), pp. 50–58, discusses the traces of Thomas North and Jacques Amyot in *Coriolanus* specifically.

18. See Bliss, *Coriolanus*, pp. 17–27.

19. See G. Miles, *Shakespeare and the Constant Romans* (1996), pp. 149–68.

20. The topic is vast. Fundamental is J. Adelman, *Suffocating Mothers: Fantasies of Maternal Origin in Shakespeare's Plays, Hamlet to* The Tempest (1992), pp. 130–65. See the concise and valuable overview in Bliss, *Coriolanus*, pp. 47–61.

21. On this aspect of Shakespeare's reading of Plutarch, see C. Pelling in S. Goldhill and E. Hall (eds.), *Sophocles and the Greek Tragic Tradition* (2009), pp. 264–88.

Notes to the Life of Coriolanus

1. *patrician house of the Marcii*: There is no ambiguity here: Plutarch specifically uses the loan word *patrikios* to indicate – erroneously – the patrician status of the Marcii (see Introduction). On the difficulties in understanding the nature of the patriciate in early Rome, see Cornell, *Beginnings of Rome*, pp. 242–56.

2. *Ancus Marcius*: The fourth king of Rome whose traditional dates are 642–617; his mother was Pompilia, the daughter of Numa (*Numa* 21).

3. *Tullus Hostilius*: Rome's third king, whose traditional dates are 673–642.

4. *best ... supply of water*: The Marcian Aqueduct, although attributed in antiquity to Ancus Marcius, was constructed in 144–140 by Quintus Marcius Rex (praetor in 144). Publius Marcius is mentioned only here (unless he is the Publius Marcius Rex, mentioned at Livy 43.1.2, who served as envoy in 171). Inasmuch as aqueducts were ordinarily dedicated by two men (*duoviri aquae perducendae*) and large building projects were family affairs, it is highly likely that Publius was Quintus' colleague in this office in 140.

5. *Censorinus*: Gaius Marcius Rutilius (consul in 310) was elected censor in 294 and 265, an unequalled feat for which he (and his descendants) acquired the surname *Censorinus*.

6.   *Gaius Marcius*: He is *Gnaeus* Marcius at Livy 2.33.3.
7.   *lost his father ... never remarried*: It was not uncommon for
     Romans to lose their father when they were relatively young; see
     R. P. Saller, *Patriarchy, Property and Death in the Roman Family*
     (1994), pp. 120–21. The decision of a mother not to remarry, no
     longer permitted in imperial Rome, was deemed laudable during
     the republic: see S. Treggiari, *Roman Marriage* (1991), pp.
     232–7.
8.   *manly valour*: The Latin word is *virtus* (*vir* means *man* or even
     hero in Latin). As the Romans became increasingly familiar with
     Greek moral philosophy, they tended to employ *virtus* where
     Greek would use *arete*, itself a philosophical term for virtue that
     could also refer to valour.
9.   *education and study ... one of them*: The importance of educa-
     tion in the perfection of character is a recurring theme in Plutarch
     (General Introduction III).
10. *He believed that mere weapons ... ready for use*: This view is
     shared by Fabius Maximus at *Fabius Maximus* 1.
11. *wrestling*: Although skill in wrestling was admirable among the
     Greeks, it never enjoyed the same status among Romans, and
     Plutarch has invented this anecdote in order to emphasize
     Coriolanus' natural excellence and contrast him with Socrates
     and Alcibiades (*Alcibiades* 6). Nevertheless, Romans were, from
     their earliest history, at least familiar with wrestling (see H. A.
     Harris, *Sport in Greece and Rome* (1972), pp. 44–74), so the
     detail is not entirely anachronistic. Wrestling recurs in the early
     development of Romulus (*Romulus* 6) and of Philopoemen
     (*Philopoemen* 3, although the Greek, himself a talented wrestler,
     rejects the sport because it is detrimental to good soldiering).
12. *Tarquinius Superbus*: Lucius Tarquinius Superbus (Tarquin the
     Proud), traditionally the last king of Rome (534–510).
13. *stake everything upon a final throw*: This image recurs at *Fabius
     Maximus* 14 and (famously) at *Caesar* 32 and *Pompey* 60. It is
     routinely regarded as an allusion to a line from Menander, from
     his *Symbol-bearer* or *Flute Girl* (fr. 59K = Athenaeus 559d), but
     the expression was a commonplace: see A. W. Gomme and F. H.
     Sandbach, *Menander: A Commentary* (1973), pp. 690–91.
14. *the battle which followed*: Plutarch's description suggests the
     (perhaps legendary) battle of Lake Regillus, fought in 499 or
     496. This conclusion, however, is made problematic by Plu-
     tarch's internal chronology. At ch. 15, in reporting Coriolanus'
     canvass, he states that Coriolanus had earned scars during his

seventeen years of military service. But, according to Dion. Hal. (7.64) and Livy (2.35), Coriolanus was exiled in 491 (*after* his failure to win the consulship). Seventeen years of military service prior to this date would put Coriolanus' first campaign near the time of the expulsion of the Tarquins, rather earlier than the battle of Lake Regillus. These confusions ultimately stem from the unhistorical nature of the Romans' traditions about the earliest years of their city.

15. *the dictator*: Aulus Postumius Albus, consul in 496.

16. *civic crown*: Plutarch also discusses the civic crown (*corona civica*) at *Moralia* 286a, though here he has additional explanations for the choice of oak as a prize.

17. *Evander*: An Arcadian hero mentioned as early as Hesiod (fr. 168 M-W = Servius Auctus, *Aeneid* 8.130). By the third century BC Roman historians had credited Evander and his Arcadian followers with settling on the Palatine Hill (e.g. Dion. Hal. 1.79.8, citing Fabius Pictor, Cincius Alimentus and the Elder Cato). Numerous Roman institutions were traced to him.

18. *oracle of Apollo*: At Delphi; reported by Herodotus (1.66), and see also *Moralia* 406e.

19. *fruit ... honey found inside them*: Gellius (5.6.12) also credits the selection of oak for the civic crown to its ancient use as a source of food. The belief that acorns could produce honey was widespread: e.g. Hesiod, *Works and Days* 233; Virgil, *Eclogues* 4.30; and Pliny, *Natural History* 11.2.

20. *Legend has it ... where their temple now stands*: This story about Castor and Pollux is also told by Cicero (*On the Nature of the Gods* 6.13.4) and Dion. Hal. (6.13.4), and again by Plutarch (*Aemilius Paullus* 25). Their temple, dedicated in 484, stood in the Roman Forum next to the Spring of Juturna.

21. *festival dedicated to the Dioscuri*: Castor and Pollux are the Dioscuri ('sons of Zeus'). The censors of 304 instituted a cavalry parade on this day, which, although it later lapsed, was revived by Augustus.

22. *They do not think of themselves ... actions excel it*: Plutarch expresses the same sentiment at *Agis* 2.

23. *Marius' motive ... please his mother*: The psychological importance of Coriolanus' devotion to his mother is Plutarch's own invention (there is nothing like it in Dion. Hal. or Livy). In this Life it provides crucial background for their climactic encounter at chs. 35–6. It is held against Coriolanus, at *Comparison Coriolanus–Alcibiades* 4–5, that he spares Rome for the sake of his

mother and not owing to genuine patriotism. Elsewhere in his Lives Plutarch observes strong attachments between his subjects and their mothers, e.g. *Tiberius Gracchus* 1, *Caesar* 7 and *Sertorius* 2.

24. *Epaminondas*: On Epaminondas see General Introduction II. Plutarch frequently cites this saying of his (*Moralia* 193a, 786d, 1098a). Coriolanus is unfavourably contrasted with Epaminondas at *Comparison Coriolanus–Alcibiades* 4.

25. *Volumnia*: In both Livy and Dion. Hal. Coriolanus' mother is named Veturia.

26. *consul Marcus Valerius*: A slip (shared with Cicero, *Brutus* 54) for *Manius* Valerius Maximus, dictator in 494.

27. *marched out of the city*: This event is known as the First Secession of the Plebs, an early phase of the Conflict of the Orders. In Plutarch's treatment here, the complaints of the plebeians as they withdraw from Rome are not wholly dissimilar from Coriolanus' at ch. 23, the major difference being that the plebeians intend no violence against their city.

28. *Sacred Mount . . . Anio*: The Sacred Mount lay beyond the River Anio (Aniene), approximately 3 miles (nearly 5 km) outside Rome. In other versions, the plebeians withdraw to the Aventine.

29. *Menenius Agrippa*: Agrippa Menenius Lanetus (consul in 503). Cicero (*Brutus* 54) and Dion. Hal. (6.71) make Manius Valerius the chief spokesman.

30. *well-known fable*: Variations on this parable include Xenophon, *Memorablia* 2.3.18; Polyaenus, *Stratagems* 3.9.22; Cicero, *On Duties* 3.22; and I Corinthians 12:2–27.

31. *tribunes of the people*: Dion. Hal. 6.89 also claims that there were originally five tribunes, but a different tradition – represented by Cicero and others, and known to Livy (2.33.3; Asconius 76–77C) – insists that at first there were only two tribunes. Diodorus (11.68.8–9) dates the institution of the tribunate to 471, and says that originally there were four tribunes.

32. *Brutus . . . Vellutus*: Lucius Junius Brutus and Lucius Sicinius Vellutus. Plutarch here follows the order given by Dion. Hal. 6.89. Cicero and his sources (Asconius 76–77C), however, name Lucius Albinius Paterculus and Sicinius, while Livy (2.33.2) names Albinus (= Albinius) and Gaius Licinius (who, in Dion. Hal., is Publius Licinius) as the first two to become tribunes.

33. *consuls*: Inasmuch as the narrative turns instantly to war with the Volscians, these must be the consuls of 493: Postumius Cominius Auruncus and Spurius Cassius Vecellinus.

34. *Volscian people*: The Volscians' presence extended from the central Apennines to the western coast of Italy, reaching from Antium to Terracina. Wars between Romans and Volscians lasted throughout the fifth century BC and well into the fourth, after which the Volscians were eventually integrated into Rome (Arpinum, the hometown of Cicero and Marius, was originally Volscian).

35. *Corioli*: Probably not a Volscian stronghold but instead a Latin city taken by the Volscians. Its exact location remains uncertain and by Pliny's day (*Natural History* 3.69) it had long ceased to exist.

36. *Titus Larcius*: Titus Larcius Flavius, consul (for the first time) in 501.

37. *as Cato insisted that a soldier should do*: See *Elder Cato* 1 and *Moralia* 199b.

38. *unwritten will*: In Roman law soldiers were permitted to make their wills 'in any way they want or can'. Wills made by soldiers when battle was imminent were *testamenta in procinctu*, a phrase explained by antiquarians as deriving from an ancient practice whereby soldiers girded up (*praecingere*) their tunics before battle: see F. Schulz, *Classical Roman Law* (1951), pp. 240–41. Plutarch here exhibits his antiquarian learning and adds what he believed to be a bit of authentic colour to his narrative (the detail is found nowhere else).

39. *Antium*: A major Volscian centre (modern Anzio).

40. *speaker's platform*: Plutarch refers to the speaker's platform in the Romans' camp – not in Rome.

41. *charger ... prize for his valour*: This reward, which diverges from the report given in Dion. Hal. 6.94, appears to be modelled on the honour accorded to Pausanias after the Greeks' victory over the Persians in the battle of Plataea (Herodotus 9.81), the effect of which, especially for a Greek reader, is to elevate Coriolanus' achievement.

42. *henceforth be named ... notable virtue*: On Roman names see General Introduction VI. Plutarch revisits this subject at *Marius* 1, and he also wrote an essay (now lost) entitled *On the Three Names* (*Catalogue of Lamprias* 100). Despite what Plutarch says here, however, Coriolanus did not receive his surname on account of his valour at Corioli: informal honorifics did not emerge until the late fourth and early third centuries, and the first time an honorific surname was officially conferred in recognition of military victory came in 201, when Scipio was given the

name Africanus for vanquishing Hannibal in the battle of Zama (Livy 30.45.7).

43. *names ... derived from some action ... Battus*: Plutarch refers, in sequence, to Ptolemy I Soter (*Saviour*; 367–282), Seleucus II Callinicus (*Nobly Victorious*; *c.* 265–225), Ptolemy VIII Euergetes II Physcon (*Bloated*; 182–116), Antiochus VIII Philometor Grypus (*Hook-nosed*; *c.* 140–96), Ptolemy III Euergetes (*Benefactor*; 284–221), Ptolemy II Philadelphus (*Sister-loving*; 308–246) and Battus II Eudaemon (*Fortunate*; early sixth century BC).

44. *Antigonus ... Lathyrus*: Antigonus Doson (*The Man Who Will Give*; *c.* 263–221) and Ptolemy X Alexander I Lathyrus (*Bean*; *c.* 140–88).

45. *Diadematus*: Lucius Caecilius Metellus Diadematus (*The Man Wearing a Diadem*; consul in 117).

46. *Celer*: Quintus Caecilius Metellus Celer (*Swift*; tribune of the people in 90 BC); Plutarch expects his reader to know or to infer that Celer means *swift* (see also *Romulus* 10).

47. *Proculus*: Although this was an extremely common surname in Rome, its etymology and significance are unclear: see I. Kajanto, *The Latin Cognomina* (1965), p. 42.

48. *Sulla ... Claudius*: Here Plutarch expects his reader to know the Latin meanings of these Roman names, which he does not explain: Sulla (*Blotchy* – discussed further at *Sulla* 2), Niger (*Black*), Rufus (*Red*), Caecus (*Blind*) and Claudius (*Crippled*).

49. *Velitrae*: Modern Velletri, it received a colony in 494 and again in 401, and was finally annexed by Rome in 338. The city was originally Volscian.

50. *clients*: The relationship between a patron (*patronus*) and his clients (*clientes*) was an unequal one but was meant to be mutually beneficial; patrons used their superior social position to look after the interests of their clients, who in exchange gave their patrons respect and loyal support. The Romans believed the institution had been established by Romulus: see *Romulus* 13 and, more extensively, Dion. Hal. 2.8–10.

51. *walk about ... without a tunic underneath it*: Plutarch attributes this information about early Rome to the Elder Cato at *Moralia* 276c–d.

52. *Anytus*: The Athenian general who in 409 failed to prevent the loss of Pylos to the Spartans; at his subsequent trial he was alleged to have bribed the jury (Pseudo-Aristotle, *The Athenian Constitution* 27.5). He remained a leading figure, however, and is familiar as a prosecutor of Socrates at his trial in 399.

53. *the companion of solitude*: This phrase occurs in Plato's letter to the Syracusan political figure Dion (*c*. 408–353), *Epistle* 4 (312c). Plutarch cites this expression again in his criticism of Coriolanus at *Comparison Coriolanus–Alcibiades* 3, as well as at *Dion* 8 and 52, and *Moralia* 69f–70a.

54. *Gelon . . . of Syracuse*: Gelon (*c*. 540–478) made himself master of Gela around 491. In 485 he became master of Syracuse as well and transferred his government there.

55. *exactly what is done by . . . the Greeks*: Distributions of subsidized and free grain, characteristic of Roman politics in the late republic and the empire, were not typical even of radical Greek democracies.

56. *aediles*: The two plebeian aediles were originally subordinates of the tribunes and, like them, their persons could not be violated. In the fourth century BC they became magistrates in their own right, with significant responsibilities, and were eventually indistinguishable in duties and status from curule aediles (which office was finally opened to plebeians). According to Dion. Hal. (7.26.3), these aediles were Titus Junius Brutus and Gaius Visellius Ruga.

57. *consuls*: The consuls of 491 were Marcus Minucius Augurinus and Aulus Sempronius Atratinus.

58. *Tarpeian Rock*: A cliff on the Capitoline from which murderers and traitors might be hurled to their deaths (*Romulus* 17–18; the practice was discontinued in AD 43).

59. *Appius Claudius*: Originally a Sabine who migrated to Rome with a large band of clients and became consul in 495; see further *Publicola* 21.

60. *centuries . . . tribes*: An anachronism. Capital cases could only be tried before the centuriate assembly, which was organized in such a way that the votes of the rich could dominate the assembly. Here, however, the tribunes resort to the more democratic tribal assembly, which in this period consisted of twenty-one tribes.

61. *Tullus Aufidius*: The manuscripts of Plutarch read Aufidius (or Autidius) Tullus, whereas Livy and Dion. Hal. call him Attius Tullus, who is also named at Plutarch, *Cicero* 1. Whether the discrepancy owes itself to textual error or not is uncertain (Plutarch's names for Coriolanus' wife and mother, after all, are unique in the tradition).

62. *'It is hard . . . life itself'*: This was a saying of Heracleitus of Ephesus (fr. 85 DK), who flourished around 500 and whose

writings survive only by way of quotations. It was popular with
Greek philosophers (e.g. it is adapted by Plato at *Republic* 375b
and *Laws* 863b and is cited by Aristotle at *Nicomachean Ethics*
1105a7, *Eudemian Ethics* 1223b22 and *Politics* 1315a29), not
least Plutarch, who returns to it at *Moralia* 457d and 755d. Its
meaning, including its likely allusion to the anger of Achilles, is
discussed by C. H. Kahn, *The Art and Thought of Heraclitus*
(1979), pp. 241–4.

63. *'Into the enemy's city . . . disguised'*: Homer, *Odyssey* 4.246.

64. *There was a certain Titus Latinus . . . without any help*: This
story was told by numerous ancient sources, sometimes in versions entirely unrelated to Coriolanus (Cicero, *On Divination*
1.55; Macrobius, *Saturnalia* 1.11.3).

65. *sacred procession . . . of Jupiter*: Jupiter was naturally central to
many religious festivals, but this event will have been the Roman
Games (*Ludi Romani*), held in early September.

66. *Any slave . . . furcifer*: Plutarch repeats this information at
Moralia 280e–f.

67. *the procession . . . enacted a second time*: Religious rituals in
Rome were vitiated, and the Romans' relationship with the gods
ruptured, by any procedural error or bad omen. The Romans
could restore their relationship with the gods, however, simply
by repeating the ritual.

68. *foresight of Numa*: See *Numa* 14.

69. *tensae*: Special carriages used to transport statues of the gods to
public spectacles.

70. *Some authorities . . . set fire to the city*: So Livy 2.37.2 and
Dion. Hal. 8.2.3–5 – and so Plutarch himself at *Comparison
Coriolanus–Alcibiades* 2.

71. *Circeii*: Modern Monte Circello. A Roman colony was believed
to have been founded there during the monarchy (Livy 1.56.3),
though other sources date Circeii's colonization to the fourth
century BC.

72. *Tolerium . . . Bola*: Four cities of Latium whose locations remain
uncertain, although it has been suggested that modern Corcolla
is Pedum.

73. *Bovillae*: Modern Frattocchie.

74. *100 stades*: Between 11 and 12 miles (approximately 18 km).

75. *Lavinium*: Modern Pratica di Mare, a city of major (especially
cultic) importance in the archaic period.

76. *they were helpless . . . previous decree of the senate*: Plutarch is
here thinking of the archaic (and not fully understood) require-

ment that decisions of popular assemblies receive the assent of the 'fathers', presumably the senatorial patricians (*patrum auctoritas*): a law of 339 required that this assent be given before the assemblies voted. This assent was probably not required for the plebeian assembly, but its measures were not universally binding until the third century BC.

77. *Fossae Cluiliae*: An ancient trench, the precise purpose and location of which remain unclear. Its proximity to the city signals Rome's heightened peril from Coriolanus.

78. *40 stades*: About 4½ miles (approximately 7⅓ km).

79. *civil rights ... to the Latins*: After the battle of Lake Regillus (note 14), the Romans concluded a treaty with the defeated Latins, the Cassian Treaty (*foedus Cassianum*: Dion. Hal. 6.95), which took its name from the consul who negotiated it – Spurius Cassius (consul for the second time in 493). This treaty provided for peace and mutual defence and stipulated means for dealing with lawsuits between Latins and Romans.

80. *order of priests ... art of divination*: Plutarch refers to the three leading priestly colleges: (i) the pontiffs (*pontifices*), (ii) the two men responsible for sacred actions (*duoviri sacris faciundis* – the number of whom during the republic was later increased to ten and then to fifteen) and (iii) the diviners or augurs (*augures*). All of these offices were routinely filled by members of the senatorial class.

81. *'Then ... this notion'*: Homer, *Odyssey* 18.158 and 21.1.

82. *'Then ... men might say'*: A slight misquotation of Homer, *Iliad* 9.459–60.

83. *'Either ... enjoined him to act'*: Homer, *Odyssey* 9.339.

84. *'Then ... stout heart'*: *Odyssey* 9.299.

85. *'Such ... strove for decision'*: Homer, *Iliad* 1.188–9.

86. *' ... but ... upright resolve'*: *Iliad* 6.161–2.

87. *Jupiter Capitolinus*: This is the temple to Jupiter Best and Greatest, on the Capitoline Hill, which was central to Roman civic religion (*Publicola* 13–15).

88. *Publicola*: He is the subject of Plutarch's *Publicola*. It is obvious that Valeria is not truly integral to the story of Coriolanus and it has been suggested that she was introduced by the first-century BC historian Valerius Antias, whose history tended to aggrandize the Valerii: see T. P. Wiseman, *Roman Drama and Roman History* (1998), p. 88.

89. *daughters of the Sabines ... peace*: Valeria refers to the aftermath of the Rape of the Sabine Women (*Romulus* 19).

90. *Fortune of Women*: The temple of the Fortune of Women (*Fortuna Muliebris*) was located 4 miles (6½ km) outside Rome on the Latin Way.

91. *'Women ... pleasing to the gods'*: This statue expresses itself differently at *Moralia* 318f–319a. Only one other statue in Plutarch speaks: the statue of Juno (*Camillus* 6).

92. *statues ... takes place inside*: See *Moralia* 397e–398b and 404b, where Plutarch discusses miraculous actions by statues.

93. *attributes of the divine ... incredibility*: Heracleitus of Ephesus (note 62), fr. 86 DK, also cited by Clement of Alexandria, *Miscellanies* 5.88.4. The original context of this fragment (and consequently the extent of its adaptation here by Plutarch) is far from clear (it is not obvious that 'attributes of the divine' was Heracleitus' subject for 'escapes'): see Kahn, *The Art and Thought of Heraclitus*, p. 212.

94. *wear mourning ... mentioned in his Life*: Numa 12.

95. *Aequians*: Little is known of them, but they, like the Volscians (and at about the same time), pushed into Latium and fought a sequence of wars against the Romans.

96. *defeated by the Romans ... obey her commands*: The Volscians began to succumb to the Romans in the fourth century BC.

CAMILLUS

Further Reading

There is no English commentary on the *Life of Camillus*. Nor has the work attracted much in the way of literary study: it figures mostly in historical inquiries or as an alternative account of the Camillus legend in historiographical treatments of Livy – or as a resource for antiquarian research. There is, however, a very useful Italian introduction with (remarkably detailed) commentary by C. Carena, M. Manfredini and L. Piccirilli (eds.), *Le Vite di Temistocle e di Camillo* (1983). The best investigations of this pairing are D. H. J. Larmour, 'Making Parallels: Synkrisis and Plutarch's *Themistokles and Camillus*', in *ANRW* 2.33.6 (1992), 4154–200, and T. Duff, 'Plutarch's *Themistocles and Camillus*', in Humble, *Plutarch's Lives*, pp. 45–86. Although rather dated, and exacting for non-experts, a good account of the development of the Camillus legend in Roman historiography is provided by A. Momigliano, 'Camillus and Concord', *CQ* 36 (1942), pp. 111–20. A. T. Grafton and N. M. Swerdlow, 'Dates and Ominous Days in

Ancient Historiography', *Journal of the Warburg and Courtauld Institutes* 51 (1988), pp. 14–42, illustrates the importance of anti-quarian investigation in *Camillus*. The significance of the Capitoline – and of the physical city of Rome in general – to Roman mentalities is made clear by C. Edwards, *Writing Rome: Textual Approaches to the City* (1996). J. H. C. Williams, *Beyond the Rubi-con: Romans and Gauls in Republican Italy* (2001), explains the Roman (and Greek) conceptions of Gauls and the various purposes, literary and cultural, to which Gauls were put. The Livian perspective is unpacked by C. Kraus, ' "No second Troy": Topoi and refounda-tion in Livy, Book V', *TAPhA* 124 (1994), pp. 267–89, while the reception of Camillus in Dionysius of Halicarnassus, Appian and Cas-sius Dio is discussed by A. M. Gowing, 'The Roman *exempla* tradition in imperial Greek historiography: the case of Camillus', in A. Feldherr (ed.), *A Cambridge Companion to the Roman Historians* (2009), pp. 332–61. G. Dumézil, *Camillus: A Study of Indo-European Religion as Roman History* (1980), investigates the underlying significance of the story of Camillus by way of comparative mythology.

Notes to the Introduction to Camillus

1. The Camillus legend is discussed by R. M. Ogilvie, *A Commen-tary on Livy, Books 1–5* (1965), pp. 626–30, 669–71, 741–3, 750–51; Cornell, *Beginnings of Rome*, pp. 310–22; S. P. Oakley, *A Commentary on Livy, Books 6–10*, vol. 1 (1997), pp. 376–9; and Forsythe, *Early Rome*, pp. 251–67.

2. This process is concisely reviewed in Momigliano, *CQ* 36, pp. 111–20 (with complete references to earlier scholarship on the matter).

3. Momigliano, *CQ* 36, pp. 111–20; Ogilvie, *Commentary on Livy, Books 1–5*, pp. 736–7; and Cornell, *Beginnings of Rome*, pp. 316–18.

4. There are useful discussions in C. A. Krauss, *Livy: Ab Urbe Con-dita, Book VI* (1994), pp. 24–7, and Oakley, *Commentary on Livy, Books 6–10*, vol. 2 (1998), pp. 35–7.

5. In addition to Dion. Hal. and Livy, Diodorus 14.113–17 is an important source for the story of Camillus. Each of these writers relied on earlier accounts, now lost or known only by occasional citation.

6. There is a good discussion of this matter in Cornell, *Beginnings of Rome*, pp. 316–17.

7.   For glimpses of rivals to Camillus, see Suetonius, *Tiberius* 3.2, and Strabo 5.2.3.

8.   See Williams, *Beyond the Rubicon*, pp. 170–82.

9.   See Edwards, *Writing Rome*, pp. 74–88.

10. In general, see Cornell, *Beginnings of Rome*, pp. 313–18, and Williams, *Beyond the Rubicon*, pp. 140–84.

11. Graeco-Roman stereotypes regarding Gauls are discussed by Williams, *Beyond the Rubicon*.

12. The others are *Alexander–Caesar*, *Phocion–Younger Cato* and *Pyrrhus–Marius*.

13. For instance, at ch. 17 (Dion. Hal. 13.12), ch. 27 (Dion. Hal. 13.7), ch. 32 (Dion. Hal. 14.2) and chs. 40–41 (Dion. Hal. 14.9).

14. Cooperation and moderation are virtues prized by Plutarch: see Duff, *Plutarch's Lives*, pp. 89–90 and 139–40. On the Conflict of the Orders, see Introduction to *Coriolanus*.

15. For example, at Livy 6.38.5 Camillus is 'filled with anger and with threats' (*plenus irae minarumque*). In his *Galba* (ch. 29), Plutarch adduces Camillus as an example of a stern disciplinarian.

16. See Pelling, *P&H*, pp. 365–6.

17. See Introduction to *Coriolanus* and Jones, 'Chronology', pp. 106–14.

18. See *Moralia* 809b–810a and 823f–825f. Important discussions of these virtues and their relevance to Plutarch's cultural and political circumstances can be found in A. E. Wardman, *Plutarch's Lives* (1974), pp. 57–63, Jones, *P&R*, pp. 111–21, and Duff, *Plutarch's Lives*, pp. 89–94.

19. See General Introduction IV.

Notes to the Life of Camillus

1.   *military tribunes with consular powers*: From 444 to 367 the Romans frequently elected military tribunes with consular powers (consular tribunes) instead of consuls. The reasons for this practice elude us, but one ancient view (reflected here) connected the office with the Conflict of the Orders; unlike the consulship, plebeians as well as patricians could be elected consular tribunes. On the Conflict of the Orders, see Introduction to *Coriolanus*.

2.   *six men instead of two*: There were not invariably six consular tribunes, although that is the most frequently attested number.

3.   *many different offices*: In addition to the offices mentioned in this chapter, Camillus was censor (see below) and (mentioned

only by Livy) *interrex* (on this office, see *Marcellus* 6) three times (in 396, 391 and 389).

4. *Furii ... first of his line to win fame*: There were already distinguished Furii by this point in Roman history. However, of Camillus' immediate origins or family line nothing was preserved or fabricated in the historians on whom Plutarch relied.

5. *Postumius Tubertus*: Aulus Postumius Tubertus was dictator in 431. Only Plutarch associates Camillus with this campaign.

6. *appointment as censor*: In 403. The connection drawn by Plutarch here with events in 431 is tenuous.

7. *consular tribune for the second time*: Camillus was consular tribune for the first time in 399, when he campaigned against the Falerians, and for the second time in 398, when he campaigned against the Capenates (see following notes).

8. *Falerians*: The inhabitants of Falerii Veteres (modern Cività Castellana) – the major city of the Faliscans – were a people who dwelt north of Veii. The Falerians were part of the Faliscan people.

9. *Capenates*: The people of ancient Capena (located not quite 3 miles or 5 km north of modern Capena); they were related in language and material culture to the Faliscans.

10. *Alban lake*: The modern Lago Albano (or Lago di Castel Gondolfo), located far to the south of Veii in Latium, near the site of Alba Longa.

11. *a marvellous prodigy ... autumn*: This is cited by numerous sources. In Dion. Hal. (12.10) it occurs during the summer.

12. *envoys*: Only Plutarch provides their names; their exact identification is uncertain. Cossius Licinius has been identified with Gnaeus Cornelius Cossus (consular tribune 406) or Publius Licinius Clavus (consular tribune 400); Valerius Potitus is either the consul of 410 or the consul of 392; Fabius Ambustus is either the consular tribune of 410 or the consular tribune of 406.

13. *Latin festivals*: The Latin Festival (*Feriae Latinae*), in honour of Jupiter Latiaris, was associated with Alba Longa and the Alban Mount, hence its relevance to the prodigy of the Alban lake.

14. *necessary sacrifices*: According to Livy (5.17.4), expiating the flawed Latin Festival entailed holding new elections, at which Camillus acted as an *interrex*.

15. *tenth year of the war ... dictator*: In 396.

16. *Cornelius Scipio*: An imperial inscription names him Publius Cornelius Maluginensis.

17. *Mater Matuta*: A divinity associated with fertility and childbirth. Her temple, elsewhere said to have been dedicated by Servius Tullius, was in the Forum Boarium. She was honoured in a festival known as the Matralia. This goddess was identified by some with Leucothea (e.g. Ovid, *Fasti* 6.545), a divinity who was early on (e.g. Homer, *Odyssey* 5.333) associated with Ino, the sister of Semele and so the aunt of Dionysus.

18. *the nursing of Dionysus . . . concubine*: At *Moralia* 267e, Plutarch associates Ino's nursing of Dionysus with the Romans' prayers to Mater Matuta for the wellbeing of their sisters' children, and at *Moralia* 267d he explains the violence done by worshippers to a slave girl by citing Ino's jealousy of her husband's slave.

19. *The Roman soldiers then seized the entrails . . . fable*: In describing this same event, Livy (5.21.8) employs a technical term for cutting out sacred entrails – *hostiae exta prosecuisset* (to whoever ritually cut out these entrails) – which Plutarch seems to have misread as *prosecutus esset* (completed). Livy characterizes this episode as a *fabula*.

20. *burst into tears*: The shedding of tears at the sight of a cataclysmic reversal of fortune displays sound Hellenic sensibilities and a correct understanding of the workings of history. Although the motif is old, its most influential instance was probably Polybius' account of Scipio Aemilianus' tears at the destruction of Carthage (38.21). Later historians, including Plutarch, put the effect to similar work (in this volume at *Marcellus* 19 and *Aemilius Paullus* 26). See further A. Rossi, *Greece & Rome* 47 (2000), pp. 56–66, and the essays by D. Lateiner and L. de Libero in T. Fögen, *Tears in the Graeco-Roman World* (2009).

21. *he turned himself to the right . . . adoration*: Plutarch makes similar observations at *Numa* 14 and *Marcellus* 6.

22. *disaster*: The word here translated *disaster* also means *fall*. Camillus' slip is a very bad omen in Livy (5.21.16) and Dion. Hal. (12.16.4–5): in each account it presages a future disgrace for Camillus, and in Livy it foretells Rome's destruction in the Gallic sack.

23. *remove the image of Juno . . . vowed*: Livy (5.21.3) includes such a vow in advance of Camillus' campaign against Veii, but Plutarch has made no prior mention of it.

24. *offered the goddess sacrifice . . . other gods of the city*: This ritual was known as *evocatio*, whereby a foreign divinity was expected to abandon its original city and accept a new home in

Rome. Veii's Juno was installed in a temple on the Aventine, where she became Rome's Juno Regina.

25. *Livy ... says ... come along with him*: This is *not* what Livy reports: in his version (5.22.5), Camillus is not present; one of the youths sent to fetch the statue asks, as a joke, if it is willing to come along, and his companions join in to give the statue's response – and only later, Livy insists, did the story emerge that the statue itself had spoken.

26. *phenomena ... recorded*: Plutarch also discusses miraculous actions by statues at *Coriolanus* 37–8.

27. *best ... the avoidance of all extremes*: Plutarch's Greek here (*to meden agan ariston*) quotes the familiar inscription on the temple of Apollo at Delphi (Plato, *Charmides* 165a: *meden agan* – 'nothing in excess'), and the sentiment is found in early poetry (Theognis 335 may be the earliest instance).

28. *celebrated his triumph ... four white horses*: Romulus (Propertius 4.1.32) and Julius Caesar (Cassius Dio 43.14.3) are also said to have celebrated triumphs in chariots drawn by four white horses, and in Ovid's *Fasti* (6.724) the triumph of the dictator Aulus Postumius Tubertus (note 5) is distinguished by white horses (their number is not specified).

29. *8 talents of gold*: An Attic talent (the measure Plutarch has in mind) weighed approximately 26 kilograms or 50 pounds.

30. *public encomium*: The first woman known to have received a public funeral oration was Popilia in 102. She was eulogized by her son, Quintus Lutatius Catulus, who was consul in that year (Cicero, *On the Ideal Orator* 2.11.44). Livy (5.50.7) explains the matrons' honour differently.

31. *three of the noblest men*: Lucius Valerius Potitus (consular tribune in 414), Lucius Sergius (consular tribune in 397) and Aulus Manlius (consular tribune in 405).

32. *Aeolian islands ... pirates*: Lipara (modern Lipari) is the largest of the Aeolian islands (modern Isole Eolie) in the Tyrrhenian Sea, off the north coast of Sicily. Lipara pursued an aggressively independent naval policy: Liparians are sometimes described as pirates (so, in relating this episode, Livy 5.28.2–4).

33. *dedication*: This dedication was kept in the treasury at Delphi that belonged to the city of Massilia (modern Marseilles) (Diodorus 1.93.4; Appian, *Italy* 8.3).

34. *Timesitheus ... honoured by the Romans*: When the Romans annexed Lipara in 252, the descendants of Timesitheus preserved their privileges (Diodorus 14.93).

35. *circumstances that required . . . proven by experience*: Plutarch adds this comment in order to explain how Camillus won election despite his unpopularity. This was Camillus' third election as consular tribune (in 394).

36. *remedy . . . humours from the state*: Plutarch also employs this metaphor from medicine at *Numa* 8 and *Coriolanus* 12. It is adapted from Plato, *Republic* 372e.

37. *indictment . . . prosecutor was Lucius Apuleius*: The trial is dated to 391. Pliny (*Natural History* 34.13) names the quaestor Spurius Carvilius as Camillus' prosecutor.

38. *like Achilles . . . laid curses . . . left the city*: See Homer, *Iliad* 1.233–44, where Achilles, insulted by Agamemnon, withdraws from battle and urges the gods to bring misfortune on his fellow Achaeans so that they will appreciate how greatly they require his valour.

39. *asses . . . denarius*: See General Introduction VI.

40. *Julius*: Gaius Julius Jullus was elected censor in 393 and died in 392.

41. *Marcus Caedicius*: A name suitable for a recipient of a prophecy of disaster (*caedes* in Latin). This divinity will receive cult status as Aius Locutius at ch. 30.

42. *Gauls . . . Celtic people*: For Graeco-Roman ideas about Gauls, see Introduction. Plutarch, like other Greek writers, tends to use Gaul and Celt interchangeably.

43. *Rhipaean mountains*: Their identity varies considerably in our Greek sources, and the geographer Strabo (8.295 and 299) goes so far as to deny their existence.

44. *Senones . . . Bituriges*: The Senones inhabited what is now Champagne and southern Burgundy; the Bituriges, parts of the Loire valley. Each name here is, owing to the condition of the manuscripts, somewhat conjectural.

45. *taste for wine*: In their excessive fondness for wine the Gauls exhibit their (stereotypical) incapacity to control their appetites.

46. *Arruns . . . into Italy*: This story was known to Polybius and the Elder Cato and variations of it are told by Livy (5.33.1–4) and Dion. Hal. (13.10). In Livy, Arruns is a citizen of Clusium and this story is (tentatively) linked to the Gallic sack of Rome.

47. *Adria*: Or Atria (modern Atri), then a coastal city but now, however, more than 12 miles (19 km) from the sea, lies in the Po valley and was possibly originally a Greek city that fell under

Etruscan control. It was, from the sixth century BC, an important port city.

48. *Etruscan Sea*: The Tyrrhenian (i.e. Etruscan) Sea.

49. *eighteen . . . cities*: Livy (5.33.9) mentions twelve cities.

50. *those events took place long ago*: Plutarch's chronology is unclear; he does not connect the story of Arruns with the fall of Rome and sets the Gauls' conquest of the Etruscan cities in the distant past, yet it is the Gallic invasion of Etruria that here (and traditionally) leads to the capture of Rome. A more detailed (though not for that reason more reliable) account is provided by Livy 5.34–5.

51. *Clusium*: Modern Chiusi.

52. *Three men of the Fabii*: Quintus Fabius Ambustus (consular tribune in 390), Kaeso Fabius (consular tribune in 404) and Numerius Fabius (consular tribune in 406), but there are difficulties attending these identifications.

53. *the Fidenates*: The people of Fidenae (modern Castel Giubileo), which was conquered by Rome in 498.

54. *the Ardeates*: The people of Ardea, a Latin city of considerable wealth. It was brought inside Rome's sphere of influence by Tarquinius Superbus and became an ally of Rome by treaty in 444.

55. *most ancient of all laws . . . the weak*: This sentiment reprises Plato, *Gorgias* 482c–486d.

56. *many denounced Fabius*: In the version recorded by Diodorus (14.113.5–6), the senate seeks to accommodate the Gauls but is thwarted by the people.

57. *Fetiales . . . justly make war*: See *Numa* 12 and notes 83–5 there.

58. *sacrifices . . . before the perils of battle*: Roman battles were preceded by ritual practices designed to diagnose whether the gods permitted them to fight on the day.

59. *River Allia*: The modern Fosso delle Bettina, which flows into the Tiber about 11 miles (18 km) north of Rome.

60. *Fabian disaster . . . had taken place*: In 477, 300 members of the Fabian clan fell in battle at the Cremera river and the catastrophe was remembered on the Day of Cremera (*dies Cremerensis*). Ovid (*Fasti* 2.195–242), diverging from the usual tradition, dates this event to 13 February.

61. *the Day of Allia*: (*Dies Alliensis*) The darkest day in Roman history, 18 July 390. Plutarch is unspecific here, possibly because he wants to exhibit his learned conclusion that the battle was fought near the time of a full moon, but it is not obvious that he diverges from the traditional date.

62. *the topic of unspeakable days ... examined elsewhere*: Hesiod
discusses the nature of various days in his *Works and Days*
(765–825). Heracleitus' reproach is not otherwise known. Ill-
omened days as well as historical synchronicities, the topics of
the following digression, invited learned investigation – and Plutarch was an expert. He recurs to these subjects frequently,
including in his (now lost) works *On Days* and *On the Works
and Days of Hesiod*. See A. T. Grafton and N. M. Swerdlow,
Journal of the Warburg and Courtauld Institutes 51 (1988), pp.
14–42.

63. *Boeotians*: Inhabitants of Boeotia, a region in central Greece
whose major city was Thebes. Plutarch's native Chaeronea was
a Boeotian city.

64. *their month ... Hecatombaeon*: Each Greek city had its own
calendar with its own months. Hippodromius and Hecatombaeon correspond very roughly with July.

65. *two glorious victories ... Thessalians*: At Leuctra (in Boeotia) in
371 the Thebans, under the command of Epaminondas, defeated
the Spartans, at that time the dominant power in Greece. Little
is known of the Thessalian commander Lattamyas. In his essay
On the Malignity of Herodotus (*Moralia* 866e), Plutarch dates
his defeat at Ceressus to just before 480 (much later than the
date indicated here).

66. *Persians were defeated ... at Marathon*: The battle of Marathon
occurred in 490. The Athenian month Boedromion corresponds
very roughly with September; on the sixth the Athenians annually offered sacrifice to Artemis in thanksgiving for their victory
over the Persians.

67. *Persians were defeated ... at ... Mycale*: In 479 the Persians
were defeated on land at Plataea (in southern Boeotia) and at sea
off Mycale (a mountain in western Anatolia, opposite Samos). In
his *Aristeides*, Plutarch dates the battle of Plataea to the fourth
of the month.

68. *also defeated at Arbela*: The battle of Arbela of 331 is better
known as the battle of Gaugamela (a site in modern Iraq, possibly Tell Gomel), Alexander the Great's decisive victory over the
Persians (*Alexander* 31).

69. *Naxos*: The largest island of the Cyclades.

70. *Chabrias*: Athenian admiral who defeated the Spartans in battle
in 376.

71. *Salamis*: The Athenians decisively defeated the Persian navy at
the battle of Salamis in 480. Elsewhere Plutarch dates the battle

to the sixteenth day of the Athenian month Munichion (*Lysander* 15, *Moralia* 349f). Plutarch's *On Days* is no longer extant.

72. *Thargelion*: This Athenian month corresponds very roughly with May.

73. *Granicus*: Alexander the Great defeated the Persians at the River Granicus (in northwest Asia Minor: the modern Biga Çayi) in 334.

74. *Carthaginians were beaten ... in Sicily*: Timoleon won this victory in 341 (*Timoleon* 27).

75. *Ephorus ... Malacas*: Ephorus (c. 405–330) was a widely influential historian of Greece. Callisthenes was the nephew of Aristotle and a historian of Alexander the Great's exploits until he was implicated in a conspiracy against the king and put to death in 327. Damastes was a fifth-century BC historian and geographer, roughly contemporary with Herodotus. For the fourth name the manuscripts divide: Malacas (*FGrH* 442), the likelier reading, was a historian of Siphnos (an island in the Cyclades) about whom very little is known; Phylarchus (*FGrH* 81), the alternative, was a third-century BC historian whose work concentrated on the period from 272 to 219 (and was much consulted by Plutarch: see *Aratus*).

76. *Metageitnion*: This Athenian month, like Panemus, corresponds very roughly with August.

77. *Antipater*: (c. 397–319) One of the successors of Alexander the Great, who crushed a Greek uprising against Macedon at the battle of Crannon (a city in Thessaly) in 322.

78. *Philip*: Philip II (382–336), the father of Alexander, made himself master of Greece at the battle of Chaeronea in 338.

79. *Archidamus*: Archidamus III, king of Sparta from 360 until his death in 338, when he was defeated in Italy while fighting in support of Tarentum (modern Taranto) against the Lucanians, an Oscan people of southern Italy.

80. *Chalcedonians*: Inhabitants of Chalcedon (modern Kadiköy), a Greek city on the Asian side of the Bosporus. According to a fragment of Arrian (*FGrH* 156 F 79), the Persian satrap Pharnabazus (late fourth and early third centuries BC) seized the boys of the city in order to make them into eunuchs.

81. *the Mysteries ... Iacchus*: The Eleusinian Mysteries took place each year in Athens, from the 14th to the 23rd of Boedromion, in the sacred precinct of Eleusis. Iacchus was a divinity celebrated in the procession from Athens to Eleusis, when participants

shouted out *iakcho iakche* (see Aristophanes, *Frogs* 316). Alexander destroyed Thebes in 335; the Macedonians installed a garrison in Athens in 322.

82. *Caepio ... Tigranes*: Quintus Servilius Caepio (consul in 106) suffered a crushing defeat at the battle of Arausio (modern Orange) on 6 October 105. On that same day in 69 BC, Lucius Licinius Lucullus (consul in 74 BC) won a brilliant victory over Tigranes (*Lucullus* 27).

83. *Attalus ... birthday*: It is unclear which Attalus Plutarch has in mind here. At *Moralia* 717e Plutarch reports a controversy over whether Pompey died on his birthday or on the day after; at *Pompey* 79 he prefers the day after.

84. *Roman Questions*: At *Moralia* 269e–270d.

85. *Vestal Virgins*: See *Numa* 9–11.

86. *with the Muses ... activates all things*: See *Numa* 8–9 and 13.

87. *everything ... kept hidden*: The objects guarded by the Vestals were secret. Nevertheless, ancient writers offered many suggestions.

88. *Palladium*: A wooden image of Pallas Athena that fell from the sky and was kept by the Trojans.

89. *Samothracian images ... came to Italy*: Dion. Hal. (1.68–9) reports how the mysteries of the Great Gods were established on Samothrace (an island in the northern Aegean) by the Arcadians, where ultimately there was a famous Panhellenic sanctuary devoted to them. Dardanus was said to have devoted a temple to these gods on Samothrace before he went on to found Troy; their sacred images were later removed to Troy and Aeneas ultimately carried them to Italy. See further H. Bowden, *Mystery Cults of the Ancient World* (2010), pp. 49–67.

90. *Quirinus*: The god came to be identified as the deified Romulus. His temple was located on the Quirinal Hill near what is now the Via del Quirinale (*Romulus* 28–9).

91. *Jars*: The Doliola was apparently a place in the Forum Boarium near the Cloaca Maxima under which were buried jars (*dolia*). Accounts of their origin and purpose varied.

92. *a Greek city*: Other sources name the Vestals' destination as Caere (modern Cerveteri), a Hellenized Etruscan city.

93. *Fabius*: The chief priest (*pontifex maximus*) was Marcus Folius (consular tribune in 433); the name, however, may have already been corrupted in Plutarch's sources.

94. *Heracleides ... Great Sea*: Heracleides of Pontus was a fourth-century BC philosopher who studied with Plato and Aristotle. His

works, especially his dialogues, which incorporated colourful mythical tales, were widely influential though they are now almost entirely lost. The Hyperboreans were a mythical people who dwelt in the very far north. The Great Sea was Heracleides' strange and apparently misleading expression for the Mediterranean.

95. *report of the city's capture by the Gauls ... Marcus*: Aristotle recorded this event in a now lost work. What Plutarch takes to be Aristotle's error owes itself to the reality that, when he wrote, Camillus had not yet been made into Rome's saviour; scholarly efforts to identify his Lucius bring varying results, though it is possible that Aristotle had in mind an account in which Lucius Albinius played a more substantial role than the one preserved in this Life and in other sources. Other early Greek sources took notice of Rome's fall, e.g. the Greek historian Theopompus (cited by Pliny, *Natural History* 3.57).

96. *Manius Papirius*: In Livy (5.41.9) he is Marcus Papirius; in Valerius Maximus (3.2.7) he is Marcus Atilius.

97. *Pontius Cominius*: At *Moralia* 324f Plutarch calls him Gaius Pontius.

98. *Carmental Gate*: The Porta Carmentalis was located at the southwest corner of the Capitol.

99. *appointed Camillus dictator*: The procedure for appointing a dictator is described in *Marcellus* 24.

100. *[So it was ... enemy]*: The sentence in brackets largely reproduces its predecessor. Plutarch cannot have intended to preserve both versions.

101. *Manlius, a former consul*: Marcus Manlius Capitolinus was consul in 392.

102. *reward ... of wine*: Cf. the reward granted Horatius Cocles at *Publicola* 16.

103. *Sulpicius*: Quintus Sulpicius Longus was consular tribune in 390.

104. *proverbial saying*: Cf. Livy 5.48.9: *vae victis*.

105. *Gabii*: A prosperous Latin city, approximately 12 miles (19 km) east of Rome. Plutarch's situation of the Gallic camp corresponds closely with Livy's (5.49.6).

106. *Ides of ... February*: Plutarch uses Quintilis instead of July. The Ides fell on 15 July: the battle of Allia took place on 18 July and the sack of Rome on the third day thereafter (ch. 22); in February the Ides also fell on the fifteenth.

107. *Rumour and Voice*: See ch. 14. Plutarch here translates *Aius Locutius*, a divinity each of whose names signifies speaking. His altar was on the Palatine.

108. *severed . . . head of all Italy*: An enduring Roman belief (Livy 1.55.5 and Dion. Hal. 4.59–61).

109. *Lucius Lucretius*: Lucius Lucretius Flavus was suffect consul in 393 (and several times thereafter a consular tribune). Plutarch suggests here that, of the senators distinguished by high office, he was the leading member (*princeps senatus*).

110. *in a spirit of religious deference . . . agreed with the god*: A common form of divination was to take up an overheard remark and apply it to one's own circumstances. Here Lucretius accepts the omen by employing the routine senatorial formula for agreeing with a preceding speaker ('I agree with so-and-so').

111. *shrine of Mars*: This was the Curia Saliorum on the Palatine, a shrine supervised by the Salii (Numa 13), a priesthood associated with the worship of Mars (Cicero, *On Divination* 1.30, and Valerius Maximus 1.8.11).

112. *augural staff . . . as Romulus . . . had done with this one*: See *Romulus* 22. The augurs employed this staff in demarcating a *templum*, a sacred precinct in the sky, in which to observe omens.

113. *Romulus vanished*: This is discussed in *Romulus* 27–9 and *Numa* 2.

114. *Sutrium*: Modern Sutri, originally an Etruscan city, about 28 miles (45 km) northwest of Rome.

115. *appointed dictator for the third time*: In 389.

116. *fabulous version*: Plutarch relates an abbreviated version of this tale at *Romulus* 29. It is also recounted (with the same uncertainty concerning the slave's name) by Macrobius, *Saturnalia* 1.11.36–40; at 3.2.11, however, Macrobius cites the historian Calpurnius Piso, who says the invaders were Etruscans.

117. *Capratine Nones*: The Nones of July fell on the seventh. This festival was also known as the *Ancillarum Feriae*, the Festival for Slave Women.

118. *recorded in his Life*: See *Romulus* 29 and *Numa* 2. In all three passages Plutarch confounds the Capratine Nones with the *Poplifugia* (The Flight of the People), which took place on 5 July and commemorated the disappearance of Romulus, but this confusion may have existed already in Plutarch's sources, inasmuch as the Poplifugia was well out of fashion by the first century BC (Varro, *On the Latin Language* 6.18).

119. *night attack . . . Capitolinus*: See ch. 27. Manlius was not the first Roman or the first in his family to have the name *Capitolinus*, which he possessed owing to the family's residence on the Capitoline.

120. *Quintus Capitolinus . . . dictator*: According to Livy (6.11.10 and 15–16), the dictator was Aulus Cornelius Cossus and Titus Quinctius Capitolinus was his master of the horse.

121. *again elected consular tribune*: In 384.

122. *prosecutors*: Manlius was prosecuted by the tribunes of the people Marcus Menenius and Quintus Publilius.

123. *the Peteline Grove*: Immediately outside the Porta Flumentana (the River Gate), where the height of the wall obscured the Capitoline.

124. *built . . . a temple to . . . Moneta*: The temple of Juno Moneta was vowed by Lucius Furius Camillus, dictator in 345, and son or grandson of Camillus.

125. *no patrician . . . dwell on the Capitol*: According to a different tradition, reflected in Livy (6.20.13), the family was obliged to surrender its use of the name *Capitolinus*.

126. *sixth time . . . consular tribune*: In 381.

127. *Lucius Furius*: Lucius Furius Medullinus.

128. *Praenestines*: Inhabitants of Praeneste (modern Palestrina), a prosperous Latin city and an important religious centre.

129. *Satricum*: Modern Le Ferriere, a Latin town frequently fought over in accounts of the fourth century BC.

130. *Tusculans*: Inhabitants of Tusculum, located near modern Frascati, 15 miles (24 km) southeast of Rome; it was a formidable Latin city in the fifth and fourth centuries. An early Roman ally, Tusculum was annexed to Rome in 381.

131. *the city was disturbed by a radical controversy*: Plutarch's narrative becomes severely concise here. From 376 to 367, Gaius Licinius Stolo and Lucius Sextius Lateranus were tribunes of the people and proposed a programme of legislation reducing debt, regulating the occupation of public land and opening the consulship to plebeians; the particulars of this episode are no longer discoverable and in any case are of dubious historicity, but the event was remembered by the Romans as a significant watershed in their history.

132. *elections were thwarted by the multitude*: No consuls or consular tribunes were elected from 375 to 371.

133. *dictator for the fourth time*: In 368, though by then the election of consular tribunes had again begun.

134. *appointed another dictator*: Publius Manlius Capitolinus. His master of the horse was named Gaius Licinius. Cassius Dio agrees with Plutarch that this was the tribune of the people Stolo,

but Livy's evidence (6.39.3) points elsewhere, probably to Gaius
Licinius Calvus (consul in 364 or 361).

135. *500 iugera of land*: Somewhat more than 300 acres; this law
actually regulated the amount of public land (i.e. land owned by
the state) that anyone could rent, not the total amount of land
that an individual could possess.

136. *appointed dictator for the fifth time*: In 367.

137. *River Anio*: The modern Aniene, which ultimately joins the Tiber.

138. *thirteen years after Rome was sacked*: Presumably Plutarch
meant to write *twenty-three* not *thirteen*.

139. *exempting priests ... against the Gauls*: This was a state of
emergency called a *tumultus Gallicus* by the Romans. Plutarch
mentions it again at *Marcellus* 3.

140. *Velitrae*: Modern Velletri, a Volscian town located in Latium,
perhaps most famous as the birthplace of the emperor
Augustus.

141. *temple ... forum and the place of assembly*: The temple of Concord was situated at the foot of the Capitoline, overlooking the
Roman Forum, where it is still evident.

142. *add a day to ... the Latin Festival*: According to Livy (6.42.12),
an additional day was added to the Roman Games, not to the
Latin Festival.

143. *Marcus Aemilius ... plebeian consul*: In 366 the patrician consul
was *Lucius* Aemilius Mamercinus; his plebeian colleague was
Lucius Sextius Lateranus.

144. *the very next year*: In 365, the year after the first plebeian actually held his consulship (not the year after his election).

FABIUS MAXIMUS

Further Reading

There is a useful Italian commentary by P. A. Stadter, R. Guerrini and
A. Santoni, *Plutarco, Vite Parallele: Pericle e Fabio Massimo* (1991).
Without question, the most important interpretative essay on this Life
is P. A. Stadter, 'Plutarch's Comparison of Pericles and Fabius Maximus', in Scardigli, *Essays*, pp. 155–64. More recently, R. Scuderi,
'L'*humanitas* di Fabio Massimo nella biografia plutarchea', *Athen-
aeum* 98 (2010), pp. 467–88, provides a close reading of the whole of
the Life. The virtue of mildness, crucial to Fabius' character, is
explained by H. Martin, 'The Concept of Praotes in Plutarch's Lives',

GRBS 3 (1960), pp. 65–73. This Life has an obvious relationship with *Marcellus*, which is discussed (in German) by H. Beck, 'Interne Synkrisis bei Plutarch', *Hermes* 130 (2002), pp. 467–89. The conflicting strands of Fabius' reputation in the Roman tradition are examined by M. B. Roller, 'The consul(ar) as *exemplum*: Fabius *Cunctator*'s paradoxical glory', in H. Beck, A. Duplá, M. Jehne and F. Pina Pola (eds.), *Consuls and Res Publica: Holding High Office in the Roman Republic* (2011), pp. 182–210.

On the historical background, see A. Goldsworthy, *The Punic Wars* (2000), and J. Briscoe, 'The Second Punic War', in *CAH* viii (1989), pp. 44–80. An important review of the so-called Fabian strategy is offered by P. Erdkamp, 'Polybius, Livy and the Fabian Strategy', *Ancient Society* 22 (1992), pp. 127–47. In view of Polybius' importance, there is much to be gleaned from the relevant portions of Walbank, *Commentary*, vols. 1 and 2. Livy's view of Fabius is well treated by D. S. Levene, *Livy on the Hannibalic War* (2010), pp. 111–18, 198–210 and 229–31.

Notes to the Introduction to Fabius Maximus

1. For the likeliest reconstruction of Fabius' immediate family, see G. V. Sumner, *The Orators in Cicero's Brutus: Prosopography and Chronology* (1973), pp. 30–32.
2. H. H. Scullard in *CAH* vii.2 (1989), pp. 486–572.
3. Briscoe in *CAH* viii, pp. 44–80.
4. The particulars of Fabius' strategy were unclear even to Polybius and Livy: see Erdkamp, *Ancient Society* 22, pp. 127–47.
5. Pliny, *Natural History* 22.6–10; and Gellius 5.6.10.
6. By contrast, Polybius (3.87.6) praised Fabius' intelligence (*phronēsis*), a view also embraced by Roman writers (e.g. Cicero, *Against Verres* 2.5.25; Nepos, *Hannibal* 5.1). In Plutarch, however, Fabius is depicted as a slow learner (ch. 1).
7. See also *Comparison Pericles–Fabius Maximus* 3.
8. Martin, *GRBS* 3, pp. 65–73.
9. Plutarch did not invent Fabius' indifference to public opinion: it was highlighted in his sources. Ennius (*Annals* 363–9, see Skutsch, p. 102), after describing Fabius as the man who saved Rome by delaying (see above), goes on to say: 'He would not put hearsay before our safety, and this is why the glory of this hero shines even more greatly now than it did in the past.' This characterization of Fabius was taken up by Polybius (3.105.8), Livy (44.22.10) and subsequent writers.

10. Fabius' caution is emphasized throughout (chs. 5, 10, 19, 25, 26).

11. Pelling, *P&H*, pp. 243–7, examines the importance of these qualities in *Philopoemen* and *Titus Flamininus* (see also Introductions to these Lives).

12. Some of Fabius' anti-Scipionic activities in chs. 25–6 (e.g. his attempt to persuade Crassus to take the command and his attempt to dissuade young men from joining Scipio) are also unique to Plutarch's account.

13. For instance, Polyaenus (*Stratagems* 8.14.2) preserves a fictitious encounter between the two (which tends to Fabius' advantage).

14. Livy 28.40–45; see Levene, *Livy on the Hannibalic War*, pp. 111–18.

15. Cicero, *On Old Age* 10–13, where the Elder Cato is the speaker. It is probably on the basis of this essay that Plutarch frequently cites Fabius as an important role model for the youthful Cato, e.g. *Elder Cato* 3, *Moralia* 791a and 805f. *On Old Age* may also be Plutarch's source for the nature of Fabius' oratory in ch. 1.

16. For Fabius' and Pericles' leonine nature and physical peculiarity see ch. 1; *Pericles* 3. For their monarchical power see chs. 3–4 and 8–9; *Pericles* 7, 9, 16, 30. On their eschewing of superstition see chs. 4–5; *Pericles* 6, 38. On oratory see ch. 1; *Pericles* 8, 15. This catalogue of parallels could be extended: see Stadter, in Scardigli, *Essays*, pp. 155–64.

17. Polybius' treatment of the Second Punic War extends through Books 3 to 16, although Books 6 and 12 are digressions. Livy's account of the war runs from Book 21 to 30. Fabius' first consulship goes unmentioned by Polybius but was included in Livy, *Summary of Book* 20. Plutarch's use of Livy is confirmed by his mistranslation at ch. 3 (note 15 below).

18. These arguments are summarized in B. Scardigli, *Die Romerbiographien Plutarchs: ein Forschungsbericht* (1979), pp. 35–7, and rejected by R. Flacelière and E. Chambry, *Plutarque, Vies*, vol. 3 (1969), pp. 61–4. Fabius Pictor, whom Plutarch cites at *Romulus* 3, was no doubt a useful repository of information about Fabius' family, even if other sources existed.

19. None of the fragments of Poseidonius dealing with either Fabius or Marcellus can be attributed to a specific work: see I. G. Kidd, *Posidonius*, vol. 2 (1988), pp. 896–902, and Introduction to *Marcellus*.

20. Little is known of either. For Silenus see *FGrH* 175. For Sosylus see *FGrH* 176; he is criticized by Polybius at 3.20.5.

21. Chs. 20 and 27 overlap with reports in Valerius Maximus. They do not correspond very neatly, but even when Plutarch explicitly cites Valerius (e.g. in *Marcellus* 30) he repeats him inaccurately.

22. Nepos, *Letters to Atticus* 18.4; cf. Livy 22.31.11.

Notes to the Life of Fabius Maximus

1. *Such was the man Pericles . . . down to us*: This constitutes Plutarch's transition from his *Pericles* to its Roman match.

2. *Fodii . . . Fabii*: This is a false etymology, as is the explanation preserved in Festus 87, which derives the name from *fovea* (ditch), 'because the first of this line was born when Hercules lay with a woman in a ditch'. Another, more plausible, etymology (Pliny, *Natural History* 18.10) connects the name with *faba* (bean).

3. *Rullus . . . Maximus*: Quintus Fabius Maximus Rullianus held five consulships, the first in 322, and was dictator at least once; many of the details of his career remain uncertain. *Maximus* means greatest.

4. *fourth in descent . . . subject of this Life*: That is, Rullianus was Fabius' great-grandfather. According to Livy (30.26.8) he was his grandfather, but this is probably incorrect.

5. *Verrucosus . . . wart*: The Latin word for wart is *verruca*.

6. *Ovicula*: Apart from Plutarch, only the anonymous *On Illustrious Men* 43.1 mentions this nickname.

7. *freedom from over-mastering passions . . . in all circumstances*: Plutarch's description of the young Fabius is adapted from Plato's discussion of the qualities that best suit the character of a future Guardian in his *Republic* (503c–d).

8. *oration over his son . . . consul*: Fabius' son was consul in 213 (ch. 24). In his *On Old Age* (12), Cicero mentions this oration and claims that it was in general circulation; he also describes Fabius' style as marked by maxims. For more on Fabius' oratory, see Cicero, *Brutus* 57 and 77.

9. *triumph over the Ligurians*: In 233. The Ligurians dwelt in what is now southeastern France and extended themselves into the regions south of the River Po in Italy. They were enemies of the Romans until their final suppression near the end of the second century BC.

10. *battle of the River Trebia*: Plutarch leaps forward to 218. Trebia (modern Trebbia) is a river that flows into the Po near Piacenza.

11. *Antium*: Modern Anzio.

12. *Falerii*: Falerii Veteres (modern Città Castellana).

13. *consul Gaius Flaminius . . . few years before*: As consul in 223, Gaius Flaminius won a sensational victory over the Insubrians, for which he celebrated a triumph (*Marcellus* 4). Flaminius was again consul in 217.

14. *like Camillus . . . her very walls*: See *Camillus* 29.

15. *leapt on his horse . . . thrown . . . on his head*: This appears to be Plutarch's mistranslation of Livy 22.3.11: 'He leapt upon his horse, when suddenly the beast stumbled and unseating the consul threw him *over its* head' (*ipse* [i.e. Flaminius] *in equum insiluisset, equus repente corruit consulemque lapsum super caput effudit*). Polybius does not mention Flaminius' spill.

16. *near Lake Trasimene in Etruria*: The precise site of this battle is uncertain.

17. *Pomponius*: Marcus Pomponius, whose exact identity is uncertain because at this time several senators bore this name.

18. *Marcus Minucius*: Marcus Minucius Rufus, who had been consul in 221. He was not selected by Fabius but rather was elected by the assembly (Polybius 3.87, Livy 22.8.7).

19. *senate's permission to use a horse*: The dictator needed the people's permission to mount a horse, but this request was routine (Livy 23.14.2).

20. *attended by . . . twenty-four lictors*: A dictator was entitled to twenty-four lictors; consuls were entitled to twelve.

21. *surviving consul . . . private citizen*: Gnaeus Servilius Geminus was the remaining consul in 217. He was ordered by Fabius to meet him without his lictors (Livy 22.11.5–6), but he did not become a private citizen; he commanded a fleet at Ostia and by the end of the year was in command of an army.

22. *Sibylline Books*: See *Publicola*, note 121.

23. *sacrifice to the gods . . . bounds of Italy*: This practice, which required a vote of the people, was known as *ver sacrum* ('sacred spring'; Livy 22.10).

24. *musical . . . festival*: These were the Roman Games (*Ludi Romani*) or Great Games (*Ludi Magni*), held in September in honour of Jupiter Best and Greatest.

25. *sestertia . . . obols*: A *sestertium* (plural: *sestertia*) was equivalent to 1,000 sesterces, and so the sum of the Romans' expense was 83,583 (plus one-third) denarii; Plutarch normally equates, as here, the Roman denarius with the Attic drachma (two obols is a third of a drachma). According to Livy (23.10), the cost was 333,333 and one-third asses, a different (and smaller) amount but one

that also emphasizes in its components the number three. In actuality, the denarius was not created until 211.

26. *nature of the number three ... elements of every number*: These ideas are associated with Pythagoreanism; see *Moralia* 288d, 374a and 744b.

27. *pedagogue*: A slave who attended his master's children on walks, especially to and from school, and kept them out of trouble. At *Marcellus* 9, Hannibal is said to fear Fabius as he would fear a pedagogue.

28. *Casinum*: Modern Cassino.

29. *Casilinum*: Modern Capua (not to be confused with ancient Capua).

30. *Olthornus ... Vulturnus*: Modern Volturno. Polybius (3.92.1) calls this river the Athyrnus.

31. *Hannibal ... gave orders ... no damage done*: Plutarch discovered Hannibal's stratagem in his sources (e.g. Livy 22.23), but it supplied a welcome parallel with Pericles: the Spartans planned to spare Pericles' property when they invaded Attica, but Pericles announced that, were that the case, he would give these lands to the state (*Pericles* 33).

32. *Metilius*: Marcus Metilius, tribune of the people in 217.

33. *exchange of prisoners of war ... cowardice*: According to Livy (22.23), Fabius was simply following a practice begun in the First Punic War.

34. *instructions to sell his estates*: These were the estates spared by Hannibal (explicit at Livy 22.23).

35. *he feared the consequences of ... his failure*: Plutarch also cites this remark at *Moralia* 195c.

36. *when all the rest have their functions suspended*: This view was held in antiquity (e.g. Polybius 3.87.8; Cicero, *On the Laws* 3.9), but it is clear that in practice the other magistrates continued to function, even if they remained subordinate to the dictator.

37. *the penalty ... inflicted on his son*: When Titus Manlius Torquatus was consul for the third time (in 340), he put his son to death for disobeying his order not to engage the enemy in single combat, although his son had been victorious (Livy 8.7).

38. *same powers as the dictator*: Minucius was thus made a second dictator and so styled himself at the time (as epigraphical evidence indicates, see *ILS* 11).

39. *a similar situation arose after ... Cannae*: This took place in the next year (chs. 15–16).

40. *Marcus Junius ... second dictator*: Marcus Junius Pera, who had been consul in 230, was named dictator immediately after the Romans' defeat at Cannae (chs. 15 and 16). Later, in 216 while Junius remained dictator, Marcus Fabius Buteo, who had been consul in 245, was also named dictator (without a master of the horse).

41. *Diogenes the philosopher*: Diogenes the Cynic (*c.* 412–324), who was well known for his idiosyncratic lifestyle.

42. *a truly good man ... nor disgraced*: The sentiment was no doubt common, even if Plutarch's formulation does not recur elsewhere. Plutarch's good man here is very much like Aristotle's 'great-souled man' (*Nicomachean Ethics* 1124a1–9).

43. *he preferred to command a part of the army ... by turns*: So also Livy (22.27), whereas in Polybius (3.103.7–8) it is Minucius who chooses to divide the army. In Livy, and unlike here, Fabius takes the second and third legions.

44. *allied troops*: The Romans' allies (*socii*) were actually subject states in Italy that were obliged to provide soldiers who fought alongside the Roman army.

45. *the Numidian cavalry*: One of the great strengths of Hannibal's army.

46. *he struck his thigh*: A Homeric touch. This is how heroes express their anguish (e.g. *Iliad* 12.162, 15.397, 16.125). Neither Polybius nor Livy reports this detail.

47. *'Haven't I kept telling you ... furious storm?'*: Repeated at *Moralia* 195d. Here Hannibal finds the right metaphor for Fabius' strategy, thereby correcting Minucius at ch. 5.

48. *'Patrons' ... liberty*: Livy (22.29) provides the same detail, but naturally without an explanation of the term *patron*. It was always a mark of deference to address someone as *patronus*. Free men in Rome (especially men of modest standing) routinely formed voluntarily and unequal relationships with elite figures, who acted as their benefactors and whom they addressed as patrons, but this institution (often referred to as *clientela*) was not the same as the bond between a freed slave and his or her ex-master (who was also addressed as patron). Livy probably had the former relationship in mind.

49. *After this ... consuls were once more elected*: Fabius laid down his dictatorship in 217. At the time, Servilius Geminus remained consul. A suffect consul, to replace Flaminius, was elected: Marcus Atilius Regulus, who had been consul in 227; he took command of Fabius' army. Plutarch's formulation is misleading.

50. *then came the year ... consulship*: In 216 Gaius Terentius Varro and Lucius Aemilius Paullus were consuls. Although tradition is hostile to Terentius Varro – Livy (22.15.18) claims that he was the son of a butcher – it appears that his approach to the war was in fact sanctioned by the senate; after the defeat at Cannae, the senate and people voted its thanks to him (Livy 22.61.14) and he remained an active commander and diplomat throughout the war.

51. *88,000 men*: Different figures are supplied by Polybius (3.107.9) and Livy (22.36.4).

52. *Aemilius Paullus*: He had also been consul in 219, when, in conjunction with his colleague, he won a major victory in the Second Illyrian War, for which both celebrated triumphs. In the following year, Aemilius' colleague was convicted of embezzling spoils from that war. In the process, Aemilius' reputation was damaged although he was not himself convicted of wrongdoing and therefore was not, as Plutarch claims, fined (Livy 22.35.3). This man is the father of the subject of Plutarch's *Aemilius Paullus*.

53. *River Aufidus*: The modern Ofanto, in southern Italy.

54. *Cannae*: Its location remains uncertain, but it was perhaps near the modern Canosa.

55. *I may refer the reader to those historians ... the war in detail*: The chief extant accounts of the rout at Cannae are Polybius 3.110–17 and Livy 22.43–50.

56. *Venusia*: Modern Venosa.

57. *Cornelius Lentulus*: Gnacus Cornelius Lentulus was a tribune of the soldiers. He was later elected consul for 201.

58. *It is said ... captured*: Slightly different figures are provided by Polybius (3.117.3–4) and Livy (22.49.15–18).

59. *Barca the Carthaginian*: In Livy (22.51.2–4) it is Maharbal who makes this observation.

60. *Capua*: Modern Santa Maria de Capua Vetere; it remained a wealthy and powerful city until the fifth century of our era (when it was sacked by Vandals). Livy (22.61.11) provides a detailed list of Hannibal's new allies.

61. *'It is no small evil ... to put friends to the test'*: From an unknown tragedy; see fr. 993 in C. Collard and M. Cropp, *Euripides: Fragments*, vol. 2 (2008).

62. *disasters of the Gallic invasion*: See *Camillus* 20. Livy (22.50.1) also compares the defeat at Cannae with the disaster at the Allia.

63. *He placed guards ... lament the dead*: Fabius, who was a private citizen in 216, in fact recommended these measures in the senate, which body then decreed them (Livy 22.55).

64. *festival of Ceres*: This was a celebration for women, many of whom would have been barred from participation because they were in mourning; see B. S. Spaeth, *The Roman Goddess Ceres* (1996), pp. 11–15.

65. *all the rites . . . were duly performed*: Plutarch here passes over the Romans' resort to human sacrifice, urged by the Sibylline oracles, in the aftermath of Cannae (Livy 22.57.6).

66. *Pictor*: Quintus Fabius Pictor, Rome's first historian (see General Introduction V). The result of his consultation is reported at Livy 23.11.

67. *two . . . Vestal Virgins*: Livy (22.57.2–3) tells us that they were named Opimia and Floronia. The man who seduced Floronia was flogged to death. Plutarch describes the traditional punishment of Vestals at *Numa* 10.

68. *'mighty in combat' . . . 'lovers of battle'*: Plutarch uses these same Homeric phrases (e.g. *Iliad* 3.36 and 16.65) to describe Marcellus at *Marcellus* 1. For the sentiments of this chapter, see also *Marcellus* 9.

69. *Poseidonius tells us . . . sword of Rome*: Plutarch also cites Poseidonius at *Marcellus* 9. Marcellus and Fabius are contrasted elsewhere (Livy 24.9.7–11; Cicero, *In Defence of Marcellus* 5.10), but the application of this metaphor ('Fabius the shield . . . Marcellus the sword of Rome') is preserved only in Plutarch. The original Poseidonian context is unknown, which is true for all fragments of Poseidonius dealing with either Fabius or Marcellus; see Kidd, *Posidonius*, vol. 2, pp. 896–902.

70. *each . . . elected consul five times*: Fabius was consul in 233, 228, 215, 214 and 209; Marcellus in 222, 215, 214, 210 and 208. Fabius held no command between 212 and 210. From 216 until the time of his death, Marcellus held either a consular or proconsular command, but from the end of 214 through to 211 he was in charge of the siege of Syracuse, not fighting Hannibal in Italy.

71. *Marcellus was killed*: In 208 (*Marcellus* 29).

72. *Metapontum*: Modern Metaponto, southern Italy.

73. *ambush . . . near the city*: This took place in 209 (Livy 27.16).

74. *Marsian soldier*: The Marsians were a people of central Italy who were closely allied with Rome. In *On Illustrious Men* (43.5) this man is called Marius Statilius. In Valerius Maximus 7.3.7 he is a citizen of Nola.

75. *Lucanian*: An inhabitant of Lucania (modern Basilicata), a region in southern Italy; many Lucanians fought with Hannibal against the Romans.

76. *Such is the account ... of this episode*: See also *Moralia* 195e, Valerius Maximus 7.3.7 and *On Illustrious Men* 43.5.

77. *Tarentum*: Modern Tarnto. Originally a Spartan colony, it became a leading power in southern Italy. It was conquered by Rome and became a Roman ally in 270.

78. *Tarentum ... lost by treachery*: Tarentum defected to Hannibal in 212 (Livy 25.7–11) but the Romans continued to hold the city's acropolis.

79. *Bruttian*: The Bruttians were the inhabitants of what is now Calabria. They were neither Greek nor Roman and, in this period, were in fact hostile to both. During the Second Punic War they sided with Hannibal.

80. *the commonest version of the story*: This is the one told (less expansively than here) by Livy (27.15.9–11).

81. *Rhegium*: Modern Reggio di Calabria, a prosperous Greek city that had long been a Roman ally.

82. *Caulonia*: A Greek settlement in southern Italy near modern Punta Stilo. It suffered extensively during the Second Punic War and by the first century BC was abandoned.

83. *they included the worse elements ... sent home from Sicily in disgrace*: In fact these were troops sent to Italy in 210 by the consul Marcus Valerius Laevinus (Livy 26.40 and 27.12).

84. *Hercules*: The Fabii claimed to descend from Hercules (ch. 1).

85. *indicated in his Life*: Plutarch praises Marcellus' conduct at the fall of Syracuse as well as his display of Syracusan art in his *ovatio* (*Marcellus* 20–21, a passage that explicitly contrasts Fabius with Marcellus).

86. *40 stades*: Hannibal had come within 4½ miles (slightly more than 7 km) of Tarentum.

87. *a second triumph ... more magnificent than his first*: Fabius' first triumph is mentioned in ch. 2.

88. *enervated by ... plunder*: According to Livy (23.18.9–16), Hannibal's soldiers were corrupted by luxury when they wintered in Capua in 216 and 215.

89. *Marcus Livius*: His precise identity is uncertain. He is *Gaius* Livius at Polybius 8.25.2, and Appian (*Hannibalic War* 32) calls him Junius.

90. *'You are quite right ... recaptured it'*: Fabius' remark is also reported at *Moralia* 195f.

91. *marks of honour ... elect his son as consul*: This had nothing to do with Fabius' capture of Tarentum. His son was consul in 213.

92. *'You are right . . . parents and children'*: Fabius' remark is also reported at *Moralia* 196a. According to Livy (24.44.9), this episode took place in the field, when the son took command of his father's army and Fabius became his son's legate.

93. *great-grandfather of our Fabius*: See note 4.

94. *son became consul . . . served as his subordinate*: Quintus Fabius Maximus Gurges, Rullianus' son, was consul for the first time in 292, when his father served as his legate.

95. *in the triumph that followed*: In 290.

96. *authority . . . as a private individual*: A Roman father possessed total authority over his children, including his adult children, unless he legally released them from it.

97. *funeral oration . . . distributed it among his friends*: See note 8.

98. *Cornelius Scipio*: Publius Cornelius Scipio, who defeated Hannibal at the battle of Zama in 202 (and was honoured with the surname Africanus). In 210 he was voted a proconsular command and sent to Spain, where, by 206, he had driven out the Carthaginian forces there.

99. *elected consul*: For 205.

100. *Crassus*: Publius Licinius Crassus was Scipio's colleague in 205.

101. *cities of Etruria . . . loyal to him*: Livy (28.45) describes in detail Scipio's support from the Etrurian cities.

102. *Crassus . . . remained at home*: He did in fact leave Rome in order to campaign in Bruttium.

103. *office of high priest*: Since 212 Crassus had been *pontifex maximus*, the chief of Rome's civic religion. According to Livy (28.44.11), Crassus preferred to remain in Italy lest he be absent from the sacred responsibilities of his priestly office, although in fact nothing prohibited his leaving inasmuch as other priests could substitute for the *pontifex maximus* whenever he was away from the city.

104. *troops . . . already in Sicily*: Scipio was allocated Sicily as his province, from which base he was authorized to invade Africa.

105. *arrived . . . decisive victories*: Scipio invaded Africa in 204. Initially he enjoyed only mixed success, but in 203 he inflicted multiple defeats on Carthage and captured Syphax, king of Numidia.

106. *envoys were sent to Hannibal*: Sent by the government in Carthage.

107. *this was the moment . . . he should be recalled*: In 205, *before* the invasion of Africa, there was a serious scandal involving Scipio's legate Quintus Pleminius, in which Scipio, as his commander,

was implicated. Fabius exploited this moment to put forward a motion in the senate recalling Scipio, who was investigated and exonerated (Livy 29.16–20). Plutarch's version of this is misleading. Cf. his account of the matter in *Elder Cato* 3.

108. *Hannibal . . . sailed away from Italy*: In 203.

109. *Scipio defeated Hannibal himself*: In 202, at the battle of Zama.

110. *'righted the ship that storms so long had tossed'*: Sophocles, *Antigone* 163 (slightly adapted).

111. *Epaminondas . . . iron spit*: On Epaminondas see General Introduction II. The 'iron spit' Plutarch mentions was Spartan currency, which was valueless in the outside world.

112. *every citizen contributed . . . towards the funeral*: Valerius Maximus 5.2.3 adduces Fabius' funeral as a notable instance of gratitude; in his version, however, the people vie with one another in giving large contributions.

Notes to the Comparison of Pericles and Fabius Maximus

1. *peak of their imperial power*: By the mid-fifth century BC, Athens had transformed the Delian League, an alliance of city-states formed in order to protect Greece from Persian aggression, into what was essentially an Athenian empire: see R. Meiggs, *The Athenian Empire* (1972).

2. *Cimon*: (*c.* 510–*c.* 450) A great Athenian general, whose victories over the Persians, especially at the battle of Eurymedon in 466, made possible Athens' dominance over and exploitation of the Delian League; he is the subject of Plutarch's *Cimon*.

3. *Myronides*: Athenian general in the 450s, celebrated for his victories over the Corinthians and Boeotians.

4. *Leocrates*: An Athenian general at the battle of Plataea (479) and commander at the siege of Aegina (459/8).

5. *Tolmides*: A leading democratic politician in Athens who was frequently elected general in the 450s and 440s; he pursued an aggressively imperialist foreign policy and won numerous spectacular victories.

6. *holidays and festivals*: *Pericles* 9, discussing Pericles' use of public largesse as a means of winning political popularity.

7. *reining in . . . a people*: More than once in *Pericles* Plutarch depicts the people as a horse that needs a bridle (e.g. *Pericles* 7, 11, 15).

8. *conquest of Samos*: During 440/39 (*Pericles* 25–8).

9. *capture of Tarentum*: *Fabius Maximus* 22–3.

10. *taking of Euboea*: In 446 (*Pericles* 22–3).

11. *Fabius' seizing the cities of Campania*: In 214 Fabius and Mar-
     cellus campaigned in Campania, capturing several cities (Livy
     24.19–20, *Marcellus* 26); Plutarch, however, does not narrate
     these events in *Fabius Maximus*.

12. *the reduction of Capua ... Fulvius and Appius*: Capua was the
     chief city of Campania and was captured in 211 by Quintus Ful-
     vius Flaccus and Appius Claudius Pulcher, consuls in the previous
     year. The episode is recorded in many sources (e.g. Polybius
     9.3.1–4 and 26.4.1–10).

13. *the victory ... celebrated his first triumph*: *Fabius Maximus* 2.

14. *nine trophies*: Plutarch also mentions nine trophies at *Pericles* 38
     but in that Life describes the circumstances of only one of them
     (at *Pericles* 19); the remainder go undiscussed.

15. *snatched Minucius away ... saved an entire Roman army*:
     Fabius Maximus 11–12.

16. *when Hannibal out-generalled him ... employing oxen*: *Fabius
     Maximus* 6–7.

17. *tried to accomplish too much and lost their empire*: According to
     Thucydides (2.65.13), Pericles told the Athenians they would
     win the Peloponnesian War if they did not attempt to add to
     their empire while fighting the Spartans. He goes on to observe
     that, after Pericles' death in 429, the Athenians discarded his
     policy and for that reason were defeated in 404.

18. *by rejecting Fabius' advice ... against the Carthaginians*: *Fabius
     Maximus* 25–7.

19. *Inexperience ... robs him of his courage*: The relevance of this
     sentiment to Fabius' opposition (near the end of his long life) to
     Scipio is far from clear.

20. *he caused it ... when he was at odds with them*: The extent of
     Pericles' responsibility for the outbreak of the Peloponnesian
     War is discussed at *Pericles* 29 and 31.

21. *subversion of Cimon*: Cimon was ostracized in 461. Pericles'
     factious politics are described at *Pericles* 9–14.

22. *Thucydides*: Not the historian but the son of Melesias, and a
     very influential figure and a political enemy of Pericles; he was
     ostracized, perhaps in 443.

23. *Tolmides ... attacked the Boeotians*: In 447 Tolmides fell at the
     battle of Coronea, after which the Athenians were forced to
     evacuate Boeotia. Plutarch records Pericles' opposition to Tol-
     mides' invasion (*Pericles* 18).

24. *at his own expense he ransomed the prisoners of war*: *Fabius Maximus* 7.

25. *around 6 talents*: In his earlier narrative (see previous note) Plutarch reports that ransoming the prisoners cost Fabius 10 talents (he paid 250 drachmas for each of the 240 prisoners he ransomed, a total of 60,000 drachmas or 10 talents).

26. *kept himself honest and incorruptible*: See e.g. *Pericles* 15.

27. *Pericles' grand public works*: Described in detail at *Pericles* 12–13.

MARCELLUS

Further Reading

The only English commentary on the *Life of Marcellus* is a University of British Columbia dissertation by E. D. Clark, 'A Historical Commentary on Plutarch's *Marcellus*' (1991). In Italian there is P. Fabrini and L. Ghilli, *Plutarco, Vite parallele: Pelopida e Marcello* (1998). The philosophical basis of Plutarch's disapproval of Pelopidas and Marcellus is examined in detail by H. G. Ingenkamp, '*Moralia* in the Lives: The Charge of Rashness in *Pelopidas/Marcellus*', in A. G. Nikolaidis (ed.), *The Unity of Plutarch's Work* (2008), pp. 263–76. A strong bias on Plutarch's part against Marcellus is detected by A. Georgiadou, 'Bias and character-portrayal in Plutarch's Lives of Pelopidas and Marcellus', *ANRW* 2.33.6 (1992), pp. 4222–57, a paper that takes a somewhat different approach to the Life from the one found in this volume. On the role of Archimedes in this Life, see M. Jaeger, *Archimedes and the Roman Imagination* (2008), and especially P. Culham, 'Plutarch on the Roman Siege of Syracuse: the primacy of science over technology', in G. Italo (ed.), *Plutarco e le scienza* (1992), pp. 179–97. This Life has an obvious relationship with the (later) *Fabius Maximus*, which is discussed (in German) by H. Beck, 'Interne Synkrisis bei Plutarch', *Hermes* 130 (2002), pp. 467–89. Marcellus' incipient Hellenism and its importance for Plutarchan biography is discussed by Pelling, 'Roman heroes', pp. 199–208, and Swain, 'Culture'.

On the historical background, see the references cited in the Introduction to *Fabius Maximus*. The best account of Marcellus' Syracusan campaign remains A. M. Eckstein, *Senate and General: Individual Decision-Making and Roman Foreign Relations, 264–194 BC* (1987), pp. 135–84. Marcellus' political skills are superbly captured in an important paper by H. Flower, 'The Tradition of the *Spolia Opima*: M. Claudius Marcellus and Augustus', *Classical Antiquity* 19 (2000), pp. 34–64. Livy's view of Marcellus is well treated by D. S. Levene, *Livy on the Hannibalic War* (2010), pp. 197–214.

Notes to the Introduction to Marcellus

1. Roman campaigns in northern Italy are discussed by E. S. Stavely in *CAH* vii.2 (1989), pp. 431–6.

2. Marcellus' innovations in self-display are examined by H. Flower, *Classical Antiquity* 19 (2000), pp. 34–64.

3. On the Second Punic War, see Introduction to *Fabius Maximus*.

4. On Marcellus' Sicilian campaign, see Eckstein, *Senate and General*, pp. 135–84. Accessible accounts include M. I. Finley, *Ancient Sicily* (1968), pp. 113–21; T. A. Dorey and D. R. Dudley, *Rome Against Carthage* (1971), pp. 119–34; and A. Goldsworthy, *The Punic Wars* (2000), pp. 260–68.

5. See the important paper by T. C. Brennan in R. W. Wallace and E. M. Harris (eds.), *Transitions to Empire: Essays in Greco-Roman History, 360–146 BC, in Honor of E. Badian* (1996), pp. 315–37.

6. On Marcellus' ovation and Alban triumph see H. S. Versnel, *Triumphus: An Inquiry into the Origin, Development and Meaning of the Roman Triumph* (1970), pp. 165–71, and Beard, *Roman Triumph*, pp. 147–79. Marcellus' dedications are noticed in chs. 8 and 30; see also Cicero, *Against Verres* 2.4.21, and *The Republic* 1.21.

7. See H. Flower in U. Eigler, U. Gotter, N. Luraghi and U. Walter (eds.), *Formen römischer Geschichtsschreibung von den Anfängen bis Livius: Gattungen, Autoren, Kontexte* (2003), pp. 39–52.

8. See e.g. poetic treatments of Marcellus' death in Virgil, *Aeneid* 6.855–86; Horace, *Odes* 1.12.45–6; and Propertius 4.10.39–44.

9. An opinion Livy underscores when later (34.4.3) he puts it in the mouth of the Elder Cato.

10. On Livy's treatment of Marcellus, see Levene, *Livy on the Hannibalic War*, pp. 197–214.

11. On this point see H. Martin, *American Journal of Philology* 82 (1961), pp. 164–75.

12. On the significance of Marcellus' introduction of Greek artworks to Rome, see M. McDonnell in S. Dillon and K. E. Welch (eds.), *Representations of War in Ancient Rome* (2006), pp. 68–90.

13. See R. Seager in *CAH* vi (1994), pp. 176–86 and 187–208. The Sacred Band was an elite Theban unit consisting of 300 men.

14. See further A. Georgiadou, *Plutarch's Pelopidas: A Historical and Philological Commentary* (1997).

15. For instance, at Plutarch, *Artaxerxes* 8 and 11; see Duff, *Plutarch's Lives*, pp. 78–82.

16. See Introduction to *Coriolanus* and General Introduction III.

17. The topic of human sacrifice is raised in *Pelopidas* 21, only to be rejected as unnatural and cruel.

18. Polybius' treatment of the Second Punic War extends through Books 3 to 16, although Books 6 and 12 are digressions. Livy's account of the war runs from Book 21 to 30. Polybius (2.34–5) records the events of Marcellus' first consulship. Livy's treatment appeared in *Summary of Book 20*.

19. Lucius Coelius Antipater flourished in the second half of the second century BC. He composed a much-admired history of the Second Punic War: see *HRR*, vol. 1, pp. ccxi–ccxxxviii and 158–77.

20. Valerius Antias was active in the first century BC. He composed a history of Rome from its origins to 91 BC: see *HRR*, vol. 1, pp. cccv and 238.

21. None of the fragments of Poseidonius dealing with Marcellus can be attributed to a specific work: see I. G. Kidd, *Posidonius*, vol. 2 (1988), pp. 896–902.

Notes to the Life of Marcellus

1. *Poseidonius*: (c. 135–c. 51) The leading Greek intellectual of the first century BC, and an admired philosopher and historian (see Introduction).

2. *Marcellus ... means warlike*: In fact the name *Marcellus* is a diminutive of *Marcus*. Plutarch (or his source) incorrectly believes *Marcellus* derives from *Mars* (hence his translation). Several Roman surnames are formed from first names.

3. *'lover of battle' ... 'mighty in combat'*: Plutarch here appropriates expressions found in Homer (e.g. *Iliad* 3.36 and 16.65); he repeats them when he refers to Marcellus at *Fabius Maximus* 19.

4. *Decreed ... in arduous wars*: See *Iliad* 14.86–7. Plutarch does not finish the quotation: 'until we perish', though in fact Marcellus will die in combat.

5. *they campaigned ... under Hannibal*: Plutarch refers to the First Punic War (264–241), the Romans' wars against the Gauls in

northern Italy (238–236 and 225–220) and the Second Punic War (218–201).

6. *Otacilius*: Titus Otacilius Crassus (praetor in 217), apparently Marcellus' half-brother or adoptive brother. Plutarch refers to combat during the First Punic War.

7. *curule aedile*: Plutarch actually writes, 'aedile of the most elevated rank', by which he means curule aedile. Marcellus probably held this office before or in 226.

8. *augur ... flight of birds*: On augury see further *Numa* 7 and *Aemilius Paullus* 3.

9. *Capitolinus*: Gaius Scantinius Capitolinus. According to Valerius Maximus (6.1.7) he was a tribune of the people. It has been suggested that in fact he was a plebeian aedile.

10. *engaged in a struggle with the Gauls*: Open war broke out in 225, but it was preceded by months of preparation. On the history of Rome's conflict with the Gauls in northern Italy see Stavely in *CAH* vii.2, pp. 431–6.

11. *Insubrians ... Gaesati*: The Insubrians lived in northern Italy; they were finally subjugated by the Romans in 194. The Gaesati came from an Alpine region along the Rhône.

12. *Romans never forgot ... invasion by the Gauls*: The sack of Rome by the Gauls in 390 is narrated at *Camillus* 19–23. For the law about emergency levies in reaction to a Gallic invasion, see *Camillus* 41.

13. *Sibylline Books*: See *Publicola*, note 121.

14. *bury alive ... Cattle-market*: The sacrifices, performed in the oldest centre of the city (the Cattle-market, or Forum Boarium), were carried out in 228 and repeated in 216 (when the Romans were threatened by Hannibal, whose invasion of Italy was supported by the Gauls) and again in 113 (when again the Romans were in fear of Gallic attacks). Later Roman tradition regarded these actions as abominations and emphasized that they were prescribed by the (Greek) Sibylline oracles. In the Greek parallel to this Life (*Pelopidas* 21), the hero is shocked by a dream that seems to demand human sacrifice; the propriety of human sacrifice is debated and, in the end, the gods present an alternative. Plutarch discusses the Romans' human sacrifice further at *Moralia* 283f–284c.

15. *perform certain ceremonies ... Greeks or Gauls*: Some editors delete the reference to Greeks or Gauls. In any case, it is unclear what ceremonies Plutarch has in mind.

16. *Flaminius and Furius*: Gaius Flaminius and Publius Furius Philus were the consuls of 223.

17. *Picenum*: A region east of the Apennines, the modern Marche.

18. *Ariminum*: Modern Rimini.

19. *omens ... inauspicious ... lay down their office*: Irregularities in the auspices resulted in a magistracy that was vitiated, a religious condition which threatened future magisterial undertakings. A vitiated consul was a legitimate consul, but it was his duty to rectify the irregularity in his appointment by resigning his office.

20. *Flaminius refused to open them ... private citizen*: Flaminius' action was not illegal nor did it technically violate ritual procedures (he was not responsible for his religious jeopardy until he was made aware of it, which is possibly why he avoided reading the senate's letters, and his success in battle demonstrated the gods' unwillingness to punish him or Rome). It is by no means clear that he or his colleague abdicated, a version of events that perhaps originates in a later and very hostile literary tradition. Although his behaviour attracted disapprobation from some quarters, he was elected censor in 220.

21. *Tiberius Sempronius*: Tiberius Sempronius Gracchus, consul in 177 and 163; Tiberius' botched augury occurred during his second consulship.

22. *Scipio Nasica ... Gaius Marcius*: Publius Cornelius Scipio Nasica, who was again consul in 155, and Gaius Marcius Figulus, who was again consul in 156.

23. *Whenever a consul ... begin ... observations afresh*: In crafting his explanation, Plutarch has misunderstood the technical augural term *tabernaculum capere* (literally, 'to take possession of a tent or hut'), which actually refers to a ritual action that was a part of the taking of auspices. Tiberius' error actually lay elsewhere: after taking auspices in the Campus Martius, he re-entered the city, crossing its religious boundary (the *pomerium*), which vitiated his initial auspices; when he returned to conduct the election, he forgot to take auspices again (Cicero, *On the Nature of the Gods* 2.11). For a detailed discussion of this procedure, see J. Linderski, *ANRW* 2.16 (1986), pp. 2159–64.

24. *Cornelius Cethegus*: Marcus Cornelius Cethegus, consul in 204. He was a *flamen* (see below) but of which god is unknown.

25. *Quintus Sulpicius*: Apart from his removal from a flaminate, nothing further is known of him.

26. *flamines*: Special priests devoted to a single deity. There were three major *flamines* (the *flamen Dialis*, *flamen Martialis* and *flamen Quirinalis*, devoted to Jupiter, Mars and Quirinus respectively); there were also twelve minor *flamines*. The *apex*, a

special piece of pointed headwear ('peaked cap'), was a distinctive part of their official dress. Cf. *Numa* 7.

27. *Minucius the dictator*: The dictator was actually Quintus Fabius Maximus, probably in 221, though the date is uncertain. The squeaking of a shrew-mouse was a common omen (Pliny, *Natural History* 8.233).

28. *Gaius Flaminius*: This is the consul of 223, whose victory over the Insubrians was mentioned above.

29. *interreges*: In the absence of consuls to conduct elections, the patricians in the senate selected one of their own to serve, for five days, as *interrex*. The first *interrex* chose his successor, who then held elections (or, if that was for some reason impossible, selected yet another *interrex*), until new consuls were elected. In this instance, however, an interregnum was apparently unnecessary because Flaminius and his colleague did not abdicate before the end of their consular year (note 20).

30. *Marcellus ... Gnaeus Cornelius*: Marcellus and Gnaeus Cornelius Scipio were consuls in 222 and not replacement consuls in 223.

31. *Marcellus stirred up the people's indignation ... continue the war*: So Polybius 2.34.1.

32. *a peace was made ... stirred up the Insubrians*: This is not in Polybius, and its obvious purpose is to justify the Romans' continuation of hostilities.

33. *Acerrae*: Modern Pizzighettone.

34. *Britomartus*: At Livy, *Summary of Book* 20, he is named Viridomarus. Nothing further is known about him.

35. *Clastidium*: Modern Casteggio.

36. *Romans always turn in this way ... worship to the gods*: Cf. *Numa* 14 and *Camillus* 5.

37. *Jupiter Feretrius*: See chs. 7 and 8 below and *Romulus*, note 74.

38. *I am the third Roman commander to do this*: See ch. 8 below.

39. *Mediolanum*: Modern Milan.

40. *Romulus ... spoils of Acron of Caenina*: See *Romulus* 16.

41. *Cornelius Cossus ... spoils of Tolumnius*: The year in which Aulus Cornelius Cossus was consul was controversial in antiquity, but 428 seems likeliest. He slew Lars Tolumnius, king of Veii.

42. *Greek ... absorbed into Latin*: Plutarch refers elsewhere to the early Roman use of Greek (*Romulus* 15 and *Numa* 7).

43. *spolia opima*: Plutarch also discusses the institution and etymology of *spolia opima* ('the first and finest of spoils') at *Romulus*

16. On Marcellus' deployment of this institution for his own glorification, see Flower, *Classical Antiquity* 19, pp. 34–64.

44. *Numa Pompilius . . . commentaries*: The sacred books of Numa are described at *Numa* 22.

45. *asses*: An *as* was a bronze coin of modest value.

46. *thank-offering*: The Romans also sent a thank-offering to Delphi at *Camillus* 8.

47. *Hiero*: Hiero II (reigned *c.* 271–215), see Introduction.

48. *Hannibal . . . invaded Italy*: In 218.

49. *Marcellus . . . in command of a fleet*: As praetor (for the second time) in 216.

50. *defeat at Cannae*: In 216 Hannibal inflicted a crushing defeat on the armies commanded by both consuls at Cannae in southeast Italy. It was, at that time, the worst loss ever suffered by the Romans. Plutarch offers an account of this battle at *Fabius Maximus* 14–17.

51. *Canusium*: Modern Canosa.

52. *Fabius Maximus*: Quintus Fabius Maximus is the subject of *Fabius Maximus*.

53. *both as consuls together*: Fabius Maximus and Marcellus were consuls together only in 214.

54. *pedagogue*: A slave who attended his master's children on walks, especially to and from school, and kept his wards out of trouble. At *Fabius Maximus* 5, Fabius is mocked by his soldiers as Hannibal's pedagogue.

55. *Poseidonius says . . . inflicted them on him*: Plutarch also cites Poseidonius at *Fabius Maximus* 19. Only Plutarch cites Poseidonius for this observation, although Marcellus and Fabius are contrasted elsewhere (Livy 24.9.7–11; Cicero, *The Republic* 5.10). The original Poseidonian context is unknown, which is true for all fragments of Poseidonius dealing with either Fabius or Marcellus; see Kidd, *Posidonius*, vol. 2, pp. 896–902.

56. *Neapolis . . . Nola*: Neapolis (modern Naples), and Nola, a city located to the east of Naples, were by this period under Roman domination, but Hannibal's presence in Italy gave each an opportunity, unwelcome to Rome, for independence. Marcellus was active in this part of Italy, especially in Nola, in 215 and 214.

57. *the senate*: Plutarch means the senate of Nola (this is made clear in the parallel narrative in Livy: e.g. 23.14).

58. *Bandius*: Plutarch calls him this, but in Livy (23.14–16) he is Lucius Bantius.

59. *Aemilius Paullus*: Lucius Aemilius Paullus was consul for the second time in 216, when he fell in the fighting at Cannae.

60. *Livy ... confirms ... they had suffered*: The reference is to Livy 23.16.

61. *one of the consuls was killed*: Lucius Postumius Albinus, consul in 215.

62. *Marcellus ... voluntarily resigned his office*: Marcellus behaves correctly, and, as is the normal practice, this consulship counts to his credit. Fabius Maximus was elected consul in Marcellus' place.

63. *the following year*: In 214.

64. *Hieronymus*: Hiero died in 215. He was succeeded by his young grandson Hieronymus – here described as tyrant rather than king – who was only fifteen years old. He was persuaded by his advisers to transfer the city's loyalty to Hannibal and, after a very brief reign, was assassinated.

65. *Appius Claudius*: Appius Claudius Pulcher, praetor in 215 and later consul in 212. He continued, as propraetor (see General Introduction VI), under Marcellus' command in 214 and 213.

66. *Hippocrates, a general of the Syracusans*: The Syracusan government, after the assassination of Hieronymous, was directed by an executive board of generals (*strategoi*), annual magistrates elected by the people. On Hippocrates see Introduction.

67. *captured the city*: Marcellus took Leontini (modern Lentini) in late 214.

68. *all the deserters ... put to death*: Livy (24.30.6) mentions the execution of 2,000 Roman deserters.

69. *siege-engine ... eight galleys lashed together*: Polybius 8.6 (who is vaguely followed at Livy 24.34) has a different account of Marcellus' siege-engines: there, Marcellus deploys four sets of dual galleys lashed to one another, each set bearing its own siege-engine.

70. *Eudoxus ... Archytas*: Eudoxus of Cnidus (*c.* 390–*c.* 340), distinguished philosopher, mathematician, geographer and (especially) astronomer. Archytas of Tarentum (d. *c.* 350), Pythagorean philosopher and mathematician and regarded as the father of mechanics, not least owing to his solution to the problem of *doubling the cube* (see following note).

71. *solve the problem ... geometrical figures*: Plutarch has in mind the problem, important in ancient mathematics, of *doubling the cube*, that is, for any cube with a given volume, to articulate mathematically the dimensions of a cube with double that vol-

ume. The problem of doubling the cube is equivalent to that of finding two mean proportionals between a given line segment and a line segment of twice the length: if *a* and *b* are two straight lines, such that *b* is twice the length of *a*, and if *x* and *y* are the two mean proportionals (that is, if $a:x = x:y = y:b$), then *x* is the length of the side of a cube which has twice the volume of the cube for which *a* is the length of its side. Plutarch recurs to this celebrated problem at *Moralia* 386e, 579b and 718e–f. On this problem, its significance and solutions see C. A. Huffman, *Archytas of Tarentum: Pythagorean, Philosopher and Mathematician King* (2005), pp. 342–401.

72. *both mathematicians . . . mechanical means*: We do not know how Eudoxus solved this problem. Contrary to Plutarch's assertion here, Archytas solved it through pure geometry.

73. *Plato was indignant . . . purity of geometry*: Plutarch is our only source for this, cf. *Moralia* 718e–f.

74. *Archimedes . . . a relative*: Only Plutarch asserts this. Other sources claim that Archimedes' origins were modest, e.g. Cicero, *Tusculan Disputations* 5.23.

75. *sambuca . . . musical instrument of that name*: A triangular instrument with several strings. The siege-engine in combination with the ships supporting it resembled a triangle owing to its inclined ladder, designed to allow soldiers to storm a city's steep walls.

76. *talents*: An Attic talent weighed approximately 26 kilograms or 50 pounds.

77. *scorpions*: The name given to Archimedes' small arrow-firing catapults; see Walbank, *Commentary*, vol. 2, p. 75.

78. *Briareus*: One of the so-called Hundred-Handers of Greek mythology, primordial monsters with a hundred arms and fifty heads.

79. *sambuca . . . in disgrace*: *Sambuca* refers both to the instrument and its player, and that is the sense here: Archimedes, in this witticism, has contrived a kind of symposium – out of which he has driven Marcellus' (objectionable) *sambuca*-player. Polybius (8.6.6) tells the joke more neatly because he does not wrap it in a clever reference to Greek mythology (possibly Plutarch's own embroidery).

80. *would not deign . . . any writings on his mechanical discoveries*: This is untrue, though perhaps Plutarch was unaware of Archimedes' essays on mechanics; see E. J. Dijksterhuis, *Archimedes* (1938), pp. 21–9.

81. *cylinder enclosing a sphere . . . the contained*: Archimedes discovered that the ratio between the two is 3 to 2. On Archimedes'

tomb and its significance, see Jaeger, *Archimedes and the Roman Imagination*, pp. 32–47.

82. *Megara*: Megara Hyblaea, about 14 miles (22½ km) north of Syracuse, was founded by the Megarians (of the Greek mainland) in the eighth century BC.

83. *Acrillae*: Modern Chiaramonte Gulfi.

84. *Some while afterwards*: The siege of Syracuse lasted more than two years. Here Plutarch abruptly shifts to the conclusion of the campaign.

85. *Damippus*: An envoy acting between Syracuse and King Philip V of Macedon, with whom the Romans were also at war (the First Macedonian War, 214–205). Because of that conflict the Romans hoped to win the goodwill of Sparta (Livy 25.23), hence the international significance of these negotiations, in which Plutarch has no real interest.

86. *Hexapyla*: This was the great northern gate of Syracuse, through which one entered the region of the city known as Tyche (see following note).

87. *whole city . . . Tyche*: Syracuse was a huge city composed of several quite large regions. Its original districts were Achradina and the island of Ortygia, but, as it expanded northwards, the city took in new districts called Tyche and Neapolis. See R. J. Evans, *Syracuse in Antiquity: History and Topography* (2009).

88. *Marcellus . . . wept*: Cf. *Camillus* 5, with note 20.

89. *except . . . to the Roman treasury*: Marcellus also preserved the property of Syracusans who had fought on the Roman side (Livy 25.31).

90. *Enna*: A city in central Sicily (modern Enna), whose inhabitants were massacred by a Roman garrison during the war against Syracuse; according to Livy (24.37–9), whose account of the incident endeavours to be apologetic, the brutality of this action led other Sicilian cities to go over to the side of the Carthaginians.

91. *Engyium . . . the Mothers*: Engyium was in central Sicily. Its cult of the Mothers is mentioned elsewhere (Diodorus 4.79.5–7; Cicero, *Against Verres* 2.4.97).

92. *Meriones*: A Cretan warrior who fought with the Greeks at Troy; he figures prominently in Homer's *Iliad*.

93. *this is the story . . . from Poseidonius*: His tale seems to have had less to do with Marcellus than with Nicias, whose histrionics, as Kidd points out, are no less effective on the Roman than on his fellow-townsmen; see Kidd, *Posidonius*, vol. 2,

pp. 898–9. Plutarch has put the story, and Poseidonius' authority, to a new purpose here.

94. *the Romans recalled Marcellus ... against Hannibal*: This is a bit misleading. When elected consul for 210, Marcellus received Sicily as his consular province and his colleague received the war against Hannibal; owing to the Syracusans' complaints about Marcellus (see below), they arranged an exchange (Livy 26.29).

95. *Epaminondas*: On Epaminondas see General Introduction II.

96. *'a dancing-floor of Ares'*: Also cited at *Moralia* 193e.

97. *'an arsenal of war'*: Citing Xenophon, *A History of My Times* 3.4.17.

98. *'a sanctuary of Ares who revels in war'*: Plutarch cites Pindar, *Pythian Odes* 2.1–2, dedicated to Hiero I. There is some irony in the fact that Pindar's lines actually describe Syracuse.

99. *'Let us leave ... these angry gods of theirs!'*: See *Fabius Maximus* 22 (where Fabius does remove a giant statue of Hercules) and *Moralia* 195f.

100. *he paraded ... gods*: By stripping statues from temples and carrying them in his victory celebrations, Marcellus paraded gods along with his mortal captives.

101. *'rough ... on great occasions noble'*: From the lost tragedy *Licymnius*; see fr. 473 in C. Collard and M. Cropp, *Euripides: Fragments*, vol. 1 (2008).

102. *Fabius Maximus ... Greek art*: Plutarch revisits his comparison of Marcellus and Fabius at *Fabius Maximus* 22, where he explicitly commends Marcellus' conduct at the fall of Syracuse and compliments his 'extraordinary mildness and humanity'. The relationship between these two Lives has been closely examined by H. Beck in A. Barazanò, C. Bearzot and F. Landucci Gattinoni (eds.), *Modelli eroici dall'antichità all cultura europea: alle radici della casa comune europea* (2003), pp. 239–63.

103. *a third triumph*: We know only of Marcellus' triumph in 222 (ch. 8). Marcellus is again said to have celebrated three triumphs at *Comparison Pelopids–Marcellus* 3.

104. *Alban Mount ... ovatio*: On the technical matters associated with Marcellus' ovation and his Alban triumph, see Introduction.

105. *flute ... averse to ... war*: At *Pelopidas* 19 Plutarch underlines the association of the flute with Aphrodite and Harmony (her daughter by Ares). Aphrodite's aversion to warfare is also discussed by Plutarch at *Moralia* 759e. The Roman goddess Venus, by contrast, was sometimes associated by the Romans with

victory in war (e.g. in her guise as Venus Erycina during the Punic Wars, or in the late republic as Venus Victrix).

106. *euasmos . . . twisted by the Greeks . . . ovatio*: The Greek word *euasmos* refers to the shout *euae!*, which is a part of the celebration of the god Dionysus, whereas Latin *ovatio* derives from *ovare*, meaning *to shout* or *rejoice*. The false etymology criticized here occurs in Dion. Hal. 5.47.2, although Plutarch's explanation is also incorrect.

107. *instructions laid down . . . a cock*: Also noted at *Moralia* 238f.

108. *exploit . . . by means of . . . intelligence*: At ch. 29 Hannibal will bring about Marcellus' death by way of deception.

109. *fourth term as consul*: In 210.

110. *his enemies*: It is clear from Livy's (very different) account of this episode that Marcellus was facing criticism from Marcus Cornelius Cethegus (consul in 204) and Titus Manlius Torquatus (consul for the first time in 235); see Livy 26.26 and 32.

111. *fellow-consul*: Marcus Valerius Laevinus, who, in Livy's account, was the one unavailable when the Sicilians first arrived.

112. *seating himself . . . in his curule chair . . . charges*: Plutarch represents this matter as if it were a trial, thereby creating a parallel with Pelopidas' trial at *Pelopidas* 25. In Livy (26.29–32), what is at issue is the formalization of Marcellus' disposition of Syracuse after its defeat.

113. *constant benefactor*: This is the first instance known to us of a Roman conqueror's becoming the benefactor and patron of a community conquered by him, and the Claudii Marcelli continued in that role. Valerius Maximus (4.1.7) cites Marcellus' behaviour here as an example of Roman moderation.

114. *garlands . . . sacrifices to the gods*: Syracuse also commemorated its conquest by Rome in an annual festival in honour of Marcellus, the *Marcellia* (Cicero, *Against Verres* 2.4.151).

115. *principal Samnite cities*: Salapia (modern Trinitapoli), Marmoreae and Meles (Livy 27.1).

116. *Gnaeus Fulvius*: Consul in 211; his command in Apulia had been extended by the senate.

117. *when these letters were read . . . alarm*: Livy (27.2) says simply that the Romans continued to fear for the future.

118. *Numistro*: Modern Muro Lucano.

119. *Quintus Fulvius dictator*: Quintus Fulvius Flaccus was consul for the first time in 237; he was to be appointed dictator in order to conduct the elections.

120. *derivation ... declare*: This is the etymology given by Cicero, *The Republic* 1.63, and Varro, *On the Latin Language* 5.81.

121. *This is the derivation ... edicta*: Both etymologies are also canvassed at Dion. Hal. 5.73.

122. *proconsul for the following year*: In 209.

123. *Fabius Maximus*: Consul again in 209.

124. *Sinuessa*: Modern Mondragone.

125. *Publicius Bibulus*: Gaius Publicius Bibulus, described by Livy (27.20) as Marcellus' personal enemy.

126. *indictment ... drawn up*: This was not an actual indictment or trial; Bibulus had drafted a bill abrogating Marcellus' command (Livy 27.20–21). Again, Plutarch contrives a parallel with *Pelopidas* (cf. note 112).

127. *consul for the fifth time*: In 208.

128. *Honour ... Valour*: Honos and Virtus were closely linked in Roman sensibilities; *honos* was also the word for an elected office, like the consulship, and so these qualities encapsulated aristocratic excellence in Rome. Marcellus vowed this temple first at the battle of Clastidium and again at Syracuse. He attempted to fulfil his vow by restoring an existing temple of Honos and dedicating it to both Honos and Virtus. In the end, a separate chapel was added for Virtus and the completed temple was dedicated in 205 by Marcellus' son. It was located outside the Porta Capena and decorated with artworks from Syracuse.

129. *that year was filled with prodigies*: At *Pelopidas* 31 bad omens presage the death of Pelopidas.

130. *his colleague*: Titus Quinctius Crispinus.

131. *Bantia ... Venusia*: Modern Banzi and Venosa.

132. *Epizephyrian Locrians*: The people of Locri Epizephyrii (modern Gerace), in southern Italy, who had defected to Hannibal in 214.

133. *Petelia*: Modern Strongoli, a city that remained loyal to Rome during the Second Punic War. These troops were not Marcellus': they had been dispatched from Tarentum (Livy 27.26).

134. *'not fire ... hinder fate'*: A fragment of Pindar from an unknown work, fr. 232 in W. H. Race, *Pindar*, vol. 2 (1997).

135. *his son*: Marcus Claudius Marcellus, the future consul of 196.

136. *Fregellae*: A Roman colony established in 328 on a site near modern Ceprano.

137. *removed his signet ring*: Hannibal took the ring in order to forge letters under Marcellus' name, but his plan was foiled by Crispinus (Livy 27.28).

138. *This . . . is the account . . . ceremony*: Valerius Maximus (6.1.external 6) reports that Hannibal gave Marcellus an honourable funeral, and Livy's account (27.28), though briefer, is similar. Nepos' biography of Marcellus is lost, as is Augustus' funeral oration for his nephew and son-in-law, Marcus Claudius Marcellus (see below).

139. *Cabiri in Samothrace*: At Samothrace there was a famous Panhellenic sanctuary devoted to the Great Gods, who included divinities known as the Cabiri. The Cabiri, whose precise identities remained mysterious even in antiquity, were also worshipped in shrines elsewhere in Greece, including Plutarch's Boeotia (*Aemilius Paullus* 23); see H. Bowden, *Mystery Cults of the Ancient World* (2010), pp. 49–67.

140. *Lindus*: A major Rhodian city and the site of an important cult of Athena.

141. *that Marcellus*: Marcus Claudius Marcellus, born in 42 BC, was the son of Augustus' sister, Octavia, and Gaius Claudius Marcellus, consul of 50 BC. He was favoured by Augustus, married his daughter Julia and was widely viewed as his successor. He died while holding the office of aedile in 23 BC, an event commemorated by Virgil (*Aeneid* 6.860–66) and Propertius (3.18).

142. *dedicated a library . . . theatre*: The Library of Marcellus was part of the Portico of Octavia; it burned down in AD 79 but was restored by Domitian (Suetonius, *Domitian* 20). The nearby Theatre of Marcellus, a structure begun by Julius Caesar, was completed by Augustus and named for his nephew (and still stands). The Hellenic quality of these two constructions – a library and a theatre – reprise Marcellus' introduction of Greek material culture (and its related values) to Rome. Plutarch often adduces a hero's descendants to give a positive finish to a Life (Pelling, *P&H*, p. 369).

Notes to the Comparison of Pelopidas and Marcellus

1. *Marcellus . . . massacred their populations*: Unlike the Life itself, where Marcellus' justice and mercy are emphasized (e.g. ch. 20), in the *Comparison* Plutarch allows that Marcellus could exhibit cruelty.

2. *treated the Orchomenians as they did*: In 364, after the deaths of Epaminondas and Pelopidas, the Thebans defeated and sacked the city of Orchomenus (Diodorus 15.79.3–6).

3. *slain by the tyrant*: In 364 Pelopidas fell in battle against Alexander of Pherae, although the outcome of the battle was a victory for Thebes (Introduction and *Pelopidas* 32).

4. *battles of Leuctra and Tegyra*: See Introduction.
5. *put an end to the tyrants of Thebes*: In 379/8 Pelopidas staged a coup d'état that liberated Thebes; the exciting and colourful story is told at *Pelopidas* 7–11.
6. *Polybius, Hannibal . . . he confronted Scipio*: On Polybius' hostility towards Marcellus, see Introduction. The victory of Scipio Africanus at Zama was decisive in the Second Punic War, but Polybius seems to go to some trouble to underline Africanus' distinctive achievement on account of his friendship with Scipio Aemilianus, who, through adoption, was Africanus' grandson.
7. *Livy . . . Juba*: On Plutarch's sources see Introduction. Caesar, here, refers to Augustus. In his *Life of Hannibal* (5.4), Nepos claims that the man was never defeated in Italy, but he may have put forward a different version in his (now lost) *Life of Marcellus*.
8. *Eurotas*: Sparta was located on the west bank of the Eurotas (modern Evrotas), and, until the Thebans managed it, no one in the Greek world had imagined that any hostile force could actually penetrate the Spartans' own borders. However, it was Pelopidas and Epaminondas together who led the Theban army into Spartan territory, as Plutarch makes clear at *Pelopidas* 24.
9. *credited to Epaminondas*: At the battle of Leuctra, Epaminondas was in command, while Pelopidas, who led the Sacred Band (Introduction to *Marcellus*, note 13), was his subordinate. At *Pelopidas* 23, however, Plutarch insists that they shared in the glory of the Thebans' victory.
10. *Chrysantes in The Education of Cyrus*: Plutarch refers to Xenophon, *Education of Cyrus* 4.1.3.
11. *to seek vengeance*: Alexander of Pherae had previously captured, imprisoned and mistreated Pelopidas (*Pelopidas* 27–9).
12. *'if he must die . . . valorously'*: From an unknown tragedy: see fr. 994 in Collard and Cropp, *Euripides: Fragments*, vol. 2.
13. *buried by his allies*: *Pelopidas* 33–4.

ARATUS

Further Reading

Aratus has mostly been studied as a source for the history of the period it covers. There is a useful commentary in Italian (mostly historical in its focus) by M. Manfredini and D. P. Orsi, *Le vite di Arato e di Artaserse* (1987). Still worth consulting, though in many respects dated, is the commentary by W. H. Porter, *Plutarch's Life of Aratus* (1937). Important aspects of characterization in *Aratus* are briefly discussed by Pelling, *P&H*, pp. 288–91. There is an excellent biography of Aratus by F. W. Walbank, *Aratos of Sicyon* (1933). The larger historical background to this Life is covered by J. A. O. Larsen, *Greek Federal States: Their Institutions and History* (1968), and F. W. Walbank, 'Macedonia and Greece' and 'Macedonia and the Greek Leagues', in *CAH* vii.1 (1984), pp. 221–56 and 446–81. For the history of Sicyon, the most recent treatment is Y. A. Lolos, *Land of Sikyon: Archaeology and History of a Greek City-State* (2011). C. B. Champion, *Cultural Politics in Polybius's Histories* (2004), especially pp. 122–43, examines Polybius' representation of the Achaean League, which lies in the background of Plutarch's narrative here.

Notes to the Introduction to Aratus

1. The basic account remains Larsen, *Greek Federal States: Their Institutions and History*. See also Walbank in *CAH* vii.1, pp. 221–56 and 446–81.
2. See the examination of the Aetolian League by J. B. Scholten, *The Politics of Plunder: Aitolians and their Koinon in the Early Hellenistic Era, 279–218 BC* (2000).
3. Polybius (2.40.2) describes Aratus as 'the originator and creator' of the league.
4. See A. Griffin, *Sikyon* (1982), p. 81.
5. The details of the Achaean League's constitution are uncertain: see Walbank, *Commentary*, vol. 3, pp. 406–14.
6. Walbank in *CAH* vii.1, pp. 247–48, puts these attacks *after* Aratus' voyage to Egypt, which he dates to 251/50, in which case Aratus could have been fighting a Macedonian garrison on behalf of Egypt (although Plutarch's narrative at the very least suggests a longer passage of time between the liberation of Sicyon and Aratus' journey to Ptolemy II).
7. Cleomenes III (*c.* 260–222), whose career and revolutionary designs are the subject of Plutarch's *Cleomenes*. See P. Cartledge and A. Spawforth, *Hellenistic and Roman Sparta: A Tale of Two Cities* (2nd edn, 2002), pp. 49–58.
8. This was the advice of Demetrius of Pharus, by now Philip's closest adviser (Polybius 5.101.7). Modern scholars divide over whether this was Philip's real motive in concluding the Social War: see A. M. Eckstein, *Rome Enters the Greek East: From Anarchy*

    to Hierarchy in the Hellenistic Mediterranean, 230–170 BC (2008), pp. 78–83.

9. See R. M. Errington in *CAH* viii (1989), pp. 94–106; Eckstein, *Rome Enters the Greek East*, pp. 78–91.

10. Plutarch's *Artaxerxes* is also a solitary biography, on which see J. Mossman in Humble, *Plutarch's Lives*, pp. 145–68.

11. The prestige associated in imperial times with having distinguished ancestors from the classical past is discussed by C. Jones in T. Whitmarsh (ed.), *Local Knowledge and Microidentities in the Imperial Greek World* (2010), pp. 111–24.

12. See General Introduction II and *Moralia* 814b–c.

13. This important point is made and elaborated by A. Wardman, *Plutarch's Lives* (1974), pp. 40–41.

14. Does the youthfulness of Plutarch's audience also help to explain his (perhaps amusingly) graphic discussion of the symptoms of Aratus' alleged cowardice at ch. 29?

15. Plutarch often stresses the importance of a sound Greek education (or, more often, the effect of its absence) in his assessment of the character of his Roman heroes (General Introduction III), but education is equally important in the development of his Greek heroes: see Duff, *Plutarch's Lives*, pp. 74–8. Although Aratus received a liberal education (ch. 3), he did not go far enough in his philosophical studies. In this he was like Pelopidas (*Pelopidas* 4) and Philopoemen (*Philopoemen* 4), who studied philosophy too selectively.

16. On Plutarch's characterization of Aratus and its didactic function in this Life, see Pelling, *P&H*, pp. 288–91.

17. Cf. Plutarch's verdict on Aratus' liberation of Corinth at ch. 16: 'Aratus' success surpassed theirs [i.e. Pelopidas' and Thrasybulus'] in that he acted, not against fellow-Greeks, but against a foreign and alien power.'

18. Sources for the career of Aratus are reviewed by Walbank, *Aratos of Sicyon*, pp. 3–21.

19. See G. Marasco in G. Marasco (ed.), *Political Autobiographies and Memoirs in Antiquity* (2011), pp. 104–17.

20. Polybius 2.40.2, 24.6.5, 28.6.9, 28.13.9–13, 29.24.1–8 and 30.13.32.

21. Polybius 2.37–80 (the rise of the Achaean League to the end of the Cleomenean War); 4.3–37, 4.57–87, 5.1–30 and 5.91–105 (the Social War); 8.12 (death of Aratus).

22. On Phylarchus, see *FGrH* 81; T. W. Africa, *Phylarchus and the Spartan Revolution* (1961); and especially P. Pédech, *Trois*

historiens méconnus: Théopompe, Duris, Phylarque (1989), pp. 391–493.

23. See *FGrH* 306.

Notes to the Life of Aratus

1. *Polycrates*: A descendant of Aratus, probably identical with the local dignitary Tiberius Claudius Polycrates (*Syll.* 846); Plutarch also mentions him at *Moralia* 409c and 667c–671b.

2. *Chrysippus*: (*c.* 280–206) An influential Stoic philosopher, whom Plutarch cites frequently in his *Moralia*.

3. *Dionysodorus of Troezen*: A grammarian who flourished in the second half of the third century BC; among other interests, he was a student of proverbs. Troezen (modern Trizina) was a city in the northeast Peloponnese.

4. '*Who will praise . . . sons?*': Cicero cites the opening words of this proverb at *Letters to Atticus* 1.19.10.

5. '*exhibits . . . of his forefathers*': Slightly adapted from Pindar, *Pythian Odes* 8.43–4.

6. *mark of a man . . . superior to everyone else*: Plutarch remarks on this baleful effect of self-love (*philautia*) at *Moralia* 471d (see also 468e).

7. *Sicyon's . . . constitution . . . demagogues*: Sicyon was ruled by tyrants during its early history, but in 417 Sparta imposed an oligarchy (Thucydides 5.81.2), which was itself replaced in the 360s by a short-lived democracy that later sources regarded unfavourably (Diodorus 15.70.3; Xenophon, *A History of My Times* 7.1.44–7.3.12); thereafter Sicyon reverted to tyranny. See Griffin, *Sikyon*, pp. 40–81.

8. *Cleon*: The tyrant was assassinated in 275 or 274.

9. *Timocleides and Cleinias . . . chief magistrates*: The chief magistracy in Sicyon was that of general (*strategos*). A different version of events is reported by Pausanias (2.8.2).

10. *murdered Cleinias*: In 264.

11. *Argos*: About 25 miles (40 km) south of Sicyon.

12. *hatred of tyrants*: At this time, however, Argos, too, was ruled by a tyrant, either by Aristippus or his son Aristomachus (ch. 25), who was certainly tyrant by 249.

13. *pentathlon*: The ancient pentathlon comprised the long jump, javelin throw, discus throw, sprint and wrestling. Aratus also won a chariot race at Olympia (Pausanias 6.12.5).

14. *exercise with a mattock*: This form of exercise is also mentioned by Athenaeus (518d).
15. *insufficiently diligent ... political affairs*: Polybius (4.8.2), however, describes Aratus as a good speaker.
16. *Memoirs*: See Introduction.
17. *Abantidas ... assassinated*: At the end of 252 or the beginning of 251.
18. *Deinias*: Possibly Deinias of Argos, a Greek historian (ch. 29).
19. *Aristotle the dialectician*: Nothing further is known of him.
20. *Periander*: Tyrant in Corinth from *c.* 627 to 587, known both for cruelty and wisdom.
21. *Orontes*: Probably a Persian satrap, but the name is too common for a specific identification.
22. *Alcmaeon, the son of Amphiaraus*: These are mythological figures. Amphiaraus was one of the Seven against Thebes and met his death betrayed by his wife; their son was therefore obliged to kill his mother and was subsequently tortured by the Furies until he was ritually purified.
23. *Myrsilus*: Myrsilus of Methymna flourished around 250. He wrote a history of Lesbos and *Historical Paradoxes*, a (now lost) collection of unexpected or unbelievable occurrences.
24. *during which time ... plans against it*: This is our only reference to Aetolian aggression against Nicocle. On the Aetolians see Introduction.
25. *the kings ... friends and hosts*: Important individuals in different cities or states often enjoyed a relationship, known as *xenia* or *guest-friendship*, whereby they looked after one another's interests in their respective communities. Although the relationship was strictly voluntary, it tended to extend from one generation to the next. Cleinias had been the guest-friend of both the king of Macedon and the king of Egypt.
26. *Antigonus*: This is Antigonus Gonatas (*c.* 320–239), the king of Macedon.
27. *Ptolemy*: Ptolemy II Philadelphus (308–246), the king of Egypt.
28. *Aristomachus*: Nothing more is known of him, unless he is the Sicyonian Aristomachus mentioned in *Syll.* 458.
29. *Ecdelus*: (sometimes called Ecdemus) Helped to liberate Megalopolis from tyranny and Cyrene to form a new constitution (Polybius 10.22.2, Pausanias 8.49.2). He was a teacher of Philopoemen (*Philopoemen* 1).

30. *Arcadian*: A person from Arcadia, the central region of the Peloponnese, where a distinct dialect of Greek was spoken.

31. *Megalopolis*: An Arcadian city (modern Megalopoli) in the central Peloponnese which was founded in the fourth century BC and soon became the largest of the Arcadian cities. Ultimately it was the leading city in the Achaean League (see *Philopoemen*).

32. *Arcesilaus the Academic*: Arcesilaus of Pitane (315–241) was a Platonist who became head of the Academy around 260. Sceptical in inclination, he was the founder of the Middle Academy.

33. *one of the exiles*: Plutarch includes in his account the names of several otherwise unknown Sicyonians, whose role in liberating their city was no doubt mentioned in Aratus' *Memoirs*.

34. *steal the king's horses*: Unless Aratus' story was false in every particular, Antigonus Gonatas apparently maintained prized horses in Sicyon, which was famous for the quality of its grazing land; see Griffin, *Sikyon*, p. 30.

35. *tower of Polygnotus*: Its location is unknown but presumably it lay to the north of Argos, on the road to Nemea, which was about halfway between Argos and Sicyon.

36. *Ecdelus*: See ch. 5.

37. *Technon*: Aratus' slave (ch. 5).

38. *his friends*: Naturally Aratus still had friends resident in Sicyon.

39. *as far away as Corinth*: The distance between the two cities is nearly 10 miles (16 km).

40. *the event . . . civil bloodshed*: Aratus liberated Sicyon in 251. The nature of his political authority after the liberation of Sicyon is unclear in our sources. Strabo (8.382) calls him both liberator and tyrant.

41. *Antigonus . . . regained*: Whether or not Antigonus Gonatas regarded Nicocles as his agent in Sicyon is a topic that divides scholars. In any case, at the time of Sicyon's liberation he sent Aratus a gift of 25 talents (ch. 11).

42. *former farms . . . strife and faction*: The restored exiles were in conflict with the current holders of their properties, who were naturally unwilling to relinquish them.

43. *Sicyon joined the Achaean League*: This happened in 251.

44. *Achaean League . . . nor great power*: Polybius (2.38–42) provides a brief history of the Achaeans and their league; see Introduction. The Dorians were one of the major ethnicities into which the Greeks were divided; the Achaeans were another.

45. *In his very nature . . . opportunities*: A similar sketch of Aratus' character is offered by Polybius (4.8); see also ch. 29.

46. *events ... in the open ... heralds*: That is, in open warfare; a formal state of war was announced by a herald.

47. *when one lacks a sound philosophical education ... numerous examples*: Aratus' liberal education (ch. 3) apparently did not extend to philosophical studies. The importance of philosophical training is a recurring theme in Plutarch (General Introduction III).

48. *Dyme ... Tritaea*: Two Achaean cities (modern Kato Achaia and Tritaia), both in the western Peloponnese.

49. *the king*: Plutarch writes just 'the king', but here he can mean only Antigonus Gonatas (see M. Holleaux, *Hermes* 41 (1906), pp. 475–8). Antigonus hoped to bring Aratus within his orbit, and there is evidence that he succeeded: Aratus went on to scheme against Alexander of Corinth (note 82), who had recently rebelled against Antigonus (ch. 18).

50. *Methone*: Presumably modern Modon, at the extreme southwest of the Peloponnese, but this is not near the Gulf of Malia (Malea).

51. *Hydria*: Modern Hydra, an island south of Argos.

52. *enemy territory ... a garrison there*: Antigonus is now an enemy because this episode comes after his enemy Alexander of Corinth (note 82) became an ally of the Achaeans. It was perhaps this change in the political landscape that required Aratus to look towards Egypt instead of Macedon for patronage. In any case, Plutarch has displaced this episode.

53. *Timanthes*: Perhaps the painter mentioned again in ch. 32.

54. *Roman ship*: A commercial vessel not a military one.

55. *Caria*: A region in southwest Asia Minor.

56. *drawings ... from Greece*: It was natural for guest-friends (ch. 4) to exchange gifts. It is an indication of Aratus' personal wealth that, even while a teenaged exile in Argos, he could send presents of exquisite art to the Egyptian king.

57. *Pamphilus ... Melanthus*: Pamphilus of Sicyon was a distinguished painter of the fourth century BC; Melanthus was his son: see Pliny, *Natural History* 35.76–7, and Griffin, *Sikyon*, pp. 148–9.

58. *Sicyon's ... paintings*: Their history is reviewed by Griffin, *Sikyon*, pp. 147–57.

59. *Apelles*: Apelles of Colophon was the most famous of ancient painters. He flourished in the late fourth century BC.

60. *Aristratus*: Mentioned by Demosthenes (18.48 and 18.294–5) but is not there called a tyrant.

61. *Philip*: Philip II (382–336) was king of Macedon and father of Alexander the Great.

62. *Polemon*: A geographer of the second century BC; a section of his (now lost) work dealt with Sicyon and in particular with Sicyonian art.

63. *Neacles*: The leading Sicyonian artist of his day; see Pliny, *Natural History* 35.102–3, and Griffin, *Sikyon*, pp. 152–3.

64. *remainder ... instalments*: The payments were extended as a means of ensuring Aratus' continued loyalty; Ptolemy's successor paid Aratus an annual subsidy of 6 talents (ch. 41).

65. *arbiter ... harmony to the city*: Cicero (*On Duties* 81–2) provides a somewhat fuller account of Aratus' procedure in resolving these matters, concluding (at *On Duties* 83): 'What a great man, and one worthy to have been born in our republic!'

66. *Pillars of Heracles*: These are the promontories at the Straits of Gibraltar and a routine literary expression for the far west or even the ends of the world.

67. *Saviour Gods*: Although this expression often refers to the Dioscuri, it is also widely used to refer to local tutelary gods and that may be the case here.

68. *during the banquet ... as a friend*: This anecdote is dubious and difficult to date. One proposal is that this episode occurred during the Isthmian Games of 250, but that leaves little time for Aratus to have made his visit to Egypt. If later, however, then it must have taken place after the death of Alexander of Corinth in 245. By then, Ptolemy II had also died (in 246) and there was a new king on the Egyptian throne. In that same year Aratus was general of the Achaeans.

69. *Ptolemy*: Because Antigonus' effort to discredit Aratus cannot be securely dated (see above), it is unclear whether this is Ptolemy II or Ptolemy III Euergetes (*c.* 284–221).

70. *elected general ... for the first time*: For 245/4.

71. *Locris and Calydon*: Locris Ozolia and Calydon lie across the Gulf of Corinth from Achaea.

72. *they were defeated*: The Boeotians, encouraged by the Achaeans to resist the Aetolians, had detached Phocis from the Aetolians, which naturally prompted retaliation. The Boeotians turned to the Achaeans for aid. In the aftermath of their defeat at Chaeronea the Boeotians became allies of the Aetolians (Polybius 20.4).

73. *Chaeronea*: Located in northwest Boeotia, this was Plutarch's native city.

74. *boeotarch*: The chief magistrate elected each year by the Boeotian League. Even on the basis of our meagre references to the

man, it is clear that Aboeocritus was a distinguished person: see Walbank, *Commentary*, vol. 3, p. 67.

75. *once again general*: For 243/2.

76. *the Acrocorinth*: A steep and almost impregnable cliff overlooking the city of Corinth.

77. *Chares*: (*c.* 400–*c.* 325) While serving as a mercenary to the rebellious satrap Artabazus he defeated the army of the Persian king, Artaxerxes III, in 356 (Diodorus 16.22.1–2).

78. *the Great King*: This is the standard means in Greek of referring to the king of Persia.

79. *Pelopidas ... Thrasybulus ... slayer of tyrants*: Pelopidas (*c.* 410–364) liberated Thebes from tyrants in 379 (*Pelopidas* 7–14); Thrasybulus (d. 388) liberated Athens from a narrow oligarchy when he defeated the Spartan-installed oligarchy known as the Thirty Tyrants in 403. Plutarch also pairs up their achievements at *Pelopidas* 13.

80. *the Isthmus*: I.e. the Isthmus of Corinth.

81. *the younger Philip*: Philip V (238–179), king of Macedon and a principal figure in this Life (chs. 46–54). On the so-called 'fetter of Greece', see further *Flamininus* 10.

82. *the Acrocorinth belonged to Alexander*: Alexander had commanded the garrison at the Acrocorinth as an officer of Antigonus Gonatas (who was also his uncle), but around 249 he revolted, made himself independent and formed an alliance with the Achaean League. He died in 245. See the discussion by Walbank in *CAH* vii.1, pp. 247–8.

83. *Nicaea*: Livy (35.26.5) may refer to this Nicaea (though Livy calls her the wife of Craterus, Alexander's father). If this is the same woman, she will very likely have been in her early forties.

84. *Demetrius*: Demetrius II (*c.* 276–229), father of Philip V; he became king of Macedon in 239.

85. *Amoebeus*: A celebrated citharoedus (that is, a singer who accompanied himself on the cithara); see *Moralia* 443a and Athenaeus 14.623d.

86. *Persaeus*: Persaeus of Citium (*c.* 306–*c.* 243), a Stoic philosopher who was a ward and later a pupil of Zeno. When Zeno was invited to the court of Antigonus Gonatas, Persaeus was sent instead and there became an influential courtier.

87. *after Alexander made an alliance ... desisted*: See notes 52 and 82.)

88. *after they had stolen some gold ... business*: It was their intention to exchange gold coins for silver ones, which would be less incriminating. The brothers involved in this theft and the following episode are not otherwise known.

89. *burglars and traitors alike*: A pun – the word used here for burglar literally describes someone who penetrates the walls of a private house, to be contrasted with someone who betrays a city's or a citadel's walls (i.e. a traitor).

90. *Phocion ... Epaminondas*: Phocion the Good (402–318), a leading Athenian statesman and general; his integrity is stressed at *Phocion* 18, 21 and 30 (and see also *Alexander* 39). On Epaminondas see General Introduction II. His incorruptibility is attested at *Philopoemen* 3 and *Alexander* 39.

91. *Ornis*: Greek for *bird*; the location of this place is unknown.

92. *sanctuary of Hera*: Both Herodotus (5.92) and Pausanias (2.4.6) mention a temple to Hera at Corinth, but its location is unknown.

93. *Archelaus*: Not otherwise known.

94. *Aratus' army arrived from Sicyon*: Aratus captured the Acrocorinth in the summer of 243.

95. *holding his spear ... rest ... on his weapon*: A familiar posture in Greek sculpture; Plutarch's description here is perhaps inspired by a statue of Aratus.

96. *restored the keys ... since the days of Philip*: This is our sole evidence for this claim, but Philip II may well have taken control of the Acrocorinth after the battle of Chaeronea in 338.

97. *Theophrastus*: Otherwise unknown.

98. *Cenchreae*: One of Corinth's ports (modern Kechries); it lay on the Saronic Gulf about 4¼ miles (7 km) southeast of the city. According to Pausanias (2.8.4 and 7.8.3), Persaeus did not escape but was killed in the fighting.

99. *'this doctrine of Zeno's ... young Sicyonian'*: Zeno of Citium (334–262) was the founder of Stoicism and the teacher of Persaeus (note 86). He put much emphasis on the wise man and his perfections (Diogenes Laertius 7.116–26), including the view that the wise man was infallible and therefore expert in important matters (7.122) and capable of doing all things well (7.125). Persaeus does not here impugn Aratus, but instead offers himself as a proof that a wise man may still be a poor general.

100. *This anecdote ... related by numerous authors*: Athenaeus (4.162d) attributes the sentiment that only the wise man can be a good general to a dialogue by Persaeus. Plutarch's anecdote is not attested elsewhere.

101. *Lechaeum*: A Corinthian port (modern Lechaio), about 3 miles (4 km) west of the city on the Gulf of Corinth.

102. *Philopoemen . . . 'the last of the Greeks'*: Philopoemen was Aratus' successor as the leading figure in the Achaean League (see *Philopoemen*). The saying cited by Plutarch is repeated at *Philopoemen* 1, and occurs also at Pausanias 8.52.1.

103. *Megara*: A city on the Isthmus of Corinth, lying opposite the island of Salamis.

104. *Troezen and Epidaurus*: A city (modern Trizina) near Argos and another (modern Epidavros) lying on the Saronic Gulf.

105. *reason to . . . revolt*: Aratus invaded Attica in 242. At this time, Athens was under Macedonian hegemony.

106. *Ptolemy*: Ptolemy III Euergetes. The position of *hegemon* seems in this instance to have been purely honorary. Ptolemy provided Aratus an annual subsidy of 6 talents (ch. 41), although around 225 he transferred it to Cleomenes (Polybius 2.51).

107. *ally . . . increase of the Achaean League*: Plutarch concentrates his narrative on the expansion of the Achaean League. He does not report that, in reaction to Aratus' success, Macedon aligned itself with the Aetolian League or that, in response to this, the Achaean League and Sparta made an alliance; see Walbank in *CAH* vii.1, pp. 251–5.

108. *Aristomachus*: He had aided Antigonus Gonatas in his attempts to defeat Alexander of Corinth (*Inscriptiones Graecae* II (2nd edn, 1940), 774) and remained a Macedonian ally (the alliance with Macedon continued with his son: ch. 26). Around 241 the Achaean League made peace with Macedon and Aetolia. If this plot was formed afterwards, Aratus' covert involvement was a provocation.

109. *Aeschylus and Charimenes*: Both otherwise unknown.

110. *Aristippus*: He and his successor, Aristomachus (ch. 29), were sons of the assassinated Aristomachus.

111. *Aratus called up . . . Argives themselves*: Aratus attempted to exploit Aristomachus' assassination to seize Argos, but was unsuccessful. This occurred in 240, after peace had been established with Macedon, and the Achaean League's naked aggression (Aratus was general at the time) threatened to rupture the accord – hence the Mantineans' condemnation of the league. Aratus also attacked the Piraeus (ch. 33), another piece of naked aggression despite the peace with Macedon.

112. *habituated to their servitude . . . over to his side*: This reaction on the part of the Argives, along with their inaction when later

the Achaeans attempted to liberate them (ch. 27), perhaps suggests that the people of Argos were disinclined to be brought into the Achaean League.

113. *Mantineans*: People of Mantinea, an Arcadian city in the central Peloponnese.

114. *30 minas*: This amounts to half a talent, a modest sum for a state to be fined.

115. *He would then retreat ... like a serpent*: Plutarch repeats this passage, nearly word for word, at *Moralia* 781d–e.

116. *perpetual authority ... to this present day*: See chs. 1 and 54 (which reprises the sentiment of this passage).

117. *Nemean Games*: Panhellenic games managed by Argos and held every other year at the sanctuary of Zeus at Nemea.

118. *the tyrant attacked him ... until nightfall*: This assault, like the battles described in chs. 28–9, very likely happened in 235 (*after* the death of Antigonus Gonatas in 239, which is not mentioned by Plutarch until ch. 34).

119. *Chares*: The modern River Charadros.

120. *Cleonae*: A city close to Nemea and southwest of Corinth (modern Archaies Kleones).

121. *Not long after this*: Still the year 235.

122. *Mycenae*: A major power in prehistoric Greece and in Homeric legend; located 6 miles (11 km) north of Argos, it was by this period a modest city.

123. *Deinias*: Deinias of Argos composed a history (now lost) of Argos down to his own times. He may be the same Deinias who helped to assassinate Abantidas of Sicyon (ch. 3), in which case he was an older contemporary of Aratus.

124. *Agias*: Not otherwise known but very likely the Macedonian commander of 'the king's troops' mentioned in this sentence. This king was Demetrius II not Antigonus Gonatas (the episode took place after Antigonus' death).

125. *the younger Aristomachus*: See note 110.

126. *vertigo*: This word, Greek *iliggos*, can also refer to bowel trouble.

127. *Lydiades*: (d. 227) He became tyrant of Megalopolis around 244, perhaps with Macedonian assistance.

128. *enrolled ... in the Achaean League*: In 235, around which time Cleomenes became king in Sparta (see Introduction).

129. *elected him general*: For 234/3.

130. *ambitious nature ... against the Lacedaemonians*: Lacedaemonian is another expression for Spartan. Lydiades' expedition was not merely a matter of personal competitiveness: Megalopolis

had a tradition of hostility against Sparta. Aratus' opposition was apparently enough to block this initiative.

131. *general for a second time*: For 232/1.

132. *general ... for the third time*: For 230/29.

133. *his own character was artificial*: See also ch. 35. This view of Lydiades, attributed to the Achaeans and no doubt derived from Aratus' *Memoirs*, was not necessarily Plutarch's own (ch. 37, *Cleomenes* 6 and *Moralia* 552b).

134. *cuckoo ... hawk*: That cuckoos could change into hawks was deemed by some to be a biological reality: see e.g. Aristotle, *Animal History* 563b.

135. *do battle ... territory*: In 241. At this time Megara was part of the Achaean League.

136. *Agis*: Agis IV (*c.* 262–241), who became king in Sparta around 244. Plutarch wrote a *Life of Agis*.

137. *Lacedaemonians ... urging ... to fight*: Aratus had sought help from Sparta, at the time an ally of the Achaean League, but in the end he courteously dismissed Agis, who was, according to Plutarch (*Agis* 15), unperturbed by Aratus' unwillingness to fight.

138. *policy*: The advantage of Aratus' policy here is not immediately obvious, unless Plutarch is anticipating Aratus' détente with Aetolia in ch. 33.

139. *Geranian mountains*: In the Isthmus of Corinth, southwest of Megara.

140. *Pellene*: An Achaean city near Sicyon. Its location was near the modern village of Zugra.

141. *wooden image ... reason*: Polyaenus (*Stratagems* 8.59) tells a roughly similar story involving a priestess of Athena.

142. *Aratus mentions nothing like any of this*: It seems he was generally unimpressed by prodigies and related matters (ch. 43).

143. *Timanthes*: Possibly Aratus' friend, mentioned in ch. 12.

144. *Pantaleon*: The son of Pleuron, he was general in the Aetolian League five times during the period 240–210.

145. *alliance between the two leagues*: Made apparently after the death of Antigonus in 239; it may have been stimulated by that event. Thereafter both leagues were hostile to Demetrius II.

146. *liberate Athens*: Aratus' previous assault on Athens is described in ch. 24.

147. *truce ... attempt to capture the Piraeus*: In 239 the Achaean League initiated an aggressive policy against Macedonian allies in Greece, especially against Athens and Argos, which ruptured

the peace established around 241. The Achaean campaign against Athens was assisted by the Aetolians, whose naval forces also raided Attica.

148. *attack on the Acrocorinth*: See ch. 18.

149. *Thriasian plain*: Immediately to the west of Athens.

150. *for this injury*: See also *Cleomenes* 16.

151. *Antigonus died*: Antigonus Gonatas died in 239.

152. *Phylacia ... Bithys*: The location of Phylacia is uncertain but it lay in Achaea. This was a Macedonian invasion, which probably took place in 233. No more is known about Bithys, unless he is the Bithys who was the recipient of an honorary decree by the Athenians (*Syll.* 476).

153. *Diogenes*: A major figure in Athens during this time and instrumental in the city's regaining its independence. He was honoured as the city's benefactor and granted a special seat in the theatre; a festival and a gymnasium were also named in his honour. But little more is known of him.

154. *the Academy*: Plato's Academy lay approximately a mile (2 km) outside Athens' walls. This was another Achaean assault which failed to take the city.

155. *death of Demetrius*: In 229. In the immediate aftermath, Macedon was beset by numerous military crises and this led to the Athenians' defection. Despite Aratus' exertions, Athens did not join the Achaean League.

156. *another man*: Lydiades, during his third and final generalship in 230/29.

157. *Munychia ... Sunium*: A steep, fortified hill in the Piraeus (modern Kastella), and a headland (modern Cape Sounion), at the southernmost tip of Attica.

158. *Aegina ... Hermione*: Aegina is an island in the Saronic Gulf. Hermione (modern Ermioni), a town near Argos, was ruled by the tyrant Xenon, who abdicated and led his city into the Achaean League; this was probably in the aftermath of Argos' union with the Achaean League (Polybius 2.44.6, Strabo 8.7.3, and see ch. 35).

159. *neighbouring enemies*: The Dardanians, who dwelt north of Macedon and with whom the Macedonians were in continual conflict.

160. *Aratus ... long-standing pursuit*: See chs. 25–9.

161. *to emulate Lydiades*: See ch. 30.

162. *At this time*: In 229.

163. *Phlius*: At about this time Cleonymus, the tyrant of Phlius (a city to the south of Sicyon), abdicated and joined the Achaean League.

164. *general*: Lydiades was general in 230/29, followed by Aratus in 229/8 and Aristomachus in 228/7.

165. *invade Laconia*: Argos, like Megalopolis and other new additions to the league, was traditionally hostile to Sparta. By 228 the Achaeans had declared war on Sparta (Polybius 2.46.6).

166. *Aratus to come . . . from Athens*: Where he was helping to settle the financial aspects of Athens' liberation from Macedonian control.

167. *Cleomenes*: Cleomenes III (*c.* 260–222) became king of Sparta around 235. He is the subject of Plutarch's *Cleomenes*. Although the war between Cleomenes and the Achaean League was crucial to Aratus' subsequent career (see below), Plutarch says little about its origins.

168. *Pallantium*: (Pallantion) An Arcadian city, west of Tegea, near modern Tripoli.

169. *Aratus prevented . . . engaging him in battle*: See also *Cleomenes* 4.

170. *twelfth time*: It was actually Aratus' tenth term as general, 227/6. That year Lydiades was elected *hipparch*, the second highest office in the league.

171. *Lycaeum*: (Modern Diaphorti) A mountain in Arcadia. Aratus fled from this battle in 227.

172. *made . . . full citizens*: Aratus' treatment of resident aliens (also reported by Polybius 2.57) is unclear. It has been suggested that, in addition to a garrison, Achaean settlers were introduced: Walbank, *Commentary*, vol. 1, p. 263.

173. *Aratus gained . . . victorious*: Polybius (4.8.4) includes this feat among Aratus' most significant military achievements.

174. *ambushed by Cleomenes and fell*: See also *Cleomenes* 6.

175. *Aegium*: Located on the Gulf of Corinth, the capital of the Achaean League (modern Aigio).

176. *continue this war . . . own means for doing so*: It appears from the sequel (ch. 38) that this decree was not enforced.

177. *Orchomenus*: Arcadian Orchomenus (there was also a Boeotian city with this name) near modern Kalpaki.

178. *Megistonous*: A rich landowner, he was the husband of Cleomenes' mother, Cratesicleia; he was later ransomed. See also ch. 41.

179. *battle . . . victory*: Neither *Cleomenes* 6 nor Polybius 2.51.3 mentions Aratus' victory at Orchomenus. In any event, Cleomenes did not allow the Achaeans to capture the town.

180. *general*: Elected for 225/4. This was the first generalship of Timoxenus, a protégé of Aratus. He was general several more times (certainly in 221/20 and 216/15).

181. *ephors*: Each year the Spartans elected ten ephors. They, and not the kings of Sparta, were the city's chief magistrates, and in 227 the ephors opposed Cleomenes' ambitions for Sparta.

182. *complete control of Sparta*: In 227 Cleomenes seized power in Sparta (aided by Megistonous) and over the course of the next year instituted revolutionary social reforms; see Cartledge and Spawforth, *Hellenistic and Roman Sparta*, pp. 49–58. One significant result of these reforms was a dramatic increase in Sparta's available military manpower.

183. *menace the Achaeans . . . over the league*: In the winter of 226/5, after inflicting a serious defeat on the Achaeans (chs. 39 and 41). At this time, Ptolemy III was the nominal leader of the league (ch. 24); at the same time, he was and remained Cleomenes' ally, indicating that there was no rift as a result of Cleomenes' demands.

184. *affairs of state . . . leaves the rudder to someone else*: Plutarch applies the same metaphor to Aratus at *Cleomenes* 15.

185. *allowing Macedonian garrisons to be installed*: Plutarch is referring to Aratus' decision to ally the Achaean League with Macedon (ch. 42).

186. *Illyrians and Gauls*: The army Antigonus Doson led in the war against Cleomenes included Gallic troops and Illyrians commanded by an Illyrian ruler, Demetrius of Pharus (modern Hvar); see ch. 50 and Polybius 2.65.2–4. The Illyrians were a large group of related peoples inhabiting the western Balkans.

187. *the Heracleidae*: According to myth, the descendants of Heracles returned to the Peloponnese and divided its territories among themselves, thereby establishing the regional authority of various Dorian states (Diodorus 4.57–8), including Sparta, whose kings were believed to derive from the Heracleidae. Cleomenes emphasized his descent from Heracles (*Cleomenes* 13).

188. *Cleomenes . . . promised . . . bestowing*: Cleomenes' offer to the Achaeans is described at *Cleomenes* 15.

189. *Antigonus*: Antigonus Doson (c. 263–221), who in 229 succeeded Demetrius II (who was his cousin), first as regent for Philip V but then as king in his own right.

190. *offer him the Acrocorinth as payment*: See ch. 42.

191. *Aesop's fable ... bridles*: A version of this fable is also reported at Aristotle, *Rhetoric* 1393b, and Horace, *Epistles* 1.10.34–8.

192. *Polybius ... says ... negotiations with Antigonus*: Polybius 2.47. It was in reaction to Cleomenes' revolution and Sparta's greater military resources that Aratus began to look towards a Macedonian alliance.

193. *an appeal to Antigonus*: Megalopolis had also enjoyed good relations with Macedon before it was drawn into the Achaean League. Polybius (2.48–51) describes this embassy, which took place in 227, as well as subsequent negotiations with Antigonus.

194. *Phylarchus*: Third-century BC historian (whose works are now lost); see Introduction.

195. *Cleomenes recaptured it*: Mantinea was taken in 226 (a year before Timoxenus was elected general).

196. *battle near Hecatombaeum*: In 226. Hecatombaeum was in the territory of Dyme (modern Kato Achaia).

197. *invited Cleomenes ... accept leadership of the league*: Plutarch here conflates two meetings between Cleomenes and the league. In late 226, the league was prepared to accept Cleomenes' terms at an emergency session held at Lerna (*Cleomenes* 15), but this was cancelled when Cleomenes fell ill. Another meeting was arranged for the summer of the next year, to be held at Argos, but Aratus, no doubt fearing a favourable outcome for Cleomenes, managed to forestall it (the details related at *Cleomenes* 17 differ from the account here).

198. *Lerna*: Modern Myli Navpliou, on the Gulf of Argos.

199. *close ... to capturing the city of Sicyon*: See ch. 40.

200. *Achaean commander*: Not the Achaean general Timoxenus (although the word used here by Plutarch is *strategos*, which could refer to the Achaean general) but the Achaean commander on the spot (*Cleomenes* 17).

201. *Pheneus ... Penteleium*: An Arcadian town (modern Feneos), at the foot of Mt Cyllene, and a fortress, presumably located on Mt Penteleium (modern Mt Pentelikon).

202. *Peloponnese ... disrupted by revolutionaries*: In Sparta, Cleomenes had redistributed land and regulated debts, policies which many in the Achaean cities believed might be extended to them if he were in authority (*Cleomenes* 17).

203. *invested with absolute power*: It was probably at this point that Aratus was named general with absolute authority and granted

a bodyguard, although Plutarch does not mention this until ch. 41.

204. *simmering hostility ... oppressed by it*: It is probably the case that it was by now known that the league had decided to offer Antigonus control of the Acrocorinth, which the Corinthians regarded as a betrayal.

205. *Acte*: The east coast of the Argolid peninsula. That is, Cleomenes gained Epidaurus, Troezen and Hermione.

206. *For thirty-three years*: Plutarch's reckoning is faulty: his narrative has reached 225, but Aratus held his first generalship in 245 and, prior to that, had liberated Sicyon in 251. Neither date yields a span of thirty-three years. Plutarch offers the same figure at *Cleomenes* 16.

207. *the Aetolians ... refused him*: Although they were Achaean allies (ch. 33).

208. *Eurycleides and Micion*: Brothers who were the leading Athenian statesmen in the second half of the third century BC. They cooperated with Diogenes in the liberation of Athens (ch. 34) and afterwards pursued a policy of strict neutrality.

209. *Tripylus*: Not otherwise known.

210. *Ptolemy ... each year paid ... 6 talents*: By this point Ptolemy had transferred Aratus' subsidy to Cleomenes.

211. *an assembly ... summoned Aratus to attend*: In the spring of 224.

212. *his son ... a young man*: Aratus' son was also named Aratus (chs. 49–51). He was later general of the league, in 219/18.

213. *federal magistrates*: These were the ten *damiorgoi*, who were elected annually and ranked next in importance to the general and *hipparch* of the league; see Larsen, *Greek Federal States: Their Institutions and History*, pp. 221–3.

214. *Pegae*: A port on the Gulf of Corinth, northwest of Megara on the Isthmus of Corinth.

215. *Antigonus was still young*: He was born *c.* 263 and so was possibly not yet forty.

216. *their struggle ... was a difficult one*: Plutarch's focus is on Corinth, but this city's fortifications were part of Cleomenes' defence of the Isthmus, which Antigonus and the Achaeans failed to penetrate.

217. *Aristotle of Argos*: Apart from his role in this episode, he is not otherwise known.

218. *1,500 soldiers*: A force of Achaeans was also sent under Timoxenus' command (Polybius 2.53.2).

219. *rushed to the aid of . . . Argos*: Megistonous had been dispatched to relieve Argos but was defeated and killed in battle.

220. *Cleomenes withdrew to Mantinea*: A fuller account is provided in *Cleomenes* 20; see also Polybius 2.53.

221. *Aratus was elected . . . by the Argives*: It is unclear how Aratus qualified for an elected office in Argos, though under the circumstances his immediate patronage may have been more attractive to the Argives than constitutional niceties.

222. *the tyrant*: Aristomachus. He had cooperated with Cleomenes in the defection of Argos from the Achaean League.

223. *episode did great damage . . . so lawless a fashion*: This criticism of Aratus was included in his history by Phylarchus and is the object of a lengthy rebuttal by Polybius (2.59–60).

224. *Orchomenus*: Aratus had once taken this city (ch. 38) but Cleomenes had recovered it. In 223 Antigonus captured it (Polybius 2.54.10–11 and 4.9).

225. *neither write . . . without Antigonus' permission*: This restriction is not otherwise attested but perhaps was a condition of the Achaean League's membership in the Hellenic League, founded by Antigonus in 224 (see Introduction). Plutarch does not actually comment on the establishment of the Hellenic League in this Life.

226. *furnish supplies . . . for Macedonian soldiers*: This was certainly the case in 218, when Philip V was king (Polybius 5.1.10–12). These payments were owed only when the Macedonian army was fighting on the league's behalf. They appear, however, to have been a new policy that helped to preserve the Achaean League's status as an ally, not a subject, of Macedon: see Walbank in *CAH* vii.1, p. 478.

227. *games in Antigonus' honour . . . city*: After the battle of Sellasia (ch. 46), Antigonus was celebrated throughout Greece. Aratus established a festival in his honour, the *Antigonea* (Polybius 28.19.3, 30.29.3; and *Cleomenes* 16). Antigonus was at Sicyon during the winter of 224/3.

228. *statues . . . removed from view*: Presumably when Argos joined the Achaean League (ch. 35). These tyrants had been Macedonian allies.

229. *captured the Acrocorinth*: An act of aggression against Macedon (chs. 18–24).

230. *behaviour . . . towards Mantinea*: Mantinea was sacked in 223 in retribution for a massacre of Achaean settlers there when the city went over to Cleomenes in 226 (ch. 39). See also *Cleomenes*

23 and Polybius 2.54.11–12 and 2.56–8 (in which Polybius reacts to Phylarchus' treatment of this event).

231. *'in the midst of necessity . . . sweet'*: Semonides fr. 590 in D. A. Campbell, *Greek Lyric*, vol. 3 (1991).

232. *Mantinea . . . Antigonea . . . today*: In AD 125 Hadrian restored the city's original name.

233. *'lovely Mantinea'*: *Iliad* 2.607.

234. *Cleomenes . . . defeated in . . . battle*: The battle of Sellasia (modern Oinountas) was the decisive battle of the war, fought in July 222.

235. *Cleomenes . . . sailed for Egypt*: He committed suicide in Alexandria.

236. *Philip . . . a young man*: In 222 Philip V was sixteen years old.

237. *death of Antigonus*: In 221.

238. *Patrae . . . Dyme*: (Modern Patras) patrae in the northern Peloponnese, and Dyme were both members of the Achaean League.

239. *invaded Messenia and ravaged it*: See also Polybius 4.6–11 and 15. Messenia was in the southwest Peloponnese. Long dominated by Sparta, this region was liberated by the Thebans in the fourth century BC, when its leading city, Messene, was founded. Aetolian raids commenced in 221, when Messenia, which was not a member of the Hellenic League, expressed interest in joining (Polybius 4.5.8), but this invasion took place in 220.

240. *Caphyae*: (Kephyai) An Arcadian city near Orchomenus.

241. *the king's goodwill and loyalty to Aratus*: The Hellenic League declared war against Aetolia in 219. In what follows, Plutarch devotes scant attention to the events of this war, focusing instead on Aratus' relationship with Philip.

242. *It was then*: During the campaign of 219 and the subsequent winter.

243. *Apelles and Megaleas*: Important courtiers, Apelles was one of the king's guardians and Megaleas was the king's minister for official correspondence (Polybius 4.76.1 and 4.87.8). These and other advisers pressed Philip to exploit the war in order to reduce the Achaean League to a condition of complete dependency on Macedon, and it is this policy that brought them into conflict with Aratus.

244. *Eperatus*: Eperatus of Pharae was elected general for 218/17, ahead of Timoxenus, Aratus' candidate (Aratus did not put himself forward although he was eligible).

245. *Philip then perceived the magnitude of his error*: That year Philip had a very successful campaign against Elis (modern Ilida), in the

northwest Peloponnese, but during that time he realized that Eperatus was less able to manage Achaean affairs than was Aratus, with whom he thereafter consulted.

246. *Lacedaemonians ... wronged him*: Following violent civil disruptions in Sparta in 220, Philip was urged towards very harsh treatment of the city by some of his advisers; others, however, persuaded the king to be moderate. Polybius (4.22–4) infers the counsel of Aratus from Philip's wise decision.

247. *Cretans ... to his side in only a few days*: In 219 (Polybius 4.53–5).

248. *Once they went so far ... 20 talents*: In 218 (Polybius 5.15 provides a much fuller account).

249. *Later ... put them to death*: In 218, perhaps in response to a conspiracy, several courtiers were executed; Apelles (and his son) and Megaleas committed suicide (Polybius 5.28).

250. *his wife*: The younger Aratus' wife was Polycrateia, who left Sicyon to become Philip's wife and the mother of Perseus, his successor as king (Livy 27.31.8).

251. *first exhibited suspicious behaviour*: Polybius cites Philip's behaviour at Messene as the beginning of a change for the worse in his character. The events described here took place in 215, after the conclusion of the war with Aetolia in 217; Polybius' account (7.10–12), now fragmentary, was Plutarch's source for this episode.

252. *the Ithomatas*: Messene (note 239) was located on the western slope of Mt Ithome, which was strongly fortified. The Ithomatas was a citadel atop this mountain.

253. *Demetrius*: An Illyrian ruler of Pharus, who had been an ally and adviser to Antigonus Doson. He fought the Romans during the Second Illyrian War (219) and subsequently fled to the court of Philip, where he became his closest adviser. He died in 214 in an attack on Messene.

254. *Phocis ... Acarnania*: Regions of central Greece, one on the Gulf of Corinth between Aetolia and Boeotia, the other in northwest Greece; Acarnania was west of Aetolia and lay along the Ionian Sea.

255. *all ... obey you*: Aratus alludes to Philip's stature as *hegemon* of the Hellenic League, since the Boeotian, Phocian and Acarnanian leagues were all members.

256. *'There are, Philip ... master there'*: Plutarch's version of Aratus' response is more ambitious in scale and sentiment than Polybius' (7.12.5–7).

257. *Epirus ... expedition*: In 214, Philip, who was by then an ally of
Hannibal, campaigned in Illyria, where he came into conflict
with Roman forces and precipitated the First Macedonian War
(214–205). Epirus is en route to Illyria.

258. *pressed by the Romans ... failure*: Philip attacked the city of
Apollonia, in Illyria (its site is near modern Vlore), but when he
was surprised by the praetor Marcus Laevinus, he was forced to
destroy his fleet in order to escape (Livy 20.40).

259. *Messenians ... ravaging their lands*: In 214 Demetrius of Pharus,
with Philip's support, tried to capture Messenia (Polybius
3.19.11; cf. Pausanias 4.29.1–5, confusing this Demetrius with
Philip's son) but fell in the attempt. Thereafter, Philip made his
own advance (Polybius 8.8); on the date, see Walbank, *Commentary*, vol. 2, p. 78. The significance of this episode for Aratus'
relationship with Philip Plutarch found in Polybius (8.12.1).

260. *he had become aware ... household*: See ch. 49 and note 250.

261. *Philip ... inexplicable transformation ... perversity*: Plutarch
was, however, open to the idea that one's character could suffer
a change: see C. Gill, CQ 33 (1983), pp. 469–87.

262. *Taurion*: Installed by Antigonus Doson, probably in 222, as the
commander of Macedonian forces in the Peloponnese and Antigonus' official representative in Greek affairs. As such, he worked
closely with all the Achaean generals.

263. *seventeenth time*: In 213/12. This should have been Aratus'
sixteenth term as general; however, Aratus' extraordinary appointment as general with full powers, in 225/4 (ch. 40), may have led
Plutarch to add an extra term. Few modern historians credit the
belief that Aratus (and his son) were poisoned by Philip (which
is not to say that Philip was above such conduct).

264. *ancient law ... observed*: Nevertheless, Euphron, a fourth-
century BC politician, had been buried in the market-place
(Xenophon, *A History of My Times* 7.3.12).

265. *the Pythia*: This was the priestess at Delphi who, while in a
trance, received the oracle of Apollo, which was then reported to
the priests at Delphi, who furnished it in verse form.

266. *Do you wish ... sky or sea*: It has been suggested that the trans-
mission of this oracle is faulty and that there is a lacuna between
lines two and three; see H. W. Parke and D. E. W. Wormell, *The
Delphic Oracle* (1956), vol. 1, p. 260, and vol. 2, p. 145.

267. *offer him sacrifices*: Aratus came to be remembered as a hero
who was a son of Asclepius (Pausanias 2.10.3).

268. *Daesius ... Anthesterion*: Anthesterion corresponds roughly to February. At *Camillus* 19 Plutarch equates Daesius with Thargelion (roughly the month of May), but there he has in mind the Macedonian Daesius, which was different from the Sicyonian Daesius.

269. *Soteria*: That is, the Festival of Salvation; Aratus was revered as the city's saviour and was celebrated in sacrifices performed by the priest of Zeus the Saviour.

270. *Artists of Dionysus*: Highly esteemed professional guilds of itinerant actors and musicians; they were active as early as the third century BC and continued to be prominent well into the imperial period.

271. *The gymnasiarch*: A prominent civic official responsible for a city's gymnasium or gymnasia, an important institution of education as well as physical training for the young.

272. *deprived of ... his empire ... hostage*: This was the result of the Second Macedonian War (200–197): see *Flamininus* 7–9. The son who went to Rome was Demetrius (c. 207–180): see *Aemilius Paullus* 8 and *Flamininus* 9. A full account of the settlement is provided by Polybius (18.39.5–6 and 18.44.2–7); Philip was actually allowed to retain six ships.

273. *a son*: Demetrius (see previous note).

274. *his other son ... Gnathaenion*: This story is repeated at *Aemilius Paullus* 8, but Perseus was not the illegitimate son of a seamstress: he was Philip's son by Polycrateia (note 250).

275. *royal line ... came to its end*: Perseus was defeated by Aemilius Paullus in the Third Macedonian War (171–168); see *Aemilius Paullus*.

PHILOPOEMEN

Further Reading

There is no English commentary on *Philopoemen*, but there is an excellent one in Italian: C. Pelling and E. Melandri, *Plutarco, Vite Parallele: Filopemene e Tito Flaminino* (1997). There is also a very good, if now somewhat dated, biography by R. M. Errington, *Philopoemen* (1969). On the historical background, see E. S. Gruen, *The Hellenistic World and the Coming of Rome* (1984), P. Cartledge and A. Spawforth, *Hellenistic and Roman Sparta: A Tale of Two Cities* (2nd edn, 2002), A. M. Eckstein, *Rome Enters the Greek East: From*

Anarchy to Hierarchy in the Hellenistic Mediterranean, 230-170 BC (2008), and P. J. Burton, *Friendship and Empire: Roman Diplomacy and Imperialism in the Middle Republic (353-146 BC)* (2011). Plutarch's view of this period has been re-examined by J. M. Bremer, 'Plutarch and the "Liberation of Greece"', in L. de Blois, J. Bons, T. Kessels and D. M. Shenkeveld (eds.), *The Statesman in Plutarch's Works*, vol. 2: *The Statesman in Plutarch's Greek and Roman Lives* (2005), pp. 257–67. There are also very helpful chapters in *CAH*: F. W. Walbank, 'Macedonia and Greece', vii.1 (1984), pp. 221–56, and 'Macedonia and the Greek Leagues', vii.1, pp. 446–81; R. M. Errington, 'Rome and Greece to 205 BC', viii (1989), pp. 81–106, and 'Rome Against Philip and Antiochus', viii, pp. 244–89. More detailed coverage is available by consulting Walbank, *Commentary*, vols. 2 and 3, and J. Briscoe, *A Commentary on Livy, Books 31-33* (1973), *Books 34-37* (1981) and *Books 38-40* (2008).

There are several excellent interpretative studies of this Life: S. Swain, 'Plutarch's *Philopoemen* and *Flamininus*', *Illinois Classical Studies* 13 (1988), pp. 335–47, and Swain, *H&E*, pp. 145–50 and 172–3; J. J. Walsh, 'Syzygy, Theme and History: A Study in Plutarch's *Philopoemen* and *Flamininus*', *Philologus* 136 (1992), pp. 208–33; Duff, *Plutarch's Lives*, pp. 267–9; and Pelling, *P&H*, pp. 243–8 and 350–53.

Notes to the Introduction to Philopoemen

1. See Jones, 'Chronology', p. 111.
2. See *Philopoemen* 1, *Aratus* 24 and Pausanias 8.52.1.
3. On Polybius' bias, see A. M. Eckstein, *Moral Vision in the Histories of Polybius* (1995), pp. 30–34.
4. For the historical background to affairs in the Peloponnese in the generation preceding Philopoemen, including the organization of the Achaean League, its relationship with Aetolia and Sparta, and its alliance with Macedon, see Introduction to *Aratus*.
5. The *hipparch* was second in authority only to the league's *strategos*, or general. On Philopoemen's activities in Crete, see Errington, *Philopoemen*, pp. 13–48; and Cartledge and Spawforth, *Hellenistic and Roman Sparta*, pp. 66–7.
6. On Philopoemen's military reforms, see J. A. O. Larsen, *Greek Federal States: Their Institutions and History* (1968), p. 375; and Errington, *Philopoemen*, pp. 51–4, 62–7.
7. Machanidas had seized power in Sparta by 211; see Cartledge and Spawforth, *Hellenistic and Roman Sparta*, pp. 65–9. On the

First Macedonian War (214–205), see Errington in *CAH* viii (1989), pp. 94–106.

8. Nabis was a major figure both in Sparta and the larger Greek world; see Cartledge and Spawforth, *Hellenistic and Roman Sparta*, pp. 59–79.

9. This is the necessary inference from Polybius 16.27.1–4.

10. On diplomatic events leading to the Second Macedonian War, see Eckstein, *Rome Enters the Greek East*, pp. 230–70.

11. See Errington, *Philopoemen*, pp. 36–48.

12. See Introduction to *Flamininus*.

13. See chs. 14–15, Livy 35.37.1–3 and Pausanias 8.50.10–8.51.1; and see further Errington, *Philopoemen*, pp. 105–12.

14. See Errington in *CAH* viii, pp. 274–89; and see Introduction to *Flamininus*.

15. Cf. Livy 38.30–34. See Errington, *Philopoemen*, pp. 144–7; and Cartledge and Spawforth, *Hellenistic and Roman Sparta*, pp. 77–80.

16. On these events, see Larsen, *Greek Federal States: Their Institutions and History*, pp. 449–54; Errington, *Philopoemen*, pp. 173–215; and Eckstein, *Rome Enters the Greek East*, pp. 360–61.

17. Cf. Livy 39.49–50; Pausanias 4.29.11 and 8.51.5. Errington, *Philopoemen*, pp. 191–3, argues that Philopoemen was not in fact executed but died of wounds he received when he was captured, but this view has not been widely accepted.

18. On the association of *philonikia* and *philoneikia* ('contentiousness') in Plutarch's day, see Pelling, *P&H*, p. 347. In the passage just quoted, Plutarch diverges from his sources: Polybius (18.46.13–15) and Livy (33.33.5–8), in their treatments of this same episode, focus on Roman virtue and power.

19. On Philopoemen's contentiousness (*philonikia/philoneikia*) see chs. 3 and 17, and *Comparison Philopoemen–Flamininus* 1; and see also Pelling, *P&H*, pp. 243–8, 350–53.

20. *Coriolanus–Alcibiades* was composed late in the series of *Parallel Lives*: see Jones, 'Chronology', p. 111. On Coriolanus' great nature and its moral hazards, see Introduction to his Life.

21. *Phronēma*, to be sure, has more than one connotation, but it sometimes appears amid the terminology marking out great natures: e.g. *Coriolanus* 15 and Plato, *Republic* 494b; see further Duff, *Plutarch's Lives*, pp. 83–4. Its association with anger and contentiousness in this Life suggests that idea here.

22. On the importance of education and culture (*paideia*) in the perfection of character in Plutarch's Lives, see General Introduction III.

23. On this point see Swain, *H&E*, p. 150.
24. See P. S. Derow in *CAH* viii, pp. 290–323.
25. For more on Phylarchus, see Introduction to *Aratus*.

Notes to the Life of Philopoemen

1. *Cleander*: Mentioned also by Polybius (10.22.1) and Pausanias (8.49.2); his exile from Mantinea, an Arcadian city in the central Peloponnese, probably belongs around 253/2.
2. *Megalopolis*: See *Aratus*, note 31.
3. *Craugis*: From a distinguished family (Polybius 10.22.1, Pausanias 8.49.2). Nothing else is known about him.
4. *Homer's tale of ... Achilles*: Iliad 9.438–95. Like Cleander, Phoenix was an exile who took special care of a child because of his ties with the father (in Achilles' case, Peleus), though that was not quite a 'guardianship' inasmuch as Peleus was still alive.
5. *Ecdelus and Demophanes*: See *Aratus* (ch. 5, mentioning only Ecdelus) and Polybius 10.22.2. Pausanias (8.49.2) refers to them as Ecdelus and Megalophanes.
6. *Arcesilaus*: Arcesilaus of Pitane (315–241) became head of the Academy in Athens around 260.
7. *Aristodemus*: Called 'Aristodemus the Good', he became tyrant of Megalopolis during the Chremonidean War (268–261). The date of his expulsion is unknown.
8. *Aratus ... Nicocles, tyrant of Sicyon*: Aratus liberated Sicyon in 251 (*Aratus* 5–9).
9. *Cyrene*: An important Greek city in northern Africa (modern Shahhat in Libya). During this period the city often fell under the influence of the Ptolemies. Its short-lived liberation occurred sometime between 253 and 247, but the entire episode remains obscure; see Walbank, *Commentary*, vol. 2, p. 224.
10. *'the last of the Greeks'*: Also cited at *Aratus* 24 and Pausanias 8.52.1. The unnamed Roman may have intended it less as praise of Philopoemen than denigration of his successors.
11. *statue at Delphi*: Presumably the statue mentioned at ch. 10.
12. *Megara*: A city on the Isthmus of Corinth, lying opposite the island of Salamis.
13. *guest-friend*: Important individuals in different cities or states often enjoyed a relationship, known as *xenia* or *guest-friendship*, whereby they looked after one another's interests in their respective communities.

14. *broad Doric*: This would not be Philopoemen's natural dialect, which presumably was Arcadian. Perhaps he is simply making himself out to be a real yokel or, more likely, the assumed Doric accent plays on the famous Spartan simplicity of dress.

15. *in the schools*: In the philosophical schools (where Aratus was also discussed: *Aratus* 29).

16. *Epaminondas*: On Epaminondas, see General Introduction II.

17. *training and diet diverge widely*: The contrast drawn here between an athlete's and a soldier's regimen is closely based on Plato, *Republic* 3.403e–404b.

18. *raids . . . into Laconia*: Megalopolis had been founded in 369 as a counterweight to Sparta, and the hostility of the two cities remained strong (*Aratus* 30).

19. *spare time . . . public affairs*: Cf. Plutarch's description of Cato's lifestyle in Tarentum at *Elder Cato* 3.

20. *Tactics of Evangelus*: Presumably Hellenistic but its precise date is unknown; also mentioned by Aelian (*Tactics* 1) and Arrian (*Tactics* 1).

21. *histories of Alexander's campaigns*: Of these there were many, most of them now lost; see A. B. Bosworth, *From Arrian to Alexander: Studies in Historical Interpretation* (1988).

22. *phalanx*: The rectangular infantry formation that characterized ancient Greek and Macedonian warfare.

23. *Cleomenes*: Cleomenes III (*c.* 260–222) became king of Sparta around 235. He is an important figure in *Aratus*, see Introduction there; he is also the subject of Plutarch's *Cleomenes*. He captured Megalopolis in autumn 223. For fuller accounts see *Cleomenes* 44–6 and Polybius 2.55.6–8 and 2.61.5–2.62.

24. *Messene*: See *Aratus*, note 239.

25. *offering to restore . . . its territory*: The condition was that Megalopolis should abandon the Achaean League and ally with Sparta.

26. *not giving back the city . . . within his power*: See also *Cleomenes* 45.

27. *These arguments*: Described in more detail at Polybius 2.61.1.

28. *Antigonus*: Antigonus Doson (*c.* 263–221) led an alliance of Macedonians and Achaeans against Cleomenes; see *Aratus* 38–46 and Introduction to that Life.

29. *marched . . . against . . . Sellasia*: In 222. Fuller accounts of this decisive battle can be read at *Cleomenes* 49 and Polybius 2.66–70; see also *Aratus* 46. A detailed modern reconstruction of the course

of the battle is provided by W. K. Pritchett, *Studies in Ancient Greek Topography*, vol. 1 (1965), pp. 59–70.

30. *among the cavalry*: Probably an error. Polybius (2.66.6–7) seems to show that the Achaean (and Megalopolitan) contingent were infantry, not cavalry. As an officer, Philopoemen will anyway have served on horseback (Polybius 2.69.1), and if Plutarch is wrong this may explain his mistake.

31. *Illyrians*: A large group of related peoples inhabiting the western Balkans.

32. *Their . . .*: Plutarch's Greek is unclear here but presumably he refers exclusively to the Achaeans (cf. *Cleomenes* 49 and Polybius 2.66.10–2.67.1).

33. *Eucleidas*: After Cleomenes deposed his royal colleague Archidamus in 227, he appointed his brother in his place. Eucleidas fell in the fighting at Sellasia.

34. *At this point . . . outwards*: Pausanias (8.49.6) puts this episode after the battle.

35. *Antigonus . . . win the battle*: Like Polybius (2.66–8), Plutarch suggests that Philopoemen's personal bravery turned the battle, but that is an exaggeration; see Errington, *Philopoemen*, pp. 20–23.

36. *a . . . lad*: Philopoemen was thirty or thirty-one at the time and so hardly a lad (the Greek word indicates a youth of not more than twenty), but it suited the Macedonian commanders, in making their excuse to the king, to exaggerate his youth.

37. *'That lad . . . a great general'*: Plutarch improves on Polybius' version of Antigonus' bon mot; see Polybius 2.68.1–2.

38. *a long time*: Philopoemen was in Crete from 221 to 211.

39. *hipparch*: Philopoemen was *hipparch* in 210/9.

40. *exercise . . . authority*: Polybius (10.22.9) makes even clearer the political clout of the Achaean League's cavalry class.

41. *nimble . . . at will*: For the details of the cavalry's exercises see Walbank, *Commentary*, vol. 2, pp. 225–9.

42. *battle . . . Larissus*: This battle took place in 209, during the First Macedonian War (214–205), when the Aetolians were allied with Rome against Macedon and the Achaean League. The Larissus is a small river that marked the border between Elis and Achaea.

43. *Eleian hipparch Damophantus*: Elis (modern Ilida) was both a region and a city in the northwest Peloponnese. Damophantus is known only from this episode.

44. *power . . . to the Achaean League*: See Introduction to *Aratus*.

45. *When land forms . . . stable and hard*: Plutarch's explanation of the origin of this sacred island (by which he means the *Insula Tiberina* and not the *Isola Sacra* located near Ostia) at *Publicola* 8.

46. *cities . . . from their tyrants*: See Introduction to *Aratus*.

47. *the whole Peloponnese . . . single power*: A vision realized by Philopoemen when he incorporated Sparta into the Achaean League (ch. 15).

48. *While Aratus was still alive*: He died in 213 (*Aratus* 52).

49. *Ptolemy . . . Antigonus . . . Greek affairs*: Ptolemy III and Antigonus Doson were each named leader (*hegemon*) of the Achaean League; thereafter Antigonus and later Philip V held the position of *hegemon* of the Hellenic League (Introduction to *Aratus*).

50. *Aratus . . . a reputation . . . his own Life*: See especially *Aratus* 10, 12, 13, 15 and 43; his ineffectuality in warfare is emphasized in *Aratus* 10 and 29.

51. *reformed . . . tactics and weaponry*: He did this during his first term as general (*strategos*) in 208/7, see Walbank, *Commentary*, vol. 2, pp. 280–82.

52. *in the Macedonian fashion*: In the Macedonian phalanx, infantrymen locked shields and wielded long pikes, creating a formidable battle array that impressed even the Romans; see the description at *Flamininus* 8.

53. *Thericlean cups*: Thericles was a much-admired Corinthian potter and a skilled engraver of bowls made from precious metals; he lived in the late fifth and early fourth centuries BC. He also gave his name to a distinctive shape of pottery: see W. Miller, *TAPhA* 52 (1921), pp. 119–31. Thericlean bowls also make an appearance in the triumph of Aemilius Paullus at *Aemilius Paullus* 33, where again they connote luxury.

54. *Achilles' new arms . . . using them*: *Iliad* 19.15–23.

55. *Machanidas*: He had seized power in Sparta by 211 and thereafter pursued an aggressive policy of territorial expansion.

56. *invaded Mantinea*: In June 207; a fuller account of this battle is provided by Polybius (11.11–18).

57. *light cavalry*: Literally *Tarentines*, which is a technical term for this brand of light cavalry; see Walbank, *Commentary*, vol. 1, p. 529.

58. *hoplites*: Greek infantrymen, named from the type of shield they carried (called a *hoplon*).

59. *Simmias and Polyaenus*: Unknown except for this episode.

60. *bronze statue*: The inscription from the base of this statue survives and reads:

> Erected by the league of the Achaeans in honour of Philopoemen, son of Craugis, to commemorate his courage and his goodwill towards the league. (*Syll.* 625)

This is probably the statue mentioned in ch. 2.

61. *Nemean festival*: Panhellenic games held every other year at the sanctuary of Zeus at Nemea.

62. *general for the second time*: In 206/5, and so these are the Nemean Games of 205.

63. *Pylades*: A citizen of Megalopolis, according to Pausanias (8.50.3), and the most renowned lyre-player of his day – the winner of a victory at the Pythian Games.

64. *Timotheus' Persians*: Timotheus of Miletus (*c.* 450–360), a distinguished lyre-player and an innovative and influential poet. Large portions of his poem *Persians* survive in a papyrus. The poem is an account of the battle of Salamis. This opening line, which presumably refers to Themistocles, is Timotheus, fr. 788, in D. A. Campbell, *Greek Lyric*, vol. 5 (1993).

65. *One example . . .*: The following three examples are recounted similarly, and in the same order, by Pausanias (8.50.4–5).

66. *assassins to Argos . . . reputation among the Greeks*: Pausanias (8.50.4) has the assassins sent to Megalopolis, not Argos; Justin (*Epitome of Pompeius Trogus* 29.4.11) also briefly tells the story. The episode is unlikely and is in any case undatable.

67. *Boeotians . . . besieging Megara . . . take it quickly*: More details are provided at Polybius 20.6.7–12. The incident remains undated.

68. *Nabis . . . captured Messene*: Probably in summer 201. Nabis made himself sole king in Sparta after Machanidas' death in 207 (ch. 10), after which he initiated profound social reforms and expanded Spartan power both in the Peloponnese and in Crete. He was assassinated in 192.

69. *Lysippus*: General in 202/1 but otherwise unknown.

70. *Philopoemen went anyway . . . liberated*: Plutarch recurs to this at his *Comparison Philopoemen–Flamininus* 3; he also mentions the episode at *Moralia* 817e.

71. *second spell in Crete*: Philopoemen went to Crete in 200 or 199, returning in 194 or early 193, which puts him outside Greece during the Second Macedonian War (200–197).

72. *Gortyn*: Philopoemen had assisted Gortyn (modern Gortyna), a major city in central Crete, during his first period in Crete. Gortyn remained in conflict with its principal rival, Cnossus, and Nabis, whose influence extended into Crete, supported Cnossus against Gortyn. Presumably Philopoemen was in Crete both to aid Gortyn and oppose Nabis' interests there. See Errington, *Philopoemen*, pp. 36–48.

73. *other men to be their generals*: If Plutarch's statement here reflects Philopoemen's true or likely motive, then either he failed in his next bid for the generalship of 199/8, which was held by Aristaenus, or, taken less literally, was dissatisfied with the results of the elections for 200/199; see Errington, *Philopoemen*, pp. 73–5. But this explanation may be nothing more than Plutarch's own surmise, based on his belief that 'Philopoemen was no friend of leisure' or his assumption that Aristaenus was Philopoemen's political enemy (ch. 13).

74. *Ptolemy*: Possibly Ptolemy V (210–180), if this anecdote is correctly associated with Polybius 22.3.7–9, where this Ptolemy's prowess is praised in Philopoemen's presence. During Ptolemy V's reign, Egypt suffered significant reverses and loss of territories.

75. *Megalopolitans ... tried to exile him ... Aristaenus*: They tried to exile Philopoemen during Aristaenus' generalship of 199/8. Aristaenus, a citizen of Megalopolis, was also general of the Achaean League in 196/5, 188/7 and 186/5. He was a staunch proponent of a pro-Roman policy for the Achaean League (ch. 17).

76. *he incited ... the Achaeans*: These events must have taken place soon after Philopoemen's return in 194 or early 193, but little about them can be recovered; see Errington, *Philopoemen*, pp. 90–91. In any case, Philopoemen was elected general for 193/2, so his political influence in the league was by then clearly robust, whether or not these intrigues made any difference outside Megalopolis (at ch. 14 Plutarch observes that Philopoemen returned from Crete with a brilliant reputation).

77. *Titus*: Titus Quinctius Flamininus, the subject of the Roman Life in this pairing. Philip was decisively defeated at the battle of Cynoscephalae in 197 (*Flamininus* 7–8).

78. *Nabis was at war ... with Rome*: In 195 Rome and her Greek allies went to war with Nabis in order to force him to surrender Argos. He was ultimately forced to capitulate and to surrender all possessions outside Laconia. Most of his Peloponnesian holdings, including Argos, became part of the Achaean League.

In 193 Nabis attempted to recover his former coastal territories, in particular Gytheum (modern Gytheio), which precipitated a war with the Achaean League (it immediately sent ambassadors to Rome and to Flamininus for consultation on the matter). The events of this chapter took place in 192.

79. *elected to a command*: Philopoemen was general for 193/2.

80. *sea battle*: Livy (35.25–30) gives an extended account of the battle and its sequel; see also Pausanias 8.50.7–10.

81. *match that of Epaminondas*: In 364/3 Epaminondas led a naval expedition to Greek cities in the east, intending to detach them from their alliance with Athens, but little came of it (Diodorus 15.78.4–15.79). The idea that the mission met with deliberate failure is decidedly improbable.

82. *in Plato's phrase*: Plato, *Laws* 4.706b–c, quoted again at *Themistocles* 4.

83. *Philopoemen . . . was quite convinced*: The more extended version at Livy 35.25 suggests that Plutarch is here misleadingly abbreviating his source's account. Philopoemen was in fact reluctant to fight at sea before the allied Roman fleet arrived, but felt that he had no alternative, an attitude that would not suit Plutarch's picture of a Philopoemen resolutely independent of Rome.

84. *ship . . . not sailed for forty years*: Livy (35.26.5) says that it had been captured *eighty* years before. The two notices are compatible, however, since it may well have sailed in some form after its capture.

85. *the siege of Gytheum*: Begun in 193, the city fell to Nabis in 192 (though Plutarch does not mention that here). In the end, however, Philopoemen inflicted a serious and crippling defeat on Nabis (in the battle described in this chapter), after which Flamininus intervened to settle hostilities (Livy 35.25–30).

86. *Philopoemen halted the pursuit . . . near the city*: Plutarch here simplifies an extremely complicated account; the exchange in fact lasted two days (Livy 35.27.14–35.29.7) and the pursuit also had several phases (35.29.8–35.30.13), of which Plutarch selects only the last.

87. *piled honours upon him . . . irritation*: See *Flamininus* 13. The idea of the two men's competition for honour and Flamininus' consequent jealousy is reported elsewhere, e.g. Livy 35.30.13 and 35.47.4 (both notices probably derive from Polybius).

88. *consul*: Flamininus was consul in 198 and afterwards proconsul until 194, when he returned to Rome. In 192 he was acting as a

Roman ambassador (*legatus*) in the east. The word used by Plutarch here, *hypatos*, can refer to a consul, proconsul or an ex-consul.

89. *a single decree*: Plutarch refers to the proclamation of 196 (see *Flamininus* 10–11).

90. *terms . . . brought the war to an end*: In early summer 192.

91. *Nabis met his death . . . Aetolians*: Nabis was assassinated in summer 192. The Aetolians had for some time encouraged Nabis to adopt an anti-Roman policy. His willingness to accept the protection offered him by Flamininus, however, made it appear to them that he had switched sides.

92. *Philopoemen . . . attacked in force*: This invasion occurred in summer 192. Livy (35.36–35.37.1–3) has a fuller account.

93. *the Spartan nobility . . . an embassy to inform him*: This incident, whereby the Spartan elite attempted to win Philopoemen's support on some issue, remains an unclear one. It is probably to be connected with the perturbation in Sparta that Plutarch mentions in ch. 16 (which took place during the generalship of Diophanes in 192/1): see Pausanias 8.51.2. This episode is also found in Polybius (20.12), but in an isolated fragment. In any case, Plutarch is uninterested in the political context: his emphasis is on Philopoemen's incorruptibility.

94. *the reality of virtue, not just the semblance*: This is an allusion to Aeschylus, *Seven Against Thebes* 592, referring to the seer Amphiaraus: 'to be best, not to seem so, that is his desire'. The same passage is quoted more fully in *Aristeides* and by Plato (*Republic* 362a–b).

95. *Spartiates*: These were full Spartan citizens and something of an elite within Lacedaemonian society.

96. *Timolaus*: Mentioned in the same context at Polybius 20.12.2, otherwise unknown.

97. *congress*: Scholars disagree over whether this a reference to Sparta's senate (the Gerousia) or to the assembly of the Achaean League, which seems more likely if Sparta was in danger of 'punishment' during Diophanes' generalship (ch. 16 and note 93).

98. *agitation was afoot in Sparta*: Although we are poorly informed about political conditions in Sparta in these years, it is nonetheless clear that Sparta remained restive, a condition that resulted in revolt against the Achaean League in 189; see Cartledge and Spawforth, *Hellenistic and Roman Sparta*, pp. 78–9.

99. *Diophanes*: General in 192/1. In the past he had been a political associate of Philopoemen, but after this incident political

differences persisted between them (Livy 38.32.6 and Polybius 22.10.4–14); see Walbank, *Commentary*, vol. 3, p. 93.

100. *Antiochus*: On Antiochus III (*c.* 242–187), his empire and his war with Rome, see Errington in *CAH* viii, pp. 244–89; S. Sherwin-White and A. Kuhrt, *From Samarkhand to Sardis: A New Approach to the Seleucid Empire* (1993), pp. 188–216; and Eckstein, *Rome Enters the Greek East*, pp. 145–50, 306–41. He was at war with the Romans from 191 until 188 (*Flamininus* 9 and 15 and *Elder Cato* 12–14).

101. *joined Titus ... marched ... on Sparta itself*: Early in 191.

102. *the Roman consul*: Flamininus was still acting as a Roman ambassador (*legatus*), see note 88.

103. *He went to Sparta ... private citizen though he was*: Plutarch returns to this at *Comparison Philopoemen–Flamininus* 3.

104. *Time passed ... against the Spartans*: Plutarch here simplifies what was in fact a complex (and still poorly understood) sequence of events, a fuller account of which is provided at Livy 38.30–34. Internal discord at Sparta resulted in an attempt, in 189, to recover some of the city's losses in the settlement of 195, an act of rebellion that inevitably provoked an Achaean response: see Cartledge and Spawforth, *Hellenistic and Roman Sparta*, pp. 78–9; and Briscoe, *A Commentary on Livy, Books 38–40*, pp. 110–18. Plutarch, then, is misleading when he reduces the matter to a mere grievance. At *Comparison Philopoemen–Flamininus* 1 he goes further and attributes Philopoemen's actions at this point simply to anger.

105. *general at the time*: In 189/8. Plutarch has displaced these events, which belong after some of those of ch. 17.

106. *Aristocrates*: (*FGrH* 591) A Spartan historian and antiquarian about whom very little is known. Plutarch also cites him at *Lycurgus* 4 and 31. Polybius' account of this event is lost, but see Livy 38.33.10–11. These deaths occurred in spring 188, when the Spartans surrendered to Philopoemen.

107. *given Spartan citizenship*: Evidently Nabis had enfranchised some of Sparta's helots (or serfs) (Pausanias 8.51.3 and Livy 38.34.2).

108. *a portico in Megalopolis*: One that the Spartans had destroyed and Philopoemen now restored (Pausanias 8.30.7 and Livy 38.34.7).

109. *the Spartan system of education*: Plutarch describes it (the *agoge*) at *Lycurgus* 16–24.

110. *Years later ... re-established their traditional one*: At an uncertain date after 146. This restoration was limited and incomplete, see Cartledge and Spawforth, *Hellenistic and Roman Sparta*, pp. 201–7.

111. *When war broke out in Greece ... Antiochus*: The Romans' war with Antiochus lasted from 191 until 188. Plutarch now reverts to the events of 192 (and subsequently), adjusting his focus to Philopoemen's relations with Rome.

112. *Philopoemen was a private citizen*: Philopoemen did not become general again until 191/90; when the war broke out, Diophanes was general.

113. *Chalcis*: Modern Chalkida, the most important city in Euboea.

114. *Syrians*: Plutarch refers here to Antiochus' troops. See *Flamininus* 16 and Livy (36.11.1–4) for lurid details of Antiochus' luxury during the winter of 192/1, but much of this is exaggeration. After all, Antiochus had captured Chalcis despite Roman and Achaean garrisons (Livy 35.50.3–4).

115. *victory*: Plutarch has in mind the Romans' victory at Thermopylae in 191, after which the war against Antiochus was carried on in Asia, although hostilities against his allies, the Aetolians, persisted until 189.

116. *the Romans ... more involved in Greek affairs*: For an account of Rome's increasing and increasingly overbearing involvement in Greek affairs, see Derow, *CAH* viii, pp. 290–303.

117. *matters were approaching ... cycle of Fortune needed to reach*: It is unclear but likely that Plutarch has in mind Aemilius Paullus' victory at the battle of Pydna in 168, an event which Polybius described as the culmination of the work of Fortune in making Rome the political master of the inhabited world (Polybius 1.1.5, 3.1.9–10 and 29.21). Plutarch shares the view that Rome's domination of Greece was part of a providential design: see Swain, *H&E*, pp. 154–5.

118. *Aristaenus of Megalopolis*: See note 75.

119. *'My dear man ... destiny?'*: Polybius (24.13.6) supplies a similar but less pointed version of Philopoemen's remark. However, in Polybius the opposition between Aristaenus' Roman policy and Philopoemen's is less sharply drawn than in Plutarch: see Eckstein, *Moral Vision in the Histories of Polybius*, pp. 163–4.

120. *Manius*: Manius Acilius Glabrio, consul of 191, was the victor at Thermopylae.

121. *demand ... allow the Spartan exiles to return*: This demand seems to have come in autumn 191 (Livy 36.35.7). Political

discord within Sparta had created several waves of exiles, some of whom were connected with Philopoemen (Livy 38.31.1).

122. *he restored the exiles himself*: At least some of the exiles were restored when Philopoemen was again general in 189/8, but this was not 'the following year'.

123. *general ... for the eighth time*: Philopoemen's final generalship was for 183/2. It is unclear when during his term in office he met his death.

124. *nemesis*: Both a goddess and an abstract concept, Nemesis was the personification of divine retribution.

125. *Deinocrates*: A leading Messenian statesman and a friend of Flamininus. Our fullest account of him comes from Polybius (23.5.1–18); see Walbank, *Commentary*, vol. 3, pp. 220–23, and *Flamininus* 17.

126. *rebellion from the Achaean League*: In 191 Messene had been compelled to join the league.

127. *Colonides*: Livy (39.49.1) names this village Corone (modern Petalidi); Colonides is about 9 miles (15 km) to the south of Corone.

128. *on hearing this he hurried to Megalopolis*: Achaean forces had already been sent into Messene (Pausanias 4.29.11, 8.51.5) but Plutarch here stresses Philopoemen's rush to the scene. At *Comparison Philopoemen–Flamininus* 1 this action is cited as the precipitate of his anger.

129. *covering more than 400 stades in a ... day*: Philopoemen travelled more than 44 miles (71 km), which is approximately the distance between the two cities.

130. *hill of Evander*: The site is unknown and is possibly a mistake for Mt Eva in Messene (Pausanias 4.31.4).

131. *Back in the city*: Messene.

132. *a mood of generosity spread among the ordinary people*: Pausanias (8.51.6) describes a meeting of the assembly in which Deinocrates and the rich pressed for execution and the popular party urged mercy.

133. *freedom ... by expelling ... Nabis*: In 201 (ch. 12).

134. *Deinocrates was afraid of delay ... before the Achaeans could intervene*: Livy (39.49–50) has a more complicated sequence of events.

135. *any news about ... Lycortas*: This is unclear as it stands. An advance force of Achaeans had been sent to Messene under the command of Lycortas (note 128), and this explains Philopoemen's question. Lycortas (d. *c.* 167), the father of the historian Polybius, was already a leading figure in the Achaean League.

136. *elected Lycortas as their general*: He was elected to fill out the remainder of Philopoemen's term (183/2).

137. *invaded Messenia ... enter the city*: Plutarch severely abbreviates the account given at Polybius 23.16.

138. *those who had voted ... killed by them*: The text is uncertain here, but it is clear from Polybius (23.16.13) that some Messenians were obliged to take their own lives (Pausanias 8.51.8 insists that only Deinocrates committed suicide).

139. *Polybius*: The historian, son of Lycortas, who was born *c.* 208 and would have been about twenty-five at the time.

140. *statues erected ... honours voted by the cities*: See Diodorus 29.18.

141. *destruction of Corinth*: During the Achaean War in 146.

142. *Polybius opposed the man's slanderous charges*: The controversy over Philopoemen's statues, including an account of Polybius' defence, is reported at Polybius 39.3.1–11. The hostile Roman is also anonymous there.

143. *Mummius ... commissioners*: Lucius Mummius was consul in 146 and was the Roman commander in the Achaean War. After his victory, a commission of ten senators was sent to aid him in organizing affairs in Greece.

TITUS FLAMININUS

Further Reading

There is no English commentary on *Titus Flamininus*, but there is an excellent one in Italian: C. Pelling and E. Melandri, *Plutarco, Vite Parallele: Filopemene e Tito Flaminino* (1997). There is also a good biography in German by R. Pfeilschifter, *Titus Quinctius Flamininus: Untersuchungen zur römischen Griechenlandpolitik* (2005). Flamininus has attracted much attention from historians writing in English. A classic and accessible introduction is provided by E. Badian, 'Titus Quinctius Flamininus: Philhellenism and *Realpolitik*', in C. G. Boulter and D. W. Bradeen (eds.), *Lectures in Memory of Louise Taft Semple, Second Series, 1966–70* (1973), pp. 271–327. See also E. Badian, 'The Family and Early Career of T. Quinctius Flamininus', *JRS* 61 (1971), pp. 102–11, and J. J. Walsh, 'Flamininus and the Propaganda of Liberation', *Historia* 45 (1996), pp. 344–63. The particulars of Flamininus' settlement of Greek communities in the aftermath of the war are examined by D. Armstrong and J. J. Walsh, 'SIG 593. The Letter of Flamininus to Chyretiae', *Classical Philology* 81 (1986), pp. 32–43.

On the historical background, and for important interpretative studies of this Life, see Further Reading for *Philopoemen*.

Notes to the Introduction to Titus Flamininus

1. That the rise of Rome was favoured by the gods is axiomatic in Plutarch: see Swain, *H&E*, pp. 151–61.
2. See Introduction to *Philopoemen*.
3. See e.g. *Moralia* 813e and General Introduction II.
4. In 208 Marcellus was killed while campaigning against Hannibal in southern Italy (*Marcellus* 29). Plutarch does not mention Flamininus' quaestorship, which is noted only by Livy (32.7.9). On the Second Punic War, see Introductions to *Fabius Maximus* and *Marcellus*.
5. Fabius Maximus recovered Tarentum for Rome in 209; see *Fabius Maximus* 21–3. Thereafter, it was assigned to the praetor Quintus Claudius. E. Badian has suggested that this man was in fact a Kaeso Quinctius Flamininus and the uncle of Flamininus, but the matter can only remain speculative; see Badian, 'The Family and Early Career of T. Quinctius Flamininus', *JRS* 61, pp. 106–10.
6. It was expected that a man be forty-two or older when he was elected consul, but the circumstances of the Second Punic War resulted in more than one anomalous election: e.g. Scipio Africanus (elected consul for 205 at the age of thirty), Publius Sulpicius Galba (consul for the first time in 211, having held no curule magistracy) and Lucius Cornelius Lentulus (became consul in 199 after holding a special command in Spain).
7. See R. M. Errington in *CAH* viii (1989), pp. 94–106. The political situation in Greece leading up to this war plays an important part in *Aratus*.
8. The origins of the Second Macedonian War remain controversial. See Errington in *CAH* viii, pp. 244–89, and A. M. Eckstein, *Rome Enters the Greek East: From Anarchy to Hierarchy in the Hellenistic Mediterranean, 230–170 BC* (2008).
9. See Livy 32.10 and Diodorus 28.11. By the second century BC 'the freedom of the Greeks' was a political ideal that had long ago been reduced to a slogan and exploited in international politics: see E. S. Gruen, *The Hellenistic World and the Coming of Rome* (1984), pp. 132–57, and D. Sviatoslav, *The Greek Slogan of Freedom and Early Roman Politics in Greece* (2011), especially pp. 151–99.

10. See Polybius 18.33–9 and Livy 33.11–13.

11. On Antiochus III, see *Philopoemen*, note 100. The deployment of the notion 'the freedom of the Greeks' in Rome's diplomatic competition with Antiochus is discussed by R. Seager, *CQ* 31 (1981), pp. 106–12.

12. See Livy 35.23.5–8, 35.31–3 and 35.48–50.

13. See Polybius 23.4.1–15, 23.5 and Livy 39.48.2–4. After the death of Nabis in 192, Sparta was forcibly absorbed into the Achaean League. Subsequent Spartan resistance incurred harsh treatment (Introduction to *Philopoemen*).

14. Demetrius (*c.* 207–180) had gone to Rome as a hostage at the end of the Second Macedonian War (ch. 9), but owing to Philip's loyalty in the war against Antiochus he was released in 190. Demetrius urged a pro-Roman policy in Macedon, which led eventually to his execution as a traitor in 180, although the veracity of the ancient tradition on this matter has been doubted by modern historians (e.g. Hammond–Walbank, p. 490). The episode is told at length and with dramatic flair by Livy (40.5–24); Polybius' account (23.3.4–9, 23.7 and 23.10) is fragmentary.

15. See Duff, *Plutarch's Lives*, pp. 83–7. This view was not original to Plutarch (see e.g. Aristotle, *Nicomachean Ethics* 2.7.1107b27 –1108a1).

16. See Introduction to *Coriolanus*.

17. See Pelling, 'Roman Heroes', pp. 199–232, and Swain, 'Culture', pp. 229–64.

18. The similarity of the deaths of Philopoemen and Hannibal is discussed by Pelling, *P&H*, pp. 351–2.

19. See Swain, *H&E*, p. 148.

20. See Polybius 18.46.13–15 and Livy 33.33.5–8.

21. See Swain, *H&E*, p. 149.

22. See *HRR*, vol. 1, pp. cci–cciii and 143–7.

Notes to the Life of Titus Flamininus

1. *bronze statue . . . Circus*: The Circus Flaminius was built in the south part of the Campus Martius in 221. Opposite was a temple of Apollo Medicus, built in 431, and evidently adorned with a statue ransacked from Carthage in 146.

2. *Hannibalic War*: In 208. The war is the Second Punic War (218–201).

3. *Marcellus . . . killed*: Narrated at *Marcellus* 29.

4. *Tarentum ... captured for the second time*: This Greek city in southern Italy was captured by Hannibal in 212 and recovered by Fabius Maximus in 209 (*Fabius Maximus* 21–2). Flamininus became its governor, with the military authority of a praetor, in 205 (Livy 29.13.6) and remained in command there until at least 203 and possibly until 202. This was a singular appointment for a man of his age.

5. *Narnia and Cosa*: Narnia (modern Narni) was in Umbria, Cosa (near modern Ortabello) in Etruria, modern Tuscany. Plutarch errs here: Flamininus was not involved in establishing colonists in either city. In 201 he served on a commission assigning land holdings in Italy (Livy 31.4.3), and in 200 he was part of a commission adding colonists at Venusia (Livy 31.49.6).

6. *tribunate ... aedileship*: Flamininus held the quaestorship at an unknown date but probably in 205. It was customary for a candidate for the consulship to have held the praetorship. The aedileship and tribunate were never either customary or obligatory requirements, and in any case, since Flamininus was a patrician, he was ineligible for the tribunate.

7. *Fulvius and Manius*: So Livy 32.7.8–11. Neither of the tribunes (Marcus Fulvius and Manius Curius in Livy) can be identified with certainty.

8. *laws and precedents*: Laws and customs (*leges et mores*) alike defined the Roman constitution. The tribunes' objections in this instance were fair ones, but there was nothing objectionable in leaving the final say to the sovereign people. The senate's decision reflects the degree of support Flamininus already enjoyed in that body.

9. *Sextus Aelius*: Sextus Aelius Paetus, consul of 198.

10. *not yet thirty years old*: The precise date of Flamininus' birth is uncertain. Plutarch here assumes a birth date of around 229. Polybius (18.12.5) describes him as still 'not more than thirty' a year later, in 198. In Livy (33.33.3) Flamininus is about thirty-three in 196.

11. *war against ... Macedonians*: The Second Macedonian War, which had begun in 200; see Introduction. Roman magistrates were ordinarily assigned their provinces by lottery.

12. *their first practical exposure*: Plutarch here overlooks the First Macedonian War (214–205).

13. *foreigners*: Plutarch does not often refer to the Romans as foreigners (but see also chs. 5 and 11 and *Comparison Philopoemen-Flamininus* 1) and here he may be depicting the attitude of

contemporary Greeks, especially those who urged their countrymen to remain as independent from Rome as possible
(Philopoemen is an example of this point of view: e.g. *Philopoemen* 17).

14. *Sulpicius*: Publius Sulpicius Galba Maximus, the consul of 200,
had previously held the consulship in 211. He arrived in Macedon in autumn 200.

15. *Publius Villius*: Publius Villius Tappulus, the consul of 199. He
arrived in Macedon late in the year and was confronted by a
mutiny on the part of Roman troops.

16. *Lucius*: Lucius Quinctius Flamininus, consul in 192 (chs. 18–19).

17. *Scipio's army ... Africa*: This is Scipio Africanus, whose Spanish
campaign against Hasdrubal ended with his victory at Ilipa (in 207
or 206) and whose victory over Hannibal at Zama in 202 effectively concluded the Second Punic War (*Fabius Maximus* 25–7).

18. *3,000 in number*: Livy 32.9.1 mentions this force, adding at
32.9.6 that Flamininus' total army numbered 8,000 infantry and
500 cavalry; these were reinforcements to the Roman army
already present in Macedon.

19. *crossed ... to Epirus*: In early May 198, where Flamininus took
over command from Villius Tappulus.

20. *Apsus*: Actually the Romans were encamped on the Aoüs river
(the modern Vjosë). The Apsus (modern Seman) is a little to the
north, at its conjunction with the River Dren.

21. *Narrows*: Both proper name and description, here and at ch. 5;
for the topography of this site, see Hammond–Walbank, pp.
424–6.

22. *Narrows at Tempe*: The Vale of Tempe (modern Tembi),
renowned in Greek literature as a favourite haunt of Apollo and
the Muses, is a gorge in northern Thessaly between Mt Olympus
and Mt Ossa (modern Mt Kissavos); the Peneius river runs
through it.

23. *Dassaretis by Lyncus ... straightforward road*: Dassaretis is the
region southwest of Lake Lychnitis, Lyncus a region in ancient
Macedon (now divided between the Republic of Macedonia and
Greece) to the east of Lake Lychnitis. This route had already
been followed by Sulpicius Galba in 199 (Livy 31.33.4–6); see
N. G. L. Hammond, *JRS* 56 (1966), pp. 39–54 (pp. 43–4 explain
this route).

24. *entry through the gorge*: Plutarch here omits a forty-day delay
and a conference between Philip and Flamininus at which the
king proposed peace terms (Livy 32.10).

25. *herdsmen*: Livy (32.11.1) makes it a single shepherd, sent by Charops (whom he calls Charopus). Polybius (27.15.2) also notes that Flamininus owed his victory to Charops; cf. Diodorus 30.5 and Appian, *Macedonian Affairs* 6. Other sources agree with Plutarch that there were several shepherds: Ennius, *Annals* 340–42 (see Skutsch, p. 99); the anonymous *On Illustrious Men* 51.

26. *Charops son of Machatas*: See Walbank, *Commentary*, vol. 3, pp. 313–14. He had already been of service to the Romans in this war. His grandson, who was reared in Rome and became fluent in Latin, was destined to become a staunch if unscrupulous Roman partisan in Epirote affairs (Polybius 27.15.1–16).

27. *led the way in chains*: A regular precaution paralleled elsewhere in the case of unfamiliar guides.

28. *moon . . . at its fullest*: This detail allows the battle to be dated to around 25 June 198. The details of the battle are provided by Hammond–Walbank, pp. 424–6.

29. *moved his whole force at dawn*: Livy (32.12.1) makes Flamininus wait for a smoke signal before launching his attack.

30. *headlong flight*: Although Flamininus successfully dislodged Philip, his losses were probably heavier than the Macedonians', though this goes unmentioned in the sources, which tend to be pro-Roman. This victory was instrumental, however, in rousing Roman support on the part of the Aetolians and in bringing the Achaean League over to the Roman side: see Hammond–Walbank, pp. 424–8.

31. *Philip . . . like a man in retreat . . . to the Romans*: Livy (32.13.5–8) makes it clear that Philip's strategy was to minimize any advantage the Romans could draw from their inevitable occupation of Thessaly, which he nonetheless continued to defend through garrisons, even inflicting a serious defeat on Flamininus at Artax (Livy 32.17.4–32.18.1).

32. *as soon as . . . cities came over to him*: This is less than entirely accurate. The Romans were not instantly welcomed everywhere in Thessaly, and they sacked the city of Phaloria (Livy 32.15.3).

33. *cities came over to him . . . full of . . . enthusiasm*: Although the Achaean League came over to the Roman side, not all of its members were enthusiastic. Representatives of Dyme, Megalopolis and Argos walked out of the Achaean assembly to avoid being implicated in the vote for a Roman alliance (Livy 38.22.9–12, cf. Pausanias 7.8.1–2), and the still-garrisoned Corinth remained loyal to Philip (Livy 32.23.5–6), as did Chalcis; Argos soon went over to Philip (Livy 32.25), and remained in his

control until he handed it over to Nabis at the end of the year (Livy 32.38).

34. *the Achaeans ... making war*: Livy (32.19–32.23.3) provides a fuller account of this debate.

35. *Opuntians*: The inhabitants of Opus (perhaps modern Atalanti), who were divided over accepting an Aetolian or Roman garrison to replace their current Macedonian garrison; the richer faction favoured Rome, and imposed their will (Polybius 18.10.4; Livy 32.32.1–5, 32.38.9).

36. *when from a lookout point ... battle array*: In 280; for his remark see *Pyrrhus* 16.

37. *champion of freedom*: The first mention of this important concept for this Life.

38. *Philip seemed ready to come to terms ... refused*: Plutarch's account is misleading here. Negotiations for peace took place at the Conference of Nicaea in November 198, for which Polybius (18.1–10) offers a very full account. Its result was a truce, while representatives of all parties put their positions before the senate in Rome, a development that was unwelcome to some Greek states (Polybius 18.9, Livy 32.36). As a condition of this truce, Philip removed his garrisons from Phocis and Locris. In any case, it is clear that Flamininus exploited the truce in order to secure the extension of his command (ch. 7).

39. *with one exception*: The following episode took place in early spring 197 (Livy 33.1–2).

40. *Brachyllas*: A prominent Theban ally of Antigonus Doson and subsequently Philip V (who was at this time not in Thebes but with Philip: Polybius 18.1.2). He was eventually assassinated in 196, with Flamininus' connivance (Polybius 18.43.10).

41. *He responded to them ... until his soldiers could come up from their march*: Whereas here Flamininus' action seems like an improvisation, at Livy 33.1–2 it represents a preconceived plot.

42. *Attalus*: Attalus I of Pergamum (269–197), whose long-standing enmity with Philip had made him a loyal ally of Rome; he was now giving Flamininus valuable naval aid.

43. *ambassadors to Rome ... representatives of his own*: Plutarch recurs to the Conference of Nicaea, where this was agreed (ch. 5).

44. *peace came about through Titus' efforts*: The senate was uninterested in peace (Polybius 18.11, Livy 32.37), which left very little for Flamininus' friends to do in this regard. But it is significant that he was continued in his command, which perhaps was owing as much to his recent successes as to his machinations.

45. *Philip's army ... a similar size*: The Romans' forces probably outnumbered the Macedonians', although full and precise figures are a bit difficult to tease from the varying accounts in our sources (Hammond–Walbank, pp. 436–7).

46. *Scotussa*: A town in Thessaly, west of modern Volos, near which the decisive battle of Cynoscephalae was fought in spring 197 (Polybius 18.18–33, Livy 33.3–11). The topography and details of this battle are discussed at Hammond–Walbank, pp. 432–43, and, in close detail, by N. G. L. Hammond, *JHS* 108 (1988), pp. 60–82. Plutarch's account is in important respects abbreviated.

47. *Alexander*: Alexander the Great (356–323), whose most important conquest was over the Persians.

48. *fairest of theatres ... best of adversaries*: Plutarch attributes to Flamininus sentiments different from what one finds at Polybius 18.23.3–6 or Livy 33.8.

49. *high burial mound outside his camp*: On this mound, see W. K. Pritchett, *Studies in Ancient Greek Topography*, vol. 2 (1969), p. 139. Plutarch will have seen the mound and may here preserve an associated oral tradition (no other source comments on a speech by Philip). Philip's soldiers took his situation on the top of a burial mound as a bad omen.

50. *'Dog's Heads' ... shape*: The shapes of the ridges, when viewed from a certain angle, are in fact vaguely similar to the shape of a dog's head; see Hammond, *JHS* 108, pp. 80–81.

51. *The phalanx is like ... individual power*: Appended to his account of this battle, Polybius (18.28–32) contrasts the merits of the legion and the phalanx.

52. *The dead ... captured*: Plutarch takes these figures from Polybius (18.27.6), who adds that 700 Romans fell.

53. *people blamed the Aetolians*: Polybius (18.27.3–5) states that the Romans resented the Aetolians' plundering but says nothing about their blaming them for Philip's escape.

54. *Aetolians ... cause ... irritation to Titus*: Both Polybius (18.34) and Livy (33.11) comment on Flamininus' resentment of the Aetolians.

55. *Aetolians ... claiming the victory for themselves*: In his account of this battle, Plutarch has omitted the important contribution made by the Aetolians (Polybius 18.22.4–5).

56. *unburied*: The fallen Macedonians remained unburied for six years, until 191, when they were finally buried on the orders of King Antiochus (Livy 36.8.3–6).

57. *Emathia*: Originally the region between the Axius and the Hali-
    acmon rivers, the name became a widely used poetic expression
    for Macedon or Thessaly.

58. *Unwept ... swift deer*: *Palatine Anthology* 7.247. See A. S. F.
    Gow and D. L. Page, *The Greek Anthology: Hellenistic Epi-
    grams* (1965), pp. 319–21.

59. *Alcaeus' work*: Alcaeus of Messene, *fl. c.* 200, was the author of
    over twenty surviving epigrams, several of which are marked by
    invective against Philip.

60. *a sheer bare stake of wood – for Alcaeus*: That is, a stake is there
    for Alcaeus to be impaled on (by Philip). This epigram is in
    Palatine Anthology, appendix 16.26B; see D. L. Page, *Further
    Greek Epigrams* (1981), pp. 321–2.

61. *no attention ... to the Aetolians*: The Aetolians wanted Philip
    deposed and expected to make extensive territorial gains in the
    settlement of the war, thereby becoming the major Greek power
    in central Greece. Flamininus and the senate, however, were
    loath to see any state in this region grow too strong, and this was
    the origin of their conflict.

62. *Philip ... came to settle terms*: A peace conference was held at
    Tempe, described in detail by Polybius (18.36–40).

63. *terms ... hostage in Rome*: The terms, both of an immediate
    armistice and of the final peace, are reported at Polybius 18.39.5–
    6 and 18.44.2–7, Plutarch's source here. Plutarch is in error on
    the number of ships Philip could retain: he was allowed six. On
    Philip's son Demetrius (*c.* 207–180), see Introduction, note 14.

64. *Antiochus' court*: A mistake. Hannibal only reached there in
    195. On Antiochus III, see *Philopoemen*, note 100.

65. *universal empire ... target was Rome*: Antiochus' imperial
    ambitions are emphasized by Polybius (11.34.14–16), and
    (according to Polybius 18.39) Flamininus' fear of Antiochus was
    considered by some to have been a factor in his decision to make
    peace with Philip. See further Eckstein, *Rome Enters the Greek
    East*, pp. 145–50, 306–41 (discussing the war).

66. *ten commissioners ... advised Titus*: It was routine for senat-
    orial commissioners to be sent to assist in making the final
    arrangements after a war of this magnitude. They arrived in win-
    ter 197 or perhaps as late as spring 196 with a senatorial decree,
    but the men on the spot were granted a degree of discretion in its
    execution (Polybius 18.44–5). This decree demanded that Philip
    hand over to Rome any Greek cities garrisoned by him.

67. *Corinth ... Demetrias*: Garrisons in these three cities had given Philip a decisive strategic advantage in Greek affairs. The strategic importance of the Acrocorinth in the Peloponnese is emphasized at *Aratus* 16; Chalcis (modern Chalkida) was the most important city in Euboea, and its position was important for Philip's control of central Greece; Demetrias, a city founded by Demetrius Poliorcetes, was located in eastern Greece, in Magnesia near the modern city of Volos, and was of strategic significance in Magnesia and Thessaly.

68. *that was Philip's phrase*: So Polybius 18.11.5; cf. *Aratus* 16.

69. *old collar ... heavier than before*: At *Moralia* 855a Plutarch attributes this expression to Philip, when he is warning the Greeks against appealing to the Romans.

70. *free these cities ... from their garrisons*: In fact only Corinth was freed; Acrocorinth, Chalcis and Demetrias remained under Flamininus' control (Polybius 18.45.2, Livy 33.31.11).

71. *Isthmian Games*: Panhellenic games held at the Isthmus of Corinth in late June and early July 196.

72. *already had peace ... celebrating at the festival*: At Polybius 18.46.1–2 and Livy 33.23.3, by contrast, the spectators are keen to learn what the Romans' final disposition of Greek affairs will be.

73. *consul*: At this time Flamininus was actually proconsul instead of consul.

74. *Corinth ... Perrhaebia*: This is a list of regions whose cities had been dominated by Macedon.

75. *ravens ... fell down into the stadium*: This story is also told by Valerius Maximus (4.8.5). Birds were reported to have fallen similarly on other occasions (*Pompey* 25, Livy 29.25.3–4).

76. *whirling of the air ... turbulence ... as on the sea*: Plutarch also explains the phenomenon at *Pompey* 25.

77. *press of the crowd ... life was in danger*: No hostility was involved.

78. *fate of Greece*: Plutarch also muses on the causes of Greek decline at ch. 15. See also *Timoleon* 29 and *Moralia* 401c–d. In *Flamininus* he diverges from his sources: instead of reflecting on Greek history in their accounts of this episode, Polybius (18.46.13–15) and Livy (33.33.5–8) concentrate on Roman virtue and power.

79. *Agesilaus ... Alcibiades*: Agesilaus (*c.* 445–359), king of Sparta and a leading military figure of his time; Lysander (d. 395), a Spartan general, hero of the Peloponnesian War and a proponent

of Spartan imperialism; Nicias (*c.* 470–413), an Athenian general and statesman who commanded Athens' ill-fated attempt to conquer Sicily; and Alcibiades (451–404), an Athenian general and political figure, notorious for his intrigues – domestic and international – during the Peloponnesian War. Each is the subject of a Plutarchan Life.

80. *Marathon ... Cyprus*: The battles of Marathon (490), Salamis (480), Plataea (479) and Thermopylae (480) were fought against the Persians in the First and Second Persian Wars. Cimon (*c.* 510–*c.* 450) was an Athenian statesman and general who won a major victory over the Persians at the battle of Eurymedon (466) and died, in 451 or 450, while campaigning on Cyprus against the Persians; he is the subject of a Plutarchan Life.

81. *an ancient shared ancestry*: The historical relationship between Greeks and Romans, defined in the multiple explanations of Rome's founding, was controversial in Greece. Elsewhere, Plutarch can describe Rome as a Greek city (*Camillus* 22).

82. *Titus ... missions*: Although Plutarch puts Flamininus in charge here, this was actually the collaborative work of the proconsul and the senatorial commission (ch. 10). A fuller and more accurate account is provided by Polybius (18.48.1–3).

83. *Lentulus ... Bargylia*: Publius Cornelius Lentulus (praetor in 203) was sent first to Bargylia (modern Asar in Turkey), then on to Antiochus himself. The freedom of the Greeks announced by the Romans included the Greek cities in Asia (Polybius 18.44), an unmistakable challenge to Antiochus.

84. *Stertinius*: Lucius Stertinius had been appointed through special legislation to a proconsular command in Spain (Livy 31.50.11), but nothing further is known of his career.

85. *Publius Villius*: Publius Villius Tappulus had been consul in 199.

86. *removing the garrisons and restoring ... to the peoples*: Plutarch is our only source for this action by Flamininus.

87. *In Argos ... freedom to the Greeks*: Late summer or early autumn in 195. Plutarch is misleading here. The proclamation at Argos was not a simple repetition of the one at Corinth but related especially to the freedom of Argos itself (Livy 34.41.1–3).

88. *from city to city ... affection*: Flamininus' jurisdiction is described at Livy 34.48.2. The nature of Flamininus' activities in Greece at this time is illustrated by an inscription recording his instructions to the city of Chyretiae (modern Domeniko) in Perrhaebia (*Syll.* 593; see R. K. Sherk, *Rome and the Greek East to the Death of Augustus* (1984), p. 5, for translation and commentary).

89. *Xenocrates*: Xenocrates of Chalcedon, head of the Academy 339–314, during which time he was a resident alien (*metic*) in Athens.

90. *Lycurgus*: (*c.* 390–*c.* 325) An important Athenian statesman. Among his significant contributions to Athens, and relevant to this anecdote, were his policies to increase Athens' revenues.

91. *God's assistance*: That the rise of Rome was favoured by the gods is axiomatic in Plutarch: see Swain, *H&E*, pp. 151–61.

92. *Sons of Zeus*: These are the Dioscuri, children of Zeus and Tyndarus' wife Leda, hence their address as *Tyndarids*.

93. *Aeneadae*: The descendants of Aeneas, i.e. the Romans.

94. *Nero*: In AD 67 Nero gave Greece freedom from direct rule and exemption from tribute (*Syll.* 814).

95. *as I have said*: At ch. 10.

96. *Nabis*: On Nabis and the war with him, see *Philopoemen* 12–15. The war began in 195 before the proclamation in Argos took place.

97. *he came to terms ... slavery*: See *Philopoemen* 15, where Plutarch attributes Flamininus' decision to end the war to his jealousy of Philopoemen.

98. *this Arcadian fellow*: Plutarch here recalls his own formulation at *Philopoemen* 15.

99. *abandoned the war ... suffering*: Similarly at Livy 34.49.1–3.

100. *1,200 of them*: Valerius Maximus (5.2.6) sets the number at 2,000, but Plutarch's figure is taken from the calculations of Polybius (preserved for us at Livy 34.50.7): the Achaeans paid 5 minas per head, and the total amount paid was 100 talents. As there are 60 minas in every talent, the total number of slaves must have been 1,200.

101. *triumph ... celebrated*: In 194.

102. *glorious sight*: A fuller description of the triumph is provided at Livy 34.52.

103. *Tuditanus*: This name has been garbled in our manuscripts, but Tuditanus is the likeliest reading here. Several editors, however, prefer to emend to read Antias, a reference to Valerius Antias (ch. 18). Gaius Sempronius Tuditanus was consul in 129 and subsequently celebrated a triumph. He wrote a work on the Roman magistracies as well as a history, the scope and scale of which are irrecoverable. See *HRR*, vol. 1, pp. cci–cciii and 143–7.

104. *Philippics*: Macedonian gold coins of a type first minted by Philip II (hence their name).

105. *owed . . . 1,000 talents*: See ch. 9.

106. *later persuaded to remit payment*: In 191 or 190, in recognition of Philip's loyalty and to assure its continuance during the war with Antiochus.

107. *his son*: On Demetrius see ch. 9. His restoration, like the remission of tribute, was intended to secure Macedonian loyalty.

108. *Antiochus' arrival in Greece*: In autumn 192 Antiochus crossed to Demetrias. He did not, as Plutarch indicates here, bring a large army but instead only 10,000 infantrymen, as well as a modest cavalry contingent and six elephants, all transported on sixty ships (Livy 35.43.6).

109. *long-standing . . . hostility towards the Roman people*: See chs. 9–10. A full account of the Aetolians' diplomatic machinations is provided by Livy (34.49.5–6 and 35.12).

110. *Manius Acilius . . . his legate*: Manius Acilius Glabrio was consul in 191. Flamininus was appointed by the senate to serve as a legate in this campaign (Livy 36.1.8); although Plutarch fails to mention it, he was already on the spot, having been sent east with other senatorial envoys to try to diffuse Aetolian agitation and rally the Greeks against Antiochus (Livy 35.23.5–8). The Elder Cato took part in this campaign as a tribune of the soldiers (*Elder Cato* 12–14).

111. *Antiochus was defeated at Thermopylae*: In 191. See further *Elder Cato* 13–14.

112. *sailed . . . to Asia*: Antiochus retreated to Asia Minor, where in 190 he was decisively defeated at the battle of Magnesia.

113. *the consul Manius divided up the Aetolians . . . allowing King Philip to destroy others*: More details are provided by Polybius (20.9–11) and Livy (36.27–9). In exchange for his assistance, Philip was allowed by the Romans to make territorial gains in Thessaly.

114. *Dolopians . . . Aperantians*: People of Dolopia (modern Evrytania), a region north of Aetolia between Epirus and Thessaly. Reference to Magnesians raises the possibility of Philip's recovering Demetrias (ch. 10). The Athamanians lived in western Thessaly and the Aperantians occupied a region southwest of Dolopia.

115. *Heraclea and was besieging Naupactus*: Heraclea Trachinia was about 4 miles (6½ km) west of Thermopylae. The Romans completed their siege in 191 (Livy 36.22–4). Naupactus (modern Nafpaktos) lies at the entrance to the Gulf of Corinth. This campaign is described more fully by Polybius (20.11.11) and Livy (36.30 and 36.33).

116. *intercede with the consul*: That is, with Manius Acilius Glabrio.

117. *the besieged people of Naupactus . . . anger*: A fuller account is provided at Livy 36.35.1–4.

118. *The result was . . . moderate treatment*: See Livy 36.35.6. In fact the senate's terms were anything but moderate (Polybius 21.2, Livy 37.1.5) and the embassy came to nothing.

119. *infuriated . . . because of the marriage . . . in progress*: Chalcis had fallen to Antiochus at the end of 192 (Livy 35.51). The marriage took place early in 191 (Polybius 20.8, Livy 36.11). Cleoptolemus is otherwise unknown.

120. *Manius immediately moved on Chalcis*: This move into Euboea came directly after Thermopylae, and predated Manius' confrontations with the Aetolians.

121. *accompanied by Titus*: Livy (36.21.3) notes Glabrio's swift move into Euboea and his moderation towards the towns of Euboea, but makes no mention of Flamininus' intercession.

122. *consecrated . . . votive offerings to Titus*: Epigraphic evidence confirms the honours to Flamininus at Chalcis: e.g. *Inscriptiones Graecae* XII (1915), 9.233 and 931.

123. *Delphinium*: A shrine to Apollo at Delphi.

124. *clashed with . . . Diophanes*: For the brush with Philopoemen see ch. 13 (and *Philopoemen* 15). His clash with Diophanes, who was general of the Achaeans in 192/1, is reported more fully at Livy 36.31.8.

125. *anger was not deep-seated . . . pointed remarks*: This recalls Flamininus' characterization in ch. 1.

126. *Zacynthus*: The southernmost of the western Greek islands. The Achaeans had taken possession of Zacynthus after the battle of Thermopylae, but the Romans now claimed it and the matter was discussed at a conference held in 191 (Livy 36.31–2), at which Flamininus issued this bon mot.

127. *'You'll be in danger . . . Peloponnese'*: Also reported at *Moralia* 197b and Livy 36.32.6–8.

128. *meeting . . . to discuss terms for a . . . peace*: At Nicaea in 198 (cf. ch. 5). Plutarch draws this story from Polybius (18.7.5–6); he reports it again at *Moralia* 197b.

129. *Deinocrates*: A leading Messenian statesman and a friend of Flamininus, but also responsible for the death of Philopoemen (*Philopoemen* 20). Our fullest account of him comes from Polybius (23.5.1–18); see Walbank, *Commentary*, vol. 3, pp. 220–23. His embassy to Rome dates to 183.

130. *envoys from Antiochus*: At Aegium in November 192 (Livy 35.48–50). The remark ('So you too, you men of Achaea . . .') is also preserved at *Moralia* 197c.

131. *censor*: Flamininus won a fiercely contested election to become censor for 189.

132. *Marcellus*: Marcus Claudius Marcellus, the consul of 196. His father, consul for the first time in 222, is the subject of Plutarch's *Marcellus*.

133. *Terentius Culleo*: Probably Quintus Terentius Culleo, the praetor of 187. This is the only reference to this measure and so its purpose is not entirely clear (Plutarch's description is not especially helpful): perhaps it required the censors to enrol the sons of freedmen as a remedy for recent abuses of the census.

134. *Scipio . . . Cato*: On Scipio Africanus, see note 17. Since the time of his censorship in 199, Scipio had been the leading man in the senate (*princeps senatus*) and here Titus extends that honour. Cato is the subject of *Elder Cato*. His bad relations with Scipio are related in *Elder Cato* 3, 11, 15 and 18.

135. *excellence and pre-eminence*: Scipio was named *princeps senatus* for the third time during Flamininus' censorship (Livy 38.28.2). This event is simply the spark for Plutarch's story about Lucius Scipio, since it did not occur until Cato's censorship in 184.

136. *Lucius Flamininus*: Lucius Quinctius Flamininus, the consul of 192 (ch. 3). The following incident is related in more than one variation; *Elder Cato* 17; Cicero, *On Old Age* 42; and Livy 39.42.5–39.43.5.

137. *provincial governor*: Lucius Flamininus was assigned Italy and Gaul as his province in 192.

138. *lictor*: A consul was attended by twelve lictors, who carried his fasces.

139. *Valerius Antias*: A Roman historian of the first century BC (his precise dates are unknown); see Introduction to *Romulus*.

140. *wife and children*: In actuality Livy's Cato mentions only the Gaul's wife (39.42.10).

141. *Lucius . . . as a favour to his boyfriend*: So Livy 39.42.7–12, where the man is a Gallic noble.

142. *said . . . to aggravate his charge*: Plutarch is sufficiently aware of rhetorical technique to distrust invective.

143. *condemned prisoner*: Cf. Cicero, *On Old Age* 42.

144. *censor*: In 184, along with Lucius Valerius Flaccus (*Elder Cato* 16–19).

145. *challenged ... truth of anything that had been said*: Cato was challenging Lucius to make a *sponsio*, i.e. to swear on oath that the charge was false (Livy 39.43.5).

146. *Cato's old enemies*: Of whom he had many. See *Elder Cato* 19 and Livy 39.44.8–9 for the opposition he confronted during his censorship; Flamininus' opposition is not specifically cited by Livy.

147. *lawsuits against him*: *Elder Cato* 15 mentions the many lawsuits Cato faced during his career (but there is no mention of Flamininus).

148. *I cannot describe this ... his punishment*: Plutarch does not often intrude into his narrative so explicitly as this. Here he criticizes Flamininus for persisting in his anger, which, as Plutarch has informed the reader, was contrary to his natural inclination (ch. 17).

149. *front seats ... special dress*: These senatorial seats were introduced only in 194 (Livy 34.44.5). Senators wore distinctive shoes and tunics adorned by a broad purple stripe.

150. *one occasion ... sit with them*: This incident is also described at *Elder Cato* 17.

151. *served a further term as tribune*: That is, as a tribune of the soldiers. Plutarch is the only evidence for this, but it is credible: at this time distinguished men, even ex-consuls, served as military tribunes (as the Elder Cato did in 191).

152. *youthfulness ... hounded Hannibal*: This is misleading. In 183, when Flamininus hounded Hannibal (see below), he was still only forty-six.

153. *Hannibal had fled ... from ... Carthage*: On account of Roman pressure, in 195.

154. *battle in Phrygia*: The battle of Magnesia of 190, which in fact took place in Lydia rather than Phrygia. The terms of Antiochus' subsequent peace with Rome, settled in the Treaty of Apamea in 188, required him to hand over Hannibal (Livy 38.38.18).

155. *Prusias*: Prusias I Cholus (*c.* 230–182), king of Bithynia. Hannibal arrived at his court in 188. From 187 to 183 Prusias was at war with Rome's ally Eumenes II of Pergamum, in which war Hannibal won at least one victory for Prusias. In the end, however, the Romans stepped in, sending Flamininus to settle the war to Eumenes' advantage.

156. *some other matter*: See previous note.

157. *infuriated ... would not relent*: Livy (39.51.2–3) leaves open the possibility that the initiative for Hannibal's death came from Prusias himself, eager as he was to gratify Flamininus and

Rome. If Plutarch knew this version (and he probably did), he ignored it.

158. *Libyssa*: Modern Gebze, on the Propontis (or Sea of Marmara).

159. *Themistocles . . . bull's blood*: Themistocles (*c.* 524–459), Athenian politician and general and the subject of Plutarch's *Themistocles*; this story is reported at *Themistocles* 31. Midas was a legendary king of Phrygia, who killed himself when threatened by the Cimmerians in the early seventh century BC; Plutarch mentions the story at *Moralia* 168f. Bull's blood, of course, is not poisonous.

160. *Livy says*: Livy 39.51.9–10.

161. *'men who sent secretly to Pyrrhus . . . poison him'*: Told more fully at *Pyrrhus* 21. This happened in 279, at which point Pyrrhus was indeed victorious, having defeated the Romans at Heraclea in 280.

162. *meeting in Ephesus*: This event, probably a fiction, is reported in several sources (e.g. Livy 35.14.5–12) and is routinely dated to 193.

163. *Africanus*: The use of the name is pointed, since Scipio was surnamed Africanus on account of his victory over Hannibal.

164. *Aristonicus . . . Eumenes*: Aristonicus (d. 128) may have been an illegitimate son of Eumenes II of Pergamum. After the death of Attalus III, who left the kingdom to Rome, he led an insurrection (133–129), during which he asserted his royal claim and enrolled soldiers from every social order, including slaves. In the end, he was defeated and executed in Rome. The allegation that he was the son of a lyre-player may be nothing more than contemporary propaganda.

165. *Mithridates . . . land and sea*: Mithridates VI of Pontus fought a series of wars with Rome. During the First Mithridatic War (88–85) he fought both Lucius Cornelius Sulla (*c.* 138–78), the future dictator, and Gaius Flavius Fimbria, a mutinous officer later forced to commit suicide by Sulla. The Second Mithridatic War (83–81) was waged by Lucius Licinius Murena, who went on to become consul in 62 BC. During the Third Mithridatic War (73–63), Mithridates fought first Lucius Licinius Lucullus, the consul of 74 BC, and then Pompey the Great.

166. *Gaius Marius . . . in Rome*: (*c.* 157–86) The great general, six times consul, was driven from Rome by Sulla in 88. He then endured a degrading escape and exile in Libya, until his return in 87, when he cruelly purged his enemies; see Plutarch's *Marius* 40–44.

167. *some people say . . . embassy . . . Hannibal's death*: This is the version of Valerius Antias, as reported at Livy 39.56.7, according to whom Lucius Cornelius Scipio Asiaticus, consul of 190 and victor of Magnesia, and Publius Cornelius Scipio Nasica, consul of 191, were the other members of this embassy (they were respectively the brother and cousin of Scipio Africanus).

168. *a peaceful death*: Flamininus died in 174. We are no better informed than Plutarch about his final years.

Notes to the Comparison of Philopoemen and Titus Flamininus

1. *many others*: Presumably men like the ones mentioned at *Flamininus* 11 (i.e. Agesilaus, Lysander, Nicias and Alcibiades).

2. *gone away to Crete*: Philopoemen's second spell in Crete, 200/199–194/3 (*Philopoemen* 13).

3. *set her peoples . . . free*: *Flamininus* 7–8 (victory at Cynoscephalae) and 10–12 (the liberation of the Greeks announced in 196).

4. *Philopoemen killed more Greeks . . . than Titus killed Macedonians*: Neither Life has given many casualty numbers and in any case Plutarch is probably relying as much on his impressions as his calculations.

5. *one man's . . . the other's*: Flamininus' . . . Philopoemen's.

6. *anger was swift*: *Flamininus* 1 and 17; Plutarch here ignores Flamininus' conduct in chs. 17–21.

7. *Titus ensured . . . Aetolians*: *Flamininus* 9 (Philip) and 15 (Aetolians).

8. *Philopoemen was led . . . contributions they paid*: *Philopoemen* 13.

9. *he had once been a benefactor . . . constitution itself*: *Philopoemen* 10 and 14–16.

10. *thought to have thrown away his life in . . . contentiousness*: *Philopoemen* 18–20. Plutarch is here more unequivocal than in his narrative, where he stressed Philopoemen's precipitate vigour in more generous tones.

11. *guided by . . . an eye for safety*: These were important considerations for Plutarch; see Introduction to *Marcellus*.

12. *struggle with Philip . . . in two contests*: *Flamininus* 3–5 and 7–8.

13. *he fought his wars . . . and he defeated both*: *Philopoemen* 7, 13 (Crete) and 14–16 (Sparta).

14. *Philopoemen made his own innovations . . . organization*: *Philopoemen* 7 and 9.

15. *many great deeds of Philopoemen*: For example at *Philopoemen* 7 and 10.

16. *Archedamus*: Three times general of the Aetolians, he commanded Aetolian troops at the battle of Cynoscephalae; eventually he was accused of anti-Roman sentiments and joined Perseus (*Aemilius Paullus* 23).

17. *mocked him for this . . . deep in prayer*: He delivered this insult at a conference in 192, when both the Aetolians and Romans were soliciting the aid of the Achaean League (Livy 35.48.12–13). The comment was manifestly unfair, and was intended to be unfair, as Plutarch will have known, but he nonetheless includes it here without further commentary.

18. *all Titus' noble achievements . . . commander or ambassador*: Inescapably so, inasmuch as it was only by way of such positions that Flamininus had any authority to act in Greece (Plutarch is not very interested in Flamininus' senatorial career in Rome).

19. *as a private citizen . . . saved the city*: *Philopoemen* 12 (Nabis expelled) and 16 (Diophanes and Flamininus barred).

20. *differences hard to evaluate . . . we shall not seem to go wrong*: Plutarch also suggests a draw between his two heroes in the *Comparisons* of *Cimon and Lucullus* and *Lysander and Sulla*.

ELDER CATO

Further Reading

A. E. Astin's *Cato the Censor* (1978) is an excellent (if somewhat apologetic) biography; in addition to Cato's political career, Astin devotes considerable (and still important) attention to his literary works. D. Sansone, *Plutarch: The Lives of Aristeides and Cato* (1989), is a very helpful commentary and I have made much use of it. On the history of this period, see, in addition to Astin's biography, W. V. Harris, 'Roman Expansion in the West', in *CAH* viii (1989), pp. 107–62, and, in the same volume, A. E. Astin, 'Roman government and politics, 200–134 BC', pp. 163–96. On Cato's diplomatic activities during the war against Antiochus, see J. Linderski, *Roman Questions II: Selected Papers* (2007), pp. 61–87. The most important ancient sources for this period are Polybius and Livy, which means there is much to be learned from Walbank, *Commentary*, vols. 1–3, and J. Briscoe, *A Commentary on Livy, Books 31–33* (1973), *Books 34–37* (1981) and *Books 38–40* (2008).

Astin provides a good introduction to Cato's writings. On the *On Agriculture*, see A. Dalby, *Cato On Farming, De Agricultura: A Modern Translation and Commentary* (1998). The remaining fragments of Cato's writings are assembled in P. Cugusi and M. T. Sblendorio Cugusi, *M. Porcio Catone Censore* (2001); see also the more specialized volumes of M. Chassignet, *Caton: les origines (fragments)* (1986), and M. T. Sblendorio Cugusi, *M. Porci Catonis Orationum Reliquiae* (1982). Cato's cultural circumstances and his contributions to Roman literary and political traditions are discussed by E. S. Gruen, *Culture and National Identity in Republican Rome* (1992), and E. Sciarrino, *Cato the Censor and the Beginnings of Latin Prose* (2011).

Notes to the Introduction to Elder Cato

1. Fronto, *Preface to his History (Principia Historiae)* 4.

2. Cicero's devotion to Cato's memory is discussed by H. van der Blom, *Cicero's Role Models: The Political Strategy of a Newcomer* (2010).

3. Cato's actual words are preserved at Pliny, *Natural History* 29.14.

4. The ideology of the New Man remained an issue in the Rome of Plutarch's day, when the typical New Man was now a provincial, including Greek provincials: see R. Syme, *Tacitus* (1958), pp. 566–84; and A. R. Birley, *Zeitschrift für Papyrologie und Epigraphik* 116 (1997), pp. 209–45.

5. See their Lives in this volume. Cato's service is mentioned in neither.

6. See Nepos, *Cato* 1.2. This episode is not mentioned by Plutarch.

7. Plutarch does not mention Cato's aedileship (Livy 32.7.13; Nepos, *Cato* 1.3), but this office was very useful to anyone hoping to advance to the consulship.

8. E. Badian, *Publicans and Sinners* (1972), pp. 32–4.

9. J. S. Richardson, *Hispaniae: Spain and the Development of Roman Imperialism, 218–82 BC* (1986), p. 95.

10. See Livy 37.57.9–37.58.2. Plutarch does not mention Cato's failure in 189.

11. See E. Sciarrino in W. Dominik and J. Hall (eds.), *A Companion to Roman Rhetoric* (2007), pp. 54–66.

12. On Hadrian's preference for Cato: *The Augustan History; Life of Hadrian* 16.6; on Favorinus' fondness for Cato: Gellius 14.2.21; on Sulpicius Apollinaris': Gellius 13.18, 13.20.5–17;

on Marcus Aurelius': e.g. Fronto, *Epistle to Marcus Aurelius* 2.1 (van den Hout). The reception of Cato's works is surveyed in W. Suerbaum, *Die archaische Literatur: von den Anfängen bis Sullas Tod* (2002), pp. 413–18.

13. See D. Feeney, *Literature and Religion at Rome* (1998), pp. 50–53.

14. See R. MacMullen, *Historia* 40 (1991), pp. 419–38; T. Habinek and A. Schiesero (eds.), *The Roman Cultural Revolution* (1997); and A. Wallace-Hadrill, *Rome's Cultural Revolution* (2008).

15. See Astin, *Cato the Censor*, pp. 157–81; Gruen, *Culture and National Identity in Republican Rome*, pp. 52–83; and Sciarrino, *Cato the Censor and the Beginnings of Latin Prose*, pp. 117–60. It is relevant to this Life that in Plutarch's own day there were Romans who made a show of despising philosophy and philosophizing, sometimes with the Elder Cato in mind: see Syme, *Tacitus*, pp. 553–63.

16. On this narrative device in Plutarch see Pelling, *P&H*, p. 369.

17. See Introduction to *Philopoemen*.

18. See chs. 15 and 18 and especially *Comparison Aristeides–Elder Cato* 5. On Plutarch's objections to contentiousness, see Pelling, *P&H*, pp. 243–7, examining the importance of these qualities in *Philopoemen* and *Titus Flamininus* (the same qualities play important roles in *Fabius Maximus*). See also Introduction to *Philopoemen*.

19. See *Comparison Aristeides–Elder Cato* 5; on *praotes*, see General Introduction III.

20. On Cicero's dialogue, see J. G. F. Powell, *Cicero: Cato Maior de Senectute* (1988).

Notes to the Life of Elder Cato

1. *Tusculum*: Modern Frascati, about 15 miles (24 km) southeast of Rome.

2. *country of the Sabines*: A region northeast of Rome (modern Sabina). Sabines played an important role in Rome's legendary history (e.g. in the rape of the Sabine women and through kings like Titus Tatius and Numa) and by Cato's day had become a byword for austerity and old-fashioned virtue.

3. *Cato soon acquired this title*: See Introduction.

4. *not Cato, but Priscus*: Although it was a quite common surname, the Porcii never used *Priscus*, which can mean 'old-fashioned' or 'elder'. Perhaps Plutarch saw Cato so described in one of his

Latin sources (as a means of distinguishing him from the Younger Cato: ch. 27).

5.   *catus*: Both Catus and Cato exist as surnames.

6.   *Red-haired ... turn you away from the gate*: This epigram is mentioned only here. Its author focuses on Cato's aggressive personality, which in these lines renders him more frightening than the mythical three-headed dog Cerberus. Persephone was queen of the underworld.

7.   *services ... a fee of any kind*: This was nothing unusual: Roman advocates did not accept fees. The point is introduced here to correspond with the same habit on the part of Aristeides (*Aristeides* 3).

8.   *Hannibal ... laying all Italy waste*: In 217, the year in which Hannibal won his victory at Lake Trasimene. Hannibal's war in Italy is central to *Marcellus* and *Fabius Maximus*, both in this volume.

9.   *such an appearance ... cold steel*: Also cited at *Coriolanus* 8 and *Moralia* 199b.

10. *vinegar*: Plutarch has in mind *posca*, wine of the cheapest sort mixed with water, the standard drink of the Roman soldier on campaign.

11. *his estate*: This is Cato's Sabine estate. Both its situation near Curius' farm and Cato's admiration for the man are discussed by Cicero at *On Old Age* 16 and 35.

12. *Manius Curius ... three triumphs*: Manius Curius Dentatus (d. 270) was several times consul (in 290, 284, 275 and 274) and censor in 272. He celebrated two triumphs in 290 (Livy, *Summary of Book* 20) and his third in 275.

13. *It was here ... possess it himself*: This anecdote, also reported at *Moralia* 194e–f, was frequently repeated (e.g. Cicero, *On Old Age* 56, *The Republic* 3.40; Valerius Maximus 4.3.5; and Pliny, *Natural History* 19.87). One of Curius' triumphs was over the Samnites, but it is not easy to attach a date to this story, which is almost certainly unhistorical. Curius' incorruptibility was celebrated by Ennius (*Annals* 456, see Skutsch, p. 112): 'whom no man could conquer with iron or with gold'.

14. *Fabius Maximus captured ... Tarentum*: In 209 (*Fabius Maximus* 21–2).

15. *Tarentum ... young man*: Cato was about twenty-five at this time. His presence at Tarentum is mentioned only in Cicero's *On Old Age* (11, 39, 41), which is Plutarch's source here. Cicero's information is not credited by every historian, largely on account

of the fictitious story, repeated here, about Cato's encounter with Nearchus, but there is no obvious reason to doubt that Cato served under Fabius.

16. *Nearchus*: Unknown, apart from his mention in Cicero (see previous note).

17. *which Plato also upholds*: See Plato, *Timaeus* 69d. Plutarch recurs to this passage at *Moralia* 13a, 554f and 1107a.

18. *he did not study Greek ... until he was an old man*: This is the standard view of Cato's Greek reading; see Cicero, *Academic Questions* 2.5, *The Republic* 5.2, *On Old Age* 26; Nepos, *Cato* 3.2; Valerius Maximus 8.7.1; and Quintilian 12.11.23. But it is obvious that Plutarch recognized in Cato's writings a high degree of Greek influence.

19. *Thucydides*: (c. 455–c. 400) The great historian of the Peloponnesian War. At *Brutus* 66 Cicero compares the style of Cato's *Origins* with Thucydides', a comparison he later rejects (in the voice of Atticus) at *Brutus* 294.

20. *Demosthenes*: (384–322) The greatest of the Athenian orators. Traces of his influence on Cato are discussed by Astin, *Cato the Censor*, p. 149.

21. *his writings are often enriched by ideas ... translated from it*: Plutarch is probably referring to the totality of Cato's reported sayings and not simply to his published collections of aphorisms (Cicero, *On Duties* 1.104, *On the Ideal Orator* 2.271).

22. *Flaccus Valerius*: Lucius Valerius Flaccus. Like Cato he was consul in 195 and censor in 184, when he was named 'the leading man of the senate' (*princeps senatus*). On the family of the Valerii, see *Publicola* 1.

23. *it was Cato's practice ... same wine*: Cf. Plutarch's account of Philopoemen's lifestyle at *Philopoemen* 4.

24. *military tribune ... quaestor*: Cato served as tribune of the soldiers under Marcellus at the siege of Syracuse in 214, and was later elected quaestor for 204, when he served under Scipio Africanus.

25. *served as his colleague ... censor*: See chs. 10 and 16.

26. *Fabius Maximus*: (c.275–203) The subject of Plutarch's Life. Cato's esteem for Fabius is mentioned at Cicero, *On Old Age* 10.

27. *Scipio ... Africanus*: Publius Cornelius Scipio, who defeated Hannibal at the battle of Zama in 202 and was honoured with the surname Africanus.

28. *This distinguished man ... jealous of him*: See *Fabius Maximus* 25.

29. *Scipio's quaestor ... squandering ... pay upon his troops*: Financial administration was one of the central responsibilities of a quaestor.

30. *Cato ... left Scipio's army*: It would have been an outrage for a quaestor to desert his commander and in fact Cato did not (Livy 29.25.10). Plutarch's story is a fiction: see Astin, *Cato the Censor*, pp. 12–15.

31. *denounce the general ... active service*: Scipio was criticized for his failure to restrain the excesses of his subordinate Quintus Pleminius, an event that Fabius and others tried to use as an excuse to recall him (Livy 29.8–22). Their complaint was amplified by protests concerning Scipio's lifestyle. In the end, Scipio was exonerated. See also *Fabius Maximus* 25.

32. *tribunes were sent out*: The senate dispatched a commission, which included two tribunes of the people, to investigate the matter.

33. *came to be known as the Roman Demosthenes*: So also Appian, *Wars in Spain* 39.160 and Diodorus 34/35.

34. *His powers of expression ... his rarity*: In other words, the young needed no convincing that eloquence was worth cultivating. A simple lifestyle, by contrast, did not have the same attraction – hence Cato's singular reputation.

35. *He tells us ...*: The following assertions by Cato derive ultimately from his oratory, perhaps his speech *On his own Expenditure*; see Astin, *Cato the Censor*, p. 107. The cost of an ordinary soldier's outfit was 100 drachmas, equivalent in Plutarch to 100 denarii: see Badian, *Publicans and Sinners*, pp. 21–2.

36. *drank the same wine as his rowers*: This boast by Cato is often repeated (e.g. Pliny, *Natural History* 14.91; Valerius Maximus 4.3.11; and Frontinus, *Stratagems* 4.3.1). While travelling to and from Spain during his consulship, Cato was satisfied to drink the same wine as the rowers of his transports.

37. *dinner ... 30 asses for it*: In Cato's day an *as* was a tenth of a denarius; 30 asses was a very modest sum for an aristocrat's evening meal.

38. *none of his villas had plastered walls*: Meaning that Cato's villas lacked wall paintings.

39. *labourers ... useless mouths*: So Cato in *On Agriculture* 2.7.

40. *nothing is cheap ... only an as*: Also quoted by Seneca, *Moral Epistles* 94.27.

41. *the people of Athens ... mules ... further service*: This story is also found at *Moralia* 970a–b; Aristotle, *Animal History* 6.24;

Pliny, *Natural History* 8.175; and Aelian, *On the Nature of Animals* 6.49.

42. *Cimon's race-horses ... Olympia*: Cimon (*c.* 585–*c.* 523), prominent Athenian noble and father of the famous general Miltiades. His Olympic victories are mentioned by Herodotus (6.103.2–3).

43. *Xanthippus ... abandoning Athens*: Xanthippus, an Athenian politician and general, was victor at the battle of Mycale in 479; the father of Pericles (note 58). This story, associated with the Athenians' evacuation of their city before the battle of Salamis in 480, is told at Plutarch, *Themistocles* 10.

44. *Attic bushels*: An Attic bushel was about 40 litres (about 9 US dry gallons).

45. *governor of Sardinia*: As praetor in 198.

46. *a single public slave*: This does not mean that Cato travelled without slaves of his own or even without his official retinue: Plutarch is here emphasizing how little Cato incurred in the way of expenses borne by his province.

47. *exemplary ... severity*: By contrast, Livy (32.27.3–4) indicates that Cato was considered too severe, especially in matters of economy.

48. *Plato remarks of Socrates*: Plato, *Symposium* 215a–e and 221d–222a.

49. *Lysias*: (459–*c.* 380) One of the canonical Attic orators, known especially for his pure and plain style of Greek, on which ground Plutarch rejects any comparison with Cato's emotional style. In his *Brutus* (63–4), Cicero complains that his contemporaries adore Lysias but ignore Cato, but later, in the voice of Atticus, he undermines the comparison (293–4).

50. *those ... better qualified ... Roman oratory*: Although Plutarch was quite capable of reading Latin, because he lacked a natural fluency he avoided making stylistic judgements about Latin authors (*Demosthenes* 2).

51. *words ... throw light on his character*: For this sentiment, cf. *Alexander* 1, where Plutarch alludes to the science of physiognomy, through which an individual's character was diagnosed from his physical appearance; see S. Swain (ed.), *Seeing the Face, Seeing the Soul: Polemon's Physiognomy from Classical Antiquity to Medieval Islam* (2007). For a discussion of physiognomy in Plutarchan biography, see W. J. Tatum, *JHS* 116 (1996), pp. 135–51.

52. *'pay more for a fish than ... an ox'*: Fish were delicacies, whereas the ox, in this saying, is for working and not for eating. This

remark occurs in various versions (e.g. *Moralia* 198d, 688b; Polybius 31.25.5; Diodorus 31.24, 37.3.6; and Pliny, *Natural History* 9.67). We learn later (ch. 21), however, that Cato invested in fisheries.

53. *Themistocles*: (*c.* 524–459) An Athenian statesman and general; the subject of Plutarch's *Themistocles*, and paired with *Camillus*, the latter in this volume. Cato's remark is repeated at *Moralia* 198d. Themistocles' is cited at *Themistocles* 18, *Moralia* 1c and 185d.

54. *expected to be attended . . . by lictors, in case they should go astray*: Lictors walked in front of magistrates carrying their fasces, hence Cato's biting remark.

55. *He . . . found fault . . . constantly electing the same men*: Cato delivered a speech entitled *Ne quis iterum consul fieret* (*That no one be made consul a second time*), from which this complaint may be drawn; see Astin, *Cato the Censor*, p. 120.

56. '*The sea . . . without any difficulty at all*': Cato's criticism is that the man in question had to sell the estate in order to pay for his decadent lifestyle.

57. *Eumenes of Pergamum*: Eumenes II (d. 158) was king of Pergamum from 197. He was a strong friend and ally of Rome in the war against Antiochus and in the Third Macedonian War. Thereafter, however, the senate began to cool towards Eumenes, favouring his brother Attalus instead. Eumenes visited Rome in 172, the likely occasion of Cato's remark.

58. *Epaminondas . . . Pericles*: On Epaminondas see General Introduction II. Pericles (*c.* 495–429), Athenian statesman and general, who guided Athens at the acme of its power and during the early years of the Peloponnesian War. He is the subject of Plutarch's *Pericles*.

59. *Manius Curius*: See note 12.

60. *Hamilcar Barca*: (*c.* 275–228) Carthaginian general and politician, prominent in the First Punic War and the Carthaginian conquest of Spain; he was the father of Hannibal.

61. *he would rather do what was right . . . unpunished*: Also cited at *Moralia* 198d.

62. *he was prepared to forgive . . . except his own*: Also cited at *Moralia* 198e.

63. *sent three ambassadors to Bithynia*: Sent in 149 (the year of Cato's death) in order to prevent a war between Bithynia and Pergamum.

64. *a delegation . . . a heart*: Early Romans often associated the heart with intelligence. The remark was well known: see e.g. Polybius 36.14.2 and Livy, *Summary of Book 20*.

65. *Scipio . . . approached him . . . exiles from Achaea*: See also *Moralia* 199e. These Greek exiles were leading Achaeans deported to Italy in 167 after the Third Macedonian War (Polybius was in fact one of them). They were allowed to return to Greece in 150 or 149. Here, Scipio Africanus is Polybius' friend Scipio Aemilianus, consul in 147 and in 134.

66. *'poor old Greeks . . . buried . . . their own'*: Of the original thousand who were deported, only about 300 were by this point still alive (Pausanias 7.10.12).

67. *Odysseus . . . Cyclops' cave . . . left behind*: The reference is to Odysseus' escape from the man-eating Polyphemus in Book 9 of the *Odyssey*.

68. *blush rather than turn pale*: See also *Moralia* 29e, 198e and 528f. Blushing was the mark of a wholesome sense of propriety and shame, whereas a pallor, which often indicated illness or disease, was routinely the sign of an intense sexual infatuation.

69. *used his hands . . . when it came to fighting*: Also cited at *Moralia* 198e. Cato's point is that soldiers should not steal from one another while on the march and should not run away during combat.

70. *'everything . . . devoted to the belly'*: During his censorship, Cato removed Lucius Veturius from the equestrian ranks because he was excessively fat; see Gellius 7.22 and 17.2.

71. *palate was so much more . . . developed than his heart*: Also cited at *Moralia* 14d. Once again, 'heart' refers to intelligence.

72. *a lover's soul lives in the body of his beloved*: See also *Moralia* 759c. This is unclear. Possibly Cato's point is that a lover is useless as a soldier because his soul, which in Latin will have been *animus*, also meaning courage, has escaped his own body – the excellent suggestion of Sansone, *Plutarch: The Lives of Aristeides and Cato*, p. 212.

73. *intestate for a whole day*: Wills were important in Roman society and to die intestate was disgraceful; see E. Champlin, *Final Judgements: Duty and Emotion in Roman Wills, 200 BC–AD 250* (1991). Still, Cato's regrets here seem fairly minor, which was presumably the point.

74. *'Old age is vile . . . vice'*: Also cited at *Moralia* 199a, 784a and 829f.

75. *allotted the province . . . known as Nearer Spain*: In 195. Cato's province was Hispania Citerior, Nearer Spain. He was still consul when he went to his province, although his delay in departing Rome had been lengthy. His Spanish campaign is described at Livy 34.8–21.

76. *Celtiberians*: A populous and warlike people inhabiting north central Spain; they were finally subdued by Scipio Aemilianus in 133.

77. *pay barbarians to come to their rescue*: In fact Cato's opponents had hired Celtiberian mercenaries, and Cato attempted to detach them by way of this payment (Livy 34.19.4). In the end, however, they refused. See Astin, *Cato the Censor*, pp. 43–4.

78. *If the Romans won . . . to pay it*: Repeated at *Moralia* 199c and also preserved by Frontinus, *Stratagems* 4.7.35.

79. *In the battle . . . successful*: We know of no battle following these negotiations and in fact it appears Cato withdrew to fight elsewhere (Livy 34.19.9).

80. *Polybius records . . .*: This section of Polybius is lost but the information is also reported at Livy 34.17.11 and Appian, *Wars in Spain* 41.

81. *Baetis*: The modern Guadalquivir, but Plutarch is in error here: the cities in question were actually north of the River Ebro; see Walbank, *Commentary*, vol. 3, p. 63.

82. *captured more cities than he stayed days in Spain*: This improbable claim is also cited at *Moralia* 199c.

83. *a pound of silver*: According to Livy (34.46.3), Cato distributed 270 asses to each soldier, a far smaller quantity of money than Plutarch mentions, but still a very generous bounty by the standards of the day; see Astin, *Cato the Censor*, p. 53.

84. *'I do not blame . . . most greedy'*: See also *Moralia* 199d.

85. *Paccius*: Known only from this passage.

86. *Scipio . . . governor of the province*: Although Scipio Africanus was again consul in 194, he had nothing to do with Spain in that year. Instead, he campaigned in northern Italy. Plutarch (like Nepos, *Cato* 2.2) has confused Africanus with Publius Cornelius Scipio Nasica, who was praetor in 194 when he was governor of Farther Spain (Hispania Ulterior). There he won a major victory and was afterwards elected consul for 191 (and celebrated a triumph in that year).

87. *Scipio . . . cut short Cato's term of office*: The issue between the two remains unclear but it appears that Scipio complained about the way in which Cato departed his province.

88. *Lacetanians*: A tribe dwelling on the northeast coast of Spain (Livy 34.20). Nothing further is known about Cato's execution of deserters, unless Plutarch has in mind Cato's execution of outlaws mentioned by Livy (34.21).

89. *Cato ... honoured with a triumph*: In 194. It is described by Livy (34.46.2–3).

90. *Sempronius ... Danube*: Tiberius Sempronius Longus was consul in 194. He, along with Scipio Africanus, campaigned in northern Italy. It is just possible that Cato moved directly from his triumph into service as Sempronius' legate (though Plutarch is our only evidence for it), but he certainly did not make his way along the Danube or into Thrace (since Sempronius did not campaign there).

91. *military tribune under Manius Acilius*: Manius Acilius Glabrio, consul in 191. Like Cato, Glabrio was a New Man. It appears that Valerius Flaccus also served as a tribune of the soldiers in this war (Polybius 20.10.10). Other ex-consuls on Glabrio's staff included Titus Flamininus and Sempronius Longus.

92. *Antiochus the Great*: Antiochus III, see *Philopoemen*, note 100.

93. *Seleucus Nicator*: Seleucus I Nicator ('the Conqueror'; *c.* 358–281) was the founder of the Seleucid empire.

94. *restoration of Greek liberties ... domination of Philip of Macedon*: Titus Quinctius Flamininus, consul in 198, defeated Philip V in 197 and thereafter proclaimed the freedom of the Greeks (*Flamininus* 10).

95. *as I have described ... in his Life*: At *Flamininus* 15.

96. *Cato was responsible ... to the side of Rome*: Perhaps derived from misleading self-advertisement on Cato's part. These cities were members of the Achaean League, which had been persuaded by Flamininus to side with the Romans (Livy 35.48–50).

97. *he clung to Roman forms*: Valerius Maximus 2.2.2 indicates that it became customary for Romans to address Greek audiences in Latin.

98. *Postumius Albinus ... ignorance of the language*: Aulus Postumius Albinus was praetor in 155. He composed a (now lost) history of Rome in Greek, in the preface for which he apparently apologized for any infelicities. Cicero (*Brutus* 81) praises his literary gifts and high culture.

99. *decree of the Amphictyony*: The Amphictyonic League was an association of Greek states that supervised the sanctuary at Delphi, adduced by Cato for its authority in matters important to Greek (but not Roman) culture. Cato's remark is also preserved at *Moralia* 199e, Polybius 39.1 and Gellius 11.8.

100. *from the heart*: Implying intelligence rather than sentimentality (cf. note 64).

101. *Antiochus had blocked . . . attack him in Greece*: Plutarch here adapts Cato's own version of his involvement in this campaign, which is quite different from Livy's (36.15–19), itself derived from Polybius' now lost account. In reality, Antiochus was aware that his position could be compromised and had guarded against it. Cato was dispatched by Glabrio to attack the Aetolians who were protecting the pass for Antiochus. A modern reconstruction of this battle is provided by W. K. Pritchett, *Studies in Ancient Greek Topography*, vol. 1 (1965), pp. 71–82. See also Briscoe, *Commentary on Livy, Books 34–37*, pp. 241–50.

102. *Leonidas' defences*: King Leonidas of Sparta was outflanked and his force cut down by the Persians at the battle of Thermopylae of 480 (Herodotus 7.206–28). Once again, according to Plutarch, Cato is inspired by Greek precedent.

103. *Lucius Mallius*: (or Manlius) Unidentified.

104. *heights of Mount Callidromus*: The ridge between the River Asopus and Thermopylae.

105. *Firmum*: Modern Fermo. These troops were Italian allies.

106. *never stinted his own praise*: Livy describes Cato as 'in no way whatsoever inclined to stint in self-praise' (Livy 34.15.9: *haud sane detrectator laudum suarum*).

107. *he was dispatched to Rome*: Glabrio first sent Lucius Cornelius Scipio, consul in 190 and brother of Scipio Africanus, to the senate, then, a few days later, he sent Cato, who arrived first (Livy 36.21.4–8).

108. *Brundisium*: Modern Brindisi in southern Italy.

109. *Petillius' prosecution of Scipio*: In 187, two tribunes, each named Quintus Petillius, began to attack Scipio Africanus for irregularities associated with his brother's campaign against Antiochus the Great. Livy (38.54.2; cf. Gellius 4.18.7–12) believed that Cato was behind them. Eventually, both brothers Scipio were brought to trial, though the dates remain uncertain. Indeed, the so-called Trials of the Scipios, already a matter of confusion in the ancient sources, remain problematic. In the end, however, Scipio Africanus retired from Rome to his estate in Liternum, where he died in 183. A recent review of the evidence is provided by Briscoe, *Commentary on Livy, Books 38–40*, pp. 170–208.

110. *intervention of the tribunes*: The Scipios were assisted by the tribune Tiberius Sempronius Gracchus, later to be consul in 177 and

163. He was the father of the Gracchi (see Plutarch's *Tiberius Gracchus* and *Gaius Gracchus*). His tribunate was probably in 187.

111. *nearly fifty impeachments*: Forty-four according to Pliny (*Natural History* 7.100).

112. *'It is hard for a man ... before another'*: Also cited at *Moralia* 784d.

113. *age of ninety*: Cato, who died in 149, lived to be eighty-five, not ninety, though Livy (39.40) makes the same mistake and is no doubt Plutarch's source here.

114. *impeached Servius Galba*: In 149 a tribune proposed legislation to try Servius Sulpicius Galba for alleged enormities committed during his praetorship in 151. Cato spoke in support of the proposal, the last speech of his career. In the end, however, the proposal failed and Galba went on to become consul in 144. Plutarch's error here stems from Livy's mistaken account (39.40.12). See Astin, *Cato the Censor*, pp. 111–12.

115. *Nestor ... his life spanned three generations*: The wise Nestor is so described at *Iliad* 1.250–52 and *Odyssey* 3.345. Cicero made the comparison at *On Old Age* 31.

116. *the younger Scipio*: Plutarch refers to Scipio Aemilianus, who was the son of Lucius Aemilius Paullus, the subject of the last Life in this volume.

117. *candidate for the censorship*: Cato was consul in 195 and elected censor in 184 (censors entered office immediately upon election). He had previously been an unsuccessful candidate in the elections in 189.

118. *crowning honour ... of a political career*: See Lintott, *Constitution*, pp. 115–20.

119. *chose two officials ... a plebeian*: Since 339, one of the censors had to be plebeian (in 131, for the first time, both censors were plebeian). On the distinction between patrician and plebeian, see Introduction to *Coriolanus*.

120. *degrade a Roman knight*: A member of the equestrian order could be deprived of his horse if he was disabled (in which case it was done without disgrace) or if he was deemed physically or morally unfit for the order (in which case it was a disgrace for the knight so degraded).

121. *censors ... expel a senator ... disorderly life*: The first act of the censors was to establish the senate's membership. Senators could be expelled if their wealth fell below a minimum qualification or if their character was deemed unfit for membership.

122. *when Cato became a candidate*: This election was fiercely contested: see Livy 39.40–39.41.4 (which was very likely Plutarch's source here).

123. *hydra-like*: Alluding to the Hydra of Lerna, a mythical many-headed creature that sprouted new heads whenever one was cut off. It was finally slain by Heracles.

124. *As soon as he was elected*: For the details of Cato's censorship, see Livy 39.42.5–39.44.9 with Briscoe, *Commentary on Livy, Books 38–40*, pp. 357–67.

125. *leading man in the senate*: That is, *princeps senatus*. Valerius succeeded Scipio Africanus in this position.

126. *Lucius Quinctius*: Lucius Quinctius Flamininus, consul in 192. His expulsion from the senate is also described by Plutarch at *Flamininus* 18–19.

127. *Cicero . . . gives the same details*: Cicero, *On Old Age* 42.

128. *Livy . . . in a speech of Cato's own*: Livy 39.42.8–12; at 39.43.1, Livy makes it clear he had read Cato's speech.

129. *judicial wager*: See *Flamininus*, note 145.

130. *expelled another senator . . . daughter*: Also reported at *Moralia* 139e and Ammianus Marcellinus 28.4.9. Manilius is named only here and must be an error, since no praetor by that name is known from years prior to 184. It has been suggested that the man in question was actually a *Manlius*, a correction which yields several possible identifications.

131. *Lucius Scipio*: Lucius (note 107) was victor over Antiochus the Great at the battle of Magnesia in 190 and celebrated a triumph in 189.

132. *the great Africanus*: Scipio Africanus died in 183 before the end of Cato's censorship.

133. *imposed a tax . . . extravagant habits*: Plutarch here relies on Livy 39.44.1–3; see the discussion by Briscoe, *Commentary on Livy, Books 38–40*, pp. 363–4. Cato's action was irregular and punitive, hence the hostility it provoked.

134. *Ariston*: Probably Ariston of Chios, a third-century BC Stoic philosopher whose writings concentrated on ethics.

135. *Scopas*: Scopas of Crannon in Thessaly was a sixth-century BC tyrant famous for his wealth.

136. *Titus*: Titus Flamininus. Plutarch also cites Flamininus' opposition to Cato at *Flamininus* 19, though Livy (39.44.8–9) says nothing about Flamininus in his account of the opposition to Cato during his censorship.

137. *fine him 2 talents*: There is no evidence, apart from this passage, that Cato was in fact fined by the tribunes; see Astin, *Cato the Censor*, p. 86.

138. *Basilica Porcia*: This building stood to the west of the senate-house. Its name derives from the name of Cato's family (Porcius). It was destroyed by fire in 52 BC.

139. *the temple of Health*: This is the temple of Salus on the Quirinal Hill. The statue, which is otherwise unknown, was probably erected after Cato's lifetime. On honorific statues in the early and middle republic, see P. Stewart, *Statues in Roman Society: Representation and Response* (2003), pp. 28–35.

140. *effigies ... carried in their hearts*: The sentiment and language are Platonic (Plato, *Philebus* 39b).

141. '*I had far rather ... why there is one*': Also cited at *Moralia* 198e, 820b and Ammianus Marcellinus 14.6.8.

142. *his wife*: Her name was Licinia (inferred from the name of her son, see below). Plutarch's is our only account of her.

143. *nothing ... to admire in Socrates ... half-witted*: Cato's criticism of Socrates is adduced in ch. 23. Socrates' wife, Xanthippe, was proverbially shrewish (e.g. Diogenes Laertius 2.36–7).

144. *his son*: Marcus Porcius Cato Licinianus (*c.* 192–152). He lived to become praetor-elect and a learned authority on Roman law (his writings remained influential even in the imperial period).

145. *suckled the child herself*: Although the employment of wet-nurses was common, it was routinely suggested that it was a good practice for women to nurse their own children. (Plutarch's wife breast-fed her children: *Moralia* 609e.)

146. *the river*: Presumably the Tiber.

147. *his historical books*: These are not the same as Cato's *Origins*, which was composed during his old age (Nepos, *Cato* 3.3).

148. *the general custom ... ashamed to show themselves naked*: Cf. *Moralia* 274a and Cicero, *On Duties* 1.129.

149. *Romans adopted from the Greeks ... women*: Plutarch here contrasts Greek with Roman habits, to the credit of the Greeks. The Romans built baths throughout their empire, and they became popular in Greece. Mixed bathing, however, which first appeared during the empire, remained rare and was deemed decadent; see G. G. Fagan, *Bathing in Public in the Roman World* (1999), pp. 26–9. Roman baths were in any case deemed by some to be pleasant but less than wholly salubrious, an attitude made clear in the funerary epitaph of one Tiberius Claudius

Secundus (*ILS* 8157): 'Baths, wine and sex wreck our bodies, but baths, wine and sex make life worth living.'

150. *his son ... excellent soldier ... Perseus*: This exploit is also narrated at *Aemilius Paullus* 21.

151. *a letter has come down to us*: Cato addressed several works, including more than one public letter, to his son; see Astin, *Cato the Censor*, pp. 182–4.

152. *when he had become more prosperous*: Cato's urgent elegance here contrasts with his representation in chs. 3–4, where one gets the impression that Cato's austerity was a permanent condition. In these chapters, however, Plutarch is reporting the impression Cato makes on others and Cato's own claims about his lifestyle.

153. *contrived to provoke quarrels ... among his slaves*: Cato says just the opposite at *On Agriculture* 5.1, but his views on the matter may have been inconsistent.

154. *agriculture ... a source of income*: This is not meant to be flattering. Agriculture was deemed the most honourable source of wealth; although in practice Roman senators were not above engaging in business practices like the ones mentioned in this chapter, Cato's brand of capitalism was in principle regarded as unsuitable for an aristocrat (see e.g. Cicero, *On Duties* 1.150–51). In the preface to his *On Agriculture*, Cato writes:

> Commerce can be very profitable, were it not so hazardous, and the same is true of money-lending, were it honourable. Our ancestors held this view ... when they offered praise to a good man, they called him 'a good farmer' ... farmers make the bravest and strongest soldiers ... and their livelihood is at once the most venerable and most assured of them all.

155. *bought ... fisheries*: At ch. 8 Cato decries the Romans' appetite for fish delicacies.

156. *workshops*: The correct reading of this word is uncertain.

157. *ruined by the whims of Jupiter*: As the god of weather, Jupiter could determine the success or failure of agricultural investments.

158. *lend money ... the most disreputable form of speculation*: Cato equated money-lending with murder (Cicero, *On Duties* 2.89; see also Cato, *On Agriculture* 61).

159. *one share ... agency of ... one of his freedmen*: Roman senators were forbidden by law from owning transport ships, a restriction Cato skirted by letting his freedman own the share on his behalf.

160. *tried to encourage his son ... capital ... not of a man*: Plutarch presumably draws this from one of Cato's works addressed to his son (note 151).

161. *Carneades*: (214–129) One of the leading philosophers of his day, famous for his dialectical and rhetorical skills. In Rome he delivered, on consecutive days, speeches for and against justice, philosophizing of a kind unlikely to appeal to Cato.

162. *Diogenes*: Diogenes of Babylon (*c*. 240–152), the leading Stoic of his time.

163. *ambassadors from Athens*: This embassy, which also included the Peripatetic philosopher Critolaus, came to Rome in 155. At the time Cato was seventy-eight or seventy-nine years old.

164. *sent to plead ... judgement against them*: For unknown reasons, the Athenians had raided the territory of the town of Oropus (modern Skala Oropou), which appealed to the senate to intervene. The senate appointed the city of Sicyon to decide the matter. The Athenians did not appear to make their defence and the Sicyonians fined Athens 500 talents. The embassy of 155 persuaded the senate to reduce the fine to 100 talents.

165. *Gaius Acilius*: A senator who wrote (in Greek) a history of Rome from its earliest times down to his own day; it appeared around 142.

166. *opposed ... to the study of philosophy*: In Plutarch's own day there were Romans who made a show of despising philosophy and philosophizing, sometimes with the Elder Cato in mind; see Syme, *Tacitus*, pp. 553–63.

167. *Isocrates*: (436–338) An important orator and rhetorician whose views on style were highly influential.

168. *disciples ... until they were old men*: According to Isocrates himself (*To Antipater* 4.87–8), his pupils remained with him three or four years.

169. *Minos ... in Hades*: In Greek myth, King Minos became one of the judges of the dead in the underworld.

170. *if ever the Romans ... lose their empire*: Cato's words are preserved at Pliny, *Natural History* 29.14. Presumably they come from one of Cato's writings dedicated to his son.

171. *Hippocrates' celebrated reply*: Hippocrates of Cos lived in the second half of the fifth century BC and was the most famous physician of antiquity. Here, Plutarch alludes to a letter, one of many pseudepigraphic works attributed to Hippocrates, addressed to an official of the Persian king Artaxerxes I: see Letters 3–8 in E. Littré, *Oeuvres completes d'Hippocrate*, vol. 9 (1861),

pp. 316–19. Plutarch does not explicitly claim here that Cato was aware of this letter (nor is it mentioned in Pliny's report of Cato's hostility towards Greek physicians: see *Natural History* 29.14), but by mentioning it he at least raises the possibility that it is by way of his familiarity with Greek literature that Cato formulates his hostility to Greek physicians.

172. *book of recipes . . . perfect health*: See A. Cruse, *Roman Medicine* (2004), especially pp. 52–60.

173. *walking towards the forum . . . in the usual way*: Grand figures in Roman society were routinely escorted from their homes to the forum by their friends, as well as their clients, for whom it was a gesture of their respect. On patrons and clients in Rome, see *Romulus* 13 and, more extensively, Dion. Hal. 2.10.

174. *Salonius*: Not otherwise known, but he is subsequently described as having been one of Cato's scribes, presumably, in view of *Comparison Aristeides–Elder Cato* 6, a scribe who worked with Cato during one or more of his magistracies. Scribes were far from poor men, some even possessed the wealth of a knight: see E. Badian, *Klio* 71 (1989), pp. 582–603. Astin, *Cato the Censor*, p. 105, however, believes Salonius was one of Cato's freedmen.

175. *'you have been a model son . . . serve my country'*: At *Comparison Aristeides–Elder Cato* 6, Plutarch judges this remark insincere (and Cato's behaviour in this entire matter disgraceful).

176. *Peisistratus*: Tyrant in Athens from *c.* 546 until his death in 527. His two marriages are discussed at Pseudo-Aristotle, *The Athenian Constitution* 17.3–4. Peisistratus' explanation of his second marriage is not elsewhere recorded. His sons were Hippias and Hipparchus, who ruled together in Athens after Peisistratus' death.

177. *a son . . . after his father-in-law*: The boy's name was Marcus Porcius Cato Salonianus.

178. *his first-born son died during his praetorship*: So also Livy, *Summary of Book 20*, but Cicero (*Tusculan Disputations* 3.70) and Gellius (13.20.9) say that Marcus died while praetor-elect.

179. *Lucius Lucullus . . . Metellus Pius*: Lucius Licinius Lucullus (*c.* 117–57 or 56) was consul in 74 BC and is the subject of Plutarch's *Lucullus*; his withdrawal from public life is described at *Lucullus* 38–9. Quintus Caecilius Metellus Pius (*c.* 130–63) was consul in 80 BC; after his triumph in 71 BC, he retired from public life.

180. *Scipio Africanus . . . in untroubled retirement*: Plutarch's characterization of Scipio's opponents here colours Cato's actions in ch. 15.

181. *Dionysius*: Dionysius I of Syracuse (*c.* 430–367) was tyrant in Syracuse from 405 until his death. Once, when he was besieged by Carthaginians and considered surrendering his tyranny, this remark by one of his friends ('absolute power is the best winding-sheet') convinced him to carry on. This anecdote is repeated at *Moralia* 783c, Isocrates, *Archidamus* 44–5, and Diodorus 14.8.5 and 20.78.2.

182. *discourses on ... histories*: For a survey of Cato's literary output, see Astin, *Cato the Censor*, pp. 131–56 and 182–266.

183. *treatise on farming ... includes recipes*: Cato's *On Agriculture* is his only work that survives in its entirety. The recipes mentioned by Plutarch are found at sections 7, 76, 99 and 143.

184. *He always invited his friends ... praise or blame*: Here, Plutarch relies on Cicero, *On Old Age* 45–6.

185. *destruction of Carthage*: Carthage was captured and destroyed in 146 by Scipio Aemilianus during the Third Punic War (149–146).

186. *Cato ... sent ... on a diplomatic mission*: In 153.

187 *Masinissa*: (238–148) He became an ally of Rome during the Second Punic War.

188. *defeat ... at the hands of Scipio Africanus*: Plutarch refers to Scipio's victory at the battle of Zama in 202. On the Second Punic War, see Introduction to *Fabius Maximus*.

189. *'Carthage must be destroyed!'*: Cato's most famous or notorious saying, but its common Latin formulation – *Carthago delenda est* – does not appear in any ancient source.

190. *Publius Scipio Nasica*: Publius Cornelius Scipio Nasica Corculum was consul in 162, censor in 159 and consul for a second time in 155; he was later *pontifex maximus* and the leading man of the senate (*princeps senatus*). His role in the battle of Pydna is described by Plutarch in *Aemilius Paullus* 15–18, 21 and 26.

191. *He died ... after it had begun*: In 149.

192. *a man who was still young*: Cato refers to Scipio Aemilianus, who was only thirty-nine when he conquered Carthage.

193. *'Only his wisdom ... shadows'*: Odyssey 10.495.

194. *Cato left ... his first son ... already dead*: In fact, Cato Licinianus left two sons. They were (i) Marcus Porcius Cato, consul in 118, who was a distinguished orator whose speeches were still being read during the empire (Gellius 13.20), and (ii) Gaius Porcius Cato, consul in 114 (who is never mentioned in this Life). Plutarch makes several errors in these final lines and it is possible

that the passage is defective: see M. Szymański, *Hermes* 125 (1997), pp. 384–6.

195. *Salonius died ... in office as praetor*: Plutarch is our only source for his praetorship and his evidence has been doubted by some.

196. *his son Marcus ... became consul*: This is incorrect. Marcus Porcius Cato Salonianus had two sons: (i) Marcus Porcius Cato, who was tribune of the people in 99 BC and died while a candidate for the praetorship, possibly in 93 BC, and (ii) Lucius Porcius Cato, consul in 89 BC.

197. *This Marcus was the grandfather of Cato the Philosopher*: This Marcus, the tribune of 99 BC, was not the grandfather but the father of 'Cato the Philosopher', that is, of the Younger Cato, Marcus Porcius Cato (95–46 BC), the opponent of Caesar, and the subject of Plutarch's *Life of the Younger Cato*.

Notes to the Comparison of Aristeides and Elder Cato

1. *highest census classification ... 200*: These census brackets were established by Solon (*Solon* 18; see also Pseudo-Aristotle, *The Athenian Constitution* 7.3); they indicate, by way of agricultural production, the profitability of an individual's assets.

2. *Curius ... Fabricius ... Atilius*: On Manius Curius Dentatus, see *Elder Cato* 2. Gaius Fabricius Luscinus was consul in 282 and 278. Gaius Atilius Regulus was consul in 257 and 250, and was said to have been found sowing his fields when visited by an official delegation (Cicero, *Defence of Roscius Amerinus* 50; Pliny, *Natural History* 18.20; and Valerius Maximus 4.4.5).

3. *when he began his political career ... 5 talents*: Plutarch repeats this at *Themistocles* 25.

4. *Scipio ... Galba ... Flamininus*: On Scipio Africanus, see *Elder Cato* 3 and 11; on Galba, see *Cato* 15; and on Flamininus, see *Cato* 17 and 19.

5. *Marathon ... Plataea*: The battles of Marathon (490) and Plataea (479) were important Greek victories over the Persians.

6. *one of ten generals*: Each year the Athenians elected ten generals (*strategoi*).

7. *one of two censors ... eminent rivals*: On Cato's election as censor, see *Cato* 16.

8. *Miltiades*: (*c.* 550–489) The mastermind of the Athenian victory at Marathon.

9.   *Salamis*: The battle of Salamis (480) was a major Greek victory over the Persians. On Themistocles, see *Cato*, note 53.

10.   *'won the noblest of victories'*: Plutarch quotes from Herodotus (9.64.1). Pausanias (d. *c.* 470) was the Spartan general who commanded the Greeks at Plataea.

11.   *Sophanes ... Cynaegeirus*: So Herodotus: see Herodotus 9.74.1 (Sophanes); Herodotus 8.84.1, 8.93.1 and Plutarch, *Themistocles* 14 (Ameinias); Herodotus 6.111.1 (Callimachus); and Herodotus 6.114 (Cynaegeirus, who was also the brother of Aeschylus).

12.   *Cato ... consul during the war in Spain*: *Cato* 10–11.

13.   *at Thermopylae ... only to the front*: *Cato* 13–14.

14.   *Scipio*: Lucius Cornelius Scipio, consul in 190, and the brother of Africanus; he defeated Antiochus at the battle of Magnesia.

15.   *in politics ... faction of Themistocles*: *Aristeides* 7.

16.   *Antipater' ... talent for persuasion*: Antipater (*c.* 397–319) was a distinguished Macedonian general, first under Philip II and then Alexander the Great. He was also a student of Aristotle and left behind two volumes of letters addressed to his son Cassander, in which he made this assessment of his teacher (the original context is made clear when Plutarch reports this same view at *Comparison Coriolanus–Alcibiades* 3).

17.   *man's highest virtue ... a household*: See Aristotle, *Nicomachean Ethics* 1094b8–9 and *Politics* 1252a5, 1253a37.

18.   *when Lycurgus banished ... iron spoiled by fire*: Plutarch's *Lycurgus* 9.

19.   *by citizens who were helpless ... extremely rich*: *Lycurgus* 8.

20.   *justice were to blame ... possessor*: Plutarch here adapts some of Thrasymachus' criticisms of justice from Plato, *Republic* 343c–e.

21.   *Yet ...*: In what follows Plutarch wishes to demonstrate, on the authority of Hesiod and Homer, that justice is *not* incompatible with successful domestic economy. In other words, it was not owing to his *justice* that Aristeides remained poor.

22.   *Hesiod, in numerous passages ... injustice*: Plutarch does not have specific passages in mind: the whole of Hesiod's *Works and Days* concerns the relationship between justice and domestic economy. He condemns idleness at line 311.

23.   *hard work ... arrows*: *Odyssey* 14.222–5.

24.   *men who neglect ... one and the same*: That is not the actual point of the speaker in the *Odyssey*. Still, by quoting Homer,

however inappropriately, Plutarch thereby arrogates his authority, not an uncommon move in ancient arguments.

25. *how it is most beneficial . . . family*: Plutarch borrows this observation not from medical writings but from Plato, *Protagoras*
334b–c.

26. *made no provisions . . . own burial*: Aristeides 27.

27. *down to the fourth generation*: Cato 27 (with note 197). Plutarch counts inclusively and so Cato's great-grandsons constitute
the fourth generation.

28. *descendants of Aristeides . . . public grants*: Aristeides 27.

29. *Poverty is never dishonourable . . . foolishness*: Pericles expresses
a similar sentiment at Thucydides 2.40.1.

30. *Poverty . . . a man who is temperate . . . great nature*: A similar
sentiment is expressed at *Moralia* 823c.

31. *not wealth but self-sufficiency . . . service to the state*: Plutarch's
language here reprises his description of Cato at Cato 4 and 8,
though here he is speaking about Aristeides.

32. *it is the one . . . most perfect and god-like*: A similar view is
expressed by Socrates at Xenophon, *Memorabilia* 1.6.10. Cf.
Plutarch's criticism of Cato at Cato 21 for his view that it is the
man who increases his inheritance who is god-like.

33. *mark of distinction . . . plastered walls*: Cato 3–4 (though Plutarch
does not tell us there that Cato refrained from wearing purple).

34. *a man who claims . . . boils them himself*: It is Manius Curius
and not Cato who does this at Cato 2.

35. *while his wife is busy baking bread*: This (unlikely) feature of
Cato's home life has not been mentioned before, but it recalls
Plutarch's description of Phocion's wife at *Phocion* 18.

36. *value of a single as*: Cato 4.

37. *what practices . . . rich most quickly*: Cato 21.

38. *Aristeides proclaimed . . . glory in it*: Aristeides 25.

39. *he could . . . have enriched himself . . . a single tent*: Plutarch
describes the wealth left behind at Marathon by the retreating
Persians at *Aristeides* 5.

40. *Xerxes*: (519–465) The king of Persia who invaded Greece in
480. The Persian empire at the time was more extensive even
than Antiochus' kingdom.

41. *incessant boasting . . . superior to everyone else*: Cato 14 and 19.

42. *He . . . insists that glorifying oneself . . . is disgusting*: We do not
know from which speech Plutarch extracted this sentiment.

43. *a modest indifference to glory . . . envy*: Here Plutarch recurs to
virtues and vices central to his moral outlook: mildness (*praotes*)

is a crucial virtue (see General Introduction III), whereas ambition (*philotimia*) often degenerates into harshness (*philoneikia*); see Introductions to *Philopoemen* and *Flamininus*.

44. *Aristeides saved Athens . . . when he was general*: Aristeides 8.
45. *Cato . . . opposition to Scipio . . . embezzlement*: Cato 3, 15 and 24.
46. *self-restraint*: (*sophrosyne*) A cardinal virtue for Plutarch, as for all Greek moralists.
47. *he chose as his father-in-law . . . honour*: Cato 24.

AEMILIUS PAULLUS

Further Reading

The only extensive commentary on the *Life of Aemilius Paullus* is (in Dutch) by C. Liedmeier, *Plutarchus' Biographie van Aemilius Paullus: Historische Commentar* (1935). W. Rieter, *Aemilius Paullus: Conqueror of Greece* (1988), is a careful study of Aemilius' portrayal by ancient writers, including Polybius, Livy and Plutarch. For the history of the Third Macedonian War, consult Hammond–Walbank, pp. 488–558, and P. S. Derow, 'Rome, the fall of Macedon and the sack of Corinth', in *CAH* viii (1989), pp. 290–323. There is also much to be learned from P. J. Burton, *Friendship and Empire: Roman Diplomacy and Imperialism in the Middle Republic (353–146 BC)* (2011), and Walbank, *Commentary*, vol. 3.

Plutarch's prologue is discussed by Duff, *Plutarch's Lives*, pp. 30–34, and A. J. Zadorojnyi, '*Hosper en esoptro*: the rhetoric and philosophy of Plutarch's mirrors', in Humble, *Plutarch's Lives*, pp. 169–96. Interpretive studies of this Life include S. C. R. Swain, 'Plutarch's Aemilius and Timoleon', *Historia* 38 (1989), pp. 314–34; Swain, *H&E*, pp. 151–4; L. Holland, 'Plutarch's *Aemilius Paullus* and the Model of the Philosopher Statesman', in L. de Blois, J. Bons, T. Kessels and D. M. Shenkeveld (eds.), *The Statesman in Plutarch's Works*, vol. 2: *The Statesman in Plutarch's Greek and Roman Lives* (2005), pp. 269–79; and W. J. Tatum, 'Another Look at *Tyche* in Plutarch's *Aemilius Paullus–Timoleon*', *Historia* 59 (2010), pp. 448–61.

Notes to the Introduction to Aemilius Paullus

1. On the design of Polybius' *Histories*, see F. W. Walbank, *Selected Papers: Studies in Greek and Roman History and Historiography* (1985), pp. 325–43, and B. McGing, *Polybius' Histories*

(2010), pp. 17–50. The importance of Pydna is unmistakable (Polybius 1.1.5, 3.1.9–10, 29.21).

2.   On chance and Macedon's rise, see Polybius 29.21.5–6.

3.   Or so we naturally assume. The relevant section of Polybius' *Histories* is lost, but this is how Aemilius is uniformly represented elsewhere in sources that almost certainly depend on Polybius' account (Livy 45.41, Diodorus 31.11 and *Aemilius Paullus* 36).

4.   See General Introduction V.

5.   For Aemilius' being hailed as *imperator*, see *ILS* 15. His *supplicatio* is reported at Livy 37.58.5. But he did not receive a triumph: see J. Briscoe, *A Commentary on Livy, Books 34–37* (1981), p. 392.

6.   Livy 39.32.5, with T. R. S. Broughton, *Candidates Defeated in Roman Elections: Some Ancient Roman 'Also-Rans'* (1991), pp. 6–7.

7.   See Hammond–Walbank, pp. 488–558; Derow in *CAH* viii, pp. 303–19.

8.   Eumenes II of Pergamum played a leading role (Livy 42.11–13).

9.   In his speech *On Behalf of the Rhodians*, delivered in 167 (cited by Gellius 6.1.3 = Cato, fr. 164, in H. Malcovati, *Oratorum Romanorum Fragmenta* (4th edn, 1967)). Greek expectations at the time of the Third Macedonian War are discussed by A. M. Eckstein, *Rome Enters the Greek East: From Anarchy to Hierarchy in the Hellenistic Mediterranean, 230–170 BC* (2008), pp. 369–71.

10. See Derow in *CAH* viii, pp. 290–323.

11. Jones, 'Chronology', pp. 108–9.

12. On *Aemilius Paullus'* Greek pairing, *Timoleon*, see below.

13. Plutarch recurs to these ideas more than once. At *Moralia* 85a–b his readers are urged, before any action, to

> ask, 'What would Plato have done in this situation, what would Epaminondas have said . . . ?', as though standing before a mirror,

cf. *Moralia* 455e–456b. See Duff, *Plutarch's Lives*, pp. 30–34; and Zadorojnyi in Humble, *Plutarch's Lives*, pp. 169–96.

14. Swain, *Historia* 38, pp. 314–34, and Tatum, *Historia* 59, pp. 448–61.

15. Plutarch does not fail to register disapproval when the Romans sack seventy cities in Epirus, but he attributes responsibility for

this to the senate and not to Aemilius, for whom it was 'a duty . . . entirely contrary to his mild and just nature' (ch. 30).

16. Also reprised at *Comparison Aemilius Paullus–Timoleon* 2. Aemilius is praised for these qualities by Polybius (31.22.1–8) in his final commentary on his character.

17. Aemilius' inexplicable divorce of Papiria is not criticized but glossed by way of an anecdote about how often motives for divorce are legitimate but undetectable (ch. 5).

18. See Hammond–Walbank, pp. 532–3.

19. See J. Geiger in Scardigli, *Essays*, pp. 184–90.

20. See R. J. A. Talbert, *Timoleon and the Revival of Greek Sicily* (1974); and H. D. Westlake in *CAH* vi (1994), pp. 693–722.

21. See especially Swain, *Historia* 38, pp. 314–34.

22. See General Introduction III.

23. Timoleon's distinction in this regard is discussed by Swain, *H&E*, pp. 154–5.

24. In the biography of Timoleon by Cornelius Nepos, for instance, his good fortune is a matter of celebration: each of his greatest victories, according to Nepos (*Timoleon* 4–5; cf. Diodorus 16.66.1–5), occurred on his birthday, irrefutable evidence of his *fortuna* and *felicitas*.

25. On Timaeus, see General Introduction V.

26. See Tatum, *Historia* 59, pp. 448–61. At his *Comparison Aemilius Paullus–Timoleon* 2, however, Plutarch prefers Aemilius to Timoleon. For all Timoleon's merits, the biographer explains, his character lacked greatness.

27. *FGrH* 233.

28. *FGrH* 169.

Notes to the Life of Aemilius Paullus

1. *LIFE OF AEMILIUS PAULLUS*: *Aemilius Paullus* and *Timoleon* are transmitted with the Roman Life preceding the Greek one, which is also true for *Coriolanus–Alcibiades* and *Sertorius–Eumenes*. Not every editor, however, is persuaded that this represents Plutarch's intention and, as a consequence, some transpose this first chapter – the prologue to the entire pairing – to the beginning of *Timoleon*. Owing to the order of the Lives accepted here, the closing *Comparison* follows the Greek and not the Roman Life; consequently, it is included with the *Life of Timoleon* in *Plutarch: The Age of Alexander*.

2. *'his god-like aspect and magnificent size'*: Priam admires Achilles in these terms, *Iliad* 24.630.

3. *'Ah! . . . can one obtain?'*: From Sophocles' lost play *The Drummers* (*Tympanistae*), fr. 636 in H. Lloyd-Jones, *Sophocles: Fragments* (2003).

4. *Democritus . . . unlucky*: Democritus of Abdera, a fifth-century BC philosopher, best known as one of the founders of atomism. According to his physical system, sight results from the impact on the soul of *eidola* (or *images*: the word used by Plutarch here), thin atomic films shed from the surfaces of all objects, including people. These images endure as they break down, appearing as visions and dreams. The view cited here is also reported at *Moralia* 419a, and, employing nearly the same terminology, by Sextus Empiricus (*Against Mathematicians* 9.19 = DK B 166).

5. *you*: Quintus Sosius Senecio, consul in AD 99 and 107, to whom Plutarch dedicated his *Parallel Lives*, as well as other works; see General Introduction I.

6. *Aemilius . . . son of . . . Pythagoras*: See *Numa* 8.

7. *on account of . . . overall charm*: Plutarch here cites a tradition that derived the name *Aemilius* (or *Aimilius*, as the name frequently appears in inscriptions) from Greek *haimilios*, which means *wheedling* (not always in a negative sense). At *Numa* 8, it is Numa's own son who is named Mamercus (after the son of Pythagoras) and who evinces this charm. But there were various stories of the family's origin: at *Romulus* 2 Plutarch mentions an Aemilia who was the daughter of Aeneas and the mother of Romulus.

8. *Lucius Paullus*: Consul (for the second time) in 216, the year in which he fell at the battle of Cannae (*Fabius Maximus* 14–16). His colleague was Gaius Terentius Varro.

9. *Scipio*: Publius Cornelius Scipio, who defeated Hannibal at the battle of Zama in 202 and was honoured with the surname Africanus (*Fabius Maximus* 25–7).

10. *He refused . . . no part in that*: Aemilius' unwillingness to court popularity by pleading in the courts or by glad-handing and charming the public is a recurring motif, also emphasized at ch. 38. This is exactly how Polybius (31.23.11) portrays Aemilius' son, the young Scipio Aemilianus, and Plutarch's depiction of the father is probably influenced by Polybius' treatment of the son.

11. *curule magistracies . . . twelve competitors*: Plutarch is our only source for the number and quality of Aemilius Paullus' competitors. The curule magistracies were the curule aedileship, praetorship and consulship. The election took place in 193.

12. *augurs*: The most important of the Romans' priestly colleges. Augury was a crucial element in the Roman constitution: see Lintott, *Constitution*, pp. 185–6, *Romulus* 9 and *Moralia* 286a–c. We do not know when Aemilius became an augur.

13. *define religion . . . service to the gods*: A familiar sentiment: see Plato, *Euthyphro* 14c–d, and the Pseudo-Platonic *Definitions* 413a.

14. *Antiochus the Great*: On Antiochus III, see *Philopoemen*, note 100.

15. *fasces*: Bundles of rods, capped with a two-headed axe, symbolizing a magistrate's or promagistrate's legal and military power (*imperium*); they were carried by lictors, who preceded magistrates during their public movements.

16. *praetor . . . level of a consul's*: Aemilius was elected praetor for 191 and assigned the province of Farther Spain (where military campaigning had persisted since the third century BC). In this period, governors in Spain were granted the military authority of a consul (and were denominated *proconsuls*): see T. C. Brennan, *The Praetorship in the Roman Republic* (2000), p. 163. Plutarch is mistaken in seeing this as a special honour for Aemilius. His command was extended through 189. In 190 he suffered defeat, but rebounded with victory in the following year, for which his troops hailed him as a victorious general (*imperator*) and Rome offered thanksgivings to the gods (Livy 37.58.5). The tradition that he was also awarded a triumph for this campaign (Velleius Paterculus 1.9.3) is probably false.

17. *restore his wife's dowry . . . barely sufficed to do so*: In Rome, although a husband had full financial control of his wife's dowry during their marriage, it reverted to his wife upon divorce or death; see S. Treggiari, *Roman Marriage* (1991), pp. 323–64. Polybius (18.35, where he too relates the difficulty his heirs had in restoring his wife's dowry) also praises Aemilius' financial rectitude.

18. *Maso*: Gaius Papirius Maso, a patrician who was consul in 231.

19. *Scipio . . . Fabius Maximus*: The 'famous Scipio' is Publius Cornelius Scipio Aemilianus, consul in 147 and 134. He destroyed Carthage and Numantia and was much admired by later generations. Plutarch's first pairing in his *Parallel Lives* probably included his biography (see General Introduction II). Quintus Fabius Maximus Aemilianus, his elder brother, was consul in 145. Each served under Aemilius in the campaign against Perseus (chs. 15 and 22).

20. *story about divorce . . . it blisters*: Plutarch repeats this story at *Moralia* 141a.

21. *gave in adoption to ... illustrious families*: Adoptions along these lines were not uncommon among the Roman aristocracy, especially when they helped to preserve the name and fortune of a distinguished family: see H. Lindsay, *Adoption in the Roman World* (2009).

22. *adopted by Fabius Maximus*: Aemilius' oldest son was in fact adopted by a son or grandson of this Fabius Maximus; see A. E. Astin, *Scipio Aemilianus* (1967), p. 13.

23. *son of Scipio Africanus*: He suffered from poor health which excluded a public career; he was, however, an augur and a writer of some distinction (Cicero, *Brutus* 77; Velleius Paterculus 1.10.3).

24. *one married the son of Cato*: See *Elder Cato* 20 (where this daughter is named Tertia). This Cato served under Aemilius in the campaign against Perseus (ch. 21).

25. *Aelius Tubero*: Quintus Aelius Tubero, who served under Aemilius in the campaign against Perseus (ch. 28). His son became a distinguished philosopher and jurist.

26. *elected consul*: Aemilius was consul for the first time in 182, rather late for a patrician elected praetor in 191. It is clear that he had been a frequent candidate before this success: see Livy 39.32.5, with Broughton, *Candidates Defeated in Roman Elections*, pp. 6–7. Both consuls of 182 campaigned against the Ligurians, peoples who dwelt in what is now southern France and extended themselves to the regions south of the River Po in Italy.

27. *Pillars of Heracles*: See *Aratus*, note 66.

28. *achievements of ... first consulship*: Aemilius' command was continued into 181, when he won a major victory over the Inguani, a Ligurian tribe, for which he was awarded a triumph.

29. *went so far as to announce his candidature*: Plutarch is our sole source for this and he may in fact be thinking of Aemilius' unsuccessful bids for the consulship *before* 182.

30. *Perseus*: (212–*c.* 165) The last king of Macedon (reigned 179–168), against whom Rome waged the Third Macedonian War (see Introduction).

31. *the generals*: Plutarch has in mind chiefly Publius Licinius Crassus (consul in 171), Aulus Hostilius Mancinus (consul 170) and Quintus Marcius Philippus (consul 169), although few of Rome's commanders in the east distinguished themselves in the first years of the war (ch. 9).

32. *Antiochus ... confined ... to Syria*: After he was defeated in 190, the Romans deprived Antiochus of his possessions north of the Taurus mountains, but he continued to rule over a vast empire that ranged from Syria and Palestine to southern Turkey and to Iran and central Asia.

33. *the Romans had defeated Philip*: In the Second Macedonian War (200–197), the Romans defeated Philip V of Macedon (ch. 8 and *Flamininus* 7–8).

34. *crushed Hannibal*: See *Marcellus* and *Fabius Maximus* for events of the Second Punic War (218–201).

35. *Antigonus*: Antigonus 'the One-Eyed' (c. 382–301).

36. *Demetrius*: Demetrius I, known as *Poliorcetes* ('the Besieger of Cities'; 336–283), is the subject of Plutarch's *Demetrius*.

37. *Antigonus surnamed Gonatas*: Antigonus Gonatas (c. 320–239). The meaning of *Gonatas* is unknown. See, further, Introduction to *Aratus*.

38. *Philip*: Philip V (238–179), the father of Perseus.

39. *Doson ... promises that he failed to fulfil*: Antigonus Doson (that is, Antigonus, *The Man Who Will Give*, though it is uncertain exactly why he was so called; c. 263–221). See, further, Introduction to *Aratus*.

40. *Scotussa*: A town in Thessaly, west of modern Volos. The battle of Cynoscephalae was fought near there in spring 197 (*Flamininus* 8).

41. *Demetrius*: (c. 207–180) He had gone to Rome as a hostage at the end of the Second Macedonian War (*Flamininus* 9), but owing to Philip's loyalty in the war against Antiochus he was released in 190. Demetrius urged a pro-Roman policy in Macedon, which led eventually to his execution as a traitor in 180, although the veracity of the ancient tradition on this matter has been doubted by modern historians (e.g. Hammond–Walbank, p. 490). The episode is told at length and with dramatic flair by Livy (40.5–24); Polybius' account (23.3.4–9, 23.7 and 23.10) is fragmentary.

42. *It is alleged ... Gnathaenion*: The same story is told in *Aratus* 54 (whereas at Livy 39.53.3 and 40.9.2, Perseus' mother is a concubine of Philip). In reality, Perseus' mother was Polycrateia, an Argive woman who had been married to the son of Aratus but was seduced by Philip V (*Aratus* 49).

43. *Publius Licinius*: Publius Licinius Crassus, consul in 171.

44. *cavalry battle ... prisoners*: The battle of Callicinus was fought near the Thessalian town of Sycurium (the precise location of which remains uncertain but was somewhere near modern

Sykourion), for which Livy (42.60.1) offers different casualty figures (at *Moralia* 197f, however, Plutarch reports the same figures as Livy).

45. *Oreus*: A city, better known as Histiaea, on the northern coast of Euboea, where Lucius Hortensius, praetor in 170, was taken by surprise.

46. *Hostilius . . . Elimiae*: Aulus Hostilius Mancinus (note 31) tried to enter Macedon from Thessaly by way of the Volustana Pass. Elimiae was a town on the Macedonian side of the pass. Plutarch's is the only extant notice of this event.

47. *Dardanians*: An Illyrian people inhabiting the southern Balkans who were long-standing enemies of the Macedonians.

48. *Basternae*: A nomadic tribe shifting along the lower Danube and often employed by Philip V and Perseus against the Dardanians. Here (and elsewhere) they are thought of as Gauls, but this owes itself more than anything else to the Greeks' and Romans' lack of precision in ethnographic matters (Introduction to *Camillus*).

49. *Illyrians*: A large group of related peoples inhabiting the western Balkans. On Genthius see ch. 13.

50. *come to the forum*: Candidates for high office circulated in the forum, greeting voters and publicizing the depth of their support.

51. *Campus Martius*: Consuls were elected by the centuriate assembly, which convened on the Campus Martius (Field of Mars), the area where today one finds (among other features) the Pantheon and the Piazza Navona.

52. *drawing of lots . . . command*: In fact lots were drawn in the ordinary way and there is no indication that Aemilius was viewed by voters as the inevitable commander for the war against Perseus (Livy 44.17.7–10).

53. *Cicero . . . On Divination*: See *On Divination* 1.103 and 2.83; cf. Valerius Maximus 1.5.3 and Plutarch, *Moralia* 197f–198a. Cicero and Valerius Maximus name the puppy *Persa*, which need not but can refer to Perseus. Plutarch eliminates the ambiguity.

54. *he had sought his first consulship . . . need for a general*: Also found at *Moralia* 197f.

55. *Roman camp . . . safely*: Mancinus (note 31) had installed the Romans at Heracleum, a fortified site at Platamona, between the base of Mt Olympus and the sea.

56. *the Maedi*: A people living in northeastern Macedon, in the valley of the River Strymon. The Basternae (note 48) were encamped at Desudaba, the exact location of which is unknown.

57. *He refused to pay*: After consulting his advisers, Perseus proposed employing 5,000 cavalrymen, an offer which the Basternae ultimately rejected (Livy 44.26–7).

58. *the Romans . . . had mustered 100,000 men*: This (approximate) figure refers to the entirety of the Roman war effort, including Lucius Anicius' campaign against the Illyrians (ch. 13) and the naval command of Gnaeus Octavius (ch. 26). Aemilius made a strong case for reinforcements before he set out for Macedon (Livy 44.18.1–5 and 44.20.2–7).

59. *some Lydian or Phoenician*: This is unattractive ethnic stereotyping. Plutarch evokes the fabulous wealth of Lydia, and its monarch, Croesus, as well as the trade and commerce of the Phoenicians (ignoble even if profitable activities so far as Greek and Roman aristocrats were concerned).

60. *whose nobility he claimed to share*: The Antigonids (falsely) claimed descent from Philip II and his son Alexander the Great.

61. *Philip's gold*: Philip was notorious for his use of bribery, e.g. *Moralia* 178b, 856b; Diodorus 16.3, 16.54; Cicero, *Atticus* 1.16.12; and Horace, *Odes* 3.16.3.

62. *Alexander . . . at the start of his expedition to India . . . bonds*: Plutarch recounts this episode at *Alexander* 57.

63. *deprived . . . of his 300 talents*: Perseus paid Genthius 10 talents but, after Genthius molested the Roman ambassadors, withheld the remainder (Livy 44.27.8–12).

64. *Lucius Anicius*: Lucius Anicius Gallus, praetor in 169, defeated and captured Genthius, who, along with his family, was paraded in Anicius' triumph.

65. *a secure position*: Perseus' camp, on the River Elpeus (modern Mavrolongos), was indeed well fortified and well supplied. At the same time, Perseus was aware of its vulnerabilities: he had to defend against a Roman landing to the north of his position and had to protect the pass at Petra (note 67), through which an army could make its way to his rear (the means by which Aemilius soon dislodged Perseus: chs. 15–16). At this point in the narrative, Aemilius had advanced from Heracleum through the Tempe Pass to the opposite side of the Elpeus (a movement not mentioned by Plutarch).

66. *There are some . . . who deny . . . stops*: This outbreak of hydrological polemic is a bit surprising. Plutarch here criticizes the belief that subterranean waters are formed by the condensation of air in the cold depths of the earth (just as above the earth rain results from the condensation of cooled air), a view associated

with Aristotle (*Meteorology* 349b20 and 349b23–350a14; and Seneca the Younger, *Natural Questions* 3.9). Instead, he prefers the theory that subterranean reservoirs account for these waters, an idea Plutarch apparently associates with Plato (*Phaedrus* 111c–113c, with Aristotle, *Meteorology* 355b34–356b2). Here, then, we have an outburst of Plutarch's Platonism – there was nothing at all like this in his sources – in the midst of his historical narrative. Its purpose is probably to lend a whiff of Hellenic science to Aemilius' actions.

67. *Perrhaebia . . . Petra*: Perrhaebia is the region west of Mt Olympus. The pass at Petra, located between Olympus and Mt Titarios, could be reached by way of the Pythium, the site of a sanctuary to Apollo (near modern Hagioi Apostoli). Perseus had in fact anticipated Aemilius' manoeuvre by garrisoning both the Pythium and the pass (Livy 44.32.9 and 44.35.11).

68. *Scipio, surnamed Nasica . . . in the senate*: Publius Cornelius Scipio Nasica Corculum was consul in 162 and again in 155, and, as Plutarch correctly notes, was a leading political figure (especially in the 140s BC). At *Elder Cato* 27 he opposes Cato's insistence that Carthage be destroyed.

69. *Polybius reports . . .*: This section of Polybius is lost, but according to Livy (44.35.11), who probably draws on Polybius, the force was composed of 5,000 men.

70. *provided by Nasica . . . in a short letter*: Plutarch prefers Nasica here presumably because he was an eyewitness to the events, but there are sound reasons for rejecting his account in favour of the version recoverable from Polybius and Livy: see Hammond–Walbank, pp. 545–6. We do not know to which of the Hellenistic kings Nasica addressed his public letter.

71. *mixed . . . contingent commanded by Harpalus*: Mentioned only here.

72. *Xenagoras . . . made this measurement*: If Xenagoras used Attic feet, his measurement was 2066 metres (6788 feet), to which one should add the elevation of Pythium (approximately 900 metres or 2953 feet), to get 2966 metres (9741 feet). The correct figure is 2985 metres (9793 feet). Xenagoras is not otherwise known.

73. *Hail, O lord!*: The epigram seems to address the god Apollo.

74. *no mountain has a height . . . exceeding 10 stades*: Cf. Cleomedes (an astronomer writing around AD 325) 1.56: 'for neither does the height of any mountain nor the depth of any sea exceed 5 stades and 10 plethra, as measured by a plumb-line'.

75. *This is where Nasica spent the night*: Their journey to this point took two days to complete, not one, as Plutarch here indicates. During the two days it took Nasica to reach the pass, Roman light-armed troops attacked Perseus' forces, often with severe losses (Livy 44.35.16–19).

76. *Milo*: He is called Midon at Livy 44.32.9. Perseus' command was logistically impossible: Milo could never have covered the distance to the pass in time to confront the Romans.

77. *Polybius reports . . .*: The accounts of both Polybius and Livy are missing for this episode.

78. *Pydna*: A Greek city in Macedon, located near its modern namesake, north of the Pierian Plain near the Thermaic Gulf.

79. *His position*: Perseus camped to the south of Pydna, with his forces facing south (and awaiting the Romans' advance).

80. *near the end of summer*: On the eve of the battle there was an eclipse (ch. 17), which can be dated to 21 June 168; however, at that time the Roman calendar was not in phase with the seasons (the pre-Julian Roman calendar required routine recalibration with the seasons, corrections not always dutifully or correctly carried out). Livy (44.37.8) gives the date as 3 September, and this may explain Plutarch's confusion.

81. *Aeson . . . Leucus . . . difficulties*: The rivers are the modern Ayios Dimitrios and Ayios Yeorios respectively. Perseus intended to meet the Romans on his side of these rivers (hence their difficulty for the Romans, who would have to cross them).

82. *'Yes of course . . . battle formation'*: Also reported at *Moralia* 198a.

83. *ordered his vanguard . . . fortifications*: This manoeuvre became a celebrated one; see Frontinus, *Stratagems* 3.20.

84. *During the night*: Of 21 June. Plutarch agrees with Livy (44.40.2) in setting the eclipse and final battle immediately after Aemilius' arrival, but according to Zonaras (9.23) there was a delay of several days, and there are good reasons to prefer his (less dramatic) account: see N. G. L. Hammond, *JHS* 104 (1984), pp. 43–4.

85. *the moon . . . disappeared from sight*: The story of this eclipse is variously told (e.g. Polybius 29.16 and Livy 44.37.5–8). A good discussion of the reliability of its variations is provided by A. C. Bowen in C. J. Tuplin and T. E. Rihll (eds.), *Science and Mathematics in Ancient Greek Culture* (2002), pp. 76–111.

86. *in accordance with their custom . . . torches*: Plutarch is our only source for this Roman practice.

87. *morning light . . . fighting*: The Roman battle array faced east.
88. *an unbridled horse . . . caused the battle to begin*: Livy (44.40.3) and Zonaras (9.23) agree that the battle began as the result of chance (and in this they probably agree with Polybius). Only Plutarch attributes the battle to a ruse. A frieze on Aemilius' victory monument at Delphi (ch. 28) depicts, in the centre of the battle, a fleeing horse, which Plutarch (who will have viewed it) perhaps interpreted as evidence of a ruse (in a Life that persistently seeks to avoid giving undue prominence to accidental good luck).
89. *Thracians under Alexander's command*: This Alexander is mentioned only here.
90. *the Paeonians*: People of a region in northern Macedon, originally independent but incorporated into the kingdom by Philip II.
91. *Bronze Shields*: An elite unit of heavily armed infantrymen (Polybius 2.66.5 and 4.67.6).
92. *Poseidonius*: This historian is otherwise unknown.
93. *the Paelignians*: A people of central Italy, inhabiting the modern Abruzzo, who were long-standing allies of Rome. Salvius' action is mentioned by Frontinus (*Stratagems* 2.8.5).
94. *the Marrucinians*: Another tribe of central Italy, who lived along the Adriatic coast (largely in what is now the province of Chieti).
95. *Marcus . . . son-in-law of Aemilius*: See ch. 5. Marcus Cato did not marry Aemilius' daughter until after the battle of Pydna (*Elder Cato* 20).
96. *25,000 . . . according to Nasica, eighty*: Livy (44.42.7–9) offers slightly different figures.
97. *ninth hour . . . tenth*: The battle took place between three and four in the afternoon.
98. *120 stades*: Slightly more than 13 miles (21 km).
99. *younger one . . . little more than a boy*: That is, Scipio Aemilianus (ch. 5). According to Livy (44.54.3), he was seventeen years old.
100. *the Scipio who . . . destroyed Carthage and Numantia*: Scipio Aemilianus destroyed Carthage in 146 and Numantia (modern Garray, a city in Spain) in 133.
101. *postponed for another time*: Until ch. 35.
102. *Pella*: The chief city of Macedon and the site of a royal palace.
103. *men of the infantry*: These survivors were light-armed soldiers; the infantry that manned the Macedonian phalanx had been cut down.

104. *Evander*: The commander of Perseus' Cretan mercenaries and a trusted agent; he once attempted, on Perseus' behalf, to assassinate King Eumenes of Pergamum (Livy 42.15.3). Perseus put him to death on Samothrace when his past assault on Eumenes II became a political liability (45.5.2–14).

105. *Archedamus*: Aetolian statesman and general; he commanded Aetolian troops under Flamininus in 197 (Polybius 18.21.5), but in 169 was denounced as anti-Roman (28.4.8) and so joined Perseus (Livy 43.21.9, 44.43.6).

106. *Neon*: A Theban statesman with pro-Macedonian sentiments (Polybius 20.5.14, 27.1.2), he fled to Perseus at the outbreak of the war (27.2.8). After the war, he was executed by the Romans at Amphipolis (Livy 45.23.3).

107. *Amphipolis . . . Galepsus*: Cities east of modern Thessaloniki.

108. *playing the part of a Cretan*: Plutarch plays on the proverb 'all Cretans are liars' (e.g. Titus 1:12).

109. *sanctuary of the Cabiri*: See *Marcellus*, note 139. At this point in Plutarch's text there is a lacuna, filled in by some manuscripts with *the Dioscuri*, but the more likely supplement (the one accepted here) is *the Cabiri*. However, the Cabiri were sometimes identified with the Dioscuri.

110. *informed of the victory*: The news is brought by the Dioscuri at Cicero, *On the Nature of the Gods* 2.6; Valerius Maximus 1.8.1; Pliny, *Natural History* 7.86; and Florus 1.28.14–15. Livy (45.1.1–5), like Plutarch, is unspecific.

111. *battle was fought*: This battle took place in the sixth century BC between Epizephyrian Locris and Croton; see also Cicero, *On the Nature of the Gods* 2.6; Strabo 6.261; and Justin, *Epitome of Pompeius Trogus* 20.3.9. The River Sagra has not been identified.

112. *battle . . . Plataeans*: The Greeks defeated the Persians in simultaneous battles on or about 27 August in 479, one of which took place at Plataea in Boeotia, the other at Mycale in Asia Minor. According to Herodotus (9.100; see also Diodorus 11.35.1–3), it was the participants in the battle of Mycale who learned of the victory at Plataea on the same day (not the other way round, as Plutarch has it here).

113. *Romans defeated the Tarquins . . . Dioscuri*: The (probably legendary) battle of Lake Regillus took place in 499 or 496 (*Coriolanus* 3). The involvement of the Dioscuri is also related at Cicero, *On the Nature of the Gods* 2.6, 3.11 and 3.13; and Dion. Hal. 6.13.

114. *Ahenobarbus*: Suetonius (*Nero* 1) says that this man was Lucius Domitius, the first of the Domitii Ahenobarbi, of which family Nero was the last.

115. *Antonius ... defeat*: In AD 88 Lucius Antonius Saturninus, the commander of Upper Germany, rebelled against Domitian but was defeated by Aulus Lappius Maximus, who commanded in Lower Germany (Suetonius, *Domitian* 6.2; Cassius Dio 67.11.1).

116. *victory ... stades*: The decisive battle occurred somewhere along the Rhine, probably near Mainz, which is only about 5,192 stades (597 miles) from Rome.

117. *Gnaeus Octavius*: Praetor in 168, consul in 165. Plutarch's formulation is a bit misleading inasmuch as Octavius' was an independent command, for which he earned a triumph (although he was naturally expected to cooperate with the consul).

118. *His children*: Perseus' eldest son, Philip, was not captured by Ion (Livy 45.6.9–10).

119. *with tears in his eyes*: See *Camillus* 5, with note 20.

120. *Tubero*: Aemilius' son-in-law, Quintus Aelius Tubero (chs. 5 and 28).

121. *The legacy of Alexander ... collapsed in a single hour*: The battle of Pydna was fought within an hour (ch. 22).

122. *busied himself ... humane*: Aemilius' command was extended into 167 so that he could oversee the disposition of Macedon. The Romans sacked several cities, and their settlement of the kingdom, while formulated in terms that stressed freedom and liberation, was in many respects severe: see Hammond–Walbank, pp. 558–69; and Derow in *CAH* viii, pp. 316–19.

123. *tall square pillar ... statue of himself*: Remains of this monument still exists in Delphi, see Hammond–Walbank, pp. 613–17.

124. *at Olympia ... the Zeus of Homer*: Pheidias was the leading sculptor of the fifth century BC. His statue of Zeus at Olympia was widely admired, as was his statue of Athena in the Parthenon in Athens. According to Strabo (8.30), Pheidias, when asked how he chose his model for the statue of Zeus, responded that he was inspired by Homer's lines at *Iliad* 1.528–30:

> Zeus, son of Cronos, nodded his dark brows. The divine hair on the king of gods fell forward, down over his immortal head, shaking Olympus to its very base.

125. *commissioners arrived from Rome*: It was routine for the senate to send commissioners to assist in making the final arrangements

after a war of this magnitude. Their identities are listed at Livy 45.17.1-4.

126. *the same intelligence ... a good symposium ... companions*: Plutarch repeats this saying at *Moralia* 615e-f; also cited by Polybius (30.14) and Livy (45.32.11).

127. *his quaestors*: We do not know their identities.

128. *as I said earlier*: In ch. 5, though there Tubero is *one* of sixteen relations.

129. *Epirus*: The region stretching from the Ionian Sea in the west to the Pindus mountains to the east, and in the north from south-western Albania to the Gulf of Arta in the south. It was dominated in the fourth century BC by the Molossians, whose kingdom was closely associated with Macedon. By Aemilius' day, however, the region, including the Molossians, had united to form the Epirote League. During the Third Macedonian War, the Molossians sided with Perseus, and it was against the Molossian cities that Aemilius marched after the war.

130. *at the expense of the cities*: Plutarch does not observe that these cities had been allies of Perseus in the war, an omission which puts the senate's decision in an even worse light inasmuch as a reader might be forgiven for not recognizing how it marked a continuation of the war against Perseus (the region had in fact been pacified by Anicius before Aemilius' arrival: Livy 45.26.3-11).

131. *each Roman soldier received ... so meagre a profit*: Livy (45.34.5) reports that each cavalryman received 400 denarii and each infantryman 200 denarii. Plutarch's figure (Plutarch tends to equate a denarius with a drachma) is clearly much lower and it has been suggested that it refers to the profits of individual pillaging and does not include the wholesale plundering carried out under the terms of Aemilius' decree to the cities.

132. *Oricum*: Now Orikum, in southwestern Albania.

133. *his desire for a triumph*: The senate endorsed triumphs for Anicius, Octavius Gnaeus and Aemilius and entrusted the tribunes of the people to put forward enabling legislation (Livy 45.35.4). Tiberius Sempronius (not otherwise known) was the tribune who put forward the appropriate legislation for Aemilius' triumph (Livy 45.36.1). On this process, see Beard, *Roman Triumph*, pp. 202-3; and M. R. P. Littenger, *Contested Triumphs: Politics, Pageantry, and Performances in Livy's Republican Rome* (2008), pp. 33-53.

134. *Servius Galba*: Servius Sulpicius Galba, destined for the consulship of 144 and one of the leading orators of his day (Cicero, *Brutus* 85-90).

135. *the Capitol*: That is, the *area Capitolina*, the open space in front of the temple of Jupiter Best and Greatest, on the south summit of the Capitoline Hill. This is where Sempronius had decided to conduct the vote. Aemilius could not be there himself, since, while awaiting a triumph, he had to remain outside the city.

136. *the assembly*: This was a meeting of the plebeian assembly, the voting units of which were tribes (not dissimilar from modern voting precincts). The decision of the first tribe was often very influential among remaining voters.

137. *The multitude . . . could do nothing*: The multitude are helpless in this instance because Aemilius' soldiers have occupied the Capitol and intimidated all other voters (Livy 45.36.6).

138. *Marcus Servilius*: Marcus Servilius Pulex Geminus, consul in 202.

139. *Illyrians . . . Libyans*: By Illyrians, Servilius refers to Anicius' triumph over the Illyrian king Genthius. Although the manuscripts read *Ligurians* it is usually corrected to *Libyans* (i.e. Africans) and construed as a reference to Scipio Africanus' triumph over King Syphax of Numidia. In Livy's version of this speech (45.39.3 and 7) he mentions each of these triumphs but says nothing about Ligurians. This is almost certainly correct, although it must be observed that Aemilius had previously been allowed to triumph over the Ligurians in 181 (ch. 6).

140. *when . . . rumour . . . reached the city*: See ch. 24.

141. *a man*: Sulpicius Galba.

142. *Three days were devoted to . . . the triumph*: In September 167. Plutarch's is the most extended account we possess. Another version (Diodorus 31.8.10–12) varies from this one.

143. *Thericlean bowls*: See *Philopoemen*, note 53.

144. *as Homer says . . . now in the other*: Here Plutarch distils Achilles' advice to Priam at *Iliad* 24.525–51, in which Priam is encouraged to bear the death of his son Hector with resolution.

145. *already said*: At ch. 5.

146. *addressed them*: Aemilius surrendered his public authority with the conclusion of his triumph and therefore did not have the right to summon the people. He was allowed to address the people by a sympathetic tribune of the people, Marcus Antonius (Livy 45.40.9).

147. *brought the war to its . . . conclusion*: At the battle of Pydna.

148. *carcer*: Located at the base of the Capitoline Hill and used in the republic for detentions and executions, not as a prison. According to Diodorus (31.9), Perseus was deposited in a ghastly

dungeon in Alba Fucens (near the modern Massa d'Albe) in central Italy, from which he was rescued through the intervention of Aemilius.

149. *in a peculiar ... way ... died*: Diodorus (31.9) also preserves this story.

150. *Alexander*: Nothing more is known of this Alexander. Magisterial scribes, though not grand personages, were nonetheless often wealthy and influential: see E. Badian, *Klio* 71 (1989), pp. 582–603.

151. *the people no longer had to pay taxes*: The annual tax on Romans' property (*tributum*) was discontinued after 167. Other forms of taxation, however, subsisted.

152. *Hirtius ... Caesar*: Aulus Hirtius and Gaius Vibius Pansa were consuls in 43 BC. They campaigned with Caesar's heir, Octavian (later Augustus), against Mark Antony in the conflict at Mutina.

153. *Appius ... Scipio Africanus*: In 142 Appius Claudius Pulcher, consul in 143, competed with Scipio Aemilianus for the censorship. Although the Romans elected two censors, only one of them could be a patrician, and, because both Claudius and Scipio were patricians, they were necessarily competing against one another. Appius lost, but was elected censor for 136.

154. *your son is being conducted ... by Aemilius the auctioneer and Licinius Philonicus*: It was a recognized asset, during electoral campaigns, to be accompanied in the forum by men of distinguished status, especially nobles and former consuls, hence the force of Appius' jibe: an auctioneer in Rome may have been wealthy, but he was undistinguished, and the otherwise unknown Licinius Philonicus has a name suggesting that he is a freedman. The details of Scipio Aemilianus' election to the censorship are discussed by Astin, *Scipio Aemilianus*, pp. 111–13.

155. *elected him censor*: Aemilius was censor in 164.

156. *depriving him of his horse*: By depriving anyone of his public horse, the censors removed him from the equestrian order, to which order the sons of senators also belonged. On the responsibilities of censors, see Lintott, *Constitution*, pp. 115–20.

157. *Marcus Aemilius Lepidus*: Consul in 187 and censor in 179, from which time he was *princeps senatus* (the leading man of the senate) until his death in 152.

158. *Marcius Philippus*: Quintus Marcius Philippus, consul in 186.

159. *Elea*: Modern Castellammare della Bruca, a Greek city in southern Italy.

160. *a . . . ritual required his presence*: It is not known what ritual Plutarch has in mind, but in any case he here reprises the theme of Aemilius' religiosity, emphasized at ch. 3.

161. *he died*: In 160.

162. *Iberians . . . Macedonians*: These were the populations conquered by Aemilius during his praetorship and his two consulships (chs. 4, 6 and 10–26). In 171 Aemilius had served as an advocate of the Spanish provinces when they complained about the conduct of their Roman governors (Livy 43.2.5–12).

163. *His estate . . . 370,000 drachmas*: Polybius (31.28.3) says that Aemilius' estate was valued at 'more than 60 talents', which comes to 360,000 drachmas (on drachmas see General Introduction VI). Presumably Plutarch's exact figure is intended to correspond with Polybius' inexact one.

164. *which he left to his two sons*: Although from a legal perspective Aemilius died without sons of his own, he was free to dispose of his property as he pleased and in Rome the legal conditions of adoption did not annihilate the natural affections between fathers and their biological sons. The two brothers celebrated lavish funeral games in honour of their father, for which Terence's comedy *The Brothers* was commissioned.

PENGUIN CLASSICS

THE RISE OF THE ROMAN EMPIRE
POLYBIUS

> 'If history is deprived of the truth,
> we are left with nothing but an idle, unprofitable tale'

In writing his account of the relentless growth of the Roman Empire, the Greek statesman Polybius (*c.* 200–118 BC) set out to help his fellow-countrymen understand how their world came to be dominated by Rome. Opening with the Punic War in 264 BC, he vividly records the critical stages of Roman expansion: its campaigns throughout the Mediterranean, the temporary setbacks inflicted by Hannibal and the final destruction of Carthage in 146 BC. An active participant in contemporary politics, as well as a friend of many prominent Roman citizens, Polybius was able to draw on a range of eyewitness accounts and on his own experiences of many of the central events, giving his work immediacy and authority.

Ian Scott-Kilvert's translation fully preserves the clarity of Polybius' narrative. This substantial selection of the surviving volumes is accompanied by an introduction by F. W. Walbank, which examines Polybius' life and times, and the sources and technique he employed in writing his history.

Translated by Ian Scott-Kilvert
Selected with an introduction by F. W. Walbank

PENGUIN CLASSICS

THE LETTERS OF THE YOUNGER PLINY

> 'Of course these details are not important enough for history …
> you have only yourself to blame for asking for them'

A prominent lawyer and administrator, Pliny (*c.* AD 61–113) was also a prolific letter-writer, who numbered among his correspondents such eminent figures as Tacitus, Suetonius and the Emperor Trajan, as well as a wide circle of friends and family. His lively and very personal letters address an astonishing range of topics, from a deeply moving account of his uncle's death in the eruption that engulfed Pompeii and observations on the early Christians – 'a desperate sort of cult carried to extravagant lengths' – to descriptions of everyday life in Rome, with its scandals and court cases, and of his own life in the country. Providing a series of fascinating views of imperial Rome, his letters also offer one of the fullest self-portraits to survive from classical times.

Betty Radice's definitive edition was the first complete modern translation of Pliny's letters. In her introduction, she examines the shrewd, tolerant and occasionally pompous man who emerges from these.

Translated with an introduction by Betty Radice

THE STORY OF PENGUIN CLASSICS

Before 1946 ... 'Classics' are mainly the domain of academics and students; readable editions for everyone else are almost unheard of. This all changes when a little-known classicist, E. V. Rieu, presents Penguin founder Allen Lane with the translation of Homer's *Odyssey* that he has been working on in his spare time.

1946 Penguin Classics debuts with *The Odyssey*, which promptly sells three million copies. Suddenly, classics are no longer for the privileged few.

1950s Rieu, now series editor, turns to professional writers for the best modern, readable translations, including Dorothy L. Sayers's *Inferno* and Robert Graves's unexpurgated *Twelve Caesars*.

1960s The Classics are given the distinctive black covers that have remained a constant throughout the life of the series. Rieu retires in 1964, hailing the Penguin Classics list as 'the greatest educative force of the twentieth century.'

1970s A new generation of translators swells the Penguin Classics ranks, introducing readers of English to classics of world literature from more than twenty languages. The list grows to encompass more history, philosophy, science, religion and politics.

1980s The Penguin American Library launches with titles such as *Uncle Tom's Cabin*, and joins forces with Penguin Classics to provide the most comprehensive library of world literature available from any paperback publisher.

1990s The launch of Penguin Audiobooks brings the classics to a listening audience for the first time, and in 1999 the worldwide launch of the Penguin Classics website extends their reach to the global online community.

The 21st Century Penguin Classics are completely redesigned for the first time in nearly twenty years. This world-famous series now consists of more than 1300 titles, making the widest range of the best books ever written available to millions – and constantly redefining what makes a 'classic'.

The Odyssey continues ...

The best books ever written

PENGUIN 🐧 CLASSICS

SINCE 1946

Find out more at www.penguinclassics.com